Applied ADO.NET: Building Data-Driven Solutions

MAHESH CHAND
AND
DAVID TALBOT

APress Media, LLC

Applied ADO.NET: Building Data-Driven Solutions

Copyright © 2003 by Mahesh Chand and David Talbot
Originally published by Apress in 2003

ISBN 978-1-59059-073-7   ISBN 978-1-4302-0759-7 (eBook)
DOI 10.1007/978-1-4302-0759-7

Trademarked names may appear in this book. Rather than use a trademark symbol with every occurrence of a trademarked name, we use the names only in an editorial fashion and to the benefit of the trademark owner, with no intention of infringement of the trademark.

Technical Reviewer: Philip Pursglove

Editorial Directors: Dan Appleman, Gary Cornell, Jason Gilmore, Simon Hayes, Karen Watterson, John Zukowski

Managing Editor: Grace Wong

Project Manager: Tracy Brown Collins

Development Editor: Philip Pursglove

Copy Editor: Kim Wimpsett

Compositor: Diana Van Winkle, Van Winkle Design Group

Artist and Cover Designer: Kurt Krames

Indexer: Ron Strauss

Production Manager: Kari Brooks

Manufacturing Manager: Tom Debolski

The information in this book is distributed on an "as is" basis, without warranty. Although every precaution has been taken in the preparation of this work, neither the author nor Apress shall have any liability to any person or entity with respect to any loss or damage caused or alleged to be caused directly or indirectly by the information contained in this work.

The source code for this book is available to readers at http://www.apress.com in the Downloads section.

To uncles Banshi Lal and Rajbir Singh Malik for their support and guidance.
—Mahesh Chand

For Nadia whose patience has carried me through this book.
—David Talbot

NOTE *Some documentation and authors represent the Sql data provider as the* SqlClient *data provider. This may be because the Sql data provider is defined in the* SqlClient *namespace.*

For this example, you'll learn how to build an application that uses OleDb data providers to access an Access 2000 database. In the "Using a DataSet to Read Data" section, you'll learn how to create an application that uses Sql data providers to access a SQL Server 2000 database.

Adding Namespace References

After you've chosen your data provider, you need to add references to the assembly and include the namespaces in your project. The System.Data.dll assembly defines ADO.NET namespaces. You can add references to the project using the Project ➤ Add Reference option. The .NET tab of the Add Reference dialog box lists all the available .NET assemblies (see Figure 1-14). Select the System.Data.dll assembly.

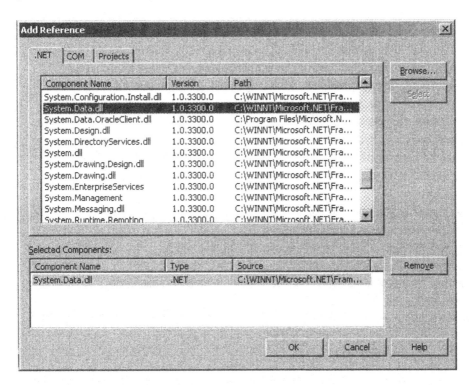

Figure 1-14. Adding a reference to the System.Data.dll *assembly*

After selecting the System.Data.dll assembly, click the Select button and then the OK button. This action adds the System.Data assembly and related namespace references to your project.

After adding a reference to the assembly, you need to include namespaces in your project by using the Imports directive. The Imports directive imports a namespace definition in a project. The following code shows how to import the System, System.Data, System.Data.Common, and System.Data.OleDb namespaces:

```
Imports System
Imports System.Data
Imports System.Data.OleDb
Imports System.Data.Common
```

NOTE *If you are using the Sql data provider, you need to include the* System.Data.Sql *namespace. If you are using the Odbc data provider, you need to include the* System.Data.Odbc *namespace.*

Establishing a Connection

Now, the next step is to create a Connection object. You create a Connection object using the data provider's Connection class. In the following code, the OleDbConnection class creates a connection with an Access 2000 database. The OleDbConnection constructor takes one parameter of a string type. This string is called connectionString, and it has two parts. First, it has a provider, and second, it has the path of the data source. As you can see, the following code uses the Microsoft.Jet.OLEDB.4.0 provider and the northwind.mdb data source:

```
Dim connectionString As String
'Create connection and command objects
connectionString = "Provider=Microsoft.JET.OLEDB.4.0;" & _
"data source=C:\\Northwind.mdb"
Dim conn As OleDbConnection = New OleDbConnection(connectionString)
'Open connection
conn.Open()
```

NOTE *In this sample, the* northwind.mdb *database path is* "C:\\northwind.mdb". *You can use any database you want. You just need to change the path and name of the database and change the table names you are using in the SQL statements to access the data.*

Creating a Command or DataAdapter Object

Next, you need to create a DataAdapter or Command object. You create a Command object by using the OleDbCommand class. (You'll see a DataAdapter object in the SQL Server example at the end of this chapter; see the "Using a DataSet to Read Data" section.)

The OleDbCommand constructor takes two parameters. The first is a SQL query, and the second is the Connection object. You can create a SELECT SQL query from the Customers table in the Northwind database. The following code shows how to create a Command object:

```
Dim sql As String
sql = "SELECT CustomerID, ContactName, ContactTitle FROM Customers"
Dim cmd As OleDbCommand = New OleDbCommand(sql, conn)
```

Filling Data to a DataSet or DataReader Object

The next step is to open the connection by calling the Open method of the Connection object and reading data from the Command object. The ExecuteReader method, OleDbCommand, returns data in an OleDbDataReader object. A DataReader object is used to read fast and forward only cached data. The following code shows this:

```
Dim reader As OleDbDataReader = cmd.ExecuteReader()
```

Displaying Data

The next step is to perform some operation on the data. In this example, you'll write data out to the console. The Read method of OleDbDataReader reads data. The DataReader class has a number of methods that return different types of data (for example, GetString and GetInteger). These methods take the index of the field from which you want to read data. The following code reads data from two fields of the Customers table, whose indexes are 0 and 1:

```
While reader.Read()
Console.Write(reader.GetString(0).ToString() + " ,")
Console.Write(reader.GetString(1).ToString() + " ,")
Console.WriteLine("")
End While
```

Closing the Connection

Finally, the last step is to close the reader and connection objects by calling their Close methods:

```
reader.Close()
conn.Close()
```

NOTE *You must always close an open* DataReader. *We discuss* DataReaders *in more detail in the "The DataReader: An Easy Walk Through the Data" section of Chapter 4.*

Creating a Simple ADO.NET Application

Now, let's use all of the previous steps and write a console-based application to read data and display it on the console. In this application, you'll read data from the Northwind database's Customers table and display it on the console.

In this example, you'll use VS .NET to create a console application by selecting Visual Basic Projects and then choosing the Console Application template from the Templates listing. Name your project FirstAdoNetApp1.

After creating the project, add the Listing 1-1 source code to the project. As you can see from this listing, first you import the required namespace. Second, you create a connection and create an OleDbConnection object by passing the connection string as only one argument. Next, you construct a SELECT statement and create an OleDbCommand object by passing the SQL statement and connection object. Then you open the connection by calling the OleDbConnection.Open method. Once a connection is opened, you can execute SQL statement by simply calling the ExecuteXXX methods of the DataReader. As you can see, the code calls the

ExecuteReader method, which returns data in an OleDataReader object. Then you read data from the DataReader and display it on the console. The last step is to close the DataReader and the connection. You do this by calling the Close methods of OleDbDataReader and OleDbConnection objects.

Listing 1-1. Your ADO.NET Application

```
Imports System
Imports System.Data
Imports System.Data.OleDb
Imports System.Data.Common


Module Module1
  Sub Main()
    Dim connectionString As String
    Dim sql As String
    'Create connection and command objects
ConnectionString = "Integrated Security=SSPI; Initial Catalog=Northwind; " & _
"Data Source=localhost;"
    Dim conn As OleDbConnection = New OleDbConnection(connectionString)
    sql = "SELECT CustomerID, ContactName, ContactTitle FROM Customers"
    Dim cmd As OleDbCommand = New OleDbCommand(sql, conn)
    'Open connection
    conn.Open()
    'Call ExecuteReader
    Dim reader As OleDbDataReader = cmd.ExecuteReader()
    Console.WriteLine("Contact Name, Contact Title")
    Console.WriteLine("=======================")
    'Read data until reader has data
    While reader.Read()
      Console.Write(reader.GetString(0).ToString() + " ,")
      Console.Write(reader.GetString(1).ToString() + " ,")
      Console.WriteLine("")
    End While
    ' Close reader and connection
    reader.Close()
    conn.Close()
  End Sub
End Module
```

Now compile and run the project. You should see data on the console (see Figure 1-15).

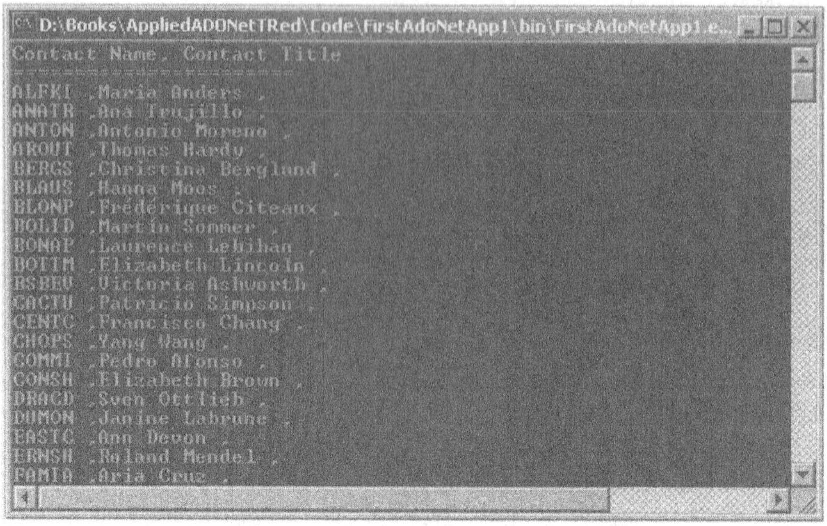

Figure 1-15. Displaying data on the console using DataReader

Using a DataSet to Read Data

You just saw an example of working with an Access 2000 database. For variety, you'll now see an example of using a SQL Server database. Instead of writing a console-based application, this time you'll create a Windows Forms application and use the VS .NET IDE.

In this application, you'll use the SQL Server Northwind database. You'll read data from the Customers table using the same CustomerId, ContactName, and ContactTitle columns you selected in Listing 1-1 and display data in a DataGrid control.

Begin your first ADO.NET application by launching VS .NET and by creating a new project using File ➤ New ➤ Project. Choose Visual Basic Projects and select the Windows Application template from the available templates, name your project DataGridSamp, and click OK.

Clicking the OK button creates a Windows application project. Now you read data from the SQL Server Northwind database and display data in a DataGrid control. This example shows the Customers table data in a DataGrid control.

Drag a DataGrid control from the Toolbox onto the form using Toolbox ➤ Window Forms and then resize it. Also drag a Button control onto the form and assign it a Text property of Fill. Now double-click the button to write a click event handler for the button. Fill data from a database to the DataGrid on the Fill button click event handler.

To access SQL Server, you use the Sql .NET data provider, which is defined in the System.Data.SqlClient namespace. Before adding this namespace class, you need to import the namespace using the Imports statement. Add the following two lines in the beginning of your application:

```
Imports System.Data
Imports System.Data.SqlClient
```

You implement your ADO.NET routine inside this method. To retrieve data from the database, you first need to connect to the database using a Connection object. The DataAdapter is the bridge between the data source (sql) and the DataSet (memory). The DataAdapter is constructed with two elements in this example: a SQL SELECT command to tell the DataAdapter which data to extract into the DataSet and the Connection object to tell the DataAdapter how to connect to the data source. In this example, select the CustomerId, ContactName, and ContactTitle column data from the Customers table. After creating a DataAdapter, the next step is to create and fill data from a DataAdapter to a DataSet, which you do by making a call to the Fill method of DataAdapter. The Fill method takes two parameters: a DataSet and a database table name.

Finally, you'll want to display the data from the Customers table in the DataGrid control. You do this by simply binding the DataSet to the DataGrid through its DefaultViewManager (Chapters 2 and 4 discuss DataViewManager in more detail) by using the DataGrid's DataSource property. You just set the DataSource property of the DataSet's DefaultViewManager.

Listing 1-2 shows the button click event handler. As you can see, this code creates a connection using the localhost server and the Northwind database, and you create a DataAdapter using the Customers table. After that, create a DataSet object and call the DataAdapter's Fill method. After that, bind DataSet.DefaultViewManager to the DataGrid using the DataSource property of the DataGrid.

Listing 1-2. Viewing Data from a SQL Server Database to a DataGrid Control

```
Private Sub Button1_Click(ByVal sender As System.Object, _
ByVal e As System.EventArgs) Handles Button1.Click
    ' Create a Connection Object
    Dim ConnectionString As String
    Dim sql As String

ConnectionString = "Integrated Security=SSPI; Initial Catalog=Northwind; " & _
"Data Source=localhost;"
    Dim myConnection As SqlConnection = New SqlConnection()
    myConnection.ConnectionString = ConnectionString
    sql = "SELECT CustomerID, ContactName, ContactTitle FROM Customers"
    Dim adapter As SqlDataAdapter = New SqlDataAdapter(sql, myConnection)
    ' Construct the DataSet and fill it
    Dim dtSet As DataSet = New DataSet("Customers")
    adapter.Fill(dtSet, "Customers")
    ' Bind the Listbox to the DataSet
    DataGrid1.DataSource = dtSet.DefaultViewManager

End Sub
```

Now compile and run the project. Press the Fill button. The output of the program should look like Figure 1-16.

Figure 1-16. Output of the ADO.NET application in a DataGrid control

CAUTION *Make sure your SQL Server is running and the name of the SQL Server is correct. If you're not using a local server, you need to pass the correct server name, with valid a user ID and password. We discuss using user IDs and passwords in a connection in Chapter 4. If SQL Server isn't running, you will get an exception.*

Summary

This chapter introduced the basics of ADO.NET and its components. You learned why ADO.NET is a much better data access technology than previous technologies. ADO.NET provides data providers such as OleDb, Sql, and Odbc to work with OLE-DB, SQL Server, and ODBC data sources, respectively. After that, you learned about various ADO.NET objects such as Connection, Command, DataAdapter, DataReader, DataSet, and DataView as well as the relationships between them. For example, DataSet is a collection of DataTable objects. A DataTable can attach to a DataView, which can later be bound with data-bound controls. Further, using a DataView's filter and sort properties, you can provide different views of a DataSet and a DataView.

At the end of this chapter, you learned how to write a simple application to read data from Microsoft Access and SQL Server databases using ADO.NET.

Chapter 2 is heavily based on the VS .NET IDE. It covers how to take advantage of VS .NET IDE wizards and utilities to develop database applications without writing much code. You'll probably find this chapter exciting because you'll learn to build fully functioning database applications by simply writing a couple of lines of code.

CHAPTER 2

Data Components in Visual Studio .NET

IN THE PREVIOUS chapter, you saw the basics of the ADO.NET model and its components and how they are connected to each other in the ADO.NET architecture. The
Visual Studio .NET (VS .NET) Integrated Development Environment (IDE) provides design-time support to work with data components. In this chapter, you'll
learn how to use these data components in the VS .NET IDE at design-time to
create database applications. Using ADO.NET components (also referred to as
data components) is similar to using any Windows control. You just drag the component from the Toolbox to a form, set its properties and methods, and you're up
and running.

We start this chapter with the Server Explorer, a useful tool for creating
database applications. We focus on developing database applications quickly
using data components in VS .NET without writing a lot of code. We also provide a
step-by-step tutorial to help you develop and run a project. After that, we discuss
the Connection, DataAdapter, Command, DataSet, and DataView components in more
detail. After finishing this chapter, you'll have a good understanding of data components and how to work with them in VS .NET.

Creating an ADO.NET Project

Begin your project by launching the VS .NET IDE and choosing New ➤ Project
from the Project menu. Choose Visual Basic Projects from Project Types and then
pick the Windows Application template. If you like, type an appropriate name into
the Name field for your first ADO.NET application and click OK. Our project name
is MyFirstADONetApp.

Using the Server Explorer

The Server Explorer is new to VS .NET; it enables you to manage your database servers and connections. You can use the Server Explorer to add a new server or a data connection to your list. The Server Explorer allows you to view, add, edit, and delete data in a tabular grid. The Server Explorer also allows you to create and delete database objects such as tables, stored procedures, views, and triggers.

NOTE *If you've ever used Open Database Connectivity (ODBC) data source names (DSNs) in your applications, then you might be familiar with the traditional Windows ODBC Administration. With ODBC Administration, you created DSNs using ODBC drivers for a data source and then connected your application using this DSN. Now, you'll hardly use ODBC Administration at all because the Server Explorer provides connection management services.*

OK, let's see how to use the Server Explorer. You can open the Server Explorer by clicking the View ➤ Server Explorer menu item.

TIP *The use of the Server Explorer isn't limited to SQL Server databases. You can add any type of database, including MySQL and Access.*

When you open the Server Explorer, you'll see two root nodes: Data Connections and Servers. Initially, the Data Connections node has no items listed under it, but the Servers node displays all the available servers. By expanding the Servers node, you can see all the servers and services running on your machine. The SQL Servers node of the Server Explorer lists all the available SQL Servers running on that machine.

If you don't have any servers listed in your Servers list, you can right-click the Servers node and select the Add Server menu option. This option allows you to add new servers to the list. You can also unregister a server by right-clicking it and selecting the "Unregister Server" menu option.

You can also manage services running on your server. If you expand the Services node, you'll see a list of services running on your system. By right-clicking a service, you can even start and stop a service using the Server Explorer.

To view and managed database objects such as tables, views, or stored procedures, you can simply expand the database server name listed under the Data Connections node. After that you can expand Tables, Views, and Stored Procedures nodes. To view, delete, and update a database table, you right-click the table and use the available options.

Adding a New Connection

Adding a new connection is the next step after adding a server (if you're using a server) to the Server Explorer. You add a new connection to your list by right-clicking the Data Connections node and choosing the Add Connection option. This brings up a Data Link Properties Wizard. By default, the Connection tab is active, but you may want to click the Provider tab. The first tab of this wizard, Provider, displays all the data source providers installed on your machine; this is where you select your database provider. The list could contain any OLE-DB provider, Jet OLE-DB, or other data driver available on your computer.

The second tab of this wizard, Connection, lets you pick your server and corresponding data source. The drop-down list displays all the available servers. Our server is a SQL Server with the default name localhost. After selecting a server, the Database drop-down list displays all the available databases on the server. Select the Northwind database in this example. You can also pick what security mode you want to use for your connection on this tab. You can use the user ID and password of a SQL Server or use the Windows NT Integrated security option. By clicking the Test Connection button, you can make sure your database connection is working. If you've provided an incorrect user ID or password, the test will throw an error.

The third tab, Advanced, is for setting connection timeout and access permissions. You can give this connection read, write, or other permissions using the Advanced tab. The last tab, All, shows you all properties of the connection in a list, such as server name, connection timeout, data source, initial catalog (database name), security, and other network options. You can also edit this data from this tab by just double-clicking a particular property and editing the value of it.

After adding a data connection, you'll see that the wizard adds a node (Servername.DatabaseName.dbo) to the Data Connections root node. If you expand this node, you can see the database objects such as tables, views, stored procedures, and functions.

Managing and Viewing Data

As mentioned earlier, the Server Explorer not only lets you add server and database connections, but it also lets you manage and view data. You can add, update, and delete data from a database. Of course, you must have read and write permissions on the server to read and write data. The Server Explorer also provides options for creating new databases and objects, including tables, views, stored procedures, and so on. You can do this from both root nodes (Data Connections or Servers).

The Server Explorer shows database objects in a tree structure. Each database is a tree node of the server. As you expand the Northwind database node, for example, you can see its children listed as tables, stored procedures, and views.

If you expand this connection by double-clicking it, you'll notice it shows tables, views, and stored procedures. You can further expand these items to see them in more detail.

NOTE *We discuss stored procedures and views in more detail in Chapter 11.*

Besides showing a list of database objects such as tables, views, stored procedures, and functions, the Server Explorer also lets you retrieve, add, edit, and delete data from a data source. You can always double-click to view the data of a table. Alternatively, right-clicking a database object (such as a table) provides you menu options based on the selection. For example, you can right-click and then select the Retrieve Data from Table menu option to retrieve data from that table.

Now, if you retrieve data from the Employees table by double-clicking or using the Retrieve Data from Table option, data will be displayed in an editable grid. You can edit this data at any time—again, assuming you have the correct permissions. For example, to delete a row or a collection of rows, select the rows and hit Delete or right-click the selected rows and then hit the Delete option. The right-click option of the grid also provides you options to move to the grid's first, next, previous, and last records.

Using Visual Data Components

At this time, ADO.NET has three base data providers and multiple add-on data providers to work with various kinds of data sources, including SQL Server, OLE-DB data sources, and ODBC data sources. What do we mean by *base* data providers? Well, initially Microsoft released only three data providers; now, based on additional requirements, Microsoft and third parties are adding new data providers to the library. For example, Microsoft, Oracle, and Core Lab Software Development provide three different data providers for the Oracle database. (We discuss these new data providers in later chapters.) The main class hierarchy model of these data providers remains the same, so programmers will have no problem switching between data providers. Some of these data providers are OleDb, Sql, Odbc, and Oracle. In this chapter, we concentrate on the OleDb and Sql data providers. Later chapters discuss the ODBC, Oracle, and other data providers.

TIP *You can even write your own custom data provider. ADO.NET provides a set of interfaces, which you must implement to write your own data provider. Chapter 13 of this book covers writing custom data providers.*

You can use the data provider components at design-time in VS .NET. The data provider components are available at design-time via the Toolbox. The Toolbox's Data tab shows you the available data controls in VS .NET. Some of the components you may see are `DataSet`, `DataView`, `SqlConnection`, `SqlCommand`, `SqlDataAdapter`, `OleDbConnection`, `OleDbCommand`, `OleDbDataAdapter`, `OdbcCommand`, `OdbcCommandBuilder`, `OdbcConnection`, and `OdbcDataAdapter`. These components are available only when you're in a design view.

TIP *You can open Toolbox by using the View ➤ Toolbox menu item.*

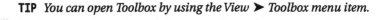

As mentioned briefly in Chapter 1, the .NET Framework Library contains many ADO.NET data providers, including OleDb, Sql, and Odbc. The OleDb data provider wraps up the native OLE-DB COM Application Programming Interface (API) for working with OLE-DB data sources. To access an OLE-DB data source, you need to install an OLE-DB data provider for that database. Sql data providers work with SQL Server 7 or later databases. Odbc data providers wrap up the ODBC API to work with ODBC data sources (with the help of the ODBC Administration and ODBC drivers). Chapter 4 discusses these data providers in more detail. Microsoft and other vendors might introduce more data providers, which you can add to the library later.

In the .NET Framework, each of these data providers has its own namespaces. For instance, the System.Data.OleDb namespace consists of classes belonging to the OleDb data providers. All of these namespace classes start with OleDb. The Microsoft.Data.ODBC and System.Data.SqlClient namespaces consist of classes belonging to the Odbc and Sql data providers, respectively. Similar to OleDb, classes in Odbc start with Odbc, and classes in SqlClient start with Sql.

In VS .NET, some of these classes (or objects) are available from the Toolbox; you can drag them onto a form like any other Windows control in the Toolbox. These controls are called *data components*.

VS .NET also provides a set of data-bound controls. The DataGrid, ListBox, and DataList are good examples of some of these data-bound controls. It's fairly easy to work with these controls. You just set a few properties, and they're ready to display your data. For example, setting a DataGrid control's DataSource property displays data from a DataSet object. We use these data-bound controls in the examples throughout this book. In the next section, we discuss how you can add these components to your Windows Forms applications and set their properties and methods at design-time with the help of the .NET wizards.

Understanding Data Connections

To connect to a data source, the first thing you need to learn about is a *data connection*.

Each data provider has a Connection class, and if you're using the VS .NET IDE, you can see these class objects as components in the Data tab of the Toolbox. For example, the SqlConnection, OdbcConnection, and OleDbConnection class objects represent a connection for the Sql, Odbc, and OleDb data providers, respectively:

- SqlConnection creates and manages SQL Server database connections.

- OdbcConnection creates and manages connections to ODBC data sources.

- OleDbConnection creates and manages connections to OLE-DB data sources.

In the VS .NET IDE, you can create a Connection in many ways. You can use the IDE to add a Connection object to a project, create it programmatically, or use DataAdapters that automatically create a Connection object for you. In this chapter, we concentrate on adding a connection through the VS .NET IDE.

IDE vs. Manual Coding

In some cases, you may not know if you should use the IDE or write code manually. Actually, creating a connection and other objects such as a Command manually is usually much better. Those types of objects only require a few lines of code, and creating them manually allows you to know where the code is and what it means. If you use the VS .NET IDE, it adds a connection and other data components but sometimes also writes lots of code that is difficult to understand. For example, adding a DataAdapter adds a great deal of code that you may not need. If you want to modify it, you'll almost certainly get lost if you don't have a lot of experience.

Now, your next question probably is, "Why do I need to use the IDE at all?"

Well, the IDE may help you if you don't know how to create connection strings and other objects because it writes code for you. Basically, the IDE is useful for part-time ADO.NET developers—those who write non-database-related code but occasionally use ADO.NET. It's also useful for beginners, who want to have their application ready and running in no time. But after completing this book, I bet you'll hate using IDE.

The easiest way to add a connection to a project in VS .NET is to drag a connection component (SqlConnection, OleDbConnection, or OdbcConnection) from the Toolbox's Data tab to a form. After that, you can set the connection's properties using the Properties window. For this demonstration, drop a SqlConnection from the Toolbox onto the form. You can set the SqlConnection properties from the Properties window by right-clicking the SqlConnection and selecting the Properties menu item.

Note that the default connection name is the class name with a unique name appended to it. Because this is the first connection, the name is sqlConnection1.

As you can see in the Properties window, a connection's properties include Database, ConnectionTimeout, DataSource, PacketSize, WorkstationId, Name, and ConnectionString.

NOTE *The connection properties depend on the data provider. Some properties may not be available for some data providers. For example, the* WorkstationId *property is available in Sql data providers but not in OleDb or ODBC data providers.*

Understanding Connection Strings

The ConnectionString property is the main property of a connection. By clicking the drop-down list of the ConnectionString property, you can see all the available data connections. If you don't have a data connection, you can use its New Connection option, which launches the Data Link Properties Wizard. (Refer to the earlier "Using the Server Explorer" section for more information.)

For this example, we use the database server name MCB instead of localhost. The SQLConnection string for server MCB looks like following:

```
data source=MCB;initial catalog=Northwind;integrated security=SSPI;" & _
"persist security info=False;workstation id=MCB;packet size=4096
```

NOTE *In Chapter 4, we discuss a connection and its properties in more detail and show how to set them programmatically. You can also use a user ID and password in a connection string.*

Working with SQL DataAdapters

A DataAdapter is another important component of a data provider. Similar to a connection, each data provider has a corresponding DataAdapter class. All DataAdapters in ADO.NET work in same way, which means if you know how to work with Sql DataAdapters, you can use OleDb, ODBC, and other DataAdapters easily. The SqlDataAdapter, OleDbDataAdapter, and OdbcDataAdaper classes represent DataAdapter components in Sql, OleDb, and Odbc data providers, respectively.

Besides creating a DataAdapter programmatically (see Chapter 4 for more details), VS .NET provides various ways to create DataAdapters. Two common ways are by using the Server Explorer and by using the Data Adapter Configuration Wizard.

Creating DataAdapters with the Server Explorer

It's easy to create a DataAdapter using the Server Explorer. You just drag and drop database objects to a form and the IDE takes care of everything for you. The IDE writes code that you can use programmatically or bind data controls at design-time. To add a new connection to a project, expand your database in the Server Explorer, and drag a table from the Server Explorer to your form. For this example, expand the Northwind database in the Server Explorer and drop the Employees table to the form.

This action adds a SqlConnection and SqlDataAdapter object to the project. You can even drag selected columns or stored procedures onto the form. The VS .NET IDE takes care of the rest. Right-click the form and choose View Code to examine the code generated by the wizard; in this example, you'll see one SqlConnection component and one SqlDataAdapter component along with a set of SqlCommand components:

```
Friend WithEvents SqlSelectCommand1 As System.Data.SqlClient.SqlCommand
  Friend WithEvents SqlInsertCommand1 As System.Data.SqlClient.SqlCommand
  Friend WithEvents SqlUpdateCommand1 As System.Data.SqlClient.SqlCommand
  Friend WithEvents SqlDeleteCommand1 As System.Data.SqlClient.SqlCommand
  Friend WithEvents SqlConnection1 As System.Data.SqlClient.SqlConnection
  Friend WithEvents SqlDataAdapter1 As System.Data.SqlClient.SqlDataAdapter
```

You'll also see that the IDE writes SQL statements and sets the CommandText property of SqlCommand objects. Once you have a DataAdapter, you can use it to populate DataSets and work with its properties. (We discuss DataSet basics and how to construct them manually in Chapter 4.) With the VS .NET IDE, you can even generate DataSets using the visual representation of the DataAdapter. (We discuss how to populate a DataSet using VS .NET IDE wizards in the "Generating Typed DataSets Using a DataAdapter" section of this chapter.)

Creating DataAdapters with the Data Adapter Configuration Wizard

The Data Adapter Configuration Wizard is a powerful tool to develop database applications. To see how you can create DataAdapters using this wizard, you'll create a new Windows Forms–based project in the following step-by-step sections.

In this first project, you'll learn how to create SQL DataAdapters, read data from a SQL Server data source, and display the data from a DataAdapter to a DataGrid control. After completing these steps, you'll see how easy it is to develop database applications using the Data Adapter Configuration Wizard.

Step 1: Selecting a Project Template

To create a new Windows application using VS .NET, select File ➤ New ➤ Project ➤ Visual Basic Projects ➤ Windows Application. Next, select an appropriate directory and type your project name.

Step 2: Adding a DataGrid Control to the Form

Now add a DataGrid control to the form. You do this by just dragging a DataGrid control from the Toolbox's Windows Forms category to the form and resizing it.

Step 3: Adding a DataAdapter Component

Next, drag a SqlDataAdapter control from the Toolbox's Data category to the form. As you drop the SqlDataAdapter the Data Adapter Configuration Wizard pops up. The following sections walk you through this wizard.

Welcome Page

The first page of this wizard is just a welcome screen. Click the Next button to move to the next screen.

Choose Your Data Connection Page

The second page of the wizard lets you create a new connection or pick from a list of available connections on your machine. All available connections are listed in the drop-down list. If you don't have any connections listed in the list, you can click the New Connection button, which launches the Data Link Properties Wizard (discussed previously in the "Adding a New Connection" section).

Choose a Query Type

The next page of the wizard is for selecting a SQL query type. If you see this page, three options are available for the SQL Server connection:

- The Use SQL Statement option allows you to create a new SQL query.

- The Create New Stored Procedure option allows you to create a new stored procedure.

- The Use Existing Stored Procedure option allows you to select a stored procedure from the existing stored procedures.

NOTE *The last two options aren't available for databases that don't support stored procedures.*

Generate the SQL Statement

The next page of the Data Adapter Configuration Wizard lets you build a SQL statement or a stored procedure. You can type a SQL statement directly into the text box, or you can click the Query Builder button to use the Query Builder to build your SQL statement.

Query Builder

The Query Builder option lets you pick tables from your data source. First, select the Employees table to read in the Employee data. You actually have the option of selecting as many as tables you want, but for now select only one table and click the Add button. After clicking the Add button, the Query Builder provides you with an option to select columns of the table. You can check *(All Columns) to select all the columns of a table, or you can check only the columns you want to participate in the SQL statement.

If you've ever used the New Query Wizard in Microsoft Access, you'll find that the Query Builder is similar to it. In Access, you can create queries by dragging tables and their columns to the grid (or checking the columns), and the Query Builder builds a SQL query for your action.

In this sample, select EmployeeID, FirstName, and LastName from the Employees table to build your SQL statements. The SQL statement after selecting these three columns looks like this:

```
SELECT EmployeeID, LastName, FirstName FROM Employees
```

You can even type this SQL statement directly into the text box.

NOTE *You can even write your own SQL statement if you don't want to use the Query Builder. For performance reasons, if you only want few columns, then use column names instead of using SELECT * statements.*

One more button is available on this page: Advanced Options. By clicking the Advanced Options button, you launch the Advanced SQL Generation Options page. On this page, there are three options: Generate Insert, Update, and Delete Statements; Use Optimistic Concurrency; and Refresh the DataSet. By default all three options are checked. If you don't want to generate INSERT, UPDATE, or DELETE SQL statements, you should uncheck the first check box.

By default, ADO.NET uses optimistic concurrency. If you don't want your program to implement optimistic concurrency, you should uncheck the second check box.

View Wizard Results

The View Wizard Results page shows you the action being taken by the wizard. If everything went well, the wizard generates a message saying, "The data adapter... was configured successfully." For this example, the Details section shows that the wizard has generated SQL SELECT, INSERT, UPDATE, and DELETE statements and mappings.

Now you can click the Finish button to complete the process.

Currently, if you examine the design surface at the bottom of the Form window, you'll see two components: sqlConnection1 and sqlDataAdapter1. The wizard sets the properties of these components for you. Now you can use the DataAdapter to populate your DataSets. Don't forget to resize the DataGrid you added to the project.

Step 4: Setting and Reviewing DataAdapter Properties

Now that you have a DataAdapter on your form, let's look at the SqlDataAdapter component properties. You can see its properties by right-clicking the adapter and selecting the Properties menu item. The wizard also shows the available command properties, including InsertCommand, DeleteCommand, SelectCommand, and UpdateCommand.

You can set DataAdapter properties by clicking these properties. . A DataAdapter has four SqlCommand properties—SelectCommand, DeleteCommand, InsertCommand, and UpdateCommand—that all execute SQL commands on the data source. For example, if you look at the SelectCommand property, you'll see the SQL SELECT statement.

NOTE *Chapter 4 covers* SelectCommand, InsertCommand, UpdateCommand, *and* DeleteCommand *in more detail.*

From the Properties window, you can also set CommandText, CommandType, Connection, and other properties. If you double-click CommandText, it pops up the Query Builder where you can rebuild your query.

The TableMapping class represents a mapping of DataColumns in the data source to DataColumns in the DataSet. We discuss DataTables and table mappings in more detail in Chapters 3 and 4. If you click the TableMappings property (which is a collection of TableMapping objects), it brings up the Table Mappings dialog box.

....

Question and Answer

Question: Why do I need table mappings? I've also heard of column mapping. What is it?

Answer: Sometimes, you won't want to display your actual table names and their columns as defined in a database. For instance, say you have a MyTable table with two fields, a0 and a1. The table stores a customer's information, and the fields a0 and a1 store customer names and addresses. If you display your table in data components such as a DataGrid, it will display the table name as MyTable and the column names as a0 and a1, which makes no sense to user.

Using table mappings, you can change the table name to Customers Table. Using column mapping, you can change the columns' names to Customer Name and Customer Address. After this mapping, DataGrid will display the table name as Customers Table and the columns as Customer Name and Customer Address, which make more sense to a user. We discuss table and column mappings in Chapter 3 in more detail.

....

If you click the TableMappings property, it opens the Table Mappings dialog box. The Table Mappings dialog box has two columns: Source Table and Dataset Table (see Figure 2-1). If you have more than one table in a DataAdapter, you'll see all the tables listed in the Source Table list box. By default the source table Table is listed in the list box. The Source Table column is a list of actual columns, and the Dataset Table column is a list of the column names used in the DataSet. By default, DataSet columns names are the same as the source table. This is useful when you want to use different names in a program. You can change DataSet columns by editing the column itself. Of course, you can't change source columns, but you can reorder them by using the Column Mappings drop-down list.

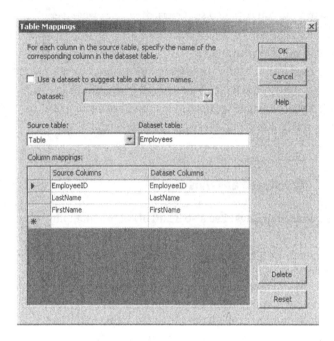

Figure 2-1. Table Mappings dialog box

By using this dialog box, you can even delete columns from your mapping using the Delete button.

Step 5: Reviewing Other Options

If you look closely at the DataAdapter's Properties window, you'll see three links: Configure Data Adapter, Generate Dataset, and Preview Data.

The Configure Data Adapter option calls the Data Adapter Configuration Wizard, discussed earlier in this chapter. If you want to reset the wizard to change your options, you can use this link.

The Generate Dataset option lets you generate a DataSet for this DataAdapter. The Generate DataSet option provides you with options that allow you to select whether you want to use an existing DataSet or create a new DataSet. The Existing option is available only when a typed DataSet is available in your project.

Create a new DataSet with the default name DataSet1. (You can change the DataSet name if you want.) Clicking the OK button adds a typed DataSet (DataSet1.xsd) to the project.

Question and Answer

Question: What's a typed `DataSet`? Are there other types of `DataSets`?

Answer: There are two types of `DataSets`: typed and untyped. A typed `DataSet` is represented by an Extensible Markup Language (XML) schema. See the "Typed and Untyped DataSets" section of Chapter 3 for more information.

Actually, the Generate DataSet option adds a class `DataSet1` to your project, which is inherited from `DataSet`. If you go to the Class View, you can see the `DataSet1` class and its members.

The Preview Data option enables you to view the `DataSet` schema. You can even preview the data in the `DataSet` by pressing the Fill button, which opens the Data Adapter Preview dialog box (see Figure 2-2).

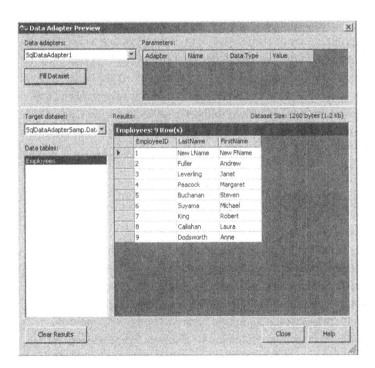

Figure 2-2. Previewing data for the `DataAdapter`

The Fill Dataset button in Figure 2-2 fills data into a grid based upon the current state of the SelectCommand in the DataAdapter. The Parameters grid displays available parameters if a DataAdapter has any. The Clear Results button clears the records.

Step 6: Reviewing the Source Code

Now it's time to examine the code and see what the wizard has done for you automatically. You can see the source code by right-clicking the form and selecting the View Source option.

NOTE *You should take the time to look at the code so you know what goes under the hood when you use the IDE to write your code. It'll help you in the long run.*

All source code generated by the Windows form designer is defined in the InitializeComponent method of the file. Right-click your form and choose View Code. Upon examining the source code, you'll see where the wizard has added two components, sqlConnection1 and sqlDataAdapter1, to your source file as well as four SqlCommand components. Scroll down to the Windows Designer Generated Code option and expand it. This reveals the contents of the InitializeComponent routine (see Listing 2-1).

Listing 2-1. Added Sql Server Provider Components

```
Friend WithEvents DataGrid1 As System.Windows.Forms.DataGrid
  Friend WithEvents SqlDataAdapter1 As System.Data.SqlClient.SqlDataAdapter
  Friend WithEvents SqlSelectCommand1 As System.Data.SqlClient.SqlCommand
  Friend WithEvents SqlInsertCommand1 As System.Data.SqlClient.SqlCommand
  Friend WithEvents SqlUpdateCommand1 As System.Data.SqlClient.SqlCommand
  Friend WithEvents SqlDeleteCommand1 As System.Data.SqlClient.SqlCommand
  Friend WithEvents SqlConnection1 As System.Data.SqlClient.SqlConnection
  Friend WithEvents DataSet11 As MyFirstADONetApp.DataSet1
  <System.Diagnostics.DebuggerStepThrough()> Private Sub InitializeComponent()
    Me.DataGrid1 = New System.Windows.Forms.DataGrid()
    Me.SqlDataAdapter1 = New System.Data.SqlClient.SqlDataAdapter()
    Me.SqlSelectCommand1 = New System.Data.SqlClient.SqlCommand()
    Me.SqlInsertCommand1 = New System.Data.SqlClient.SqlCommand()
    Me.SqlUpdateCommand1 = New System.Data.SqlClient.SqlCommand()
```

```
Me.SqlDeleteCommand1 = New System.Data.SqlClient.SqlCommand()
Me.SqlConnection1 = New System.Data.SqlClient.SqlConnection()
```

Search for the ConnectionString by hitting Ctrl+F to bring up VS .NET's Find dialog box. If you examine the InitializeComponent() method, you'll see that the wizard sets SqlConnection's ConnectionString property to the following:

```
Me.SqlConnection1.ConnectionString = _
"data source=localhost;initial catalog=Northwind;" & _
"integrated security=SSPI;persist " & _
"security info=False;workstation id=MCB;packet size=4096"
```

It also sets the CommandText property of the SqlCommand with the corresponding SELECT, INSERT, UPDATE, and DELETE SQL statements. The Connection property of SqlCommand is set to SqlConnection:

```
Me.SqlSelectCommand1.CommandText = "SELECT EmployeeID, LastName, " & _
    "FirstName FROM Employees"
    Me.SqlSelectCommand1.Connection = Me.SqlConnection1
```

If you examine Listing 2-2, you'll see that DataAdapter is connected to a Connection through data commands, and the TableMapping property is responsible for mapping tables and their columns. Note that the table mappings between DataSet columns and DataSource columns generated by the wizard have exactly the same column names.

Listing 2-2. DataAdapter *Connection through* TableMapping

```
Me.SqlDataAdapter1.DeleteCommand = Me.SqlDeleteCommand1
    Me.SqlDataAdapter1.InsertCommand = Me.SqlInsertCommand1
    Me.SqlDataAdapter1.SelectCommand = Me.SqlSelectCommand1
    Me.SqlDataAdapter1.TableMappings.AddRange( _
    New System.Data.Common.DataTableMapping() { _
    New System.Data.Common.DataTableMapping("Table", "Employees", _
    New System.Data.Common.DataColumnMapping() { _
    New System.Data.Common.DataColumnMapping("EmployeeID", "EmployeeID"), _
    New System.Data.Common.DataColumnMapping("LastName", "LastName"), _
    New System.Data.Common.DataColumnMapping("FirstName", "FirstName")})})
    Me.SqlDataAdapter1.UpdateCommand = Me.SqlUpdateCommand1
```

It looks like the wizard did a lot of the work for you!

Step 7: Filling the DataGrid Control with Data

Until now, you haven't had to write a single line of code. Now, though, you'll add few lines of code and then you'll be all set to see the data from your data source. Now you have two options. First, you can use the typed DataSet to read the data, and second, you can create a DataSet object programmatically and fill it using the SqlDataAdapter's Fill method.

You'll create a DataSet object programmatically and use it to fill data in a DataGrid. Add the code in Listing 2-3 to the form load event handler. As you can see, this code creates a DataSet object and fills it by calling SqlDataAdapter's Fill method. The Fill method of SqlDataAdapter fills data from a DataAdapter to the DataSet. You call the Fill method in the FillDBGrid method. Once you have a DataSet containing data, you can do anything with it, including creating views for that data. In this example, you set a DataGrid control's DataSource property to the DataSet.DefaultViewManager, which binds the DataSet object to the DataGrid control.

Listing 2-3. Form's Load Event Handler

```
Private Sub Form1_Load(ByVal sender As System.Object, _
  ByVal e As System.EventArgs) Handles MyBase.Load
    Dim ds As DataSet = New DataSet()
    SqlDataAdapter1.Fill(ds)
    DataGrid1.DataSource = ds.DefaultViewManager
  End Sub
```

Another option is to use the typed DataSet you generated using the Generate DataSet option. The wizard added an instance of DataSet1 called DataSet11 to the project. Now just call the Fill method of DataAdapter and bind the DataSet's default view to the DataGrid. Just write the following two lines on the form load event handler:

```
SqlDataAdapter1.Fill(DataSet11)
DataGrid1.DataSource = DataSet11.DefaultViewManager
```

Finally, build and run the project using either of the two methods. The result looks like Figure 2-3. Easy, huh?

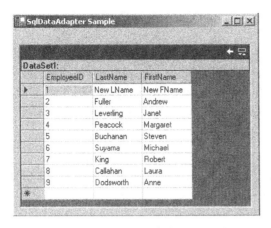

Figure 2-3. Output of the Employee data to a DataGrid *control*

Using DataSet and DataView Components

After discussing DataAdapters and data connections, you should have a pretty good idea of how to take advantage of the VS .NET design-time support to develop data-bound Windows Form database applications.

The DataSet and DataView components are two powerful and easy-to-use components of the ADO.NET model. In this section, you'll learn how to utilize DataSet and DataView components at design-time. In Chapter 4, we discuss their properties and methods in more detail and show how to use them programmatically. The DataSet and DataView components fall into the *disconnected* components category, which means you can use these components with or without data providers. We discuss disconnected data components in Chapter 3.

Understanding Typed DataSets in VS .NET

There are two types of DataSets: typed and untyped. As discussed in Chapter 1 (and in more detail in Chapter 4), a *typed* DataSet has an XML schema attached to it. The XML schema defines members for a DataSet corresponding to database table columns, and you can access data through these columns. *Untyped datasets* are ones that are created at runtime and don't have a schema attached to them. In the following section, we show you how you can generate typed datasets using a VS .NET wizard.

Generating Typed DataSets Using a DataAdapter

As you saw earlier, you can generate typed datasets by using the Generate Dataset option from a DataAdapter's Properties dialog box. And as mentioned earlier, the Generate DataSet option adds an XML schema to the project and also adds a class to the project inherited from the DataSet class. The designer looks like Figure 2-4.

Figure 2-4. A DataSet's *Properties window showing a typed* DataSet

Again, you can see a typed DataSet's properties by right-clicking the DataSet and using the Properties menu option.

Every DataSet generated by the IDE creates an XML schema for the DataSet. If you look at the bottom of the Properties window of a DataSet, you'll see two links: View Schema and DataSet Properties. The View Schema option lets you view the DataSet schema, and the DataSet Properties hyperlink lets you set the DataSet properties. By following these links you can also set the DataSet's column names and other properties.

Now you can use this DataSet as discussed earlier.

Adding a Typed DataSet

In the previous discussion, you saw how you can generate DataSet objects from a DataAdapter. There are also other ways to create a typed DataSet object.

You can click the Project menu and choose Add New Item. This brings up the Add New Item window where you'll find the DataSet template (see Figure 2-5). The default name of the DataSet template is DataSet1.xsd, but you can change it by entering something in the Name text box.

After adding the DataSet, the designer creates an XSD (XML Schema) file and adds it your project area. By default the schema is empty the first time you add a DataSet schema using the Add New Item. You can see the contents of a DataSet schema by double-clicking DataSet1.xsd in the Solution Explorer. As you can see from Figure 2-6, the designer has two options: the Server Explorer and the Toolbox. If you click the Server Explorer link, it launches the Server Explorer. The XML designer has its own Toolbox, which contains various XML schema items.

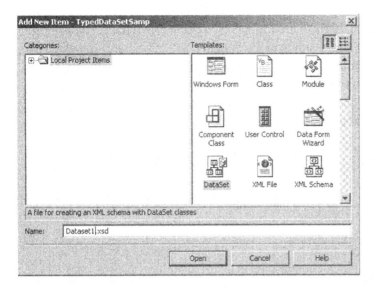

Figure 2-5. Creating a typed DataSet *from the Add New Item window*

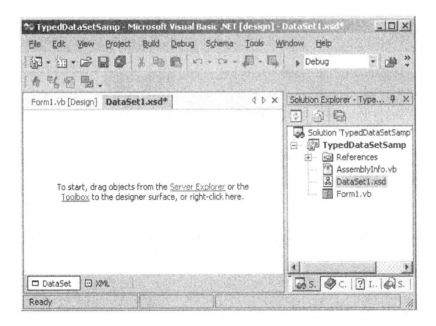

Figure 2-6. Empty Dataset1.xsd *in the VS .NET IDE*

The next step is to fill this XML schema with data and connect to a database. The easiest way to do this is to use the Server Explorer. Open the Server Explorer by clicking the Sever Explorer link in the designer. You can expand any database and simply drop a database object such as a table, a view, or a stored procedure on the designer from the Server Explorer. You can even drop multiple database objects. To keep it simple, drop only one table, the Employees table from the SQL Server Northwind database.

Dragging the Employees table to the designer adds one XML schema (see Figure 2-7).

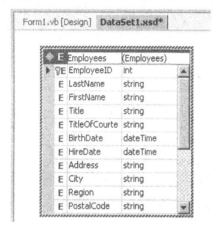

Figure 2-7. Design view of the DataSet*'s XML schema*

It also automatically adds the typed DataSet class that inherits from DataSet. If you go to the Class View, you can see the DataSet1 class. If you expand this class, you'll notice this class is derived from the DataSet class. You can explore the code added by the designer. However, you'll never use these class members directly.

Once you have a typed DataSet, you can bind it to any data-bound control (as discussed earlier in this chapter).

Understanding the DataView

A DataView represents a view of a DataSet object.

Question and Answer

Question: Why do I need a DataView when I can use a DataSet's
DefaultViewManager?

Answer: Actually, the DefaultViewManager provides a view of all the available
tables in a DataSet. What if you want to display only one table? Or what if you
want to filter or sort data?

A DataView provides you with Filter and Sort properties; by using them you
can filter and sort the data. There are many occasions when you don't want all
data from a table. You can apply a filter criteria on a DataView and bind the DataView
to the data-bound controls. You can also separate multiple tables of a DataSet by
associating each table with a DataView1. For example, you can create a DataSet with
three tables and create three different DataView objects for each table. Once you
have a DataView object, you can attach it with any data-bound control, such as a
DataGrid or a ComboBox control using the data-bound control's DataSource property.
Or you can filter only records based on a date or an ID.

NOTE *In this chapter, we concentrate on the VS .NET part of* DataView. *We
discuss the* DataView *class and its members in more detail in Chapter 4.*

Creating and attaching a DataView with a data source is simple in the designer.
In this sample, you'll create and attach a DataView with a DataSet. Before creating a
DataView, though, you need to have a DataSet.

First, you create a DataAdapter by simply dragging a database table from the
Server Explorer to the form. This action adds a Connection and a DataAdapter to the
application and makes them available at design-time. Second, you generate a
DataSet from a DataAdapter by selecting the Generate Dataset menu option
available after right-clicking the DataAdapter.

Now you need to add a DataView. You simply drag a DataView by dragging
the DataView control from Toolbox ➤ Data onto your form. This action adds a
DataView1 to the project.

Next, attach DataView1 to the DataSet. You can do that by simply setting the
Table property of the DataView. The Table property of DataView1 lists the DataSet and
DataSet tables. In this case, select DataSet11.Employees as the Table property of
DataView1 (see Figure 2-8).

Figure 2-8. DataView *Properties window*

This is where the DataView is useful. The DataView has two properties: Sort
and RowFilter. The Sort property takes an expression with the name of the column
followed by the sort order. For example, if you want to sort data based on the
FirstName column in ascending order, you set the FirstName ASC string as the Sort
property of DataView.

The RowFilter property filters the data of a DataView. This property works as a
WHERE clause of the SELECT statement. The RowFilter property takes an expression
with the column name and the criteria. For example, if you want to retrieve
records where the country is USA, you simply set "Country='USA'" as the filter.
As you can see in Figure 2-8, we set the RowFilter and Sort properties.

NOTE *To sort in descending order, use* DESC *instead of* ASC.

Once you have a DataView, you can bind it to a data-bound control such as a DataGrid by setting data-bound control's DataSource property. To test this, you can drop a DataGrid control onto the form and set DataGrid's DataSource property as DataView1. You can simply set that from the Properties window of DataGrid.

Now if you compile and run your project, you'll only see USA records sorted on the FirstName column (see Figure 2-9).

	EmployeeID	LastName	FirstName	Title	TitleOfCourte	BirthDate
▶	2	Fuller	Andrew	Vice Presiden	Dr.	2/19/195:
	3	Leverling	Janet	Sales Repres	Ms.	8/30/196:
	8	Callahan	Laura	Inside Sales	Ms.	1/9/1958
	4	Peacock	Margaret	Sales Repres	Mrs.	9/19/193:
	1	New LName	New FName	Sales Repres	Ms.	12/8/194!
*						

Figure 2-9. Sorted and filtered data in a DataGrid

Using the Data Form Wizard

The Data Form Wizard is one most useful tools for developing database applications. You can use the Data Form Wizard to develop your database application with viewing, updating, and deleting capabilities. This is probably the fastest way to develop database applications in .NET (unless you're an extremely fast typist!).

In the following sections, you'll use the Data Form Wizard to write a fully functional database application including features such as inserting, updating, and deleting data without writing a single line of code. In this simple example, you'll use the familiar Northwind database, and you'll use both the Customers and Orders tables to build a data relationship between table data.

First, you'll create a Windows application. Second, you'll add a Data Form Wizard to it and then call the Data Form Wizard from the main application. Like many parts of this book, this topic is in the form of tutorial. Just follow the simple steps, and in a few minutes you'll be able to run the application.

Step 1: Selecting a Project Template

Create a new Windows project by selecting File ➤ New Project ➤ Visual Basic Projects ➤ Windows Application and typing **MyDataFormWizardSamp** as your application name.

Step 2: Adding a Data Form Wizard Item

Now add a Data Form Wizard by selecting Project ➤ Add New Item ➤ Data Form Wizard from the available templates. You can type **DataForm1.vb** as the name of your DataForm class in the Name field of the dialog box (see Figure 2-10). (If you're using C# language, the filename would be DataForm1.cs.)

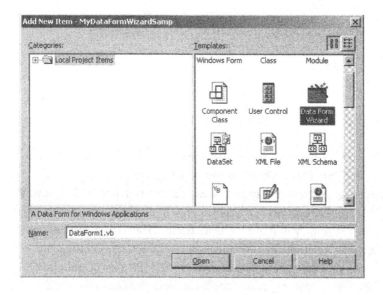

Figure 2-10. Adding a Data Form Wizard

Now click Open, which calls the Data Form Wizard.

Step 3: Walking through the Data Form Wizard

The first page of the wizard is a welcome page telling you what the wizard is about to do.

Step 4: Choosing the DataSet You Want

On the second page of the wizard, you can choose a DataSet name that will later be used to access the data. You can either create a new DataSet name or select an existing one. If there's no DataSet available in the project, the Use the Following Dataset Named option is disabled. For this test, type **MyDS** as the DataSet name in the Create a New Dataset Named option and move to the next page by clicking the Next button.

Step 5: Choosing a Data Connection

The next page of the wizard asks you to provide a connection. The combo box displays your available connections. If you didn't create a connection, use the New Connection button, which launches the Server Explorer discussed earlier in this chapter. You'll select the usual database, Northwind. If you followed the Server Explorer discussion in the beginning of this chapter, you should have a Northwind connection in the list. If you don't have any connection listed in this list, create a new connection using the Northwind SQL Server database.

Step 6: Choosing Tables or Views

The next page of the wizard lets you pick the tables and views you want to connect to the DataSet. As you can see in Figure 2-11, we selected the Customers and Orders tables in the Available Items list on this page and use the > button to add these tables to the Selected Items list.

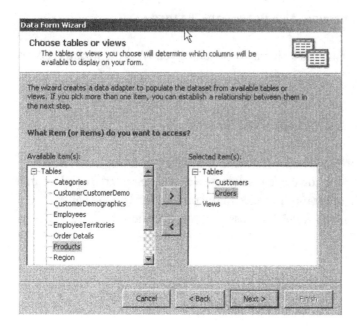

Figure 2-11. Choosing tables and views

Now you're ready to create a relationship between these two tables.

Step 7: Creating a Relationship between Tables

The next page of the wizard lets you define a relationship between the Customers and Orders tables. It's useful to provide a relationship between tables when you have a master-detail relationship in the database. In other words, a customer may have many orders associated with it, so there's a relationship through the CustomerID in the Orders table joined to information about the customer in the Customers table. Now, say you want to see all the orders of a customer based on the CustomerID. If you do this manually, you need to write code to select data from the Orders table to correspond to a CustomerID and then fill data to the form. If you use the Data Form Wizard instead, it does everything for you. Cool, huh?

This is the same step you're going to see on the Create a Relationship between Tables page of the wizard. You're going to create a relationship between the Customers and Orders tables based on the CustomerID. Name the relationship between the Customers and Orders table `CustOrderRelation`. You also need to pick the associated primary key and foreign key that links the parent to the child table. Once you've chosen the joining key (CustomerID), you have to press the > button to tell the wizard that you want to add it.

When you run the final program, you'll see how you can filter all orders for a customer based on the CustomerID. As you can see from Figure 2-12, you need to pick one table as parent and another table as a child based on the relationship between them. In this example, the Customers table is the parent table, and the Orders table is the child table.

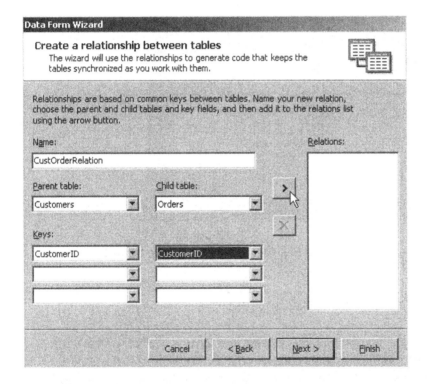

Figure 2-12. Selecting Customers as the parent and Orders as the child table to create the CustOrderRelation *relationship*

Step 8: Choosing Tables and Columns to Display on the Form

The next page of the wizard lets you select which tables and columns you want to show on the form. For this example, select all the columns from both of the tables (this is the default selection). As you can see in Figure 2-13, the Customers table is the master, and the Orders table is the detail table. On this page, you can select whatever column you want to display on the form.

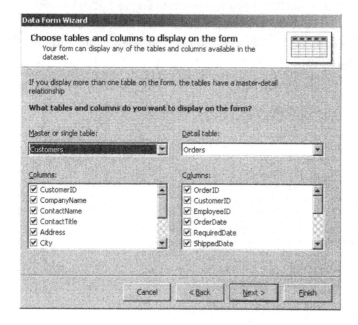

Figure 2-13. Choosing columns to display on the Data Form Wizard

Step 9: Choosing the Display Style

This page is an important part of creating your form. Actually, the Data Form Wizard adds a Form with some controls on it and writes code to fill, update, delete, and navigate data. There are two ways to view the data, and you choose your option on this page. These two options are as follows:

- All Records in a Grid

- Single Record in Individual Controls

Figure 2-14 displays these options.

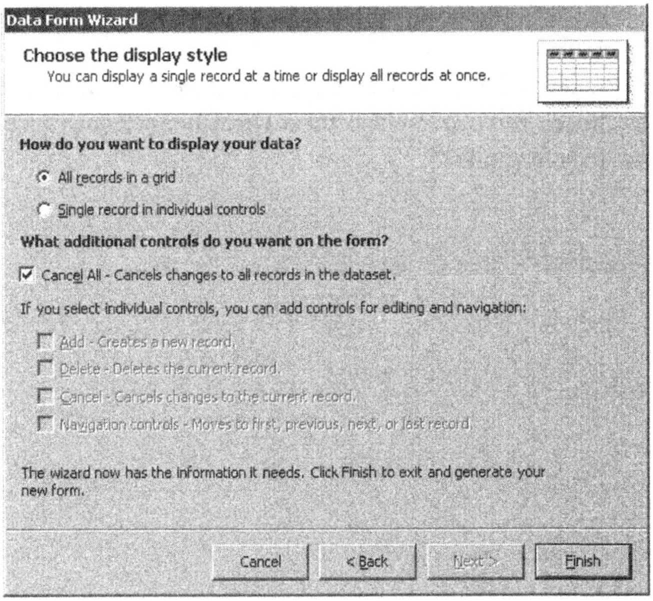

Figure 2-14. Choosing between a grid and individual controls on the Data Form Wizard

The output of All Records in a Grid looks like Figure 2-15. After that you can resize or move the controls on the form.

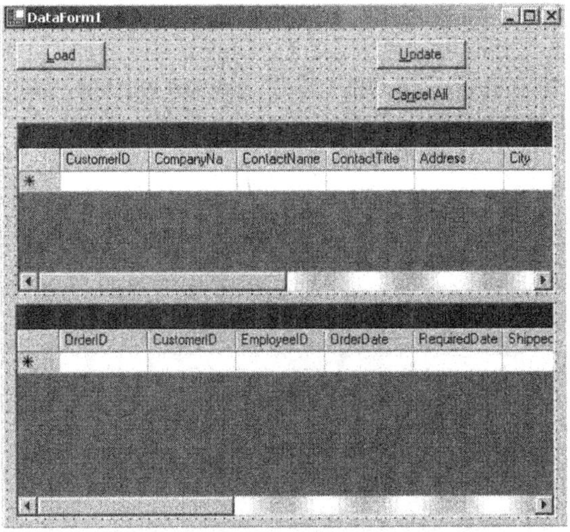

Figure 2-15. Grid DataForm *output*

The second option, Single Record in Individual Controls, shows data in text boxes and provides you with navigation controls. As you can see from Figure 2-16, the Single Record in Individual Controls option activates Add, Delete, Cancel, and Navigation Controls check boxes. You can uncheck these check boxes if you don't want to add those features to your project.

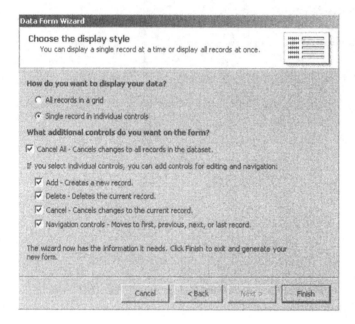

Figure 2-16. The Single Record in Individual Controls option

The form generated by this option looks like Figure 2-17. As you can see, each column of the table has a field on the form.

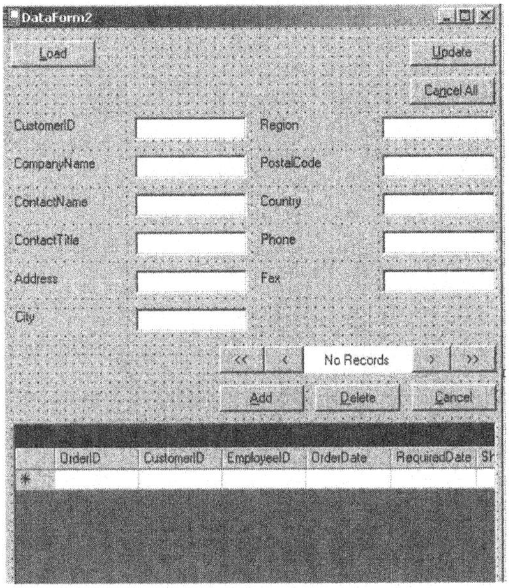

Figure 2-17. Data Form Wizard–generated form for the Single Record in Individual Controls option

After selecting the data display style, click the Finish button. The Data Form Wizard adds the Windows form DataForm1 and the class DataForm1.vb corresponding to it.

Step 10: Calling the Data Form Wizard Form from the Application

Now you need to change one more thing. You need to call the DataForm1 form. Generally, you call a DataForm from a menu or a button click event handler. Say you've added two DataForm objects, DataForm1 and DataForm2, using both the options. The code in Listing 2-4 calls DataForm1.

Listing 2-4. Calling DataForm1 *from a Button Click*

```
Private Sub Button1_Click(ByVal sender As System.Object, _
   ByVal e As System.EventArgs) Handles Button1.Click
     Dim dfw1 As DataForm1 = New DataForm1()
     dfw1.Show()
   End Sub
```

Listing 2-5 calls DataForm2 from a button click handler.

Listing 2-5. Calling DataForm2 *from a Button Click*

```
Private Sub Button2_Click(ByVal sender As System.Object, _
  ByVal e As System.EventArgs) Handles Button2.Click
    Dim dfw2 As DataForm2 = New DataForm2()
    dfw2.Show()
  End Sub
```

NOTE *If you have modified the name of your Data Form Wizard–generated form, you need to call that form instead of* DataForm1 *and* DataForm2.

Step 11: Viewing the Output

When you run any of the modes (DataGrid mode or individual column mode), you'll see Load and Update buttons. The Load and Update buttons load and update the data, respectively, and Cancel All cancels all the operations. The neat thing is if you move into the top grid, corresponding information changes in the bottom grid.

After compiling and running your application, you'll notice that without writing a single line of code, you just created a fully functional database application.

The Load button on the individual control form loads the data, and the Add, Update, and Delete buttons on the form inserts, updates, and deletes records, respectively.

Data Form Wizard: Looking under the Hood

You just saw how you can develop fully functional database applications with the help of the Data Form Wizard. Now let's see what the wizard does for you in the actual code. (The inherent beauty of the VS .NET IDE is that it magically hides all the messy code for you.) The wizard adds two items to your project: MyDS.xsd and DataForm1.vb.

Understanding MyDS.xsd

MyDS.xsd is an XML schema for the DataSet you've added to the project. (It's similar to the one discussed in the "Understanding Typed DataSets in VS .NET" section of this chapter.)

Understanding DataForm1.vb

The second item added by wizard is the DataForm1 class, a class derived from System.Windows.Forms.Form. The DataForm1 class defines the class's entire functionality:

```
Public Class DataForm1
    Inherits System.Windows.Forms.Form
```

The btnUpdate_Click and btnLoad_Click methods are the event handlers for the Update and Load buttons, respectively. As you can see from Listing 2-6, the btnLoad_Click method calls LoadDataSet, and the btnUpdate_Click method calls the UpdateDataSet method.

Listing 2-6. The Load and Update Button Click Event Handlers

```
Private Sub btnUpdate_Click(ByVal sender As System.Object, _
  ByVal e As System.EventArgs) Handles btnUpdate.Click
    Try
      'Attempt to update the datasource.
      Me.UpdateDataSet()
    Catch eUpdate As System.Exception
      'Add your error handling code here.
      'Display error message, if any.
      System.Windows.Forms.MessageBox.Show(eUpdate.Message)
    End Try

  End Sub
  Private Sub btnLoad_Click(ByVal sender As System.Object, _
  ByVal e As System.EventArgs) Handles btnLoad.Click
    Try
      'Attempt to load the dataset.
      Me.LoadDataSet()
    Catch eLoad As System.Exception
      'Add your error handling code here.
      'Display error message, if any.
      System.Windows.Forms.MessageBox.Show(eLoad.Message)
End Try
```

The `LoadDataSet` method loads the data from the data source into the controls by calling `FillDataSet` (see Listing 2-7). As you can see from the code, it assigns the MyDS `DataSet` generated by the Data Form Wizard as a temporary `DataSet` and fills it using the `FillDataSet` method.

Listing 2-7. `LoadDataSet` Method Generated by the Data Form Wizard

```
Public Sub LoadDataSet()
    'Create a new dataset to hold the records returned
    'A temporary dataset is used because filling the existing dataset would
    'require the databindings to be rebound.
    Dim objDataSetTemp As MyDataFormWizardSamp.MyDS
    objDataSetTemp = New MyDataFormWizardSamp.MyDS()
    Try
        'Attempt to fill the temporary dataset.
        Me.FillDataSet(objDataSetTemp)
    Catch eFillDataSet As System.Exception
        'Add your error handling code here.
        Throw eFillDataSet
    End Try
    Try
        'Empty the old records from the dataset.
        objMyDS.Clear()
        'Merge the records into the main dataset.
        objMyDS.Merge(objDataSetTemp)
    Catch eLoadMerge As System.Exception
        'Add your error handling code here.
        Throw eLoadMerge
    End Try
End Sub
```

The `FillDataSet` fills the `DataSet` from the `DataAdapter` by calling the `Fill` method on each `DataAdapter`. Note that with the Data Form Wizard, a `DataAdapter` is created for each table—one `DataAdapter` for the Customers table and one `DataAdapter` for the Orders table. Both `DataAdapters` fill the same `DataSet`. Listing 2-8 shows the `FillDataSet` method.

NOTE *One thing you may notice is that the Data Form Wizard uses the OleDb provider to write the Data Form Wizard code.*

Listing 2-8. The FillDataSet *Method Generated by the Data Form Wizard*

```
Public Sub FillDataSet(ByVal dataSet As MyDataFormWizardSamp.MyDS)
    'Turn off constraint checking before the dataset is filled.
    'This allows the adapters to fill the dataset without concern
    'for dependencies between the tables.
    dataSet.EnforceConstraints = False
    Try
       'Open the connection.
       Me.OleDbConnection1.Open()
       'Attempt to fill the dataset through the OleDbDataAdapter1.
       Me.OleDbDataAdapter1.Fill(dataSet)
       Me.OleDbDataAdapter2.Fill(dataSet)
    Catch fillException As System.Exception
       'Add your error handling code here.
       Throw fillException
    Finally
       'Turn constraint checking back on.
       dataSet.EnforceConstraints = True
       'Close the connection whether or not the exception was thrown.
       Me.OleDbConnection1.Close()
    End Try

End Sub
```

The UpdateDataSource method updates the data source from the DataSet. This method is called by the UpdateDataSet method and utilizes the Update command of the DataAdapters. Listing 2-9 shows the UpdateDataSource method.

Listing 2-9. The UpdateDataSource *and* UpdateDataSet *Methods Generated by the Data Form Wizard*

```
    Public Sub UpdateDataSet()
'Create a new dataset to hold the changes that have been made to the main dataset.
    Dim objDataSetChanges As MyDataFormWizardSamp.MyDS = _
    New MyDataFormWizardSamp.MyDS()
    'Stop any current edits.
    Me.BindingContext(objMyDS, "Customers").EndCurrentEdit()
    Me.BindingContext(objMyDS, "Orders").EndCurrentEdit()
    'Get the changes that have been made to the main dataset.
    objDataSetChanges = CType(objMyDS.GetChanges, MyDataFormWizardSamp.MyDS)
    'Check to see if any changes have been made.
    If (Not (objDataSetChanges) Is Nothing) Then
      Try
        'There are changes that need to be made, so attempt to update"
        'calling the update method and passing the dataset and any parameters.
        Me.UpdateDataSource(objDataSetChanges)
        objMyDS.Merge(objDataSetChanges)
        objMyDS.AcceptChanges()
      Catch eUpdate As System.Exception
        'Add your error handling code here.
        Throw eUpdate
      End Try
      'Add your code to check the returned dataset for any errors"
      'pushed into the row object's error.
    End If
  End Sub


  Public Sub UpdateDataSource(ByVal ChangedRows As MyDataFormWizardSamp.MyDS)
    Try
      'The data source only needs to be updated if there are changes pending.
      If (Not (ChangedRows) Is Nothing) Then
        'Open the connection.
        Me.OleDbConnection1.Open()
        'Attempt to update the data source.
        OleDbDataAdapter1.Update(ChangedRows)
        OleDbDataAdapter2.Update(ChangedRows)
      End If
    Catch updateException As System.Exception
      'Add your error handling code here.
      Throw updateException
    Finally
```

```
    'Close the connection whether or not the exception was thrown.
    Me.OleDbConnection1.Close()
  End Try
End Sub
```

The btnCancelAll_Click method is the Cancel All button click handler, which calls the DataSet's RejectChanges method (see Listing 2-10).

Listing 2-10. Cancel All Button Click Event Handler

```
Private Sub btnCancelAll_Click(ByVal sender As System.Object, _
  ByVal e As System.EventArgs) Handles btnCancelAll.Click
    Me.objMyDS.RejectChanges()
End Sub
```

Summary

Congratulations! You've now completed one more step toward understanding ADO.NET and its components. After completing this chapter, you should have a good idea of how to write database applications using the VS .NET IDE.

In this chapter, you learned about visual data components in VS .NET. The Server Explorer is a handy utility added to VS .NET IDE to help you manage your database connections.

DataAdapters let you connect to a data source at design-time and populate DataSet objects. In addition, DataAdapters also allow you to add, update, and delete data through data command objects. The VS .NET IDE also lets you generate typed DataSets, which are DataSets with properties of tables and columns specific to a data source.

A DataView is a bindable view of a DataSet. You can sort and filter a DataSet with a DataView and use it to bind to a graphical component in many of the Windows form controls.

Finally, the Data Form Wizard is a useful tool for generating full-fledged database applications with features such as inserting, deleting, and updating in no time.

In the next chapter, we discuss ADO.NET disconnected classes and components.

CHAPTER 3

ADO.NET in Disconnected Environments

IN CHAPTER 1 and Chapter 2, you learned about ADO.NET, and you learned how to use ADO.NET components with Visual Studio (VS) .NET. You also learned how to write code that binds ADO.NET components to data-bound controls and how to use VS .NET's Integrated Development Environment (IDE) wizards to write full-fledged database applications.

In this chapter, you'll get a broad view of the ADO.NET architecture and the basic building blocks of ADO.NET in a disconnected environment. Now, the first question on your mind might be, "What is a disconnected environment?" Generally, when we talk about ADO.NET and data access, we're talking about data stored in a database server such as a SQL Server or Oracle. Actually, ADO.NET not only provides a way to work with databases, it also allows you to access various kinds of data sources and even in-memory representations of data. In-memory data is stored in a system's memory and erased when an application is closed. Data that is held in-memory is referred to as a *disconnected environment*.

Why use in-memory data? Well, there may be occasions when you don't want to store data in a database but you want to perform some actions such as adding, deleting, sorting, and searching data, and once you're done, you don't care what happens to the data. This scenario would be perfect for working with disconnected data.

 NOTE *In Chapter 4, we will concentrate on working with connected data, where data will be stored in a database. In the connected environment, you use a data provider to connect to a database and read and write data using the data provider classes.*

ADO.NET *disconnected classes* are basic building blocks of the ADO.NET architecture. The classes are independent of data providers and data sources. In other words, you can use these classes with data providers as well as without data providers.

ADO.NET data providers are sets of classes designed to work with multiple data sources to provide the best of all the database access technologies. ADO.NET provides many data providers to work with different kinds of data sources, including OleDb, ODBC, and Sql.

NOTE *You can access SQL Server 6.5 or previous versions using ODBC or OleDb data providers.*

Although ADO.NET is a new programming model, it still uses old native data access technologies to access different data sources. For example, OleDb data providers use the native OLE DB Application Programming Interface (API) to access OLE DB data sources. Similar to OLE DB data sources, ODBC data providers use ODBC drivers and the ODBC Administration to access ODBC data sources. ADO.NET data providers wrap up these technologies for easier programming.

So, what's new in ADO.NET? That is a good question. Weren't you using the ODBC and OLE DB APIs in previous data access technologies? You're right. ADO.NET uses the same native API. The only difference is, ADO.NET provides high-level, object-oriented classes that are easy to program and understand. Further, all the data providers supply the same programming model. So, if you know how to write applications using OleDb data providers, you'll be able to write applications using ODBC or Sql providers in no time. It's just a matter of changing the class names and connection strings. When working with SQL Server databases, the Sql data provider is much more efficient and faster in comparison to the OleDb or ODBC data providers. Unlike ODBC and OleDb data providers, which use ODBC and OLE DB data layers to connect to a SQL Server database, the Sql data provider uses the native SQL Server layer to connect to the databases. We discuss this in more detail in later chapters.

Understanding the ADO.NET Architecture

You briefly looked at the ADO.NET architecture in Chapter 1. Now you'll see a broad view of the ADO.NET architecture and learn how disconnected and connected components (classes) provide access to multiple data sources. In this section, we talk about objects in general.

Figure 3-1 shows the basic architecture of the ADO.NET model. As you can see, the entire ADO.NET model sits between the data source and client applications that can be built using Windows Forms, Web Forms, or even console-based applications. The Connection is the first component that talks to a data source. In ADO.NET, each data provider (OleDb, Sql, Odbc, or Oracle) has its own Connection class. The Connection component is a mediator between a DataAdapter or a Command component. The DataAdapter components create SQL INSERT, SELECT, UPDATE, and DELETE statements that add, read, update, and delete data from a data source, respectively. Not only does a DataAdapter create these SQL statements, it also executes these statements. Basically, a DataAdapter (with the help of Command) physically updates and reads data from a data source. In Figure 3-1, an arrow shows this flow of data.

You can use the Command components with or without a DataAdapter. You can directly execute commands and read data in a DataReader, which provides a read-only, forward-only fast access to data. This is best when you need to read data in applications that are not data-bound. You can also see from Figure 3-1 that all arrows are double-sided arrows except the arrow connecting a DataReader and Command. A double-sided arrow means data transfer is possible on both sides. A DataReader can only read data, which is why the DataReader has only a one-sided arrow. This shows that you can fill a DataReader from the Command, but you can't send back data from a DataReader to the Command.

A DataAdapter sits between a data source and a DataSet. It provides Fill and Update methods to fill a DataSet from a data source based on the SELECT statement, and the Update method saves a DataSet's changes to the data source. The DataSet plays a vital role in data-bound Graphical User Interface (GUI) applications to display and manipulate data. Not only does it provide fast data manipulation using Extensible Markup Language (XML) schemas, it also provides multiple views of data that can be bound with multiple Windows Forms and Web Forms data-bound controls.

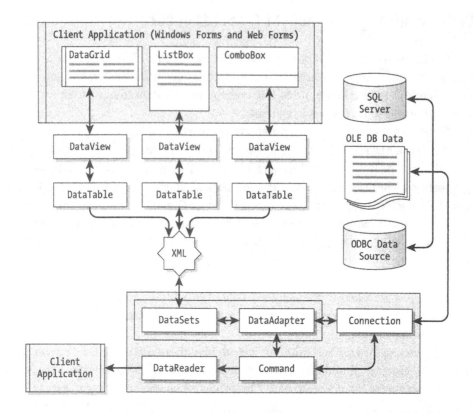

Figure 3-1. ADO.NET architecture

A DataSet is a collection of DataTable components. A DataTable represents a table in a data source. You can apply a filter or do sorts on a table. You can bind a DataTable to data-bound controls such as a DataGrid, DataList, ListBox, or ComboBox using DataView. You can also apply sorts and filters on a DataView. As you can see from Figure 3-1, there are three DataSets represented and three DataTables. Each DataTable binds to different data-bound controls using different DataViews.

This section gave you an overview of the ADO.NET architecture. We discuss these controls in more detail throughout this chapter and Chapter 4, depending on their category.

Exploring the ADO.NET Class Hierarchy

Before you start swimming in the deep ocean of ADO.NET, you need to take a quick look at the ADO.NET class hierarchy provided by the .NET Runtime Class Library (also known as *Base Class Library,* or BCL). These classes represent ADO.NET components.

All ADO.NET functionality in the .NET Runtime Class Library is defined in three general namespaces and a number of provider-specific namespaces. `System.Data` and `System.Data.Common` are two general namespaces common to all data providers. The `System.Data.SqlTypes` namespace is a SQL Server–specific namespace. The remainder of the functionality is defined in the data provider–specific namespaces; some of them are `System.Data.OleDb`, `System.Data.ODBC`, and `System.Data.SqlClient`.

The `System.Data` namespace defines classes that you can use with all the data providers or without data providers at all. This namespace also defines interfaces that are base classes for the data provider classes. Figure 3-2 shows the `System.Data` namespace's class hierarchy.

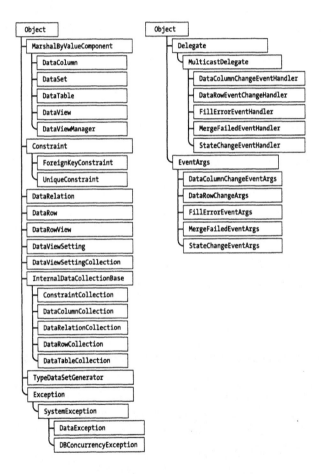

Figure 3-2. The `System.Data` *namespace class hierarchy*

The `System.Data.Common` namespace defines classes common to all data providers. Figure 3-3 shows the `System.Data.Common` namespace hierarchy.

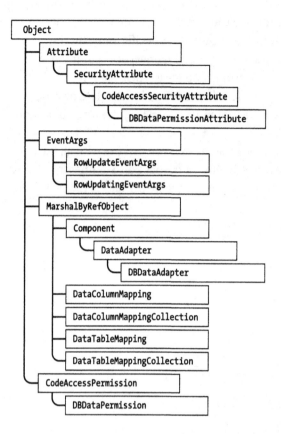

Figure 3-3. The `System.Data.Common` *namespace hierarchy*

The `System.Data.SqlTypes` namespace defines classes for native SQL Server data types that provide type-safe conversion between the .NET data types and the SQL Server native data types. Figure 3-4 shows the `System.Data.SqlTypes` namespace hierarchy.

In addition to these three namespaces, there are a number of provider-specific namespaces. The class hierarchy models of these namespaces are similar except for the name of the class. The classes defined in the provider-specific namespaces start with the data provider name. For example, the Sql data provider classes start with `Sql`, and the OleDb data provider classes start with `OleDb`. The `Command` object class of the Sql data provider is `SqlCommand`, and the `Command` object class of the OleDb data provider is `OleDbCommand`.

In this section, you'll see only the `System.Data.OleDb` namespace class hierarchy because all the data providers (including `System.Data.Sql` and `System.Data.Odbc`) implement the same class hierarchy model (with minor changes). Figure 3-5 shows the `System.Data.OleDb` namespace hierarchy.

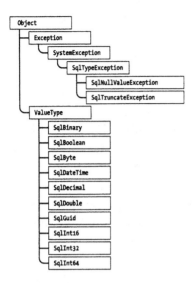

Figure 3-4. The `System.Data.SqlTypes` *namespace hierarchy*

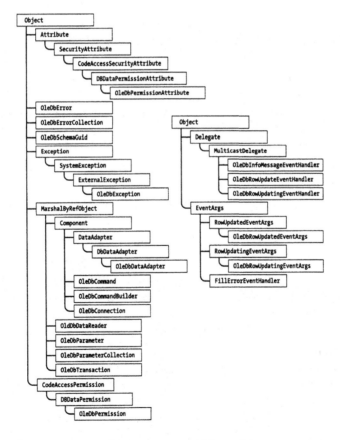

Figure 3-5. The `System.Data.OleDb` *namespace hierarchy*

We discuss these namespaces and their classes in more detail throughout this chapter and Chapter 4.

Choosing a Data Provider

As you saw earlier, many data providers are available in ADO.NET. There may be cases when you can access a data source using more than one data provider. Now the question arises: Which one is better? When choosing a data provider, the main criteria of selection is performance and multiple data source connectivity.

In brief, to work with SQL Server 7 or later databases, the Sql data provider is the best choice. The Sql data provider bypasses many layers and directly connects to the internal layer of the infrastructure. Not only that, but the Sql data provider provides classes that help you to convert from native SQL Server data types to the .NET data types, and vice versa.

OleDb data provider uses native OLE DB providers to access OLE DB data sources. OleDb data providers are useful because some database providers don't implement ODBC drivers to connect to a database through ODBC.

The Odbc data provider provides a way to work with different kinds of data sources through ODBC drivers. ODBC is an older data access technology, but many applications still use ODBC to access data sources. ODBC data providers provide a way to access ODBC data sources through ODBC drivers and ODBC Administration. Database venders generally provide the ODBC drivers. Using ODBC you can access any data source for which you have an ODBC driver installed.

In general, Odbc data provider connectivity is faster than OLE-DB because of OLE DB's COM nature, which is very "chatty." Sql data provider is faster than ODBC to work with SQL Server databases. But ODBC is useful when you need to write a generic class that can access multiple data sources through ODBC. For example, say you're writing an application that can work with multiple back-end servers including SQL Server, Oracle, Access, and MySql. When you install these back-end servers, you also install the ODBC driver for these databases. So, you can write a generic application that accesses these data sources based on the ODBC Data Source Name (DSN). You can also pass the driver and data source information in the application itself, but the user has to only create a DSN from ODBC, and the application can use that DSN as the connection string in the application for the Odbc data provider.

Understanding ADO.NET Disconnected Classes

ADO.NET disconnected classes are the basic building blocks of the ADO.NET architecture. These classes loosely couple with data providers. The System.Data namespace defines these classes.

The System.Data Namespace

The System.Data namespace consists of classes that are the basic building blocks of the ADO.NET architecture. These classes are also known as *disconnected classes* because they store disconnected data and can work without data providers.

Table 3-1 describes some of the common classes of the System.Data namespaces. We discuss these classes in more detail throughout this chapter.

Table 3-1. The System.Data *Namespace Classes*

CLASS	DESCRIPTION
Constraint, ConstraintCollection, UniqueConstraint, ForeignKeyConstraint	Constraints are rules set on a database table and its columns to help maintain the integrity of the data or to enforce business rules. The Constraint class object represents a constraint that you can apply on a DataColumn object. Some of these constraints are primary key, uniqueness, and foreign key. The ConstraintCollection class represents a collection of constraints for a DataTable. UniqueConstraint and ForeignKeyConstraint represent unique and foreign key constraints.
DataColumn, DataColumnCollection	The DataColumn object represents a column of a table. DataColumnCollection represents a collection of columns of a table.
DataRelation, DataRelationCollection	The DataRelation object represents a parent/child relationship between two DataTable objects. DataRelationCollection represents a collection of DataRelation.
DataRow, DataRowCollection	A DataRow object represents a row of a table, and DataRowCollection represent a collection of rows.
DataRowView	DataRowView represents a view of DataRow. It's useful when you want to attach a DataRow with data-bound controls such as a DataGrid.

(continued)

Table 3-1. The System.Data *Namespace Classes (continued)*

CLASS	DESCRIPTION
DataSet	In ADO.NET, a DataSet object is a replacement of the ADO recordset and represents an in-memory cache of data. A DataSet is a collection of DataTable objects.
DataTable, DataTableCollection	A DataTable object represents an in-memory cache of a table, and DataTableCollection is a collection of one or more DataTable objects.
DataView	Represents a data-bindable, customized view of a DataTable for sorting, filtering, searching, editing, and navigation.
DataViewManager	The DefaultViewManager represents the default view of a DataSet or DataTableCollection.

The System.Data namespace also defines many enumerations and delegates that we discuss throughout this chapter.

Once you have an idea of what classes the System.Data.Common namespace constaints, you'll have no problem understanding how to use these classes in a sample application.

The System.Data.Common Namespace

As its name says, the System.Data.Common namespace contains classes shared by the .NET data providers. Some of these classes are the base classes for the .NET data provider classes. Table 3-2 defines some of these classes.

Table 3-2. The System.Data.Common *Namespace Classes*

CLASS	DESCRIPTION
DataAdapter	The DataAdapter class represents a DataAdapter that works as a bridge between a data source and DataSet. It implements the Fill and Update methods. The Fill method fills data from a data source to a DataSet using Command objects. This class is a base class for the DbDataAdapter class, which itself is a base class for the OleDbDataAdapter, SqlDataAdapter, and ODBC DataAdapter classes. These classes are discussed in the "The DataAdapter: Adapting to Your Environment" section of Chapter 4.

(continued)

Table 3-2. The `System.Data.Common` *Namespace Classes*

CLASS	DESCRIPTION
DataColumnMapping	If you don't want to use the default column names of a table to access these columns, you can define your own names. You map your custom names with the original column names through DataAdapters and use these names in your application. The SourceColumn and DataSetColumn properties of this class represent the source column name and DataSet column name.
DataColumnMappingCollection	Collection of DataColumnMapping objects.
DataTableMapping	You can even map a database table to a DataTable and use this DataTable as the source in your applications. The ColumnMappings property returns DataColumnMappingCollection for the DataTable. The DataSetTable and SourceTable properties represent the DataTable and source tables.
DataTableMappingCollection	Collection of DataTableMapping objects.
DbDataAdapter	Inherited from DataAdapter, this class implements the IdbDataAdapter interface. This class is used as the base class of a data provider's DataAdapter classes.
DBDataPermission	Ensures that data providers have security to access data. This class is a base class from the OleDbDataPermission, OdbcDataPermission, and SqlDataPermission classes.

Working with DataTables

A DataTable object represents a database table. A data table is a collection of columns and rows. The DataRow object represents a table row, and the DataColumn object represents a column or a field of the table. Assuming you haven't imported, reengineered, or otherwise "inherited" a database and its DataTables, the first step to working with these three objects is to create a DataTable schema, which is defined by the DataColumnCollection object. You use the Add method of DataColumnCollection to add columns to the collection. The Columns property of the DataTable object represents the DataColumnCollection, which is a collection of DataColumn objects in a DataTable. You use a DataRow object to add data to a DataTable. The DataRowCollection object represents a collection of rows of a DataTable object, which can be accessed by its Rows property.

Figure 3-6 shows the relationship between the DataTable, the DataRow, and the DataColumn.

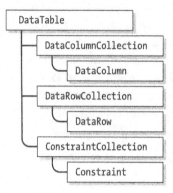

Figure 3-6. Relationship between the DataTable, *the* DataRow, *and the* DataColumn

A database table schema is the structure or design of the table, which includes table columns, their types, relationships, and constraints. You can view a database schema from the Server Explorer as well as from other places such as the SQL Server Enterprise Manager or Visio. To view a table schema from the Server Explorer, simply right-click the table in the Server Explorer and then click the Design Table menu item. You'll see the Column Name, Data Type, Length, and Allow Nulls columns. These columns represent the name, data type, length, and whether the column allows null values, respectively. The Columns area represents the properties of a column; you can see and specify the description, default value, formula if any, and other properties of a column.

NOTE *A database table column is also called a* field.

So, when we talk about creating a DataTable, we mean building a database table (in memory, of course) and its schema using the DataTable and the DataColumn objects. Based on a column requirement, you can also apply constraints on a column. A *constraint* is a rule that restricts adding unwanted data to a column. For example, the uniqueness of a column means that a column can't have duplicate values. You'll see constraints in more detail in Chapter 8. After creating a data table schema, the next step is to add DataRows to the DataTable. You use DataRows using the DataRow object. A DataRow object represents a row in a table.

TIP *To see data in the Customers table, double-click the Customers table in the Server Explorer.*

OK, now you'll learn how to accomplish this task in ADO.NET using the DataTable, DataColumn, and DataRow objects. First we discuss the DataColumn and the DataRow objects, followed by the DataRelation and the DataTable objects. Then, you'll create a sample project containing all these objects to build a DataTable and add data to it programmatically.

The DataColumn

To understand a DataTable, you must first understand DataRows and DataColumns. As you can see from Figure 3-6, the DataColumnCollection type returns a collection of columns that you can access through the Columns property of the DataTable.

The DataColumnCollection object represents a collection of columns attached to a DataTable. You add a DataColumn to the DataColumnCollection using its Add method. The DataColumn object represents a column of a DataTable. For example, say you want to create a Customers table that consists of three columns: ID, Address, and Name. So, you create three DataColumn objects and add these columns to the DataColumnCollection using the DataTable.Column.Add method.

The DataColumn has some properties. These properties describe a column, such as its uniqueness, what kind of data you can store in that column, its default value, its caption, its name, and so on. Table 3-3 describes some of the DataColumn class members.

Table 3-3. The DataColumn *Class Properties*

PROPERTIES	DESCRIPTION
AllowDBNull	Both read and write; represents whether the column can store null values
AutoIncrement	Represents whether column's value is auto increment
AutoIncrementSeed	Starting value of auto increment, applicable when AutoIncrement is True
AutoIncrementStep	Indicates the increment value
Caption	Caption of the column
ColumnMapping	Represents the MappingType of the column
ColumnName	Name of the column
DataType	Data type stored by the column
DefaultValue	Default value of the column
Expression	Represents the expression used to filter rows, calculate values, and so on
MaxLenght	Represents maximum length of a text column
ReadOnly	Represents if a column is read only
Unique	Indicates whether the values in a column must be unique

Creating a DataColumn

The DataColumn class provides five overloaded constructors to create a DataColumn. By using these constructors you can initialize a DataColumn with its name, data type, expressions, attributes, and any combination of these.

This is the format for creating a DataColumn with no arguments:

```
public DataColumn()
```

For example:

```
Dim dtColumn As DataColumn =  New DataColumn()
```

This is the format for creating a DataColumn with the column name:

```
Public DataColumn(String)
```

where String is the column name. For example:

```
// Create Quantity Column
DataColumn qtCol = new DataColumn("Quantity");
```

This is the format for creating a DataColumn with the column name and its type:

```
Public DataColumn(String, Type)
```

where String is the column name and Type is the column data type.

This is the format for creating a DataColumn with the column name, its type, and its expression:

```
Public DataColumn(String, Type, String)
```

where first String is the column name, Type is the data type, and the second String is an expression.

For example:

```
Dim myDataType As System.Type
myDataType = System.Type.GetType("System.String")
Dim dtColumn As DataColumn =  New DataColumn("Name",myDataType)
```

This is the format for creating a DataColumn with the column name, expression, and MappingType:

```
public DataColumn(String, Type, String, MappingType);
```

where String is the column name, Type is the data type, the second String is an expression, and MappingType is an attribute.

In the following example, strExpr is an expression, which is the result of the Price and the Quantity column multiplication:

```
// Creating an expression
string strExpr = "Price * Quantity";
// Create Total Column, which is result of Price*Quantity
DataColumn totCol = new DataColumn("Total", myDataType, strExpr,
MappingType.Attribute);
```

NOTE *As you can see from the previous code, the expression* strExpr *is a multiplication of the* Price *and* Quantity *columns. The* Price *and* Quantity *columns must exist in the table before you use them in an expression. Otherwise, the compiler will throw an exception of "column not found."*

Listing 3-1 summarizes all the constructors. As you can see, dcConstruc-torsTest creates the Price, Quantity, and Total columns of a DataTable, which later is added to a DataSet. The DataSet binds to a DataGrid using the SetDataBinding method.

Listing 3-1. Creating Columns Using Different DataColumn *Constructors*

```
Private Sub dcConstructorsTest()
    ' Create Customers table
    Dim custTable As DataTable = New DataTable("Customers")
    Dim dtSet As DataSet = New DataSet()
    ' Create Price Column
    Dim myDataType As System.Type
    myDataType = System.Type.GetType("System.Int32")
    Dim priceCol As DataColumn = New DataColumn("Price", myDataType)
    priceCol.Caption = "Price"
    custTable.Columns.Add(priceCol)
    ' Create Quantity Column
    Dim qtCol As DataColumn = New DataColumn()
    qtCol.ColumnName = "Quantity"
    qtCol.DataType = System.Type.GetType("System.Int32")
    qtCol.Caption = "Quantity"
    custTable.Columns.Add(qtCol)
    ' Creating an expression
    Dim strExpr As String = "Price * Quantity"
    ' Create Total Column, which is result of Price*Quantity
    Dim totCol As DataColumn = New DataColumn("Total", myDataType, strExpr, _
                                        MappingType.Attribute)
    totCol.Caption = "Total"
    ' Add Name column to the table.
    custTable.Columns.Add(totCol)
    ' Add custTable to DataSet
    dtSet.Tables.Add(custTable)
    ' Bind dataset to the data grid
    DataGrid1.SetDataBinding(dtSet, "Customers")
End Sub
```

To test this source code, you need to create a Windows application with a form and a DataGrid control on it. After that you can call dcConstructorsTest from either Form_Load or the button click event handler:

```
Private Sub Form1_Load(ByVal sender As System.Object, _
  ByVal e As System.EventArgs) Handles MyBase.Load
    dcConstructorsTest()
  End Sub
```

Setting DataColumn Properties

The DataColumn class provides properties to set a column type, name, constraints, caption, and so on. You already saw a list of DataColumn properties in Table 3-3. You'll now learn how to use these properties to get and set their values.

Listing 3-2 creates a column with a name ID and sets its DataType, ReadOnly, AllowDBNull, Unique, AutoIncrement, AutoIncremetnSeed, and AutoIncrementStep properties.

Listing 3-2. Creating a DataColumn and Setting Its Properties

```
Dim IdCol As DataColumn =  New DataColumn()
IdCol.ColumnName = "ID"
IdCol.DataType = Type.GetType("System.Int32")
IdCol.ReadOnly = True
IdCol.AllowDBNull = False
IdCol.Unique = True
IdCol.AutoIncrement = True
IdCol.AutoIncrementSeed = 1
IdCol.AutoIncrementStep = 1
```

As you can see from Listing 3-2, this code sets the AutoIncrement property as True along with the AutoIncrementSeed and AutoIncrementStep properties. The AutoIncrement property sets a column value as an auto number. When you add a new row to the table, the value of this column is assigned automatically depending on the values of AutoIncrementStep and AutoIncrementSeed. The first value of the column starts with AutoIncrementSeed, and the next value will be the previous column value added to the AutoIncrementStep. In this code, the ID number value starts with 1 and increases by 1 if you add a new row to the table. If you set the AutoIncrementStep value to 10, the value of the auto number column will increase by 10.

Having a primary key in a table is a common practice to maintaining the data's integrity. A primary key in a table is a unique key that identifies a DataRow. For example, in the Customers table, each customer should have a unique ID. So, it's always a good idea to apply a primary key constraint on the ID table. The properties AllowDBNull as False and Unique as True set a key value as the primary key, and you use the PrimaryKey property of a DataTable to assign a DataTable's primary key. Listing 3-2 shows the AllowDBNull as False and the Unique property as True. Now you'll set DataTable's PrimaryKey property as the ID column (see Listing 3-3).

Listing 3-3. Setting a DataColumn as the Primary Key

```
' Make the ID column the primary key column.
Dim PrimaryKeyColumns() As DataColumn =  New DataColumn(1) {}
PrimaryKeyColumns(0) = custTable.Columns("ID")
custTable.PrimaryKey = PrimaryKeyColumns
```

Adding a DataColumn to a DataTable

You add a DataColumn to a DataTable using the DataTable.Column.Add method. The Add method takes one argument of the DataColumn type. Listing 3-4 creates two data columns, Id and Name, and adds them to the DataTable custTable.

Listing 3-4. Creating the Id and Name Data Columns of the Customers Table

```
Dim custTable As DataTable =  New DataTable("Customers")
Dim IdCol As DataColumn =  New DataColumn()
custTable.Columns.Add(IdCol)
Dim nameCol As DataColumn =  New DataColumn()
custTable.Columns.Add(nameCol)
```

Now you'll put all the pieces together (see Listing 3-5). In Listing 3-5, you create a Customers table with the columns ID, Name, Address, DOB (date of birth), and VAR where ID is a primary key. Name and Address are string types. DOB is a date type field, and VAR is a Boolean type field.

NOTE *To test this program, create a Windows application and add a* DataGrid *control to the form.*

Listing 3-5. Creating a Table Using DataTable *and* DataColumn

```vb
Private Sub CreateCustTable()
    ' Create a new DataTable
    Dim custTable As DataTable = New DataTable("Customers")
    ' Create ID Column
    Dim IdCol As DataColumn = New DataColumn()
    IdCol.ColumnName = "ID"
    IdCol.DataType = Type.GetType("System.Int32")
    IdCol.ReadOnly = True
    IdCol.AllowDBNull = False
    IdCol.Unique = True
    IdCol.AutoIncrement = True
    IdCol.AutoIncrementSeed = 1
    IdCol.AutoIncrementStep = 1
    custTable.Columns.Add(IdCol)
    ' Create Name Column
    Dim nameCol As DataColumn = New DataColumn()
    nameCol.ColumnName = "Name"
    nameCol.DataType = Type.GetType("System.String")
    custTable.Columns.Add(nameCol)
    ' Create Address Column
    Dim addCol As DataColumn = New DataColumn()
    addCol.ColumnName = "Address"
    addCol.DataType = Type.GetType("System.String")
    custTable.Columns.Add(addCol)
    ' Create DOB Column
    Dim dobCol As DataColumn = New DataColumn()
    dobCol.ColumnName = "DOB"
    dobCol.DataType = Type.GetType("System.DateTime")
    custTable.Columns.Add(dobCol)
    ' VAR Column
    Dim fullTimeCol As DataColumn = New DataColumn()
    fullTimeCol.ColumnName = "VAR"
    fullTimeCol.DataType = Type.GetType("System.Boolean")
    custTable.Columns.Add(fullTimeCol)
    ' Make the ID column the primary key column.
    Dim PrimaryKeyColumns() As DataColumn = New DataColumn(1) {}
    PrimaryKeyColumns(0) = custTable.Columns("ID")
    custTable.PrimaryKey = PrimaryKeyColumns
    ' Create a dataset
    Dim ds As DataSet = New DataSet("Customers")
    ' Add Customers table to the dataset
    ds.Tables.Add(custTable)
    ' Attach the dataset to a DataGrid
    dataGrid1.DataSource = ds.DefaultViewManager
End Sub
```

The output of Listing 3-5 looks like Figure 3-7, which shows a table with empty columns in a DataGrid controlempty columns in a DataGrid control.

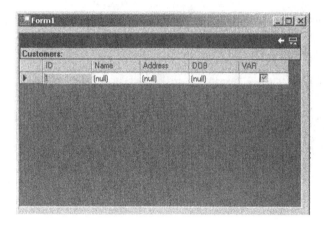

Figure 3-7. The DataGrid view of an empty DataTable

More DataColumn Properties

You just saw some common properties of the DataColumn class, and you learned how to create and add a DataColumn to a DataTable. But guess what? DataColumn isn't finished yet. It has more to offer. Now let's see the remaining properties of DataColumn.

The ColumnMapping property of DataColumn represents how a DataColumn is mapped in a DataSet and how the value of the column will be written when a DataSet is saved in XML format using the WriteXml method of DataSet. The ColumnMapping takes a value of MappingType enumeration. The MappingType enumeration has four values: Attribute, Element, Hidden, and SimpleContent, which are mapped to an XML attribute, element, internal structure, and XmlText (respectively). Listing 3-6 shows you how to use the ColumnMapping property.

Listing 3-6. Using the ColumnMapping Property of DataColumn

```
Dim custTable As DataTable = New DataTable("Customers")
Dim nameCol As DataColumn = New DataColumn("Name", _
Type.GetType("System.Int32"), MappingType.Attribute)
nameCol.DataType = Type.GetType("System.String")
nameCol.ColumnMapping = MappingType.Element
custTable.Columns.Add(nameCol)
DataGrid1.DataSource = custTable
```

So far you saw how to create a new table column, set its various properties, and add it to a table. But what if you wanted to store some custom information about a column, such as a description? Guess what? You can do it. The Extended-Properties property of DataColumn lets you read and write custom properties about a DataColumn. The ExtendedProperties property takes a value of type PropertyCollection, which is inherited from the HashTable class. A hash table is a table that stores data in a key/value pair. The PropertyCollection class defines methods to add, clear, and remover properties to a collection. Some of the PropertyCollection class properties are Count, IsFixedSize, IsReadOnly, IsSynchronized, Item, Keys, and Values. Listing 3-7 creates a column and adds four custom properties to it. After that, the code removes the Description property and displays the rest of the properties using the ExtendedProperties property of DataColumn.

Listing 3-7. Adding and Removing Custom Properties

```
Dim custTable As DataTable = New DataTable("Customers")
Dim nameCol As DataColumn = New DataColumn("Name", _
  Type.GetType("System.Int32"), MappingType.Attribute)
' Add custom properties
nameCol.DataType = Type.GetType("System.String")
nameCol.ExtendedProperties.Add("Description", "The Name Column")
nameCol.ExtendedProperties.Add("Author", "Mahesh Chand")
nameCol.ExtendedProperties.Add("UserId", "MCB")
nameCol.ExtendedProperties.Add("PWD", "Password")
custTable.Columns.Add(nameCol)
' Remove Author property
nameCol.ExtendedProperties.Remove("Author")
' Read custom properties
Dim str As String
Dim i As Integer
str = nameCol.ExtendedProperties("Description").ToString()
str = str + ", " + nameCol.ExtendedProperties("UserId").ToString()
str = str + ", " + nameCol.ExtendedProperties("PWD").ToString()
MessageBox.Show(str)
```

The Ordinal property (read only) of DataColumn returns the position of a column in a DataColumnCollection, and the MaxLength (get and set both types) property represents the maximum length of a column. Listing 3-8 shows how to use the Ordinal and MaxLength properties.

Listing 3-8. Using the Ordinal *and* MaxLength *Properties*

```
Dim custTable As DataTable = New DataTable("Customers")
Dim nameCol As DataColumn = New DataColumn("Name", _
Type.GetType("System.Int32"), MappingType.Attribute)
custTable.Columns.Add(nameCol)
nameCol = New DataColumn()
nameCol.DataType = Type.GetType("System.String")
nameCol.Caption = "New Column"
nameCol.ColumnName = "Col2"
nameCol.MaxLength = 240
custTable.Columns.Add(nameCol)
Dim str As String
str = "Ordinal " + nameCol.Ordinal.ToString()
str = str + " ,Length " + nameCol.MaxLength.ToString()
MessageBox.Show(str)
```

The DataRow

A DataRow represents a row of data in a DataTable. You add data to the DataTable
using the DataRow object. A DataRowCollection object represents a collection of
DataRows of a DataTable. You use the DataTable's NewRow method to return a DataRow
object, add values to the DataRow, and add the row to the DataTable again by using
DataRowCollection's Add method.

Table 3-4 describes DataRow class properties, and Table 3-5 describes the
methods.

Table 3-4. The DataRow *Class Properties*

PROPERTY	DESCRIPTION
Item	Represents an item of a row
ItemArray	Represents all values in a row
RowState	Indicates the current state of a row
Table	Returns the DataTable to which this row is attached

Table 3-5. The DataRow *Class Methods*

METHOD	DESCRIPTION
AcceptChanges	Commits all the changes made to this row
BeginEdit	Starts an edit operation on a row
CancelEdit	Cancels the current edit on a row
Delete	Deletes a DataRow
EndEdit	Ends the current edit on a row
GetChildRows	Returns child rows of a DataRow
GetParentRows	Returns parent rows of a DataRow.
RejectChanges	Rejects all the changes made since last AcceptChanges

You access DataRow members through the DataTable columns. A column acts as an item of the row. For example, if a DataTable has three columns such as Id, Name, and Address, then a row will have three members: Id, Name, and Address. You access DataTable members using the column names. For example, Listing 3-9 sets values of the Id, Name, and Address columns.

Listing 3-9. Setting the Values of the Id, Address, and Name Columns of a DataRow

```
Dim row1 As DataRow =  custTable.NewRow()
row1("id") = 1001
row1("Address") = "43 Lanewood Road, Cito, CA"
row1("Name") = "George Bishop "
```

After setting a row member's values, you add the row to the row collection with the DataTable.Rows.Add method. The following code adds a row to the collection:

```
custTable.Rows.Add(row1)
```

The RejectChanges method of the DataRow rejects recent changes on that row. For example, if you have recently added row1 to the DataTable, then calling the RejectChanges method as follows:

```
row1.RejectChanges()
```

won't add the row to the DataTable.

You can also delete a row from a `DataTable` by calling the `DataRow`'s `Delete` method:

```
Row1.Delete()
```

CAUTION *The* `RejectChanges` *and* `Delete` *methods may not work together if you're applying both methods on the same row because* `RejectChanges` *doesn't add a row to the* `DataTable`.

Listing 3-10 shows a program that creates a `DataTable` with three columns (Id, Name, and Address) and adds three rows to the `DataTable`. At the end, this program attaches the newly created `DataTable` to a `DataGrid` control using a `DataSet`.

CAUTION *As you can see from Listing 3-10, the Id column of the Customers table is read only (the* `ReadOnly` *property is* `True`*). That means you won't be able to add data to the table. If you want to add data from the front end, you need to set the* `ReadOnly` *property to* `False`.

Listing 3-10. Adding Rows to a `DataTable` *Using* `DataRow`

```
' This method creates Customers table
  Private Sub CreateCustomersTable()
    ' Create a new DataTable.
    Dim custTable As System.Data.DataTable = New DataTable("Customers")
    Dim dtColumn As DataColumn
    ' Create id Column.
    dtColumn = New DataColumn()
    dtColumn.DataType = System.Type.GetType("System.Int32")
    dtColumn.ColumnName = "id"
    dtColumn.Caption = "Cust ID"
    dtColumn.ReadOnly = True
    dtColumn.Unique = True
    ' Add id Column to the DataColumnCollection.
    custTable.Columns.Add(dtColumn)
    ' Create Name column.
    dtColumn = New DataColumn()
    dtColumn.DataType = System.Type.GetType("System.String")
    dtColumn.ColumnName = "Name"
```

```vb
dtColumn.Caption = "Cust Name"
dtColumn.AutoIncrement = False
dtColumn.ReadOnly = False
dtColumn.Unique = False
' Add Name column to the table.
custTable.Columns.Add(dtColumn)
' Create Address column.
dtColumn = New DataColumn()
dtColumn.DataType = System.Type.GetType("System.String")
dtColumn.ColumnName = "Address"
dtColumn.Caption = "Address"
dtColumn.ReadOnly = False
dtColumn.Unique = False
' Add Address column to the table.
custTable.Columns.Add(dtColumn)
' Make the ID column the primary key column.
Dim PrimaryKeyColumns() As DataColumn = New DataColumn(1) {}
PrimaryKeyColumns(0) = custTable.Columns("id")
custTable.PrimaryKey = PrimaryKeyColumns
' Instantiate the DataSet variable.
Dim ds As DataSet = New DataSet("Customers")
' Add the custTable to the DataSet.
ds.Tables.Add(custTable)
' Add rows to the custTable using its NewRow method
' I add three customers with thier addresses, name and id
Dim row1 As DataRow = custTable.NewRow()
row1("id") = 1001
row1("Address") = "43 Lanewood Road, Cito, CA"
row1("Name") = "George Bishop "
custTable.Rows.Add(row1)
Dim row2 As DataRow = custTable.NewRow()
row2("id") = 1002
row2("Name") = "Rock Joe "
row2("Address") = "King of Prusssia, PA"
custTable.Rows.Add(row2)
Dim row3 As DataRow = custTable.NewRow()
row3("id") = 1003
row3("Name") = "Miranda "
row3("Address") = "279 P. Avenue, Bridgetown, PA"
custTable.Rows.Add(row3)
'row3.RejectChanges()
'row2.Delete()
' Bind dataset to the data grid
dataGrid1.DataSource = ds.DefaultViewManager
End Sub
```

The output of the program looks like Figure 3-8.

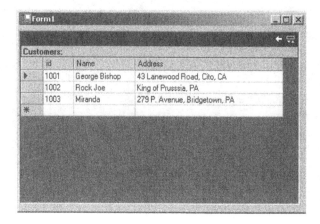

Figure 3-8. A DataTable *with three rows*

NOTE *To run this program, create a Windows application and drop a* DataGrid *control on the form. After that you can either call* CreateCustomersTable *in Listing 3-3 from the form's* Load *event or from a button click handler. You can write a* Load *event by double-clicking on the form or by opening the Properties window.*

If you uncomment row3.RejectChanges() and row2.Delete() at the end of Listing 3-10, the RejectChanges method rejects the addition of row 3, and the Delete method deletes row 2.

Listing 3-11. Calling DataRow's RejectChanges *and* Delete *Methods*

```
row3.RejectChanges()
row2.Delete()
```

The DataRowState enumeration returns the current state of a row. It's useful during operations when you want to know the current state of a row. Table 3-6 lists the values of the DataRowState enumeration.

Table 3-6. The DataRowState *Enumeration Members*

MEMBER	DESCRIPTION
Added	Row has been added, and AcceptChanges has not been called.
Deleted	Row was deleted using the Delete method.
Detached	Row was created but deleted before it was added to the collection.
Modified	Row has been modified, but AcceptChanges has not been called yet.
Unchanged	Row has not changed since the last AcceptChanges was called.

The RowState property of a DataRow returns the DataRowState enumeration. You can use this to find out the current state of a row. For example, Listing 3-12 calls RowState just after the Delete and RejectChanges methods.

Listing 3-12. Calling the RowState *Property*

```
row3.RejectChanges()
MessageBox.Show(row2.RowState.ToString())
row2.Delete()
MessageBox.Show(row3.RowState.ToString())
```

The DataRelation

To provide data integrity and consistency, you should use relationships between two tables. You achieve this relationship by defining a primary key in one table and using a foreign key in the other table. Say a customer has multiple orders; the Customers table stores the customer details, and the Orders table stores all the order details. To avoid the redundancy of data, you define the primary key of the Customers table as a foreign key in the Orders table.

> **NOTE** *In general this relationship is called the* parent/child, *or* master/details, relationship.

In this example, the Customers table is also the *parent* table, and the Orders table is also the *child* table. The ParentRelations property of DataTable represents the parent relationship, and ChildRelations represents the child relationship.

CAUTION *The data type of both columns, which you're linking through a relationship in the Customers and the Orders tables, must be identical.*

You can also access this relationship though a DataSet using its Relations property. To create a relationship between two columns, you create two DataColumn objects and pass them as DataRelation arguments.

Listing 3-13 shows you how to create a customer/order relationship between the Customers and Orders table through the Customers table's id column, referenced as CustId in the Orders table. The DataRelation constructor takes three arguments: the name of the relationship, the first DataColumn, and the second DataColumn. After that you call DataTable's ParentRelation.Add method with DataRelation as an argument. (Listing 3-15 shows the full source code of this example.) In this code, dtSet is a DataSet object, which we discuss in the following section.

Listing 3-13. Creating a Customer/Order Relationship Using DataRelation

```
Private  Sub BindData()
    Dim dtRelation As DataRelation
    Dim CustCol As DataColumn = dtSet.Tables("Customers").Columns("id")
    Dim orderCol As DataColumn = dtSet.Tables("Orders").Columns("CustId")
    dtRelation = New DataRelation("CustOrderRelation", CustCol, orderCol)
    dtSet.Tables("Orders").ParentRelations.Add(dtRelation)
    dataGrid1.SetDataBinding(dtSet,"Customers")
End Sub
```

The DataTable

In the previous sections you've seen that columns and rows are the building blocks of a DataTable. You need to work with the DataColumn and DataRow objects to create DataTables and add data to them. Besides creating a DataTable schema and adding rows to it, a DataTable has more to offer. The DataTable object represents a DataTable.

First you'll take a look at the DataTable class properties and methods. Table 3-7 describes some common DataTable properties, and Table 3-8 summarizes some of the common DataTable methods.

Table 3-7. The DataTable *Class Properties*

PROPERTIES	DESCRIPTION
Columns	Represents all table columns
Constraints	Represents all table constaints
DataSet	Returns the DataSet for the table
DefaultView	Customized view of the DataTable
ChildRelation	Returns child relations for the DataTable
ParentRelation	Returns parent relations for the DataTable
PrimaryKey	Represents an array of columns that function as primary key for the table
Rows	All rows of the DataTable
TableName	Name of the table

Table 3-8. The DataTable *Class Methods*

METHOD	DESCRIPTION
AcceptChanges	Commits all the changes made since the last AcceptChanges was called
Clear	Deletes all DataTable data
Clone	Creates a clone of a datatable including its schema
Copy	Copies a DataTable including its schema
NewRow	Creates a new row, which is later added by calling the Rows.Add method
RejectChanges	Rejects all changes made after the last AcceptChanges was called
Reset	Resets a DataTable's original state
Select	Gets an array of rows based on the criteria

The DataTable class provides methods and properties to remove, copy, and clone data tables. Not only that, but you can also apply filters on a DataTable. The Constraints property provides access to all the constraints that a DataTable has. You can also access the child/parent relationship using ChildRelation and ParentRelation. Now we'll create two tables—Customers and Orders—and set a relationship between them. To test this application, you build a Windows application using Visual Basic and add a DataGrid control to the form. After that you call the CreateCustomersTable, CreateOrdersTable, and BindData methods from the form constructor after InitializeComonent. The form constructor looks like Listing 3-14.

Listing 3-14. Form's Constructor Calling CreateCustomersTable, CreateOrdersTable, *and* BindData

```
Private Sub Form1_Load(ByVal sender As System.Object, _
   ByVal e As System.EventArgs) Handles MyBase.Load
     CreateCustomersTable()
     CreateOrdersTable()
     BindData()
   End Sub
```

You also need to add a DataSet variable, dtSet, in the beginning of your form:

```
Public Class Form1
   Inherits System.Windows.Forms.Form
   Private dtSet As System.Data.DataSet
```

In Listing 3-15, the CreateCustomersTable method creates the Customers data table with Id, Name, and Address columns and adds three data rows to it. The CreateOrdersTable method creates the Orders table with OrderId, CustId, Name, and Description columns and adds data to it. The BindData method creates a customer/orders relationship and binds the data to a DataGrid control using DataSet.

Listing 3-15 shows all three CreateCustomerTable, CreateOrdersTable, and BindData methods.

Listing 3-15. Customer/Orders Relationship Example

```
Private Sub CreateCustomersTable()
  ' Create a new DataTable.
  Dim custTable As System.Data.DataTable = New DataTable("Customers")
  ' Create id, Name, and Address Columns and
  ' add these columns to custTable
  ' See source code for details
  ' Make the ID column the primary key column.
  Dim PrimaryKeyColumns() As DataColumn = New DataColumn(1) {}
  PrimaryKeyColumns(0) = custTable.Columns("id")
  custTable.PrimaryKey = PrimaryKeyColumns
  ' Instantiate the DataSet variable.
  dtSet = New DataSet("Customers")
  ' Add the custTable to the DataSet.
  dtSet.Tables.Add(custTable)
  ' Add rows to the custTable using its NewRow method
  ' I add three customers with thier addresses, name and id
  ' See source code for details
End Sub
```

```vb
' This method creates Orders table with
Private Sub CreateOrdersTable()
  ' Create Orders table.
  Dim ordersTable As DataTable = New DataTable("Orders")
  ' Create OrderId, Name, CustId, Description columns
  ' Add them to ordersTable
  ' See source code for more details
  ' Add ordersTable to the dataset
  dtSet.Tables.Add(ordersTable)
  ' Add two rows to Customer Id 1001
  dtRow = ordersTable.NewRow()
  dtRow("OrderId") = 0
  dtRow("Name") = "ASP Book"
  dtRow("CustId") = 1001
  dtRow("Description") = "Same Day"
  ordersTable.Rows.Add(dtRow)
  dtRow = ordersTable.NewRow()
  dtRow("OrderId") = 1
  dtRow("Name") = "C# Book"
  dtRow("CustId") = 1001
  dtRow("Description") = "2 Day Air"
  ordersTable.Rows.Add(dtRow)
  ' Add two rows to Customer Id 1002
  dtRow = ordersTable.NewRow()
  dtRow("OrderId") = 2
  dtRow("Name") = "Data Quest"
  dtRow("Description") = "Monthly Magazine"
  dtRow("CustId") = 1002
  ordersTable.Rows.Add(dtRow)
  dtRow = ordersTable.NewRow()
  dtRow("OrderId") = 3
  dtRow("Name") = "PC Magazine"
  dtRow("Description") = "Monthly Magazine"
  dtRow("CustId") = 1002
  ordersTable.Rows.Add(dtRow)
  ' Add two rows to Customer Id 1003
  dtRow = ordersTable.NewRow()
  dtRow("OrderId") = 4
  dtRow("Name") = "PC Magazine"
  dtRow("Description") = "Monthly Magazine"
  dtRow("CustId") = 1003
  ordersTable.Rows.Add(dtRow)
  dtRow = ordersTable.NewRow()
```

```
    dtRow("OrderId") = 5
    dtRow("Name") = "C# Book"
    dtRow("CustId") = 1003
    dtRow("Description") = "2 Day Air"
    ordersTable.Rows.Add(dtRow)
End Sub


' This method creates a customer order relationship and binds data tables
' to the data grid cotnrol using dataset.
Private Sub BindData()
  Dim dtRelation As DataRelation
  Dim CustCol As DataColumn = dtSet.Tables("Customers").Columns("id")
  Dim orderCol As DataColumn = dtSet.Tables("Orders").Columns("CustId")

  dtRelation = New DataRelation("CustOrderRelation", CustCol, orderCol)
  dtSet.Tables("Orders").ParentRelations.Add(dtRelation)
  DataGrid1.SetDataBinding(dtSet, "Customers")
End Sub
```

As you can see from the `CreateCustomersTable` method in Listing 3-15, it creates the Customers table using `DataTable` and adds the Id, Name and Address columns to the table. You use `DataColumn` to add these columns. The Id column has properties such as `ReadOnly` and `Unique`. As discussed earlier, to add a column to a `DataTable`, you create a `DataColumn` object, set its properties, and then call the `DataTable.Coumns.Add` method. Similar to the id column, you add two more columns, Name and Address, of string type to the table. After that you make the id column the primary key by setting `DataTable.PrimaryKey` as the id column:

```
PrimaryKeyColumns(0) = custTable.Columns("id")
 custTable.PrimaryKey = PrimaryKeyColumns
```

After creating a `DataTable` you add it to a `DataSet` using the `DataSet.Tables.Add` method. This method takes one argument of type `DataTable`:

```
dtSet = New DataSet("Customers")
dtSet.Tables.Add(custTable)
```

Now, the last step is to add data to `DataTable`. You add data using `DataRow`. First, you create a `DataRow` object using `DataTable`'s `NewRow` method, add data to a `DataRow`'s items, and add `DataRow` to the `DataTable` using the `DataTable.Rows.Add` method. You'll follow the same method for the second table in `CreateOrdersTable` to create the Orders table. The Orders table has the fields OrderId, Name, Description, and

CustId. The BindData method creates a relationship by using DataRelation and binds the id column of the Customers tables to the CustId column of the Orders table. The name of the relationship is CustOrderRelation. After that you bind DataTable to the DataGrid using the SetDataBinding method.

The output of Listing 3-15 looks like Figure 3-9.

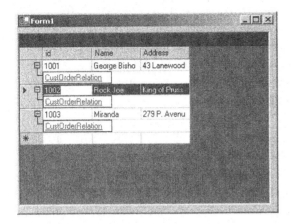

Figure 3-9. A DataGrid with data relations

If you click the CustOrderRelation link, the output looks like Figure 3-10.

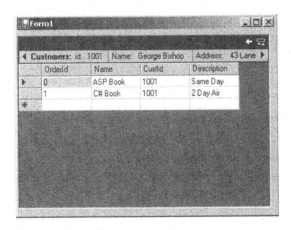

Figure 3-10. Orders record for Customers id 1001

As you can see from Figure 3-10, DataGrid shows all the orders for Customer id 1001.

More DataTable Operations

Adding and deleting are two common operations when working with databases. You've already learned about how to add data to a DataTable using a DataRow. In this section you'll see how to add, delete, sort, and search data programmatically. You'll keep all data in memory in the form of DataTables, but you'll also see a Save option, which will save data in XML format. This is a simple Windows Forms application.

The first step is to build a GUI (see Figure 3-11). To build this GUI, you create a Windows Application project. After that, add a DataGrid control, four Button controls, seven TextBox controls, five GroupBox controls, and some Label controls. Then adjust them on your form. You can also change the background color of the controls.

In this application, we show you all basic common operations such as adding, deleting, sorting, and searching rows. The Add Row button reads the name and address, adds a new row in the DataTable, and displays the added row in the DataGrid. The Delete Rows button deletes rows based on the entered criteria. To delete rows, you enter the column name and value, and the Delete Rows button will delete all the rows that meet the criteria. The Search button reads column name and values entered in the text boxes and returns data that matches the criteria. The Apply Sort button reads a column and sorts rows based on that column. The Save method saves the current data of the DataTable to an XML document.

NOTE *You don't have to create the same form as shown in Figure 3-11. The only thing you need to have is a* DataGrid *with the same number of* TextBox *and* Button *controls.*

Now, you change the names of the form controls and add the DataSet variable dtSet and the DataTable variable custTable to the beginning of the form. Besides the variables defined for the controls (see the MoreDataTableOpsSamp sample available with the source code for details), add two variables of type DataTable and DataSet, as shown in Listing 3-16.

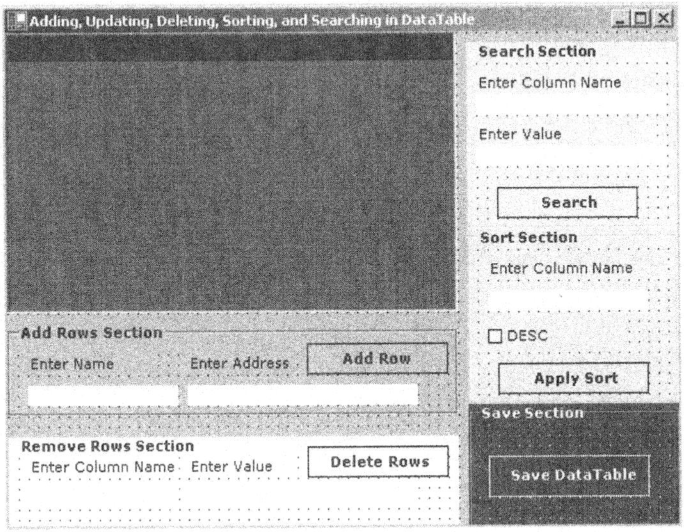

Figure 3-11. Add, delete, sort, and search operations in a DataTable

Listing 3-16. Class-Level DataTable *and* DataSet *Variables*

```
Private custTable As DataTable
Private dtSet As DataSet
```

Now you create the Customers table with three columns: id, Name, and Address. You've already learned how to add columns to a DataTable using a DataColumn and binding it to a DataGrid. The CreateCustomersTable method creates the Customers table. After creating the Customers table, you add the DataTable to the DataSet using the DataSet.Tables.Add method. The CreateCustomersTable method looks like Listing 3-17.

Listing 3-17. The CreateCustomersTable *Method*

```
' This method creates Customers table
  Private Sub CreateCustomersTable()
    ' Create a new DataTable.
    custTable = New DataTable("Customers")
    Dim dtColumn As DataColumn
    ' Create id Column
    dtColumn = New DataColumn()
    dtColumn.DataType = System.Type.GetType("System.Int32")
```

```
            dtColumn.ColumnName = "id"
            dtColumn.AutoIncrement = True
            dtColumn.AutoIncrementSeed = 100
            dtColumn.AutoIncrementStep = 1
            dtColumn.Caption = "Cust ID"
            dtColumn.ReadOnly = True
            dtColumn.Unique = True
            ' Add id Column to the DataColumnCollection.
            custTable.Columns.Add(dtColumn)
            ' Create Name column.
            dtColumn = New DataColumn()
            dtColumn.DataType = System.Type.GetType("System.String")
            dtColumn.ColumnName = "Name"
            dtColumn.Caption = "Cust Name"
            dtColumn.AutoIncrement = False
            dtColumn.ReadOnly = False
            dtColumn.Unique = False
            ' Add Name column to the table.
            custTable.Columns.Add(dtColumn)
            ' Create Address column.
            dtColumn = New DataColumn()
            dtColumn.DataType = System.Type.GetType("System.String")
            dtColumn.ColumnName = "Address"
            dtColumn.Caption = "Address"
            dtColumn.ReadOnly = False
            dtColumn.Unique = False
            ' Add Address column to the table.
            custTable.Columns.Add(dtColumn)
            ' Make the ID column the primary key column.
            Dim PrimaryKeyColumns() As DataColumn = New DataColumn(1) {}
            PrimaryKeyColumns(0) = custTable.Columns("id")
            custTable.PrimaryKey = PrimaryKeyColumns
            ' Instantiate the DataSet variable.
            dtSet = New DataSet("Customers")
            ' Add the custTable to the DataSet.
            dtSet.Tables.Add(custTable)
            RefreshData()
        End Sub
```

At the end of the `CreateCustomersTable` method you call the `RefreshData` method, which refreshes the `DataGrid` contents and fills them with the current data of the `DataTable` by setting `DataGrid`'s `DataSource` property to the `DataSet`'s `DefaultViewManager`. The `RefreshData` method looks like the following:

```
Private Sub RefreshData()
    dataGrid1.DataSource = dtSet.DefaultViewManager
End Sub
```

As you can see from Figure 3-12, the Add Row button adds a new row to the Customers' `DataTable` with the Name and Address columns reading from the Name and Address text boxes. The Delete Rows button deletes the row number inserted in the Enter Row # text box. The Search button searches and returns rows that contain the name entered in the Enter Name text box of the Search group box.

OK, now it's time to write code for the button event handlers. You can write button event handlers by double-clicking the buttons or using the Properties windows. First, you write the event handler for the Add Row button with the handler name `AddRow_Click`. After that, write event handlers for the Delete Rows and Search buttons; the event handler names for these buttons are `DeleteRow_Click` and `SearchButton_Click`, respectively.

You add a new row to the `DataTable` using `DataRow` and call the `Add` and `AcceptChanges` methods of the `DataTable`. Listing 3-18 shows the Add Row button click event handler.

As you can see, the code adds Name as TextBox4.Text and Address as TextBox4.Text.

You call `NewRow` of `DataTable` to add a new row to `DataTable`, set its field values, and call the `DataTable.Rows.Add` method to add it. After the `Add` method, you also call `DataTable.AcceptChanges` method to save the changes. At the end, you call the `RefreshData` method to fill the `DataGrid` with the records.

Listing 3-18. The `AddRowBtn_Click` *Method*

```
Private Sub AddRowBtn_Click(ByVal sender As System.Object, _
   ByVal e As System.EventArgs) Handles AddRowBtn.Click
    ' Add rows to the custTable using its NewRow method
    ' I add three customers with thier addresses, name and id
    Dim myDataRow As DataRow = custTable.NewRow()
    myDataRow("Name") = TextBox4.Text.ToString()
    myDataRow("Address") = TextBox5.Text.ToString()
    custTable.Rows.Add(myDataRow)
    custTable.AcceptChanges()
    RefreshData()
End Sub
```

If you add six rows to the DataTable using the Add Row button, the result looks like Figure 3-12.

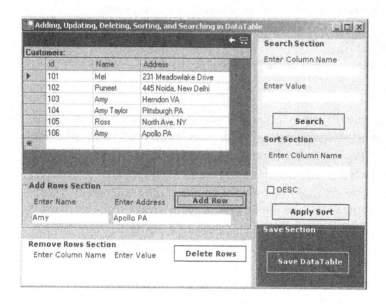

Figure 3-12. Adding rows to the DataTable

The Delete Rows button deletes the records from a column that matches the given criteria. The Remove Rows Section takes a column name and column value, and the Delete Rows button click event handler removes the rows from the DataTable.

The DeleteRowsBtn_Click method is the click event handler for the Delete Rows button (see Listing 3-19). As you can see, the code uses the Select method of DataTable. The Select method of DataTable takes a criterion and returns the rows that meet the given criteria. In this case, you pass a column name and its value as a criterion. The Select method returns all the matching rows in an array of DataRow. Once you've retrieved these rows, you call DataRow.Delete method to delete the rows one by one, followed by a call of DataRow.AcceptChanges method to save the changes.

In the end, you call the RefreshData method to refresh the grid.

Listing 3-19. The DeleteRow_Click *Method*

```
Private Sub DeleteRowsBtn_Click(ByVal sender As System.Object, _
  ByVal e As System.EventArgs) Handles DeleteRowsBtn.Click
    Dim str As String = TextBox7.Text + "='" + TextBox6.Text + "'"
    Dim rows() As DataRow = custTable.Select(str)
    ' If no record found
    If rows.Length = 0 Then
      MessageBox.Show("Record not found!")
      Return
    End If
    Dim i As Integer
    For i = 0 To rows.Length - 1 Step i + 1
      rows(i).Delete()
      rows(i).AcceptChanges()
    Next
    RefreshData()
End Sub
```

As you can see from Figure 3-13, if you enter column name as **Name** with the value **Puneet**, then the Delete Rows button removes the row with Id = 102.

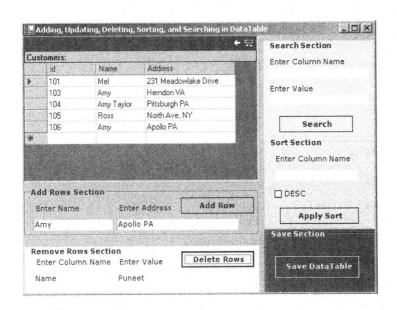

Figure 3-13. Deleting rows from the DataTable

You just saw the usage of the DataTable.Select method, which sorts and filters the DataTable rows. The Select method has four overloaded forms. The Select method can take an expression with optional sort and row state parameters.

A *filter* is a conditional statement that uses the SELECT…WHERE clause to select conditional data from the database. All SQL conditional operators are valid in the filter string. For example, to filter rows where the id is greater than 22, the filter string will be Id>22; for selecting records with the name Ross, the filter string will be Name='Ross'. The SeachBtn_Click method searches for the criteria you specify on the form. As you can see from Listing 3-20, the code first calls the Select method with the given criteria, which returns an array of DataRow objects. It creates a new DataTable called searchTable and adds all rows returned by the Select method to this DataTable, and it later binds the searchTable to DataGrid to view the rows.

Listing 3-20. The SearchButtonClick *Method*

```
Private Sub SearchBtn_Click(ByVal sender As System.Object, _
  ByVal e As System.EventArgs) Handles SearchBtn.Click

    Dim searchTable As DataTable = New DataTable("SortTable")
    searchTable = custTable.Clone()
    Dim str As String = TextBox1.Text & " ='" & TextBox2.Text + "'"
    Dim rows() As DataRow = custTable.Select(str)
    ' If no record found
    If rows.Length = 0 Then
      MessageBox.Show("Name not found!")
      Return
    End If
    Dim i As Integer
    For i = 0 To rows.Length - 1 Step i + 1
      Dim row As DataRow = searchTable.NewRow()
      row("Name") = rows(i)("Name")
      row("Address") = rows(i)("Address")
      searchTable.Rows.Add(row)
    Next
    Dim sortdtSet As DataSet = New DataSet("SortedData")
    sortdtSet.Tables.Add(searchTable)
    DataGrid1.DataSource = sortdtSet.DefaultViewManager
End Sub
```

Now using the Search Section text boxes, you can search for records with the name Amy by entering **Name** in the Enter Column Name box, entering **Amy** in the Enter Value box, and clicking the Search button. The result looks like Figure 3-14.

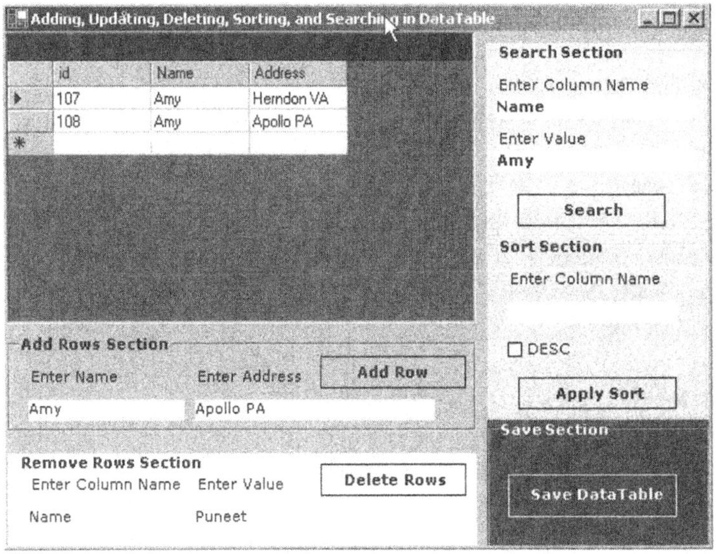

Figure 3-14. Result of clicking the Search button for Name="Amy"

Now using the Select method, you can also sort the data of a DataTable. As you can see from Figure 3-14, the Sort Section has a DESC check box and an Enter Column Name text box. If the DESC check box is clicked, rows will be sorted in descending order; otherwise, the default order is ascending. A filter followed by values ASC and DESC sorts the rows filtered using the Select method.

Listing 3-21 shows the code written on the Sort button click event handler. As you can see, first the code builds a filter string, checking whether the DESC check box is checked. After that it simply calls the Select method with the filter string and creates a new DataTable from the rows returned by the Select method and binds the new DataTable to the grid.

Listing 3-21. Sorting Data Using the Select *Method*

```
Private Sub SortBtn_Click(ByVal sender As System.Object, _
  ByVal e As System.EventArgs) Handles SortBtn.Click

    Dim sortTable As DataTable = New DataTable("SortTable")
    sortTable = custTable.Clone()
    Dim strSort As String = TextBox3.Text
    If (CheckBox1.Checked) Then
      strSort = strSort & " DESC"
    Else
```

```
        strSort = strSort & " ASC"
      End If
      Dim rows() As DataRow = _
      custTable.Select(String.Empty, strSort)
      Dim i As Integer
      For i = 0 To rows.Length - 1 Step i + 1
        Dim row As DataRow = sortTable.NewRow()
        row("Name") = rows(i)("Name")
        row("Address") = rows(i)("Address")
        sortTable.Rows.Add(row)
      Next
      Dim sortdtSet As DataSet = New DataSet("SortedData")
      sortdtSet.Tables.Add(sortTable)
      DataGrid1.DataSource = sortdtSet.DefaultViewManager
    End Sub
```

To sort the records, you enter the column name **Name** and check the DESC
check box. Now, if you click the Apply Sort button, you'll see the records are sorted
on the name. If you uncheck the DESC check box, you'll see the rows sorted in
ascending order.

The last thing to do in this example is to create the Save button. The DataSet
class provides methods to read and write XML documents. The WriteXml method
of DataSet saves data to an XML document. (We discuss XML and ADO.NET in
more detail in Chapter 6.)

Listing 3-22 shows the Save method button click event handler. As you can see,
the code calls a SaveFileDialog and reads the name and path of the file. You can
browse the path where you want to save the file. After saving data, if you open the
XML file, you'll see all data from the DataTable is stored in this file.

Listing 3-22. Saving a DataTable *Data in an XML Document*

```
  Private Sub SaveBtn_Click(ByVal sender As System.Object, _
  ByVal e As System.EventArgs) Handles SaveBtn.Click
    Dim fdlg As SaveFileDialog = New SaveFileDialog()
    fdlg.Title = "Applied ADO.NET Save File Dialog"
    fdlg.InitialDirectory = "c:\\"
    fdlg.Filter = "XML files (*.xml)|*.*|All files (*.*)|*.*"
    If fdlg.ShowDialog() = DialogResult.OK Then
      dtSet.WriteXml(fdlg.FileName)
    End If
  End Sub
```

The Row and Column Collections

Do you remember the Rows and Columns property of DataTable? As mentioned earlier, the Columns property of DataSet, represented by a DataColumnCollection object, stands for all columns of a DataTable. The Rows property of DataTable represents a collection of rows of a DataTable. Generally, you access the rows and columns collections through the Rows and Columns properties of a DataTable. You've already seen how to add columns and rows to a DataTable in the previous sections. In the following sections, we discuss the methods and properties.

The DataRowCollection Class

The Count property of DataRowCollection returns the total number of rows in a collection. The following code reads the total number of rows in custTable:

```
Dim rows As DataRowCollection = custTable.Rows
Dim counter As Integer
counter = rows.Count
```

The Clear method of DataRowCollection removes all the rows in a collection and sets the Rows count to zero:

```
Dim rows As DataRowCollection = custTable.Rows
rows.Clear()
```

The Remove and RemoveAt methods remove a specified DataRow based on the DataRow and its index, respectively.

The Contains method looks for a primary key value in the collection. This method returns True if a collection finds the specified value in the primary key column. The Contains method takes an argument of an object type.

The Find method is one more useful method of DataRowCollection; it searches for a row in the collection. Similar to the Contains method, the Find method also takes an argument of object type, which means Find can be used to find any types of values.

Listing 3-23 checks if the row collection's primary key column contains value 1002. If it does, it uses the Find method, which returns a DataRow and calls the DataRowCollection.Remove method to remove the row from the collection.

Listing 3-23. Using the Contains, Find, *and* Remove *Method of* DataRowCollection

```
Dim rows As DataRowCollection = custTable.Rows
Dim row As DataRow
If rows.Contains(1002) Then
    row = rows.Find(1002)
    rows.Remove(row)
    MessageBox.Show("Row Removed")
Else
    MessageBox.Show("Row not found")
End If
```

As you saw in earlier sections, the Add method of DataRowCollection adds a new row at the end of a collection. But what if you want to insert a row between two rows? The InsertAt method does the trick for you and inserts a row at the specified index, and the row at the index becomes the next row. Listing 3-24 inserts and removes rows at the specified index using the InsertAt and RemoveAt methods.

Listing 3-24. Using the InsertAt *and* RemoveAt *Methods*

```
Dim newRow As DataRow
newRow = custTable.NewRow()
newRow("id") = 1005
newRow("Address") = "New Address"
newRow("Name") = "New Name"
rows.InsertAt(newRow, 3)

If (Not rows(1).IsNull("id")) Then
    rows.RemoveAt(1)
End If
```

The DataColumnCollection Class

Similar to DataRowCollection, the Count property of DataColumnCollection returns the number of columns in a collection. You already saw in previous samples that you can use the Add method to add a new column to a collection.

You can use the CanRemove method to find out if a column can be removed from a collection. It returns True if a column can be removed from a collection; otherwise, it returns False. This method performs several operations to make sure the column exists in the table and it's not involved in a constraint or relation. The Contains method checks if a column with a given name exists in the collection.

The Remove and RemoveAt methods remove a column from a collection. The Remove method takes a parameter of type DataColumn or a name of the column. Listing 3-25 uses some of these methods.

Listing 3-25. Removing a Column from a Collection

```
Dim cols As DataColumnCollection = custTable.Columns
Dim str As String
str = cols.Count.ToString()
MessageBox.Show(str)
If cols.Contains("Name") Then
  If cols.CanRemove(cols("Name")) Then
    cols.Remove("Name")
  End If
End If
```

The RemoveAt method removes a column at the given index. The Clear method removes all the columns from a column collection. The following codes uses these two methods:

```
cols.RemoveAt(2)
cols.Clear()
```

The DataRow States and Versions

A DataRow changes its states as you work on it. The RowState property of DataRow represents the state of a row, which is a type of DataRowState enumeration. The DataRowState enumeration has five members:

- The Added state means the row has been added to a collection and the DataRow.AcceptChanges method hasn't been called yet.

- The Deleted state means the row was deleted using DataRow.Delete.

- The Detached state means the row has been created but not added to a collection.

- The Modified state means the row has been changed, and DataRow.AcceptChanges has not been called yet.

- The Unchanged state means that DataRow.AcceptChanges has been called but the row wasn't changed.

You can examine the state of a DataRow after any operation on the row. Listing 3-26 uses the RowState property to determine the state of a row.

Listing 3-26. Determining the State of a Row

```
Dim row As DataRow
row = custTable.NewRow()
MessageBox.Show(row.RowState.ToString())
row("id") = 1007
row("Name") = "Noak "
row("Address") = "Tame Lack, NJ"
custTable.Rows.Add(row)
MessageBox.Show(row.RowState.ToString())
custTable.Rows.Remove(row)
custTable.AcceptChanges()
```

The DataRowView is one more important class you should know when working with tables and rows. You can create a DataRowView that corresponds to a DataRow, which you can then bind to data-bound controls directly.

A DataRowView class represents a customized view of a DataRow, which can be bound to data-bound controls such as a DataGrid. When you work with a DataRow (update data of a DataRow), the DataRow has different versions. These states are represented by a DataRowVersion enumeration, which has four values: Current, Default, Proposed, and Original. The version of a DataRow changes when you call the BeginEdit, CancelEdit, and EndEdit methods of DataRow as well as the AcceptChanges and RejectChanges methods of DataTable.

After calling DataRow.BeginEdit and changing the value of a row, both the Current and Proposed values become available. After calling DataRow.CancelEdit, the Proposed value isn't available. After a call of DataRow.EndEdit, the Current value becomes the Proposed value, and the Proposed value becomes unavailable. The call of DataRow.AcceptChanges means the original value becomes identical to the Current value. A call of DataTable.RejectChanges means the Proposed value is removed. The version becomes Current.

The DataView property of DataRowView class returns a DataView object for a row, which can be bound to data-bound controls. The IsEdit and IsNew properties represent whether a row is in edit mode or new mode, respectively. The DataRow property returns the DataRow being viewed, and the RowVersion property returns the version of a row.

The BeginEdit method starts editing a row, and the CancelEdit method cancels editing. The Delete method deletes a row, and the EndEdit method ends the editing. Listing 3-27 starts editing a row and later calls the CancelEdit and EndEdit methods, followed by the AcceptChanges method.

Listing 3-27. Editing Rows Using BeginEdit, CancelEdit, *and* EndEdit *Methods*

```
Dim row As DataRow
  row = custTable.NewRow()
  MessageBox.Show(row.RowState.ToString())
  row("id") = 1007
  row("Name") = "Noak "
  row("Address") = "Tame Lack, NJ"
  custTable.Rows.Add(row)
  MessageBox.Show(row.RowState.ToString())
  custTable.Rows.Remove(row)
  custTable.AcceptChanges()

  ' Start Editing the Row
  custTable.Rows(0).BeginEdit()
  custTable.Rows(0)("id") = 1008
  custTable.Rows(0)("Name") = "New Name"
  custTable.Rows(0)("Address") = "New Address"
  ' Find out DataRowVersion
  If custTable.Rows(0).HasVersion(DataRowVersion.Proposed) Then
    MessageBox.Show(DataRowVersion.Proposed.ToString())
  End If
  If custTable.Rows(0).HasVersion(DataRowVersion.Original) Then
    MessageBox.Show(DataRowVersion.Original.ToString())
  End If
  ' Cancel the edit.
  custTable.Rows(0).CancelEdit()
  ' BeginEdit again
  custTable.Rows(0).BeginEdit()
  custTable.Rows(0)("id") = 1008
  custTable.Rows(0)("Name") = "New Name"
  custTable.Rows(0)("Address") = "New Address"
  custTable.Rows(0).EndEdit()
  custTable.Rows(0).AcceptChanges()
DataGrid1.DataSource = custTable
```

Using DataSet, DataView, and DataViewManager

As you saw in Chapter 2, ADO.NET provides components to view data in data-bound controls. You just drag and drop controls to a form, set their properties, and bind them to data-bound controls. Then you're all set to run your programs. The DataView and DataViewManager classes fall into this category. You can use these classes to represent different views of a DataTable based on different filter and sort criterion. You can use these classes either at design-time or at runtime.

A DataSet is a key component in the ADO.NET data model. It's an in-memory representation of one or multiple DataTables, relations, and constraints. A DataSet stores data from a data source and provides data to the client applications (Web Forms or Windows Forms). A DataSet's contents can be bound to data-bound controls. (We discuss the DataSet class in more detail in "The DataSet: The Heart of ADO.NET."

The DataView is useful when you need to bind a DataTable or multiple DataTable objects with data-bound controls. You can also represent multiple views of the same data by applying a filter and sort on a DataTable, and you can bind these multiple views to different data-bound controls such as DataGrid, DataList, ComboBox, and ListBox controls.

Figure 3-15 shows the relationship between a DataSet, DataTable, DataView, and Windows and Web Forms controls. As you can see, a DataSet contains three DataTable objects, which are represented by three different views. You can bind the three different DataView objects to different data-bound controls to represent data in different ways.

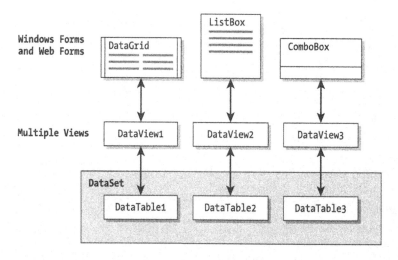

Figure 3-15. Relationship between the DataSet, DataTable, *and* DataView

The DataSet: The Heart of ADO.NET

A DataSet object plays a vital role in the ADO.NET component model. A DataSet represents a disconnected cache of data in the form of tables, rows, columns, or XML schemas. If you've ever programmed a database application in previous versions of VS, you're probably familiar with *recordsets*. A recordset object was a way to represent data in your programs. Similar to a recordset, a DataSet represents data in your applications. Once you've constructed a DataSet, you can get or set data in your application or your data source. As mentioned earlier, the DataSet works in both connected and disconnected environments. A DataSet communicates with a DataAdapter and calls the DataAdapter's Fill method to fill data from a DataAdapter. You can fill a DataSet object with multiple tables or stored procedures with the aid of the DataAdapters. You'll see how a DataSet works in a connected environment to access data from multiple data sources in the next chapter. In this section, you'll see how it works with DataTable and DataView objects. (We discuss DataAdapter in more detail in Chapter 4.) Once data is filled to a DataSet from a DataAdapter, you can view it in Windows or Web applications by binding data to data-bound controls through a DataView. You can generate one or multiple views for a DataTables based on the filter and sort criteria.

Figure 3-16 shows the relationship between DataSet, DataAdapter, and DataView objects.

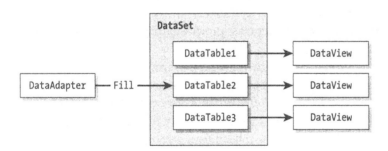

Figure 3-16. The relationship between DataSet, DataAdapter, *and* DataView *objects*

As you saw earlier, a DataSet can have multiple DataTable objects. The DataTableCollection object represents all DataSet objects related to a DataSet. The Tables property of the DataSet represents the collection of DataTable objects. The tables relate to each other with DataRelation objects, discussed earlier.

DataRelationCollection represents all the available relations in the DataSet. The Relations property represents the DataRelationCollection of a DataSet. A DataSet object stores data in XML format. An XML schema represents a DataSet. A DataSet also defines methods to read and write XML documents. The ReadXml method reads an XML document and fills the DataSet with the XML data, and the WriteXML method writes DataSet data to an XML document. This class also defines the methods ReadXmlSchema and WriteXmlSchema to read and write XML schema.

Creating a DataSet

The DataSet class provides three overloaded constructors to create a DataSet object. You create a DataSet with or without passing a DataSet name in the DataSet contructor. The following code creates two DataSet objects in different ways:

```
Dim dtSet1 As DataSet
dtSet1 = New DataSet("DataSet1")
Dim dtSet2 As DataSet = New DataSet("DataSet2")
```

The DataSet Properties

You just learned how to create a DataSet object. In most cases, you'll probably create a DataSet and use the DataAdapter's Fill and Update methods to fill and save data from a data source. But the DataSet class provides properties that you can get and set as needed.

The CaseSensitive property indicates whether the string comparison within DataTable objects is case sensitive. This property affects how sorting, searching, and filtering operations are performed on DataTable objects of a DataSet, when lyou use the Select method of DataTable to filter and sort data. By default the lCaseSensitive property is False. Use the following to set it to True:

```
DtSet1.CaseSensitive =  True
```

The DataSetName property represents the name of a DataSet. The following code first sets a DataSet name and then displays it in a message box:

```
Dim dtSet1 As DataSet
dtSet1 = New DataSet("DataSet1")
dtSet1.DataSetName = "CustomDataSet"
MessageBox.Show(dtSet1.DataSetName.ToString())
```

The DefaultViewManager (read only) property returns a custom view of the data of a DataSet. (We discuss this in more details in "The DefaultViewManager.")

The EnforceConstraints property is a Boolean type property, which makes sure constraint rules are followed when data of a DataSet is being updated. The default value of the EnforceConstraints property is True. If you don't want the Update method to check the constraints, just set this property as False.

Do you remember the ExtendedProperties property of the DataTable? The ExtendedProperties property attaches some additional custom information about a DataTable. Similar to the DataTable, the DataSet also provides the ExtendedProperties property. Listing 3-28 sets and reads the custom properties of a DataSet.

Listing 3-28. Setting and Reading Custom Properties of a DataSet

```
Dim dtSet1 As DataSet
dtSet1 = New DataSet("DataSet1")
dtSet1.DataSetName = "CustomDataSet"
dtSet1.ExtendedProperties.Add("Description", "The Name Column")
dtSet1.ExtendedProperties.Add("Author", "Mahesh Chand")
dtSet1.ExtendedProperties.Add("UserId", "MCB")
dtSet1.ExtendedProperties.Add("PWD", "Password")
' Remove Author property
dtSet1.ExtendedProperties.Remove("Author")
' Read custom properties
Dim str As String
Dim i As Integer
str = dtSet1.ExtendedProperties("Description").ToString()
str = str + ", " + dtSet1.ExtendedProperties("UserId").ToString()
str = str + ", " + dtSet1.ExtendedProperties("PWD").ToString()
MessageBox.Show(str)
```

The HasErrors property finds out if any of the rows of a DataSet has any errors. The DataTable also provides this property to check if a particular row has any errors. (We show you how to use this property in a moment.)

A CultureInfo object contains the data about a machine locale. The Locale property gets and sets this data. The following code uses this property to read the information:

```
Dim cInfo As System.Globalization.CultureInfo
cInfo = dtSet1.Locale
Console.WriteLine(cInfo.DisplayName, cInfo.EnglishName)
```

As mentioned earlier (and in more detail in Chapter 6), a DataSet is represented by an XML schema, which has a namespace and prefix. The Namespace and Prefix properties represent the namespace and prefix of the schema, respectively. These properties are both readable and writeable:

```
dtSet1.Namespace = "CustDSNamespace"
dtSet1.Prefix = "CustPrefix"
```

The Relations property returns a collection of relations that a DataSet has. (We discuss this property in later sections and in Chapter 4.)

As discussed earlier, the Tables property of a DataSet represents a collection of DataTables attached to a DataSet. The Tables property is of type DataTableCollection, which was discussed earlier. The DataTableCollection class provides methods to add and remove DataTable objects to a collection.

Attaching a DataTable to a DataSet

You've already seen how to create a DataTable and add columns and rows to a DataTable by using the DataRow and DataColumn. As mentioned earlier, a DataSet is a collection of DataTable objects. The Tables property of DataSet gets all the attached DataTables of a DataSet. The Tables property, which is a type of DataTableCollection, also adds DataTable objects to a DataSet and removes them. Listing 3-29 creates four DataTable objects and adds them to a DataSet using the DataSet.Tables.Add method. The DataSet is bound to a DataGrid to view the contents in a DataGrid.

In this code, custTable is a DataTable created using the methods discussed.

Listing 3-29. Adding DataTable Objects to a DataSet

```
Dim tbl1 As DataTable = New DataTable("One")
Dim tbl2 As DataTable = New DataTable("Two")
Dim tbl3 As DataTable = New DataTable("Three")
Dim dtSet1 As DataSet = New DataSet("CustDtSet")
dtSet1.Tables.Add(custTable)
dtSet1.Tables.Add(tbl1)
dtSet1.Tables.Add(tbl2)
dtSet1.Tables.Add(tbl3)
DataGrid1.DataSource = dtSet1.DefaultViewManager
```

The output of Listing 3-29 looks like Figure 3-17. If you click a DataTable link, you can see the data of the DataTable (if it has any).

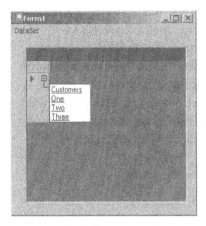

Figure 3-17. Attaching DataTables *to a* DataSet

Copying, Cloning, and Clearing DataSets

The Clear method removes all the rows from a DataSet; however, it does not destroy the structure of a DataSet. The Copy method copies the contents with schema of a DataSet to another DataSet. The Clone method only copies the structure of a DataSet to another. Listing 3-30 uses all three members.

Listing 3-30. Using Copy, Clone, *and* Clear *Methods of* DataSet

```
Dim dtSet1 As DataSet = New DataSet("CustDtSet")
dtSet1.Tables.Add(custTable)
Dim dtSet2 As DataSet = New DataSet()
dtSet2 = dtSet1.Clone()
dtSet2 = dtSet1.Copy()
dtSet1.Clear()
```

Getting Changed Rows of a DataSet

So far, we've talked about filling data from a DataAdapter to a DataSet and saving data back to a data source using the Update method of DataSet. The Update method takes a DataSet and saves its results in a data source. A DataAdapter belongs to a data provider, so we discuss it in Chapter 4.

The GetChanges method helps you find the changed data of a DataSet so you can send only changed data back to the data source instead of sending an entire DataSet. It helps to reduce the network traffic and make the save process faster.

The GetChanges method returns a DataSet, which contains all the changes made to a DataSet since it was last loaded or the AcceptChanges method was called.

The GetChanges method has two overloaded forms. The first form takes no parameters and returns all the results. The second form lets you filter the results based on the row states, and it takes a parameter of type DataRowState.

The HasChanges method determines if a DataSet has any changes since it was last saved or loaded. The following snippet shows how to use the HasChanges and GetChanges methods (you'll see these methods in more detail in Chapter 4).

```
If Not dtSet1.HasChanges(DataRowState.Modified) Then Exit Sub
Dim dtSet2 As DataSet
dtSet2 = dtSet1.GetChanges(DataRowState.Modified)
SqlDbDataAdapter1.Update(dtSet2)
```

Merging a DataRow, DataTable, or a DataSet

The Merge method merges two DataSet objects and saves the results in one DataSet. The Merge method has seven overloaded forms. These forms allow you to merge a DataRow, a DataTable, and a DataSet with an existing DataSet. The first parameter of the Merge method is a DataRow, DataTable, or DataSet. The second optional parameter is a Boolean type—a True value indicates that the changes should be preserved and False indicates that changes won't be preserved. The third optional parameter is a type of MissingSchemaAction, which indicates what action should be taken when the schema of added DataRow, DataTable, or DataSet does not match the schema of the current DataSet. The MissingSchemaAction enumeration has four values: Add, AddWithKey, Error, and Ignore. The Add value adds necessary columns to complete the schema. The AddWithKey value adds the necessary information with a primary key. The Error value generates an error. The Ignore value ignores the extra columns.

Listing 3-31 merges two DataSet objects. The custTable and ordersTables are two DataSet objects created by the CreateCustomersTable() and CreateOrdersTable() methods, as discussed in "The DataSet: The Heart of ADO.NET" section.

Listing 3-31. Merging Two DataSets

```
Dim dtSet1 As DataSet = New DataSet("EmpDataSet")
Dim dtSet2 As DataSet = New DataSet("OrdersDataSet")
dtSet1.Tables.Add(custTable)
dtSet2.Tables.Add(ordersTable)
dtSet1.Merge(dtSet2, False, MissingSchemaAction.Add)
DataGrid1.DataSource = dtSet1.DefaultViewManager
```

As mentioned, the Merge method also lets you merge an array of a DataRow or a DataTable object. Listing 3-32 shows you how to merge rows and a DataTable with a DataSet.

Listing 3-32. Merging DataRow and DataTable Objects

```
Dim str As String = "OrderId >= 2 "
Dim rows() As DataRow = ordersTable.Select(str)
dtSet1.Tables.Add(custTable)
dtSet2.Tables.Add(ordersTable)
dtSet1.Merge(rows)
dtSet1.Merge(ordersTable, True, MissingSchemaAction.Ignore)
```

Other DataSet Methods

There are a few more DataSet methods left to discuss. The AcceptChanges method saves all the changes made to a DataSet since it was loaded or the last time AcceptChanges was called. The RejectChanges method rolls back all the changes made to a DataSet since it was created or the last time AcceptChanges was called. These methods are discussed in more details in next chapter.

The ReadXml and ReadXmlSchema methods read an XML document and XML schema document, respectively. The WriteXml and WriteXmlSchema methods save DataSet data to XML document and XML schema document, respectively. (We discuss these methods in Chapter 6 in more detail.)

Typed and Untyped DataSets

As you may recall from earlier discussions, there are two kinds of a DataSet: typed or untyped. A typed DataSet first comes from the DataSet class and then uses an XML schema (.xsd file) to generate a new class. You saw how to create a typed DataSet using VS .NET in Chapter 2. An untyped DataSet has no built-in schema. You create an instance of a DataSet class and call its methods and properties to work with the data sources. All elements of an untyped DataSet are collections. In this chapter, you'll work with untyped DataSets.

Both kinds of DataSet have their own advantages and disadvantages. Typed DataSets take less time to write applications but offer no flexibility. They're useful when you already know the schema of a database. The biggest advantage of typed DataSets is the VS .NET IDE support. As you saw in Chapter 2, you can drag a database table, its columns, or stored procedures to a form in your application, and the IDE generates typed DataSet for you. After that, you can bind these DataSets to the controls. However, there are many occasions when you don't know the schema of a database. In those cases, the untyped DataSets are useful. The untyped DataSets also provide the flexibility of connecting with multiple data sources. And you can use them without the VS .NET IDE.

The DataView

Another powerful feature of ADO.NET is the ability to create several different views of the same data. You can sort these views differently and filter them on different criteria. They can contain different row state information.

A DataView represents a customized view of DataTable that you can bind to Windows Forms and Web Forms controls. Using DataView sort and filter features, you can also have multiple views of a single DataTable. Using RowFilter and Sort properties, you can apply a filter on a DataView and sort its contents before binding it to a data-bound control. The AddNew method adds a new row to a DataView, and the Delete method deletes a row from a DataView. You can use the Find and FindRows methods to search for rows based on the defined criteria.

Table 3-9 describes some of the DataView properties, and Table 3-10 describes some of its methods.

Table 3-9. The DataView *Class Properties*

PROPERTY	DESCRIPTION
AllowDelete	Indicates whether deletes are allowed.
AllowEdit	Indicates whether edits are allowed.
AddNews	Indicates whether new rows can be added.
ApplyDefaultSort	Indicates whether to use default sort. True means use the default sort and False means no.
Count	Represents the number of records in a DataView after RowFilter and RowStateFilter have been applied.
DataViewManager	DataViewManager associated with this view.
Item	Represents an item of a row.
RowFilter	Represents the expression used to filter rows to view in the DataView.
RowStateFilter	You can use a row state filter using this property.
Sort	Represents the sort column and sort order.
Table	DataTable attached with this view.

Table 3-10. The DataView *Class Methods*

METHOD	DESCRIPTION
AddNew	Adds a new row to the DataView
BeginInit	Begins the intialization if a data view was previously used
EndInit	Ends the initialization started by BeginInit
Delete	Deletes a row
Find	Finds a row in the DataView based on the specified criteria
FindRows	Returns an array of rows based on the specified criteria

Creating a DataView

The DataView constructor allows you to create a DataView object from a DataTable, which you can use with or without a DataSet. In Listing 3-33, the custTable and ordersTable are two DataTable objects. As you can see, the code creates a DataView directly from a DataTable and creates a second DataView through a DataSet.

Listing 3-33. Creating DataView *Objects from a* DataTable

```
' Creating a DataView from DataTable
Dim dtView1 As DataView = New DataView(custTable)
' Creating a DataView through  DataSet
Dim dtSet1 As DataSet = New DataSet()
dtSet1.Tables.Add(ordersTable)
Dim dtView2 As DataView = New DataView(dtSet1.Tables(0))
```

Binding a DataView with a data-bound control is pretty easy. You set the DataSource and DisplayMember properties of a data-bound control. For example, the following code binds two DataView objects with a DataGrid and a ListBox control.

```
DataGrid1.DataSource = dtView1
ListBox1.DataSource = dtView2
ListBox1.DisplayMember = "Name"
```

Chapter 7 discusses data-bound controls in more detail.

Adding, Editing, and Deleting Data Using DataView

The AddNew method of a DataView, which returns a DataRowView, adds a new row to the DataView. The AddNew method is followed by a call of EndEdit. The BeginEdit and EndEdit pair edits the values of a row. The AllowDelete, AllowNew, and AllowEdit properties allow deleting, adding, and updating in a DataView if they're set to True.

The Delete method of a DataView deletes a row specified by the index of the row. The Count property returns the total number of rows in a DataView.

Listing 3-34 uses the previously discussed methods and properties to add, delete, and edit rows of a DataView.

Listing 3-34. Adding, Updating, and Deleting Rows of a DataView

```
' Creating a DataView from DataTable
Dim dtView1 As DataView = New DataView(custTable)
' Creating a DataView through  DataSet
Dim dtSet1 As DataSet = New DataSet()
dtSet1.Tables.Add(ordersTable)
Dim dtView2 As DataView = New DataView(dtSet1.Tables(0))
' Set AllowDelete, AllowNew and AllowEdit to true
dtView1.AllowDelete = True
dtView1.AllowNew = True
dtView1.AllowEdit = True
' Edit the data of first row
dtView1(0).BeginEdit()
dtView1(0)("Name") = "Edited Name"
dtView1(0)("Address") = "Edited Address"
dtView1(0).EndEdit()
' Delete the first row from DataView
' the Delete method takes an index of row starting
' at 0
If dtView1.AllowDelete Then
  dtView1.Delete(0)
End If
' Add a new row
Dim drv As DataRowView = dtView1.AddNew
' Change values in the DataRow.
drv("id") = 1010
drv("Name") = "New Name"
drv("Address") = "New Address"
drv.EndEdit()
' Count number of rows
MessageBox.Show(dtView1.Count.ToString())
```

Searching and Sorting Data Using DataView

Searching and sorting are two major operations that a DataView does to filter data. The Sort property of DataView sorts rows of a DataView. The Sort property takes a string value, which contains the sort criteria with one or more than one DataTable columns separated by a comma (,) and followed by ASC or DESC, where ASC is for sorting rows in ascending order and DESC for sorting rows in descending order. The following code shows how to use one or more than one column with the ASC and DESC options:

```
dtView1.Sort = "Name, Address ASC"
dtView1.Sort = "Name DESC"
```

The RowFilter property of a DataView filters the rows depending on the given criteria. The RowFilter takes a criteria, which contains columns and their values. The following code returns all rows that contain Name column values of Miranda:

```
dtView1.RowFilter = "Name = 'Miranda'"
```

Besides the Sort and RowFilter properties, the DataView class provides Find and FindRow methods to find rows. The Find method requires a Sort field and takes a parameter of type Object or an array of Object. The FindRow method returns an array of DataRowView, whose column matches the specified sort key value.

Listing 3-35 uses the Find method to find the value "Data Quest" in the column Name, which returns an index of the row.

Listing 3-35. Finding Rows in a DataView *Using the* Find *Method*

```
' Creating a DataView from DataTable
Dim dtView1 As DataView = New DataView(custTable)
' Creating a DataView through  DataSet
Dim dtSet1 As DataSet = New DataSet()
dtSet1.Tables.Add(ordersTable)
Dim dtView2 As DataView = New DataView(dtSet1.Tables(0))
dtView2.Sort = "Name"
Dim val As Object = "Data Quest"
Dim pos As Integer = dtView2.Find(Val)
MessageBox.Show(pos.ToString())
```

The DataViewManager

A DataViewManager contains a collection of views of a DataSet—one view for each DataTable in the DataSet. The DataViewManager has a DataViewSettings property that enables the user to construct a different view for each DataTable in the DataSet. If you want to create two views on the same DataTable, you need to create another instance of the DataViewManager and construct the DataViewSettings for that particular view. Then you construct a DataView using the DataViewManager. For example, in the Orders DataSet, you may want to filter out the orders with an EmployeeID of 4 and sort the orders by the date they were shipped. You can retrieve records for EmployeedId = 4 sorted on the date they were shipped using the sort and filter properties of the DataSet and attaching the filtered and sorted data to a DataView or a DataViewManager.

To construct a DataViewManager, you can either use the Default constructor or pass in a DataSet object. For example:

```
view = new DataViewManager ()
```

or, for example:

```
view = new DataSetView(myDataSet)
```

The DataViewManager has a few properties you need to know about to utilize it effectively. Table 3-11 shows the main properties.

Table 3-11. DataSetView *Properties*

PROPERTIES	DESCRIPTION
DataSet	The DataSet being viewed of type DataSet.
DataViewSettings	Contains the collection of TableSetting objects for each table in the DataSet. The TableSetting object contains sorting and filtering criteria for a particular table.

DataViewManager contains the CreateDataView method, which allows you to create a DataView object for a particular table in your DataSet. You can construct the DataView for the table with the DataViewManager's DataViewSettings for the particular DataTable of the DataSet. You can also adjust settings for the DataView by assigning filter and sort properties directly in the DataView.

You'll see DataView and DataViewManager objects in the sample applications in Chapter 4.

Summary

In this chapter you learned about the ADO.NET model class hierarchy. ADO.NET consists of three general namespaces and many data provider namespaces. There are two general namespaces—System.Data and System.Data.Common—and a SQL Server–specific namespace called System.Data.SqlTypes. The System.Data namespace defines classes that are the basic building clocks of the ADO.NET model. The System.Data.Common namespace defines classes shared by all data providers. The System.SqlTypes namespace defines classes that convert from SQL native data types to .NET data types.

You can divide ADO.NET classes into two categories: disconnected and connected. You can use disconnected classes with or without data providers, but connected classes work with the data providers. Some of the disconnected classes are DataSet, DataTable, DataRow, DataColumn, DataView, and DataViewManager.

In this chapter, you saw how to work with these disconnected classes. You learned how to create in-memory tables with the help of the DataTable, DataRow, and DataColumn classes. After that you worked with the DataView, DataSet, and DataViewManager classes.

Chapter 4 covers the ADO.NET data providers and working with ADO.NET in a connected environment.

CHAPTER 4

ADO.NET in Connected Environments

As MENTIONED EARLIER, you can divide ADO.NET functionality into two categories: connected and disconnected. In Chapter 3, you examined the disconnected functionality provided by the .NET Framework that resides in the System.Data and System.Data.Common namespaces. In disconnected environments, the data is stored in memory.

In this chapter, we explain ADO.NET functionality in connected environments, which means reading and storing data in data sources. Specifically, you access data from a data source and save data back to the data source with the help of a bridge between the application and the data source; in ADO.NET this bridge is a *data provider*. ADO.NET provides many data providers for different data sources to make data access fast, reliable, and easy to use. Each data provider has data components (classes) that let you connect to a data source, as well as read, write, add, delete, and update data. In this chapter, you'll learn about these components and how to work with them.

So what are the ADO.NET data providers? Technically, an ADO.NET data provider is a set of classes that enables you to connect to a data source in order to read and write data from a data source. A data provider also has components that serve as conduits between the data source and the DataSet. In this way, the architecture isolates the manipulation of data from the data source.

Understanding the Generic Data Provider Model

Let's examine a generic data provider model before looking at specific data providers. Figure 4-1 shows a generic class model of a data provider. The same component model applies to all of the data providers, with minor changes. All data providers implement a similar class hierarchy model, so once you're comfortable with one data provider, you can easily manipulate the other data providers in no time. It's usually just a matter of changing the class names and the connection string.

The Connection component of a data provider is the first component, and it communicates with a data source. A DataAdapter sits between a DataSet and the data source and passes data back and forth. The DataAdapter's Fill method fills data from a data source to a DataSet, and the Update method of the DataAdapter saves changes from a DataSet to a data source. In Chapter 3, you saw how to use the data once you have it in a DataSet through the DataTable, DataRow, and DataColumn objects.

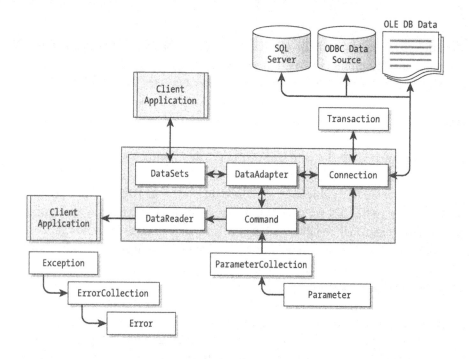

Figure 4-1. A generic data provider model

The Command and CommandBuilder objects are two more important components of a data provider. A Command component uses SQL queries to transfer data back and forth from a data source to an application and vice versa. A Command or CommandBuilder object can use a DataAdapter or a DataReader. The DataReader is a fast, read-only gateway of data.

You'll begin your understanding of the ADO.NET data providers by examining the Sql data provider defined in the System.Data.SqlClient namespace. This namespace contains the classes necessary to manipulate the data providers.

Importing a Namespace

Before anything else, you need to decide what data provider you'll use in your applications. Once you've decided, you need to include the namespace in your applications so the namespace objects are available to you. You include a namespace by adding an Imports directive, followed by the namespace, to your project. The following lines import the System.Data, System.Data.Common, System.Data.SqlClient, and System.Data.OleDb namespaces of ADO.NET:

```
Imports System.Data
Imports System.Data.Common
Imports System.Data.SqlClient
Imports System.Data.OleDb
```

In later chapters, we discuss other data providers—such as Odbc and Oracle—and their related namespaces.

You can also access a namespace's objects by specifying the full namespace when you declare the objects. For example, the following code accesses the SqlConnection class of the System.Data.SqlClient namespace (in this case, you don't need to use the Imports statement):

```
Dim conn As SqlConnection = New SqlClient.SqlConnection()
```

The previous code is equivalent to the following code:

```
Imports System.Data.SqlClient
Dim conn As SqlConnection = New SqlConnection()
```

Exploring the System.SqlClient Namespace

In this chapter, we use the SQL Server database as the data source to test the code samples. Hence, we use the System.Data.SqlClient (or just SqlClient) namespace most of the time. Before going any further, let's explore the SqlClient namespace and see what it has to offer.

Table 4-1 describes the SqlClient namespace classes.

Table 4-1. Sql Data Provider Classes

CLASS	DESCRIPTION
SqlClientPermission	Makes sure the user who is accessing the data has permission to access a data source.
SqlClientPermissionAttribute	Sets permission attributes.
SqlCommand	Represents a SQL statement or stored procedure. Data can be returned in a DataReader by calling its ExecuteReader method.
SqlCommandBuilder	Provides a mechanism to generate automatic commands for a table.
SqlConnection	Represents a Connection object. This is first class you need to use to connect to a data source.
SqlDataAdapter	Set of commands that provides a link between SqlConnection and DataSet.
SqlDataReader	Reads data in a forward-only direction through SqlCommand.
SqlError	Collects error and warnings returned by the data source.
SqlErrorCollection	Collects errors generated by Sql data providers.
SqlException	Exception handling class designed for Sql data sources.
SqlInfoMessageEventArgs	Provides data for the InfoMessage event.
SqlParameter	This class represents a parameter used in SqlCommand.
SqlParameterCollection	A collection of parameters.
SqlRowUpdateEventArgs	Provides data for the RowUpdated event.
SqlRowUpdatingEventArgs	Provides data from the RowUpdating event.
SqlTransaction	A transaction that can be processed at a data source.

Like the Sql data provider, the OleDb, ODBC, and other data providers implement the same class hierarchy model. Programmatically, the only difference is the prefix for each data provider namespace and the connection string. Internally, each data provider uses a different native data access technology to access the data source. For example, the OleDb provider classes begin with OleDb, the Sql Server provider namespace classes start with Sql, and the ODBC provider classes begin with Odbc. The System.Data classes have no provider-specific prefix, of course, because the classes defined in the System.Data and System.Data.Common namespaces are used in memory and are shared by all the providers.

The way ADO.NET works is that once you've connected to a database and dumped the data into the in-memory object (known as the DataSet), you can disconnect from the database and manipulate the data until you're ready to write it back to the database. The data provider classes serve as a bridge for moving data back and forth between memory and the database. In the next section we discuss how to initially connect to a database using these providers and how to implement the data provider classes to allow data to use this efficient bridge.

In the sections that follow we describe how to connect to various databases with the data providers. Then we show you how to use the data provider classes to execute queries and stored procedures. Also, you'll learn how these powerful classes work together and how the data providers differ in certain capabilities. You'll also learn how to do transaction locking, batch transactions, and transaction rollbacks.

The Connection: Connecting to a Data Source

As you saw in Figure 4-1, the first object that interacts with a data source is the Connection object. You can bypass a Connection object by using a DataAdapter directly, but in that case a DataAdapter uses the Connection internally. The Connection class has a different name depending upon the data provider. The Connection class for OleDb, Sql, and Odbc are OleDbConnection, SqlConnection, respectively.

Creating a Connection

The SqlConnection class provides two forms of constructors. The first doesn't take any parameters, and the second takes a parameter of a connection string that points to the database to which you want to attach. The connection string contains the server name, database name, user ID, password, and more.

Listing 4-1 creates SqlConnection objects using both constructors.

Listing 4-1. Creating SqlConnection *Objects*

```
Dim connString As String = "user id=sa;password=password;" & _
    "initial catalog=northwind;data source=Northwind;Connect Timeout=30"
Dim conn1 As SqlConnection = New SqlConnection(connString)
Dim conn2 As SqlConnection = New SqlConnection()
conn2.ConnectionString = connString
```

After creating a connection, you call its Open method, and when you're done with the connection, you call the Close method.

Understanding the Connection Properties and Methods

The Connection class (SqlConnection in this case) has a connection string that contains a server and a database name. The connection string will vary depending upon the provider used. The connection string will typically contain a group of property-value pairs to describe how to connect to a database. For the OleDbConnection class, you have properties such as Provider and DataSource. For the SqlConnection class, you have the server name, initial catalog, user ID, and password. Table 4-2 describes the Connection class properties. (Based on the data provider, some of these properties may not be applicable.)

A typical connection for SQL Server may also contain the security type, the workstation ID, and even the network packet size. The following code is a connection string for a SQL Server called MCB:

```
connectionString =
    "data source=MCB;initial catalog=Northwind;"
    + "integrated security=SSPI;persist security info=False;"
    + "workstation id=MCB;packet size=4096";
```

Table 4-2. Connection *Object Properties*

PROPERTY	DESCRIPTION
ConnectionString	The connection string.
ConnectionTimeOut	Waiting time while establishing a connection.
DataBase	Name of the current database.
DataSource	Filename of the data source.
Provider	Name of the OLE DB provider. This property is not available for the Sql and ODBC data providers.
State	Current state of the connection of type ConnectionState.
PacketSize	Size of network packets. This is only available to Sql data providers.
ServerVersion	SQL Server version. This is only available to Sql data providers.
WorkStationId	Database client ID. This is only available to Sql data providers.

The Connection can have different states such as open, closed, connecting, and so on. The ConnectionType enumeration defines the members of the ConnectionState. Table 4-3 describes its members.

Table 4-3. The ConnectionType *Enumeration Members*

MEMBER	DESCRIPTION
Broken	Connection is broken after it was opened. This may be caused by network failure.
Closed	Connection is closed.
Connecting	Opening a new connection.
Executing	The connection is executing a command.
Fetching	Retrieving data from a data source.
Open	Connection is open and ready to use.

Table 4-4 describes the Connection class methods. You'll see some of these methods throughout this chapter. The purpose of this table is to give you an idea of available methods.

Table 4-4. The Connection *Class Members*

METHOD	DESCRIPTION
BeginTransaction	Begins a database transaction.
ChangeDatabase	Changes databases for an open connection.
Close	Closes an open connection.
CreateCommand	Creates and returns a Command objects depends on the data provider. For example, OleDbConnection returns OleDbCommand, and SqlConnection returns SqlCommand.
Open	Opens a new connection.
ReleaseObjectPool	Represents that the connection pooling can be cleared when the provider is released. This is only available for OleDb data providers.

Opening and Closing a Connection

As you can see from Listing 4-1, the code creates two Connection objects: conn1 and conn2. It creates conn1 with no connection string. If you create a Connection object with no connection string, you must set its ConnectionString property before you call the Open method of the Connection object. The code creates the conn2 object with a connection string as an argument. As you can see from the connection string, it consists of a provider name and data source.

NOTE *All the providers construct their connections in the same way. The thing that makes the connection construction different from other different providers is the* ConnectionString. *For example, the* SqlClient *namespace doesn't need to specify a provider string because Sql Server is always the database when using this class.*

After creating a Connection object, you call its Open method to open a connection. The Open method doesn't take any arguments. The following code opens a connection:

```
conn.Open()
```

When you're done with the connection, you call its Close method to release the connection. The Close method also doesn't take any arguments. The following code closes a connection:

```
conn.Close()
```

Listing 4-2 opens a connection with the Access 2000 Northwind database that resides in the C:\ directory. As you can see, you check the connection state to see if the connection is already opened (which is impossible in this code) or closed.

Listing 4-2. Connecting to an OleDb Database and Reading the OleDbConnection
Properties

```
' Create a Connection Object
    Dim ConnectionString As String = "Provider=Microsoft.Jet.OLEDB.4.0;" & _
              "Data Source=c:\\Northwind.mdb"
    Dim conn As OleDbConnection = New OleDbConnection(ConnectionString)
    ' Open the connection
    If conn.State <> ConnectionState.Open Then
      conn.Open()
      MessageBox.Show("Connection state: " + conn.State.ToString())
    End If
    ' Show the connection properties
    MessageBox.Show("Connection String :" + conn.ConnectionString & _
              ", DataSource :" + conn.DataSource.ToString() & _
              ", Provider :" + conn.Provider.ToString() & _
              "," + conn.ServerVersion.ToString() & _
              "," + conn.ConnectionTimeout.ToString())

    ' Close the connection
    If conn.State = ConnectionState.Open Then
      conn.Close()
      MessageBox.Show("Connection state: " + conn.State.ToString())
    End If
    ' Dispose the connection
    If (Not conn Is Nothing) Then
      conn.Dispose()
    End If
```

CAUTION *To utilize connection resources properly, it's always recommended to close open connections and dispose of connections explicitly if you don't intend to use them again. If you don't dispose of connections, the garbage collector will take care of it; however, the garbage collector waits for a certain interval of time. To force the garbage collector to dispose of connections, you call the* Dispose *method of the* SqlConnection. *The call to the* Dispose *method destroys the connection resource immediately.*

You can also use the OleDb data provider to connect to SQL Server or other databases if you have an OLE DB data provider installed for that database. Listing 4-3 shows the connection for a SQL Server using the OleDb data provider.

Listing 4-3. Connecting to a SQL Server Using the OleDb Data Provider

```
' Create a Connection Object
    Dim ConnectionString As String = "Provider=SQLOLEDB.1;" & _
          "Integrated Security=SSPI;" & _
          "Persist Security Info=false;" & _
          "Initial Catalog=Northwind;" & _
          "Data Source=MCB;"
    Dim conn As OleDbConnection = New OleDbConnection(ConnectionString)
    ' Open the connection
    If conn.State <> ConnectionState.Open Then
      conn.Open()
      MessageBox.Show("Connection state: " + conn.State.ToString())
    End If
```

Now you'll connect to a SQL Server database using the Sql data provider. For this example, you'll use the SQL Server 2000 Northwind database. Listing 4-4 shows the connection with the SQL Server database. As you can see, the code first constructs a connection string with the SQL Server name MCB and the database name Northwind. It uses Windows security in this connection, but depending on your SQL Server setup you could alternatively use a SQL Server login and password. After constructing a connection string, it calls the Open method to open the connection. After that it reads the connection properties and displays them in a message box. In the end, it calls the Close method to close the connection and the Dispose method to get rid of the connection resources.

Listing 4-4. Connecting to a SQL Server and Reading the SqlConnection *Properties*

```
' Create a Connection Object
    Dim ConnectionString As String = "Integrated Security=SSPI;" & _
              "Initial Catalog=Northwind;Data Source=MCB;"
    Dim conn As SqlConnection = New SqlConnection(ConnectionString)
    ' Open the connection
    If conn.State <> ConnectionState.Open Then
      conn.Open()
      MessageBox.Show("Connection state: " + conn.State.ToString())
    End If
```

```
' Show the connection properties
MessageBox.Show("Connection String :" + conn.ConnectionString & _
            ", Workstation Id:" + conn.WorkstationId.ToString() & _
            ", Packet Size :" + conn.PacketSize.ToString() & _
            ", Server Version " + conn.ServerVersion.ToString() & _
            ", DataSource :" + conn.DataSource.ToString() & _
            ", Server Version:" + conn.ServerVersion.ToString() & _
            ", Connection Time Out:" + conn.ConnectionTimeout.ToString())


' Close the connection
If conn.State = ConnectionState.Open Then
  conn.Close()
  MessageBox.Show("Connection state: " + conn.State.ToString())
End If
' Dispose the connection
If (Not conn Is Nothing) Then
  conn.Dispose()
End If
```

You can even pass a user ID and password in a connection string. For example, the following connection string uses a user ID and password:

```
Dim ConnectionString As String = "user id=sa;password=pass;" & _
            "Initial Catalog=Northwind;Data Source=MCB;"
```

NOTE *As you can see, we used MCB as the data source name. You can use localhost as your local server.*

Understanding Connection Pooling

Connection pooling is a mechanism to utilize and share connection resources already available in a connection pool. In general, if an application needs a connection, it creates a new connection. There's a whole process of establishing a new connection. When the application is done using a connection, it closes the connection. Connection pooling plays a vital role in a three-tier development. For example, in a three-tier development, say you're using a Web server. The opening and closing of a connection consumes time and server resources in this scenario.

Now say the application executes only a SELECT statement, which returns only a few records from the database. It may be possible that establishing a connection with the server may take more time than executing the query. This situation gets worse when there are hundreds of users accessing the same server. Another scenario is that a user logs into a server and then stays connected, never logging out. So, having a connection open until a user logs out is not a feasible solution.

So how does connection pooling help in this scenario? In the .NET Framework, when an application closes a connection, the connection goes to a pool of available connections and stays active for a certain interval of time even after you close the connection. When a user connects, the provider compares the connection string to the connection strings in the pool. If the string matches, then a connection is returned from the pool instead of creating and opening a new connection.

The connection pooling mechanism works differently for different data providers. The Connection class defines members that allow you to pool connection resources manually.

OLE DB provides automatic connection pooling (also known as *session pooling*), which is handled by OLE DB core components through its providers.

In ADO, you set the value of the OLE DB Services parameter, which includes connection pooling as well. This is an ADO connection string passed to the Open method of an OLEDBConnection:

```
Dim conn As OLEDBConnection =  Nothing
Conn.Open("DSN=LocalServer;UID=sa;PWD=;OLE DB Services=-1")
```

Table 4-5 describes the values for the OLE DB Services parameter.

Table 4-5. The OLE DB Services Settings

SERVICES ENABLED	VALUE
All services (default)	"OLE DB Services = -1;"
All services except pooling	"OLE DB Services = -2;"
All services except pooling and auto enlistment	"OLE DB Services = -4;"
All services except client cursor	"OLE DB Services = -5;"
All services except client cursor and pooling	"OLE DB Services = -6;"
No services	"OLE DB Services = 0;"

For example, the following string disables the connection pooling:

```
Dim connString As String = "Provider = SQLOLEDB OLE DB Services = -2;" & _
"Data Source = MCB; Integrated Security = SSPI "
```

ADO .NET manages connection pooling automatically when you call the Close or Dispose method of a Connection object. Once a pool is created, you can add connections to this pool until the pool reaches its maximum size. You can define the maximum size of a connection pool using the connection string. If a pool reaches its maximum size, the next added connection will join a queue and wait until the pool releases an existing connection.

You create a pool when you call the Open method of a connection based on the connection string. If you're using the same database for two Connection objects, but the connection string is different (including spaces and single characters), each connection will be added to a different pool. For example, Listing 4-5 creates two connections: conn1 and conn2. The ConnectionString1 and ConnectionString2 connection strings are different for both connections. Because these connections have different connection strings, they'll be added to two different pools.

Listing 4-5. Creating Two Connections with Different Strings

```
' Create a Connection Object
Dim ConnectionString1 As String = "Integrated Security=SSPI;" & _
"Initial Catalog=Northwind;" & _
"Data Source=MCB;"
Dim conn1 As SqlConnection = New SqlConnection(ConnectionString1)
' Create a Connection Object
Dim ConnectionString2 As String = "Integrated Security=SSPI;" & _
    "Initial Catalog=Pubs;" & _
    "Data Source=MCB;"
Dim conn2 As SqlConnection = New SqlConnection(ConnectionString2)
' Open connections
conn1.Open()
conn2.Open()
MessageBox.Show("Connection1 " + conn1.State.ToString())
MessageBox.Show("Connection2 " + conn2.State.ToString())
' some code
conn1.Close()
conn2.Close()
MessageBox.Show("Connection1 " + conn1.State.ToString())
MessageBox.Show("Connection2 " + conn2.State.ToString())
```

CAUTION *You must always call the* Close *or* Dispose *method of* Connection *to close the connection. Connections that are not explicitly closed are not added or returned to the pool.*

Even though the .NET Framework automatically manages connection pooling, you can customize the connection pooling properties programmatically by passing them in a connection string or by setting them using the Connection properties. A typical connection string with connection pooling parameters looks like the following:

```
Dim ConnectionString As String = "user id=sa;password=pass;" & _
            "Initial Catalog=Northwind;Data Source=MCB;" & _
    "Pooling='true';Connection Reset='false';" & _
    "Connection Lifetime=5;Min Pool Size=3;Max Pool Size=20;"
```

Some of the pooling settings are in the form of key-value pairs (see Table 4-6).

Table 4-6. Connection Pooling Settings

KEY	DESCRIPTION
Connection Lifetime	Connection creation time is compared with the current time, and if time span exceeds the Connection Lifetime value, the object pooler destroys the connection. The default value is 0, which will give a connection the maximum timeout.
Connection Reset	Determines whether a connection is reset after it was removed from the pool. The default value is True.
Max Pool Size	Maximum number of connection allowed in the pool. The default value is 100.
Min Pool Size	Minimum number of connections allowed in the pool. The default value is 0.
Pooling	When True (the default), the connection is drawn from the pool or created if necessary.

The OleDbConnection class provides a ReleaseObjectPool method you can use to free resources reserved for a connection. You call this method when this connection won't be used again. To call ReleaseObjectPool, first you call the Close method. Listing 4-6 shows how to use ReleaseObjectPool.

Listing 4-6. Calling ReleaseObjectPool

```
' Connection and SQL strings
Dim ConnectionString As String = "Provider=Microsoft.Jet.OLEDB.4.0;" & _
"Data Source=c:\\Northwind.mdb"
Dim SQL As String = "SELECT OrderID, Customer, CustomerID FROM Orders"
' Create connection object
Dim conn As OleDbConnection = New OleDbConnection(ConnectionString)
conn.Open()
' do something
conn.Close()
OleDbConnection.ReleaseObjectPool()
' Dispose the connection
If (Not conn Is Nothing) Then
conn.Dispose()
End If
```

Using the CreateCommand and ChangeDatabase Methods

The SqlConnection class provides two more useful methods: the CreateCommand and ChangeDatabase methods. The CreateCommand method creates a SqlCommand object, which will be associated with the Connection object. In general, when you create a SqlCommand object, you need to pass a SqlConnection argument to connect to a connection, but if you use the CreateCommand method of SqlConnection, you don't need to do so.

The following code creates a SqlCommand using the CreateCommand method of an already existing SqlConnection object:

```
Dim cmd As SqlCommand = conn.CreateCommand()
cmd.CommandText = "SELECT * FROM Customers"
' Do something with the command
```

We discuss SqlCommand in more detail in the following section.

The ChangeDatabase method of the SqlConnection object is a relief to developers who frequently have to change the database to which they're connected. This feature was missing in previous technologies, and the only way out of this problem was to disconnect the connection and then reconnect to the new database. The ChangeDatabase method does the same thing, but it does so internally so that developers can continue using the same SqlConnection object. The following code opens a connection to the Northwind database and later changes the database source using the ChangeDatabase:

```vb
' Create a Connection Object
Dim ConnectionString As String = "Integrated Security=SSPI;" & _
          "Initial Catalog=Northwind;Data Source=MCB;"
Dim conn As SqlConnection = New SqlConnection(ConnectionString)
    ' Open the connection
    conn.Open()
    conn.ChangeDatabase("pubs")
    ' Do something with the command
    MessageBox.Show(conn.Database.ToString())
    ' Close the connection and call Dispose
    conn.Close()
    conn.Dispose()
```

The Command: Executing SQL Statements

The Command object allows you to directly execute SQL statements such as INSERT, SELECT, UPDATE, and DELETE against a data source for reading, writing, and updating a database. You can also use the Command object to execute stored procedures. The SqlCommand, OleDbCommand, and OdbcCommand classes represent the Command objects in the Sql, OleDb, and ODBC data providers, respectively.

Table 4-7 describes some of the more important properties of the Command class for the Sql data provider. The CommandText listed in this table can contain either a SQL statement or a stored procedure name. The CommandType determines which one of these forms the CommandText takes.

Table 4-7. The Command Properties

PROPERTY	DESCRIPTION
CommandText	Could be a SQL statement, a stored procedure, or a database table name depending on the CommandType
CommandTimeout	Wait time before terminating the execute command
CommandType	An enumeration of values Text, StoredProcedure, or TableDirect
Connection	A Connection representing the ActiveConnection
DesignTimeVisible	Indicates whether the command should be visible at design-time
Parameters	A collection of parameters (SqlParameterCollection)
Transaction	A transaction
UpdateRowSource	Represents how command results are applied to a DataRow when used by the Update method

Listing 4-7 creates a SqlCommand object, sets its properties, and then reads back its properties to display them. You'll see the rest of the properties—such as Transaction—in the related sections of this chapter.

Listing 4-7. Setting and Getting SqlCommand *Properties*

```
' Connection and SQL strings
    Dim ConnectionString As String = "Integrated Security=SSPI;" & _
            "Initial Catalog=Northwind;Data Source=MCB;"
    Dim SQL As String = "SELECT * FROM Orders"
    ' Create connection object
    Dim conn As SqlConnection = New SqlConnection(ConnectionString)
    ' Create command object
    Dim cmd As SqlCommand = New SqlCommand()
    cmd.Connection = conn
    cmd.CommandText = SQL
    cmd.CommandTimeout = 30
    cmd.CommandType = CommandType.Text
    ' Open connection
    conn.Open()
    ' Read Command properties
    Dim str As String
    str = "Connection String: " + cmd.Connection.ConnectionString.ToString()
    str = str + " , SQL Statement :" + cmd.CommandText
    str = str + " , Timeout :" + cmd.CommandTimeout.ToString()
    str = str + " , CommandTyoe:" + cmd.CommandType.ToString()
    MessageBox.Show(str)
    ' close connection
    conn.Close()
    'Dispose
 conn.Dispose()
```

Creating a Command Object

There are a number of ways to construct a Command object. You can create a Command and set its connection and SQL string, or you can create a Command by passing the connection string and SQL string as parameters of the Command constructor.

The following examples show you three different ways to create a Command object. This code constructs a connection and a SQL string:

```
' Connection and SQL strings
Dim ConnectionString As String = "Integrated Security=SSPI;" & _
        "Initial Catalog=Northwind;Data Source=MCB;"
' Create connection object
Dim conn As SqlConnection = New SqlConnection(ConnectionString)
Dim SQL As String = "SELECT * FROM Orders"
```

Now create a SqlCommand object using a constructor with no arguments. Later you set SqlCommand's Connection and CommandText properties to connect to a Connection and set the SQL statement, which this command will be executing:

```
' Create command object
Dim cmd1 As SqlCommand = New SqlCommand()
cmd1.Connection = conn
cmd1.CommandText = SQL
cmd1.CommandTimeout = 30
cmd1.CommandType = CommandType.Text
```

In the second form, you create a SqlCommand object by directly passing a SQL query and the SqlConnection object as the first and second arguments:

```
// Create command object
Dim cmd2 As SqlCommand = New SqlCommand(SQL, conn)
```

The third way of creating a Command object is to create a command by just passing a SQL query as the argument and setting its Connection property later:

```
// Create command object
Dim cmd3 As SqlCommand = New SqlCommand(SQL)
cmd3.Connection = conn
```

Listing 4-8 shows you how to connect to the Northwind SQL Server database, read all the records from the Orders table, and output the first and second field's data to the console. The new things you'll notice in this code are ExecuteReader and SqlDataReader. A SqlDataReader is a DataReader class, and ExecuteReader fills data from a data source to the DataReader based on the SQL query. (We discuss DataReader classes in the next section.)

Listing 4-8. Using `SqlCommand` *to Read Data from a Database*

```
' Connection and SQL strings
Dim ConnectionString As String = "Integrated Security=SSPI;" & _
        "Initial Catalog=Northwind;Data Source=MCB;"
Dim SQL As String = "SELECT * FROM Orders"
' Create connection object
Dim conn As SqlConnection = New SqlConnection(ConnectionString)
' Create command object
Dim cmd As SqlCommand = New SqlCommand(SQL)
cmd.Connection = conn
' Open connection
conn.Open()
' Call command's ExecuteReader
Dim reader As SqlDataReader = cmd.ExecuteReader()
While reader.Read()
  If Not reader.IsDBNull(0) Then
    Console.Write("OrderID:" + reader.GetInt32(0).ToString())
    Console.Write(" ,")
    Console.WriteLine("Customer:" + reader.GetString(1).ToString())
  End If
End While
' close reader and connection
reader.Close()
conn.Close()
'Dispose
conn.Dispose()
```

The output of Listing 4-8 will list records from the Customers table to the console.

Creating and Using OleDbCommand

Like the `SqlCommand` object, you create OleDb and ODBC `Command` objects by using the `OleDbCommand` and `OdbcCommand` classes. You can pass the same arguments as discussed previously. The only difference is the connection string. For example, Listing 4-9 uses `OleDbCommand` and `OleDbConnection` to connect to a SQL Server database. As you can see, the only changes are the class prefixes and the connection string. Similarly, you can use the `OdbcCommand` object.

Listing 4-9. Using OleCommand *to Access an Access Database*

```
' Connection and SQL strings
    Dim ConnectionString As String = "Provider=Microsoft.Jet.OLEDB.4.0;" & _
    "Data Source=c:\\Northwind.mdb"
    Dim SQL As String = "SELECT * FROM Orders"
    ' Create connection object
    Dim conn As OleDbConnection = New OleDbConnection(ConnectionString)
    ' Create command object
    Dim cmd As OleDbCommand = New OleDbCommand(SQL)
    cmd.Connection = conn
    ' Open connection
    conn.Open()
    ' Call command's ExecuteReader
    Dim reader As OleDbDataReader = cmd.ExecuteReader()
    While reader.Read()
      Console.Write("OrderID:" + reader.GetInt32(0).ToString())
      Console.Write(" ,")
      Console.WriteLine("Customer:" + reader.GetString(1).ToString())
    End While
    ' close reader and connection
    reader.Close()
    conn.Close()
conn.Dispose()
```

Using the CommandType Enumeration

The CommandType enumeration decides what type of object a command will be executed as. The CommandType enumeration can have any of the three values defined in Table 4-8.

Table 4-8. The CommandType *Enumeration Members*

MEMBERS	DESCRIPTION
StoredProcedure	The name of the stored procedure.
TableDirect	The CommandText property should be set to the table name, and all rows and columns in the table will be returned.
Text	A SQL text command.

As you can see from Table 4-8, you can call a stored procedure, use TableDirect, or execute a SQL command. We present these options individually in the following sections.

Calling a Stored Procedure

Calling stored procedures using the Command object is similar to executing a SQL query. This section gives you a quick overview of how to execute stored procedures. (We cover stored procedures in more detail in Chapter 11.)

You need to set the CommandType property of a Command object before calling a stored procedure. By default, the CommandType property is Text. If you want to call a stored procedure, you need to set the CommandType to StoredProcedure and the CommandText to the stored procedure name. After that you can call the ExecuteReader method or other methods. You can also pass parameters to the procedure by setting parameter values in the Command and then calling ExecuteReader on the Command object. Alternatively, you can pass a procedure name as a string when creating a Command object. Listing 4-10 shows the settings of the CommandType and CommandText properties of SqlCommand. As you can see, it calls an existing SQL Server Northwind database stored procedure, Sales By Year.

Listing 4-10. Calling a Stored Procedure Using SqlCommand

```
' Create a SqlCommand with stored procedure as string
Dim cmd As SqlCommand = New SqlCommand("Sales By Year", conn)
' set Command's CommandType as StoredProcedure
cmd.CommandType = CommandType.StoredProcedure
```

NOTE *Executing stored procedures can be helpful in improving the performance of an application in multiuser and Web applications because a stored procedure executes on the server itself.*

The Northwind database in SQL Server contains a few stored procedures. One is called Sales By Year (see Listing 4-11).

Listing 4-11. The Sales By Year *Stored Procedure in the Northwind Database*

```
SELECT Orders.ShippedDate, Orders.OrderID, "Order Subtotals".Subtotal,
DATENAME(yy,ShippedDate) AS Year
FROM Orders INNER JOIN "Order Subtotals" ON Orders.OrderID =
 "Order Subtotals".OrderID WHERE Orders.ShippedDate
 BETWEEN  @Beginning_Date AND @Ending_Date
```

This stored procedure takes two parameters, Beginning_Date and Ending_Date. The procedure selects all of the orders between these two dates. It also performs a join with the Order Subtotals from the Order Subtotal view, which calculates the subtotals of each. If you want to execute this stored procedure in ADO.NET, you just create a Command object of type StoredProcedure and then call the Command object's ExecuteReader method. You then cycle through the results in the reader that you're looking for from your stored procedure. Listing 4-12 executes a stored procedure that selects all the orders in July and displays their order IDs.

Listing 4-12. Executing and Reading the Results of a Stored Procedure

```
Dim ConnectionString As String = "Integrated Security=SSPI;" & _
        "Initial Catalog=Northwind;Data Source=MCB;"
    Dim SQL As String = "SELECT * FROM Orders"
    ' Create connection object
    Dim conn As SqlConnection = New SqlConnection(ConnectionString)
    ' Create a SqlCommand with stored procedure as string
    Dim cmd As SqlCommand = New SqlCommand("Sales By Year", conn)
    cmd.Connection = conn
    ' set Command's CommandType as StoredProcedure
    cmd.CommandType = CommandType.StoredProcedure
    ' Create a SqlParameter and add a parameter
    Dim parm1 As SqlParameter = cmd.Parameters.Add("@Beginning_Date", _
    SqlDbType.DateTime, 20)
    parm1.Value = "7/1/1996"
    Dim parm2 As SqlParameter = cmd.Parameters.Add("@Ending_Date", _
    SqlDbType.DateTime, 20)
    parm2.Value = "7/31/1996"
    ' Open connection
    conn.Open()
    ' Call ExecuteReader to execute the stored procedure
    Dim reader As SqlDataReader = cmd.ExecuteReader()
    Dim orderlist As String = ""
    ' Read data from the reader
```

```
While reader.Read()
  Dim result As String = reader("OrderID").ToString()
  orderlist += result + " "
End While
' close the connection and reader
reader.Close()
conn.Close()
conn.Dispose()
' Print data on the console
Console.WriteLine("Orders in July")
Console.WriteLine("================")
Console.WriteLine(orderlist)
```

If you wanted to look at the subtotals along with the orders, you'd just add a DataReader index for dereferencing the subtotal and concatenate with the order ID. Listing 4-13 shows the new DataReader loop.

Listing 4-13. Adding the Subtotal Listing to the Output of the Stored Procedure Results

```
While reader.Read()
 Dim nextID As String = reader("OrderID").ToString()
 Dim nextSubtotal As String = reader("Subtotal").ToString()
 orderlist += nextID + ", " + nextSubtotal + ", "
End While
```

The result of replacing this line of code in Listing 4-13 gives output that returns order IDs and subtotals in the month of July in the Northwind database.

Using TableDirect

You can also use the TableDirect CommandType to read information directly from a table. You need to make two changes in the example to execute a table by setting TableDirect. First, you need to set Command's CommandText property to the table name; second, you need to set the CommandType property to CommandType.TableDirect.

The following code reads the Customers table and sets the CommandType property to CommandType.TableDirect:

```
cmd.CommandText = "Customers"
cmd.CommandType = CommandType.TableDirect
```

Listing 4-14 reads information from the Customers table by setting the TableDirect method and displaying it on the console.

Listing 4-14. Using TableDirect *to Read a Table*

```
' Create a Connection Object
    Dim ConnectionString As String = "Provider=Microsoft.Jet.OLEDB.4.0;" & _
    "Data Source=c:\\Northwind.mdb"
    Dim conn As OleDbConnection = New OleDbConnection(ConnectionString)
    Dim cmd As OleDbCommand = New OleDbCommand()
    cmd.Connection = conn
    cmd.CommandText = "Customers"
    cmd.CommandType = CommandType.TableDirect
    conn.Open()
    Dim reader As OleDbDataReader = cmd.ExecuteReader()
    Console.WriteLine("Customer Id, Contact Name, Company Name")
    Console.WriteLine("=======================================")
    While reader.Read()
      Console.Write(reader("CustomerID").ToString())
      Console.Write(", " + reader("ContactName").ToString())
      Console.WriteLine(", " + reader("CompanyName").ToString())
    End While
    ' release objects
    reader.Close()
    conn.Close()
conn.Dispose()
```

Executing a Command

You just saw the ExecuteReader method, which reads data from a data source and fills the DataReader object depending on the data provider. Besides ExecuteReader, the Command object defines three more execute methods. These methods are ExecuteNonQuery, ExecuteScalar, and ExecuteXmlReader. The ExecuteReader method produces a DataReader, which is the solution for streaming data through ADO.NET. (We discuss the DataReader in more details in "The DataReader: Walking through the Data.")

The ExecuteNonQuery method allows you to execute a SQL statement or a Command object with the CommandText property and a SQL statement without using a DataSet. This method doesn't take any parameters and returns the number of rows affected by the execute operation.

For example, you could have an UPDATE, INSERT, or DELETE statement in your CommandText and then call ExecuteNonQuery to execute it directly on your database.

Listing 4-15 shows how to insert a row into the Northwind database using the ExecuteNonQuery method. You can even use UPDATE and DELETE SQL queries to update and delete data from a database. (We use these statements in later examples.) In this example, you create an INSERT query and call ExecuteNonQuery.

Listing 4-15. Adding Records to a Table Using the INSERT *SQL Statement*

```
' Create a Connection Object
Dim ConnectionString As String = "Integrated Security=SSPI;" & _
    "Initial Catalog=Northwind;Data Source=MCB;"
Dim conn As SqlConnection = New SqlConnection(ConnectionString)
 open an existing Connection to the Database and Create a
' Command Object with it:
conn.Open()
Dim cmd As SqlCommand = New SqlCommand("Customers", conn)
' Assign the SQL Insert statement we want to execute to the CommandText
cmd.CommandText = "INSERT INTO Customers" & _
  "(Address, City, CompanyName, ContactName, CustomerID)" & _
   "VALUES ('111 Broad St.', 'NY', 'Xerox', 'Fred Biggles', 1400)"
' Call ExecuteNonQuery on the Command Object to execute insert
Dim res As Integer
res = cmd.ExecuteNonQuery()
Console.WriteLine("Affected Rows :" + res.ToString())
' release objects
conn.Close()
conn.Dispose()
```

NOTE *If you're deleting, inserting, and updating data with known parameters, using* Execute *methods is faster than using* DataAdapter's Update *method.*

ExecuteScalar is a handy method for using a SQL statement that retrieves a single value. A good example of this is retrieving the number of rows from a database. Listing 4-16 retrieves the total number of rows from the Customers table. Then you assign the SQL command for getting the row count in Customers to the Command object, and you call ExecuteScalar to retrieve the counter.

Listing 4-16. Using the ExecuteScalar *Method to Retrieve a Single Value*

```
' Create a Connection Object
Dim ConnectionString As String = "Integrated Security=SSPI;" & _
        "Initial Catalog=Northwind;Data Source=MCB;"
    Dim conn As SqlConnection = New SqlConnection(ConnectionString)
    ' open an existing Connection to the Database and Create a
    ' Command Object with it:
    conn.Open()
    Dim cmd As SqlCommand = New SqlCommand("Customers", conn)
    ' Assign the SQL Insert statement we want to execute to the CommandText
    cmd.CommandText = "SELECT Count(*) FROM Customers"
    ' Call ExecuteNonQuery on the Command Object to execute insert
    Dim res As Integer
    res = cmd.ExecuteScalar()
    Console.WriteLine("Total Rows :" + res.ToString())
    ' release objects
    conn.Close()
conn.Dispose()
```

If you run Listings 4-17, it will display only the total row number on the console.

Using Other Command Methods

The Cancel method of a SqlCommand object tries to cancel an execute operation. If there's no execute operation or the Cancel method fails to cancel the execution, nothing happens.

The CreateParameter method creates a SqlParameter object.

The Prepare method creates a prepared version of the command. It doesn't affect the operation if CommandType is TableDirect. Before calling this method, you need to specify the data type of each parameter in the statement to be prepared.

The ResetCommandTimeout method resets the command timeout value to the default value, which is 30 seconds.

We use these methods in later examples.

The DataReader: Walking through the Data

As discussed earlier in this chapter, there are two common ways to fetch data from a data source: using a DataSet and using a DataReader. A DataReader provides an easy way for the programmer to read data from a database as if it were coming from a stream. The DataReader is the solution for forward-streaming data through ADO.NET. The DataReader is also called a *firehose cursor* or *forward, read-only cursor* because it moves forward through the data. The DataReader not only allows you to move forward through each record of a database, but it also enables you to parse the data from each column.

Similar to other data components, each data provider has a DataReader class. For example, OleDbDataReader is the DataReader class for OleDb data providers. Similarly, SqlDataReader and ODBC DataReader are DataReader classes for the Sql and ODBC data providers, respectively.

Initializing a DataReader

As you saw previously, you call the ExecuteReader method of the Command object, which returns an instance of the DataReader. For example, you use the following code:

```
Dim cmd As SqlCommand = New SqlCommand(SQL, conn)
' Call ExecuteReader to return a DataReader
Dim reader As SqlDataReader = cmd.ExecuteReader()
```

Once you're done with a DataReader, call the Close method to close a DataReader:

```
reader.Close()
```

Understanding DataReader Properties and Methods

Table 4-9 describes the DataReader properties, and Table 4-10 describes the DataReader methods.

Table 4-9. The DataReader *Properties*

PROPERTY	DESCRIPTION
Depth	Indicates the depth of nesting for a row
FieldCount	Returns number of columns in a row
IsClosed	Indicates whether a DataReader is closed
Item	Gets the value of a column in native format
RecordsAffected	Number of rows affected after a transaction

Table 4-10. The DataReader *Methods*

METHOD	DESCRIPTION
Close	Closes a DataReader object.
IsDBNull	Represents whether a column contains null values.
Read	Reads the next record in the DataReader.
NextResult	Advances the DataReader to the next result during batch transactions.
GetXXX	There are dozens of GetXXX methods. These methods read a specific data type value from a column. For example, GetChar will return a column value as a character and GetString as a string.

Reading with the DataReader

Once a DataReader is initialized, you can utilize its various methods to read your data records. Foremost, you can use the Read method, which, when called repeatedly, continues to read each row of data into the DataReader object. The DataReader also provides a simple indexer that enables you to pull each column of data from the row. Listing 4-17 is an example of using the DataReader in the Northwind database for the Customers table and displaying data on the console.

As you can see, you use similar steps as in previous examples. Initially, you create a Connection object, create a Command object, call the ExecuteReader method, call the DataReader's Read method until the end of the data, and then display the data. At the end, you release the DataReader and Connection objects.

Listing 4-17. DataReader *Reads Data from a SQL Server Database*

```
' Create a Connection Object
Dim ConnectionString As String = "Integrated Security=SSPI;" & _
    "Initial Catalog=Northwind;Data Source=MCB;"
Dim conn As SqlConnection = New SqlConnection(ConnectionString)
Dim SQL As String = "SELECT * FROM Customers"
' open a connection
conn.Open()
Dim cmd As SqlCommand = New SqlCommand(SQL, conn)
' Call ExecuteNonQuery on the Command Object to execute insert
Dim res As Integer
' Call ExecuteReader to return a DataReader
Dim reader As SqlDataReader = cmd.ExecuteReader()
Console.WriteLine("Customer ID, Contact Name," & _
```

```
"Contact Title, Address")
Console.WriteLine("====================================")
While reader.Read()
 If Not reader.IsDBNull(0) Then
   Console.Write(reader("CustomerID").ToString() + ", ")
  Console.Write(reader("ContactName").ToString() + ", ")
  Console.Write(reader("ContactTitle").ToString() + ", ")
   Console.WriteLine(reader("Address").ToString() + ", ")
End If
End While
Console.WriteLine("Affected Records: " & _
'reader.RecordsAffected.ToString())
' release objects
conn.Close()
conn.Dispose()
```

Figure 4-2 shows the output of Listing 4-17.

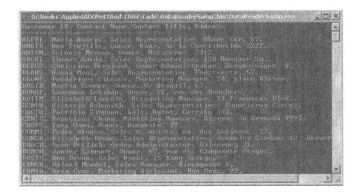

Figure 4-2. Output of the Customers table from the DataReader

SqlDataReader provides many Read methods, which allow you to get the value of a column as a specific type. For instance, you could rewrite this line from the previous example:

```
Dim str As String =  reader("CustomerID").ToString()
```

as this:

```
Dim str As String =  reader.GetString(0)
```

With the GetString method of CustomerID, you don't need to do any conversion, but you do have to know the zero-based column number of CustomerID (which, in this case, is zero).

Interpreting Batches of Queries

The DataReader also has methods that enable you to read data from a batch of SQL queries. The following is an example of a batch transaction on the Customers and Orders tables. The NextResult method allows you to obtain each query result from the batch of queries performed on both tables. In this example, after creating a Connection object, you set up your Command object to do a batch query on the Customers and the Orders tables:

```
Dim cmd as SqlCommand = new SqlCommand(
  "SELECT * FROM Customers;SELECT * FROM Orders",
  conn )
```

Now you can create the Reader through the Command object. You then use a result flag as an indicator to check if you've gone through all the results. Then you loop through each stream of results and read the data into a string until it reads 10 records. After that, you show results in a message box (see Listing 4-18).

After that you call the NextResult method, which gets the next query result in the batch. The result is processed again in the Read method loop. The code displays data from both tables.

Listing 4-18. Executing Batches Using DataReader

```
' Create a Connection Object
Dim ConnectionString As String = "Integrated Security=SSPI;" & _
    "Initial Catalog=Northwind;Data Source=MCB;"
Dim conn As SqlConnection = New SqlConnection(ConnectionString)
Dim SQL As String = "SELECT * FROM Customers; SELECT * FROM Orders"
' open a connection
conn.Open()
Dim cmd As SqlCommand = New SqlCommand(SQL, conn)
' Call ExecuteNonQuery on the Command Object to execute insert
Dim res As Integer
' Call ExecuteReader to return a DataReader
Dim reader As SqlDataReader = cmd.ExecuteReader()
Dim str As String = ""
Dim counter As Integer
```

```
Dim bNextResult As Boolean = True
While bNextResult = True
  While reader.Read()
   str += reader.GetValue(0).ToString() + " ,"
   counter = counter + 1
  If counter = 10 Then
    Exit While
  End If
End While
 MessageBox.Show(str)
bNextResult = reader.NextResult()
End While
' release objects
conn.Close()
conn.Dispose()
```

TIP *One of the commonly asked questions on ADO.NET-related discussion forums and newsgroups is about when to use* DataReader *vs. when to use a* DataSet. *Here is a simple answer: You use a* DataReader *instead of a* DataSet *when you need read-only data and you don't need to alter the data. See the "Using a DataSet vs. Using a DataReader" section for a more in-depth answer.*

Understanding Command Behaviors

The ExecuteReader method of a Command object such as SqlCommand has two over-loaded forms, as shown:

```
Overloads Public Function ExecuteReader() As SqlDataReader
Overloads Public Function ExecuteReader(CommandBehavior) As SqlDataReader
```

The first form doesn't take any arguments, but the second form takes an argument of type CommandBehavior. The Command behavior can control the action and return data as a result of executing a Command.

The default value passed in the ExecuteReader is CommandBehavior.Default, which returned the same results as ExecuteReader with no arguments.

When CommandBehavior.CloseConnection is passed in ExecuteReader, the associated Connection object is closed when the DataReader is closed. In this case, you don't have to call SqlConnection.Close explicitly.

You can fetch only a single row from a database by executing a SqlCommand. The CommandBehavior.SingleRow value passed in ExecuteReader returns the single row from a table instead of the result set.

CommandBehavior.SequentialAccess provides a way for the DataReader to handle rows that contain large binary values (BLOB data) such as images or memo fields. SequentialAccess values enable DataReader to load data as a stream of bytes or characters.

By setting the CommandBehavior.KeyInfo value, the DataReader doesn't return data. It returns the table column and primary key information instead. This is useful when you're collecting metadata.

The CommandBehavior.SchemaOnly value returns column information only.

The DataAdapter: Adapting to Your Environment

As you saw in Figure 4-1, a DataAdapter plays a vital role in the ADO.NET architecture. It sits between a data source and a DataSet, and it passes data from the data source to the DataSet, and vice versa, with or without using commands. Now you'll use disconnected classes such as DataSet, DataTable, DataView, and DataViewManager to write interactive database applications based on Windows Forms and Web Forms.

The DataAdapter enables you to connect to a database and specify SQL strings for retrieving data from or writing data to a DataSet. As you know, a DataSet represents in-memory cached data. An in-memory object frees you from the confines of the specifics of a database and allows you to deal with the data in memory. The DataAdapter serves as an intermediary between the database and the DataSet.

Constructing a DataAdapter Object

The DataAdapter constructor has many overloaded forms. You can create a DataAdapter using a constructor with no arguments, pass a Command object, pass a Command object with Connection object as arguments, or use a combination of these. You can also specify a SQL statement as a string for querying a particular table or more than one table. You can also specify the connection string or a Connection object to connect to the database. Listing 4-19 creates four SqlDataAdapter instances with different approaches. As you can see, the code first creates and opens SqlConnection and SqlCommand objects. Later you use these two objects to create DataAdapters. The first DataAdapter, da1, takes only one parameter of type SqlCommand. Because SqlCommand already has a SqlConnection, there's no need to specify a connection explicitly with the DataAdapter. The second DataAdapter, da2, is created using no argument, and later its SelectCommand property is set to a

SqlCommand. The third DataAdapter, da3, takes a string argument as a SQL statement and a second argument as SqlConnection. The last DataAdapter takes both string arguments, one containing the SQL statement and the second containing the connection string.

Listing 4-19. Creating SqlDataAdapter *Instances*

```
' Create a Connection Object
Dim ConnectionString As String = "Integrated Security=SSPI;" & _
    "Initial Catalog=Northwind;Data Source=MCB;"
Dim conn As SqlConnection = New SqlConnection(ConnectionString)
Dim SQL As String = "SELECT * FROM Customers"
' open a connection
conn.Open()
Dim cmd As SqlCommand = New SqlCommand(SQL, conn)
' Creating SqlDataAdapter using different constructors
Dim da1 As SqlDataAdapter = New SqlDataAdapter(cmd)
Dim da2 As SqlDataAdapter = New SqlDataAdapter()
da2.SelectCommand = cmd
Dim da3 As SqlDataAdapter = New SqlDataAdapter(SQL, conn)
Dim da4 As SqlDataAdapter = New SqlDataAdapter(SQL, ConnectionString)
```

As discussed, there's no difference between creating OleDb, Sql, and Odbc DataAdapters. The only difference is the connection string. For example, Listing 4-20 shows you how to create an OleDbDataAdapter object. Listing 4-20 uses the Access 2000 Northwind database and accesses all records of the Orders table by using a SELECT * SQL query.

Listing 4-20. Executing a SELECT * *Statement Using* OleDbDataAdapter

```
' Create a Connection Object
Dim ConnectionString As String = "Provider=Microsoft.Jet.OLEDB.4.0;" & _
"Data Source=c:\\Northwind.mdb"
Dim SQL As String = "SELECT * FROM Orders"
Dim conn As OleDbConnection = New OleDbConnection(ConnectionString)
' Open the connection
conn.Open()
' Create an OleDbDataAdapter object
Dim adapter As OleDbDataAdapter = New OleDbDataAdapter()
adapter.SelectCommand = New OleDbCommand(SQL, conn)
```

You can also use a DataAdapter's Command properties by using the Command object with OleDbDataAdaper. For example, the following code uses OleDbCommand to set the SelectCommand property of the DataAdapter. You can see that OleDbDataAdapter has no arguments as its constructor:

```
' Create an OleDbDataAdapter object
Dim adapter As OleDbDataAdapter =  New OleDbDataAdapter()
adapter.SelectCommand = New OleDbCommand(SQL, conn)
```

Understanding DataAdapter Properties

As you start working with DataAdapters, you need take a quick look at the DataAdapter properties and methods. The DataAdapter has four properties that are Command objects; they represent the ways it can query, insert, delete, and update the database.

Table 4-11 describes SqlDbDataAdapter class properties, and Table 4-12 shows the OleDbDataAdapter properties.

Table 4-11. The SqlDataAdpater *Class Properties*

PROPERTY	DESCRIPTION
AcceptChangesDuringFill	The AcceptChanges method of a DataRow saves the changes made to a DataRow. The True value of this property makes a call to the DataRow's AcceptChanges property after it has been added to the DataTable. The False value doesn't. The default value is True.
ContinueUpdateOnError	The True value of this property keeps the update process continuing even if an error occurred in a DataRow. The False value generates an exception. The default value is False.
DeleteCommand	Represents a DELETE statement or stored procedure for deleting records from the data source.
InsertCommand	Represents an INSERT statement or stored procedure for inserting a new record to the data source.
MissingSchemaAction	Determines the action to be taken when incoming data doesn't have a matching schema. This is a type of MissingMappingAction enumeration, which has three values: Error, Ignore, and Passthrough. The Error value generates an exception, the Ignore value maps the unmatched columns or tables, and the Passthrough value adds the source column or source table created to the DataSet using its original name.

Table 4-11. The SqlDataAdpater *Class Properties (Continued)*

PROPERTY	DESCRIPTION
MissingActionSchema	Determines the action to be taken when a DataSet schema is missing. This is a type of MissingSchemaAction enumeration, which has three values: AddWithKey, Error, and Ignore. AddWithKey adds the necessary columns and primary key information, Error generates an exception, and Ignore ignores the extra columns.
SelectCommand	Represents a SELECT statement or stored procedure for selecting records from a data source.
UpdateCommand	Represents an UPDATE statement or stored procedure for updating records in a data source.
TableMappings	Represents a collection of mappings between an actual data source table and a DataTable object.

Table 4-12. OleDbDataAdapter *Command Properties with Examples*

PROPERTY	EXAMPLE
SelectCommand	cmd.SelectCommand.CommandText = "SELECT * FROM Orders ORDER BY Price";
DeleteCommand	cmd.DeleteCommand.CommandText = "DELETE FROM Orders WHERE LastName ='Smith'";
InsertCommand	cmd.InsertCommand.CommandText = "INSERT INTO Orders VALUES (25,'Widget1','Smith')";
UpdateCommand	cmd.UpdateCommand.CommandText = "UPDATE Orders SET ZipCode='34956' WHERE OrderNum =14";

Listing 4-21 sets some of the SqlDataAdapter properties.

Listing 4-21. Using SqlDataAdapter *Properties*

```
' Create an OleDbDataAdapter object
Dim adapter As SqlDataAdapter = New SqlDataAdapter()
adapter.SelectCommand = New SqlCommand(SQL, conn)
adapter.AcceptChangesDuringFill = True
adapter.ContinueUpdateOnError = True
adapter.MissingSchemaAction = MissingSchemaAction.Error
adapter.MissingMappingAction = MissingMappingAction.Error
```

Understanding DataAdapter Methods

The DataAdapter class provides many useful methods. For instance, the Fill method of the DataAdapter fills data from a DataAdapter to the DataSet object, and the Update method stores data from a DataSet object to the data source.

Table 4-13 describes some of the OleDbDataAdapter methods.

Table 4-13. The DataAdapter *Methods*

METHOD	DESCRIPTION
Fill	Fills data records from a DataAdapter to a DataSet object depending on the selection query.
FillSchema	This method adds a DataTable to a DataSet and configures the schema to match that in the data source.
GetFillParameters	This method retrieves parameters that are used when a SELECT statement is executed.
Update	This method stores data from a DataSet to the data source.

Filling the DataSet

The Fill method is the primary method for bringing data into a DataSet from a data source. This command uses the SelectCommand SQL statement to fill a DataSet memory structure consisting of DataTables, DataRows, DataColumns, and DataRelations. The Fill method has eight overloaded forms. Using these methods, you can fill a DataSet from a DataAdapter by selecting a particular table, selecting a range of rows, and selecting rows based on the CommandBehavior. The following shows different overloaded forms of the Fill method defined in the DbDataAdapter class:

```
Overloads Overrides Public Function Fill(DataSet) As Integer _
Implements IDataAdapter.Fill
Overloads Public Function Fill(DataTable) As Integer
Overloads Public Function Fill(DataSet, String) As Integer
Overloads Overridable Protected Function Fill(DataTable, IDataReader) _
  As Integer
Overloads Overridable Protected Function Fill(DataTable, _
IDbCommand, CommandBehavior) As Integer
Overloads Public Function Fill(DataSet, Integer, Integer, String) _
  As IntegerOverloads
```

```
Overridable Protected Function Fill(DataSet, String, IDataReader, _
 Integer, Integer) As IntegerOverloads
Overridable Protected Function Fill(DataSet, Integer, Integer, _
 String, IDbCommand, CommandBehavior) As Integer
```

The following form of the Fill method selects or refreshes rows in a specified range in the DataSet:

```
Overloads Public Function Fill( _
   ByVal dataSet As DataSet, _
   ByVal startRecord As Integer, _
   ByVal maxRecords As Integer, _
   ByVal srcTable As String _
) As Integer
```

In this example, dataSet is a DataSet, startRecord is the zero-based record number to start with, maxRecords is the maximum number of records to retrieve, and srcTable is the name of the source table to use for table mapping. The following code calls the same overloaded method to get or refresh rows from the 9th position to the 15th position of the Orders table. In other words, it fills the DataSet with seven rows if found in the table:

```
adapter.Fill(ds, 9, 15, " Orders")
```

You can use a DataSet directly or a DataTable to fill or refresh the data of a DataSet. Listing 4-22 calls the Fill method to fill data to a DataSet, which later can bind with data-bound controls.

Listing 4-22. Calling a DataAdapter*'s* Fill *Method*

```
' Create an OleDbDataAdapter object
  Dim adapter As SqlDataAdapter = New SqlDataAdapter()
  adapter.SelectCommand = New SqlCommand(SQL, conn)
  ' Create DataSet Object
  Dim ds As DataSet = New DataSet("Orders")
  ' Call DataAdapter's Fill method to fill data from the
  ' DataAdapter to the DataSet
  adapter.Fill(ds)
```

Adding a DataTable to a DataSet

The FillSchema method adds a DataTable to a DataSet. The FillSchema method has two arguments; the first is DataTable, and the second is SchemaType. The SchemaType argument defines the handling of existing schema. It has two values: Mapped and Source. The SchemaType.Mapped value means you can apply any existing table mapping to the incoming schema and configure the DataSet with the transformed schema. The SchemaType.Source value means you can ignore any table mappings on the DataAdapter and configure the DataSet using the incoming schema without applying any transformations.

Listing 4-23 uses the FillSchema method to add a DataTable to a DataSet.

Listing 4-23. Using the FillSchema *Method of* SqlDataAdapter

```
' Create an OleDbDataAdapter object
Dim adapter As SqlDataAdapter = New SqlDataAdapter()
adapter.SelectCommand = New SqlCommand(SQL, conn)
' Create DataSet Object
Dim ds As DataSet = New DataSet("Orders")
' Call DataAdapter's Fill method to fill data from the
' DataAdapter to the DataSet
adapter.Fill(ds)
' Adding a DataTable to the DataSet
Dim table As DataTable() = _
adapter.FillSchema(ds, SchemaType.Mapped, "Categories")
```

Looking at a DataAdapter Example

Now you'll create your first sample using DataAdapters. In this example, you'll learn how to create DataAdapters using the Sql and OleDb data providers and fill data from a DataAdapter to a DataGrid control.

First, create a Windows application using Visual Basic Projects and add two Button controls and a DataGrid control to the form by dragging the controls from the Toolbox. Second, set both buttons' Name property; use OleDbDataAdapter and SqlDataAdapter. Next, set the Text properties to OleDbDataAdapter and SqlDataAdapter. After setting these properties, the form will look like Figure 4-3. As you can see, there are two buttons, shown as OleDbDataAdapter and SqlDataAdapter.

Now add button click event handlers for both the OleDbDataAdapter and SqlDataAdapter buttons. You can add a button click event handler either by double-clicking the button or by using the Events tab of the Properties window.

On the OleDbDataAdapter button click event handler, you'll write code to read data from an OleDb data source and fill data to the DataGrid control. On the SqlDataAdapter button click event handler, you'll write code to read data from a SQL Server data source and fill data to the DataGrid.

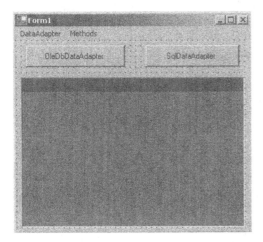

Figure 4-3. Creating a Windows Forms application and adding controls to the form

Listing 4-24 shows the source code for the OleDbDataAdapter button click, and Listing 4-25 shows the source code for the SqlDataAdapter button click. As you can see, you follow the same steps as before. Open a connection, create a DataAdapter object with a SELECT string, create a DataSet object, call a DataAdapter's Fill method to fill the DataSet, and bind the DataSet to the DataGrid control using the DataGrid.DataSouce property of DataSet.DefaultViewManager, which represents the default view of a DataSet object.

Listing 4-24. Displaying the Orders Table Data in a DataGrid Using OleDbDataAdapter

```
Private Sub OleDbDataAdapter_Click(ByVal sender As System.Object, _
 ByVal e As System.EventArgs) Handles OleDbDataAdapter.Click
    ' Create a Connection Object
    Dim ConnectionString As String = "Provider=Microsoft.Jet.OLEDB.4.0;" & _
    "Data Source=c:\\Northwind.mdb"
    Dim SQL As String = "SELECT * FROM Orders"
    Dim conn As OleDbConnection = New OleDbConnection(ConnectionString)
    ' Open the connection
    conn.Open()
    ' Create an OleDbDataAdapter object
```

```
    Dim adapter As OleDbDataAdapter = New OleDbDataAdapter()
    adapter.SelectCommand = New OleDbCommand(SQL, conn)
    ' Create DataSet Object
    Dim ds As DataSet = New DataSet("Orders")
    ' Call DataAdapter's Fill method to fill data from the
    ' DataAdapter to the DataSet
    adapter.Fill(ds)
    ' Bind data set to a DataGrid control
    DataGrid1.DataSource = ds.DefaultViewManager
End Sub
```

The output of Listing 4-24 looks like Figure 4-4.

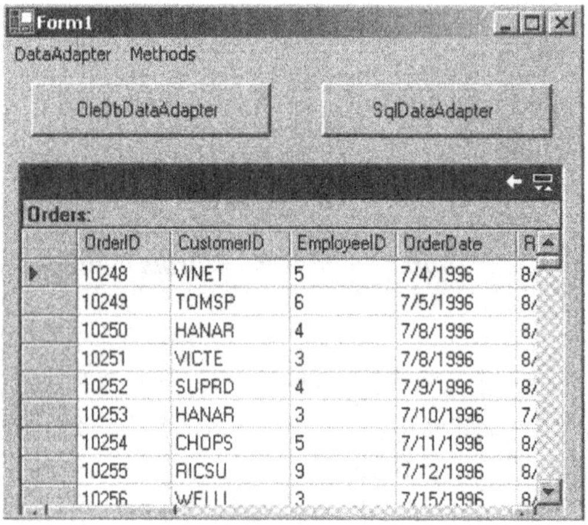

Figure 4-4. Filling data from an Access database to a DataGrid *control using* OleDbDataAdapter

Listing 4-25. Displaying the Customers Table's Data in a DataGrid *Using* SqlDataAdapter

```
Private Sub SqlDataAdapter_Click(ByVal sender As System.Object, _
  ByVal e As System.EventArgs) Handles SqlDataAdapter.Click
    ' Create a Connection Object
    Dim ConnectionString As String = "Integrated Security=SSPI;" & _
        "Initial Catalog=Northwind;Data Source=MCB;"
    Dim conn As SqlConnection = New SqlConnection(ConnectionString)
    Dim SQL As String = "SELECT * FROM Customers"
    ' Open the connection
    conn.Open()
```

```
    ' Create an OleDbDataAdapter object
    Dim adapter As SqlDataAdapter = New SqlDataAdapter()
    adapter.SelectCommand = New SqlCommand(SQL, conn)
    ' Create DataSet Object
    Dim ds As DataSet = New DataSet("Orders")
    ' Call DataAdapter's Fill method to fill data from the
    ' DataAdapter to the DataSet
    adapter.Fill(ds)
    ' Adding a DataTable to the DataSet
    Dim table As DataTable() = _
      adapter.FillSchema(ds, SchemaType.Mapped, "Categories")
    ' Bind data set to a DataGrid control
    DataGrid1.DataSource = ds.DefaultViewManager
End Sub
```

The output of Listing 4-25 looks like Figure 4-5.

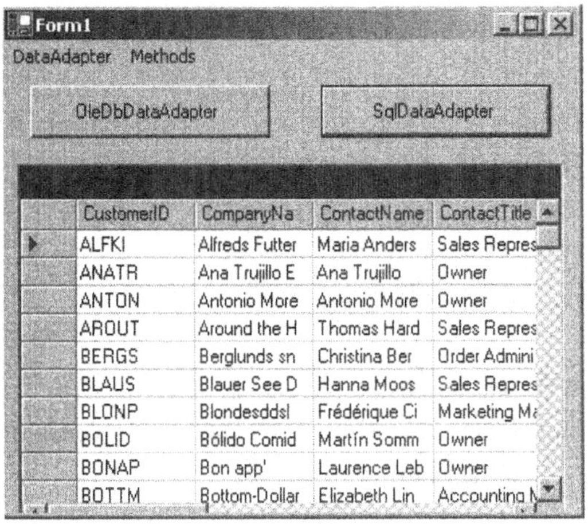

Figure 4-5. Filling data from a SQL Server database to a DataGrid *control using* SqlDataAdapter

Filling the DataAdapter from a Recordset

Because Microsoft realized it would be difficult for some developers to let go of their ADO recordsets (or perhaps they have some legacy applications or components that would be difficult to convert), the DataAdapter's Fill method also allows you to fill a DataSet with an ADO recordset. You can't, however, go the other way and fill a recordset with a Dataset. The Fill method appends rows from the recordset to the existing `DataSet`'s `DataTable`. If a primary key exists for the `DataRows` in the `DataSet`, then the `Fill` method will attempt to update rows from the recordset with a matching primary key. You can call the recordset with the lfollowing code:

```
OleDbDataAdapter1.Fill(ds, anADORecordset, SourceTableName)
```

Updating the Database Using the Update Method

The architecture of a `DataAdapter` has been designed so that you can make any changes you want to the data in a filled `DataSet`, without affecting the database until you call the `Update` method. When `Update` is called, the `DataAdapter` will attempt to execute each query (UPDATE, INSERT, DELETE) on every row of the `DataSet` that has been updated, inserted, and deleted. For example, if you call `Delete` on a row in the `DataSet`, then when `Update` is called on the `DataAdapter`, the `DeleteCommand` of the `DataAdapter` will be called using the particular row in the `DataSet`.

NOTE *Keep in mind that this* Update *is different from a SQL* UPDATE *statement.*

To delete a row, you create an `SqlCommand` object with a DELETE statement and set the `DeleteCommand` property of the `DataAdapter`. Listing 4-26 creates a `SqlCommand` object with a DELETE statement where EmployeeId = 10.

Listing 4-26. Setting the DeleteCommand *Property of* DataAdapter

```
' Set DeleteCommand property
adapter.DeleteCommand = New SqlCommand(
    "DELETE from Employees where EmployeeID = 10", conn)
```

Also, you need to create a parameter for the command that maps to the EmployeeID in the database. (We discuss parameters in more depth in the "Staying within the Parameters" section of this chapter.)

Listing 4-27 shows an example that creates and sets parameter properties for the Sql data provider.

Listing 4-27. Creating a SqlParameter

```
Dim workParam As SqlParameter = Nothing
adapter.DeleteCommand = New SqlCommand( _
"DELETE from Employees where EmployeeID = 10", conn)
 workParam = adapter.DeleteCommand.Parameters.Add( _
"@EmployeeID", OleDbType.Integer)
workParam.SourceColumn = "EmployeeID"
workParam.SourceVersion = DataRowVersion.Original
```

Now you create a DataSet and fill it with the employees from the Employees table in the Northwind database, as shown in Listing 4-28.

Listing 4-28. Calling the Fill *Method of a* DataAdapter

```
Dim ds As DataSet = New DataSet("EmployeeSet")
adapter.Fill(ds, "Employees")
```

Now you're prepared to delete data from a table using a DataTable. By calling Delete on the last row in the Rows collection, you *mark* the last row as deleted. To cause the actual deletion to take place in the Northwind database, you need to call Update on the adapter. This causes the adapter to go through each changed row of the DataSet and see which command needs to be called on that row. In the case of the last row in the Employees table, you call the DeleteCommand (see Listing 4-29).

Listing 4-29. Removing a Row and Calling the Update *Method of a* DataAdapter

```
Dim Dt As DataTable = ds.Tables("Employees")
Dim lastRow As Integer = Dt.Rows.Count - 1
Dim firstName As String = Dt.Rows(lastRow)("FirstName").ToString()
Dim lastName As String = Dt.Rows(lastRow)("LastName").ToString()
Dt.Rows(Dt.Rows.Count - 1).Delete()
adapter.Update(ds, "Employees")
```

Listing 4-30 shows the code that calls the Update method to delete a row from a DataSet and updates it back to the database using DataApdater's Update method.

Listing 4-30. Calling a DataAdapter's Update *Method*

```
Dim ConnectionString As String = "Integrated Security=SSPI;" & _
        "Initial Catalog=Northwind;Data Source=MCB;"
```

```
Dim conn As SqlConnection = New SqlConnection(ConnectionString)
Dim adapter As SqlDataAdapter = New SqlDataAdapter()
Dim workParam As SqlParameter = Nothing
adapter.DeleteCommand = New SqlCommand( _
"DELETE from Employees where EmployeeID = 10", conn)
workParam = adapter.DeleteCommand.Parameters.Add( _
"@EmployeeID", OleDbType.Integer)
workParam.SourceColumn = "EmployeeID"
workParam.SourceVersion = DataRowVersion.Original
adapter.SelectCommand = New SqlCommand("SELECT * FROM Employees", conn)
Dim ds As DataSet = New DataSet("EmployeeSet")
adapter.Fill(ds, "Employees")
Dim Dt As DataTable = ds.Tables("Employees")
Dim lastRow As Integer = Dt.Rows.Count - 1
Dim firstName As String = Dt.Rows(lastRow)("FirstName").ToString()
Dim lastName As String = Dt.Rows(lastRow)("LastName").ToString()
Dt.Rows(Dt.Rows.Count - 1).Delete()
adapter.Update(ds, "Employees")
DataGrid1.DataSource = ds.DefaultViewManager
' release objects
conn.Close()
conn.Dispose()
```

Table and Column Mapping

One of the important properties of the DataAdapter is the TableMappings property. This property contains a collection of DataTableMapping objects (from the System.Data.Common namespace). The DataAdapter uses the DataTableMapping object to map the table name of the data source to the DataTable name of the DataSet. In general, the names for both sources can be the same.

For example, Listing 4-31 constructs the Northwind database's Order Table Mapping and adds it to the DataAdapter.

Listing 4-31. Using DataTableMapping *to Map the Orders Table of Northwind*

```
' Create a Connection Object
    Dim ConnectionString As String = "Integrated Security=SSPI;" & _
    "Initial Catalog=Northwind; Data Source=MCB;"
    Dim conn As SqlConnection = New SqlConnection(ConnectionString)
    ' Open the connection
    conn.Open()
    ' Create a DataTableMapping object
    Dim dtMapping As DataTableMapping =
        New DataTableMapping("Orders", "mapOrders")
    Dim adapter As SqlDataAdapter =
        New SqlDataAdapter("Select * From Orders", conn)
    ' Call DataAdapter's TableMappings.Add method
    adapter.TableMappings.Add(dtMapping)
    ' Create a DataSet Object and call DataAdapter's Fill method
    ' Make sure you use new name od DataTableMapping i.e., MayOrders
    Dim ds As DataSet = New DataSet()
    adapter.Fill(ds, "mapOrders")
    DataGrid1.DataSource = ds.DefaultViewManager
    'Dispose
    conn.Close()
    conn.Dispose()
```

The default mapping for a DataTable is the Table alias. If you use this mapping name, then you don't need to mention the table in the Fill method. Listing 4-32 shows an example using DataTableMapping with the Table option.

Listing 4-32. Using DataTableMapping *with the* Table *Option*

```
' Create a Connection Object
    Dim ConnectionString As String = "Integrated Security=SSPI;" & _
    "Initial Catalog=Northwind; Data Source=MCB;"
    Dim conn As SqlConnection = New SqlConnection(ConnectionString)
    ' Open the connection
    conn.Open()
    ' Create a DataTableMapping object
Dim dtMapping As DataTableMapping =
        New DataTableMapping("Table", "mapOrders")
    Dim adapter As SqlDataAdapter =
        New SqlDataAdapter("Select * From Orders", conn)
    ' Call DataAdapter's TableMappings.Add method
```

```
    adapter.TableMappings.Add(dtMapping)
    ' Create a DataSet Object and call DataAdapter's Fill method
    ' Make sure you use new name od DataTableMapping i.e., MayOrders
    Dim ds As DataSet = New DataSet()
    adapter.Fill(ds)
    DataGrid1.DataSource = ds.DefaultViewManager
    'Dispose
    conn.Close()
    conn.Dispose()
```

DataTables are not the only things aliased in ADO.NET. You can also alias the DataColumns using DataColumnMapping objects. Why do you want column mapping? Let's say you have a table that has column names such as a1, a2, and so on, but when a user views the data in data-bound controls, you want to display some meaningful names such as CustomerName and so on.

Data column mapping allows you to customize a DataSet's column names, which internally are mapped with a table columns. You can achieve this by using DataAdapter.DataTableMapping.ColumnMapping. The DataColumnMapping property of DataTableMapping is a collection of column mappings. You use the Add method of DataColumnCollection, which adds a column mapping. The Add method takes a column name of the source table and a DataSet column name. Listing 4-33 maps the OrderId, ShipName, ShipCity, and OrderDate columns of the Orders table to mapID, mapName, mapCity, and mapDate, respectively.

Listing 4-33. Using DataColumnMapping

```
' Create a Connection Object
    Dim ConnectionString As String = "Integrated Security=SSPI;" & _
    "Initial Catalog=Northwind; Data Source=MCB;"
    Dim conn As SqlConnection = New SqlConnection(ConnectionString)
    ' Open the connection
    conn.Open()
    ' Create a DataTableMapping object
    Dim dtMapping As DataTableMapping = New DataTableMapping("Table", "Orders")
    Dim adapter As SqlDataAdapter = New SqlDataAdapter _
    ("SELECT OrderID, ShipName, ShipCity, OrderDate FROM Orders", conn)
    ' Call DataAdapter's TableMappings.Add method
    adapter.TableMappings.Add(dtMapping)
    dtMapping.ColumnMappings.Add(New DataColumnMapping("OrderID", "mapID"))
    dtMapping.ColumnMappings.Add(New DataColumnMapping("ShipName", "mapName"))
    dtMapping.ColumnMappings.Add(New DataColumnMapping("ShipCity", "mapCity"))
    dtMapping.ColumnMappings.Add(New DataColumnMapping("OrderDate", "mapDate"))
```

```
' Create a DataSet Object and call DataAdapter's Fill method
' Make sure you use new name od DataTableMapping i.e., MayOrders
Dim ds As DataSet = New DataSet()
adapter.Fill(ds)
DataGrid1.DataSource = ds.DefaultViewManager
'Dispose
conn.Close()
conn.Dispose()
```

Figure 4-6 displays the results of Listing 4-33.

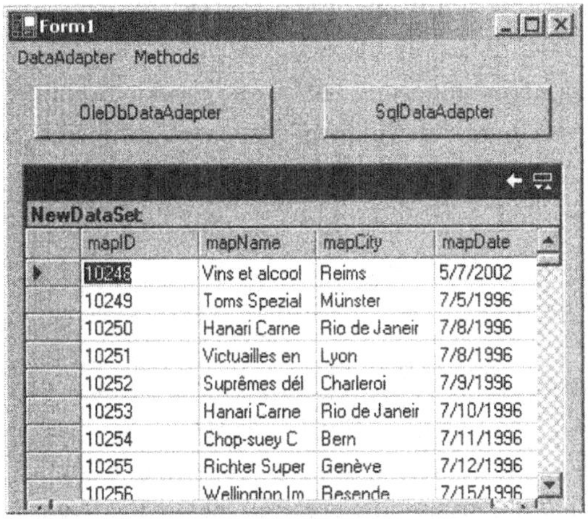

Figure 4-6. Column mapping

The IDE automatically generates much of the mappings, so you don't have to worry about them. But, occasionally, you may want to choose your own schema names for your DataSet that map back to the data source.

CommandBuilder: Easing the Work of Programmers

Sometimes creating SQL statements can be a lengthy job when dealing with many columns in a table. A CommandBuilder object reduces the burden of creating SQL statement for you. In other words, the CommandBuilder object helps you generate UPDATE, DELETE, and INSERT commands on a single database table for a DataAdapter. The OleDbCommandBuilder, SqlCommandBuilder, and OdbcCommandBuilder classes represent the CommandBuilder object in the OleDb, Sql, and Odbc data providers (respectively).

Creating a CommandBuilder Object

Creating a CommandBuilder object is pretty simple. You pass a DataAdapter as an argument of the CommandBuilder contructor. For example:

```
// Create a command builder object
SqlCommandBuilder builder = new SqlCommandBuilder(adapter);
```

Using SqlCommandBuilder Members

The DataAdapter property of a CommandBuilder represents the DataProvider attached to a CommandBuilder object for which automatic SQL statements are generated. The GetDeleteCommand, GetUpdateCommand, and GetInsertCommand methods return the Delete, Update, and Insert commands in the form of a Command object. The RefreshSchema method refreshes the database schema.

Using SqlCommandBuilder

Now you'll see how to use the SqlCommandBuilder in an application. You can use the OleDbCommandBuilder and OdbcCommandBuilder classes in the same way.

As usual, you create a connection to the database and use it to create the adapter object. The adapter is constructed with the initial query for the Employees table as well as with the database connection.

Next, you construct the CommandBuilder by passing the DataAdapter into its constructor. The act of creating the CommandBuilder automatically causes the UPDATE, INSERT, and DELETE commands to be generated for the adapter. The following code creates two SqlCommandBuilder objects:

```
Dim adapter As SqlDataAdapter = New SqlDataAdapter(SQL, conn)
  Dim builder1 As SqlCommandBuilder = New SqlCommandBuilder()
  builder1.DataAdapter = adapter
  Dim builder2 As SqlCommandBuilder = _
  New SqlCommandBuilder(adapter)
```

Next, fill the DataSet using the adapter and create an instance of the Employees DataTable from the DataSet:

```
Dim ds As DataSet = New DataSet("EmployeeSet")
adapter.Fill(ds, "Employees")
```

Now, insert a new DataRow into the DataTable in memory and populate a row with your desired values using the DataTable's AddNew method. After that you call the DataRowCollection.Add method to add the row to the DataTable:

```
' Create a data table object and add a new row
    Dim EmployeeTable As DataTable = ds.Tables("Employees")
    Dim row As DataRow = EmployeeTable.NewRow()
    row("FirstName") = "Rodney"
    row("LastName") = "DangerField"
    row("Title") = "Manager "
    EmployeeTable.Rows.Add(row)
```

Finally, you call DataAdapter's Update method to update the DataTable changes to the data source:

```
// Update data adapter
adapter.Update(ds, "Employees");
```

Listing 4-34 shows the full source code for creating and using a CommandBuilder object.

Listing 4-34. Creating and Using the SqlCommandBuilder *Class*

```
    Dim ConnectionString As String = "Integrated Security=SSPI;" & _
        "Initial Catalog=Northwind;Data Source=MCB;"
Dim conn As SqlConnection = New SqlConnection(ConnectionString)
    Dim SQL As String = "SELECT * FROM Employees"
    ' open a connection
    conn.Open()
    Dim adapter As SqlDataAdapter = New SqlDataAdapter(SQL, conn)
    Dim builder1 As SqlCommandBuilder = New SqlCommandBuilder()
    builder1.DataAdapter = adapter
    Dim builder2 As SqlCommandBuilder = _
    New SqlCommandBuilder(adapter)
    ' Create a command builder object
    Dim builder As SqlCommandBuilder = New SqlCommandBuilder(adapter)
    ' Create a dataset object
    Dim ds As DataSet = New DataSet("EmployeeSet")
    adapter.Fill(ds, "Employees")
    ' Create a data table object and add a new row
    Dim EmployeeTable As DataTable = ds.Tables("Employees")
    Dim row As DataRow = EmployeeTable.NewRow()
```

```
row("FirstName") = "Bill"
row("LastName") = "Harvey"
row("Title") = "President"
EmployeeTable.Rows.Add(row)
' Update data adapter
adapter.Update(ds, "Employees")
' Dispose
conn.Close()
conn.Dispose()
```

As you can see from Listing 4-34, you didn't have to figure out how to create InsertCommand for the Employees table because the CommandBuilder did it for you. All you had to do was add a row to the DataSet and invoke an Update on the DataAdapter. You may argue that the InsertCommand is automatically generated by VS .NET with the DataAdapter configurer, but the CommandBuilder works with the SelectCommand you choose for the adapter, so you can change the SelectCommand on the fly and reuse the CommandBuilder at runtime.

Note that you should call the RefreshSchema method of the CommandBuilder if the SelectCommand of the associated DataAdapter changes. The RefreshSchema rebuilds the other command structures (InsertCommand, DeleteCommand, UpdateCommand) of the DataAdapter.

Staying within the Parameters

ADO.NET wraps a class around the parameters used for each column of the database. You can use the parameters in conjunction with SelectCommand to help you to select data for the DataSet. You also use it in conjunction with the other commands of the CommandDataSet (InsertCommand, UpdateCommand, DeleteCommand) to place data into the DataSet. These are generated automatically when you insert a OleDbDataAdapter component from the Toolbox.

The OleDbType describes the type information for the parameter. It consists of everything from strings to Global Unique Identifiers (GUIDs).

The Sql data provider has a SqlDbType, and the Odbc data provider has an OdbcType. These type names and definitions differ, depending upon the provider you're using; for example, the Money type is the same in Odbc and Sql data providers, but it's called Currency in OleDb data providers.

Not only does a parameter have a DbType property, but a parameter has a Direction (input, output), Size, and even a Value. Table 4-14 describes the SqlParameter properties.

Table 4-14. The SqlParameter *Class Properties*

PROPERTY	DESCRIPTION
DbType	Represents the DbType of the parameter.
Direction	Represents the direction of a parameter. A parameter can be input-only, output-only, bi-directional, or a stored procedure.
IsNullable	Represents whether a parameter accepts null values.
OleDbType	Represents the OleDbType of the parameter.
Offset	Represents the offset to the Value property.
ParameterName	Represents the name of the parameter.
Precision	Represents the maximum number of digits used to represent the Value property.
Scale	Represents the decimal places to which Value is resolved.
Size	Represents the maximum size in bytes a column can store.
SourceColumn	Represents the source column mapped to the DataSet.
SourceVersion	Represents the DataRow version.
SqlDbType	Represents the SqlDbType of the parameter
Value	Represents the value of the parameter.

Now you're going to see the construction of parameters using the Integrated Development Environment (IDE) as well as manually. Listing 4-35 shows the construction of an OleDbParameter generated by the IDE for the Northwind database. All commands have a collection of parameters; in this example, the parameter ContactName is being added to a command used for deleting from the database.

Listing 4-35. Creating a Parameter

```
Me.oleDbDeleteCommand2.Parameters.Add(New
System.Data.OleDb.OleDbParameter("ContactName",
System.Data.OleDb.OleDbType.Char, 30,
System.Data.ParameterDirection.Input, False,
((System.Byte)(0)), ((System.Byte)(0)),
"ContactName", System.Data.DataRowVersion.Original,
Nothing))
```

Luckily, the IDE automatically generates the parameters for you; as you can see, this is a lot of code to write for just one parameter. Imagine if you had to manually deal with a database table of 50 parameters!

You need to create and add parameters to the command for each parameter reference that appears in the SQL command. If the SQL command only describes a single row insert or update, then you don't have parameters. But, more often than not, when you're using DataSets, DataTables, and DataRows, you'll need parameters because these in-memory structures operate on several rows.

Parameters appear in a SQL Server INSERT command proceeded by an @ sign, as shown in the following code:

```
sqlInsertCommand1.CommandText =
@"INSERT INTO Customers(CustomerID, CompanyName, ContactName)"+
" VALUES (@CustomerID, @CompanyName, @ContactName)"
In OleDb, parameters appear as question marks such as:
oleDbInsertCommand2.CommandText =
"INSERT INTO Customers(Address, City, CompanyName, ContactName)"+
" VALUES (?, ?, ?, ?)"
```

To add the parameter @CustomerID to the InsertCommand of the SqlDataAdapter, simply call Add on the command's ParameterCollection. This will return a parameter in which you can further assign properties, such as:

```
SqlParameter  workParam = theSqlServerAdapter.InsertCommand.
            Parameters.Add("@CustomerID", SqlDbType.Int)
```

Two other crucial properties are the name of the column that the parameter is mapping to and the RowVersion. Typically, it's good to give the parameter the same name as the column of the database to avoid the confusion:

```
workParam.SourceColumn = "CustomerID"
workParam.SourceVersion = DataRowVersion.Original
```

The SourceVersion can be either Current or Original. The SourceVersion property helps the DataAdapter's Update command decide which value version to load when executing the SQL UpdateCommand on the database. (InsertCommand and DeleteCommand ignore the SourceVersion.) The SourceVersion property comes in handy when you're updating a row whose primary key you may want to change. If the value is DataRowVersion.Original, then the primary key will retain its original value.

You just saw an example of a parameter generated by the VS .NET IDE. It's always a better idea to write your own code if you really want to know what goes under the hood. So, let's create parameters and use them in a SqlCommand. The following code creates a parameter by reading a value from a TextBox control and

deletes the record from the Categories table that matches the `CategoryID` as
`TextBox1.Text`:

```
dim strId as string = TextBox1.Text
   dim sql = "DELETE Categories WHERE CategoryID=@catID"
   dim cmd as SqlCommand = new SqlCommand(sql, conn)
   cmd.Parameters.Add("@catID", strId)
   cmd.ExecuteNonQuery()
```

As you can see, the `Parameters` property of `SqlCommand` returns an object of type
`SqlParameters`, which represents a collection of parameters. It provides an `Add`
method to add a parameter to the collection.

Now let's construct a `SqlCommand` with an UPDATE SQL statement using three
parameters. The following code creates and adds three parameters to the collection. The code also constructs an UPDATE SQL statement with parameters and
calls the `ExecuteNonQuery` method to execute the command:

```
dim strId as string = TextBox1.Text
   dim strCatName as string = TextBox2.Text
   dim strDesc as string = TextBox3.Text
   dim sql = "UPDATE Categories SET CategoryName=@catName, " & _
   " Description=@desc WHERE CategoryID=@catID"
   dim cmd as SqlCommand = new SqlCommand(sql, conn)
   cmd.Parameters.Add("@catID", strId)
   cmd.Parameters.Add("@catName", strCatName)
   cmd.Parameters.Add("@desc", strDesc)
   cmd.ExecuteNonQuery()
```

You can even directly assign parameter values by using the `Value` property. For
example, the following code adds two parameters to the command with the values
`NewCategory` and `New Description`:

```
cmd.Parameters.Add("@CategoryName", SqlDbType.VarChar, 80).Value = _
"NewCategory"
cmd.Parameters.Add("@Description", SqlDbType.Int).Value = _
"New Description"
```

The DataSet in Connected Environments

In Chapter 3, you saw how to create and use DataSet objects in disconnected environments. You saw how to use a DataSet's properties and how to fill, delete, and update data using DataTable objects. In the following sections, you'll see how to work with DataSets in connected environments. Instead of using a DataTable, you'll use a DataAdapter to fill and save data from a DataSet to a data source.

As mentioned, the Fill method of a DataAdapter fills data from a data source to a DataSet. Once the DataSet is filled with data, you can do any operation on this data. This data is disconnected data, and there's no connection between a DataSet and a data source until you finally call the Update method of a DataAdapter. The Update method of a DataAdapter saves the DataSet changes to the data source. You saw these Fill and Update methods in "The DataAdapter: Adapting to Your Environment."

Filling a DataSet from Multiple Tables

You saw how to fill a DataSet from a table in many of the previous samples. Now, there may be times when you'll want to view data from multiple tables in data-bound controls. If you remember ADO, you used SQL JOIN statements to fill a recordset from multiple tables.

In ADO.NET, there are different ways you can fill data from multiple tables depending on your requirements. If you want to view data from multiple tables in multiple data-bound controls, the simplest way is create a DataAdapter for each table and fill a DataSet from a DataAdapter and use the DataSet to bind data to the controls. Listing 4-36 simply creates two SqlDataAdapter objects using two different SqlCommand objects and then fills two different DataSet objects (which you later bind to two separate DataGrid controls).

Listing 4-36. Filling Data from Multiple Tables

```
Dim ConnectionString As String = "Integrated Security=SSPI;" & _
    "Initial Catalog=Northwind;Data Source=MCB;"
Dim conn As SqlConnection = New SqlConnection(ConnectionString)
conn.Open()
Dim adapter1 As SqlDataAdapter = New SqlDataAdapter()
Dim adapter2 As SqlDataAdapter = New SqlDataAdapter()
adapter1.SelectCommand = New SqlCommand("SELECT * FROM Customers")
adapter2.SelectCommand = New SqlCommand("SELECT * FROM Orders")
adapter1.SelectCommand.Connection = conn
```

```
adapter2.SelectCommand.Connection = conn
Dim ds1 As DataSet = New DataSet()
Dim ds2 As DataSet = New DataSet()
adapter1.Fill(ds1)
adapter2.Fill(ds2)
DataGrid1.DataSource = ds1.DefaultViewManager
DataGrid2.DataSource = ds2.DefaultViewManager
' Dispose
conn.Close()
conn.Dispose()
```

Now what if you want to fill a DataSet with data from multiple tables? Actually, that's pretty easy, too. If you remember the Merge method of the DataSet from Chapter 3, you'll learned how to merge two DataSet objects. You can use the same method to fill data from two different tables in two different DataSet objects and later call the Merge method, which merges one DataSet into another. Listing 4-37 fills two DataSet objects from two different tables—Customers and Orders—and later one DataSet merges into another. After that you just bind the final DataSet to a DataGrid control, which displays data from both tables.

Listing 4-37. Merging Two DataSet Objects

```
Dim adapter As SqlDataAdapter = New SqlDataAdapter()
    adapter.SelectCommand = New SqlCommand("SELECT * FROM Customers")
    adapter.SelectCommand.Connection = conn
    Dim ds1 As DataSet = New DataSet()
    adapter.Fill(ds1)
    adapter.SelectCommand = New SqlCommand("SELECT * FROM Orders")
    adapter.SelectCommand.Connection = conn
    Dim ds2 As DataSet = New DataSet()
    adapter.Fill(ds2)
    ds1.Merge(ds2, False, MissingSchemaAction.Add)
DataGrid1.DataSource = ds1.DefaultViewManager
```

NOTE *The* Merge *method has seven overloaded forms. Using this method, you can even merge* DataRow *and* DataTable *objects with a* DataSet.

Using a SQL Statement to Read Data from Two or More Tables

Using a SQL statement is the simplest way to put data from multiple tables into a DataSet. The following code selects data from the Customers and Orders tables and fills it to a single DataSet:

```
Dim conn As SqlConnection = New SqlConnection(ConnectionString)
SQL = "SELECT * FROM Customers; SELECT * FROM Orders"
conn.Open()
Dim adapter As SqlDataAdapter = New SqlDataAdapter(SQL, conn)
Dim ds As DataSet = New DataSet("CustOrdersDataSet")
adapter.Fill(ds)
```

Adding, Updating, and Deleting Data through the DataSet

You add, edit, and delete data in a DataSet through DataSet objects. As you know, a DataSet is a collection of DataSet objects. The DataSet's Rows and Columns properties represent the collection of a DataSet's rows and columns, which are represented by the DataRowCollection and DataColumnCollection objects. The DataRowCollection and DataColumnCollection classes provide methods to add and delete rows and columns, respectively (see Chapter 3 for more details). You can add a new row to a DataTable using its NewRow method, which takes a DataRow as an argument. To update a DataRow's data (through DataTable), you first get a DataRow based on the index of the row and edit its values. The Delete method of a DataRow deletes a row. Listing 4-38 adds, updates, and deletes data of a DataSet through a DataTable and a DataRow.

Listing 4-38. Adding, Editing, and Deleting a DataSet Rows

```
Dim adapter As SqlDataAdapter = New SqlDataAdapter(SQL, conn)
    ' Create a command builder object
    Dim builder As SqlCommandBuilder = New SqlCommandBuilder(adapter)
    ' Create a dataset object
    Dim ds As DataSet = New DataSet()
    adapter.Fill(ds, "Employees")
    ' Create a data table object and add a new row
    Dim EmployeeTable As DataTable = ds.Tables("Employees")
    Dim row As DataRow = EmployeeTable.NewRow()
```

```
row("FirstName") = "New Name"
row("LastName") = "Mr. Last"
row("Title") = "New Employee"
EmployeeTable.AcceptChanges()
EmployeeTable.Rows.Add(row)
' Get the last row
Dim editedRow As DataRow = EmployeeTable.Rows _
(EmployeeTable.Rows.Count - 1)
editedRow("FirstName") = "Edited Name"
editedRow("LastName") = "Mr. Edited"
editedRow("Title") = "Edited Employee"
EmployeeTable.AcceptChanges()
' Delete a row. Last row - 1
Dim deletedRow As DataRow = EmployeeTable.Rows _
(EmployeeTable.Rows.Count - 2)
deletedRow.Delete()
EmployeeTable.AcceptChanges()
' Save changes to the database
adapter.Update(ds, "Employees")
```

Accepting and Rejecting Changes through the DataSet

The DataSet class provides methods that allow you to make sure if you want to save changes or reject changes made to a DataSet since it was loaded or the last time AcceptChanges was called. The AcceptChanges method saves the changes, and the RejectChanges method rejects (rolls back) all the changes made to the DataSet. Listing 4-39 shows you how to use these methods to accept and reject changes.

Listing 4-39. Using the AcceptChanges *and* RejectChanges *Methods of a* DataSet

```
Dim adapter As SqlDataAdapter = New SqlDataAdapter(SQL, conn)
    ' Create a command builder object
    Dim builder As SqlCommandBuilder = New SqlCommandBuilder(adapter)
    ' Create a dataset object
    Dim ds As DataSet = New DataSet()
    adapter.Fill(ds, "Employees")
    ' Create a data table object and add a new row
    Dim EmployeeTable As DataTable = ds.Tables("Employees")
    Dim row As DataRow = EmployeeTable.NewRow()
    row("FirstName") = "New Name"
    row("LastName") = "Mr. Last"
```

```
row("Title") = "New Employee"
EmployeeTable.Rows.Add(row)
' Update data adapter
  If MessageBox.Show("Do you want to save change?", _
      "DataSet AcceptReject Methods", _
      MessageBoxButtons.YesNo, MessageBoxIcon.Question) _
    = DialogResult.Yes Then
  ds.AcceptChanges()
Else
  ds.RejectChanges()
End If
adapter.Update(ds, "Employees")
```

Saving Changed Data Only

As you know, you fill a DataSet using the Fill method of a DataAdapter, modify its contents, and call the Update method to save changes made to a DataSet. This method sends the entire DataSet data back to the database. This scenario may affect the performance and increase network congestion when working with large data—especially over the Web.

Wouldn't it be nice if you could send only the changed data of a DataSet back to the database instead of sending the entire contents of a DataSet? The DataSet provides methods that allow you to find out the changed rows and retrieve changed rows only. The HasChanges method of the DataSet returns True if it finds any changes based on the DataRow's state, represented by the DataRowState enumeration. The GetChanges method returns the changed rows since a DataSet was loaded or AcceptChanges was last called and returns the changed data in a DataSet. Now you just need to call the DataAdapter's Update method with the DataSet object returned by the GetChanges method, which will send this DataSet's contents back to the database.

Listing 4-40 shows you how to call the GetChanges method and save only the modified rows back to the database.

Listing 4-40. Saving Only Modified Rows of a DataSet

```
' See if DataSet has changes or not
    If Not ds.HasChanges(DataRowState.Modified) Then Exit Sub
    Dim tmpDtSet As DataSet
    ' GetChanges for modified rows only.
    tmpDtSet = ds.GetChanges(DataRowState.Modified)
    If tmpDtSet.HasErrors Then
      MessageBox.Show("DataSet has errors")
      Exit Sub
    End If
    adapter.Update(tmpDtSet)
```

Using a DataSet vs. Using a DataReader

When should you use a DataSet and when should you use a DataReader? This question comes up on almost every ADO.NET-related discussion forum or news-group. There are several differences between the two:

Accessing performance: A DataReader provides a read-only, forward-only view of data and is faster than a DataSet because it's only reading data. In other words, you can only read data using a DataReader. A DataSet provides both read and write access to data.

Data-bound connectivity: A DataReader doesn't provide any direct data-bound connectivity, which makes it less flexible than a DataSet. A DataSet is a versatile and flexible control, which allows both data read and write options and provides way to add, edit, delete, and view data in data-bound controls with little effort.

Connected state: A DataReader is always in a connected state. This means if you're using a DataReader, there's always a connection established between the reader and the database, until you close the DataReader. A DataSet stores data in a disconnected state in Extensible Markup Language (XML) format. Once you fill data from a data source to a DataSet, there's no connection between a DataSet and the database. A connection is established when you read or updated data again.

You should now have an idea of when to use a DataReader and when to use a DataSet.

Fetching Data Based on Wildcard Characters

The SELECT...LIKE SQL statement is useful when you want to select rows based on a wildcard string. For example, say you want to get all rows of the Employees table where an employee's first name starts with *C* and ends with *a*. You build a SQL statement like so:

```
Dim sql as string = SELECT * FROM Employees WHERE FirstName LIKE 'C%a'
```

Another useful example of LIKE is when you want to select all the employees whose first name contains the string *gar*. You can build a SELECT statement as follows:

```
Dim sql as string = SELECT * FROM Employees WHERE FirstName LIKE '%gar%'
```

Now you can use this SELECT statement in a DataReader or DataAdapter to retrieve the data from a database.

The DataView in Connected Environments

In Chapter 3, you learned how a DataView is useful to sort, filter, and view data based on different selection criteria. You also saw how to add, edit, and delete data from a DataView. In Chapter 3, you saw all of this in disconnected data. Also, you created DataView objects from DataTable objects. In the following sections, you'll see how to work with DataView objects in a connected environment. You'll also learn how to search and sort data based on criteria and how to create different views of the same data.

You simply create a DataView from a DataTable, which can be retrieved using the Tables property of a DataSet. The following code creates a DataView from the first table of a DataSet and binds a DataView to the DataGrid control:

```
Dim dtView1 As DataView = New DataView(ds.Tables(0))
DataGrid1.DataSource = dtView1
```

Creating Multiple Views

The main features of a DataView is that it's easily bound to controls, and it provides filter and sort properties, which allow you to create different views of the same data. To see how to use DataViews, let's create a Windows application. After creating a Windows application, you'll add two DataGrid controls, four TextBox controls, two CheckBox controls, and a Button control and arrange them as shown in Figure 4-7. The Load Data button loads data from the Northwind SQL Server database's Orders table.

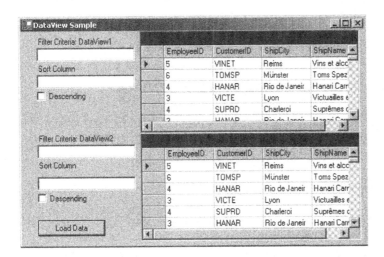

Figure 4-7. Default multiple views application

Now, if you enter the filter and sort criteria from both DataGrid controls, the data is filtered and sorted based on the criteria. For example, Figure 4-8 shows the criteria and the result of clicking the Load Data button.

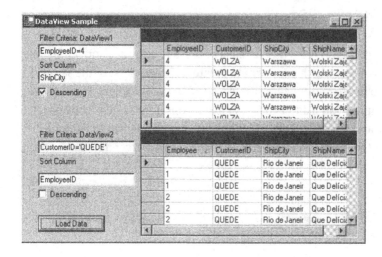

Figure 4-8. Multiple views with different filter and sorting criteria

Now let's examine the code. Listing 4-41 shows the private members.

Listing 4-41. Private Members

```
Private ConnectionString As String = "Integrated Security=SSPI;" & _
        "Initial Catalog=Northwind;Data Source=MCB;"
  Private conn As SqlConnection
  Private SQL As String = _
  "SELECT EmployeeID, CustomerID, ShipCity, ShipName FROM Orders"
  Private adapter As SqlDataAdapter
  Dim ds As DataSet = New DataSet()
```

Listing 4-42 shows the code of the Load Data button's click event handler. As you can see, the code creates two different DataView objects from the DataSet and sets their RowFilter and Sort properties based on the data entered on the form. In the end, you bind each DataView object to a separate DataGrid control.

Listing 4-42. The Load Data Button's Click Event Handler

```
Private Sub LoadDataBtn_Click(ByVal sender As System.Object, _
  ByVal e As System.EventArgs) Handles LoadDataBtn.Click
    conn = New SqlConnection(ConnectionString)
    Try
      conn.Open()
      adapter = New SqlDataAdapter(SQL, conn)
```

```vb
      adapter.Fill(ds)
    Catch exp As SqlException
      exp.Message.ToString()
    End Try


    ' Create two DataView objects
    Dim dtView1 As DataView = New DataView(ds.Tables(0))
    Dim dtView2 As DataView = New DataView(ds.Tables(0))
    ' Set RowFilter and Sort proeprties of DataView1
    If (TextBox1.Text <> String.Empty) Then
      dtView1.RowFilter = TextBox1.Text
    End If
    Dim sortStr1 As String = TextBox2.Text
    If (sortStr1 <> String.Empty) Then
      If CheckBox1.Checked Then
        sortStr1 = sortStr1 + " DESC"
      Else
        sortStr1 = sortStr1 + " ASC"
      End If
      dtView1.Sort = sortStr1
    End If


    ' Set RowFilter and Sort proeprties of DataView2
    If (TextBox3.Text <> String.Empty) Then
      dtView2.RowFilter = TextBox3.Text
    End If
    Dim sortStr2 As String = TextBox4.Text
    If (sortStr2 <> String.Empty) Then
      If CheckBox2.Checked Then
        sortStr2 = sortStr2 + " DESC"
      Else
        sortStr2 = sortStr2 + " ASC"
      End If
      dtView2.Sort = sortStr2
    End If


    ' Bind both DataViews to two different DataGrids
    DataGrid1.DataSource = dtView1
    DataGrid2.DataSource = dtView2
    ' release objects
    conn.Close()
    conn.Dispose()
End Sub
```

Transactions and Concurrency in ADO.NET

Transactions are groups of database commands that execute as a package and provide an ability to commit or roll back (abort) all changes made during the transaction processing. Transaction changes will be committed if there wasn't an error during the transaction processing. If an error occurs during the transaction processing, all changes will be aborted and data will be same as it was before any transactions started. To start transaction processing, you call BeginTransaction. At the end you can call CommitTransaction or Rollback Transaction based on the status of the transactions. CommitTransaction reflects all changes to the database, and Rollback aborts all changes.

For example, say you have an application with two tables: Inventory and Orders. When a customer places an order, the Inventory table needs to be reduced. Now imagine that updating the Orders table was successful, but updating the Inventory table failed. This scenario leads to data inconsistency. To maintain the integrity of data, you could package both commands into a single transaction. If one table updated successfully and the other table didn't, the transaction could be rolled back; otherwise, the transaction could be committed.

Nested transactions are transactions within the scope an existing transaction. The changes made within the nested transactions are invisible to the top-level transactions until the nested transactions are committed. To create nested transactions, you call BeginTransaction with CommitTransaction and Rollback-Transaction within the existing transactions. For example:

```
Begin Transaction A
      Begin Transaction B
               Do something
      Commit Transaction B
Commit Transaction A
```

Savepoints are useful when you're working with nested transactions. There are occasions when you want to abort a portion of transaction, but not all of it. For example, say you're processing four commands as nested transactions, but you want to commit only two commands and abort two of them. A *savepoint* is a temporary point in the transaction that you want to save (or back up) without aborting the entire transaction. In transaction processing, you set the savepoint call and come back later when you think it's safe to process the transaction. A unique number represents the savepoint. For example:

```
Begin Transaction A
     Do something
         SetSavePoint
     Do something
Commit or Rollback Transaction A
```

Managing and writing reliable and scalable multitier distributed applications is one of the most challenging jobs for database developers. Think about multiple clients accessing same server database simultaneously—some of them are accessing data, some of them are updating the same data, and some of them are trying to delete the same data that other clients are using in their operations.

To prevent data inconsistency, it's important to provide some kind of mechanism so other users can't update data when a user is already using that data. The mechanism to deal with this situation is called *concurrency control*. Concurrency is the method by which multiple clients can access and update the same data simultaneously without being concerned that they're forcing data redundancy and inconsistency.

There are three common ways to manage concurrency:

Pessimistic concurrency control: In pessimistic concurrency, the data is unavailable to other users from the time the record is fetched by a user until it's updated in the database. This is useful when users accessing a row are going to play a major role based on the data they're accessing. Another advantage of pessimistic concurrency is less locking overhead. Once a row is locked, it's locked until the first user is done. The main drawback of this type of concurrency is that data is not available to other users. For example, if a user accessing data left his terminal, other users have to wait for him to release the connection.

Optimistic concurrency control: In optimistic concurrency, data is available all the time except when a user is updating the data. The update examines the row in the database and determines whether any changes have been made. In this type of concurrency, the locks are set and held only while the database is being accessed. The locks prevent other users from attempting to update records at the same instant. If other users try to update the data that is locked by first user, the update fails.

Last in wins concurrency control: In this case of concurrency control, a row is unavailable to other users only while the data is being updated. This is only useful when the last user's update counts. For example, it's useful if you're keeping track of the last winner of a race. In other words, many users are updating the same data, and the person who updates it last is the latest data. The data updated by other users will be lost. In this case, data could easily lead to inconsistencies because of network slowness when data previously posted arrives last.

NOTE *See Appendix A for more on locking, cursors, and isolation levels.*

Using Transactions in ADO.NET

ADO.NET provides a Transaction class that represents a transaction. All data providers provide their own version of the Transaction class. In the provider classes, a transaction is represented as an object returned after BeginTransaction is called on a Connection. You can commit (make permanent) or roll back (cancel and return to the original state) the transactions. Table 4-15 describes the methods for the OleDb provider's Transaction class.

Table 4-15. Methods of the Transaction *Class*

METHOD	DESCRIPTION
Commit	Commits the transaction to the database
Rollback	Rolls back a transaction to the previous database state
Begin(IsolationLevel)	Begins a nested database transaction passing the isolation level

The IsolationLevel allows you to lock your transaction in various ways. The default isolation level is ReadCommitted, which allows you to alter data during a transaction. If you use an isolation level of RepeatableRead, locks are placed on all the data, so you can't alter the data in this transaction. If you lock at the Serializable level, locks are placed on the entire DataSet, preventing changes to all the data in the DataSet. Table 4-16 describes different isolation levels.

Table 4-16. Isolation Levels Available for Transactions

ISOLATION LEVEL	DESCRIPTION
ReadCommitted (default)	Locks are shared to prevent inconsistent reads between multiple users. Data can be altered during the transaction.
ReadUncommitted	Locks are not placed on the data, so a dirty read is possible. A dirty read occurs when a transaction reads some data that has been added to the table but not committed yet.

Table 4-16. Isolation Levels Available for Transactions (Continued)

ISOLATION LEVEL	DESCRIPTION
RepeatableRead	Locks are placed on all the data of the database query, so the data can't be altered during a read.
Chaos	The changes made on transactions awaiting commitment can't be altered.
Serializable	A range lock is placed on an entire DataSet, preventing changes from being made to the DataSet
Unspecified	The IsolationLevel can't be determined.

Using Concurrency in ADO.NET

The ADO.NET model assumes that optimistic concurrency is the default concurrency model because of the disconnected nature of data in ADO.NET. A user reads data in a DataSet through a DataAdapter, and data is available to a user as a local copy of the data. The server database is available to all other users.

Even though the ADO.NET model supports optimistic concurrency by default, that doesn't mean you can't implement pessimistic concurrency in ADO.NET. The following two examples show you how to handle both cases.

Listing 4-43 shows you how to implement optimistic concurrency. You can handle the optimistic concurrency by creating an Update command that checks the database to make sure the original data of the database row hasn't changed when an immediate Update is about to be performed. It does this by creating two sets of parameters for the Update command: a current set of parameters and an original set of parameters. The original parameters maintain the data that was originally read in from the DataSet. If the data has changed in the data source, when you run the Update command with the WHERE clause filter, the filter won't find the row and an Update won't occur. If the data has not changed in the data source, then the WHERE clause will find the original row you're updating, and the row will be updated with the new data. Listing 4-43 has a built-in WHERE clause on the original data. The IDE generates parameters such as @ShipCity and @ShipDate. The framework even generates the Update command (which has been shortened in the example).

NOTE *To test these samples, create a Windows application, add references to the* System.Data *and* System.Data.SqlClient *namespaces, add two* Button *controls to the form, write code on the button event handlers, and make sure SQL Server is up and running.*

Listing 4-43. Optimistic Concurrency

```
    Private Sub TestOptimisticConcurrency()
Dim ConnectionString As String = "Integrated Security=SSPI;" & _
    "Initial Catalog=Northwind;Data Source=MCB;"
    Dim conn As SqlConnection = New SqlConnection(ConnectionString)
    conn.Open()
    Try
      Dim da As SqlDataAdapter = New SqlDataAdapter("SELECT * FROM Orders", conn)
      Dim ds As DataSet = New DataSet("test")
      Dim updateCmd As SqlCommand = New SqlCommand()
      updateCmd.CommandText = "UPDATE Orders SET CustomerID = @CustomerID," & _
      "OrderDate = @OrderDate, ShippedDate = @ShippedDate WHERE " & _
      "(OrderID = @Original_OrderID) AND (CustomerID = @Original_CustomerID " & _
      "OR @Original_CustomerID IS NULL AND CustomerID IS NULL) AND " & _
      "(OrderDate = @Original_OrderDate OR @Original_OrderDate " & _
      "IS NULL AND OrderDate IS NULL) AND (ShippedDate = " & _
      "@Original_ShippedDate OR @Original_ShippedDate IS NULL AND " & _
      "ShippedDate IS NULL); SELECT CustomerID, OrderDate, ShippedDate, " & _
      "OrderID FROM Orders WHERE (OrderID = @OrderID)"

      updateCmd.Connection = conn
      ' CustomerID parameter
      updateCmd.Parameters.Add(New SqlParameter _
          ("@CustomerID", SqlDbType.NVarChar, 5, "CustomerID"))
      ' OrderDate parameter
      updateCmd.Parameters.Add(New SqlParameter _
          ("@OrderDate", SqlDbType.DateTime, 8, "OrderDate"))
      ' ShippedDate parameter
      updateCmd.Parameters.Add(New SqlParameter _
          ("@ShippedDate", SqlDbType.DateTime, 8, "ShippedDate"))
      updateCmd.Parameters.Add(New SqlParameter _
          ("@Original_OrderID", SqlDbType.Int, 4, _
          ParameterDirection.Input, False, _
          (CType((0), System.Byte)), (CType((0), System.Byte)), _
          "OrderID", DataRowVersion.Original, Nothing))
      updateCmd.Parameters.Add(New SqlParameter _
          ("@Original_CustomerID", SqlDbType.NVarChar, _
          5, ParameterDirection.Input, False, (CType((0), System.Byte)), _
          (CType((0), System.Byte)), "CustomerID", _
          DataRowVersion.Original, Nothing))
      updateCmd.Parameters.Add(New SqlParameter _
          ("@Original_OrderDate", SqlDbType.DateTime, _
```

```
          8, ParameterDirection.Input, False, (CType((0), System.Byte)), _
          (CType((0), System.Byte)), "OrderDate", _
                  DataRowVersion.Original, Nothing))
      updateCmd.Parameters.Add(New SqlParameter _
        ("@Original_ShippedDate", SqlDbType.DateTime, _
        8, ParameterDirection.Input, False, (CType((0), System.Byte)), _
        (CType((0), System.Byte)), "ShippedDate", _
        DataRowVersion.Original, Nothing))
      updateCmd.Parameters.Add(New SqlParameter("@OrderID", _
      SqlDbType.Int, 4, "OrderID"))
      da.UpdateCommand = updateCmd
      da.Fill(ds, "Orders")
      ' update the row in the dataset
      ds.Tables("Orders").Rows(0).BeginEdit()
      ds.Tables("Orders").Rows(0)("OrderDate") = DateTime.Now
      ds.Tables("Orders").Rows(0)("ShipCity") = "Leone"
      ds.Tables("Orders").Rows(0).EndEdit()
      ' update the row in the data Source (Orders Table)
      da.Update(ds, "Orders")
      MessageBox.Show("Finished updating first row.")
      ' close connection
      conn.Close()
      conn.Dispose()
    Catch ex As SqlException
      ' close connection
      conn.Close()
      conn.Dispose()
      MessageBox.Show(ex.Message.ToString())
    End Try
  End Sub
```

Another way of handling optimistic concurrency that you may be familiar with is by checking to see if a timestamp on the data source row has changed or the row version number has changed on the row being updated.

The data providers don't really support pessimistic locking on the database because the connection to the database is not kept open, so you must perform all locking with business logic on the DataSet.

You can do a form of pessimistic concurrency, however, using ADO.NET on the data source through transactions. The way to do this is to keep the connection open on the database and create a transaction that has a certain isolation level on a row. Listing 4-44 opens a connection and creates a transaction that locks out the rows used in the Update of the Orders table in the Northwind database.

Listing 4-44. Pessimistic Concurrency

```
Private Sub TestPessimisticConcurrency()
    Dim ConnectionString As String = "Integrated Security=SSPI;" & _
    "Initial Catalog=Northwind;Data Source=MCB;"
    Dim conn As SqlConnection = New SqlConnection(ConnectionString)
    conn.Open()
    Try
        ' Create a transaction that locks the records of the query
        Dim tr As SqlTransaction = conn.BeginTransaction _
        (IsolationLevel.RepeatableRead, "test")
        ' Create a command that updates the order of
        ' the database using the transaction\
        Dim cmd As SqlCommand = New SqlCommand("UPDATE Orders SET " & _
            "ShippedDate = '5/10/01', ShipCity = 'Columbus' WHERE " & _
            "OrderID = 10248", conn, tr)
        ' Execute the update
        cmd.ExecuteNonQuery()
        ' Generate message
        MessageBox.Show("Wait for keypress...")
        ' transaction is committed As tr.Commit()
        conn.Close()
    Catch ex As SqlException
        MessageBox.Show(ex.Message.ToString())
    End Try
End Sub
```

Understanding Rollback, Commit, and Savepoints

The Sql data provider provides some additional methods for dealing with trans-
actions involving savepoints (which may not be available in all data providers).
Savepoints allow you to roll back to a "bookmarked" point in the transaction.
Table 4-17 describes these methods.

Table 4-17. Transaction *Methods in the Sql Data Provider*

METHOD	DESCRIPTION
Rollback(SavePoint)	Performs a rollback on a transaction to the previous database state.
Begin(IsolationLevel)	Begins a nested database transaction passing the isolation level.

Table 4-17. Transaction *Methods in the Sql Data Provider (Continued)*

METHOD	DESCRIPTION
Save(SavePointName)	Equivalent to the Transact-SQL SAVE TRANSACTION in the SQL Server database. Allows you to create a savepoint so that you can roll back to a particular saved state of the database.

Listing 4-45 shows an example of how you use savepoints in SQL Server. As you can see, first you establish a connection with the Northwind database and open the connection. After that, by calling BeginTransaction on the connection, you can return a SqlTransaction object, which you can use with your Command object. To establish the relationship with the Command object, you then pass the Transaction object in the constructor of Command.

Now that the transaction is tied to the Command object, you'll save the initial savepoint to the transaction and then execute the first insertion into the database. After that you assign a new SQL Insert to the Command text and save the current transaction savepoint before executing the query. This Insert puts *Bob Hope* into the database.

Finally, you assign a new SQL Insert to the Command text and save the current transaction savepoint before executing the query. This Insert puts *Fred* into the database.

Listing 4-45. Using Savepoints in the Sql Data Provider

```
Dim ConnectionString As String = "Integrated Security=SSPI;" & _
    "Initial Catalog=Northwind;Data Source=MCB;"
    Dim conn As SqlConnection = New SqlConnection(ConnectionString)
    Dim tran As SqlTransaction = Nothing

    Try
      conn.Open()
      tran = conn.BeginTransaction("Transaction1")
      Dim cmd As SqlCommand = New SqlCommand( _
      "INSERT INTO Customers (CustomerID, ContactName, CompanyName)" & _
          "VALUES (516, 'Tim Howard', 'FireCon')", conn, tran)
      ' Call Save method
      tran.Save("save1")
      cmd.ExecuteNonQuery()
      MessageBox.Show("Tim is in the Database")
      cmd.CommandText = _
      "INSERT INTO Customers (CustomerID, ContactName, CompanyName)" & _
      "VALUES (517, 'Bob Hope', 'Hollywood')"
```

```
      ' Call Save again
      tran.Save("save2")
      cmd.ExecuteNonQuery()
      MessageBox.Show("Bob is in the Database")
      cmd.CommandText = _
      "INSERT INTO Customers(CustomerID, ContactName, CompanyName)" & _
      "VALUES (518, 'Fred Astaire', 'Hollywood')"
      MessageBox.Show("Fred is in the Database")
      ' Save
      tran.Save("save3")
      cmd.ExecuteNonQuery()
      ' rollback
      tran.Rollback("save2")
      ' Commit the transaction
      tran.Commit()
      MessageBox.Show("Transaction Rolledback, only Tim Made it.")
      conn.Close()
      conn.Dispose()
  Catch exp As Exception
    If tran Is Nothing Then
      tran.Rollback()
    End If
    MessageBox.Show(exp.Message.ToString() & _
        "Transaction Rolledback, Tim didn't make it.")
  Finally
    conn.Close()
    conn.Dispose()
  End Try
```

By rolling back to the second savepoint, it's as if the second and third ExecuteNonQuery calls never happened, so the first ExecuteNonQuery that puts *Tim* in the database is the only one that actually gets committed. If there's an exception, then you can roll back the whole transaction.

Executing Batches

Another common concern for developers is the question of how to execute multiple INSERT statements in a batch. Again, using transactions, you can execute multiple queries in a batch and save or roll back changes based on some condition. For example, Listing 4-46 shows you how to execute multiple SQL queries.

Listing 4-46. Executing Multiple SQL Queries Using SqlTransaction

```
Dim ConnectionString As String = "Integrated Security=SSPI;" & _
    "Initial Catalog=Northwind;Data Source=MCB;"
    Dim conn As SqlConnection = New SqlConnection(ConnectionString)
    ' Open the connection
    conn.Open()
    ' Create SqlCommand and SqlTransaction objects
    Dim myCommand As New SqlCommand()
    Dim trans As SqlTransaction = Nothing
    ' Create a local transaction using BeginTransaction
    ' All changes inside this transaction will be saves or rollback
    ' after a call of Commit or Rollback
    trans = conn.BeginTransaction()
    myCommand.Connection = conn
    myCommand.Transaction = trans
    Try
      myCommand.CommandText = _
      "INSERT INTO Employees (FirstName, LastName, Address, City) " & _
      " VALUES ('Sundar', 'Lal','234 Lane, Rose Blvd', 'Chester')"
      myCommand.ExecuteNonQuery()
      myCommand.CommandText = _
      "INSERT INTO Employees (FirstName, LastName, Address, City) " & _
      " VALUES ('Dinesh', 'Chand', '23rd Streed, Old Road', 'Delhi')"
      myCommand.ExecuteNonQuery()
      myCommand.CommandText = _
      "INSERT INTO Employees (FirstName, LastName, Address, City) " & _
      " VALUES ('Rajesh', 'Kumar', '278 Meadowlake Drive', 'Downingtown')"
      myCommand.ExecuteNonQuery()
      If MessageBox.Show("Save Changes?", "SqlTransaction Commit Rollback", _
    MessageBoxButtons.YesNo, MessageBoxIcon.Question,
            MessageBoxDefaultButton.Button1) _
      = MessageBoxDefaultButton.Button1 Then
        ' Commit transaction and save changes
        trans.Commit()
      Else
        ' Rollback transaction
        trans.Rollback()
      End If
    Catch exp As Exception
      Dim str As String = "Message :" + exp.Message
      str = str + "Source :" + exp.Source
      MessageBox.Show(str)
```

```
Finally
  conn.Close()
  conn.Dispose()
End Try
```

Summary

In this chapter you saw the connected side of ADO.NET. The connected classes are based on the data providers. There are a number of data providers. Some of them are Sql, OleDb, and Odbc. As their names suggest, they're designed to work with a specific kind of data source. For example, the Sql data providers are designed to work with SQL Server databases, and the OleDb data providers are designed to work with OLE DB data sources. Similarly, you can use the Odbc data providers to work with any ODBC data source. Each of these data providers is best used with the associated data source. Although their names are different, all data providers work in same way.

All the data providers follow a common model. A connection is created between the data provider and the data sources. You saw how to access different kinds of data sources using different kinds of data providers. After a connection is created, a DataAdapter or a command accesses and updates the data source. A DataTable represents an in-memory cache for a database table. A DataSet is a collection of DataTables. A DataAdapter sits between a DataSet, and a data source and passes data back and forth. The Fill method of a DataAdapter fills data from a data source to a DataSet based on the SQL statement on which it was created. The Update method of a DataAdapter reflects DataSet changes to the data source. You can use commands to execute SQL statements. You can execute direct SQL commands such as INSERT, UPDATE, and DELETE to add, update, and delete data.

A DataReader is another important component used to read data from a data source through a DataAdapter. You can use the ExecuteReader method of a Command to get data in a DataReader. You can also execute stored procedures and views using a command. You also learned how to handle concurrency and locking issues using transactions in ADO.NET.

In the next chapter you'll concentrate on event handling in ADO.NET.

CHAPTER 5

Handling
ADO.NET Events

EVENTS ARE USEFUL for notifying you when some action happens to an object.
An event can have a method, called an *event handler*, associated with it. When an
event occurs, the associated event handler (method) is executed. An event can
have multiple event handlers. In Visual Basic .NET (VB .NET), you use the
AddHandler and RemoveHandler statements to add and remove event handlers.

AddHandler takes two arguments: the name of an event from an object and an
expression that evaluates to a delegate. You use the AddressOf statement to pass a
reference to the delegate. For example, the following code adds an event handler:

```
AddHandler MyObject.Event1, AddressOf Me.MyEventHandler
```

RemoveHandler disconnects an event from an event handler, and it uses the
same syntax as AddHandler. For example, the following code removes the event
handler:

```
RemoveHandler MyObject.Event1, AddressOf Me.MyEventHandler
```

> **NOTE** *If you want to learn more about events and delegates in VB .NET, see
> the VB .NET language reference in the documentation.*

In this chapter, you'll learn how you can handle events for ADO.NET objects.
As discussed in the past two chapters, you can divide ADO.NET classes into two
groups: disconnected classes and connected classes. The System.Data namespace
defines common event handlers and event argument classes for all data providers.
As you can see from Figure 5-1, event handler classes are derived from the Delegate
class and event argument classes are derived from the EventArgs class.

NOTE *ADO.NET data providers are derived from a common hierarchy, so all data providers support the same set of events.*

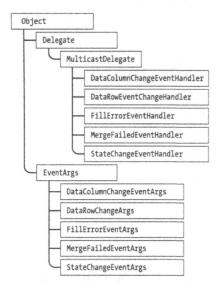

Figure 5-1. Event handler and event argument classes defined in the System.Data *namespace*

DataColumnChangeEventHandler is an event handler for DataColumn when a value is being changed for a column in a DataRow. DataRowChangeEventHandler is an event handler that handles the RowChanging, RowChanged, RowDeleting, and RowDeleted events of a DataTable. The FillErrorEventHandler is an event handler that handles a DataAdapter's Fill event. If an error occurred during the fill operation, the FillError fires, which executes FillErrorEventHandler. MergeFailedEventHandler handles the DataSet's MergeFailed event that occurs when a DataSet merge operation fails. Whenever a connection's state changes, the StateChange event occurs. StateChangeEventHandler handles this event.

Besides the event handler and event argument classes defined in the System.Data namespace, the data provider event handler and event argument classes are defined in the data provider–specific namespace. Figure 5-2 shows the OleDb data provider event handlers and event argument classes.

OleDbInfoMessageEventHandler handles the InfoMessage event of the OleDbConnection. An InfoMessage event occurs when a provider sends a warning or an informational message to the application.

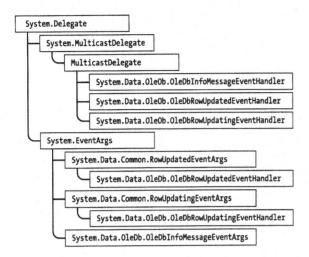

Figure 5-2. OleDb data provider event handler and event arguments

The `RowUpdated` event occurs when an `Update` method is called on a `DataAdapter`. `OleDbRowUpdatedEventHandler` handles the `RowUpdated` event of the `OleDbDataAdapter`. Apart from the `RowUpdated` event, there's one more update-related event: `RowUpdating`. As you can guess from its name, this event occurs when a row is being updated, which means before the command is executed against a data source. `OleDbRowUpdatingEventHandler` is responsible for handling this event.

In this chapter, you'll use the Sql data provider.

Working with Connection Events

The `Connection` object has two events that notify the application if a connection state changes. You can use these events to retrieve informational messages from a data source or to determine if the state of a `Connection` has changed. These two events are `InfoMessage` and `StateChange`. The `InfoMessage` event occurs when an informational message is returned from a data source. The exception handling doesn't catch these messages. The `StateChange` event occurs only when the state of a connection changes.

The `InfoMessage` event receives an `InfoMessageEventArgs` object. The `InfoMessageEventArgs` is as follows:

```
Public Delegate Sub SqlInfoMessageEventHandler( _
    ByVal sender As Object, _
    ByVal e As SqlInfoMessageEventArgs _
)
```

In this example, sender is the source of the event and *e* is an SqlInfoMessageEventArgs object that contains the event data. Table 5-1 describes the InfoMessageEventArgs properties.

Table 5-1. InfoMessageEventArgs *Properties*

PROPERTY	DESCRIPTION
ErrorCode	Returns the HRESULT following the ANSI SQL standard for the database
Errors	Returns the collection of warnings sent from the data source
Message	Returns the full text of the error
Source	Returns the name of the object that generated the error

 CAUTION *Some of these members may be different for other data providers. For example, the Sql data provider doesn't have the* ErrorCode *property.*

The StateChange event occurs when the state of a Connection changes. The StateChangeEventHandler is as follows:

```
Public Delegate Sub StateChangeEventHandler( _
    ByVal sender As Object, _
    ByVal e As StateChangeEventArgs _
)
```

As you can see from the definition of StateChangeEventHandler, this handler has a second argument called StateChangeEventArgs. You can use StateChangeEventArgs to determine the change in state of the Connection using the OriginalState and CurrentState properties. The OriginalState property represents the original state of the Connection, and the CurrentState property represents the current state of the connection. The ConnectionState enumeration defines members for connection states (see Table 5-2).

Table 5-2. The ConnectionState *Enumeration Members*

PROPERTY	DESCRIPTION
Broken	This state occurs if the connection is broken after it was opened.
Closed	The connection is closed.
Connecting	The connection is connecting to a data source.
Executing	The Connection object is executing a command.
Fetching	The Connection object is retrieving data.
Open	The connection is open.

To test events, create a Windows application and add a SqlConnection to the form by dragging a SqlConnection component from the Toolbox Data tab. Then add two Button controls to the form: an Open button and a Close button. Now write the InfoMessage and StateChange event handlers (see Listing 5-1). As you can see from Listing 5-1, you generate messages if any of the events occur.

Listing 5-1. Writing Event Handlers for the InfoMessage *and* StateChange *Events*

```
' The InfoMessage event handler
  Private Sub SqlConnection1_InfoMessage(ByVal sender As System.Object, _
  ByVal e As System.Data.SqlClient.SqlInfoMessageEventArgs) _
  Handles SqlConnection1.InfoMessage
    Dim err As SqlError
    For Each err In e.Errors
      MessageBox.Show(err.Source.ToString() + err.State.ToString() & _
        err.Source.ToString() + err.Message.ToString())
    Next
  End Sub
  'The state change event handler
  Private Sub SqlConnection1_StateChange(ByVal sender As System.Object, _
  ByVal e As System.Data.StateChangeEventArgs) _
  Handles SqlConnection1.StateChange
    MessageBox.Show("Original State: " + e.OriginalState.ToString() & _
      ", Current State :" + e.CurrentState.ToString())
  End Sub
```

Now let's write code to call these events. You write code on the Open and Close button click event handlers. On the Open button click event handler, you open a SqlConnection, and on the Close event handler, you close the connection (see Listing 5-2).

Listing 5-2. Writing Code That Executes Connection *Events*

```
' Open button click event handler
  Private Sub OpenBtn_Click(ByVal sender As System.Object, _
  ByVal e As System.EventArgs) Handles OpenBtn.Click
    ' Create a Connection Object
    Dim ConnectionString As String = "Integrated Security=SSPI;" & _
      "Initial Catalog=Northwind;Data Source=MCB;"
    SqlConnection1.ConnectionString = ConnectionString
    ' Open the connection
    If SqlConnection1.State <> ConnectionState.Open Then
      SqlConnection1.Open()
    End If
  End Sub
' Close button click event handler
  Private Sub CloseBtn_Click(ByVal sender As System.Object, _
  ByVal e As System.EventArgs) Handles CloseBtn.Click
    Try
      SqlConnection1.Close()
    Catch exp As SqlException
      MessageBox.Show(exp.Message.ToString())
    End Try
  End Sub
```

NOTE *You may notice one thing when you compile your code. Even though you added* SqlConnection *using the wizard, you still need to import the* System.Data.SqlClient *namespace using the following line:* Imports System.Data.SqlClient.

The output of clicking the Open button looks like Figure 5-3. It shows that the original state of the connection was Closed, and the current state is Open.

Figure 5-3. Output of the Open button click

The output of the Close button click looks like Figure 5-4. It shows that the original state of the connection was Open, and the current state is Closed.

Figure 5-4. Output of the Close button click

Working with DataAdapter Events

The DataAdapter has a FillError event that occurs when there's an error during a Fill method. It allows a user to determine whether a fill operation should continue. FillError may occur when data from a database can't be converted to a Common Language Runtime (CLR) type without losing precision; or it may occur when data type casting isn't valid.

FillErrorEventHandler handles the FillError event. The event handler receives an argument of type FillErrorEventArgs containing data related to this event. The FillErrorEventHandler is defined as follows:

```
Public Delegate Sub FillErrorEventHandler( _
    ByVal sender As Object, _
    ByVal e As FillErrorEventArgs _
)
```

In this example, sender is the source of the event and e is the FillErrorEventArgs that contains the event data.

Table 5-3 describes the FillErrorEventArgs properties.

Table 5-3. The FillErrorEventArgs *Members*

PROPERTY	DESCRIPTION
Continue	Represents a value indicating whether to continue the Fill operation
DataTable	Returns the data table being updated when the error occurred
Errors	Returns the errors
Values	Returns the rows being updated when the error occurred

The RowUpdated and RowUpdating events are two more events supported by a DataAdapter. The RowUpdating event occurs when an Update method is called before a command is executed against the data source. The RowUpdated event occurs when a command is executed.

The RowUpdated event handler receives an argument SqlRowUpdatedEventArgs containing data related to this event. The SqlRowUpdatedEventArgs contains the members in Table 5-4.

Table 5-4. The SqlRowUpdatedEventArgs *Members*

PROPERTY	DESCRIPTION
Command	Returns the Command object executed when Update is called
Errors	Returns errors generated during the Update operation
RecordsAffected	Returns the number of rows affected during inserting, updating, and deleting
Row	Returns the data row sent through an Update
StatementType	Returns the SQL statement type
Status	Returns the UpdateStatus of a command
TableMapping	Returns the DataTableMapping sent through an Update

Similarly to the RowUpdated event, the RowUpdating event handler receives an argument of type SqlRowUpdatedEventArgs that defines the same properties as the SqlRowUpdated with the same meaning.

To test the DataAdapter events and event handlers, create a Windows application, add a Button control to the form, and change its name to DataAdapterEventsTestBtn. Also add a SqlDataAdapter by dragging the SqlDataAdapter from the Toolbox Data tab to the form and configure the DataAdapter using the Data Adapter Configuration Wizard. Select the CompanyName, ContactName, and CustomerID columns from the Customers table. The final SELECT statement looks like the following:

```
SELECT CustomerID, CompanyName, ContactName FROM Customers
```

NOTE *See Chapter 2 for more details about the Data Adapter Configuration Wizard.*

Now add all three `FillError`, `RowUpdating`, and `RowUpdated` event handlers manually. Listing 5-3 defines the event handler bodies for these three methods.

Listing 5-3. `SqlDataAdapter` *Event Handler Bodies*

```
'FillError event handler
  Private Shared Sub FillError(ByVal sender As Object, _
  ByVal args As FillErrorEventArgs)

  End Sub

  'RowUpdating event handler
  Protected Shared Sub OnRowUpdating(ByVal sender As Object, _
  ByVal e As SqlRowUpdatingEventArgs)

  End Sub

  'RowUpdated event handler
  Protected Shared Sub OnRowUpdated(ByVal sender As Object, _
  ByVal e As SqlRowUpdatedEventArgs)

  End Sub
```

Now you need to write code on these event handlers. Listing 5-4 shows the source code for the `FillError` event. You can also use other members of `EventArgs` to get more details. This event handler will execute when an error occurs during the `Fill` method.

Listing 5-4. `DataAdapter` `FillError` *Event Handler Code*

```
'FillError event handler
  Private Shared Sub FillError(ByVal sender As Object, _
  ByVal args As FillErrorEventArgs)
    If args.Errors.GetType() Is Type.GetType("System.OverflowException") Then
      MessageBox.Show("Error in Fill operation for table " & _
                 args.DataTable.TableName & _
                 ", Error Message: " + args.Errors.Message.ToString() & _
                 ", Source: " + args.Errors.Source.ToString())
      args.Continue = True
    End If
  End Sub
```

Listing 5-5 and Listing 5-6 show the code for the RowUpdated and RowUpdating event handlers. The RowUpdated event handler is called when a row is updated using the Update method of a DataAdapter, and RowUpdating is called when a row is updating.

Listing 5-5. The RowUpdated *Event Handler*

```
'RowUpdated event handler
  Protected Shared Sub OnRowUpdated(ByVal sender As Object, _
  ByVal e As SqlRowUpdatedEventArgs)
    If e.Status = UpdateStatus.ErrorsOccurred Then
      MessageBox.Show("Error Message: " + e.Errors.Message.ToString() & _
                      ", Source: " + e.Errors.Source.ToString())
      e.Row.RowError = e.Errors.Message
      e.Status = UpdateStatus.SkipCurrentRow
    Else
      MessageBox.Show("Updated")
    End If
  End Sub
```

As you can see from Listing 5-6, you can compare the StatementType member of OleDbRowUpdatingEventArgs to the StatementType enumeration to find out the statement type. The StatementType enumeration defines Select, Insert, Update, and Delete members.

Listing 5-6. The RowUpdating *Event Handler*

```
'RowUpdating event handler
  Protected Shared Sub OnRowUpdating(ByVal sender As Object, _
  ByVal e As SqlRowUpdatingEventArgs)
    ' Inserting
    If e.StatementType = StatementType.Insert Then
      MessageBox.Show("Inserting")
    End If
    ' Updating
    If e.StatementType = StatementType.Update Then
      MessageBox.Show("Updating")
    End If
    'Deleting
    If e.StatementType = StatementType.Delete Then
      MessageBox.Show("Deleting")
    End If
    ' Selecting
```

```
    If e.StatementType = StatementType.Select Then
      MessageBox.Show("Selecting")
    End If
  End Sub
```

To test these events you can write code that fills a DataSet and calls the Update method of the DataAdapter. You add an event handler for the button by double-clicking it and writing the code in Listing 5-7. As you can see, you call AddHandler and RemoveHandler.

Listing 5-7. Calling the DataAdapter's Fill *and* Update *Methods*

```
Private Sub DataAdapterEventsTestBtn_Click(ByVal sender As System.Object, _
  ByVal e As System.EventArgs) Handles DataAdapterEventsTestBtn.Click
    ' Create InsertCommand
    SqlDataAdapter1.InsertCommand = New SqlCommand _
    ("INSERT INTO Customers (CustomerID, CompanyName)" & _
              "VALUES(@CustomerID, @CompanyName)", SqlConnection1)
    SqlDataAdapter1.InsertCommand.Parameters.Add("@CustomerID", _
    SqlDbType.VarChar, 5, "CustomerID")
    SqlDataAdapter1.InsertCommand.Parameters.Add("@CompanyName", _
    SqlDbType.VarChar, 30, "CompanyName")
    ' Opening Connection
    SqlConnection1.Open()
    ' Create and Fill DataSet
    Dim custDS As DataSet = New DataSet()
    SqlDataAdapter1.Fill(custDS, "Customers")
    ' add handlers
    AddHandler SqlDataAdapter1.RowUpdating, AddressOf OnRowUpdating
    AddHandler SqlDataAdapter1.RowUpdated, AddressOf OnRowUpdated
    ' Add a new data row and call Update method
    ' of data adapter
    Dim custRow As DataRow = custDS.Tables("Customers").NewRow()
    custRow("CustomerID") = "NEWCO"
    custRow("CompanyName") = "New Company"
    custDS.Tables("Customers").Rows.Add(custRow)
    SqlDataAdapter1.Update(custDS, "Customers")
    RemoveHandler SqlDataAdapter1.RowUpdating, AddressOf OnRowUpdating
    RemoveHandler SqlDataAdapter1.RowUpdated, AddressOf OnRowUpdated
    ' Close the connection
    SqlConnection1.Close()
    SqlConnection1.Dispose()
  End Sub
```

You can also use SelectCommand, UpdateCommand, and DeleteCommand objects to select, update, and delete data from the table. See the "The Command: Executing SQL Statements" section of Chapter 4 for more on using commands.

Now if you run the application, you'll see the insert message; if you click the button more than once, you'll get the following error message: "Violation of PRIMARY KEY constraint 'PK_Customers.' Cannot insert duplicate key in object 'Customers.'"

Working with DataSet Events

A DataSet has a MergeFailed event that occurs when merging two DataSets fails. MergeFailedEventHandler handles the MergeFailed event, which receives an argument of type MergeFailedEventArgs containing data related to this event. The MergeFailedEventHandler is defined as follows:

```
Public Delegate Sub MergeFailedEventHandler( _
    ByVal sender As Object, _
    ByVal e As MergeFailedEventArgs _
)
```

In this example, sender is the source of the event, and e is the MergeFailedEventArgs object that contains the event data.

MergeFailedEventArgs has Conflict and Table properties. The Conflict property returns a description of the merge conflict, and the Table property returns the name of the data table. Listing 5-8 shows an example of the MergeFailed event handler.

Listing 5-8. Writing Code to Call MergeFailed *Event Handler*

```
ByVal e As System.EventArgs) Handles MergetFailedEventBtn.Click
    Dim ConnectionString As String = "Integrated Security=SSPI;" & _
    "Initial Catalog=Northwind;Data Source=MCB;"
    Dim conn As SqlConnection = New SqlConnection()
    conn.ConnectionString = ConnectionString
    Dim sql As String = "SELECT * FROM Employees"
    Dim da As SqlDataAdapter = New SqlDataAdapter(sql, conn)
    Dim ds1 As DataSet = New DataSet()
    da.Fill(ds1)
```

```
sql = "SELECT * FROM Customers"
da = New SqlDataAdapter(sql, conn)
Dim ds2 As DataSet = New DataSet()
da.Fill(ds2)
' Add MergeFailed Event handler
AddHandler ds1.MergeFailed, New MergeFailedEventHandler _
(AddressOf DataSetMergeFailed)
ds1.Merge(ds2)
' Remove the MergeFailed handler
RemoveHandler ds1.MergeFailed, AddressOf DataSetMergeFailed
conn.Close()
conn.Dispose()
End Sub
' MergeFailed event handler
Private Shared Sub DataSetMergeFailed(ByVal sender As Object, _
ByVal args As MergeFailedEventArgs)
  MessageBox.Show("Merge failed for table " & args.Table.TableName & _
  "Conflict = " & args.Conflict)
End Sub
```

As you can see from Listing 5-8, you write an event handler that will be called when a `Merge` method on a `DataSet` fails.

Working with DataTable Events

A `DataTable` represents a table of a `DataSet`. A `DataTable` provides many events that can be tracked down by an application (see Table 5-5).

Table 5-5. The `DataTable` *Events*

EVENT	DESCRIPTION
ColumnChanged	This event occurs when a value of a column has been changed.
ColumnChanging	This event occurs when a new value is being added to a column.
RowChanged	This event occurs when value of a row in the table is changed.
RowChanging	This event occurs when a row in a table is changing.
RowDeleted	This event occurs when a row in a table is deleted.
RowDeleting	This event occurs when a row is being deleted.

The ColumnChangedEventHandler handles the ColumnChanged event and is defined as follows:

```
Public Delegate Sub DataColumnChangeEventHandler( _
   ByVal sender As Object, _
   ByVal e As DataColumnChangeEventArgs _
)
```

In this example, sender is the source of the event and e is DataColumnChangedEventArgs that contains the event data.

ColumnChangingEventHandler handles the ColumnChanging event and is defined as follows:

```
Public Delegate Sub DataColumnChangeEventHandler( _
   ByVal sender As Object, _
   ByVal e  As DataColumnChangeEventArgs _
)
```

In this example, sender is the source of the event and e is DataColumnChangingEventArgs that contains the event data.

Similar to these two event handlers, RowChangedEventHandler, RowChangingEventHandler, RowDeletedEventHandler, and RowDeletedEventHandler handle the RowChanged, RowChanging, RowDeleted, and RowDeleting events, respectively. Definitions of these event handlers are similar to DataColumnChangingEventHandler and DataColumnChangedEventHandler—except the EventArgs class is different.

To test these events you'll create a DataTable, add DataRows to it, and then update and delete rows from the table.

Listing 5-9 creates a DataTable, adds three columns—id, name, and address—adds data to the table and changes the column of the table. It also calls the ColumnChanged and ColumnChanging event handlers. You write the code for the ColumnChanged and ColumnChanging event handlers in the Column_changed and Column_Changing methods. You can write this code on a button click event handler.

Listing 5-9. Writing the ColumnChanging *and* ColumnChanged *Event Handlers*

```
Private Sub ColumnChange_Click(ByVal sender As System.Object, _
   ByVal e As System.EventArgs) Handles ColumnChange.Click

      Dim custTable As DataTable = New DataTable("Customers")
      ' add columns
      custTable.Columns.Add("id", Type.GetType("System.Int32"))
```

```
custTable.Columns.Add("name", Type.GetType("System.String"))
custTable.Columns.Add("address", Type.GetType("System.String"))
' add a ColumnChanged & ColumnChanging event handler for the table.
AddHandler custTable.ColumnChanged, New DataColumnChangeEventHandler _
(AddressOf Column_Changed)
AddHandler custTable.ColumnChanging, New DataColumnChangeEventHandler _
(AddressOf Column_Changing)
' add Two rows
custTable.Rows.Add(New Object() {1, "name1", "address1"})
custTable.Rows.Add(New Object() {2, "name2", "address2"})
' Save changes
custTable.AcceptChanges()
' change Address column in all the rows
Dim row As DataRow
For Each row In custTable.Rows
  row("address") = "New address"
Next row
' Removing event handlers
RemoveHandler custTable.ColumnChanged, AddressOf Column_Changed
RemoveHandler custTable.ColumnChanging, AddressOf Column_Changing
End Sub


' Column changed event handler
Private Shared Sub Column_Changed(ByVal sender As Object, _
ByVal e As DataColumnChangeEventArgs)

  MessageBox.Show("Column_Changed Event: " + " ," & _
 e.Row("name") + " ," + e.Column.ColumnName + " ," & _
  e.Row("name", DataRowVersion.Original))

End Sub
' Column Changing event handler
Private Shared Sub Column_Changing(ByVal sender As Object, _
ByVal e As DataColumnChangeEventArgs)
  MessageBox.Show("Column_Changing Event: " + " ," & _
  e.Row("name") + " ," + e.Column.ColumnName + " ," & _
  e.Row("name", DataRowVersion.Original))
End Sub
```

Listing 5-10 creates a DataTable, adds three columns—id, name, and address—adds data to the table, and changes the column of the table. It also calls the RowChanging and RowChanged event handlers.

Listing 5-10. Writing the RowChanging *and* RowChanged *Event Handlers*

```
' Row Changed and Row Changing Events Caller
Private Sub UpdateRow_Click(ByVal sender As System.Object, _
ByVal e As System.EventArgs) Handles UpdateRow.Click

    Dim custTable As DataTable = New DataTable("Customers")
    ' add columns
    custTable.Columns.Add("id", Type.GetType("System.Int32"))
    custTable.Columns.Add("name", Type.GetType("System.String"))
    custTable.Columns.Add("address", Type.GetType("System.String"))
    ' add a ColumnChanged & ColumnChanging event handler for the table.
    AddHandler custTable.RowChanged, New DataRowChangeEventHandler _
    (AddressOf Row_Changed)
    AddHandler custTable.RowChanged, New DataRowChangeEventHandler _
    (AddressOf Row_Changing)
    ' add Two rows
    custTable.Rows.Add(New Object() {1, "name1", "address1"})
    custTable.Rows.Add(New Object() {2, "name2", "address2"})
    ' Save changes
    custTable.AcceptChanges()
    ' change Address column in all the rows
    Dim row As DataRow
    For Each row In custTable.Rows
      row("name") = "New name"
    Next row
    ' Removing event handlers
    RemoveHandler custTable.RowChanged, AddressOf Row_Changed
    RemoveHandler custTable.RowChanging, AddressOf Row_Changing
End Sub
' Row Changed event handler
Private Shared Sub Row_Changed(ByVal sender As Object, _
ByVal e As DataRowChangeEventArgs)
  MessageBox.Show("Row_Changed Event:" & _
  e.Row("name", DataRowVersion.Original).ToString() & _
  e.Action.ToString())
End Sub
' Row Changing event handler
Private Shared Sub Row_Changing(ByVal sender As Object, _
ByVal e As DataRowChangeEventArgs)
  MessageBox.Show("Row_Changing Event:" & _
  e.Row("name", DataRowVersion.Original).ToString() & _
  e.Action.ToString())
End Sub
```

Listing 5-11 creates a `DataTable`, adds three columns—id, name, and address— adds data to the table, and changes a column of the table. It also calls the `RowDeleting` and `RowDeleted` event handlers.

Listing 5-11. Writing the `RowDeleting` and `RowDeleted` Event Handlers

```
' Row Deleted and Row Deleting Events Caller
Private Sub DeleteRow_Click(ByVal sender As System.Object, _
ByVal e As System.EventArgs) Handles DeleteRow.Click
   Dim custTable As DataTable = New DataTable("Customers")
   ' add columns
   custTable.Columns.Add("id", Type.GetType("System.Int32"))
   custTable.Columns.Add("name", Type.GetType("System.String"))
   custTable.Columns.Add("address", Type.GetType("System.String"))
   ' add a ColumnChanged & ColumnChanging event handler for the table.
   AddHandler custTable.RowDeleted, New DataRowChangeEventHandler _
   (AddressOf Row_Deleted)
   AddHandler custTable.RowDeleting, New DataRowChangeEventHandler _
   (AddressOf Row_Deleting)
   ' add Two rows
   custTable.Rows.Add(New Object() {1, "name1", "address1"})
   custTable.Rows.Add(New Object() {2, "name2", "address2"})
   ' Save changes
   custTable.AcceptChanges()
   ' change Address column in all the rows
   Dim row As DataRow
   ' Go through all rows
   For Each row In custTable.Rows
      ' Delete the row
      row.Delete()
   Next row
   ' Removing event handlers
   RemoveHandler custTable.RowDeleted, AddressOf Row_Deleted
   RemoveHandler custTable.RowDeleting, AddressOf Row_Deleting
End Sub
' Row Deleted event handler
Private Shared Sub Row_Deleted(ByVal sender As Object, _
ByVal e As DataRowChangeEventArgs)
   MessageBox.Show("Row_Deleted Event:" & _
   e.Row("name", DataRowVersion.Original).ToString() & _
   e.Action.ToString())
End Sub
```

```
'Row Deleting event handler
Private Shared Sub Row_Deleting(ByVal sender As Object, _
ByVal e As DataRowChangeEventArgs)
  MessageBox.Show("Row_Deleting Event:" & _
  e.Row("name", DataRowVersion.Original).ToString() & _
  e.Action.ToString())
End Sub
```

Working with XmlDataDocument Events

You must be wondering where XmlDataDocument comes from. Actually, this class works with Extensible Markup Language (XML) documents and is defined in the System.Xml namespace. So before testing this example, you must import the System.Xml namespace. (We discuss the XmlDataDocument object in Chapter 6.)

NOTE *You might want to skip this section if you're not familiar with the* XmlDataDocument *object. Chapter 6 covers* XmlDataDocument.

The XmlDataDocument events are useful when your application needs to be notified when changes are being made to an XmlDataDocument object. XmlDocument defines the XmlDataDocument events (see Table 5-6).

Table 5-6. XmlDataDocument *Events*

EVENT	DESCRIPTION
NodeChanged	Occurs when the Value of a node has been changed
NodeChanging	Occurs when the Value of a node is changing
NodeInserted	Occurs when a node inserted into another node
NodeInserting	Occurs when a node is inserting to another node
NodeRemoved	Occurs when a node has been removed
NodeRemoving	Occurs when a node is being removed

The XmlNodeChangedEventHandler method handles these (NodeChanged, NodeChanging, NodeInserted, NodeInserting, NodeRemoved, and NodeRemoving) events. The XmlNodeChangedEventHandler is defined as follows:

```
Public Delegate Sub XmlNodeChangedEventHandler( _
    ByVal sender As Object, _
    ByVal e As XmlNodeChangedEventArgs _
)
```

In this example, sender is the source of the event and e is an XmlNodeChangedEventArgs containing the event data. The XmlNodeChangedEventArgs defines properties (see Table 5-7).

Table 5-7. The XmlNodeChangedEventArgs Properties

PROPERTY	DESCRIPTION
Action	Returns a value indicating the type of node-changed event
NewParent	Returns the value of parent node after the operation is finished
Node	Returns the node that is being added, removed, or changed
OldParent	Returns the value of the parent node before operation started

Listing 5-12 handles the XmlDataDocument events. The XmlDocumentBtn_Click method creates event handlers for NodeChanged, NodeInserted, and NodeRemoved events. MyNodeChangedEvent, MyNodeInsertedEvent, and MyNodeRemoved event handlers are executed when these events are fired. You use LoadXml to load an XML fragment and then use the ReplaceChild and RemoveChild methods to replace and remove document nodes.

Listing 5-12. The XmlDataDocument Event Handling Example

```
Private Sub XmlDataDocumentBtn_Click(ByVal sender As System.Object, _
    ByVal e As System.EventArgs) Handles XmlDataDocumentBtn.Click
    Dim xmlDoc As XmlDocument = New XmlDocument()
    xmlDoc.LoadXml("<Record> Some Value </Record>")
    ' Add event handlers
    AddHandler xmlDoc.NodeChanged, AddressOf NodeChangedEvent_Handler
    AddHandler xmlDoc.NodeInserted, AddressOf NodeInsertedEvent_Handler
    AddHandler xmlDoc.NodeRemoved, AddressOf NodeRemovedEvent_Handler
```

```
Dim root As XmlElement = xmlDoc.DocumentElement
Dim str As String = root.ToString()
Dim xmlDocFragment As XmlDocumentFragment = xmlDoc.CreateDocumentFragment()
xmlDocFragment.InnerXml = _
"<Fragment><SomeData>Fragment Data</SomeData></Fragment>"
' Replace Node
Dim rootNode As XmlElement = xmlDoc.DocumentElement
rootNode.ReplaceChild(xmlDocFragment, rootNode.LastChild)
' Remove Node
Dim node As XmlNode = xmlDoc.LastChild
xmlDoc.RemoveChild(node)
' Remove event handlers
RemoveHandler xmlDoc.NodeChanged, AddressOf NodeChangedEvent_Handler
RemoveHandler xmlDoc.NodeInserted, AddressOf NodeInsertedEvent_Handler
RemoveHandler xmlDoc.NodeRemoved, AddressOf NodeRemovedEvent_Handler
End Sub
```

Listing 5-13 shows the NodeChangedEvent handler. The Node property of XmlNodeChangedEventArgs returns an XmlNode object. Using the Node property you can get more information about a node such as its parent node, value, name, namespace, and so on. (See the "Using the XmlNode Class" section of Chapter 6 to learn more about XmlNode.)

Listing 5-13. The NodeChanged *Event Handler*

```
' NodeChanged event handler
Public Sub NodeChangedEvent_Handler(ByVal src As Object, _
ByVal args As XmlNodeChangedEventArgs)
  MessageBox.Show("Node Changed Event Fired for node " + args.Node.Name)
  If args.Node.Value <> Nothing Then
    MessageBox.Show(args.Node.Value)
  End If
End Sub
```

Similar to Listing 5-13, Listing 5-14 and Listing 5-15 show event handlers for the NodeInserted and NodeRemoved events.

Listing 5-14. The NodeInserted *Event Handler*

```
' NodeInserted event handler
 Public Sub NodeInsertedEvent_Handler(ByVal src As Object, _
 ByVal args As XmlNodeChangedEventArgs)
   MessageBox.Show("Node Inserted Event Fired for node " + args.Node.Name)
   If args.Node.Value <> Nothing Then
     MessageBox.Show(args.Node.Value)
   End If
 End Sub
```

Listing 5-15. The NodeRemoved *Event Handler*

```
 ' Node Removed event handler
 Public Sub NodeRemovedEvent_Handler(ByVal src As Object, _
 ByVal args As XmlNodeChangedEventArgs)
   MessageBox.Show("Node Removed Event Fired for node " + args.Node.Name)
   If args.Node.Value <> Nothing Then
     MessageBox.Show(args.Node.Value)
   End If
 End Sub
```

Working with DataView and DataViewManager Events

The DataView and DataViewManager objects both define a ListChanged event. The ListChanged event occurs when a row is added to or deleted from a DataView or DataViewManager object. The ListChangedEventHandler method handles the ListChanged event and is defined as follows:

```
Public Delegate Sub ListChangedEventHandler( _
   ByVal sender As Object, _
   ByVal e As ListChangedEventArgs _
)
```

In this example, sender is the source of the event and e is the ListChangedEventArgs containing the event data.

The ListChangedEventArgs has the members defined in Table 5-8.

Table 5-8. The ListChangedEventArgs *Members*

MEMBER	DESCRIPTION
ListChangedType	Returns the way that list changed
NewIndex	Returns the new index of the item in the list
OldIndex	Returns the old index of the item in the list

Listing 5-16 shows the OnListChanged_Handler.

Listing 5-16. DataView OnListChanged *Event Handler*

```
Public Sub OnListChanged_Handler(ByVal src As Object, _
   ByVal args As System.ComponentModel.ListChangedEventArgs)
   MessageBox.Show("ListChanged: Type = " + args.ListChangedType & _
   ", OldIndex = " + args.OldIndex & _
   ", NewIndex = " + args.NewIndex)
  End Sub
```

To test this application, you can create a Windows application and add the code in Listing 5-17 to the form load event or a button click event handler. As you can see from Listing 5-17, the code creates a DataView object, adds a new row to the DataView, and then removes the first row from the DataView. The adding and removing of rows is responsible for firing the OnListChanged event handler.

Listing 5-17. The DataView *Event Handler Caller*

```
Dim ConnectionString As String = "Integrated Security=SSPI;" & _
   "Initial Catalog=Northwind;Data Source=MCB;"
   Dim conn As SqlConnection = New SqlConnection()
   conn.ConnectionString = ConnectionString
   ' Open the connection
   conn.Open()
   Dim sql As String = "SELECT EmployeeId, LastName, FirstName FROM Employees"
   ' Create a data adapter
   Dim da As SqlDataAdapter = New SqlDataAdapter(sql, conn)
   ' Create and Fill DataSet
   Dim ds As DataSet = New DataSet()
   da.Fill(ds, "Employees")
```

```
Dim dv As DataView = ds.Tables("Employees").DefaultView
' Add DataView Event Handlers
AddHandler dv.ListChanged, New System.ComponentModel.ListChangedEventHandler _
(AddressOf OnListChanged_Handler)

' Add a row to the DataView
dv.AllowEdit = True
Dim rw As DataRowView = dv.AddNew()
rw.BeginEdit()
rw("FirstName") = "FName"
rw("LastName") = "LName"
rw.EndEdit()
' Remove a row from the DataView
If dv.Count > 0 Then
  dv.Delete(0)
  dv(0).Row.AcceptChanges()
End If
' Close the connection
conn.Close()
conn.Dispose()
' Remove DataView Event Handlers
RemoveHandler dv.ListChanged, AddressOf OnListChanged_Handler
```

 CAUTION *As you can see from Listing 5-17, the* AcceptChanges() *method removes a row permanently from the database. If you don't want to remove the row, call* RejectChanges *instead.*

Summary

In this chapter, you learned about ADO.NET object events and how to handle them. Events are useful to notify an action taken by an object. The Connection object has two InfoMessage and StateChange events. The DataAdapter provides FillError, UpdateChanging, and UpdateChanged events. The DataSet has only one event—MergeFailed. The DataTable provides events raises during column and row changes and row deletions. XmlDataDocument provides events relating to adding, changing, and removing XML document nodes. The DataView and DataViewManager define the ListChanged event, which occurs when a row is added to or deleted from a DataView or from a DataViewManager.

After finishing this chapter, you should have a good idea of the events model of ADO.NET components and how to handle events in your applications.

In next chapter, you'll see how XML is tied to ADO.NET and how you can take advantage of the ADO.NET model to read to and write data from XML documents.

CHAPTER 6

Integrating XML with ADO.NET

THE PROGRAMMING WORLD is moving more and more toward the Web, and Extensible Markup Language (XML) is an essential part of Web-based programming. This chapter assumes you have an understanding of basic XML syntaxes and documents.

This chapter introduces the classes provided by the .NET Framework Library to work with XML documents. In this chapter, we discuss how to read from and write to XML documents using the .NET Framework Library classes. Then we discuss how to navigate through XML documents. We also discuss XML transformations. Furthermore, this chapter covers the relationship between ADO.NET and XML and shows how to mix them up and use rich ADO.NET database components to display and manipulate XML data. Finally, we cover the XPathNavigator class, which navigates XML documents.

Understanding Microsoft .NET and XML

Microsoft's .NET Framework utilizes XML features both internally and externally to transfer data between applications. In the following sections, you'll learn about the XML namespaces and classes, which you'll use in the examples throughout this chapter.

In the .NET Framework Library, the System.Xml and its four supporting namespaces define the functionality to work with XML data and documents. These namespaces are System.Xml, System.Xml.Schema, System.Xml.Serialization, System.Xml.XPath, and System.Xml.Xsl. These namespaces reside in the System.Xml.dll assembly.

> **TIP** *Covering every class defined in* System.Xml *and its related namespaces is impossible in this chapter. We cover the commonly used classes. If you want to learn more about XML in .NET, you can find many useful source code samples, articles, and tutorials on C# Corner's XML.NET section* (www.c-sharpcorner.com/xmlnet.asp).

Using the System.Xml Namespace

The System.Xml namespace defines common and major XML functionality. It defines classes for XML 1.0, XML namespaces and schemas, XPath, XSL Transformations (XSLT), Document Object Model (DOM) Level 2 Core, and Simple Object Access Protocol (SOAP) 1.1.

The following sections define some of the System.Xml namespace classes.

The XmlNode Class

The XmlNode class, an abstract base class for XmlDocument and XmlDataDocument, represents a single node in a document. This class implements methods for adding, removing, and inserting nodes into a document. This class also implements properties to get data from a node such as name, child nodes, siblings, parents, and so on.

Document Classes

The System.Xml namespace also contains classes to deal with XML documents. The XmlDocument and XmlDocumentFragment classes represent an entire XML document and a fragment of document, respectively. The XmlDocumentFragment class is useful when you're dealing with a small fragment of a document.

The XmlDataDocument class allows you to work with relational data using the DataSet object. It provides functionality to store, retrieve, and manipulate data. The XmlDocumentType class represents the type of document.

The XmlDocument and XmlDataDocument classes come from XmlNode. Besides the methods contained in XmlNode, this class implements a series of CreateXXX methods to create a document's contents such as comments, elements, text, and so on. You can even load an XML document by using its Load and LoadXml methods.

Each content type of an XML document has a corresponding class defined in this namespace. The classes are XmlAttribute, XmlCDataSection, XmlComment, XmlDeclaration, XmlEntity, XmlEntityReference, XmlProcessingInstruction, XmlText, and XmlWhitespace. All of these classes are self-explanatory. For example, the XmlAttribute and XmlComment classes represent an attribute and comment of a document. You'll see these classes throughout the examples in this chapter.

Reader and Writer Classes

Six classes (XmlReader, XmlWriter, XmlTextWriter, XmlTextReader, XmlValidatingReader, and XmlNodeReader) represent the reading and writing of XML documents.

The XmlReader and XmlWriter classes are abstract base classes that represent a reader that provides fast, non-cached, forward-only stream access to XML documents. XmlReader has three classes: XmlTextReader, XmlValidatingReader, and XmlNodeReader. As their names imply, XmlTextReader reads text XML documents, XmlNodeReader reads XML DOM trees, and XmlValidatingReader validates data using Document Type Definitions (DTDs) or schemas. This reader also expands general entities and supports default attributes. XmlWriter is an abstract base class that defines functionality to write XML. It implements methods and properties to write XML contents. The XmlTextWriter class comes from the XmlWriter class.

Other Classes

The XmlConvert class provides conversion in XML. It defines methods for converting Common Language Runtime (CLR), or .NET data types, and XML Schema Definition (XSD) types. It contains the following classes:

- XmlException defines functionality to represent detailed exceptions.

- XmlNamespaceManager resolves, adds, and removes namespaces and provides scope management for these namespaces.

- XmlLinkedNode returns the node immediately preceding or following this node.

- XmlNodeList represents a collection of nodes.

Using the System.Xml.Schema Namespace

The System.Xml.Schema namespace contains classes to work with XML schemas. These classes support XML schemas for structures and XML schemas for data types.

This namespace defines many classes to work with schemas. The discussion of these classes is beyond the scope of this book. Some of these namespace classes are XmlSchema, XmlSchemaAll, XmlSchemaXPath, and XmlSchemaType.

Using the System.Xml.Serialization Namespace

This namespace contains classes to serialize objects into XML format documents or streams.

> **NOTE** Serialization *is the process of reading and writing an object to or from a persistent storage medium such as a hard drive.*

You can use the main class, XmlSerializer, with TextWriter or XmlWriter to write the data to a document. Again, this namespace also defines many classes. The discussion of these classes is beyond the scope of this chapter.

Using the System.Xml.XPath Namespace

This namespace is pretty small in comparison to the previous three namespaces. This namespace contains only four classes: XPathDocument, XPathExression, XPathNavigator, and XPathNodeIterator.

The XPathDocument class provides fast XML document processing using the stylesheet language of XML: XSLT. This class is optimized for XSLT processing and the XPath data model. The CreateNavigator method of this class creates an instance of XPathNavigator.

The XPathNavigator class treats an XML document as a tree and provides methods to traverse through a document as tree. Its MoveXXX methods let you traverse through a document.

Two other classes of this namespace are XPathExpression and XPathIterator. XPathExpression encapsulates an XPath expression, and XPathIterator provides an iterator over the set of selected nodes.

Using the System.Xml.Xsl Namespace

The last namespace, System.Xml.Xsl, defines functionality for XSLT transformations. It supports XSLT 1.0. The XsltTransform class defines functionality to transform data using an XSLT stylesheet.

Using the Document Object Model Interfaces

You can represent an XML document in a tree structure using DOM interfaces and objects.

Microsoft .NET provides a nice wrapper around these interfaces: the DOM Application Programming Interface (API). This wrapper has a class for almost every interface. These classes hide all the complexity of interface programming and provide a high-level programming model for developers. For example, the .NET class XmlDocument provides a wrapper for the Document interface.

Besides the DOM, the Microsoft .NET XML API also provides corresponding classes for the XPath, XSD, and XSLT industry standards. These classes are well coupled with the .NET database models (ADO.NET) to interact with databases.

Looking at the XML .NET Architecture

The XML .NET API is a nice wrapper around the XML DOM interfaces and provides a higher-level of programming over XML documents. The heart of the XML .NET architecture consists of three classes: XmlDocument, XmlReader, and XmlWriter. The XmlReader and XmlWriter classes are abstract base classes that provide fast, non-cached, forward-only cursors to read and write XML data. XmlTextReader, XmlValidatingReader, and XmlNodeReader are concrete implementations of the XmlReader class. The XmlWriter and XmlNodeWriter classes come from the XmlWriter class. XmlDocument represents an XML document in a tree structure with the help of the XmlNode, XmlElement, and XmlAttribute classes.

Figure 6-1 shows a relationship between these classes and the XML .NET architecture.

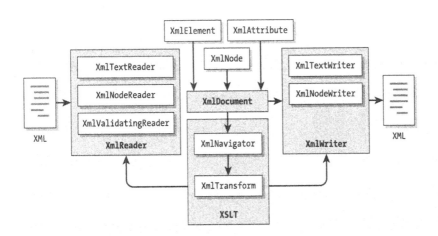

Figure 6-1. XML .NET architecture

The System.Xml.Xsl interface provides classes that implement XSLT. The Xml-Transform class implements XSLT. This class reads and writes XML data with the help of the XmlReader and XmlWriter classes.

The XPathDocument and the XPathNavigator classes provide read/write and navigation access to the XML documents.

Associated with these classes are some more powerful classes for working with XML. We discuss these classes in "Navigating in XML" and other sections of this chapter.

Adding a System.Xml Namespace Reference

Before using the System.Xml classes in your application, you may need to add a reference to the System.Xml.dll assembly and include the System.Xml namespace in your application. You can add a reference to the System.Xml.dll assembly by selecting Project ➤ Add Reference, choosing the .NET tab, and selecting System.Xml.dll from the component name listing. After adding the reference, you need to import the namespace by adding the following line:

```
Imports System.Xml
```

The abstract base classes XmlReader and XmlWriter support reading and writing XML documents in the .NET Framework.

Reading XML

As mentioned previously, XmlReader is an abstract base class for XML reader classes. This class provides fast, non-cached, forward-only cursors to read XML documents.

The XmlTextReader, XmlNodeReader, and XmlValidatingReader classes are defined from the XmlReader class. Figure 6-2 shows XmlReader and its derived classes.

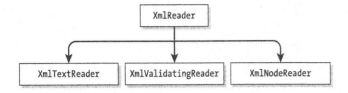

Figure 6-2. XmlReader *and its derived classes*

You use the XmlTextReader, XmlNodeReader, and XmlValidatingReader classes to read XML documents. These classes define overloaded constructors to read XML files, strings, streams, TextReader objects, XmlNameTable, and combinations of these. After creating an instance, you simply call the Read method of the class to read the document. The Read method starts reading the document from the root node and continues until Read returns False, which indicates there's no node left to read in the document. Listing 6-1 reads an XML file and displays some information about the file. In this example, we use the books.xml file. You can use any XML by replacing the string name.

Listing 6-1. Reading an XML File

```
Dim reader As XmlTextReader = New XmlTextReader("C:\\books.xml")
Console.WriteLine("General Information")
Console.WriteLine("====================")
Console.WriteLine(reader.Name)
Console.WriteLine(reader.BaseURI)
Console.WriteLine(reader.LocalName)
```

Getting Node Information

The Name property returns the name of the node with the namespace prefix, and the LocalName property returns the name of the node without the prefix.

The Item property works as an indexer and returns the value of the attribute at the specified index. The Value property returns the value of current node. You can even get the level of the node by using the Depth property, as shown in Listing 6-2.

Listing 6-2. Getting XML Node Information

```
Dim reader As XmlTextReader =  New XmlTextReader("C:\\books.xml")
While reader.Read()
      If reader.HasValue Then
            Console.WriteLine("Name: "+reader.Name)
            Console.WriteLine("Node Depth: " +reader.Depth.ToString())
           Console.WriteLine("Value: "+reader.Value)
      End If
End While
```

The NodeType property returns the type of the current node in the form of an XmlNodeType enumeration:

```
XmlNodeType type = reader.NodeType;
```

which defines the type of a node. The XmlNodeType enumeration members are Attribute, CDATA, Comment, Document, Element, WhiteSpace, and so on. These represent XML document node types.

In Listing 6-3, you read a document's nodes one by one and count them. Once the reading and counting are done, you see how many comments, processing instructions, CDATAs, elements, whitespaces, and so on that a document has and display them on the console. The XmlReader.NodeType property returns the type of node in the form of an XmlNodeType enumeration. The XmlNodeType enumeration contains a member corresponding to each node type. You can compare the return value with the XmlNodeType members to find out the node's type.

Listing 6-3. Getting Node Information

```
Sub Main()
    Dim DecCounter As Integer = 0
    Dim PICounter As Integer = 0
    Dim DocCounter As Integer = 0
    Dim CommentCounter As Integer = 0
    Dim ElementCounter As Integer = 0
    Dim AttributeCounter As Integer = 0
    Dim TextCounter As Integer = 0
    Dim WhitespaceCounter As Integer = 0
    Dim reader As XmlTextReader = New XmlTextReader("C:\\books.xml")
    While reader.Read()
      Dim nodetype As XmlNodeType = reader.NodeType
      Select Case nodetype
```

```
      Case XmlNodeType.XmlDeclaration
        DecCounter = DecCounter + 1
        Exit Select
      Case XmlNodeType.ProcessingInstruction
        PICounter = PICounter + 1
        Exit Select
      Case XmlNodeType.DocumentType
        DocCounter = DocCounter + 1
        Exit Select
      Case XmlNodeType.Comment
        CommentCounter = CommentCounter + 1
        Exit Select
      Case XmlNodeType.Element
        ElementCounter = ElementCounter + 1
        If reader.HasAttributes Then
          AttributeCounter += reader.AttributeCount
        End If
        Exit Select
      Case XmlNodeType.Text
        TextCounter = TextCounter + 1
        Exit Select
      Case XmlNodeType.Whitespace
        WhitespaceCounter = WhitespaceCounter + 1
        Exit Select
    End Select
  End While
  ' Print the info
  Console.WriteLine("White Spaces:" + WhitespaceCounter.ToString())
  Console.WriteLine("Process Instructions:" + PICounter.ToString())
  Console.WriteLine("Declaration:" + DecCounter.ToString())
  Console.WriteLine("White Spaces:" + DocCounter.ToString())
  Console.WriteLine("Comments:" + CommentCounter.ToString())
  Console.WriteLine("Attributes:" + AttributeCounter.ToString())
End Sub
```

The Case statement can have the values XmlNodeType.XmlDeclaration, XmlNodeType.ProcessingInstruction, XmlNodeType.DocumentType, XmlNodeType.Comment, XmlNodeType.Element, XmlNodeType.Text, XmlNodeType.Whitespace, and so on.

The XmlNodeType enumeration specifies the type of node. Table 6-1 describes its members.

Table 6-1. The XmlNodeType *Enumeration's Members*

MEMBER NAME	DESCRIPTION
Attribute	Attribute node
CDATA	CDATA section
Comment	Comment node
Document	Document object
DocumentFragment	Document fragment
DocumentType	The DTD, indicated by the <!DOCTYPE> tag
Element	Element node
EndElement	End of element
EndEntity	End of an entity
Entity	Entity declaration
EntityReference	Reference to an entity
None	Returned if XmlReader is not called yet
Notation	A notation in the document type
ProcessingInstruction	Represents a processing instruction (PI) node
SignificantWhitespace	Represents whitespace between markup in a mixed content model
Text	Represents the text content of an element
Whitespace	Represents whitespace between markup
XmlDeclaration	Represents an XML declaration node

Moving to a Content Node

You can use the MoveToMethod to move from the current node to the next content node of an XML document. A content's node is an item of the following type: Text, CDATA, Element, EntityReference, or Entity. So, if you call the MoveToContent method, it skips other types of nodes besides the content type nodes. For example, if the next node of the current node is PI, DxlDeclaration, or DocumentType, it'll skip these nodes until it finds a content type node. Listing 6-4 reads books.xml and moves through its nodes using the MoveToContent method.

Listing 6-4. Using the MoveToContent *Method*

```
Dim reader As XmlTextReader = New XmlTextReader("C:\\books.xml")
    While reader.Read()
      Console.WriteLine(reader.Name)
      reader.MoveToContent()
      Console.WriteLine(reader.Name)
    End While
```

Using the GetAttributes of a Node

The GetAttribute method is an overloaded method. You can use this method to
return attributes with the specified name, index, local name, or namespace
Uniform Resource Indicator (URI). You use the HasAttributes property to check if a
node has attributes, and AttributeCount returns the number of attributes on the
node. The local name is the name of the current node without prefixes. For
example, if <bk:book> represents a name of a node, where bk is a namespace and :
refers to the namespace, the local name for the <bk:book> element is *book*.
MoveToFirstAttribute moves to the first attribute. The MoveToElement method moves
to the element that contains the current attribute node (see Listing 6-5).

Listing 6-5. Using the GetAttribute *of a Node*

```
Imports System.Xml
Module Module1
  Sub Main()
    Dim reader As XmlTextReader = _
    New XmlTextReader("C:\\books.xml")
    reader.MoveToContent()
    reader.MoveToFirstAttribute()
    Console.WriteLine("First Attribute Value" + reader.Value)
    Console.WriteLine("First Attribute Name" + reader.Name)
    While reader.Read()
      If reader.HasAttributes Then
        Console.WriteLine(reader.Name + " Attribute")
        Dim i As Integer
        Dim counter As Integer = reader.AttributeCount - 1
```

```
        For i = 0 To counter
          reader.MoveToAttribute(i)
          Console.WriteLine("Name: " + reader.Name)
        Next i
        reader.MoveToElement()
      End If
    End While
  End Sub
End Module
```

You can move to attributes by using MoveToAttribute, MoveToFirstAttribute, and MoveToNextAttribute. MoveToFirstAttribute and MoveToNextAttribute move to the first and next attributes, respectively. After calling MoveToAttribute, the Name, Namespace, and Prefix properties will reflect the properties of the specified attribute.

Searching for a Node

The Skip method skips the current node. It's useful when you're looking for a particular node and want to skip other nodes. In Listing 6-6, you read the books.xml document and compare its XmlReader.name (through XmlTextReader) to look for a node with the name *bookstore* and display the name, level, and value of that node using XmlReader's Name, Depth, and Value properties.

Listing 6-6. Using the Skip *Method*

```
New XmlTextReader("C:\\books.xml")
    While reader.Read()
      ' Look for a node with name bookstore
      If reader.Name <> "bookstore" Then
        reader.Skip()
      Else
        Console.WriteLine("Name: " + reader.Name)
        Console.WriteLine("Level of the node: " + reader.Depth.ToString())
        Console.WriteLine("Value: " + reader.Value)
      End If
    End While
    reader.Close()
```

Closing the Document

Finally, you use Close to close the opened XML document.

Tables 6-2 and 6-3 describe the XmlReader class properties and methods. We already discussed some of them in the previous discussion.

Table 6-2. The XmlReader *Class Properties*

PUBLIC INSTANCE PROPERTY	DESCRIPTION
AttributeCount	Returns the number of attributes on the current node
BaseURI	Returns the base URI of the current node
Depth	Returns the level of the current node
EOF	Indicates whether its pointer is at the end of the stream
HasAttributes	Indicates if a node has attributes
HasValue	Indicates if a node has a value
IsDefault	Indicates whether the current node is an attribute generated from the default value defined in the DTD or schema
IsEmptyTag	Returns if the current node is empty or not
Item	Returns the value of the attribute
LocalName	Name of the current node without the namespace prefix
Name	Name of the current node with the namespace prefix
NamespaceURI	Namespace Uniform Resource Name (URN) of the current namespace scope
NameTable	Returns the XmlNameTable associated with this implementation
NodeType	Returns the type of node
Prefix	Returns the namespace associated with a node
ReadState	Read state
Value	Returns the text value of a node
XmlLang	Returns the current xml:lang scope
XmlSpace	Returns the current xml:space scope

Table 6-3. The XmlReader *Class Methods*

PUBLIC INSTANCE METHOD	DESCRIPTION
Close	Closes the stream and changes ReadState to Closed
GetAttribute	Returns the value of an attribute
IsStartElement	Checks if a node has start tag
LookupNamespace	Resolves a namespace prefix in the current element's scope
MoveToAttribute, MoveToContent, MoveToElement	Moves to specified attribute, content, and element
MoveToFirstAttribute, MoveToNextAttribute	Moves to the first and next attributes
Read	Reads a node
ReadAttributeValue	Parses the attribute value into one or more Text and/or EntityReference node types
ReadXXX (ReadChar, ReadBoolean, ReadDate, ReadInt32, and so on)	Reads the contents of an element into the specified type including char, integer, double, string, date, and so on
ReadInnerXml	Reads all the content as a string
Skip	Skips the current element

Understanding the XmlWriter Classes

As you saw in the "Understanding Microsoft .NET and XML" section, the XmlWriter class contains methods and properties to write to XML documents, and XmlTextWriter and XmlNodeWriter come from the XmlWriter class. Figure 6-3 shows XmlWriter and its derived classes.

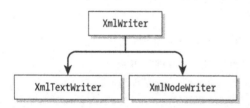

Figure 6-3. The XmlWriter *class and its derived classes*

Besides providing a constructor and three properties (WriteState, XmlLang, and XmlSpace), the XmlWriter classes have many WriteXXX methods to write to XML documents. The following sections discuss some of these class methods and properties and use them in examples of the XmlTextWriter and XmlNodeWriter classes. XmlTextWriter creates a write object and writes to the documents. The XmlTextWriter constructor can take three types of inputs: a string, stream, or TextWriter.

Setting XmlWriter Properties

The XmlWriter class contains three properties: WriteState, XmlLang, and XmlSpace. The WriteState property gets the current state of the XmlWriter class. The values could be Attribute, Start, Element, Content, Closed, or Prolog. The return value WriteState.Start means the Write method has not been called yet. In other cases, it represents what's being written. For example, the return value WriteState.Attribute means the Attribute value has been written. WriteState.Close represents that the stream has been closed by calling Close method.

Writing XML Items

As discussed earlier, an XML document can have many types of items including elements, comments, attributes, and whitespaces. Although it's not possible to describe *all* the WriteXXX methods here, we cover the most important ones.

The WriteStartDocument and WriteEndDocument methods open and close a document for writing, respectively. You must open a document before you start writing to it. The WriteComment method writes comments to a document. It takes only one string type: argument. The WriteString method writes a string to a document. With the help of WriteString, you can use the WriteStartElement and WriteEndElement method pair to write an element to a document. The WriteStartAttribute and WriteEndAttribute pair writes an attribute. WriteNode is another write method, which writes XmlReader to a document as a node of the document.

The following example summarizes these methods and creates a new XML document with some items in it such as elements, attributes, strings, comments, and so on. (See Listing 6-7 in the next section.)

In this example, you create a new XML file, c:\xmlWriterText.xml, using XmlTextWriter:

```
' Create a new file c:\xmlWriterTest.xml
    Dim writer As XmlTextWriter = _
    New XmlTextWriter("C:\\xmlWriterTest.xml", Nothing)
```

After that, add comments and elements to the document using WriteXXX methods. After that you can read the books.xml file using XmlTextReader and add its elements to xmlWriterTest.xml using XmlTextWriter:

```
' Create an XmlTextReader to read books.xml
Dim reader As XmlTextReader =  New XmlTextReader("c:\\books.xml")
While reader.Read()
        If reader.NodeType = XmlNodeType.Element Then
            ' Add node.xml to xmlWriterTest.xml usign WriteNode
            writer.WriteNode(reader, True)
        End If
End While
```

Seeing XmlWriter in Action

Listing 6-7 shows an example of using XmlWriter to create a new document and write its items. This program creates a new XML document, xmlWriterTest, in the C:\ root directory.

Listing 6-7. XmlWriter *Example*

```
Imports System.Xml
Module Module1
  Sub Main()
    ' Create a new file c:\xmlWriterTest.xml
    Dim writer As XmlTextWriter = _
    New XmlTextWriter("C:\\xmlWriterTest.xml", Nothing)
    ' Opens the document
    writer.WriteStartDocument()
    ' Write comments
    writer.WriteComment("This program uses XmlTextWriter.")
    writer.WriteComment("Developed By: Mahesh Chand.")
    writer.WriteComment("===============================")
    ' Write first element
```

```
        writer.WriteStartElement("root")
        writer.WriteStartElement("r", "RECORD", "urn:record")
        ' Write next element
        writer.WriteStartElement("FirstName", "")
        writer.WriteString("Mahesh")
        writer.WriteEndElement()
        ' Write one more element
        writer.WriteStartElement("LastName", "")
        writer.WriteString("Chand")
        writer.WriteEndElement()
        ' Create an XmlTextReader to read books.xml
        Dim reader As XmlTextReader = New XmlTextReader("c:\\books.xml")
        While reader.Read()
          If reader.NodeType = XmlNodeType.Element Then
            ' Add node.xml to xmlWriterTest.xml usign WriteNode
            writer.WriteNode(reader, True)
          End If
        End While
        ' Ends the document.
        writer.WriteEndDocument()
        writer.Close()
    End Sub
End Module
```

NOTE *In Listing 6-7, you write output of the program to a file. If you want to write your output directly on the console, pass* Console.Out *as the filename when you create an* XmlTextWriter *object. For example:* XmlTextWriter writer = new XmlTextWriter (Console.Out);.

When you open C: \xmlWriterTest.xml in a browser, the output of the program looks like Listing 6-8.

Listing 6-8. Output of the XmlWriterSample.vb *Class*

```
<?xml version="1.0" ?>
        - <!-- This program uses XmlTextWriter.
                            -->
    - <!-- Developed By: Mahesh Chand.
                    -->
```

```
- <!-- ================================
-->
- <root>
- <r:RECORD xmlns:r="urn:record">
<FirstName>Mahesh</FirstName>
<LastName>Chand</LastName>
- <bookstore>
- <book genre="autobiography" publicationdate="1981" ISBN="1-861003-11-0">
<title>The Autobiography of Benjamin Franklin</title>
- <author>
<first-name>Benjamin</first-name>
<last-name>Franklin</last-name>
</author>
<price>8.99</price>
</book>
- <book genre="novel" publicationdate="1967" ISBN="0-201-63361-2">
<title>The Confidence Man</title>
- <author>
<first-name>Herman</first-name>
<last-name>Melville</last-name>
</author>
<price>11.99</price>
</book>
- <book genre="philosophy" publicationdate="1991" ISBN="1-861001-56-6">
<title>The Gorgias</title>
- <author>
<name>Plato</name>
</author>
<price>9.99</price>
</book>
</bookstore>
</r:RECORD>
</root>
```

Using the Close Method

You use the Close method when you're done with the XmlWriter object to close the stream.

Using the XmlConvert Class

Some characters aren't valid in XML documents. XML documents use XSD types, which are different from CLR (.NET) data types. The XmlConvert class contains methods to convert from CLR types to XSD types and vice versa. The DecodeName method transfers an XML name into an ADO.NET object such as a DataTable. The EncodeName method is the reverse of DecodeName: It converts an ADO.NET object to a valid XSD name. It takes any invalid character and replaces it with an escape string. Another method, EncodeLocalName, converts unpermitted names to valid names.

Besides these three methods, the XmlConvert class has many methods to convert from a string object to Boolean, byte, integer, and so on. Listing 6-9 shows the conversion from a Boolean and DateTime object to XML values.

Listing 6-9. Using the XmlConvert *Class*

```
Dim writer As XmlTextWriter = _
    New XmlTextWriter("c:\\test.xml", Nothing)
    writer.WriteStartElement("MyTestElements")
    Dim bl As Boolean = True
    writer.WriteElementString("TestBoolean", _
    XmlConvert.ToString(bl))
    Dim dt As DateTime = New DateTime(2000, 1, 1)
    writer.WriteElementString("TestDate", _
    XmlConvert.ToString(dt))
    writer.WriteEndElement()
    writer.Flush()
    writer.Close()
```

Understanding the DOM Implementation

Microsoft .NET supports the W3C DOM Level 1 and DOM Level 2 Core specifications. The .NET Framework provides DOM implementation through many classes; XmlNode and XmlDocument are two of them. Using these two classes, you can easily traverse through XML documents in the same manner as you do in a tree.

Using the XmlNode Class

The XmlNode class is an abstract base class; it represents a node of an XML document. Because an XML document starts with a root node, the XmlNode class that corresponds to the root node represents the entire XML document's nodes. An XmlNode object can represent a node at any level. This class defines enough methods and properties to represent a document node as a tree node and traverse though it. It also provides methods to insert, replace, and remove document nodes.

The ChildNodes property returns all the child nodes of the current node. You can treat an entire document as a node and use ChildNodes to get all the nodes in a document. Also, you can use the FirstChild, LastChild, and HasChildNodes triplet to traverse from a document's first node to the last node. The ParentNode, PreviousSibling, and NextSibling properties return the parent and previous/next sibling nodes of the current node. Other common properties are Attributes, BaseURI, InnerXml, InnerText, Item, NodeType, Name, Value, and so on.

You can use the CreateNavigator method of this class to create an XPathNavigator object, which provides fast navigation using XPath. The AppendChild, InsertAfter, and InsertBefore methods add nodes to the document. The RemoveAll, RemoveChild, and ReplaceChild methods remove or replace document nodes, respectively. You'll implement these methods and properties later in this chapter.

Using the XmlDocument Class

The XmlDocument class represents an XML document. Because it's derived from the XmlNode class, it supports all tree traversal, insert, remove, and replace functionality. In spite of XmlNode functionality, this class contains many useful methods.

The DOM is a cached tree representation of an XML document. The Load and LoadXml methods of this class load XML data and documents, and the Save method saves a document.

The Load method can load a document from a string, stream, TextReader, or XmlReader. The following code loads the document books.xml from a string:

```
Dim xmlDoc As XmlDocument = New XmlDocument()
    Dim filename As String = "C:\\books.xml"
    xmlDoc.Load(filename)
xmlDoc.Save(Console.Out)
```

The following example uses the Load method to load a document from an XmlReader:

```
Dim xmlDoc As XmlDocument = New XmlDocument()
    Dim reader As XmlTextReader _
    = New XmlTextReader("C:\\books.xml")
    xmlDoc.Load(reader)
    xmlDoc.Save(Console.Out)
```

The LoadXml method loads a document from the specified string. For example:

```
xmlDoc.LoadXml("<Record> write something</Record>");
```

Saving a Document

The Save method saves a document to a specified location. The Save method takes a parameter of XmlWriter, XmlTextWriter, or a string type:

```
 Dim xmlDoc As XmlDocument = New XmlDocument()
Dim filename As String = "C:\\books.xml"
xmlDoc.Load(filename)
Dim writer As XmlTextWriter = _
New XmlTextWriter("C:\\domtest.xml", Nothing)
writer.Formatting = Formatting.Indented
xmlDoc.Save(writer)
```

You can also use a filename or Console.Out to save the output as a file or on the console:

```
xmlDoc.Save("C:\\domtest.xml")
xmlDoc.Save(Console.Out)
```

Using the XmlDocumentFragment Class

Usually, you would use the XmlDocumentFragment class when you need to insert a small fragment of an XML document or node into a document. This class also comes from the XMLNode class and has the same tree node traverse, insert, remove, and replace capabilities.

You usually create this class instance by calling XmlDocument's CreateDocumentFragment method. The InnerXml property represents the children of this node. Listing 6-10 shows an example of how to create XmlDocumentFragment and load a small piece of XML data using its InnerXml property.

Listing 6-10. The XmlDocumentFragment *Sample*

```
Dim xmlDoc As XmlDocument = New XmlDocument()
    Dim filename As String = "C:\\books.xml"
    xmlDoc.Load(filename)
    'Create a document fragment.
    Dim docFrag As XmlDocumentFragment = xmlDoc.CreateDocumentFragment()
    'Set the contents of the document fragment.
    docFrag.InnerXml = "<Record> write something</Record>"
    'Display the document fragment.
    Console.WriteLine(docFrag.InnerXml)
```

You can use XmlNode methods to add, remove, and replace data. Listing 6-11 appends a node in the document fragment.

Listing 6-11. Appending in an XML Document Fragment

```
Dim doc As XmlDocument = New XmlDocument()
doc.LoadXml("<book genre='programming'>" & _
        "<title>ADO.NET Programming</title>" & _
        "</book>")
' Get the root node
Dim root As XmlNode = doc.DocumentElement
' Create a new node.
Dim newbook As XmlElement = doc.CreateElement("price")
newbook.InnerText = "44.95"
'Add the node to the document.
root.AppendChild(newbook)
doc.Save(Console.Out)
```

Using the XmlElement Class

An XmlElement class object represents an element in a document. This class inherits from the XmlLinkedNode class, which inherits from the XmlNode, as shown in Figure 6-4.

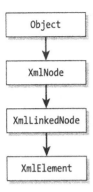

Figure 6-4. The XmlElement *class inheritance*

The XmlLinkedNode has two useful properties: NextSibling and PreviousSibling. As their names indicate, these properties return the next and previous nodes of an XML document's current node.

The XmlElement class implements and overrides some useful methods for adding and removing attributes and elements. Table 6-4 describes some of the XmlElement class methods.

Table 6-4. Some XmlElement *Class Methods*

METHOD	DESCRIPTION
GetAttribute	Returns the attribute value
HasAttribute	Checks if a node has the specified attribute
RemoveAll	Removes all the children and attributes of the current node
RemoveAllAttributes	Removes all attributes from an element
RemoveAttribute	Removes specified attributes from an element
RemoveAttributeAt	Removes the attribute node with the specified index from the attribute collection
RemoveAttributeNode	Removes an XmlAttribute
SetAttribute	Sets the value of the specified attribute
SetAttributeNode	Adds a new XmlAttribute

In the later examples, we show you how you can use these methods in your programs to get and set XML element attributes.

Adding Nodes to a Document

You can use the AppendChild method to add a node to an existing document.
The AppendChild method takes a single parameter of XmlNode type. The
XmlDocument's CreateXXX methods can create different types of nodes. For
example, the CreateComment and CreateElement methods create comment and
element node types. Listing 6-12 shows an example of adding two nodes to
a document.

Listing 6-12. Adding Nodes to a Document

```
 Dim xmlDoc As XmlDocument = New XmlDocument()
xmlDoc.LoadXml("<Record> Some Value </Record>")
' Adding a new comment node to the document
Dim node1 As XmlNode = xmlDoc.CreateComment("DOM Testing Sample")
xmlDoc.AppendChild(node1)
' Adding an FirstName to the document
node1 = xmlDoc.CreateElement("FirstName")
node1.InnerText = "Mahesh"
xmlDoc.DocumentElement.AppendChild(node1)
xmlDoc.Save(Console.Out)
```

Getting the Root Node

The DocumentElement method of the XmlDocument class (inherited from XmlNode)
returns the root node of a document. Listing 6-13 shows you how to get the root
node of a document.

Listing 6-13. Getting the Root Node of a Document

```
Dim filename As String = "C:\\books.xml"
Dim xmlDoc As XmlDocument = New XmlDocument()
xmlDoc.Load(filename)
Dim root As XmlElement = xmlDoc.DocumentElement
```

Removing and Replacing Nodes

The RemoveAll method of the XmlNode class can remove all elements and attributes of a node. RemoveChild removes the specified child only. Listing 6-14 calls RemoveAll to remove all the elements and attributes of a node.

Listing 6-14. Removing All Items of a Node

```
' Load a document fragment
   Dim xmlDoc As XmlDocument = New XmlDocument()
   xmlDoc.LoadXml("<book genre='programming'>" & _
"<title>ADO.NET Programming</title> </book>")
   Dim root As XmlNode = xmlDoc.DocumentElement
   Console.WriteLine("XML Document Fragment")
   Console.WriteLine("=====================")

   xmlDoc.Save(Console.Out)
   Console.WriteLine()
   Console.WriteLine("--------------------")
   Console.WriteLine("XML Document Fragment After RemoveAll")
   Console.WriteLine("=====================")
   'Remove all attribute and child nodes.
   root.RemoveAll()
   ' Display the contents on the console after
   ' removing elements and attributes
   xmlDoc.Save(Console.Out)
```

NOTE *You can apply the* RemoveAll *method on the* books.xml *file to delete all the data, but make sure to have a backup copy first!*

Listing 6-15 shows how to delete all the items of books.xml.

Listing 6-15. Calling RemoveAll *for* books.xml

```
Dim filename As String = "C:\\books.xml"
Dim xmlDoc As XmlDocument = New XmlDocument()
    xmlDoc.Load(filename)

    Dim root As XmlNode = xmlDoc.DocumentElement
    Console.WriteLine("XML Document Fragment")
    Console.WriteLine("=====================")

    xmlDoc.Save(Console.Out)
    Console.WriteLine()
    Console.WriteLine("---------------------")
    Console.WriteLine("XML Document Fragment After RemoveAll")
    Console.WriteLine("=====================")
    'Remove all attribute and child nodes.
    root.RemoveAll()
    ' Display the contents on the console after
    ' removing elements and attributes
    xmlDoc.Save(Console.Out)
```

The ReplaceChild method replaces an old child with a new child node. In Listing 6-16, ReplaceChild replaces rootNode.LastChild with xmlDocFrag.

Listing 6-16. Calling ReplaceChild

```
Dim filename As String = "C:\\books.xml"
    Dim xmlDoc As XmlDocument = New XmlDocument()
    xmlDoc.Load(filename)
    Dim root As XmlElement = xmlDoc.DocumentElement
    Dim xmlDocFragment As XmlDocumentFragment = xmlDoc.CreateDocumentFragment()
    xmlDocFragment.InnerXml = _
    "<Fragment><SomeData>Fragment Data</SomeData></Fragment>"
    Dim rootNode As XmlElement = xmlDoc.DocumentElement
    'Replace xmlDocFragment with rootNode.LastChild
    rootNode.ReplaceChild(xmlDocFragment, rootNode.LastChild)
    xmlDoc.Save(Console.Out)
```

Inserting XML Fragments into an XML Document

As discussed previously, the XmlNode class is useful for navigating through a document's nodes. It also provides other methods to insert XML fragments into a document. For instance, the InsertAfter method inserts a document or element after the current node. This method takes two arguments. The first argument is an XmlDocumentFragment object, and the second argument is the position where you want to insert the fragment. As discussed earlier in this chapter, you create an XmlDocumentFragment class object by using the CreateDocumentFragment method of the XmlDocument class. Listing 6-17 inserts an XML fragment into a document after the current node using InsertAfter.

Listing 6-17. Inserting an XML Fragment into a Document

```
Dim xmlDoc As XmlDocument = New XmlDocument()
    xmlDoc.Load("c:\\books.xml")
    Dim xmlDocFragment As XmlDocumentFragment = _
    xmlDoc.CreateDocumentFragment()
    xmlDocFragment.InnerXml = _
    "<Fragment><SomeData>Fragment Data</SomeData></Fragment>"
    Dim aNode As XmlNode = xmlDoc.DocumentElement.FirstChild
    aNode.InsertAfter(xmlDocFragment, aNode.LastChild)
    xmlDoc.Save(Console.Out)
```

Adding Attributes to a Node

You use the SetAttributeNode method of XmlElement to add attributes to an element, which is a node. XmlAttribute represents an XML attribute. You create an instance of XmlAttribute by calling CreateAttribute of XmlDocument. After that you call an XmlElement's SetAttribute method to set the attribute of an element. Finally, you append this new item to the document (see Listing 6-18).

Listing 6-18. Adding a Node with Attributes

```
Dim xmlDoc As XmlDocument = New XmlDocument()
    xmlDoc.Load("c:\\books.xml")
    Dim NewElem As XmlElement = xmlDoc.CreateElement("NewElement")
    Dim NewAttr As XmlAttribute = xmlDoc.CreateAttribute("NewAttribute")
    NewElem.SetAttributeNode(NewAttr)
    'add the new element to the document
    Dim root As XmlElement = xmlDoc.DocumentElement
    root.AppendChild(NewElem)
    xmlDoc.Save(Console.Out)
```

Understanding Transformation and XSLT

Extensible Stylesheet Language (XSL) is a language for expressing *stylesheets.*
Stylesheets format XML documents in a way so that the XML data can be presented in a certain structure in a browser or other media such as catalogs, books,
and so on.

The XML stylesheet processor reads an XML document (called an *XML source
tree*) and stylesheet, and it presents the document data in an XML tree format.
This processing is XSLT (see Figure 6-5).

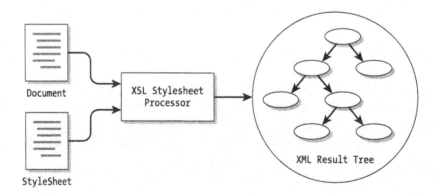

Figure 6-5. The XSL transformation

The result tree generated after the XML transformation contains element and
attribute nodes. In this tree, an object is an XML element, and properties are
attribute-value pairs.

The XSL stylesheet plays a vital role in the XSLT process. A stylesheet contains a set of tree construction rules, which have two parts. The first part is a pattern of elements in the source tree, and the second is a template for the result tree. The XSL parser reads the pattern and elements from the source tree and then generates results according to the result tree template.

Transformation is required when you need to convert an XML document into an XML schema-matching document. The XslTransform class provides the functionality to implement the XSLT specification. A separate namespace called System.Xml.Xsl defines this class. Make sure you add a reference to this namespace before using the XslTransform class. You can use the XsltException class to handle exceptions thrown by an XSLT transformation.

Using the Transform Method

The Transform method of XslTransform transforms data using the loaded stylesheet and outputs the result depending on the argument. This method has eight overloaded forms. You can write output of Transform in the form of XmlWriter, a stream, TextWriter, or XPathNavigator. (We discuss XPathNavigator in the "Navigating in XML" section of this chapter.)
Follow these steps perform the transformation:

1. First, you need to create an XslTransform object:

   ```
   Dim xslt As XslTransform =  New XslTransform()
   ```

2. Now, you load the stylesheet using the Load method:

   ```
   xslt.Load("stylesheetFrmt.xsl");
   ```

3. Finally, call the Transform method of XslTransform:

   ```
   xslt.Transform("xmlfile.xml", "file.html")
   ```

Looking at an Example

Before you use XslTransform in your application, you need to add three namespace references to your application. These namespaces are System.Xml, System.Xml.XPath, and System.Xml.Xsl. (We discuss the XPath namespace in more detail in the "Navigating in XML" section of this chapter.) Listing 6-19 uses the books.xsl schema file that comes with the .NET Software Development Kit (SDK) samples.

Listing 6-19. An XSL Transformation

```
'Create a new XslTransform object and load the stylesheet
  Dim xslt As XslTransform = New XslTransform()
  xslt.Load("c:\\books.xsl")
  'Create a new XPathDocument and load the XML data to be transformed.
  Dim mydata As XPathDocument = New XPathDocument("c:\\books.xml")
  'Create an XmlTextWriter which outputs to the console.
  Dim writer As XmlWriter = New XmlTextWriter(Console.Out)
  'Transform the data and send the output to the console.
  xslt.Transform(mydata, Nothing, writer)
```

Using ADO.NET and XML Together

So far in this chapter, you've seen how to work with XML documents. In this
section, you'll now learn how to work with XML documents with the help of
ADO.NET. There are two approaches to work with XML and ADO.NET. Using
the first approach, you can directly read XML documents by using a DataSet's
methods. Not only can you read XML documents in a DataSet, you can also update
and save XML documents by using a DataSet. Besides the DataSet object, which is
defined in the System.Data namespace, the System.Xml namespace defines classes
that can integrate ADO.NET components with XML. In this section, you'll see both
of these approaches.

Reading XML Using a DataSet

In ADO.NET, you can access the data using the DataSet class. The DataSet class
implements methods and properties to work with XML documents.

Using the ReadXML Method

ReadXml is an overloaded method; you can use it to read a data stream, TextReader,
XmlReader, or an XML file and to store data in a DataSet object, which can later be
used to display the data in a tabular format. The ReadXml method has eight overloaded forms that can accept the Stream, String, TextReader, XmlReader types of
objects as the first parameter; the second argument is of type XmlReadMode.

The XmlReadMode parameter defines the read mode with these objects. The read
mode is of type XmlReadMode. XmlReadMode specifies how to read XML data and a
relational schema into a DataSet. Table 6-5 describes the XmlReadMode members.

Table 6-5. The XmlReadMode *Members*

MEMBER	DESCRIPTION
Auto	This is the default mode. It automatically sets the best-suited mode. For example, If the data is a DiffGram, it sets XmlReadMode to DiffGram. If the DataSet already has a schema, or the document contains an inline schema, it sets XmlReadMode to ReadSchema. If the DataSet doesn't already have a schema and the document does not contain an inline schema, it sets XmlReadMode to InferSchema.
DiffGram	Reads a DiffGram.
Fragment	Reads an XML fragment.
IgnoreSchema	Ignores any inline schema. If any data doesn't match the existing schema, it's discarded.
InferSchema	If the DataSet already contains a schema, the current schema is extended by adding new tables or adding columns to existing tables.
ReadSchema	Reads an XML schema.

NOTE *See Chapter 3 and Chapter 4 for more details about the* DataSet *object.*

In the following example, create a new DataSet object and call the DataSet.ReadXml method to load the books.xml file in a DataSet object:

```
' Create a DataSet Object
Dim ds As DataSet = New DataSet()
' Fill with the data
ds.ReadXml("books.xml ")
```

Once you have a DataSet object, you know how powerful it is. Make sure you provide the correct path to books.xml.

NOTE *Make sure you add a reference to* System.Data *and the* System.Data.Common *namespace before using* DataSet *and other common data components.*

Using the ReadXmlSchema Method

The ReadXmlSchema method reads an XML schema in a DataSet object. It has four overloaded forms. You can use a TextReader, string, stream, and XmlReader. The following example shows how to use a file as direct input and call the ReadXmlSchema method to read the file:

```
Dim ds As DataSet = New DataSet()
ds.ReadXmlSchema("c:\\books.xml")
```

The following example reads the file XmlTextReader and uses XmlTextReader as the input of ReadXmlSchema:

```
' Create a dataset object
Dim ds As DataSet = New DataSet("New DataSet")
' Read xsl in an XmlTextReader
Dim myXmlReader As XmlTextReader = New XmlTextReader("c:\\books.xml")
' Call ReadXmlSchema
ds.ReadXmlSchema(myXmlReader)
myXmlReader.Close()
```

Writing XML Using a DataSet

Not only for reading, the DataSet class contains methods to write XML files from a DataSet object and fill the data to the file.

Using the WriteXml Method

The WriteXml method writes the current data (the schema and data) of a DataSet object to an XML file. By using this method, you can write data to a file, stream, TextWriter, or XmlWriter. The WriteXml method takes an argument of type Stream, String, TextWriter, or XmlWriter.

When writing XML using WriteXml, you can also specify the write mode. The second parameter of WriteXml is a type of XmlWriteMode, which specifies the write mode. XmlWriteMode specifies how to write XML data and a relational schema from a DataSet. Table 6-6 describes the XmlWriteMode members.

Table 6-6. The XmlWriteMode *Members*

MEMBER	DESCRIPTION
DiffGram	Writes a DataSet's contents including original and current values as a DiffGram.
IgnoreSchema	Writes the current contents of a DataSet as XML data, without an XSD schema. If there's no data in a DataSet, nothing is written.
WriteSchema	This is the default mode. The method writes the current contents as XML data with the relational structure as inline XSD schema. If the DataSet has only a schema with no data, only the inline schema is written. If there's no data in a DataSet, nothing is written.

Listing 6-20 creates a DataSet, fills the data for the DataSet, and writes the data to an XML file using the WriteXml method.

Listing 6-20. Using the WriteXml *Method*

```
Imports System.Data
Imports System.Xml
Imports System.IO

Module Module1
  Sub Main()
    try
    ' Create a DataSet, namespace and Student table
    'with Name and Address columns
    Dim ds As DataSet = New DataSet("DS")
    ds.Namespace = "StdNamespace"
    Dim stdTable As DataTable = New DataTable("Student")
    Dim col1 As DataColumn = New DataColumn("Name")
    Dim col2 As DataColumn = New DataColumn("Address")
    stdTable.Columns.Add(col1)
    stdTable.Columns.Add(col2)
    ds.Tables.Add(stdTable)
    ' Add Student Data to the table
    Dim NewRow As DataRow = stdTable.NewRow()
      NewRow("Name") = "Melanie Talmadge"
    NewRow("Address") = "Meadowlake Dr, Dtown"
    stdTable.Rows.Add(NewRow)
    NewRow = stdTable.NewRow()
      NewRow("Name") = "Amy Talmadge"
      NewRow("Address") = "Herndon"
```

```
        stdTable.Rows.Add(NewRow)
        ds.AcceptChanges()
        ' Create a new StreamWriter
        ' We'll save data in stdData.xml file
        Dim writer As System.IO.StreamWriter = _
        New System.IO.StreamWriter("c:\\stdData.xml")
        ' Writer data to DataSet which actually creates the file
        ds.WriteXml(writer)
        writer.Close()
        Catch exp As Exception
            Console.WriteLine("Exception: {0}", exp.ToString())
        End Try
    End Sub
End Module
```

You wouldn't believe what the WriteXml method does for you. Take a peek at the output stdData.xml file; it generates a standard XML file that looks like Listing 6-21.

Listing 6-21. WriteXml *Method Output*

```
- <DS xmlns="StdNamespace">
- <Student>
<Name>Melanie Talmadge</Name>
<Address>Meadowlake Dr, Dtown</Address>
</Student>
- <Student>
<Name>Amy Talmadge</Name>
<Address>Herndon</Address>
</Student>
</DS>
```

Using the WriteXmlSchema Method

The WriteXmlSchema method writes a DataSet structure to an XML schema. WriteXmlSchema has four overloaded methods. You can write the data to a stream, text, TextWriter, or XmlWriter. Listing 6-22 uses XmlWriter for the output.

Listing 6-22. Using the WriteXmlSchema *Method*

```
Dim ds As DataSet = New DataSet("DS")
ds.Namespace = "StdNamespace"
Dim stdTable As DataTable = New DataTable("Students")
Dim col1 As DataColumn = New DataColumn("Name")
Dim col2 As DataColumn = New DataColumn("Address")
stdTable.Columns.Add(col1)
stdTable.Columns.Add(col2)
ds.Tables.Add(stdTable)
' Add Student Data to the table
Dim NewRow As DataRow = stdTable.NewRow()
NewRow("Name") = "Melnaie Talmadge"
NewRow("Address") = "Meadowlake Dr, Dtown"
stdTable.Rows.Add(NewRow)
NewRow = stdTable.NewRow()
NewRow("Name") = "Amy Talmadge"
NewRow("Address") = "Herndon, VA"
stdTable.Rows.Add(NewRow)
ds.AcceptChanges()
Dim writer As XmlTextWriter =
    New XmlTextWriter(Console.Out)
ds.WriteXmlSchema(writer)
```

Refer to the previous section to see how to create an XmlTextWriter object.

Using XmlDataDocument and XML

As discussed earlier in this chapter, the XmlDocument class provides a DOM tree structure of XML documents. The XmlDataDocument class comes from XmlDocument, which comes from XmlNode. Figure 6-6 shows the XmlDataDocument class inheritance.

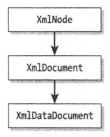

Figure 6-6. The XmlDataDocument *class inheritance*

Besides overriding the methods of XmlNode and XmlDocument, XmlDataDocument also implements its own methods. The XmlDataDocument class lets you load relational data using the DataSet object as well as XML documents using the Load and LoadXml methods. As Figure 6-7 indicates, you can use a DataSet to load relational data to an XmlDataDocument object and use the Load or LoadXml methods to load an XML document. Figure 6-7 shows the relationship between a Reader, Writer, DataSet, and XmlDataDocument.

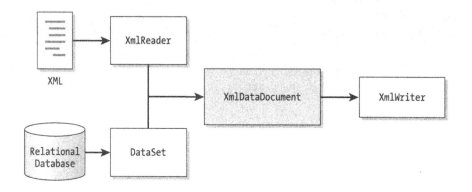

Figure 6-7. Reading and writing data using XmlDataDocument

The XmlDataDocument class extends the functionality of XmlDocument and synchronizes it with a DataSet. As you know, a DataSet is a powerful object in ADO.NET. As Figure 6-7 shows, you can take data from two different sources. First, you can load data from an XML document with the help of XmlReader, and second, you can load data from relational data sources with the help of database providers and a DataSet. The neat thing is the *data synchronization* between these two objects. If you update data in a DataSet object, you see the results in the XmlDataDocument object—and vice versa. For example, if you add a record to a DataSet object, the action will add one node to the XmlDataDocument object representing the newly added record.

Once the data is loaded, you're allowed to use any operations that you're able to use on XmlDocument objects. You can also use XmlReader and XmlWriter objects to read and write the data.

The XmlDataDocument class has a property called DataSet. It returns the attached DataSet object with XmlDataDocument. The DataSet property provides you a relational representation of an XML document. Once you have a DataSet object, you can do anything with it that you did in Chapters 3 and 4, such as binding it to data-bound controls.

You can use all the XML read and write methods of the DataSet object (such as ReadXml, ReadXmlSchema, WriteXml, and WriteXmlSchema) through the DataSet property. Refer to the DataSet read and write methods in the previous section to see how these methods are used.

Loading Data Using Load and LoadXml from the XmlDataDocument

You can use either the Load method or the LoadXml method to load an XML document. The Load method takes a parameter of a filename string, a TextReader, or an XmlReader. Similarly, you can use the LoadXml method. This method passes an XML filename to load the XML file. For example:

```
Dim doc As XmlDataDocument = New XmlDataDocument()
doc.Load("C:\\Books.xml")
```

Or you can load an XML fragment, as in the following example:

```
Dim doc As XmlDataDocument = New XmlDataDocument()
doc.LoadXml("<Record> write something</Record>")
```

Loading Data Using a DataSet

As you learned in Chapter 3, a DataSet object has methods to read XML documents. These methods are ReadXmlSchema and LoadXml. You use the Load or LoadXml methods to load an XML document the same way you did directly from XMLDataDocument. Again, the Load method takes a parameter of a filename string, TextReader, or XmlReader. Similarly, use the LoadXml method to pass an XML filename through the DataSet. For example:

```
Dim doc As XmlDataDocument =  New XmlDataDocument()
doc.DataSet.ReadXmlSchema("test.xsd")
```

or as follows:

```
doc.DataSet.ReadXml("<Record> write something</Record>")
```

Displaying XML Data in a DataSet Format

As mentioned previously, you can get a DataSet object from an XmlDataDocument object by using its DataSet property. OK, now it's time to see how to do that. The next sample shows you how easy it is to display an XML document data in a DataSet format.

You can read an XML document using the ReadXml method of the DataSet object. The DataSet property of XmlDataDocument represents the DataSet of XmlDataDocument. After reading a document in a DataSet, you can create data views from the DataSet, or you can also use a DataSet's DefaultViewManager property to bind to data-bound controls, as you can see in the following code:

```
Dim xmlDatadoc As XmlDataDocument =  New XmlDataDocument()
xmlDatadoc.DataSet.ReadXml("C:\\XmlDataDoc.xml")
 dataGrid1.DataSource = xmlDatadoc.DataSet.DefaultViewManager
```

As you can see from Listing 6-23, you create a new DataSet, Books, fill it from the books.xml file, and bind it to a DataGrid control using its DataSource property. To make Listing 6-23 work, you need to create a Windows application and drag a DataGrid control to the form. After doing that, write the Listing 6-23 code on the form load event.

Listing 6-23. XmlDataDocumentSample.vb

```
Private Sub Form1_Load(ByVal sender As System.Object, _
  ByVal e As System.EventArgs) Handles MyBase.Load
    ' Create an XmlDataDocument object and read an XML
    Dim xmlDatadoc As XmlDataDocument = New XmlDataDocument()
    xmlDatadoc.DataSet.ReadXml("C:\\books.xml")
    ' Create a DataSet object and fill it with the dataset
    ' of XmlDataDocument
    Dim ds As DataSet = New DataSet("Books DataSet")
    ds = xmlDatadoc.DataSet
    ' Attach dataset view to the DataGrid control
    DataGrid1.DataSource = ds.DefaultViewManager
  End Sub
```

If you run this program, you'll see the DataGrid filled with the data.

Saving Data from a DataSet to XML

You can save a DataSet as an XML document using the Save method of the XmlDataDocument class. Actually, XmlDataDocument comes from XmlDocument, and the XmlDocument class defines the Save method. As you know, you can use Save method to save your data in a string, stream, TextWriter, and XmlWriter.

First, you create a DataSet object and fill it using a DataAdapter. The following example reads the Customers table from the Northwind Access database and fills data from the table to the DataSet:

```
Dim sql As String = "SELECT * FROM Customers"
Dim da As SqlDataAdapter = New SqlDataAdapter(sql, conn)
' Create and fill a DataSet
Dim ds As DataSet = New DataSet()
da.Fill(ds)
```

Now, you create an instance of XmlDataDocument with the DataSet as an argument and call the Save method to save the data as an XML document:

```
Dim doc As XmlDataDocument = New XmlDataDocument(ds)
doc.Save("C:\\XmlDataDoc.xml")
```

Listing 6-24 shows a complete program. You create an XmlDataDocument object with a DataSet and call the Save method to save the DataSet data in an XML file.

Listing 6-24. Saving the DataSet *Data to an XML Document*

```
Imports System.Data
Imports System.Data.SqlClient
Imports System.Xml

Module Module1
  Sub Main()
    ' Create a Connection Object
    Dim ConnectionString As String = "Integrated Security=SSPI;" & _
      "Initial Catalog=Northwind;Data Source=MCB;"
    Dim conn As SqlConnection = New SqlConnection()
    conn.ConnectionString = ConnectionString
    ' Open the connection
    If conn.State <> ConnectionState.Open Then
      conn.Open()
    End If
```

```
      Dim sql As String = "SELECT * FROM Customers"
      Dim da As SqlDataAdapter = New SqlDataAdapter(sql, conn)
      ' Create and fill a DataSet
      Dim ds As DataSet = New DataSet()
      da.Fill(ds)
      ' Now use SxlDataDocument's Save method to save data as an XML file
      Dim doc As XmlDataDocument = New XmlDataDocument(ds)
      doc.Save("C:\\XmlDataDoc.xml")
      ' Close and dispose the connection
      If conn.State <> ConnectionState.Open Then
        conn.Open()
        conn.Dispose()
      End If
    End Sub
  End Module
```

XmlDataDocument: Looking under the Hood

After looking at Listing 6-23, which illustrates the reading of an XML document in a DataGrid control, you must be wondering how it happened. The DataSet object handles everything for you under the hood:

```
doc.DataSet.ReadXml("C:\\outdata.xml")
```

As you see in this line, you're calling the DataSet.ReadXml method to read an XML document. The DataSet extracts the document and defines tables and columns for you.

Generally, the root node of the XML document becomes a table; the document's name, namespace, namespace URI, and prefix become the DataSet's Name, Namespace, NamespaceURI, and Prefix properties, respectively. If an element's children have one or more children, they become another table inside the main table in a nested format. Anything left from the tables becomes columns of the table. The value of a node becomes a row in a table. The DataSet takes care of all of this for you.

Navigating in XML

As you saw, XmlNode provides a way to navigate DOM trees with the help of its FirstChild, ChildNodes, LastChild, PreviousNode, NextSibling, and PreviousSibling methods.

Besides XmlNode, the XML .NET has two more classes, which help you navigate XML documents. These classes are XPathDocument and XPathNavigator. The System.Xml.XPath namespace defines both of these classes.

The XPath namespace contains classes to provide read-only, fast access to documents. Before using these classes, you must add a reference to the System.Xml.XPath namespace in your application.

XPathNodeIterator, XPathExpression, and XPathException are other classes defined in this namespace. The XPathNodeIterator class provides iteration capabilities to a node. XPathExpression provides selection criteria to select a set of nodes from a document based on those criteria, and the XPathException class is an exception class. TheXPathDocument class provides a fast cache for XML document processing using XSLT and XPath.

You use the XPathDocument constructor to create an instance of XmlPathDocument. It has many overloaded constructors. You can pass an XmlReader, TextReader, or even direct XML filenames.

Using the XPathNavigator Class

The XPathNavigator class implements the functionality to navigate through a document. It has easy-to-use and self-explanatory methods. You create an XPathNavigator instance by calling XPathDocument's CreateNavigator method.

You can also create a XPathNavigator object by calling XmlDocument's CreateNavigator method. For example, the following code calls XmlDocument's CreateNavigator method to create a XPathNavigator object:

```
' Load books.xml document
Dim xmlDoc As XmlDocument = New XmlDocument()
xmlDoc.Load("c:\\books.xml")
' Create XPathNavigator object by calling CreateNavigator of XmlDocument
Dim nav As XPathNavigator = xmlDoc.CreateNavigator()
```

NOTE *Don't forget to add a reference to the* System.Xml.XPath *namespace to your project before using any of its classes.*

The XPathNavigator class contains methods and properties to move to the first, next, child, parent, and root nodes of the document.

Using XPathNavigator Move Methods

Table 6-7 describes XPathNavigator's Move methods.

Table 6-7. XPathNavigator *Members*

MEMBER	DESCRIPTION
MoveToAttribute	Moves to an attribute
MoveToFirst	Moves to the first sibling of the current node
MoveToFirstAttribute	Moves to the first attribute
MoveToFirstChild	Moves to the first child of the current node
MoveToFirstNamespace	Moves the XPathNavigator to first namespace node of the current element
MoveToId	Moves to the node with specified ID
MoveToNamespace	Moves to the specified namespace
MoveToNext	Moves to the next node of the current node
MoveToNextAttribute	Moves to the next attribute
MoveToNextNamespace	Moves to the next namespace
MoveToParent	Moves to the parent of the current node
MoveToPrevious	Moves to the previous sibling of the current node
MoveToRoot	Moves to the root node

So, with the help of these methods, you can move through a document as a DOM tree. Listing 6-25 uses the MoveToRoot and MoveToFirstChild methods to move to the root node and first child of the root node. Once you have a root, you can display corresponding information such as the name, value, node type, and so on.

Listing 6-25. Moving to Root and First Child Nodes Using XPathNavigator

```
' Load books.xml document
Dim xmlDoc As XmlDocument = New XmlDocument()
    xmlDoc.Load("c:\\books.xml")
    ' Create XPathNavigator object by calling CreateNavigator of XmlDocument
    Dim nav As XPathNavigator = xmlDoc.CreateNavigator()

    ' Move to root node
    nav.MoveToRoot()
    Dim name As String = nav.Name
    Console.WriteLine("Root node info: ")
```

```
Console.WriteLine("Base URI" + nav.BaseURI.ToString())
Console.WriteLine("Name: " + nav.Name.ToString())
Console.WriteLine("Node Type: " + nav.NodeType.ToString())
Console.WriteLine("Node Value: " + nav.Value.ToString())


If nav.HasChildren Then
  nav.MoveToFirstChild()
End If
```

Now, using the `MoveToNext` and `MoveToParent` methods, you can move through the entire document. Listing 6-26 moves though an entire document and displays the data on the console. The `GetNodeInfo` method displays a node's information, and you call it recursively.

Listing 6-26. Reading a Document Using XPathNavigator

```
Imports System.Data
Imports System.Data.SqlClient
Imports System.Xml
Imports System.Xml.XPath

Module Module1
  Sub Main()
    ' Load books.xml document
    Dim xmlDoc As XmlDocument = New XmlDocument()
    xmlDoc.Load("c:\\books.xml")
    ' Create XPathNavigator object by calling CreateNavigator of XmlDocument
    Dim nav As XPathNavigator = xmlDoc.CreateNavigator()

    ' Moce to root node
    nav.MoveToRoot()
    Dim name As String = nav.Name
    Console.WriteLine("Root node info: ")
    Console.WriteLine("Base URI" + nav.BaseURI.ToString())
    Console.WriteLine("Name: " + nav.Name.ToString())
    Console.WriteLine("Node Type: " + nav.NodeType.ToString())
    Console.WriteLine("Node Value: " + nav.Value.ToString())

    If nav.HasChildren Then
      nav.MoveToFirstChild()
      GetNodeInfo(nav)
    End If
  End Sub
End Sub
```

```
' GetNodeInfo method
Public Sub GetNodeInfo(ByVal nav1 As XPathNavigator)
   Console.WriteLine("Name: " + nav1.Name.ToString())
   Console.WriteLine("Node Type: " + nav1.NodeType.ToString())
   Console.WriteLine("Node Value: " + nav1.Value.ToString())

   ' If node has children, move to fist child.
   If nav1.HasChildren Then
     nav1.MoveToFirstChild()

     While nav1.MoveToNext()
       GetNodeInfo(nav1)
       nav1.MoveToParent()
     End While
   Else
     nav1.MoveToNext()
     GetNodeInfo(nav1)
   End If
 End Sub

End Module
```

Searching Using XPathNavigator

Select, SelectChildren, SelectAncestors, and SelectDescendents are other useful methods. Specifically, these methods are useful when you need to select a document's items based on an XPath expression. For example, you could use one when selecting nodes for the author tag only.

Now, say you want to search and display all <first-name> tag nodes in the books.xml document. In Listing 6-27, you use XPathNavigator's Select method to apply a criteria (all elements with the <first-name> tag) to read and display all the nodes.

Listing 6-27. Using XPathIterator and Select

```
' Load books.xml document
   Dim xmlDoc As XmlDocument = New XmlDocument()
   xmlDoc.Load("c:\\books.xml")
   ' Create XPathNavigator object by calling CreateNavigator of XmlDocument
   Dim nav As XPathNavigator = xmlDoc.CreateNavigator()
   ' Look for author's first name
```

```
Console.WriteLine("Author First Name")
Dim itrator As XPathNodeIterator = _
nav.Select("descendant::first-name")
While itrator.MoveNext()
  Console.WriteLine(itrator.Current.Value.ToString())
End While
```

Working with Schemas

XML schemas play a major role in the .NET Framework, and Visual Studio
.NET (VS .NET) provides many tools and utilities to work with XML. The .NET
Framework uses XML to transfer data from one application to other. XML schemas
define the structure and validation rules of XML documents. You use XML Schema
Definition (XSD) language to define XML schemas.

VS .NET provides an XML designer to work with schemas. In this section,
you'll learn how to take advantage of the VS .NET XML designer and wizards to
work with XML documents and databases.

Generating a New Schema

To generate a new schema, create a new Windows application using File ➤ New ➤
Project ➤ Visual Basic Projects ➤ Windows Application. Then just follow the steps
outlined in the following sections.

Step 1: Adding an Empty Schema

You can add an XML schema to a project by right-clicking a project and then
selecting Add ➤ Add New Item. The Add New Item option opens the Add New
Item dialog box, where you can select different templates. To add an XML schema,
you need to select the XML Schema template on this page. This page also allows
you to specify the schema name. The default schema name is XMLSchema1.xsd.
Next, click the Open button on the Add New Item page.

This action launches the XML designer, which allows you to design XML
schemas. The default XML designer page like Figure 6-8. As you can see, there are
two links available: Server Explorer and Toolbox.

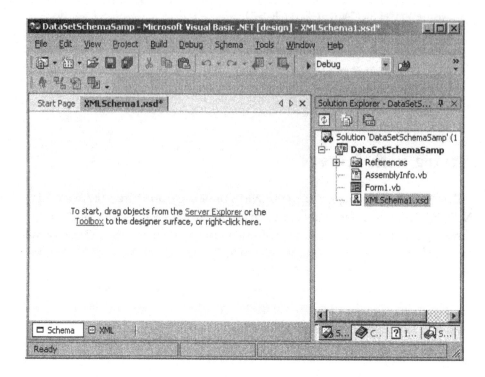

Figure 6-8. The XML designer

As you might guess, the Server Explorer link launches the Server Explorer. (See Chapter 2 to learn more about the Server Explorer.) The Toolbox link launches a Toolbox that contains the XML Schema items rather than Windows or Web controls.

If you click the XML option at the bottom of screen, you'll see that your XML looks like the following:

```xml
<?xml version="1.0" encoding="utf-8" ?>
<xs:schema id="XMLSchema1" targetNamespace="http://tempuri.org/XMLSchema1.xsd"
elementFormDefault="qualified" xmlns="http://tempuri.org/XMLSchema1.xsd"
xmlns:mstns="http://tempuri.org/XMLSchema1.xsd"
xmlns:xs="http://www.w3.org/2001/XMLSchema">
</xs:schema>
```

Step 2: Adding Schema Items

Once an empty schema is available in the XML designer, you can click the Toolbox link to open the Toolbox and add schema items (see Figure 6-9).

Figure 6-9. The XML schema Toolbox

The XML designer works in pretty much same way as the form designer. You drag components from the Toolbox to the designer, and the designer writes the code for you. As you can see in Figure 6-9, you can add an element, attribute, complexType, and other schema items to the form.

First, let's add an element to the schema, dragging it from the Toolbox. Second, set its name and type in the designer. The default element looks like Figure 6-10. If you click the right-side column of the grid, you'll see a drop-down list with element types. You can either select the type of an item from the list or define your own type (which is a *user-defined type*).

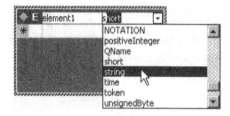

Figure 6-10. Adding a schema element and its type

For this example, define your own custom type. Define the first element as
bookstore with a custom type of bookstoretype. Figure 6-11 shows the bookstore
element of bookstoretype.

Figure 6-11. Adding a new bookstore *element*

Now add a complexType item by dragging a complexType item to the XML
designer (see Figure 6-12).

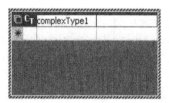

Figure 6-12. A complexType item

A complexType item can contain other types, too. You can add items to a complexType in many ways. You can either drag an item from the Toolbox to the complexType or right-click a complexType and use the Add option and its suboptions to add an item. Figure 6-13 shows different items you can add to a complexType.

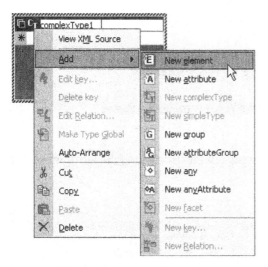

Figure 6-13. Adding other types to complexType item

You can delete items by right-clicking and selecting Delete. You can also delete the entire complexType or other schema items by right-clicking the header of an item or right-clicking the left side of the item.

Now, rename the added complexType name to book and add four element types: title, author, price, and category. Now your complexType book should now look like Figure 6-14.

	book	booktype
E	title	string
E	author	authorname
E	price	decimal
E	category	string

Figure 6-14. The book *complexType and its elements*

Next, add one more complexType author with two elements: first-name and last-name. Your final schema should now look like Figure 6-15.

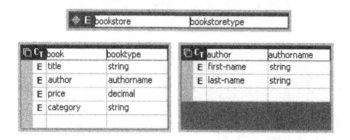

Figure 6-15. The author *and* book *complexTypes in an XML schema*

You can now see the XML code for this schema by clicking the left-bottom XML button (see Figure 6-16).

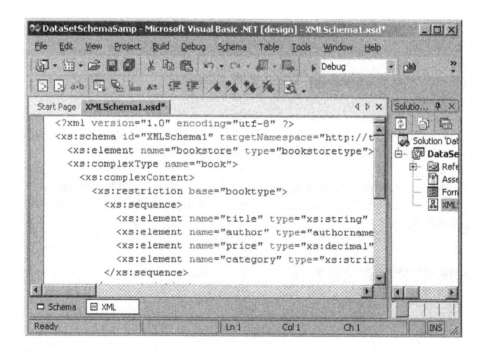

Figure 6-16. Viewing the XML code for a schema

You just saw how the VS .NET Integrated Development Environment (IDE) provides a tool to design your custom schema.

Adding Schema from a Database Objects

You can generate a typed DataSet (discussed in Chapter 4)—which actually is an XML schema—from a database table or other objects such as a view or a stored procedure. To test this option, you use the Server Explorer, which you can launch either by clicking the Server Explorer option of the XML designer or by opening it from the View ➤ Server Explorer menu item.

To create an XML schema from a database table, you simply open the Server Explorer, expand a database table, and drag a table onto the XML schema designer. For this example, drag the Employees table onto the designer. After dragging it, the XML designer generates a schema for the table (see Figure 6-17).

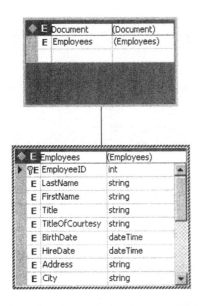

Figure 6-17. XML designer–generated schema

Listing 6-28 shows the generated XML code.

Listing 6-28. The XML Schema Generated for a Database Table

```xml
<?xml version="1.0" encoding="utf-8" ?>
<xs:schema id="XMLSchema1" targetNamespace=
"http://tempuri.org/XMLSchema1.xsd"
elementFormDefault="qualified"
xmlns="http://tempuri.org/XMLSchema1.xsd"
xmlns:mstns="http://tempuri.org/XMLSchema1.xsd"
xmlns:xs="http://www.w3.org/2001/XMLSchema"
xmlns:msdata="urn:schemas-microsoft-com:xml-msdata">
<xs:element name="Document">
<xs:complexType>
<xs:choice maxOccurs="unbounded">
<xs:element name="Employees">
<xs:complexType>
<xs:sequence>
<xs:element name="EmployeeID" msdata:ReadOnly="true"
msdata:AutoIncrement="true" type="xs:int" />
<xs:element name="LastName" type="xs:string" />
<xs:element name="FirstName" type="xs:string" />
<xs:element name="Title" type="xs:string" minOccurs="0" />
<xs:element name="TitleOfCourtesy" type="xs:string" minOccurs="0" />
<xs:element name="BirthDate" type="xs:dateTime" minOccurs="0" />
<xs:element name="HireDate" type="xs:dateTime" minOccurs="0" />
<xs:element name="Address" type="xs:string" minOccurs="0" />
<xs:element name="City" type="xs:string" minOccurs="0" />
<xs:element name="Region" type="xs:string" minOccurs="0" />
<xs:element name="PostalCode" type="xs:string" minOccurs="0" />
<xs:element name="Country" type="xs:string" minOccurs="0" />
<xs:element name="HomePhone" type="xs:string" minOccurs="0" />
<xs:element name="Extension" type="xs:string" minOccurs="0" />
<xs:element name="Photo" type="xs:base64Binary" minOccurs="0" />
<xs:element name="Notes" type="xs:string" minOccurs="0" />
<xs:element name="ReportsTo" type="xs:int" minOccurs="0" />
<xs:element name="PhotoPath" type="xs:string" minOccurs="0" />
</xs:sequence>
</xs:complexType>
</xs:element>
</xs:choice>
</xs:complexType>
```

```
<xs:unique name="DocumentKey1" msdata:PrimaryKey="true">
<xs:selector xpath=".//mstns:Employees" />
<xs:field xpath="mstns:EmployeeID" />
</xs:unique>
</xs:element>
</xs:schema>
```

Generating a Typed DataSet from a Schema

Now let's generate a typed DataSet from the schema you just added to the XML designer. The Generate Dataset option generates a typed DataSet for an XML schema. You can find the Generate Dataset option after right-clicking on the XML designer.

This action generates a DataSet class and adds it to your project. If you look in your Class View, you see the Document class derives from a DataSet and its members. The Document class looks like Figure 6-18 in the Class Wizard.

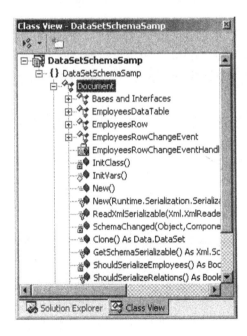

Figure 6-18. The DataSet*-derived class in the Class View*

NOTE *The Generate Dataset option may not generate a* DataSet *if an XML schema isn't designed properly.*

Once you have a DataSet object, you can use it in any way you want.

Summary

In this chapter, you learned the basics of System.Xml and it related namespaces and how XML is represented in .NET through classes such as XmlNode, XmlAttribute, XmlElement, and XmlDocument. You also learned how to read and write to these structures using the XmlReader and XmlWriter classes. Also discussed was the navigation in an XML node structure using XmlPathNavigator. Most importantly, you learned how XML applies to ADO.NET and how to use a DataSet to read and write data with XML. VS .NET provides the XML designer to work with XML. Using the XML designer, you can generate XML schemas, which later can be used to generate typed DataSets.

VS .NET provides a rich set of data-bound controls, which are very flexible and useful. In the next chapter, you'll see how to take advantage of VS .NET data-bound controls to write database applications.

CHAPTER 7

Data Binding
and Windows Forms
Data-Bound Controls

WHEN IT COMES to developing interactive database applications, it's difficult to resist using data-bound controls. Data-bound controls are easy to use, and they also provide many handy, built-in features. You used DataGrid, ListBox, and other data-bound controls in the previous chapters. In this chapter, we discuss the basics of data binding, how to use data-bound controls, and how to develop interactive database applications using these controls with a minimal amount of time and effort.

Both Windows Forms and Web Forms provide a rich set of data-bound controls, which help developers build data-driven Windows and Web applications. In this chapter, we concentrate on Windows Forms. Chapter 16 covers data binding in Web Forms.

Understanding Data Binding

So what are data-bound controls? You've already seen the DataGrid and ListBox controls in the previous chapters. You used these controls to display data from a data source. Data-bound controls are Windows controls that represent and manipulate data in Graphical User Interface (GUI) forms. Both Windows Forms and Web Forms provide a variety of flexible and powerful data-bound controls. These data-bound controls vary from a TextBox to a DataGrid.

The process of binding a data source's data to GUI controls is called *data binding*. Most of the editable Windows controls provide data binding, either directly or indirectly. These controls contain members that connect directly to a data source, and then the control takes care of displaying the data and other details. For example, to view data in a DataGrid control, you just need to set its DataSource property to a data source. This data source could be a DataSet, DataView, array, collection, or other data source. Data-bound controls can display data, and they are smart enough to display properties (metadata) of the stored data such as data relations.

You can divide data binding into two categories: simple data binding and complex data binding. In *simple data binding*, a control displays data provided by a data feed. In fact, the control itself is not capable of displaying complex data. Setting the Text property of a TextBox or Label control is an example of simple data binding. *Complex data binding*, on the other hand, allows controls to bind to multiple columns and complex data. Binding an entire database table or multiple columns of a database table to a DataGrid or a ListBox control is an example of complex data binding.

Using the Binding Class

The Binding class, defined in the System.Windows.Forms namespace, represents simple binding between the data source item and a control.

Constructing a Binding Object

The Binding class constructor, which creates an instance of the Binding class, takes three arguments: a data-bound control's property name, a data source as an Object, and a data member, usually the name of the data source columns as a string. You define the Binding class constructor as follows:

```
Public Sub New( _
    ByVal propertyName As String, _
    ByVal dataSource As Object, _
    ByVal dataMember As String _
)
```

In this syntax, dataSource can be a DataSet, DataTable, DataView, DataViewManager, any class that implements IList, and a class object. Listing 7-1 binds the Employees.FirstName column of a DataSet to the Text property of a TextBox.

Listing 7-1. Binding a TextBox Using Binding

```
Dim ds As DataSet = New DataSet()
ds = GetDataSet("Employees")
Dim bind1 As Binding
bind1 = New Binding("Text", ds, "Employees.FirstName")
```

```
TextBox1.DataBindings.Add(bind1)
```

Besides the previous two controls, you can perform simple binding on many controls including Button, CheckBox, CheckedListBox, ComboBox, DateTimePicker, DomainUpDown, GroupBox, HscrollBar, Label, LinkLabel, ListBox, ListView, MonthCalender, NumericUpDown, PictureBox, ProgressBar, RadioButton, RichTextBox, ScrollBar, StatusBar, TextBox, TreeView, and VscrollBar. Listing 7-2 binds the Text property of a ComboBox, Label, and Button control with the DataTable's LastName, City, and Country columns (respectively).

Listing 7-2. Binding Multiple Controls Using Binding

```
ComboBox1.DataBindings.Add _
    (New Binding("Text", ds, "Employees.LastName"))
TextBox2.DataBindings.Add _
    (New Binding("Text", ds, "Employees.EmployeeID"))
Label4.DataBindings.Add(
    New Binding("Text", ds, "Employees.City"))
Button1.DataBindings.Add(
    New Binding("Text", ds, "Employees.Country"))
```

Understanding the BindingsCollection Class

The BindingsCollection class represents a collection of Binding objects for a control. You access the BindingsCollection class through the control's DataBindings property. The BindingsCollection class provides members to add, count, and remove Binding objects to the collection. Listing 7-1 and Listing 7-2 used the Add method of BindingsCollection to add a Binding object to the collection.

The BindingsCollection class has three properties: Count, Item, and List. The Count property returns the total number of items in the collection. The Item property returns the Binding object at a specified index, and the List property returns all the items in a collection as an ArrayList.

The Add method of BindingsCollection adds a Binding object to the collection. The Remove method deletes a Binding object from the collection. The RemoveAt method removes a Binding object at the specified index. The Clear method removes all the Binding objects from the collection.

Listing 7-3 counts the total number of Binding objects associated with a control and removes the Binding objects from various controls.

Listing 7-3. Counting and Removing Binding Objects

```
MessageBox.Show("Total Bindings: " + _
Button1.DataBindings.Count.ToString())
TextBox1.DataBindings.RemoveAt(0)
TextBox2.DataBindings.Clear()
```

NOTE *The* BindingsCollection *class is a collection of* Binding *objects. The index of* Binding *objects in a collection is 0 based, which means the 0th item of the collection is the first item and (n–1)th item in the collection is the nth item.*

Setting Binding Class Members

The Binding class provides six properties: BindingManagerBase, BindingMemberInfo, Control, DataSource, IsBinding, and PropertyName.

BindingManagerBase represents the BindingManagerBase object, which manages the binding between a data source and data-bound controls.

The BindingMemberInfo property object is a BindingMemberInfo structure that contains the information about the binding. The BindingMemberInfo structure has three properties: BindingField, BindingMember, and BindingPath. The BindingField property returns the data-bound control's property name. BindingMember returns the information used to specify the data-bound control's property name, and BindingPath returns the property name, or the period-delimited hierarchy of property names, that precedes the data-bound object's property.

Listing 7-4 reads the bindings available on all the controls and displays their information by using the BindingMemberInfo property.

Listing 7-4. Reading All the Bindings of a Form

```
Dim str As String
  Dim curControl As Control
  Dim curBinding As Binding
  For Each curControl In Me.Controls
    For Each curBinding In curControl.DataBindings
      Dim bInfo As BindingMemberInfo = _
      curBinding.BindingMemberInfo
```

```
        str = "Control: " + curControl.Name
        str += ", BindingPath: " + bInfo.BindingPath
        str += ", BindingField: " + bInfo.BindingField
        str += ", BindingMember: " + bInfo.BindingMember
        MessageBox.Show(str)
    Next curBinding
Next curControl
```

The Control and DataSource properties return the control and data source that belong to this binding. The IsBinding property returns True if the binding is active; otherwise it returns False. PropertyName returns the name of the bound control's property that can be used in data binding. Listing 7-5 displays the DataSource and PropertyName properties of a TextBox.

Listing 7-5. Reading a TextBox *Control's Binding Properties*

```
If (TextBox1.DataBindings(0).IsBinding) Then
    Dim ds As DataSet = _
    CType(TextBox1.DataBindings(0).DataSource, DataSet)
    str = "DataSource : " + ds.Tables(0).TableName
    str += ", Property Name: " + _
    TextBox1.DataBindings(0).PropertyName
    MessageBox.Show(str)
End If
```

In addition to the previously discussed properties, the Binding class also provides two protected methods: OnParse and OnFormat. OnParse raises the Parse event, and OnFormat raises the Format event. The Parse event occurs when the value of a data-bound control is changing, and the Format event occurs when the property of a control is bound to a data value. The event handler for both the Parse and Format events receives an argument of type ConvertEventArgs containing data related to this event, which has two members: DesiredType and Value. DesiredType returns the data type of the desired value, and Value gets and sets the value of the ConvertEventArgs object.

Now let's say you want to convert text and decimal values for a Binding for a TextBox. You write the code in Listing 7-6, where you change the Binding type and add event handlers for the Binding objects for Format and Parse members.

NOTE *This listing uses the Customers table instead of Employees because the Employees table doesn't have any decimal data. If you want to use the Employees table, you could convert a Date type to a String type.*

Listing 7-6. Adding Format and Parse Event Handlers

```
Dim bind2 As Binding = New Binding _
    ("Text", ds, "customers.custToOrders.OrderAmount")
AddHandler bind1.Format, AddressOf DecimalToCurrencyString
AddHandler bind1.Parse, AddressOf CurrencyStringToDecimal
Private Sub DecimalToCurrencyString(ByVal sender As Object, _
 ByVal cevent As ConvertEventArgs)
    If Not cevent.DesiredType Is GetType(String) Then
      Exit Sub
    End If
    cevent.Value = CType(cevent.Value, Decimal).ToString("c")
End Sub
Private Sub CurrencyStringToDecimal(ByVal sender As Object, _
  ByVal cevent As ConvertEventArgs)
    If Not cevent.DesiredType Is GetType(Decimal) Then
      Exit Sub
    End If
    cevent.Value = Decimal.Parse(cevent.Value.ToString, _
    NumberStyles.Currency, Nothing)
End Sub
```

NOTE *To test this code, you need to create a* DataSet *from the Employees table of the Northwind database and use it as a data source when constructing a* Binding *object. Also, don't forget to add a reference to the* System.Globalization *namespace because the* NumberStyle *enumeration is defined in this namespace.*

Understanding the BindingManagerBase Functionality

The BindingManagerBase class is an abstract base class. You use its functionality through its two derived classes: CurrencyManager and PropertyManager.

By default data-bound controls provide neither data synchronization nor the position of the current item. The BindingManagerBase object provides the data synchronization in Windows Forms and makes sure that all controls on a form are updated with the correct data.

....

Question and Answer

Question: What is data synchronization?

Answer: Have you ever developed database applications in Visual Basic 6.0 or Microsoft Foundation Classes (MFC)? In both of those languages, a data-bound control lets you navigate through data from one record to another and update data in the controls available on the form. As you move to the next record, the next row was fetched from the data source and every control was updated with the current row's data. This process is called *data synchronization.*

....

OK, now let's say a form has three controls: a TextBox, a Label, and a PictureBox. All three controls support data binding from a DataSet, which is filled with the data from the Employees table. The TextBox control displays FirstName, the Label control displays LastName, and the PictureBox control displays Photo properties (columns) of the DataSet. All of the controls must be synchronized in order to display the correct first name, last name, and photo for the same employee.

CurrencyManager accomplishes this synchronization by maintaining a pointer to the current item for the list. All controls are bound to the current item so they display the information for the same row. When the current item changes, CurrencyManager notifies all the bound controls so that they can refresh their data. Furthermore, you can set the Position property to specify the row in the DataSet or DataTable to which the controls point. Figure 7-1 shows the synchronization process.

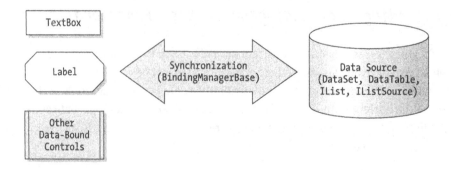

Figure 7-1. Synchronization between a data source and data-bound controls

Using the BindingManagerBase Class Members

As you learned, the Binding property returns the collection of binding objects as a BindingsCollection object that BindingManagerBase manages. Listing 7-7 creates a BindingManagerBase object for the form and reads all of the binding controls.

Listing 7-7. Reading All Controls Participating in Data Binding

```
' Get the BindingManagerBase
Dim bindingBase As BindingManagerBase = _
    Me.BindingContext(ds, "Employees")
Dim bindingObj As Binding
 ' Read each Binding object from the collection
For Each bindingObj In bindingBase.Bindings
    MessageBox.Show(bindingObj.Control.Name)
Next bindingObj
```

NOTE *To read a form's controls that are participating in data binding, you must make sure that the form's data source and control's data source are the same.*

The Count property returns the total number of rows being managed by BindingManagerBase. The Current property returns the current object, and the Position property represents (both gets and sets) the position in the underlying list to which controls bound to this data source point. We use these properties in the following sample examples.

Table 7-1 describes the `BindingManagerBase` class methods.

Table 7-1. The `BindingManagerBase` *Class Methods*

METHOD	DESCRIPTION
AddNew	Adds a new item to the list
CancelCurrentEdit	Cancels the current edit operation
EndCurrentEdit	Ends the current edit operation
GetItemProperties	Returns the list of property descriptions for the data source
RemoveAt	Deletes the row at the specified index
ResumeBinding	Resumes data binding
SuspendBinding	Suspends data binding
GetListName	Protected. Returns the name of the list
OnCurrentChanged	Raises the `CurrentChanged` event, which occurs when the bound value changes
PullData	Pulls data from the data-bound control into the data source
PushData	Pushes data from data source into the data-bound control
UpdateIsBinding	Updates the binding

Besides the properties and methods discussed previously, the `BindingManagerBase` class provides two events: `CurrentChanged` and `PositionChanged`. The `CurrentChanged` event occurs when the bound value changes, and the `PositionChanged` event occurs when the position changes.

Using CurrencyManager and PropertyManager

`CurrencyManager` manages a list of `Binding` objects on a form. It's inherited from the `BindingManagerBase` class. Besides the functionality provided by `BindingManagerBase`, the `CurrencyManager` provides two members: a `List` property and a `Refresh` method. The `List` property returns the list of bindings maintained by `CurrencyManager` as an `IList` object. To convert an `IList` to other objects, you need to cast it with the type of the object, which must implement `IList`. Some of the objects that implement `IList` are `DataView`, `DataTable`, `DataSet`, `Array`, `ArrayList`, and `CollectionBase`.

You create a `CurrencyManager` object by using the `BindingContext` object, which returns either `CurrencyManager` or `PropertyManager`, depending on the value of the data source and data members passed to the `Item` property of `BindingContext`. If the data source is an object that can only return a single property (instead of a list of objects), the type will be `PropertyManager`. For example, if you specify a `TextBox` control as the data source, PropertyManager will be returned. If the data source is an object that implements IList, IListSource, or IBindingList, such as a DataSet, DataTable, DataView, or an Array, CurrencyManager will be returned.

You can create a CurrencyManager from objects such as a DataView and vice versa. For example, the following code creates a CurrencyManager from a DataView and a DataView from a CurrencyManager:

```
Dim dv As DataView
dv = New DataView(ds.Tables("Customers"))
Dim curManager1 As CurrencyManager = DataGrid1.BindingContext(dv)
Dim list As IList = curManager1.List
Dim dv1 As DataView = CType(curManager1.List, DataView)
Dim curManager2 As CurrencyManager = Me.BindingContext(ds1)
```

Unlike CurrencyManager, PropertyManager doesn't provide any additional members besides the members provided by its base class, BindingManagerBase.

Understanding BindingContext

Each object inherited from the Control class has a BindingContext object attached to it. BindingContext manages the collection of BindingManagerBase objects for that object such as a form. The BindingContext creates the CurrencyManager and PropertyManager objects, which were discussed previously. Normally you use the Form class's BindingContext to create a CurrencyManager and PropertyManager for a form and its controls, which provide data synchronization.

The Item property of BindingContext returns the BindingManagerBase (either CurrencyManager or PropertyManager). The Contains methods returns True if it contains the specified BindingManagerBase.

Besides the Item and Contains members, the BindingContext has three protected methods: Add, Clear, and Remove. The Add method adds a BindingManagerBase to the collection, the Clear method removes all items in the collection, and the Remove method deletes the BindingManagerBase associated with the specified data source.

Building a Record Navigation System

Now let's see data binding in action. In this section, you'll develop an application that provides data synchronization. In this application, you'll build a record navigation system. The controls will display records, and then when you click the

Move Next, Move Last, Move Previous, and Move First buttons, the controls will display the respective records.

To begin, create a Windows application and design a form that looks like Figure 7-2. For this example, you don't have to place the ReadBindingMemberInfo and Remove controls. Add a ComboBox control, two TextBox controls, a ListBox control, some Label controls, and some Button controls. The Load Data button loads data to the controls and attaches Binding objects to the BindingContext. You should also add four buttons with brackets as the text (<<, <, >, >>), which represents the Move First, Move Previous, Move Next, and Move Last records.

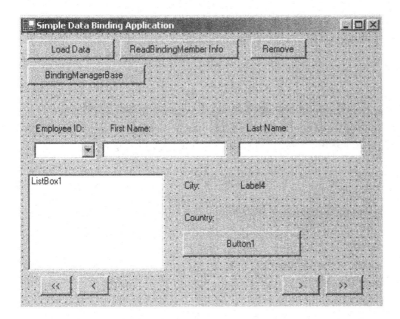

Figure 7-2. Record navigation form

NOTE *You can create your own form, but to save you some time, you can download the code from the Apress (www.apress.com) or C# Corner (www.c-sharpcorner.com) Web sites. Open the project in Visual Studio .NET (VS .NET) to understand it better.*

As usual, first you add some variables to the project, which shown in Listing 7-8. Don't forget to change your server name; the server name in this example is MCB.

Listing 7-8. Record Navigation System Variables

```
Private ConnectionString As String = "Integrated Security=SSPI;" & _
"Initial Catalog=Northwind;Data Source=MCB;"
Private conn As SqlConnection = Nothing
Private sql As String = Nothing
Private adapter As SqlDataAdapter = Nothing
Private ds As DataSet = Nothing
```

Second, you call the LoadData method on the Load Data button click:

```
Private Sub LoadBtn_Click(ByVal sender As System.Object, _
  ByVal e As System.EventArgs) Handles LoadBtn.Click
    LoadData()
End Sub
```

Listing 7-9 shows the LoadData and GetDataSet methods. The GetDataSet method returns a DataSet object from the table name passed in the method. The LoadData method creates bindings for these controls with different DataTable columns.

Listing 7-9. LoadData *and* GetDataSet *Methods*

```
Private Sub LoadData()
    Dim ds As DataSet = New DataSet()
    ds = GetDataSet("Employees")
    Dim bind1 As Binding
    bind1 = New Binding("Text", ds, "Employees.FirstName")
    TextBox1.DataBindings.Add(bind1)
    TextBox2.DataBindings.Add _
  (New Binding("Text", ds, "Employees.LastName"))
    ComboBox1.DataBindings.Add _
   (New Binding("Text", ds, "Employees.EmployeeID"))
    Label4.DataBindings.Add(New Binding("Text", ds, "Employees.City"))
    Button1.DataBindings.Add(New Binding("Text", ds, "Employees.Country"))
    ListBox1.DataSource = ds.Tables(0).DefaultView
    ListBox1.DisplayMember = "Title"
End Sub
' object based on various parameters.
Public Function GetDataSet(ByVal tableName As String) As DataSet
    sql = "SELECT * FROM " + tableName
    ds = New DataSet(tableName)
```

```
        conn = New SqlConnection()
        conn.ConnectionString = ConnectionString
        adapter = New SqlDataAdapter(sql, conn)
        adapter.Fill(ds, tableName)
        Return ds
    End Function
```

The previously discussed steps will load the first row from the Employees table to the controls. Now, the next step is to write code for the move buttons. Listing 7-10 shows the code for all four buttons—Move First, Move Next, Move Previous, and Move Last. As you can see, this code uses the `Position` and `Count` properties of `BindingManagerBase` to set the position of the new record. `Binding-Context` and other `Binding` objects manage everything for you under the hood.

Listing 7-10. Move Next, Move Previous, Move First, and Move Last Button Code

```
Private Sub MoveFirstBtn_Click(ByVal sender As System.Object, _
   ByVal e As System.EventArgs) Handles MoveFirstBtn.Click
      Me.BindingContext(Me.ds, "Employees").Position = 0
End Sub

Private Sub MovePrevBtn_Click(ByVal sender As System.Object, _
   ByVal e As System.EventArgs) Handles MovePrevBtn.Click
      Dim idx As Int32 = _
         Me.BindingContext(Me.ds, "Employees").Position
      Me.BindingContext(Me.ds, "Employees").Position = idx - 1
End Sub

Private Sub MoveNextBtn_Click(ByVal sender As System.Object, _
   ByVal e As System.EventArgs) Handles MoveNextBtn.Click
      Dim idx As Int32 = _
         Me.BindingContext(Me.ds, "Employees").Position
      Me.BindingContext(Me.ds, "Employees").Position = idx + 1
End Sub

Private Sub MoveLastBtn_Click(ByVal sender As System.Object, _
   ByVal e As System.EventArgs) Handles MoveLastBtn.Click
      Me.BindingContext(Me.ds, "Employees").Position = _
      Me.BindingContext(Me.ds, "Employees").Count - 1
End Sub
```

When you run your application, the first record looks like Figure 7-3. Clicking the Move First, Move Next, Move Previous, and Move Last buttons will navigate you through the first, next, previous, and last records of the table (respectively).

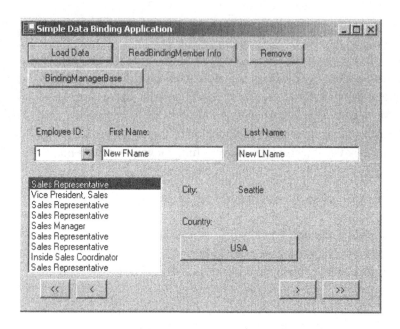

Figure 7-3. Record navigation system in action

Question and Answer

Question: When I click the move buttons, I don't see the pointer in the ListBox moving. Why not?

Answer: The ListBox control doesn't use the same binding method as simple data-bound controls such as TextBox or Label controls. We discuss this in the following section.

You just saw how to implement a record navigation system using simple data binding and simple data-bound controls. In the following section, we show you how to build a record navigation system using complex data-bound controls such as ListBox and DataGrid controls.

Working with Complex Data-Bound Controls

Unlike simple data-bound controls, the complex data-bound controls can display a set of data such as a single column or a collection of columns. The controls such as DataGrid are even able to display data from multiple tables of a database. Whereas the simple data-bound controls usually use their Text properties for binding, complex data-bound controls use their DataSource and DataMember properties.

In the following sections, we discuss some of the common complex data-bound controls such as the ComboBox, ListBox, and DataGrid.

The Role of Control Class in Data Binding

The Control class is the mother of all Windows controls. This class's basic functionality is required by visual Windows controls that are available from the Toolbox or through other wizards. The Control class handles user input through the keyboard, the mouse, and other pointing devices. It also defines the position and size of controls; however, it doesn't implement painting.

If you count the Control class members, you'll find that this class is one of the biggest classes available in the .NET Framework Library. In the following sections, you'll explore some of the data-binding functionality implemented by this class.

The Control class provides two important and useful properties, which play a vital role in the data-binding process. These properties are BindingContext and DataBinding. The BindingContext property represents the BindingContext attached to a control. As discussed earlier, BindingContext returns a single BindingManagerBase object for all data-bound controls. The BindingManagerBase object provides the synchronization for all data-bound controls. The Control class also implements the DataSourceChanged event, which raises when the data source of a control is changed. We discuss this event in more detail shortly.

Using the ListControl Class

The ListControl class is the base class for ListBox and ComboBox controls and implements the data-binding functionality. The ListControl class provides four data-binding properties: DataManager, DataSource, DisplayMember, and ValueMember.

The DataManager (read-only) property returns the CurrencyManager object associated with a ListControl class.

The DataSource property (both get and set) represents the data source for a ListControl class.

The DisplayMember (both get and set) represents a string, which specifies the property of a data source whose contents you want to display. For example, if you want to display the data of a DataTable's Name column in a ListBox control, you set DisplayMember ="Name".

The ValueMember (both get and set) property represents a string, which specifies the property of the data source from which to draw the value. The default value of this property is an empty string ("").

You'll see how to use these properties in the following samples.

ListControl DataBinding-Related Events

Besides the BindingContextChanged event, the ListControl class implements three data-binding events: OnDataSourceChanged, OnDisplayMemberChanged, and OnValueMemberChanged. The OnDataSourceChanged method raises the DataSourceChanged event. This event occurs when the DataSource property of a ListControl class is changed. The OnDisplayMemberChanged method raises the DisplayMemberChanged event, which occurs when the DisplayMember property of the control changes. The OnValueMemberChanged method raises the ValueMemberChanged event, which occurs when the ValueMember property of the control changes.

These events are useful when your program needs a notification when any of these events occur. Listing 7-11 attaches these events with event handlers. The code also shows the handler methods, which will be called when the event occurs.

Listing 7-11. Adding a ListBox *Control Event Handler*

```
' Bind data with controls
  Private Sub BindListControls()
    ComboBox1.DataSource = ds.Tables(0)
    ComboBox1.DisplayMember = "EmployeeID"
    ListBox1.DataSource = ds.Tables(0)
    ListBox1.DisplayMember = "FirstName"
    ListBox2.DataSource = ds.Tables(0)
    ListBox2.DisplayMember = "LastName"
    ListBox3.DataSource = ds.Tables(0)
    ListBox3.DisplayMember = "Title"
  End Sub
```

```
Private Sub ComboDataSourceChangedMethod(ByVal sender As Object, _
ByVal cevent As EventArgs) Handles ListBox1.DataSourceChanged
  MessageBox.Show("Data Source changed")
End Sub
Private Sub DisplayMemberChangedMethod(ByVal sender As Object, _
ByVal cevent As EventArgs) Handles ListBox1.DisplayMemberChanged
  MessageBox.Show("Display Member changed")
End Sub
Private Sub ValueMemberChangedMethod(ByVal sender As Object, _
ByVal cevent As EventArgs) Handles ListBox1.ValueMemberChanged
  MessageBox.Show("Value Member changed")
End Sub
Private Sub BindingContextChangedMethod(ByVal sender As Object, _
ByVal cevent As EventArgs) Handles ListBox1.BindingContextChanged
  MessageBox.Show("Binding Context changed")
End Sub
```

To raise these events, just change the value of the ListBox properties (see Listing 7-12).

Listing 7-12. Raising ListBox *Events*

```
Private Sub ListChangedEvents_Click(ByVal sender As System.Object, _
  ByVal e As System.EventArgs) Handles ListChangedEvents.Click
    Dim custDataSet As DataSet = New DataSet()
    sql = "SELECT CustomerID, ContactName, City FROM Customers"
    custDataSet = New DataSet("Customers")
    conn = New SqlConnection()
    conn.ConnectionString = ConnectionString
    adapter = New SqlDataAdapter(sql, conn)
    adapter.Fill(custDataSet, "Customers")
    ListBox1.DataSource = custDataSet.Tables(0)
    ListBox1.DisplayMember = "ContactName"
    ListBox1.ValueMember = "ContactName"
    conn.Close()
    conn.Dispose()
End Sub
```

Data Binding in ComboBox and ListBox Controls

Now you'll learn how to use complex data binding in a ComboBox and a ListBox control. Unlike simple data-bound controls, complex data-bound controls maintain the default binding synchronization. For instance, if you bind a data source with a ListBox and a ComboBox control, and then move from one item to another in a control, you can see the selection change in the second control respective to the item you select in the first control.

To prove this theory, you'll create a Windows application with a ComboBox and three ListBox controls. The final form looks like Figure 7-4.

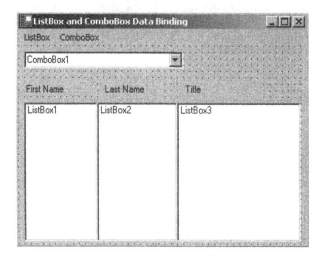

Figure 7-4. ListBox *and* ComboBox *data-binding form*

As usual, you load data in the Form_Load event. Listing 7-13 shows the event handler code, where you call the FillDataSet and BindListControl methods.

Listing 7-13. The Form Load Event Handler

```
Private Sub Form1_Load(ByVal sender As System.Object, _
  ByVal e As System.EventArgs) Handles MyBase.Load
    FillDataSet()
    BindListControls()
End Sub
```

The FillDataSet method simply opens the connection and fills data in a DataSet. Listing 7-14 shows this method.

Listing 7-14. The FillDataSet *Method*

```
' Fill DataSEt
Private Sub FillDataSet()
    ds = New DataSet()
    sql = "SELECT * FROM Employees"
    ds = New DataSet("Employees")
    conn = New SqlConnection()
    conn.ConnectionString = ConnectionString
    adapter = New SqlDataAdapter(sql, conn)
    adapter.Fill(ds, "Employees")
    conn.Close()
    conn.Dispose()
End Sub
```

The BindListControls method is where you bind the ComboBox and ListBox controls. Listing 7-15 shows the BindListControls method. As you can see, this code binds the ComboBox to the EmployeeID column and binds the three ListBox controls to the FirstName, LastName, and Title columns.

Listing 7-15. Binding ListBox *and* ComboBox *Controls*

```
' Bind data with controls
Private Sub BindListControls()
    ComboBox1.DataSource = ds.Tables(0)
    ComboBox1.DisplayMember = "EmployeeID"
    ListBox1.DataSource = ds.Tables(0)
    ListBox1.DisplayMember = "FirstName"
    ListBox2.DataSource = ds.Tables(0)
    ListBox2.DisplayMember = "LastName"
    ListBox3.DataSource = ds.Tables(0)
    ListBox3.DisplayMember = "Title"
End Sub
```

If you run the application and select any record in the ComboBox or ListBox controls, you'll see that the other controls select the correct value. For instance, if you select the sixth record in the ComboBox, all of the ListBox controls reflect this choice (see Figure 7-5).

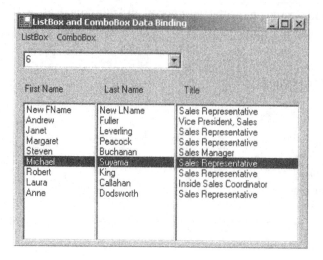

Figure 7-5. Data synchronization in ComboBox *and* ListBox *controls*

Data Binding in a DataGrid Control

The DataGrid control is much more powerful than any other data-bound control. It's also capable of displaying data relations. A DataGrid control displays data in a tabular, scrollable, and editable grid. Like other data-bound controls, a DataGrid control can display data from various sources with the help of its DataSource property. The DataSource property can be a DataTable, DataView, DataSet, or DataViewManager.

When a DataSet or a DataViewManager contains data from more than one table, you can specify what table you want to display in the DataGrid property by using the DataMember property. For example, let's say you have a DataSet that contains two tables—Customers and Orders. By default, if you bind a DataSet, it'll display data from both tables. But if you want to display data from the Customers table only, you need to set the DataMember property to the table's name. Listing 7-16 sets the DataSource and DataMember properties of a DataGrid.

Listing 7-16. Setting the DataSource *and* DataMember *Properties of a* DataGrid *Control*

```
ds = New DataSet()
sql = "SELECT * FROM Customers"
ds = New DataSet()
adapter = New SqlDataAdapter(sql, conn)
adapter.Fill(ds)
DataGrid1.DataSource = ds
DataGrid1.DataMember = "Customers"
```

You can also set the DataSource and DataMember properties by using the DataGrid control's SetDataBinding method. This method takes the first argument as a dataSource and the second argument as a dataMember. Typically, a data source is a DataSet, and the dataMember is the name of a table available in the DataSet. The following code shows how to call the SetDataBinding method of a DataGrid control:

```
DataGrid1.SetDataBinding(ds, "Customers")
```

You'll use the DataGrid control and its members throughout this chapter.

Deleting Data Binding

Removing data binding from a data-bound control is simple. The following code snippet deletes data binding from a DataGrid control:

```
DataGrid1.DataSource = null;
DataGrid1.DataMember = "";
```

The DataGrid: Super Data-Bound Control

The DataGrid control is one of the most flexible and versatile controls in Windows Forms. In this section, we discuss some of the DataGrid functionality.

The DataGrid class represents the DataGrid control in Windows Forms. Before writing any code, you'll learn about the DataGrid class properties and methods. Figure 7-6 shows a DataGrid's parent items and background, and Figure 7-7 shows some of the DataGrid parts.

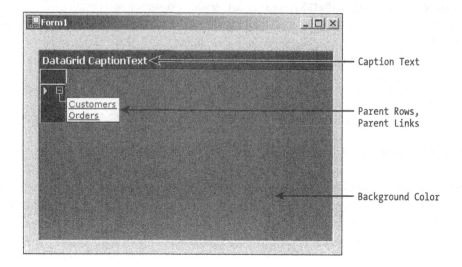

Figure 7-6. The DataGrid*'s parent items and background*

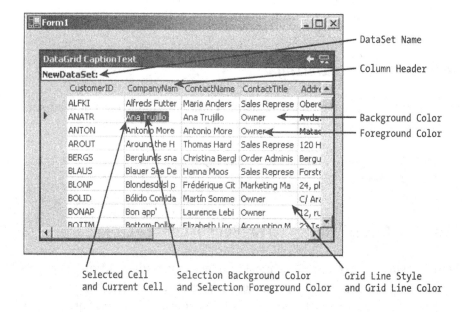

Figure 7-7. The DataGrid*'s parts*

Understanding the DataGrid Class Members

Like all other Windows controls, the DataGrid inherits from the Control class, which means that the data-binding functionality defined in the Control class is available in the DataGrid control. Besides the hundreds of members implemented in the Control class, the DataGrid provides many more members. Table 7-2 describes the DataGrid class properties.

Table 7-2. The DataGrid *Class Properties*

PROPERTY	DESCRIPTION
AllowNavigation	Indicates whether navigation is allowed. True or false. Both get and set.
AllowSorting	Indicates whether sorting is allowed. True or false. Both get and set.
AlternatingBackColor	Background color of alternative rows.
BackColor	Background color of the grid.
BackgroundColor	Color of the nonrow area of the grid. This is the background color if the grid has no rows.
BorderStyle	Style of the border.
CaptionBackColor	Background color of caption.
CaptionFont	Font of caption.
CaptionForeColor	Foreground color of caption.
CaptionText	Caption text.
CaptionVisible	Indicates whether caption is visible.
ColumnHeadersVisible	Indicates whether column headers are visible.
CurrentCell	Returns current selected cell.
CurrentRowIndex	Index of the selected row.
DataMember	Represents the data sources among multiple data sources. If there's only one data source, such as a DataTable or a DataSet with a single table, there's no need to set this property. Both get and set.
DataSource	Represents the data source such as a DataSet, a DataTable, or Ilist.
FirstVisibleColumn	Index of the first visible column.
FlatMode	FlatMode. Type of FlatMode enumeration.
ForeColor	Foreground color.
GridLineColor	Color of grid lines.

Table 7-2. The DataGrid *Class Properties (Continued)*

PROPERTY	DESCRIPTION
GridLineStyle	Style of grid lines.
HeaderBackColor	Background color of column headers.
HeaderFont	Font of column headers.
HeaderForeColor	Foreground color of column headers.
Item	Value of the specified cell.
LinkColor	Color of the text that you can click to navigate to a child table.
LinkHoverColor	Link color changes to when the mouse moves over it.
ParentRowBackColor	Background color of parent rows. Parent rows are rows that allow you to move to child tables.
ParentRowForeColor	Foreground color of parent rows.
ParentRowLabelStyle	Label style of parent rows.
ParentRowsVisible	Indicates whether parent rows are visible.
PreferredColumnWidth	Default width of columns in pixel.
PreferredRowHeight	Default height of rows in pixels.
ReadOnly	Indicates whether grid is read only.
RowHeaderVisible	Indicates whether row header is visible.
RowHeaderWidth	Width of row headers.
SelectionBackColor	Background color of selected rows.
SelectionForeColor	Foreground color of selected rows.
TableStyles	Table style. DataGridTableStyle type.
VisibleColumnCount	Total number of visible columns.
VisibleRowCount	Total number of visible rows.
HorizScrollBar	Protected. Returns the horizontal scroll bar of the grid.
VertScrollBar	Protected. Returns the horizontal scroll bar of the grid.
ListManager	Protected. Returns the CurrencyManager of the grid.

Table 7-3 describes the DataGrid class methods.

Table 7-3. The DataGrid *Class Methods*

METHOD	DESCRIPTION
BeginEdit	Starts the editing operation
BeginInit	Begins the initialization of grid that is used on a form or used by other components
Collapse	Collapses children if a grid has parent and child relationship nodes expanded
EndEdit	Ends the editing operation
EndInit	Ends grid initialization
Expand	Expands children if grid has children in a parent/child relation
GetCurrentCellBounds	Returns a rectangle that specifies the four corners of the selected cell
HitTest	Gets information when clicking on the grid
IsExpanded	True if node of the specified row is expanded; otherwise false
IsSelected	True if specified row is selected; otherwise false
NavigateBack	Navigates to the table previously displayed in the grid
NavigateTo	Navigates to the table specified by the row and relation name
ResetAlternatingBackColor	Resets the AlternatingBackColor property to the default color
ResetBackColor	Resets background color to default
ResetGridLineColor	Resets grid lines color to default
ResetHeaderBackColor	Resets header background to default
ResetHeaderFont	Resets header font to default
ResetHeaderForeColor	Resets header foreground color to default
ResetLinkColor	Resets link color to default
ResetSelectionBackColor	Resets selection background color to default
ResetSelectionForeColor	Resets selection foreground color to default
Select	Selects a specified row
SetDataBinding	Sets the DataSource and DataMember properties
UnSelect	Unselects a specified row

Besides the methods described in Table 7-3, the DataGrid class provides some protected methods (see Table 7-4).

Table 7-4. The DataGrid *Class Protected Methods*

PROTECTED METHOD	DESCRIPTION
CancelEditing	Cancels the current edit operation and rolls back all changes
GridHScrolled	Listens for the horizontal scroll bar's scroll event
GridVScrolled	Listens for the vertical scroll bar's scroll event
OnBackButtonClicked	Listens for the caption's Back button clicked event
OnBorderStyleChanged	Raises the BorderStyleChanged event
OnCaptionVisibleChanged	Raises the CaptionVisibleChanged event
OnDataSourceChanged	Raises the DataSourceChanged event
OnFlatModeChanged	Raises the FlatModeChanged event
OnNavigate	Raises the Navigate event
OnParentRowsLabelStyleChanged	Raises the ParentRowsLabelStyleChanged event
OnParentRowsVisibleChanged	Raises the ParentRowsVisibleChanged event
OnReadOnlyChanged	Raises the ReadOnlyChanged event
OnRowHeaderClick	Raises the RowHeaderClick event
OnScroll	Raises the Scroll event
OnShowParentDetailsButtonClicked	Raises the ShowParentDetailsButtonClick event
ProcessGridKey	Processes keys for grid navigation
ProcessTabKey	Gets a value indicating whether the Tab key should be processed
ResetSelection	Turns off selection for all rows that are selected

Exploring the DataGrid Helper Objects

The DataGrid class comes with 13 helper objects (classes, structures, and enumerations). What do we mean by *helper classes*? Helper classes provide simple methods to access some of the more complicated aspects of the DataGrid class. These helper objects are DataGrid.HitTestInfo, the DataGrid.HitTestType enumeration, DataGridBoolColumn, the DataGridCell structure, DataGridColumnStyle, DataGridColumnStyle.CompModSwitches, the DataGridColumnStype.DataGridColumnHeaderAccessibleObject DataGridLineStyle enumeration, the DataGridParentRowsLabelStyle enumeration, DataGridPreferredColumnWidthTypeConverter,

DataGridTableStyle, DataGridTextBox, and DataGridTextBoxColumn. We discuss some of these objects in the following section. You'll see the rest of them later in this chapter.

Understanding the DataGrid and DataGrid Column Styles

The DataGrid control hides much more functionality in it. Not only can it display data and data relations, it also provides functionality to customize its styles including color, text, caption, and font. The TableStyles property of DataGrid opens the door for formatting a grid and its columns. The GridStyles property returns an object of GridTableStyleCollection, which is a collection of DataGridTableStyle.

DataGridTableStyle represents the style of a DataTable that can be viewed in the grid area of a DataGrid. The GridTableStyles class of DataGridTableStyle represents a collection of DataGridColumnStyle. Figure 7-8 represents the relationship between the DataGrid-related style objects. We discuss these objects in more detail in the following sections.

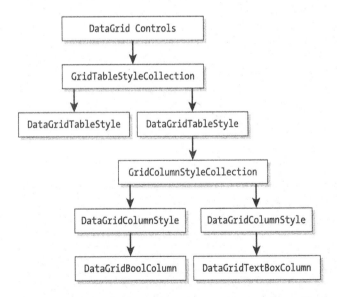

Figure 7-8. DataGrid-*related style objects*

Before you see these objects in action, you'll look at these object classes and their members briefly.

Using the DataGridTableStyle Class

The DataGridTableStyle object customizes the grid style for each DataTable in a DataSet. However, the DataGridTableStyle name is a little misleading. From its name, you would probably think the DataGridTableStyle represents the style of a DataGridTable such as its color, text, and font. Correct? Actually, DataGridTableStyle represents the grid itself. Using DataGridTableStyle, you can set the style and appearance of each DataTable, which is being displayed by the DataGrid. To specify which DataGridTableStyle is used when displaying data from a particular DataTable, set the MappingName to the TableName of a DataTable. For example, if a DataTable's TableName is Customers, you set MappingName to the following:

DataGridTableStyle.Mapping="Customers"

The DataGridTableStyle class provides similar properties and methods to those in the DataGrid class. Some of these properties are AllowSorting, AlternativeBackColor, BackColor, ColumnHeaderVisible, ForeColor, and GridColumnStyle.

Using the GridColumnStyles Property

The GridColumnStyles property returns a collection of columns available in a DataGridTableStyle as a GridColumnStylesCollection, which is a collection of Data-GridColumnStyle objects. By default all columns are available through this property.

Using the GridTableStyleCollection Members

The GridTableStyleCollection is a collection of DataGridTableStyle. The TableStyle property of DataGrid represents and returns a collection of DataGridTableStyle objects as a GridTableStylesCollection object.

TIP DataGridTableStyle *is useful when it comes to managing a* DataGrid's *style programmatically. One of the real-world usages of* DataGridTableStyle *is when you need to change the column styles of a* DataGrid *or want to move columns from one position to another programmatically.*

Unlike other collection objects, by default the GridTableStylesCollection doesn't contain any DataGridTableStyle objects. You need to add DataGridTableStyle objects to the collection. By default a DataGrid displays default settings such as color, text, font, width, and formatting. By default all columns of DataTable are displayed.

Constructing and Adding a DataGridStyle

You'll now learn how to create a DataGridTableStyle object and add it to the DataGrid's DataGridTableStyle collection. Listing 7-17 creates a DataGridTableStyle, set its properties, and adds two columns: a Boolean and a text box column. The DataGridBookColumn class represents a Boolean column with check boxes, and the DataGridTextBoxColumn represents a text box column. (We discuss these classes in the following sections.)

Listing 7-17. Creating and Adding a DataGridTableStyle

```
Private Sub AddDataGridStyleMethod()
    ' Create a new DataGrudTableStyle
    Dim dgTableStyle As New DataGridTableStyle()
    dgTableStyle.MappingName = "Customers"
    dgTableStyle.BackColor = Color.Gray
    dgTableStyle.ForeColor = Color.Wheat
    dgTableStyle.AlternatingBackColor = Color.AliceBlue
    dgTableStyle.GridLineStyle = DataGridLineStyle.None
    ' Add some columns to the style
    Dim boolCol As New DataGridBoolColumn()
    boolCol.MappingName = "boolCol"
    boolCol.HeaderText = "boolCol Text"
    boolCol.Width = 100
    ' Add column to GridColumnStyle
    dgTableStyle.GridColumnStyles.Add(boolCol)
    ' Text column
    Dim TextCol As New DataGridTextBoxColumn()
    TextCol.MappingName = "Name"
    TextCol.HeaderText = "Name Text"
    TextCol.Width = 200
    ' Add column to GridColumnStyle
    dgTableStyle.GridColumnStyles.Add(TextCol)
    ' Add DataGridTableStyle to the collection
    DataGrid1.TableStyles.Add(dgTableStyle)
End Sub
```

You can even create a DataGridTableStyle from a CurrencyManager. Listing 7-18 creates a DataGridTableStyle from a CurrencyManager and adds it the collection.

Listing 7-18. Creating a DataGridTableStyle from CurrencyManager

```
Private Sub CreateNewDGTableStyle()
    Dim curManager As CurrencyManager
    Dim newTableStyle As DataGridTableStyle
    curManager = CType _
    (Me.BindingContext(ds, "Customers"), CurrencyManager)
    newTableStyle = New DataGridTableStyle(curManager)
    DataGrid1.TableStyles.Add(newTableStyle)
End Sub
```

Using the DataGridColumnStyle Class

The DataGridColumnStyle represents the style of a column. You can attach a DataGridColumnStyle to each column of a DataGrid. The DataGrid can contain different types of columns such as a check box or a text box. As you saw earlier, a DataGridTableStyle contains a collection of DataGridColumnStyle objects, which can be accessed through the GridColumnStyles property of DataGridTableStyle. This object is pretty useful and allows many formatting- and style-related members. Table 7-5 describes the DataGridColumnStyle properties.

Table 7-5. The DataGridColumnStyle *Properties*

PROPERTY	DESCRIPTION
Alignment	Alignment of text in a column. Both get and set.
DataGridTableStyle	Returns the DataGridTableStyle object associated with the column.
HeaderText	Text of the column header. Both get and set.
MappingName	Name used to map the column style to a data member. Both get and set.
NullText	You can set the column text when the column has null values using this property. Both get and set.
PropertyDescriptor	PropertyDescriptor object that determines the attributes of data displayed by the column. Both get and set.
ReadOnly	Indicates if column is read only. Both get and set.
Width	Width of the column. Both get and set.

Besides the methods described in Table 7-6, the DataGridColumnStyle class provides a method, ResetHeaderText, which resets the header text to its default value of null.

Table 7-6. The DataGridColumnStyle *Methods*

METHOD	DESCRIPTION
Abort	Aborts the edit operation.
BeginUpdate	Suspends the painting operation of the column until the EndUpdate method is called.
CheckValidDataSource	If a column is not mapped to a valid property of a data source, this throws an exception.
ColumnStartEditing	Informs DataGrid that the user has start editing the column.
Commit	Completes the editing operation.
ConcedeFocus	Notifies a column that it must relinquish the focus to the control it's hosting.
Edit	Prepares the cell for editing a value.
EndUpdate	Resumes the painting of columns suspended by calling the BeginUpdate method.
EnterNullValue	Enters a DBNullValue into the column.
GetColumnValueAtRow	Returns the value in the specified row.
GetMinimumHeight	Returns the minimum height of a row.
GetPreferedHeight	Returns the height used for automatically resizing columns.
GetPreferedSize	Automatic size.
Invalidate	Redraws the column.
SetColumnValueAtRow	Sets a value in the specified row.
SetDataGrid	Sets the DataGrid to which this column belongs.
SetDataGridInColumn	Sets the DataGrid for the column.
UpdateUI	Updates the value of a row.

Using the DataGridBoolColumn Class

A DataGrid can contain different types of columns such as a check box or a text box. By default all columns are in a simple grid format. The DataGridBoolColumn class represents a Boolean column of a DataGrid. Each cell of a Boolean column contains a check box, which can be checked (true) or unchecked (false). The DataGridBoolColumn class is inherited from the DataGridColumnStyle class. Besides the functionality provided by the DataGridColumnStyle, it provides its own members. Table 7-7 describes the DataGridBoolColumn class properties.

Table 7-7. The DataGridBoolColumn *Properties*

PROPERTY	DESCRIPTION
AllowNull	Represents whether null values are allowed in this column or not (both get and set)
FalseValue	Represents the actual value of column when the value of column is set to False (both get and set)
NullValue	The actual value used when setting the value of the column to Value (both get and set)
TrueValue	Represents the actual value of column when the value of column is set to True (both get and set)

Listing 7-19 creates a new DataGridBoolColum and sets its properties.

Listing 7-19. Creating a DataGridBoolColumn

```
Dim dgCol As DataGridBoolColumn
    dgCol = CType(dtGrid.TableStyles _
 ("Customers").GridColumnStyles("Current"), DataGridBoolColumn)
    dgCol.TrueValue = True
    dgCol.FalseValue = False
    dgCol.NullValue = Convert.DBNull
```

Setting DataGrid Sorting and Navigation

By default, navigation and sorting is on in a DataGrid. If a DataGrid is filled with data and you click the DataGrid header, it sorts data in ascending or descending order, depending on the current state. In other words, if the data is sorted in ascending order, right-clicking the header will sort it in descending order—and vice versa. You can activate or deactivate sorting programmatically using the AllowSorting property, which is a Boolean type. The following code shows how to set the AllowSorting property:

```
' Allow Sorting
If (allowSortingCheckBox.Checked) Then
  dtGrid.AllowSorting = True
Else
  dtGrid.AllowSorting = False
End If
```

Like the `AllowSorting` property, the `AllowNavigation` property enables or disables navigation. Setting the property to `True` indicates that navigation in a `DataGrid` is allowed and setting it to `False` means that navigation is not allowed. When you change the `AllowNavigation` property, the `AllowNavigationChanged` event is fired. Perhaps you notice in the previous samples that if a `DataSet` had more than one database table, there were links to each table? When you click a table link, the `DataGrid` opens that table. If `AllowNavigation` is `False`, then no links to child tables display. Listing 7-20 uses `AllowNavigation` and also handles the `AllowNavigationChanged` event.

Listing 7-20. `AllowNavigation` *in Action*

```
' Change navigation using AllowNavigation property
  Private Sub NavigationMenu_Click(ByVal sender As System.Object, _
  ByVal e As System.EventArgs) Handles NavigationMenu.Click
    ' Change navigation. If its true, change it to false and
    ' vice versa
    If dtGrid.AllowNavigation = True Then
      dtGrid.AllowNavigation = False
    Else
      dtGrid.AllowNavigation = True
    End If
  End Sub

  Private Sub AllowNavigationEvent(ByVal sender As Object, _
  ByVal e As System.EventArgs) Handles dtGrid.AllowNavigationChanged
    Dim nav As Boolean = dtGrid.AllowNavigation
    Dim str As String = "AllowNavigationChanged event fired. "
    If (nav) Then
      str = str + "Navigation is allowed"
      NavigationMenu.Checked = True
    Else
      str = str + "Navigation is not allowed"
      NavigationMenu.Checked = False
    End If
    MessageBox.Show(str, "AllowNavigation")
  End Sub
```

Setting DataGrid Coloring and Font Styles

As mentioned, the DataGrid provides properties to set the foreground and background color of almost every part of a DataGrid such as headers, grid lines, and so on. The DataGrid also provides font properties to set the font of the DataGrid. Listing 7-21 sets Font and Color properties of a DataGrid.

Listing 7-21. Using Some of the DataGrid's Color and Font Properties

```
' Setting DataGrid's Color and Font properties
dtGrid.BackColor = Color.Beige
dtGrid.ForeColor = Color.Black
dtGrid.BackgroundColor = Color.Red
dtGrid.SelectionBackColor = Color.Blue
dtGrid.SelectionForeColor = Color.Yellow
dtGrid.GridLineColor = Color.Blue
dtGrid.HeaderBackColor = Color.Black
dtGrid.HeaderForeColor = Color.Gold
'dtGrid.AlternatingBackColor = Color.AliceBlue
dtGrid.LinkColor = Color.Pink
dtGrid.HeaderFont = New Font("Verdana", FontStyle.Bold)
dtGrid.Font = New Font("Verdana", 8, FontStyle.Regular)
```

TIP *You can customize a DataGrid and allow the user to select a color and font for each part of the DataGrid at runtime as well as at design-time using the Properties window.*

Setting Caption Properties

You just saw the Font property of the DataGrid itself. The DataGrid also provides properties to set the caption's fonts and color. For example, Listing 7-22 sets the font, background color, and foreground color of caption of the DataGrid.

Listing 7-22. The DataGrid*'s Caption Properties*

```
dtGrid.CaptionText = "Customized DataGrid"
dtGrid.CaptionBackColor = System.Drawing.Color.Green
dtGrid.CaptionForeColor = System.Drawing.Color.Yellow
dtGrid.CaptionFont = New Font("Verdana", 10, FontStyle.Bold)
```

Seeing DataGridTableStyle and DataGridColumnStyle in Action

A common use of DataGridColumnStyle is changing the positions of a DataGrid's columns programmatically. In the following sections, you'll see some common usages of DataGridTableStyle and DataGridColumnStyle.

As mentioned, you'll see some real-world uses of data-bound controls in this chapter. Specifically, you'll learn how to add check box and text box columns to a DataGrid. You also know that the GridColumnStyles property returns a collection of DataGridTableStyle as an object of GridColumnStyleCollection. Using GridColumnStyleCollection you can add and remove column styles to a collection. This is what you'll use to add new columns to a collection and attach them to a DataGridTableStyle.

To start this application, create a Windows application and define a DataSet variable as private:

```
Private ds As DataSet = Nothing
```

On the form's Load event, you call the CreateDataSet, DataGrid.SetDataBinding, and FillDataGrid methods (see Listing 7-23).

Listing 7-23. Form's Load *Method*

```
Private Sub Form1_Load(ByVal sender As System.Object, _
  ByVal e As System.EventArgs) Handles MyBase.Load
    ' Create in memory DataSet. You can even create
    ' a DataSet from a database
    CreateDataSet()
    ' Bind DataSet to DataGrid
    dtGrid.SetDataBinding(ds, "Employees")
    ' Fill data in DataGrid
    FillDataGrid()
  End Sub
```

The CreateDataSet method in Listing 7-24 simply creates a DataSet by creating a DataTable and adding three columns: EmployeeID (integer), Name (string), and StillWorking (Boolean). This method also adds four rows to the DataTable and adds the DataTable to a DataSet.

Listing 7-24. The CreateDataSet *Method*

```
' Create a DataSet with two tables and populate it.
  Private Sub CreateDataSet()
    ' Create a DataSet, add a DataTable
    ' Add DataTable to DataSet
    ds = New DataSet("ds")
    Dim EmployeeTable As DataTable = New DataTable("Employees")
    ' Create DataColumn objects and add to the DataTAable
    Dim dtType As System.Type
    dtType = System.Type.GetType("System.Int32")
    Dim EmpIDCol As DataColumn = _
    New DataColumn("EmployeeID", dtType)
    Dim EmpNameCol As DataColumn = New DataColumn("Name")
    dtType = System.Type.GetType("System.Boolean")
    Dim EmpStatusCol As DataColumn = New DataColumn("StillWorking", dtType)
    EmployeeTable.Columns.Add(EmpIDCol)
    EmployeeTable.Columns.Add(EmpNameCol)
    EmployeeTable.Columns.Add(EmpStatusCol)
    ' Add first records
    Dim row As DataRow = EmployeeTable.NewRow()
    row("EmployeeID") = 1001
    row("Name") = "Jay Leno"
    row("StillWorking") = False
    EmployeeTable.Rows.Add(row)
    ' Add second records
    row = EmployeeTable.NewRow()
    row("EmployeeID") = 1002
    row("Name") = "Peter Kurten"
    row("StillWorking") = True
    EmployeeTable.Rows.Add(row)
    ' Add third records
    row = EmployeeTable.NewRow()
    row("EmployeeID") = 1003
    row("Name") = "Mockes Pope"
    row("StillWorking") = False
    EmployeeTable.Rows.Add(row)
```

```
    ' Add fourth records
    row = EmployeeTable.NewRow()
    row("EmployeeID") = 1004
    row("Name") = "Rock Kalson"
    row("StillWorking") = True
    EmployeeTable.Rows.Add(row)
    ' Add the tables to the DataSet
    ds.Tables.Add(EmployeeTable)
End Sub
```

In Listing 7-25, the FillDataSet method creates a DataGridTableStyle and sets its properties. After that, it creates two DataGridTextBoxColumns and one DataGrid-BoolColumn and sets their properties. Also, it makes sure that the MappingName of the columns matches with the name of the columns of the DataTable. After creating each column, you add these methods to the column collection by using the DataGrid.GridColumnStyles.Add method. Finally, you add DataGridTableStyle to the DataGrid by using the DataGrid.TableStyles.Add method. After doing so, the DataGrid should have a new style with a check box and two text box columns.

Listing 7-25. The FillDataGrid *Method*

```
Private Sub FillDataGrid()
    ' Create a DataGridTableStyle and set its properties
    Dim dgTableStyle As DataGridTableStyle = New DataGridTableStyle()
    dgTableStyle.MappingName = "Employees"
    dgTableStyle.AlternatingBackColor = Color.Gray
    dgTableStyle.BackColor = Color.Black
    dgTableStyle.AllowSorting = True
    dgTableStyle.ForeColor = Color.White
    ' Create a DataGridColumnStyle. Add it to DataGridTableStyle
    Dim dgTextCol As DataGridColumnStyle = New DataGridTextBoxColumn()
    dgTextCol.MappingName = "Name"
    dgTextCol.HeaderText = "Employee Name"
    dgTextCol.Width = 100
    dgTableStyle.GridColumnStyles.Add(dgTextCol)
    ' Get PropertyDescriptorCollection by calling GetItemProperties
    Dim pdc As PropertyDescriptorCollection = Me.BindingContext _
    (ds, "Employees").GetItemProperties()
    'Create a DataGrodTextBoxColu
    Dim dgIntCol As DataGridTextBoxColumn = _
    New DataGridTextBoxColumn(pdc("EmployeeID"), "i", True)
    dgIntCol.MappingName = "EmployeeID"
```

```
      dgIntCol.HeaderText = "Employee ID"
      dgIntCol.Width = 100
      dgTableStyle.GridColumnStyles.Add(dgIntCol)
      ' Add CheckBox column using DataGridCoolColumn
      Dim dgBoolCol As DataGridColumnStyle = New DataGridBoolColumn()
      dgBoolCol.MappingName = "StillWorking"
      dgBoolCol.HeaderText = "Boolean Column"
      dgBoolCol.Width = 100
      dgTableStyle.GridColumnStyles.Add(dgBoolCol)
      ' Add table style to DataGrid
      dtGrid.TableStyles.Add(dgTableStyle)
    End Sub
```

Seeing HitTest in Action

You can use a *hit test* to get information about a point where a user clicks a control. There are many real-world usages of a hit test. For example, say you want to display two pop-up menus when a user right-clicks a certain area on a DataGrid. One area is on the DataGrid column header; this right-click pop-up menu will have options such as Sort Ascending, Sort Descending, Hide, and Find. As you can pretty guess from these names, the sort menu items will sort a column's data in ascending and descending order, the Hide menu item will hide (or delete) a column, and the Find menu item will search for a keyword in the selected column.

The second pop-up menu will pop up when you right-click any grid's cell. This menu will have options such as Move First, Move Previous, Move Next, and Move Last that will allow you to move to the first, previous, next, and last rows of a DataGrid.

Now, using only these two cases, you can find out what DataGrid part is processing the hit test action (in other words, which one is being clicked by the user). The HitTest method of DataGrid performs a hit test action.

Using the DataGrid.HitTestInfo Class

The HitTest method takes a point and returns the DataGrid.HitTestInfo object, which determines the part of a DataGrid clicked by the user. It's useful when you're designing a custom grid and want to do different things when user clicks different parts of the DataGrid.

The DataGrid.HitTestInfo class has three properties: Column, Row, and Type. The Column and Row properties represent the number of the column and row that the user has clicked. The Type property specifies the part of the DataGrid that is clicked.

The DataGrid.HitTestType enumeration is used as the Type property, which is defined in Table 7-8.

Table 7-8. The DaaGrid.HitTestType *Enumeration*

MEMBER	DESCRIPTION
Caption	Returns True if the caption was clicked.
Cell	Returns True if a cell was clicked.
ColumnHeader	Returns True if a column header was clicked.
ColumnResize	Represents the column border, the line between column headers.
None	Returns True if the background area was clicked.
ParentRow	The parent row displays information about the parent table of the currently displayed child table.
RowHeader	Returns True if the row header was clicked.
RowResize	Returns True if the line between rows.

You can also check the Type property against the combination of DataGrid.HitTestType enumeration members. Listing 7-26 is the mouse down event handler of a DataGrid, which tracks almost every portion of a DataGrid and generates a message when you right-click a DataGrid. Simply copy this code, right-click the DataGrid, and see it in action.

Listing 7-26. Seeing HitTest *in Action*

```
' DataGrid Mouse down event handler
  Private Sub dtGrid_MouseDown(ByVal sender As Object, _
  ByVal e As System.Windows.Forms.MouseEventArgs) Handles dtGrid.MouseDown
    Dim grid As DataGrid = CType(sender, DataGrid)
    Dim hti As DataGrid.HitTestInfo
    ' When right mouse button was clicked
    If (e.Button = MouseButtons.Right) Then
      hti = grid.HitTest(e.X, e.Y)
      Select Case hti.Type
        Case DataGrid.HitTestType.None
          MessageBox.Show("Background")
        Case DataGrid.HitTestType.Cell
          MessageBox.Show("Cell - Row:" & hti.Row & ", Col: " & hti.Column)
        Case DataGrid.HitTestType.ColumnHeader
          MessageBox.Show("Column header " & hti.Column)
        Case DataGrid.HitTestType.RowHeader
```

```
            MessageBox.Show("Row header " & hti.Row)
        Case DataGrid.HitTestType.ColumnResize
            MessageBox.Show("Column seperater " & hti.Column)
        Case DataGrid.HitTestType.RowResize
            MessageBox.Show("Row seperater " & hti.Row)
        Case DataGrid.HitTestType.Caption
            MessageBox.Show("Caption")
        Case DataGrid.HitTestType.ParentRows
            MessageBox.Show("Parent row")
    End Select
  End If
End Sub
```

Reshuffling DataGrid Columns

How about reshuffling or moving DataGrid columns? Reshuffling a DataGrid's columns is a simple trick. You need to find which column you want to reshuffle. You can do this by using the column name or column index. In this sample, you'll use the column index.

How about reading information about a DataGridTableStyle and its columns? The following code reads information about a grid's tables and their names:

```
Dim gridStyle As DataGridTableStyle
For Each gridStyle In DataGrid1.TableStyles
  infoStr = "Table Name: " + gridStyle.MappingName
  Dim colStyle As DataGridColumnStyle
  For Each colStyle In gridStyle.GridColumnStyles
    infoStr = "Column: " + colStyle.MappingName
  Next
Next
```

Let's see this in action. Create a Windows application, add a DataGrid control, two Button controls, two Label controls, two TextBox controls, and a ListBox control. Next, set their properties and positions. The final form looks like Figure 7-9. As you can see, to exchange two columns, you enter column index in both text boxes and click the Exchange Columns button.

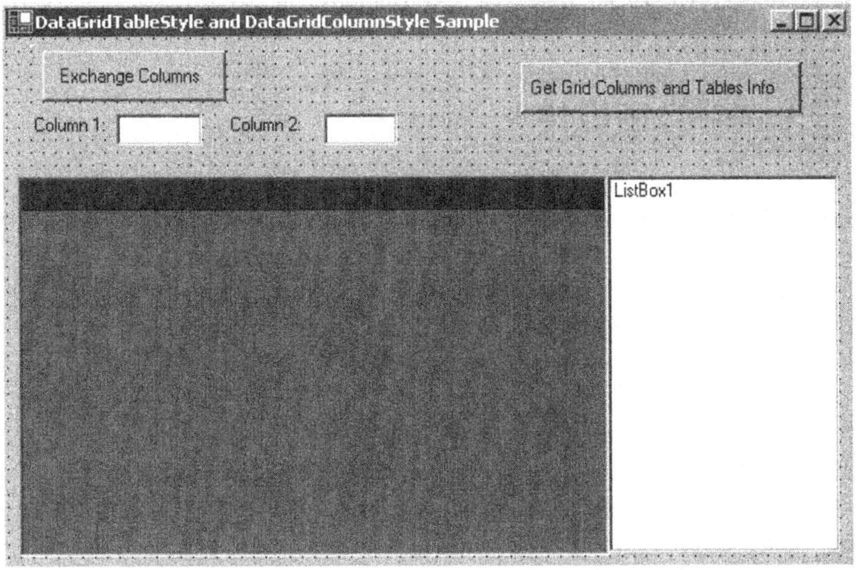

Figure 7-9. Column reshuffling form

Now let's write the code. As usual, you first define some variables:

```
' Developer defined variables
  Private conn As SqlConnection = Nothing
  Private ConnectionString As String = "Integrated Security=SSPI;" & _
     "Initial Catalog=Northwind;Data Source=MCB;"
  Private sql As String = Nothing
  Private ds As DataSet = Nothing
  Private adapter As SqlDataAdapter = Nothing
```

Next, add a new method called FillDataGrid, which fills the DataGrid from the Customers table of the Northwind database. You call the FillDataGrid method from the form's Load event handler (see Listing 7-27). You can also see from the FillDataGrid method, this code adds DataGridTableStyle to each DataTable in a DataSet.

> **CAUTION** *What if you don't add DataGridTableStyle? By default, the* DataGrid *doesn't have any* DataGridTableStyle *and uses the default* DataGridTableStyle. *To make this program work, you must add it manually.*

Listing 7-27. The FillDataGrid *and* Form_Load *Methods*

```
    Private Sub Form1_Load(ByVal sender As System.Object, _
    ByVal e As System.EventArgs) Handles MyBase.Load
      FillDataGrid()
    End Sub
  Private Sub FillDataGrid()
      sql = "SELECT * FROM Customers"
      conn = New SqlConnection(connectionString)
      adapter = New SqlDataAdapter(sql, conn)
      ds = New DataSet("Customers")
      adapter.Fill(ds, "Customers")
      DataGrid1.DataSource = ds.Tables(0).DefaultView
      ' By default there is no DataGridTableStyle object.
      ' Add all DataSet table's style to the DataGrid
      Dim dTable As DataTable
      For Each dTable In ds.Tables
        Dim dgStyle As DataGridTableStyle = New DataGridTableStyle()
        dgStyle.MappingName = dTable.TableName
        DataGrid1.TableStyles.Add(dgStyle)
      Next
      ' DataGrid settings
      DataGrid1.CaptionText = "DataGrid Customization"
      DataGrid1.HeaderFont = New Font("Verdana", 12)
    End Sub
```

Now you write code on the Exchange Columns button click event handler (see Listing 7-28). As you can see, you need to make sure that the text boxes aren't empty. After that you call the ReshuffleColumns method, which actually moves the columns from one position to another.

Listing 7-28. Exchanging the Button Click Handler

```
Private Sub ExchangeColsBtn_Click(ByVal sender As System.Object, _
ByVal e As System.EventArgs) Handles ExchangeColsBtn.Click
  If (TextBox1.Text.Length < 1) Then
    MessageBox.Show("Enter a number between 0 to 19")
    TextBox1.Focus()
    Return
  ElseIf (TextBox2.Text.Length < 1) Then
    MessageBox.Show("Enter a number between 0 to 19")
    TextBox1.Focus()
    Return
  End If
  ' Get column 1 and column 2 indexes
  Dim col1 As Integer = Convert.ToInt32(TextBox1.Text)
  Dim col2 As Integer = Convert.ToInt32(TextBox2.Text)
  ' Exchange columns
  ReshuffleColumns(col1, col2, "Customers", DataGrid1)
End Sub
```

As mentioned earlier, moving column positions in a grid involves resetting a DataGridTableStyle. As you can see from Listing 7-29, you read the current Data-GridTableStyle and create a new DataGridTableStyle. Next, you copy the entire current DataGridTableStyle including the two columns that you want to exchange and then change positions of these columns. Next, you remove the current Data-GridTableStyle from the DataGrid and apply the new DataGridTableStyle by using the DataGrid.TableStyles.Remove and DataGrid.TableStyles.Add methods.

Listing 7-29. The ReshuffleColumns *Method*

```
Private Sub ReshuffleColumns(ByVal col1 As Integer, _
ByVal col2 As Integer, ByVal mapName As String, ByVal grid As DataGrid)
  Dim existingTableStyle As DataGridTableStyle = grid.TableStyles(mapName)
  Dim counter As Integer = existingTableStyle.GridColumnStyles.Count
  Dim NewTableStyle As DataGridTableStyle = New DataGridTableStyle()
  NewTableStyle.MappingName = mapName
  Dim i As Integer
  For i = 0 To counter - 1 Step +1
    If i <> col1 And col1 < col2 Then
      NewTableStyle.GridColumnStyles.Add _
      (existingTableStyle.GridColumnStyles(i))
    End If
```

```
    If i = col2 Then
      NewTableStyle.GridColumnStyles.Add _
      (existingTableStyle.GridColumnStyles(col1))
    End If
    If i <> col1 And col1 > col2 Then
      NewTableStyle.GridColumnStyles.Add _
      (existingTableStyle.GridColumnStyles(i))
    End If
  Next
  ' Remove the existing table style and add new style
  grid.TableStyles.Remove(existingTableStyle)
  grid.TableStyles.Add(NewTableStyle)
End Sub
```

Reading information about a DataGrid's columns using a DataGridColumnStyle is simple. You just read the GridColumnStyleCollection using the GridColumnStyles property of DataGridTableStyle. Listing 7-30 reads a DataGrid's column styles and adds them to the ListBox control.

Listing 7-30. Getting a DataGrid Columns' Style Using DataGridColumnStyle

```
Private Sub GetInfoBtn_Click(ByVal sender As System.Object, _
ByVal e As System.EventArgs) Handles GetInfoBtn.Click
  Dim infoStr As String = "Visible Rows: " + _
  DataGrid1.VisibleRowCount.ToString()
  ListBox1.Items.Add(infoStr)
  infoStr = "Visible Cols: " + _
  DataGrid1.VisibleColumnCount.ToString()
  ListBox1.Items.Add(infoStr)
  infoStr = "Total Rows: " + _
  ds.Tables(0).Rows.Count.ToString()
  ListBox1.Items.Add(infoStr)
  infoStr = "Total Cols: " + _
  ds.Tables(0).Columns.Count.ToString()
  ListBox1.Items.Add(infoStr)
  ' Get all table styles in the Grid and Column Styles
  ' which returns table and column names
  Dim gridStyle As DataGridTableStyle
```

```
For Each gridStyle In DataGrid1.TableStyles
  infoStr = "Table Name: " + gridStyle.MappingName
  ListBox1.Items.Add(infoStr)
  Dim colStyle As DataGridColumnStyle
  For Each colStyle In gridStyle.GridColumnStyles
    infoStr = "Column: " + colStyle.MappingName
    ListBox1.Items.Add(infoStr)
  Next
Next
End Sub
```

Now run the application and enter **1** in the Column 1 box and enter **2** in the Column 2 box and then click the Exchange Columns buttons. You'll see both columns switched their positions. Now if you click the Get Grid Columns and Tables Info button, the output looks like Figure 7-10.

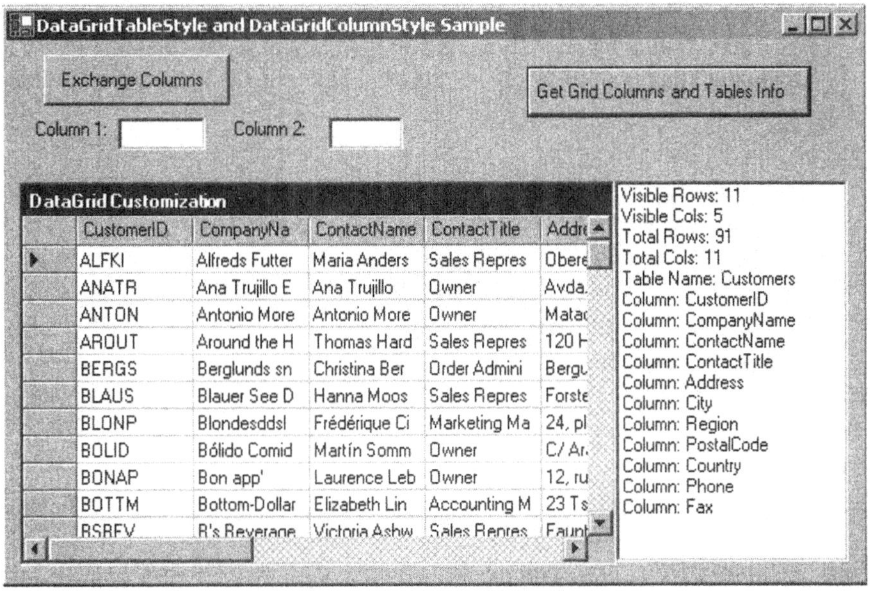

Figure 7-10. Getting a DataGrid *control's column styles*

Getting a Column Header Name

Listing 7-31 returns the column name when a user right-clicks a DataGrid column header.

Listing 7-31. Getting a DataGrid *Column Header Name*

```
Private Sub DataGrid1_MouseDown(ByVal sender As Object, _
ByVal e As System.Windows.Forms.MouseEventArgs) Handles DataGrid1.MouseDown
  Dim str As String = Nothing
  Dim pt As Point = New Point(e.X, e.Y)
  Dim hti As DataGrid.HitTestInfo = DataGrid1.HitTest(pt)
  ' If right mouse button clicked
  If e.Button = MouseButtons.Right Then
    If hti.Type = DataGrid.HitTestType.ColumnHeader Then
      Dim gridStyle As DataGridTableStyle = _
      DataGrid1.TableStyles("Customers")
      str = gridStyle.GridColumnStyles(hti.Column).MappingName.ToString()
      MessageBox.Show("Column Header " + str)
    End If
  End If
  ' If left mouse button clicked
  If e.Button = MouseButtons.Left Then
    If hti.Type = DataGrid.HitTestType.Cell Then
      str = "Column: " + hti.Column.ToString()
      str += ", Row: " + hti.Row.ToString()
      MessageBox.Show(str)
    End If
  End If
End Sub
```

Hiding a DataGrid's Columns

Now you'll learn a few more uses of a DataGrid control. Hiding a DataGrid column is simply a job of finding the right column and setting its Width property to 0. For an example, see the TotalDataGrid sample that comes with the downloads from www.apress.com.

To make your program look better, you'll create a right-click pop-up menu, as shown in Figure 7-11.

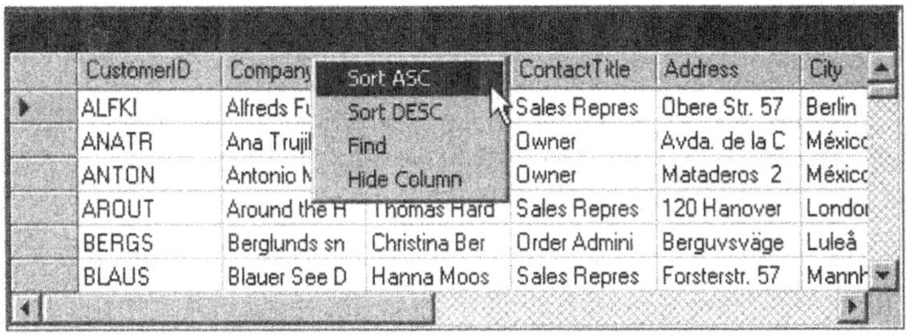

Figure 7-11. Pop-up menu on DataGrid *right-click menu*

To create a pop-up menu, you declare a ContextMenu and four MenuItem objects as sortAscMenu, sortDescMenu, findMenu, and hideMenu. You also define two more variables to store the current DataGridColumnStyle and column name as follows:

```
Private curColName As String = Nothing
Private curColumnStyle As DataGridColumnStyle
```

If DataGrid.HitTestType is ColumnHeader, you add menu items and get the current column, as shown in Listing 7-32. In this listing, you simply store the current DataGridColumnStyle and the name of the column.

Listing 7-32. Getting the Current DataGridColumnStyle

```
Case DataGrid.HitTestType.ColumnHeader
        ' Add context menus
        popUpMenu = New ContextMenu()
        popUpMenu.MenuItems.Add("Sort ASC")
        popUpMenu.MenuItems.Add("Sort DESC")
        popUpMenu.MenuItems.Add("Find")
        popUpMenu.MenuItems.Add("Hide Column")
        Me.ContextMenu = popUpMenu
        Me.BackColor = Color.Sienna
        sortAscMenu = Me.ContextMenu.MenuItems(0)
        sortDescMenu = Me.ContextMenu.MenuItems(1)
        findMenu = Me.ContextMenu.MenuItems(2)
        hideMenu = Me.ContextMenu.MenuItems(3)
        ' Find the Column header name
        Dim gridStyle As DataGridTableStyle = _
        dtGrid.TableStyles("Customers")
        curColName = gridStyle.GridColumnStyles _
        (hti.Column).MappingName.ToString()
      curColumnStyle = gridStyle.GridColumnStyles(hti.Column)
```

Finally, you write the Find menu button click event handler and set
curColumnStyle.Width to 0:

```
Private Sub hideMenuHandler(ByVal sender As System.Object, _
 ByVal e As System.EventArgs) Handles hideMenu.Click
    curColumnStyle.Width = 0
 End Sub
```

Implementing Custom Sorting in a DataGrid

By default a DataGrid provides you with sorting options when you click a DataGrid
column. But there may be occasions when you don't want to use the default
behavior and instead want to implement your own custom sorting.

In Figure 7-11, you saw the Sort ASC and Sort DESC menu options. As you
probably remember from Chapter 3 and Chapter 4, sorting is easy to implement in
a DataView. To sort a DataView, you simply set the Sort property of the DataView to
the column name and to ASC or DESC for ascending and descending sorting,
respectively. Listing 7-33 shows the Sort ASC and Sort DESC menu event handler
code.

Listing 7-33. Sorting a DataGrid *Control's Columns*

```
Private Sub SortAscMenuHandler(ByVal sender As System.Object, _
ByVal e As System.EventArgs) Handles sortAscMenu.Click
    Dim dv As DataView = ds.Tables("Customers").DefaultView
    dv.Sort = curColName + " ASC"
    dtGrid.DataSource = dv
 End Sub
 Private Sub SortDescMenuHandler(ByVal sender As System.Object, _
 ByVal e As System.EventArgs) Handles sortDescMenu.Click
   Dim dv As DataView = ds.Tables("Customers").DefaultView
   dv.Sort = curColName + " DESC"
   dtGrid.DataSource = dv
End Sub
```

Building a DataGrid Record Navigation System

Move methods are one of the features of the ADO recordset that don't appear in ADO.NET. A recordset provides MoveFirst, MoveNext, MovePrevious, and MoveLast methods to move to the first, next, previous and last record in a recordset (respectively). In this example, you'll implement move functionality in a DataGrid control.

Listing 7-34 implements move functionality in a custom recordset class called CustRecordSet.vb. (We already discussed how you can use BindingContext to move the current pointer from one position to another.) In this code, CreateRecordSet simply fills and binds a DataSet to the grid. The FirstRecord, PrevRecord, NextRecord, and LastRecord methods set the current position of the pointer to the first row, current row –1, current row +1, and the last row (respectively).

NOTE *In this example, the table name is Customers. You may want to customize the name so it can work for any database table.*

Listing 7-34. CustRecordSet.vb

```vb
Imports System.Data.SqlClient

Public Class CustRecordSet
    Private dataAdapter As SqlDataAdapter = Nothing
    Private dataSet As DataSet = Nothing
    Private dtGrid As DataGrid = Nothing
    Private frm As Form = Nothing
    Private mapName As String = Nothing

    Public Sub CreateRecordSet(ByVal conn As SqlConnection, _
    ByVal sql As String, ByVal grid As DataGrid, ByVal curForm As Form, _
    ByVal tableName As String)
        Me.dataAdapter = New SqlDataAdapter(sql, conn)
        Me.dataSet = New DataSet("Customers")
        Me.dataAdapter.Fill(Me.dataSet, "Customers")
        dtGrid = grid
        frm = curForm
        mapName = tableName
        dtGrid.DataSource = Me.dataSet
        dtGrid.DataMember = "Customers"
    End Sub
```

```
Public Sub FirstRecord()
  If frm.BindingContext(Me.dataSet, mapName) Is Nothing Then
    Return
  End If
  frm.BindingContext(Me.dataSet, mapName).Position = 0
End Sub
Public Sub PrevRecord()
  If frm.BindingContext(Me.dataSet, mapName) Is Nothing Then
    Return
  End If
  frm.BindingContext(Me.dataSet, mapName).Position -= 1
End Sub
Public Sub NextRecord()
  If frm.BindingContext(Me.dataSet, mapName) Is Nothing Then
    Return
  End If
  frm.BindingContext(Me.dataSet, mapName).Position += 1

End Sub
Public Sub LastRecord()
  If frm.BindingContext(Me.dataSet, mapName) Is Nothing Then
    Return
  End If
  frm.BindingContext(Me.dataSet, mapName).Position = _
  frm.BindingContext(Me.dataSet, mapName).Count - 1
End Sub

End Class
```

Now create a Windows application and add a DataGrid control and four Button controls (Move First, Move Next, Move Previous, and Move Last). The form's Load event calls FillDataSet, which creates a new CustRecordSet object and calls its CreateRecordSet method, which in turn fills data in a DataGrid control and binds a DataSet with the DataGrid control (see Listing 7-35).

Listing 7-35. Creating a Custom Recordset

```
' form load
  Private Sub Form1_Load(ByVal sender As System.Object, _
  ByVal e As System.EventArgs) Handles MyBase.Load
    FillDataGrid()
  End Sub
  ' Fill DataGrid
  Private Sub FillDataGrid()
    sql = "SELECT * FROM Customers"
    conn = New SqlConnection(connectionString)
    recordSet = New CustRecordSet()
    recordSet.CreateRecordSet(conn, sql, DataGrid1, Me, "Customers")
  End Sub
```

Now on the button click event handlers, simply call CustRecordSet's
FirstRecord, PrevRecord, NextRecord, and LastRecord methods, as shown in Listing
7-36.

Listing 7-36. Moving Record Button Click Event Handlers

```
' Move First button click
  Private Sub MoveFirstBtn_Click(ByVal sender As System.Object, _
  ByVal e As System.EventArgs) Handles MoveFirstBtn.Click
    recordSet.FirstRecord()
  End Sub
  ' Move Previous button click
  Private Sub MovePrevBtn_Click(ByVal sender As System.Object, _
  ByVal e As System.EventArgs) Handles MovePrevBtn.Click
    recordSet.PrevRecord()
  End Sub
  ' Move next button click
  Private Sub MoveNextBtn_Click(ByVal sender As System.Object, _
  ByVal e As System.EventArgs) Handles MoveNextBtn.Click
    recordSet.NextRecord()
  End Sub
  ' Move last button click
  Private Sub MoveLastBtn_Click(ByVal sender As System.Object, _
  ByVal e As System.EventArgs) Handles MoveLastBtn.Click
    recordSet.LastRecord()
  End Sub
```

The final application looks like Figure 7-12.

Figure 7-12. DataGrid *navigation system*

 TIP *You can implement the same functionality on a* DataGrid *control's right-click menu by adding four menu items that allow users to move to the first, next, previous, and last records of a* DataGrid. *You can even develop your own* DataGrid *component with sorting, searching, and navigating features.*

Implementing Search in a DataGrid

You just saw how to implement custom sorting in a DataGrid control. After sorting, searching is one more basic requirement of database-driven applications. There are two methods to implement search in a DataGrid control:

- Using the SELECT statement

- Using a DataSet and DataView

Searching Using the SELECT Statement

You already used search functionality in a connected environment using the SQL SELECT statement. Do you remember using a SELECT statement with a WHERE clause? In a WHERE clause, you passed the criteria specifying the data for which you're looking. If you want to search in multiple tables, you construct a JOIN query with WHERE clause. You can even search for a keyword using the SELECT...LIKE statement, which was discussed in "The DataView in Connected Environments" section of Chapter 4.

You use the SELECT statement in a DataAdapter, which reads data based on the SELECT statement and the criteria passed in it. However, using this method for searching may not be useful when you're searching data frequently—especially when you're searching data in a DataGrid. We suggest not using this method when searching data in an isolated application and there's no other application updating the data. Why? The main reason is that every time you change the SELECT statement, you need to create a new DataAdapter and fill the DataSet when you change the SELECT statement. This method is useful when there are multiple applications updating the data simultaneously and you want to search in the latest updated data.

Searching Using a DataTable and DataView

The DataTable and DataView objects provide members that can filter data based on criteria. (See "The DataView" section in Chapter 3 for more information.) You can simply create a DataView from a DataSet, set a DataView's RowFilter property to the search criteria, and then bind the DataView to a DataGrid, which will display the filtered records.

TIP *Using the same method, you can implement a Search or Find feature in a* DataGrid *control. You can also provide a Search option on a* DataGrid *control's header so that you know on which column a user has clicked.*

The new application looks like Figure 7-13. Obviously, the Search button searches the column entered in the Column Name text box for a value entered in the Value text box.

NOTE *If you search for a string, use a singe quote (') before and after the string.*

We discuss the Save method functionality in the following section.

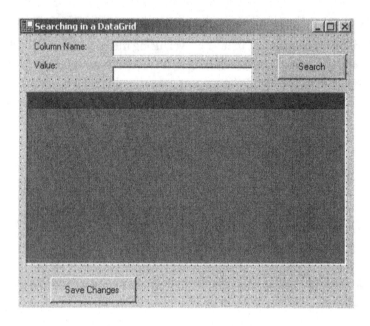

Figure 7-13. Implementing search functionality in a DataGrid *control*

After creating a Windows application and adding controls to the form, define following variables:

```
' Developer defined variables
  Private conn As SqlConnection = Nothing
  Private connectionString As String = _
    "Integrated Security=SSPI;Initial Catalog=Northwind;Data Source=MCB;"
  Private sql As String = Nothing
  Private searchView As DataView = Nothing
  Dim adapter As SqlDataAdapter = Nothing
  Dim ds As DataSet = Nothing
```

Now add the `FillDataGrid` method, which fills the `DataGrid` and creates a `DataView` called `searchView` (see Listing 7-37).

Listing 7-37. `FillDataGrid` *Method*

```
' Fill DataGrid
  Private Sub FillDataGrid()
    sql = "SELECT * FROM Orders"
    conn = New SqlConnection(connectionString)
    adapter = New SqlDataAdapter(sql, conn)
    ds = New DataSet("Orders")
    adapter.Fill(ds, "Orders")
    DataGrid1.DataSource = ds.Tables("Orders")
    searchView = New DataView(ds.Tables("Orders"))
    Dim cmdBuilder As SqlCommandBuilder = _
    New SqlCommandBuilder(adapter)
    ' Disconnect. Otherwise you would get
    ' Access violations when try multiple operations
    conn.Close()
    conn.Dispose()
  End Sub
```

Now, the next step is to set a `RowFilter` of `searchView` based on the values entered in the Column Name and Value text fields. Listing 7-38 shows the code for the Search button. As you can see, the code sets the `RowFilter` of `searchView` and binds it to the `DataGrid` to display the filtered data.

Listing 7-38. Seach Button Click Event Handler

```
Private Sub SearchBtn_Click(ByVal sender As System.Object, _
  ByVal e As System.EventArgs) Handles SearchBtn.Click
    If (TextBox1.Text.Equals(String.Empty)) Then
      MessageBox.Show("Enter a column name")
      TextBox1.Focus()
      Return
    End If
    If (TextBox2.Text.Equals(String.Empty)) Then
      MessageBox.Show("Enter a value")
      TextBox1.Focus()
      Return
    End If
    ' Construct a row filter and apply on the DataView
```

```
    Dim str As String = TextBox1.Text + "=" + TextBox2.Text
    searchView.RowFilter = str
    ' Set DataView as DataSource of DataGrid
    DataGrid1.DataSource = searchView
End Sub
```

At this time, if you run the application, the data from the Orders table is filled
in the DataGrid. If you enter **EmployeeID** in the Column Name text box and **6** in the
Value field and then click the Search button, the filtered data looks like Figure 7-14.

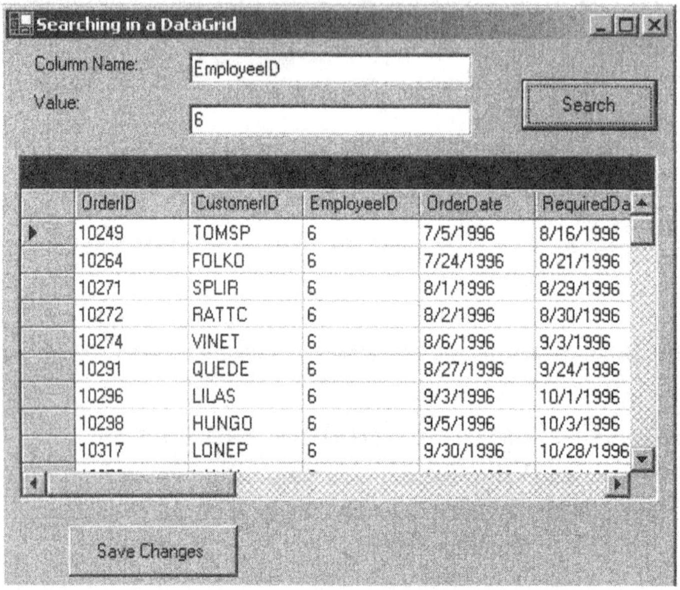

Figure 7-14. Filtered data after searching

Inserting, Updating, and Deleting Data through DataGrids

As you learned earlier, the DataGrid control is one of the most powerful, flexible,
and versatile controls available in Windows Forms. It has an almost unlimited
number of properties and methods. You can add new records, update records, and
delete existing records on a DataGrid with little effort, and you can easily save the
affected data in a database.

When a DataGrid control is in edit mode (the default mode), you can simply add a new record by clicking the last row of the grid and editing the column values. You can update data by changing the existing value of cells. You can delete a row by simply selecting a row and clicking the Delete button.

In the previous example, you used a Save Changes button on a form (see Figure 7-14). Now just write the code in Listing 7-39 on the Save Changes button click to save the data.

Listing 7-39. Saving Updated Data in a Data Source from a DataGrid *Control*

```
Private Sub SaveBtn_Click(ByVal sender As System.Object, _
  ByVal e As System.EventArgs) Handles SaveBtn.Click

    Dim changeDS As DataSet = New DataSet()
    ' Data is modified
    If (ds.HasChanges(DataRowState.Modified)) Then
      changeDS = ds.GetChanges(DataRowState.Modified)
      Dim changedRecords As Integer
      changedRecords = adapter.Update(changeDS, "Orders")
      If (changedRecords > 0) Then
        MessageBox.Show(changedRecords.ToString() & _
        " records modified.")
      End If
    End If
    ' Data is deleted
    If (ds.HasChanges(DataRowState.Deleted)) Then
      changeDS = ds.GetChanges(DataRowState.Deleted)
      Dim changedRecords As Integer
      changedRecords = adapter.Update(changeDS, "Orders")
      If (changedRecords > 0) Then
        MessageBox.Show(changedRecords.ToString() & _
        " records deleted.")
      End If
    End If
    ' Data is added
    If (ds.HasChanges(DataRowState.Added)) Then
      changeDS = ds.GetChanges(DataRowState.Added)
      Dim changedRecords As Integer
      changedRecords = adapter.Update(changeDS, "Orders")
      If (changedRecords > 0) Then
        MessageBox.Show(changedRecords.ToString() & _
        " records added.")
```

```
        End If
    End If
    ds.AcceptChanges()
    DataGrid1.Refresh()
End Sub
```

As you can see from Listing 7-39, you simply get the modified, deleted, and updated changes in a new DataSet by calling the DataSet.GetChanges method and save the changes by calling the DataAdapter.Update method. In the end, you accept the changes by calling DataSet.AcceptChanges and refresh the DataGrid control by calling the DataGrid.Refresh method.

Summary

Data-bound controls are definitely one of the greatest additions to GUI applications. In this chapter, we discussed the basics of data binding and how data binding works in Windows Forms data-bound controls and ADO.NET. We discussed some essential objects that participate in the data-binding phenomena, including Binding, BindingContext, BindingsCollection, BindingManagerBase, PropertyManager, CurrencyManager, and BindingContext.

After discussing basics of data binding and how to use these objects, you learned about some data-bound controls and how to bind data using the data-binding mechanism. You also saw some practical usage of data binding and data-bound controls; specifically, you created a record navigation system with a DataGrid control. Some of the examples discussed in this chapter included changing DataGrid styles programmatically, binding data sources to various data-bound controls, building a record navigation application, and implementing search, add, update, and delete record features in a DataGrid.

The next chapter covers constraints and data relations in more detail.

CHAPTER 8

Constraints
and Data Relations

IN CHAPTER 3, you encountered constraints and data relations. In this chapter, we discuss constraints and data relations in more detail. First, we start this chapter with a discussion of constraints and how ADO.NET constraint objects maintain data integrity. Second, we discuss data relations. An object that encapsulates a data relationship may be a new concept for many programmers.

Understanding Constraints

A *constraint* is a rule used to automatically maintain the integrity of a column's data. When we say *automatically*, we mean that the database itself makes sure the rule is being followed when changes are made to the data. For example, a UNIQUE constraint on a column makes sure that there aren't any duplicate values in a column. There are different types of constraints, including NOT NULL, UNIQUE, PRIMARY KEY, FOREIGN KEY, and CHECK constraints:

The NOT NULL constraint specifies that a column can't contain null values.

The UNIQUE constraint enforces a rule of uniqueness on a column, which means two rows of the column can't have duplicate values. A UNIQUE constraint may also apply to a combination of columns, which means the combination of the columns must be a unique value. For example, a database table can have two fields—a path and a file—and the combination of these fields must be unique to maintain the unique file entry in the database. In this case, the path or file column may have duplicate values individually, but they must be unique when used together.

A PRIMARY KEY constraint on a column or combination of columns enforces both the UNIQUE constraint and the NOT NULL constraint. This type of constraint is enforced when you need to identify column values as unique items and not null values such as a customer ID number or an order number.

The FOREIGN KEY constraint identifies the relationships between two tables. A foreign key in the first table points to a primary key in the second table. Foreign keys prevent actions that would ignore rows with foreign key values when there are no primary keys with that value. For example, the Orders table of a database may have a foreign key on the CustomerID column of the Customers table, which would prevent a user from entering an order that related to a nonexistent customer.

The CHECK constraint enforces data integrity by limiting a column's values. For example, you can specify a column type as an integer, which means only integer values can be placed in a column.

To implement many of these constraints, ADO.NET provides various classes. In the following sections, we discuss some of these classes, their members, and how to use them to implement constraints.

Implementing the Constraint Classes

The Constraint class represents a constraint and serves as a base class of the ForeignKeyConstraint and UniqueConstraint classes. This class provides three properties: ConstraintName represents the name of a constraint, ExtendedProperties represents a collection of user-defined properties, and Table represents a DataTable object to which the constraint applies. Before you learn how to implement constraints on a table, you'll look at the constraint classes.

Implementing the ForeignKeyConstraint Class

The ForeignKeyConstraint class creates a FOREIGN KEY constraint. In a primary key/foreign key relationship, first column acts as a parent column, and the second column acts as a child column. The ForeignKeyConstraint class has five overloaded constructors. Each of these constructors takes two DataColumn objects as a parent and a child column. Optionally, you can also specify the relation name.

The ForeignKeyConstraint class provides properties that can represent the relation name; the columns participating in the relationship; the accept, delete, and update rules; and so on. Table 8-1 describes the ForeignKeyConstraint class properties.

Table 8-1. The ForeignKeyConstraint *Class Properties*

PROPERTY	DESCRIPTION
AcceptRejectRule	Occurs when the AcceptChanges method of a DataTable is called. The parameter of AcceptRejectRule is represented by the AcceptRejectRule enumeration, which has two members: Cascade and None. The default action is None.
Columns	Returns the child columns of a constraint.
ConstraintName	Represents the name of the constraint.
DeleteRule	Occurs when a row is deleted. The parameter of DeleteRule is represented by the Rule enumeration, which has four members: Cascade, None, SetDefault, and SetNull. The default action is Cascade.
ExtendedProperties	Returns any user-defined properties that exist for the object.
RelatedColumns	Represents the parent column of a constraint.
Table	Returns the DataTable of a constraint.
UpdateRule	Occurs when a row is updated. The parameter of UpdateRule is represented by the Rule enumeration, which has four members: Cascade, None, SetDefault, and SetNull. The default action is Cascade.

Listing 8-1 creates a FOREIGN KEY constraint on the id column of custTable and the CustID column of ordersTable. custTable and ordersTable are two DataTable objects created by the CreateCustomersTable and CreateOrdersTable methods, respectively.

Listing 8-1. Creating a FOREIGN KEY Constraint

```
Dim custTable As DataTable = CreateCustomersTable()
Dim ordersTable As DataTable = CreateOrdersTable()
Dim parentColumn As DataColumn = custTable.Columns("id")
Dim childColumn As DataColumn = ordersTable.Columns("CustID")
Dim fkConst As ForeignKeyConstraint = New ForeignKeyConstraint _
"CustOrderConts", parentColumn, childColumn)
fkConst.DeleteRule = Rule.SetNull
fkConst.UpdateRule = Rule.Cascade
fkConst.AcceptRejectRule = AcceptRejectRule.Cascade
```

CAUTION *Be careful when using the* Cascade *action. The default action for* AcceptRejectRule *is* None, *but the default action for* UpdateRule *and* DeleteRule *is* Cascade. *Calling the* Cascade *action on* DeleteRule *deletes all the children rows, which are related using the FOREIGN KEY constraint.*

Using the UniqueConstraint Class

The UniqueConstraint object represents a UNIQUE constraint, which ensures that the value of a column is unique. Table 8-2 describes the UniqueConstraint class properties.

Table 8-2. The UniqueConstraint *Class Properties*

PROPERTY	DESCRIPTION
Columns	Returns an array of columns that this constraint affects
ConstraintName	Represents the name of the constraint
ExtendedProperties	Returns a collection of any user-defined properties that exist for the object
IsPrimaryKey	Represents whether the constraint is a primary key
Table	Returns the DataTable of a constraint

Listing 8-2 creates two UNIQUE constraints on the id column of custTable and the OrderId column of ordersTable.

Listing 8-2. Creating a UNIQUE Constraint

```
' Create unique constraints
Dim idCol As DataColumn = New DataColumn()
idCol = custTable.Columns("id")
Dim unqConst1 As UniqueConstraint = _
New UniqueConstraint("idUnqConst1", idCol)
idCol = ordersTable.Columns("OrderId")
Dim unqConst2 As UniqueConstraint = _
New UniqueConstraint("idUnqConst2", idCol)
```

NOTE *You can also set the* Unique *property of a* DataColumn *to* True *to make a column unique. Chapter 3 discusses this technique.*

Using the ConstraintCollection Class

A DataTable can have multiple constraints. The ConstraintCollection class represents a collection of constraints of a DataTable and is accessed through the Constraints property of a DataTable. This class provides two properties: List and Item. The List property returns a list of all the constraints in the collection in an ArrayList object. The Item property is the indexer for the ConstraintCollection class, which returns a constraint at a specified index.

Similar to other collection classes, the ConstraintCollection class also provides methods to add and remove items to the collection. Table 8-3 describes the ConstraintCollection class methods.

Table 8-3. The ConstraintCollection *Class Methods*

METHOD	DESCRIPTION
Add	This method adds a constraint to the collection. (The following section describes in this method in more detail.)
AddRange	Adds a collection of constraints to the existing collection.
CanRemove	Checks whether a constraint can be removed from the collection.
Clear	Removes all constraints from a collection.
Contains	Indicates whether a constraint exists in the collection. Returns True if a constraint exists; otherwise, returns False. This is useful when you need to remove or read a constraint from the collection.
IndexOf	Returns the index of a constraint in the collection. You can use the constraint name or an object.
OnCollectionChanged	An event raises when the constraint collection is changed by adding or removing constraints.
Remove	Deletes a constraint from the collection. You can specify the constraint name or an object.
RemoveAt	Removes a constraint at the specified index in the collection.

You've now seen the constraint classes and their members. Next let's put these classes together and see how to use them in applications.

Adding and Removing Constraints

You use the Add method of the ConstraintCollection to add new constraints to the collection of constraints associated with a DataTable. Listing 8-3 adds a FOREIGN KEY constraint to a collection and removes the first constraint. As you can see from the code, the Contains method returns True if the collection contains a constraint, and the CanRemove method returns True if the program can delete the constraint. The Remove method removes the constraint. You can also use the RemoveAt method if you want to delete a constraint based on the index.

NOTE *You must set the* DataSet *property* EnforceConstraints *to* True *if you want to save the constraint in a* DataSet.

Listing 8-3. Adding and Removing Constraints

```
' Create two DataTable objects
' Customer and Orders
Dim custTable As DataTable = CreateCustomersTable()
Dim ordersTable As DataTable = CreateOrdersTable()
Try
      ' Add a foriegn key constraint
      Dim parentColumn As DataColumn = custTable.Columns("id")
      Dim childColumn As DataColumn = ordersTable.Columns("CustID")
      Dim fkConst As ForeignKeyConstraint = New ForeignKeyConstraint _
   ("CustOrderConts", parentColumn, childColumn)
      fkConst.DeleteRule = Rule.SetNull
      fkConst.UpdateRule = Rule.Cascade
      fkConst.AcceptRejectRule = AcceptRejectRule.Cascade
      ordersTable.Constraints.Add(fkConst)
Catch exp As Exception
      MessageBox.Show(exp.Message)
End Try

' Create a DataSet and add DataTables to it
Dim ds As DataSet = New DataSet("CustOrderDataSet")
```

```
' Add DataTables to a DataSet
ds.Tables.Add(custTable)
ds.Tables.Add(ordersTable)
' Enforce Constraints
ds.EnforceConstraints = True


' Using Contains, CanRemove and Remove methods
' Get the first constraint
Dim cnst1 As Constraint = ordersTable.Constraints(0)
Try
     If ordersTable.Constraints.Contains(cnst1.ConstraintName) Then
       If ordersTable.Constraints.CanRemove(cnst1) Then
         ordersTable.Constraints.Remove(cnst1)
       End If
     End If
Catch myException As Exception
     Console.WriteLine(myException.Message)
End Try
```

NOTE *The* CreateCustomersTable *and* CreateOrdersTable *methods return two* DataTable *objects created programmatically. If you're using constraints in a connected environment, you can get these* DataTable *objects from a* DataSet *using* DataSet.Tables("TableName") *or* DataSet.Tables(index).

Listing 8-4 adds UNIQUE constraints to two tables.

Listing 8-4. Adding UNIQUE Constraints

```
' Create unique constraints
Dim idCol As DataColumn = New DataColumn()
idCol = custTable.Columns("id")
Dim unqConst1 As UniqueConstraint = _
New UniqueConstraint("idUnqConst1", idCol)
idCol = ordersTable.Columns("OrderId")
Dim unqConst2 As UniqueConstraint = _
New UniqueConstraint("idUnqConst2", idCol)
' Add constraints to DataTables
custTable.Constraints.Add(unqConst1)
ordersTable.Constraints.Add(unqConst2)
```

Reading All the Constraints

Reading all the constraints is pretty simple. You just read all the items in the collection. Listing 8-5 reads all the constraints of a collection.

Listing 8-5. Reading All the Constraints of a Collection

```
Dim contCollection As ConstraintCollection = _
    ordersTable.Constraints
  Dim str As String = "Number of Constraints:" & _
   contCollection.Count.ToString()
  Dim i As Integer
  Dim cnst As Constraint
  For Each cnst In contCollection
    str = str + ", "
    str = str + cnst.ConstraintName
  Next
```

Adding PRIMARY KEY Constraints

There's no specific primary key class to add a PRIMARY KEY constraint to a DataTable. The PrimaryKey property of DataTable sets the primary key of that table, and you assign a DataColumn as the PrimaryKey property. Listing 8-6 creates a DataColumnCollection and sets it as the primary key of the CustTable.

Listing 8-6. Adding a PRIMARY KEY Constaint to a DataTable

```
Dim custTable As DataTable = CreateCustomersTable()
' Make the ID column the primary key column.
Dim PrimaryKeyColumns() As DataColumn = New DataColumn(1) {}
PrimaryKeyColumns(0) = custTable.Columns("id")
custTable.PrimaryKey = PrimaryKeyColumns
```

Using SQL Statements to Add and Remove Constraints

When working in a connected environment, using SQL may be a better way to add constraints to a database table. You can add constraints to a table when you create a table or by altering an already existing table.

The CREATE TABLE SQL statement allows you to set a column as a constraint when you create a table. The CONSTRAINT keyword sets a column as the specified constraint. For example, the following SQL statement creates a table with myId as the primary key:

```
Dim sql As String = "CREATE TABLE myTable" & _
 "(myId INTEGER CONSTRAINT PKeyMyId PRIMARY KEY," & _
 "myName CHAR(50), myAddress CHAR(255), myBalance FLOAT)"
```

You can always add and delete constraints from a database table using the ALTER TABLE SQL statement. If you read the SQL documentation, you'll see that this statement allows options such as ADD CONSTRAINT and DROP CONSTRAINT to add and remove constraints.

If you're working in a connected environment and you can execute commands (through SqlCommand), using SQL statements to add and remove constraints is preferable because it entails less overhead and code and has better performance.

Understanding Data Relations

Until now it was the job of the database server to maintain data relationships, but with the flexibility of ADO.NET, now programmers can also create and maintain data relationships in a disconnected environment. A *data relationship* relates two tables to each other through their columns—for example, a customer/order relationship. The Customers table stores records of a customer, and the Orders table stores records of orders made by customers. Each customer has only one record in the Customers table, which is identified by a unique column value called Customer Id. Each order is related to a customer, which has a column that stores the customer ID. The Orders table can have multiple records for a single customer. In this scenario, the Customer Id row in the Customers table acts as a parent row, and all related rows in the Orders table act as its child rows. One condition in this example is that the data type of both the parent and row columns must be identical.

In ADO.NET, the DataRelation class represents a data relation between two DataTable objects, and the DataRelationCollection represents a collection of data relations.

In a connected environment, you can access and maintain data relations through a DataSet. The Relations property of the DataSet returns a collection of data relations associated with that DataSet in the form of a DataRelationCollection object. The ChildRelations and ParentRelations properties of a DataTable return the child relations and parent relations associated with that DataTable.

As you know from "The DataRow" section of Chapter 3, the DataRow also provides methods to return a row's parent and child rows. The GetParentRow method of a DataRow returns the parent row of a DataRow, and the GetParentRows method returns all parent rows related to a DataRow. The GetChildRows method returns all the child rows associated with a DataRow.

Understanding the DataRelation and DataRelationCollection Objects

The DataRelation class represents a parent/child relationship between two tables. The DataRelation's overloaded constructors allow you to create a DataRelation object from a parent and a child column or a collection of columns. The first argument of the constructors is the name of the relation. The second and third arguments are the parent and child column(s), respectively. The last optional argument is a Boolean type, which indicates whether you want to create a constraint.

Before you create a DataRelation, let's fill a DataSet from two tables. Listing 8-7 fills a DataSet from the Customers and Orders tables.

Listing 8-7. Filling a DataSet from Two Tables

```
' Create a Connection Object
Dim conn As SqlConnection = New SqlConnection(ConnectionString)
SQL = "SELECT * FROM Customers"
conn.Open()
Dim adapter As SqlDataAdapter = New SqlDataAdapter(SQL, conn)
Dim ds1 As DataSet = New DataSet("Customers")
adapter.Fill(ds1, "Customers")
SQL = "SELECT * FROM Orders"
adapter = New SqlDataAdapter(SQL, conn)
Dim ds2 As DataSet = New DataSet("Orders")
adapter.Fill(ds2, "Orders")
ds1.Merge(ds2)
```

Now let's create a DataRelation between the CustomerId column of the Customers table and the CustomerID column of Orders table (see Listing 8-8).

Listing 8-8. Creating a DataRelation

```
' Get the DataColumn objects from Customers
' and Orders tables of a DataSet
Dim parentCol As DataColumn = New DataColumn()
Dim childCol As DataColumn = New DataColumn()
'Retrieve columns from a DataSet
parentCol = ds1.Tables("Customers").Columns("CustomerID")
childCol = ds1.Tables("Orders").Columns("CustomerID")
Dim bConstraints As Boolean
bConstraints = True
' Create a DataRelation.
Dim CustOrderRelation As DataRelation = _
New DataRelation("CustOrdersRelation", parentCol, childCol, bConstraints)
```

Now you can add a DataRelation to a DataSet using the Add method of
DataRelationCollection, which you access through the DataSet.Relations property.
(We dicuss DataRelationCollection in a moment.) Use this code to add the
DataRelation:

```
' Add the relation to the DataSet.
ds1.Relations.Add(CustOrderRelation)
```

Even multiple sets of columns can participate in a relationship. The following
code uses two columns to participate in a data relation:

```
Dim parentCols() As DataColumn
Dim childCols() As DataColumn
parentCols(0) = DataSet1.Tables("Customers").Columns("CustID")
parentCols(1) = DataSet1.Tables("Customers").Columns("OrdID")
childCols(0) = DataSet1.Tables("Orders").Columns("CustID")
childCols(1) = DataSet1.Tables("Orders").Columns("OrdID")
Dim CustOrderRel As DataRelation
CustOrderRel = New DataRelation("CustomersOrders", parentCols, childCols)
```

After creating a DataRelation object, the next step is to see what properties
are available in the DataRelation class. Table 8-4 describes the DataRelation class
properties.

Table 8-4. The DataRelation *Class Properties*

PROPERTY	DESCRIPTION
ChildColumns	Returns all child columns of a relation
ChildKeyConstraint	Returns the FOREIGN KEY constraint of a relation if any available
ChildTable	Returns the child table (DataTable)
DataSet	Returns the DataSet to which a relation belongs
ExtendedProperties	Returns the collection of custom properties
Nested	Represents whether a DataRelation is nested (both get and set)
ParentColumns	Returns all parent columns of a relation
ParentKeyConstraint	Returns the UNIQUE constraint of the parent column
ParentTable	Returns the parent table (DataTable) of a relation
RelationName	Represents the name of the relation (both get and set)

You can also create nested data relations. For example, if in addition to the Customers and Orders tables you have an Items table that stores data related to items such as Item ID, location, and so on, then you can create one more relation between the Orders and Items tables using the same steps you took for the Customers and Orders tables.

Now you'll learn how to access a DataRelation's properties. Listing 8-9 reads the DataSet, ParentTable, ChildTable, ParentColumns, ChildColumns, and RelationName properties of DataRelation.

Listing 8-9. Getting DataRelation *Properties*

```
' Getting a DataRelation properties
    Dim dtSet As DataSet = dtRelation.DataSet
    ' Getting Tables
    Dim pTable As DataTable = dtRelation.ParentTable
    Dim chTable As DataTable = dtRelation.ChildTable
    ListBox1.Items.Add("Parent Table: " + pTable.TableName)
    ListBox1.Items.Add("Child Table: " + chTable.TableName)
    'Getting columns
    Dim parentCols() As DataColumn
    Dim childCols() As DataColumn
    parentCols = dtRelation.ParentColumns
    childCols = dtRelation.ChildColumns
    ' Print the ColumnName of each column.
    Dim i As Integer
```

```
    ListBox1.Items.Add("Parent Columns:")
    For i = 0 To parentCols.GetUpperBound(0)
        ListBox1.Items.Add(parentCols(i).ColumnName)
    Next i
    ListBox1.Items.Add("Child Columns:")
    For i = 0 To childCols.GetUpperBound(0)
        ListBox1.Items.Add(childCols(i).ColumnName)
    Next i
    ' Data relation name
ListBox1.Items.Add("DataRelation Name:" + dtRelation.RelationName)
```

You just saw how to create a DataRelation object, add it to a DataSet, and access its properties. Now let's look at the DataRelationCollection class, which is a gateway to access data relations.

The DataRelationCollection class represents a collection of DataRelation objects of a DataSet, which is accessed through the Relations property of the DataSet. The Count property of DataRelationCollection returns the number of data relations in a collection, and the Items property allows you to access a DataRelation based on the index in the collection. Like the other collection classes, this class also provides Add, Remove, and other methods. Table 8-5 describes these methods.

Table 8-5. The DataRelationCollection *Class Methods*

METHOD	DESCRIPTION
Add	Adds a DataRelation to the collection.
AddRange	Copies an array of DataRelation objects to the end of this collection.
CanRemove	Returns True if the specified DataRelation can be removed from the collection; otherwise False.
Clear	Removes all DataRelation objects from the collection.
Contains	Returns True if a collection contains the specified DataRelation. You should make sure that a DataRelation exists in the collection before calling the Remove method to avoid exceptions.
IndexOf	Returns the index of the specified data relation.
Remove	Deletes the specified data relation from the collection.
RemoveAt	Removes the data relation at the specified index.

Listing 8-10 calls the Contains, CanRemove, and Remove methods to delete a data relation from the collection.

Listing 8-10. Deleting a Data Relation from the Collection

```
Dim dtRelCollection As DataRelationCollection = dtSet.Relations
If (dtRelCollection.Contains("CustOrdersRelation")) Then
    If (dtRelCollection.CanRemove(dtRelation)) Then
        dtRelCollection.Remove(dtRelation)
    End If
End If
```

Summary

Managing data relations and constraints programmatically is a new concept for developers. In this chapter, you learned how ADO.NET helps you create and manage data relations and constraints.

Exception and error handling is another important part of programming. In next chapter, you'll learn how to handle exceptions in your code with the help of ADO.NET classes.

CHAPTER 9

ADO.NET Exception Handling

EFFECTIVE EXCEPTION AND error handling is one of the most important things to learn in order to write reliable and error-proof applications. In this chapter, we discuss how to use the exception and error handling classes provided by the .NET Framework.

If you come from a C++ background, you're probably familiar with different exception handling methods such as C++ exception handling, structured exception handling, and MFC exceptions. If you come from a Visual Basic (VB) background, you're probably familiar with the On Error statement. Although you can continue to use these techniques to handle errors, .NET implements exceptions differently. In addition, all .NET-supported languages (C# and VB .NET) share the same mechanism. Now VB developers can enjoy the same rich exception handling that C++ developers enjoy.

NOTE *Discussing .NET exception handling is beyond the scope of this book. In this chapter, we concentrate on ADO.NET exception handling classes only.*

VB .NET supports two types of exceptions—unstructured and structured. Remember using the On Error statement in VB? Using the On Error statement is unstructured handling. In other words, you place the On Error statement at the beginning of a block of code and errors are handled at the end of the block. Unstructured exception handling also employs the Error and Resume statements. All the code after the On Error statement is within the scope of the error handler. If there's another On Error statement, then that becomes the active error handler. However, structured exception handling is a better approach, and there's no reason why you should be using the On Error statement.

Structured exception handling works a little differently than unstructured handling. If you come from a C++ background, you're probably familiar with Try...Catch blocks. However, if you haven't encountered them before, it's OK—

they're simple enough. Specifically, you place the code within a Try block that you think may cause an exception, and when an exception rises, the control goes to the Catch block.

Why Use Exception Handling?

If you've been writing software for a while, you're probably familiar with why you want to handle exceptions. Whenever an exception occurs in a program, if there's no exception handling, the program crashes with system-generated messages. Unfortunately, system-generated messages are often incomprehensible. Instead of system messages, you can handle exceptions and generate user-readable messages. Let's take a simple example. Listing 9-1 opens the file c:\abc.txt.

Listing 9-1. Opening a File

```
Imports System.IO
Module Module1
  Sub Main()
      File.Open("c:\\abc.txt", FileMode.Open)
  End Sub
End Module
```

What if the file c:\abc.txt doesn't exist? Well, you get a lengthy error message, which looks like Figure 9-1.

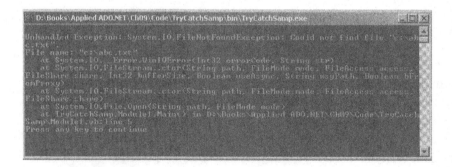

Figure 9-1. A system-generated error

Now let's modify this program little bit to make the error message more readable. As you can see from this Listing 9-2, you handle the exception using a simple Try...Catch block.

Listing 9-2. A Simple Exception Handling Block

```
Imports System.IO
Module Module1
  Sub Main()
    Try
      File.Open("c:\\abc.txt", FileMode.Open)
    Catch exp As Exception
      Console.WriteLine("Exception Ocurred :" + exp.Message.ToString())
    End Try
  End Sub
End Module
```

If you run the program, the output now looks like Figure 9-2, which not only handles the exception but also reports the cause of exception.

Figure 9-2. An exception-handled error message

Using Try...Catch Statements

Using a Try...Catch statement is pretty straightforward. First, you decide what code you want the error handler to monitor. Second, you place that code inside the Try...Catch block. When an exception occurs within that block of the code, the control goes to the Catch block and handles the exception the way you've specified. Listing 9-3 shows a simple Try...Catch block.

Listing 9-3. A Simple Try...Catch *Block*

```
Try
    ' Place your code that may generate
    ' an exception in this block.
Catch [optional filters]
    ' This code executes when the Try block fails and
' the filter on the Catch statement is true.
End Try
```

In Listing 9-3, the optional filter describes the type of error you want to handle. For example, if you want to handle memory-related exceptions, you place a memory-related filter within the block. You'll learn about filters in the "Defining Custom Filters and Error Messages" section.

Using Try...Catch...Finally Statements

The Try...Catch...Finally construct is an extended version of the Try...Catch statement. If an error occurs during the execution of any code inside the Try section, then control moves to the Catch block when the filter condition is True. The Finally block always executes last, just before the error handling block loses scope, regardless of whether an exception occurred. The Finally block is the perfect place to clean up by closing files and disposing objects. Listing 9-4 shows a simple Try...Catch...Finally statement.

Listing 9-4. The Try...Catch...Finally *Statement*

```
Try
    ' Place your code that may generate
    ' an exception in this block.
Catch [optional filters]
    ' This code executes when the Try block fails and
' the filter on the Catch statement is true.
Finally
    'Release and dispose objects here.
End Try
```

Nesting Try...Catch Statements

Can you nest Try...Catch statements? Of course you can. But the only reason you may want to use nested Try...Catch blocks is when you want to catch different types of exceptions. For example, say one block is catching memory-related exceptions, one is catching Input/Output–related exceptions, and one is catching database-related errors. In that case, nesting Try...Catch statements would be beneficial.

However, you may not need to write nested statements. Actually, you can write multiple Catch statements with a single Try statement, which may solve the problem of handling multiple types of exceptions. But it doesn't mean you can't use nested statements.

Using Try with Multiple Catch Statements

The Try...Catch statement allows you to write multiple Catch statements for a Try statement. For example, you can catch memory, Input/Output (I/O), and database-related exceptions using a simple Try statement.

Listing 9-5 shows how to use nested Try...Catch blocks and multiple Catch blocks.

Listing 9-5. Using Nested Try...Catch *and Multiple* Catch *Blocks*

```
Imports System.IO
Module Module1
  Sub Main()
    Dim filename As String = "c:\\abc.txt"
    Dim Strings As New Collection()
    ' start first try block here
    Try
      Dim Stream As System.IO.StreamReader = _
      File.OpenText(filename)
      ' start second Try block here
      Try
        While True
          Strings.Add(Stream.ReadLine())
        End While
      Catch eosExp As System.IO.EndOfStreamException
        ' Write EndOfStream exception error
      Catch IOExp As System.IO.IOException
```

```
                ' IO Eception error
                Console.WriteLine(IOExp.Message)
                Strings = Nothing
            Finally
                ' Close and dispose objects here
                Stream.Close()
            End Try
            ' end second try bkock here


            ' catch of first Try block
        Catch exp As Exception
            Console.WriteLine(exp.Message)
        Finally
            ' Close and dispose objects here of first Try
            ' block here
        End Try
        ' end first try block here
    End Sub
End Module
```

Defining Custom Filters and Error Messages

Using a Try...Catch block, you can even define your own custom filters and error messages. For example, Listing 9-6 defines a filter that fires if the counter variable is 5 or greater and then generates a custom error message.

Listing 9-6. Defining a Custom Filter and Error Message

```
Imports System.IO
Module Module1
    Sub Main()
        Dim filename As String = "c:\\abc.txt"
        Dim counter As Int16 = 10

        Try
            Dim Stream As System.IO.StreamReader = _
            File.OpenText(filename)
        Catch When counter > 5
            Console.WriteLine("Counter Out of Range")
        Finally
            ' Close and dispose objects here of first Try
```

```
      ' block here
    End Try
  End Sub
End Module
```

If you run the program, the output looks like Figure 9-3.

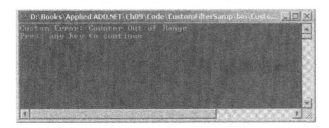

Figure 9-3. The custom error message

Understanding the Exception Classes

By now you probably have an idea of how to implement exception handling in your code. The following sections give a quick overview of the exception-related classes provided by the .NET Framework Library.

Using the Exception Class: Mother of All Exceptions

The Exception class represents errors that occur during application execution. This class is the base class for all exception classes. In the previous samples, you already saw how to create an object of the Exception class. Table 9-1 describes the Exception class properties.

Table 9-1. Exception *Class Properties*

PROPERTY	DESCRIPTION
HelpLink	Represents the link to the help file associated with the exception (both get and set)
InnerException	Returns the Exception instance that caused the current exception (get only)
Message	Returns the error message that describes the current exception (read only)

Table 9-1. Exception *Class Properties (Continued)*

PROPERTY	DESCRIPTION
Source	Represents the name of the application or object that caused the error (both get and set)
StackTrace	Returns a string of the frames on the call stack at the time the exception occurred (read only)
TargetSite	Returns the method that throws the exception (read only)

Understanding Other Exception Classes

The .NET Framework Class Library defines many exception classes, and each of them is designed to handle a specific kind of exception. For example, an IOException error is thrown when an I/O error occurs.

The SystemException class is the base class for system (runtime) errors. Some of the classes derived from SystemException are StackOverflowException, ArithmeticException, ArrayTypeMismatchException, FormatException, IOException, OutOfMemory-Exception, RankException, and TypeLoadException.

The .NET Framework Library defines hundreds of exception classes—some of which are specific to a particular operation. For example, an OutOfMemory exception is thrown when there's not enough memory to continue the execution of a program. Discussing all of the exception classes is beyond the scope of this chapter.

Exception Handling in ADO.NET

It's now time to talk about exception handling in ADO.NET. Each data provider provides three classes: Exception, Error, and ErrorCollection. For example, the SQL data provider provides the SqlException, SqlError, and SqlErrorCollection classes. You'll look at the ADO.NET-related classes and then you'll learn how to implement a few of them in your code.

If you look at the System.Data class hierarchy, you'll find many exception classes. These exception classes are accessible to all data providers through the System.Data namespace and the classes defined in this namespace. Table 9-2 briefly describes these classes.

Table 9-2. The `System.Data` *Exception Classes*

CLASS	DESCRIPTION
`ConstraintException`	This class represents an exception thrown when attempting an operation that violates a constraint.
`DataException`	This class is a base class for many database-related exception classes such as `ConstraintException`, `NoNullAllowException`, and `MissingPrimaryKey-Exception`. It's thrown when an error is generated using ADO.NET.
`DBConcurrencyException`	This exception is a result of the `DataAdapter`'s `Update` method when the affected rows after an `Insert`, `Update`, or `Delete` operation are zero because of the concurrency violation.
`DeleteRowInaccessibleException`	This exception is thrown when a program tries to delete a `DataRow` that has already been deleted.
`DuplicateNameException`	This exception is thrown when a program tries to add a duplicate database object such as a table, relation, column, or a constraint to the database schema.
`EvaluateException`	This exception is thrown when a program isn't able to evaluate the `Expression` property of a `DataColumn` object.
`InRowChangingEventException`	This exception is thrown when calling the `EndEdit` method within the `RowChanging` event.
`InvalidConstraintException`	This exception is thrown when a program tries to create an incorrect relation.
`InvalidExpressionException`	This exception is thrown when attempting to add a `DataColumn` with an invalid `Expression` property value to a `DataColumnCollection`.
`MissingPrimaryKeyException`	This exception is thrown when trying to access a row in a table that has no primary key.
`NoNullAllowedException`	This exception is thrown when a program tries to insert a null value where the `DataColumn`'s `AllowDBNull` property is `False`.
`NoNullAllowedException`	This exception is thrown when a program tries to change the value of a read-only column.
`RowNotInTableException`	This exception is thrown when a program tries to perform an operation on a row that doesn't belong to a table.
`StrongTypingException`	This exception is thrown by a strongly typed `DataSet` when the user accesses a `DBNull` value.

Table 9-2. The System.Data *Exception Classes (Continued)*

CLASS	DESCRIPTION
SyntaxErrorException	This exception is thrown when the Expression property of a DataColumn contains a syntax error.
TypedDataSetGeneratorException	This exception is thrown when a name conflict occurs while generating a strongly typed DataSet.
VersionNotFoundException	This exception is thrown when a program tries to return a version of a DataRow that has been deleted.

Recognizing SQL Server 2000 Errors

Whenever you run an invalid SQL query, SQL Server returns a formatted error message. Also, SQL Server writes these error messages to the error log and/or event log. For instance, if you select records from a database table that doesn't exist, SQL Server will return an error message including the message ID, severity level, error state, line number, and the error message. For example, if you execute the following SQL query:

```
select * from SomeTable
```

but SomeTable doesn't exist in the database, then SQL Server will return an error that looks like the following:

```
Server: Msg 208, Level 16, State 1, Line 1
Invalid object name 'SomeTable'.
```

The first part of the error is the error message number. Each error message has an associated error message number that uniquely identifies the error. Error messages number from 1 to 49,999 are reserved for SQL Server. You can also define your own custom error messages, but your message number must be fall between 50,000 and 2,147,483,647.

The second part of the message is the error severity level, which falls between 0 and 25. The error severity represents the nature of the error. Table 9-3 describes the severity levels.

Table 9-3. Severity Levels

RANGE	DESCRIPTION
0–10	These messages are not actual errors. These messages are used only for informational purposes.
11–16	Severity levels 11–16 are generated because of user problems and can be fixed by the user. For example, the error message returned in the invalid Update query, used earlier, had a severity level of 16.
17	SQL Server has run out of a configurable resource, such as locks.
18	Represents nonfatal internal software problems.
19	A nonconfigurable resource limit has been exceeded.
20	Represents a problem with a statement issued by the current process.
21	SQL Server has encountered a problem that affects all the processes in a database.
22	Represents a table or index that has been damaged.
23	Represents a suspect database.
24	Represents a hardware problem.
25	Represents some type of system error.

NOTE *Severity level errors that fall between 19 and 25 are fatal errors and can only be used via* RAISERROR *by members of the fixed database role* sysadmin *with the with* log option *required.*

The next part of SQL Server error message is the state number, which varies from 1 to 127; it represents information about the source that issued the error.

The line portion of the error message represents the source line where the actual error occurred.

The last part of the error message is the error description. The SQL Server error messages are stored in the sysmessages system table. To read all the messages from this table, you can run the following SQL query in the Query Analyzer:

```
select * from sysmessages
```

Using SQL Server Error Logs

SQL Server maintains an error log (in text format) that stores the server information and error messages. Error log files can help you track down problems or alert you to potential or existing problems. The SQL Server log files are stored in the LOG folder of the SQL Server home folder. This folder has more than one log file (usually seven), and the first of them is ERRORLOG. By default there's no extension to these files. To see their contents, you need to add a .txt extension to the file. Note that you may not be able to change the name of the log file if SQL Server is running. So, stop SQL Server before modifying or reading the log file. The partial contents of ERRORLOG looks like the following:

```
2002-10-27 13:32:00.57 server
Microsoft SQL Server  2000 - 8.00.194 (Intel X86)
Aug  6 2000 00:57:48
Copyright (c) 1988-2000 Microsoft Corporation
Personal Edition on Windows NT 5.0 (Build 2195:
Service Pack 3)
2002-10-27 13:32:00.79 server
Copyright (C) 1988-2000 Microsoft Corporation.
2002-10-27 13:32:00.79 server
 All rights reserved.
2002-10-27 13:32:00.79 server
Server Process ID is 596.
2002-10-27 13:32:00.79 server
Logging SQL Server messages in file
'D:\Program Files\Microsoft SQL Server\MSSQL\log\ERRORLOG'.
2002-10-27 13:32:00.97 server
SQL Server is starting at priority class 'normal'(1 CPU detected).
2002-10-27 13:32:02.43 server
 SQL Server configured for thread mode processing.
2002-10-27 13:32:02.57 server
Using dynamic lock allocation.
[500] Lock Blocks, [1000] Lock Owner Blocks.
2002-10-27 13:32:02.95 spid3
......
```

SQL Server also adds error messages to the Windows NT event log. You can use the Windows NT Event Viewer to view the error messages. The Windows NT Event Viewer is located in the Windows NT Administrative Tools group.

Using the SqlException Class

The SqlException class is thrown when SQL Server returns a warning or error. The SqlException class is inherited from the SystemException class, which in turn is inherited from the Exception class. Besides the Exception class members, the SqlException class defines the properties described in Table 9-4.

Table 9-4. The SqlException *Class Properties*

PROPERTY	DESCRIPTION
Class	Returns the severity level of the error.
Errors	Returns a collection of one or more SqlError objects. This property is used when you need to collect more information about the errors generated by the Sql data provider.
LineNumber	Returns the line number within the SQL command or stored procedure that generated the error.
Message	Represents human-readable text of the error.
Number	Returns a number that identifies the type of error.
Procedure	Represents the name of the stored procedure that generated the error.
Server	Represents the name of the computer running SQL Server.
Source	Returns the name of the provider.
State	Numeric error code from SQL Server that represents an error or warning.

OK, now you'll see the SqlException class in action. Listing 9-7 connects to a SQL Server called MCB, reads data from the Customers table, and then fills a DataSet.

Listing 9-7. Reading Data from a SQL Server

```
' Create a Connection Object
    Dim ConnectionString As String = "Integrated Security=SSPI;" & _
        "Initial Catalog=Northwind;Data Source=MCB;"
    Dim conn As SqlConnection = New SqlConnection(ConnectionString)
    Dim SQL As String = "SELECT * FROM Customers"
    Dim adapter As SqlDataAdapter = New SqlDataAdapter(SQL, conn)
    Dim ds As DataSet = New DataSet()

    Try
      ' open a connection
      conn.Open()
      adapter.Fill(ds, "Customers")
```

```
Catch exp As SqlException
  ' Generate error message
  Console.WriteLine("Error:" + exp.Message & _
  ", Number:" + exp.Number.ToString() & _
  ", Line Number: " + exp.LineNumber.ToString() & _
  ", Server:" + exp.Server.ToString() & _
   ", Source:" + exp.Source.ToString())
Finally
  ' Close the connection
  If conn.State = ConnectionState.Open Then
    conn.Close()
  End If
  ' Dispose the connection
  If (Not conn Is Nothing) Then
    conn.Dispose()
  End If
End Try
```

Now change the SQL Server name to MCB1. The connection string looks like following:

```
Dim ConnectionString As String = "Integrated Security=SSPI;" & _
        "Initial Catalog=Northwind;Data Source=MCB1;"
```

If you run the code after changing the SQL Server name, it generates an error that looks like Figure 9-4.

Figure 9-4. SqlException *messages for SQL Server not found*

Now let's switch the SQL Server to MCB and change the SQL string to the following:

```
Dim SQL As String = "SELECT * FROM Test"
```

The output looks like Figure 9-5.

Figure 9-5. `SqlException` *messages when a database table not found*

Using the SqlError and SqlErrorCollection Classes

The `SqlException.Errors` property returns an object of `SqlErrorCollection` class. This object is a collection of `SqlError` objects, each of which encapsulates an error or warning by SQL Server. The `Count` property of `SqlErrorCollection` returns the total number of errors in a collection, and the `Item` property returns an error at the specified index.

The `Class` property of `SqlError` represents the severity level of the error, which varies from 0 to 25. Even using the severity level, you can notify a user of the results of the error.

Messages with a severity level starting from 0 to 10 are informational and indicate a nonfatal error. Severity levels from 11 to 16 indicate a user error that can be corrected by the user. Severity levels from 17 to 25 indicate software or hardware errors, but the program can continue working. Severity level 20 or more indicates serious fatal errors and may cause damage.

Listing 9-8 uses the `SqlError` and `SqlErrorCollection` classes and handles the errors generated by the Sql data provider.

Listing 9-8. Using the `SqlError` *and* `SqlErrorCollection` *Objects*

```
Imports System.Data.SqlClient
Module Module1
  Sub Main()
    ' Create a Connection Object
    Dim ConnectionString As String = "Integrated Security=SSPI;" & _
        "Initial Catalog=Northwind;Data Source=MCB;"
    Dim conn As SqlConnection = New SqlConnection(ConnectionString)
    Dim SQL As String = "SELECT * FROM Test"
```

```
Dim adapter As SqlDataAdapter = New SqlDataAdapter(SQL, conn)
Dim ds As DataSet = New DataSet()

Try
  ' open a connection
  conn.Open()
  adapter.Fill(ds, "Customers")
Catch exp As SqlException
  ' Generate error message
Dim errs As SqlErrorCollection = exp.Errors
Dim i As Integer
Dim err As SqlError
For Each err In errs
  Console.WriteLine("Error #:" & i.ToString() & _
          ", Class:" & err.Class.ToString() & _
          ", Line Number :" & err.LineNumber & _
          ", Message:" & err.Message & _
          ", Source:" & err.Source & _
          ", Server:" & err.Server)
Next    Finally
  ' Close the connection
  If conn.State = ConnectionState.Open Then
    conn.Close()
  End If
  ' Dispose the connection
  If (Not conn Is Nothing) Then
    conn.Dispose()
  End If
End Try
End Sub
End Module
```

Summary

In this chapter, you learned about exception handling. You saw how exception handling works in .NET, and you learned how to handle exceptions in ADO.NET.

ODBC .Net data provider classes work with ODBC data sources. The good thing about ODBC connectivity is that an application can connect to multiple data sources as long as it has an ODBC driver for the data source. In next chapter, you'll learn about the ODBC .Net data provider, and you'll learn how to write applications that access various data sources.

CHAPTER 10

Working with the ODBC .NET Data Provider

IN PREVIOUS CHAPTERS, you saw how to use the Sql data provider to work with SQL Server databases. You also learned that there aren't great differences between any of the data providers. With a few minor exceptions, it's just a matter of changing class names and the connection string. You don't believe us? To prove this theory, you'll see how to use the ODBC data provider in this chapter.

The ODBC data provider uses ODBC drivers to connect to different data sources; it's useful when you're not sure what database your clients will be using in their applications. The user shouldn't have any trouble connecting as long as they have an ODBC driver for the database installed on their machine. In this chapter, you'll see how you can use the ODBC .NET data provider to work with MySQL, Oracle, Excel, and even text data files.

Using the ODBC .NET Data Provider

You read a brief discussion about the ODBC .NET data provider in Chapter 4. The ODBC .NET data provider provides access to ODBC data sources with the help of native ODBC drivers in the same way that the OleDb data provider accesses native OLE DB providers. One of the best things about working with ADO.NET data providers is that all the data providers define a similar class hierarchy. The only things you need to change are the classes and the connection string.

Before you start using the ODBC .NET data provider, let's quickly look at some installation issues.

NOTE *If you're using Visual Studio .NET (VS .NET) code name Everett, you don't need to worry about installation because the ODBC .NET data provider is already installed. You can skip the following section.*

Installing the ODBC .NET Data Provider

Unlike the Sql and OleDb data providers, the ODBC data provider is an add-on component to the .NET Framework. If the ODBC .NET provider isn't installed on your system, you can download it from the .NET Software Development Kit (SDK) and VS .NET on the Microsoft site (www.microsoft.com/data).

> **NOTE** *Microsoft VS .NET code name Everett installs the ODBC .NET data provider automatically.*

After installing the ODBC data provider, you need to customize the Toolbox to add the ODBC data components to it. You can customize the Toolbox by right-clicking the Data tab and selecting Customize Toolbox.

> **NOTE** *Make sure the Data tab is selected when you choose Customize Toolbox. Otherwise, new components will be added to the active tab.*

Next, click the .NET Framework Components tab (not the default COM components) and look for the ODBC components. Check the appropriate boxes, and then click the OK button. These check boxes are OdbcCommand, OdbcCommandBuilder, OdbcConnection, and OdbcDataAdapter.

Next, you need to add a reference to the Microsoft.Data.Odbc.dll assembly using Project ➤ Add Reference. You can use the Browse button to browse the directory. The Microsoft.Data.Odbc.dll assembly resides in the \Program Files\Microsoft.NET\Odbc.NET directory. On the Add Reference dialog box, select Microsoft.Data.Odbc.dll and then click the OK button, which adds the Microsoft.Data.Odbc namespace reference to the project. You can see the namespace reference by expanding the References node of your project in the Server Explorer.

To make sure the ODBC data provider is installed and added to your project, you can also look at the Toolbox. If the ODBC data provider is installed on your machine, the Toolbox will display the ODBC data components.

NOTE *The Toolbox's Data tab isn't available for console applications. However, you can use ADO.NET in console-based applications by writing the code manually.*

You saw how to use the SQL and OleDb data providers in previous chapters. Working with the ODBC data provider is no different from working with the Sql and OleDb data providers. Unlike the Sql and OleDb data providers, however, the ODBC data provider is defined in the `Microsoft.Data.Odbc` namespace. You must add the following reference to this namespace before you can start using the ODBC data provider classes:

```
Imports Microsoft.Data.Odbc
```

NOTE *If you're using Microsoft VS .NET code name Everett, the ODBC data provider is defined in the* `System.Data.Odbc` *namespace. Make sure you import the correct namespace.*

Understanding the ODBC .NET Data Provider

The ODBC data provider defines similar classes and a similar class hierarchy as the Sql and OleDb data providers. Further, you can use the ODBC data provider classes the same way as you've used the Sql and OleDb data provider classes. Table 10-1 defines the ODBC data provider classes.

Table 10-1. The ODBC .NET Data Provider Classes

CLASS	DESCRIPTION
OdbcCommand	Similar to OleDbCommand and SqlCommand, this class represents an SQL statement or stored procedure to execute against a data source.
OdbcCommandBuilder	Similar to OleDbCommandBuilder and SqlCommandBuilder, this class automatically generates SELECT, INSERT, UPDATE, and DELETE SQL commands.
OdbcConnection	Represents a connection.
OdbcDataAdapter	Represents a DataAdapter.

Table 10-1. The ODBC .NET Data Provider Classes (Continued)

CLASS	DESCRIPTION
OdbcDataReader	Represents a DataReader.
OdbcError	Represents errors and warnings.
OdbcErrorCollection	Represents a collection of errors and warnings.
OdbcException	Represents an ODBC Exception class.
OdbcParameter	Represents an ODBC parameter.
OdbcParameterCollection	Represents a parameter collection.
OdbcTransaction	Represents a transaction.

As you can see from Table 10-1, the ODBC data provider has many classes that are similar to the Sql and OleDb data providers. To use the ODBC data provider classes, you create a Connection object and then fill data from the Connection object to a DataAdapter or a DataReader, and they display the data.

Accessing Access Databases

Now you'll see an example of how to access data from a data source using the ODBC data provider. In this example, you'll use the Access 2000 Northwind database as the data source.

Before creating a connection, the first thing you need to set is the connection string. The connection string for OdbcConnection contains a data source driver and the data source path with an optional user ID and password. Optionally, you can also use an ODBC Data Source Name (DSN) as the connection string. You create a DSN from the ODBC Administration applet in the Windows Control Panel.

The connection string for an Oracle database looks like the following:

```
Driver={Microsoft ODBC for Oracle};Server=ORACLE8i7;UID=odbcuser;PWD=odbc$5xr
```

The connection string for a Microsoft Access database looks like the following:

```
Driver={Microsoft Access Driver (*.mdb)};DBQ=c:\\Northwind.mdb
```

The connection string for an Excel database looks like the following:

```
Driver={Microsoft Excel Driver (*.xls)};DBQ=c:\bin\book1.xls
```

The connection string for a text database looks like the following:

```
Driver={Microsoft Text Driver (*.txt; *.csv)};DBQ=c:\\
```

You can use any DSN by using the following connection string:

```
DSN=dsnname
```

The connection string for a SQL Server database looks like following:

```
"DRIVER={SQL Server};SERVER=MyServer;UID=sa;PWD=Qvr&77xk;DATABASE=northwind;";
```

Listing 10-1 reads data from the Northwind database and shows the results on the console. For this example, create a console application to test the code. As you can see from Listing 10-1, first you import the Microsoft.Data.Odbc namespace. After that you create an OdbcConnection object with the Microsoft Access ODBC driver and the Northwind database. The next step is to create an OdbcCommand object and call the ExecuteReader method, which returns an OdbcDataReader object. Finally, you read data from the DataReader and display the results on the console.

Listing 10-1. Reading Data from Northwind Using the ODBC Data Provider

```
Imports Microsoft.Data.Odbc
Module Module1
  Sub Main()
    ' Build a connection and SQL strings
    Dim connectionString As String = _
    "Driver={Microsoft Access Driver (*.mdb)};DBQ=c:\\Northwind.mdb"
    Dim SQL As String _
    = "SELECT EmployeeID, FirstName, LastName FROM Employees"
    ' Create connection object
    Dim conn As OdbcConnection = New OdbcConnection(connectionString)
    ' Create command object
    Dim cmd As OdbcCommand = New OdbcCommand(SQL)
    cmd.Connection = conn
    ' Open connection
    conn.Open()
    ' Call command's ExecuteReader
    Dim reader As OdbcDataReader = cmd.ExecuteReader()
    ' Read the reader and display results on the console
    Console.WriteLine("Employeed ID, First Name, Last Name ")
    While reader.Read()
      Console.Write(reader.GetInt32(0).ToString())
      Console.Write(", ")
```

```
        Console.Write(reader.GetString(1).ToString())
        Console.Write(", ")
        Console.WriteLine(reader.GetString(2).ToString())
      End While
      ' close reader and connection
      reader.Close()
      conn.Close()
      conn.Dispose()
    End Sub
End Module
```

The output of Listing 10-1 looks like Figure 10-1. As you can see, the program reads the EmployeeID, FirstName, and LastName fields from Employees table.

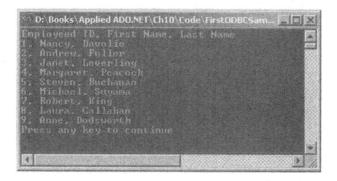

Figure 10-1. The output of Listing 10-1

Accessing MySQL Databases

MySQL is a widely used, multithreaded, multiuser, robust SQL database server. You can use MySQL for free under the GNU General Public License. You can download the MySQL database and its tools from www.mysql.com/downloads/index.html. After downloading the zipped file, you unzip it in a folder and run Setup.exe. By default the setup file installs MySQL in your C:/mysql folder. The Documentation section (www.mysql.com) has detailed instructions on how to install and register the MySQL server and its services.

NOTE *You may need Administrator rights to install and register the MySQL server and its services.*

After installing MySQL, make sure it's running. If the service isn't running, you may need to start it manually. You can start it by selecting Control Panel ➤ Administrative Tools ➤ Services, right-clicking the MySql service, and then selecting the Start menu option. This action will start MySql as a service. Because in this chapter you'll be using ODBC to connect to a MySQL database, you need to install an ODBC driver for it. You can find the most widely used ODBC driver for MySQL, MyODBC, at `www.mysql.com/downloads/api-myodbc.html`.

After downloading the zipped driver file, the obvious action is to unzip it and install it. If the driver is installed properly, you can see it from the ODBC Data Source Administrator by selecting Control Panel ➤ Data Source (ODBC). You must see MySQL in the ODBC Drivers list to proceed.

For your program, you can use any MySQL database you have on the server, but for this example, use the Northwind database. You've never heard of a MySQL version of the Northwind database, you say? Well, there isn't one. You'll convert the Access Northwind database to MySQL and then you'll use it.

To convert (or, import) the Access Northwind database, you can use a free tool called DBTools Manager. This tool provides many handy functions for MySQL developers. You can download DBTools at `www.dbtools.com.br`.

Accessing MySQL Databases

As we've been saying, working with different data sources is only a matter of changing the connection string and class names. You can access a MySQL database either using a DSN or using the database name directly in the connection string. You can use a database name directly, as shown in the following code:

```
dim connectionString as string =
"Driver={MySQL};SERVER=localhost;DATABASE=NorthwindMySQL;"
```

Or you can use an ODBC DSN, as you can see from the following code that uses TestDSN to connect to the data source:

```
Dim conn as OdbcConnection = new OdbcConnection("DSN=TestDSN")
```

To test this code, create a Windows application, add a DataGrid control to the form, and then write the code in Listing 10-2 on the Form_Load event. As you can see in Listing 10-2, this code is similar to the code you saw in Listing 10-1. It creates a Connection object, a DataAdapter, fills the DataSet from the DataAdapter, and then sets the DataSet's DefaultViewManager as the DataGrid control's DataSource property.

Listing 10-2. Accessing a MySQL Database

```
Private Sub Form1_Load(ByVal sender As System.Object, _
  ByVal e As System.EventArgs) Handles MyBase.Load
    Dim connectionString As String = _
    "Driver={MySQL};SERVER=localhost;DATABASE=NorthwindMySQL;"
    Dim conn As OdbcConnection = New OdbcConnection(connectionString)
    conn.Open()
    Dim da As OdbcDataAdapter = New OdbcDataAdapter _
    ("SELECT CustomerID, ContactName, ContactTitle FROM Customers", conn)
    Dim ds As DataSet = New DataSet("Cust")
    da.Fill(ds, "Customers")
    DataGrid1.DataSource = ds.DefaultViewManager
    conn.Close()
    conn.Dispose()
  End Sub
```

Accessing Text File Databases

To test text database connectivity, you can export the Employees table of the Northwind database using the File ➤ Export option of Access 2000. In the following section, you'll export a table to a text file, and you'll see how to use it with the ODBC DataAdapter.

Exporting an Access Table to a Text File

You can export an Access database table to a text file using the Export option. In other words, select a table and choose File ➤ Export. Another option is to right-click a table and choose the Export option from the menu.

After clicking the Export option, the dialog box that appears lets you pick a path and the file you want to export. There are many export formats available. For this example, select the Text Files option.

Next, the Export Text Wizard lets you define the format of the text file—either delimited or fixed width (see Figure 10-2).

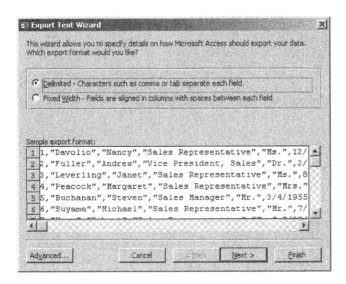

Figure 10-2. Export Text Wizard options

You can also click the Advanced button to set more options, such as specifying the delimiters and other options (see Figure 10-3).

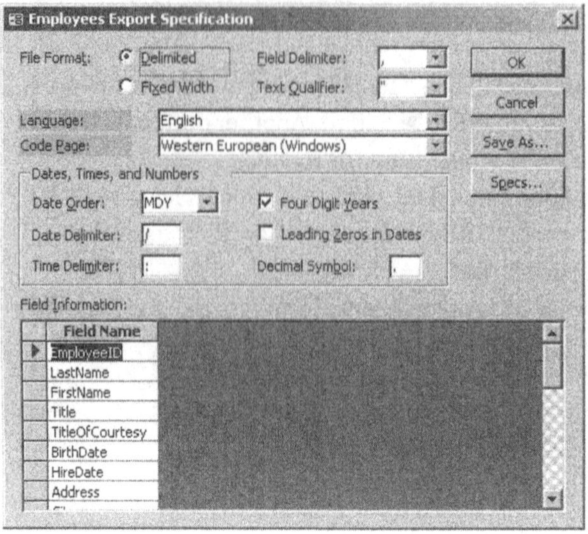

Figure 10-3. The advanced options of the Export Text Wizard

The next screen lets you pick the delimiter, including a comma, tab, semi-colon, space, and others. Figure 10-4 shows the Comma option checked.

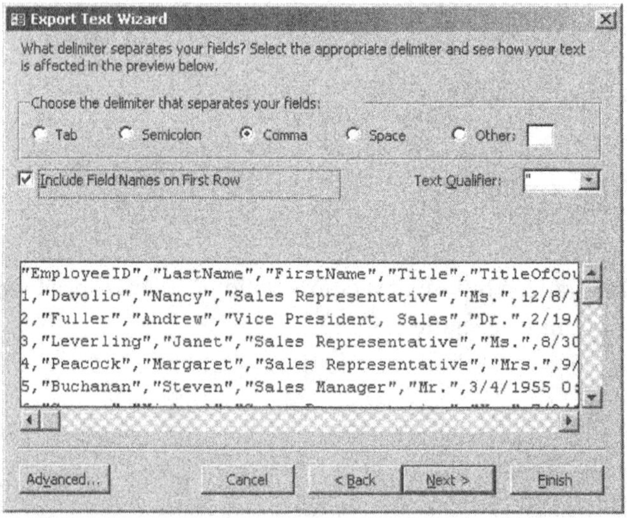

Figure 10-4. Delimiter options of the Export Text Wizard

Figure 10-4 also shows the Include Field Names on First Row check box selected. This option adds the first row of the text file as field names.

The last page of the wizard asks you for the filename of where you want to export the data. Enter the filename `C:\Employees.txt`.

Finally, click the Finish button. When the wizard is done exporting, you'll see a message saying the export is finished. Click OK and close Access.

If you view `C:\Employees.txt`, it looks like Figure 10-5.

```
Employees.txt - Notepad                                    _ □ ×
File  Edit  Format  Help
"EmployeeID","LastName","FirstName","Title","TitleofCourtesy","BirthDa
te","HireDate","Address","City","Region","PostalCode","Country","HomeP
hone","Extension","Photo","Notes","ReportsTo"
1,"Davolio","Nancy","Sales Representative","Ms.",12/8/1968
0:00:00,5/1/1992 0:00:00,"507 - 20th Ave. E.
Apt. 2A","Seattle","WA","98122","USA","(206)
555-9857","5467",,"Education includes a BA in psychology from Colorado
State University.  She also completed ""The Art of the Cold Call.""
Nancy is a member of Toastmasters International.",2
2,"Fuller","Andrew","Vice President, Sales","Dr.",2/19/1952
0:00:00,8/14/1992 0:00:00,"908 W. Capital
Way","Tacoma","WA","98401","USA","(206) 555-9482","3457",,"Andrew
```

Figure 10-5. Exported `Employees.txt` *file from* `Nothwind.mdb`

Accessing a Text File

You can access a text file using the ODBC data provider. There are two ways to access text files: You can create a DSN from the ODBC Data Source Administrator, or you can access the text file directly from your application. To create a data source for a text file, go to ODBC Data Source Admin, click the New button (or the Add button if you're using Windows XP), and select the Microsoft Text Driver (*.txt, *.csv) option (see Figure 10-6).

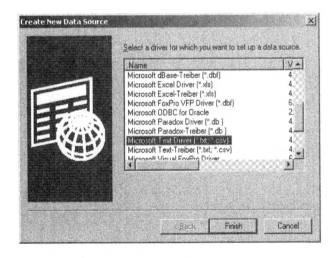

Figure 10-6. Selecting the Microsoft Text Driver (.txt, *.csv) option*

You define the DSN name and description in the ODBC Text Setup dialog box. If you don't want to use the current directory, uncheck the Use Current Directory option to enable the Select Directory button and click Options to see more options (see Figure 10-7).

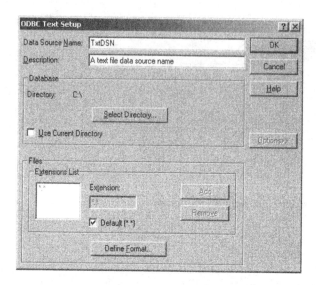

Figure 10-7. Setting the DSN name and description

Now you can select any directory you want to use. An entire text file is used as a database table (see Figure 10-8).

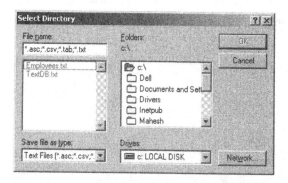

Figure 10-8. Selecting the directory and file types

You can even define different formats by using the Define Format button in the ODBC Text Setup dialog box. As you can see from Figure 10-9, all files are treated as a database table. From the Format drop-down box, you can select the type of format you want such as comma delimited or tab delimited. The Guess button assigns the column names for you. If it doesn't find a proper format file, it creates F1...Fn columns for you. You can also add, modify, and remove columns and their types.

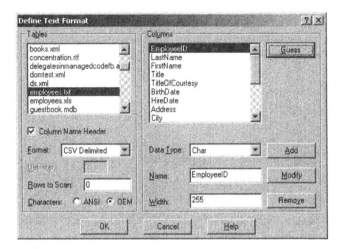

Figure 10-9. Defining a text file format and column settings

After creating a DSN, you can use it as a connection source for your connection:

```
Dim conn As OdbcConnection = New OdbcConnection("DSN=TxtDSN")
```

Another way to access text files is directly using the text ODBC driver in the connection string. For example, `ConnectionString` in the following code defines a connection with the Microsoft Text Driver and the source directory `c:\`:

```
Dim connectionString As String = _
"Driver={Microsoft Text Driver (*.txt; *.csv)};DBQ=c:\\"
```

Every .txt or .csv file in the C:\ directory will be treated as a database table, which you pass in your SQL string:

```
OdbcConnection  conn = new OdbcConnection(ConnectionString);
OdbcDataAdapter da = new OdbcDataAdapter
("Select * FROM Employees.txt", conn
```

To test this code, create a Windows application, drop a DataGrid control onto the form, and use the code in Listing 10-3 for the Form_Load event.

Listing 10-3. Accessing the TextDB.txt *File*

```
Private Sub Form1_Load(ByVal sender As System.Object, _
  ByVal e As System.EventArgs) Handles MyBase.Load
    ' Connection string for a Text File
    Dim connectionString As String = _
    "Driver={Microsoft Text Driver (*.txt; *.csv)};DBQ=c:\\"
    ' Query the Employees.txt file as a table
    Dim conn As OdbcConnection = New OdbcConnection(connectionString)
    conn.Open()
    ' Create a data adapter and fill a DataSet
    Dim da As OdbcDataAdapter = New OdbcDataAdapter _
    ("Select * FROM Employees.txt", conn)
    Dim ds As DataSet = New DataSet()
    da.Fill(ds, "TextDB")
    ' Bind the DataSet to a DataGrid
    DataGrid1.DataSource = ds.DefaultViewManager
    ' Close the connection
    conn.Close()
    conn.Dispose()
  End Sub
```

NOTE *Don't forget to add a reference to the* Microsoft.Data.Odbc *namespace.*

If you compile and run the application, you should see data in the DataGrid control.

Accessing Excel Databases

You'll now learn how to connect to Excel databases. If you don't have an Excel database, you can export data from your Northwind database to test this example. As you did in the previous section, export the Employees table from Microsoft Access by right-clicking the table and selecting the Export option. (You can also choose File ➤ Export).

When you export, make sure you select the Microsoft Excel 97–2000 (*.xls) option in the Save as Type drop-down list. For this example, save the file as Employees.xls.

Now, if you open Employees.xls, it looks like Figure 10-10.

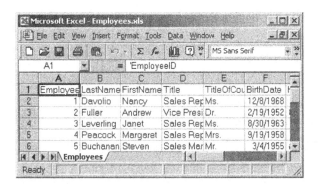

Figure 10-10. Employees.xls *data view*

Again, you can access the Excel database either by using an ODBC DSN or by passing the database name directly in the connection string. In this example, you're passing the database name directly:

```
Dim ConnectionString as string =
"Driver={Microsoft Excel Driver (*.xls)};DBQ=c:\\Employees.xls"
```

After that, the code should be familiar to you. It's the same steps as creating a DataAdapter, selecting some fields of the table, filling a DataSet from the DataAdapter, and binding data with the data-bound controls. To test this code, create a Windows application, add a DataGrid control and a ListBox control to the form, and import the Microsoft.Data.Odbc namespace. Listing 10-4 shows the full source code.

Listing 10-4. Accessing Employees.xls *Using the ODBC Data Provider*

```
private void Form1_Load(object sender, System.EventArgs e)
{
 // Connection string for ODBC Excel Driver
 string ConnectionString =
 @"Driver={Microsoft Excel Driver (*.xls)};DBQ=c:\Employees.xls";
 OdbcConnection  conn = new OdbcConnection(ConnectionString);

 // Tables in Excel can be thought of as sheets and are queried as shown
 string sql = "Select EmployeeID, FirstName, LastName FROM Employees";
 conn.Open();

 OdbcDataAdapter da = new OdbcDataAdapter(sql, conn);

 DataSet ds = new DataSet();
 da.Fill(ds, "Employees");

 dataGrid1.DataSource = ds.DefaultViewManager;
 listBox1.DataSource = ds.DefaultViewManager;
 listBox1.DisplayMember = "Employees.FirstName";
}
```

The output of Listing 10-4 looks like Figure 10-11.

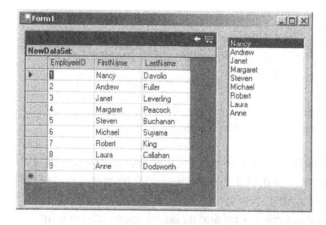

Figure 10-11. Output of Listing 10-4

Implementing Two .NET 1.1 Updates

The following two .NET version 1.1 updates affect the ODBC data provider:

Require FullTrust for OleDb, ODBC, and OracleClient: You can now use portions of System.Data in partially trusted applications, such as SQL Client. This means that it's now necessary to require FullTrust permission for OleDb, ODBC, and OracleClient. It's not possible to allow these providers to work in partially trusted scenarios because of their interaction with native pointers and Application Programming Interfaces (APIs).

Workaround: If you're using .NET Framework version 1.0 and are setting system.data.dll as allowed in partially trusted scenarios, you must modify your security settings to allow these components to work in partially trusted scenarios.

Removed an OnStateChange(Open) event from OLE DB client and ODBC client packages: The .NET Framework version 1.0 was incorrectly firing an OnStatechange(Open) event when there was an invalid connection string.

Workaround: No workaround is available for this change. Generally, this indicates that the change isn't intended to have a workaround.

Summary

The best thing about ADO.NET is that it treats all types of data sources similarly. As we've stated repeatedly, the only difference is the connection string and the class names. If you know how to build a connection string, you can use the same code to work with multiple data sources. Based on this theory, you saw how to work with the MySQL, Oracle, and Sybase databases. You also saw how to work with Excel spreadsheets and text files.

When it comes to the performance of database applications, server-side data objects such as stored procedures and views play a vital role. ADO.NET—with the help of VS .NET—provides great support for creating, managing, and executing stored procedures. The next chapter covers stored procedures and views, as well as how to write database applications using these two objects.

CHAPTER 11

Stored Procedures and Views

RELATIONAL DATABASES SUCH as SQL Server and Oracle rely on stored procedures to do repetitive tasks, so a programmer's main jobs when creating database applications are creating, debugging, and testing stored procedures (often called *stored procs*). Another database object it behooves programmers to learn is the view—or *virtual table*. In this chapter, you'll learn how to take advantage of Visual Studio .NET (VS .NET) tools to work with both stored procedures and views.

Working with Stored Procedures

User-defined stored procedures are handy for a variety of reasons. User-defined stored procs, as opposed to the built-in ones called *system* stored procedures, distribute load between a client and a database server because they reside on a database server but are executed by a client's call. Stored procedures not only provide modularity in an application design, they also provide better control, management, load distribution, and performance. In the following sections, we discuss how to create and execute stored procedures using VS .NET.

Creating a Stored Procedure

You have a variety of ways to create stored procedures. As a database administrator, you can use the database server's administrative tools (SQL Server Enterprise Manager or Oracle Enterprise Manager, for example) to create and manage stored procedures. As a programmer, you can create stored procedures programmatically by using the CREATE PROCEDURE SQL statement. In this chapter, you'll learn how to create and manage stored procedures using VS .NET.

VS .NET's Server Explorer, discussed in Chapter 2, enables you to create, update, and delete You can launch the Server Explorer by selecting View ➤ Server Explorer. After opening it, you'll see the available database servers in the list. If you expand a server tree node, you'll find the available databases and database objects on the server. You can use the database's Stored Procedures node to managed stored procedures. As you can see from Figure 11-1, the Stored Procedures node lists all the available stored procedures in the Northwind database. You can view stored procedures by double-clicking the stored procedure's name.

Figure 11-1. Viewing available stored procedures in the Northwind database

The right-click menu option allows you to create a new stored procedure and edit, delete, and execute existing stored procedures (see Figure 11-2).

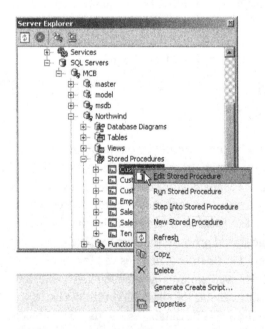

Figure 11-2. Create, edit, delete, and run stored procedure options

The Edit Stored Procedure option lets you edit a stored procedure. To edit an existing stored procedure of the Northwind database, right-click the `CustOrderHist` stored procedure, and select the Edit Stored Procedure option. The stored procedure editor opens (see Figure 11-3).

```
Form1.cs [Design]*   dbo.CustOrder...CB.Northwind)                    ◁ ▷
   ALTER PROCEDURE CustOrderHist @CustomerID nchar(5)
   AS
   SELECT ProductName, Total=SUM(Quantity)
   FROM Products P, [Order Details] OD, Orders O, Customers C
   WHERE C.CustomerID = @CustomerID
   AND C.CustomerID = O.CustomerID AND O.OrderID = OD.OrderID AND OD.
   GROUP BY ProductName
```

Figure 11-3. Stored procedure editor

NOTE *In SQL Server, the login that creates or has the ownership of a database or the administrator of the server is known as the* database owner. *In the database and its objects, the username* dbo *is always associated with the login name of the database owner.*

Now that you know how to edit an existing stored procedure, let's create a one. You can create a stored procedure by right-clicking the Stored Procedures node and selecting the New Stored Procedure option. This launches the stored procedure editor, which you use to write stored procedures. In SQL Server, dbo stands for the database owner. In Figure 11-4, the syntax `CREATE PROCEDURE dbo.StoredProcedure2` creates a stored procedure where `StoredProcedure1` is the name of the stored procedure and `dbo` is the owner of the stored procedure.

```
:s [Design]*  dbo.CustOrderHis... (MCB.Northwind)  dbo.StoredPro...MCB.Northwind)  ‹
   CREATE PROCEDURE dbo.StoredProcedure2
   /*
      (
         @parameter1 datatype = default value,
         @parameter2 datatype OUTPUT
      )
   */
   AS
      /* SET NOCOUNT ON */
      RETURN
```

Figure 11-4. Creating a stored procedure

A stored procedure can return data as a result of SELECT statement, a return code (an integer value), or an output parameter. As you can see from Figure 11-4, the section after CREATE PROCEDURE is the parameters section, which is closed with comments (/* and */). If you have no requirement for using parameters in a stored procedure, you can skip this area. The section after AS is used for the actual SQL statement, and the section after RETURN is used for returning a value when you execute a stored procedure.

Now, you can write a simple SELECT statement and save it as a stored procedure. Use this SQL statement to select three columns values for customers from the United States:

```
SELECT CustomerId, CompanyName, ContactName
FROM Customers WHERE Country ='USA'
```

You can change the stored procedure name to whatever you want; this example uses mySP (my stored procedure). The final stored procedure looks like Figure 11-5.

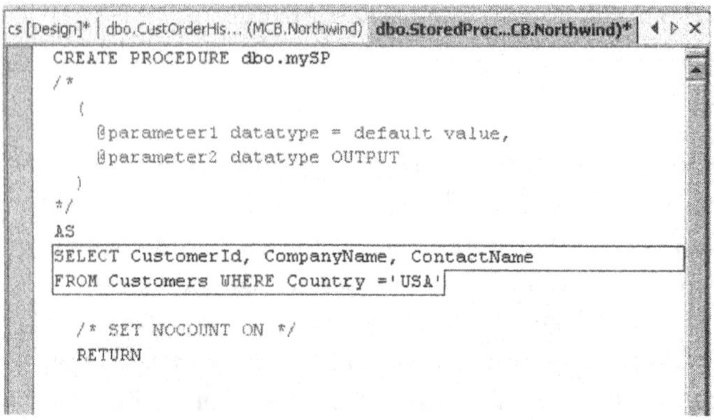

Figure 11-5. The mySP *stored procedure in the editor*

You can save a stored procedure by using File ➤ Save mySP or the Save All menu option or toolbar button. The Save option is also available after right-clicking on the stored procedure editor.

NOTE *The Save option not only creates a stored procedure, but it also changes the* CREATE PROCEDURE *statement to* ALTER PROCEDURE *because the stored procedure has already been created.*

Now, if you go to the Server Explorer and look at all the stored procedures for the Northwind database, your stored procedure should be listed. As you can see from Figure 11-6, the stored procedure mySP has three fields listed under it that appear in the SELECT statement.

Figure 11-6. The mySP *stored procedure listed for the Northwind database*

Executing a Stored Procedure from VS .NET

Executing a stored procedure in the Server Explorer is simple. You run (or execute) a stored procedure by right-clicking on the stored procedure editor and selecting Run Stored Procedure.

When you run the stored procedure mySP, the output looks like Figure 11-7.

```
Output                                                                        ×
Database Output                                                               ▼
  Running dbo."mySP".

  CustomerId CompanyName                                  ContactName
  ---------- ---------------------------------------      -------------------
  GREAL      Great Lakes Food Market                      Howard Snyder
  HUNGC      Hungry Coyote Import Store                   Yoshi Latimer
  LAZYK      Lazy K Kountry Store                         John Steel
  LETSS      Let's Stop N Shop                            Jaime Yorres
  LONEP      Lonesome Pine Restaurant                     Fran Wilson
  OLDWO      Old World Delicatessen                       Rene Phillips
  RATTC      Rattlesnake Canyon Grocery                   Paula Wilson
  SAVEA      Save-a-lot Markets                           Jose Pavarotti
  SPLIR      Split Rail Beer & Ale                        Art Braunschweiger
  THEBI      The Big Cheese                               Liz Nixon
  THECR      The Cracker Box                              Liu Wong
  TRAIH      Trail's Head Gourmet Provisioners            Helvetius Nagy
  WHITC      White Clover Markets                         Karl Jablonski
  No more results.
  (13 row(s) returned)
  @RETURN_VALUE = 0
  Finished running dbo."mySP".
```

Figure 11-7. The output of the mySP *stored procedure in VS .NET*

NOTE *Like your* SELECT *SQL statement, you can use almost any SQL statement, such as* UPDATE *and* DELETE, *in the stored procedure. (Exceptions include* CREATE TRIGGER, CREATE VIEW, CREATE DEFAULT, CREATE PROCEDURE, *and* CREATE RULE.*)*

A stored procedure can also accept input parameters. For example, the CustOrdersDetail stored procedure takes a parameter value of OrderID. Based on the OrderID value, it returns ProductName and calculates Discount and ExtendedPrice (see Figure 11-8).

```
lis... (MCB.Northwind) | dbo.mySP : Stor... (MCB.Northwind)   dbo.CustOrders...CB.Northwind)*  ◄ ▷

   ALTER PROCEDURE CustOrdersDetail @OrderID int
   AS
   SELECT ProductName,
       UnitPrice=ROUND(Od.UnitPrice, 2),
       Quantity,
       Discount=CONVERT(int, Discount * 100),
       ExtendedPrice=ROUND(CONVERT(money,
       Quantity * (1 - Discount) * Od.UnitPrice), 2)
   FROM Products P, [Order Details] Od
   WHERE Od.ProductID = P.ProductID and Od.OrderID = @OrderID
```

Figure 11-8. Stored procedure with input parameter

When you run the stored procedure, it asks you for the value of the OrderID parameter, as shown in Figure 11-9.

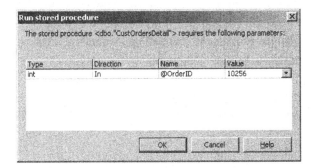

Figure 11-9. Registering a stored procedure parameter

The output of the stored procedure CustOrdersDetail looks like Figure 11-10.

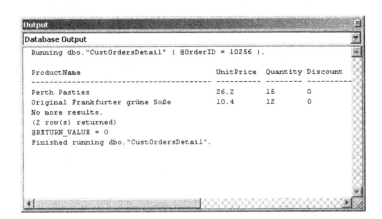

Figure 11-10. The output of stored procedure CustOrdersDetail

Executing a Stored Procedure Programmatically

As an application developer, most of the time you'll be creating and testing stored procedures programmatically. You can execute a stored procedure programmatically using the Command object. Instead of passing a SQL statement, you pass the stored procedure name as the SQL statement to execute a stored procedure. As you saw in Chapter 4, each data provider provides a Command object to execute SQL statements. The Command classes for the OleDb, ODBC, and Sql data providers are

OleDbCommand, OdbcCommand, and SqlCommand (respectively). Listing 11-1 shows how to use SqlCommand to execute a stored procedure programmatically against a SQL Server database.

There are two steps involved in executing a stored procedure from your program. First, you set the Command object property CommandText to the stored procedure name; second, you set the CommandType property to CommandType.StoredProcedure. Listing 11-1 executes the mySP stored procedure you created in the previous section. To test code in Listing 11-1, create a console application and type Listing 11-1 on the Main method. Don't forget to import the following two namespaces to the project before using Sql data provider classes:

```
Imports System.Data
Imports System.Data.SqlClient
```

Listing 11-1. Executing the mySP Stored Procedure Using the Sql Data Provider

```
Sub Main()
    ' Create a Connection Object.
    Dim ConnectionString As String = "Integrated Security=SSPI;" & _
            "Initial Catalog=Northwind;" & _
            "Data Source=localhost;"
    Dim conn As SqlConnection = New SqlConnection(ConnectionString)
    ' Open the connection
    conn.Open()
    ' Create a SqlCommand object and pass mySP as the
    ' SQL command and set CommandType property to
    ' CommandType.StoredProcedure
    Dim cmd As SqlCommand = New SqlCommand("mySP", conn)
    cmd.CommandType = CommandType.StoredProcedure
    ' Call ExecuteReader of SqlCommand
    Dim reader As SqlDataReader = cmd.ExecuteReader()
    ' Read all data and display on the console
    While reader.Read()
      Console.Write(reader(0).ToString())
      Console.Write(reader(1).ToString())
      Console.WriteLine(reader(2).ToString())
    End While
    Console.Read()
    ' Close reader and connection
    reader.Close()
    conn.Close()
  End Sub
```

Listing 11-1, creates a SqlCommand object by passing the stored procedure as the first parameter of the SqlCommand constructor and then sets the CommandType property CommandType.StoredProcedure. The result of Listing 11-1 looks like Figure 11-11.

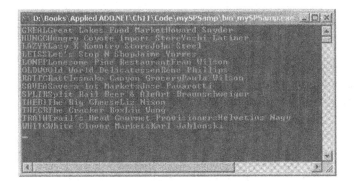

Figure 11-11. The output of stored procedure mySP

A stored procedure can also accept input, output, or both types of parameters. Next, let's modify the mySP stored procedure a little bit. This time give the user an option to select the customers based on their country. The modified stored procedure looks like Figure 11-12.

```
Module1.vb*   dbo.mySP : Sto...CB.Northwind)*              ◁ ▷ :
    ALTER PROCEDURE dbo.mySP
       (
          @country varchar(50)
       )

    AS
    SELECT CustomerId, CompanyName, ContactName
    FROM Customers WHERE Country =@country

       /* SET NOCOUNT ON */
       RETURN
```

Figure 11-12. A stored procedure with parameters

As you can see from Figure 11-12, the stored procedure selects customers based on the country entered by the user. You can use the SqlParameter class to create a parameter. The SqlParameter class has properties such as Direction and Value. The Direction property defines whether the stored procedure is an input, output, or both. It also defines whether it has a return value. The ParameterDirection enumeration defines values of Direction (see Table 11-1).

Table 11-1. The `ParameterDirection` *Members*

MEMBER	DESCRIPTION
Input	Input parameter
InputOutput	Both input and output parameter
Output	Output only
ReturnValue	Returns a value from the stored procedure

The `Value` property sets the value of the parameter. The following code adds a parameter with the value `UK`. After you execute the `mySP` stored procedure, it will return customers from the United Kingdom only:

```
'Set the SqlParameter
Dim param As SqlParameter = New SqlParameter()
param = cmd.Parameters.Add("@country", SqlDbType.VarChar, 50)
param.Direction = ParameterDirection.Input
param.Value = "UK"
```

The updated source code looks like Listing 11-2, and the output of Listing 11-2 looks like Figure 11-13. Listing 11-2 creates `SqlParameter` as the country and sets its value to `UK`. `ExecuteReader` only returns rows where `Country = "UK"`.

Listing 11-2. Using Parameters in a Stored Procedure

```
' Create a Connection Object
    Dim ConnectionString As String = "Integrated Security=SSPI;" & _
            "Initial Catalog=Northwind;" & _
            "Data Source=localhost;"
    Dim conn As SqlConnection = New SqlConnection(ConnectionString)
    ' Open the connection
    conn.Open()
    ' Create a SqlCommand object and pass mySP as the
    ' SQL command and set CommandType property to
    ' CommandType.StoredProcedure
    Dim cmd As SqlCommand = New SqlCommand("mySP", conn)
    cmd.CommandType = CommandType.StoredProcedure

    'Set the SqlParameter
    Dim param As SqlParameter = New SqlParameter()
    param = cmd.Parameters.Add("@country", SqlDbType.VarChar, 50)
    param.Direction = ParameterDirection.Input
    param.Value = "UK"
```

```
' Call ExecuteReader of SqlCommand
Dim reader As SqlDataReader = cmd.ExecuteReader()
' Read all data and display on the console
While reader.Read()
  Console.Write(reader(0).ToString())
  Console.Write(reader(1).ToString())
  Console.WriteLine(reader(2).ToString())
End While
Console.Read()
' Close reader and connection
reader.Close()
conn.Close()
```

Figure 11-13. Output of Listing 11-2

To return a value from a stored procedure, the only thing you need to do is change the stored procedure, which will store and return a value as a parameter and set the parameter's Direction property as follows:

```
' Create a SqlParameter
Dim param As SqlParameter = new SqlParameter()
param.Direction = ParameterDirection.ReturnValue
```

Also, store the command's execution results in a number variable like this:

```
param = cmd.Parameters.Add("@counter", SqlDbType.Int)
```

NOTE *See Listing 11-3 for the complete source code.*

Now you'll see an example of using `ParameterDirection.Output`. To test this source code, create a console application and these namespace references:

```
Imports System.Data
Imports System.Data.Common
Imports System.Data.SqlClient
```

Next, create a stored procedure called `AddCat1` that adds a row to the Categories table and returns the row count. Listing 11-3 defines the stored procedure.

Listing 11-3. `AddCat1` *Stored Procedure*

```
CREATE PROCEDURE AddCat1
  @CategoryName nchar(15),
  @Description char(16),
  @Identity int OUT
AS
INSERT INTO Categories (CategoryName, Description)
VALUES(@CategoryName, @Description)
SET @Identity = @@Identity
RETURN @@ROWCOUNT
```

Listing 11-4 shows how to use output parameters. Everything is similar to the previous samples except that you need to use the parameter direction `Parameter-Direction.Output`.

Listing 11-4. Executing a Stored Procedure with Output Parameter

```
' Create a Connection Object
    Dim ConnectionString As String = "Integrated Security=SSPI;" & _
            "Initial Catalog=Northwind;" & _
            "Data Source=localhost;"
    Dim conn As SqlConnection = New SqlConnection(ConnectionString)
    ' Open the connection
    conn.Open()
    Dim sql As String = _
    "SELECT CategoryID, CategoryName, Description FROM Categories"
    Dim da As SqlDataAdapter = New SqlDataAdapter(sql, conn)
    da.InsertCommand = New SqlCommand("AddCat1", conn)
    da.InsertCommand.CommandType = CommandType.StoredProcedure
```

```
    ' Create a SqlParameter
    Dim param As SqlParameter = _
    da.InsertCommand.Parameters.Add("@RowCount", SqlDbType.Int)
    param.Direction = ParameterDirection.ReturnValue
    da.InsertCommand.Parameters.Add _
("@CategoryName", SqlDbType.NChar, 15, "CategoryName")
    da.InsertCommand.Parameters.Add _
    ("@Description", SqlDbType.Char, 16, "Description")
    param = da.InsertCommand.Parameters.Add _
    ("@Identity", SqlDbType.Int, 0, "CategoryID")
    param.Direction = ParameterDirection.Output
    ' Creat a DataSet and fill it
    Dim ds As DataSet = New DataSet()
    da.Fill(ds, "Categories")
    ' Creat a DataRow and add it to the DataSet's DataTable
    Dim row As DataRow = ds.Tables("Categories").NewRow()
    row("CategoryName") = "Beverages"
    row("Description") = "Chai"
    ds.Tables("Categories").Rows.Add(row)
    ' Save changes to the database
    da.Update(ds, "Categories")
    ' Output
    Console.WriteLine(da.InsertCommand.Parameters _
    ("@RowCount").Value.ToString())
```

Understanding SQL Injection

One of the dangers of writing public Web applications is that eventually someone
will try to hack your application, especially if it contains sensitive financial information such as credit card numbers or bank account details. For hackers, one way
to try to get this information from your application is SQL *injection*. Its use isn't
necessarily limited to applications that use stored procedures, but we're presenting it here because of the way that stored procs are often used.

Let's say that the first page in the application requires users to enter a
username and password. Once the hacker has tried the usual combinations of
manager, sa, admin, and so on (you already know not to use obvious usernames
such as these, right?), he might try entering the following:

```
myusername; SELECT username FROM users
```

If the contents of the username box are passed directly into a stored proc, then the stored proc runs as normal when executed, except that the semicolon acts as a statement terminator and the additional SELECT statement also runs. Depending on what the proc returns, our hacker could now have a complete list of valid user IDs for the application. The same technique can be used for passwords, so the hacker can now log into the application as any valid user.

How do you stop this? The most obvious way to trap SQL injection is to scan every text input for a semicolon and then pass only the input before the semicolon to the stored proc. Alternatively, if you detect a semicolon, return some kind of error page to hackers that lets them know you're onto them. A more complex method of blocking SQL injection is to run stored procs from a component, rather than calling them directly from an ASP.NET page. In this way, the raw output from the stored proc isn't returned to the hacker's browser, and the hacker receives no clues about your database's structure or data.

Working with Views

A *view* is a virtual table that represents data from one or more database tables. A view can also be a partial table. You can select data from a single table or multiple tables based on the sort and filter criteria (using WHERE and GROUP BY clauses) and save data as a view. You can also set permissions on views. For example, a manager, an accountant, and a clerk of a company share the same database. The manager can access all data from different tables of the database. The accountant can access partial data from multiple tables, and the clerk can access partial data from a single table. You can create three different views based on the user rights and let the user access these views based on their rights.

In brief, the views do the following:

- Provide a security mechanism to hide certain parts of a database or database tables from certain users

- Permit users to access data in a customized way so that different users can see the same data in different ways at the same time

Creating a View

Like stored procedures, you can create and manage views from the Server Explorer. To create a view, expand a database, right-click the Views leaf, and select the New View option. This action launches a wizard that helps you pick tables. Use the Add button adds tables to the view designer (see Figure 11-14).

Figure 11-14. Adding tables to the view designer

For this example, add three tables to the designer: Customers, Orders, and Employees. Figure 11-15 shows a few columns selected from each table.

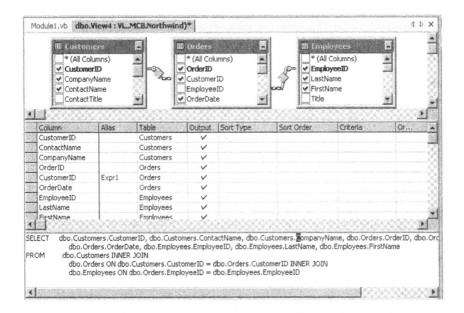

Figure 11-15. Creating a view after selecting columns from three tables

You can save a view by using the Save button, by using File ➤ Save, or by right-clicking on the view and selecting Save *ViewName* (see Figure 11-16).

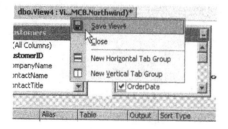

Figure 11-16. Saving a view

For this example, save the view as CustEmpView and click OK (see Figure 11-17).

Figure 11-17. Entering a name for the view

When you now see the Server Explorer views, you'll see CustEmpView listed (see Figure 11-18).

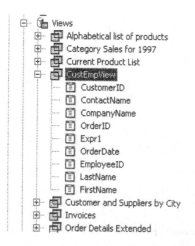

Figure 11-18. Available views in the Server Explorer

Executing a View from VS .NET

To execute a view, right-click it in the Server Explorer and select Retrieve Data from the View option. The output of CustEmpView looks like Figure 11-19.

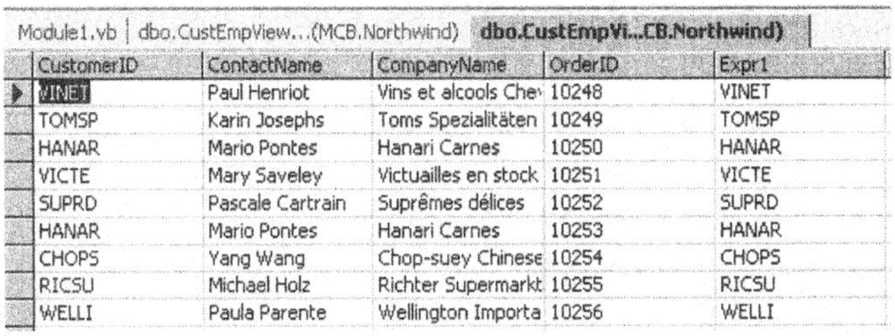

CustomerID	ContactName	CompanyName	OrderID	Expr1
VINET	Paul Henriot	Vins et alcools Che	10248	VINET
TOMSP	Karin Josephs	Toms Spezialitäten	10249	TOMSP
HANAR	Mario Pontes	Hanari Carnes	10250	HANAR
VICTE	Mary Saveley	Victuailles en stock	10251	VICTE
SUPRD	Pascale Cartrain	Suprêmes délices	10252	SUPRD
HANAR	Mario Pontes	Hanari Carnes	10253	HANAR
CHOPS	Yang Wang	Chop-suey Chinese	10254	CHOPS
RICSU	Michael Holz	Richter Supermarkt	10255	RICSU
WELLI	Paula Parente	Wellington Importa	10256	WELLI

Figure 11-19. Results of the CustEmpView *view after executing it from the Server Explorer*

Retrieving Data from a View Programmatically

In the same way that you execute a stored proc, the Command object executes a view. You can retrieve data from a view programmatically by replacing the view name with the table name in a SQL statement. Listing 11-5 shows you how to use the CustEmpView view in an application. As you can see, the code uses the CustEmpView view as the table name in the SELECT statement:

```
SELECT * FROM CustEmpView
```

To test this code, create a Windows application in VS .NET, add a DataGrid control to the form, and write the code in Listing 11-5 on the Form_Load event. Also, don't forget to import the System.Data.SqlClient namespace in the project.

Listing 11-5. Executing a View Programmatically

```
Private Sub Form1_Load(ByVal sender As System.Object, _
  ByVal e As System.EventArgs) Handles MyBase.Load
    ' Create a Connection Object
    Dim ConnectionString As String = "Integrated Security=SSPI;" & _
        "Initial Catalog=Northwind;" & _
        "Data Source=localhost;"
    Dim conn As SqlConnection = New SqlConnection(ConnectionString)
    Dim adapter As SqlDataAdapter = _
    New SqlDataAdapter("SELECT * FROM CustEmpView", conn)
    Dim ds As DataSet = New DataSet("CustEmpView")
    adapter.Fill(ds, "CustEmpView")
    DataGrid1.DataSource = ds.DefaultViewManager
End Sub
```

The output of Listing 11-5 looks like Figure 11-20.

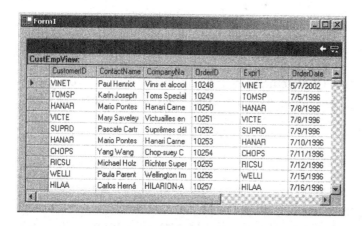

Figure 11-20. The output the CustEmpView *view from a program*

 CAUTION *The* ORDER BY, COMPUTE, COMPUTE BY, *and* INTO SQL *keywords don't work with views.*

Filling a DataSet from Multiple Views

If you want, you can fill a DataSet from multiple views. You just need to change the
SQL statement you used in Listing 11-5. For example, say you want to fill a DataSet
from the CustEmpView and Invoices views. Just replace the SQL statement in Listing
11-5 with the following:

```
Dim adapter As SqlDataAdapter = New SqlDataAdapter _
    ("SELECT * FROM CustEmpView; SELECT * FROM Invoices", conn)
```

Summary

VS .NET provides plenty of support to create and manage stored procedures and
views. This chapter discussed how you can take advantage of the VS .NET tools to
create, manage, and execute stored procedures and views. You also learned how to
work with stored procedures and views programmatically as well.

In the next chapter, we'll discuss two new data providers—Oracle and XML
.NET—and see how to use these data providers to work with Oracle databases and
XML data sources.

CHAPTER 12

Oracle, SQLXML, and Other .NET Data Providers

IN PREVIOUS CHAPTERS, we discussed the Sql, OleDb, and ODBC data providers and how to use them work with various databases including SQL Server, Access, Excel, and MySQL. As mentioned, ADO.NET is flexible enough so anyone can develop their data provider and add it to the library as an add-on.

In this chapter, you'll see some more data providers. Once you've come to grips with any one data provider, working with the rest of them is a piece of cake. All data providers implement a similar class hierarchy model with only a few changes.

Using Oracle .NET Data Providers

Besides the OleDb and ODBC providers, you can use other data providers to access an Oracle database:

- Microsoft has developed the Oracle .NET data provider (although some documentation refers to it as the *Oracle managed provider.*

- Oracle has developed the Oracle data provider for .NET or *ODP.NET.*

- CoreLab Software Development has developed the OraDirect.NET data provider.

So, why there are so many approaches to access a database? Why can't they just provide a single provider? That's the pity and beauty of software development. Users are never satisfied. No matter how good a product you develop, you'll always find somebody somewhere complaining about it. It may be a performance issue, it may lack features, or it may contain bugs.

By having the ODBC and OleDb data providers, you can leverage the existing ODBC and OLE DB technologies satisfactory to developers working with Oracle database. However, data access using OLE DB and ODBC isn't satisfactory to developers. For example, when you compare the performance of the OleDb data provider to the performance of the Sql provider.

The OleDB data provider provides data access for generic data sources and isn't designed to work with a specific database. OLE DB is a COM library, so the OleDb data provider uses COM Interop services internally to provide connectivity with Oracle databases, which causes a performance hit for each use because of moving between the managed and unmanaged spaces. On the other hand, the Oracle data provider works with Oracle databases only. Not only that, the Oracle data provider skips COM Interop services and provides database connectivity by directly using the Oracle Call Interface (OCI) as provided by Oracle client software.

NOTE *A recent survey, published in an article on MSDN (*www.microsoft.com/ indonesia/msdn/ManProOracPerf.asp*), claims that the Oracle data provider could be lot faster than the OleDb data provider.*

Microsoft's Oracle data provider is free and is included as part of Visual Studio .NET (VS .NET) 2003. If you're running VS .NET 1.0, you need to install it separately. You can download it from the Microsoft's download section (http://microsoft.com/downloads/). The ODP.NET provider from Oracle Corporation is also free. You can download it from Oracle's Web site at http://otn.oracle.com/tech/windows/odpnet/content.html. OraDirect.NET currently costs $99 and is available at www.crlab.com/products.html.

CAUTION *There may be some changes in these URLs. See the C# Corner (*www.c-sharpcorner.com*) Downloads section for the latest links.*

In this chapter, you'll use Microsoft's Oracle .NET data provider.

Adding a Reference to the Oracle .NET Data Provider

The Oracle data provider's functionality resides in the System.Data.OracleClient.dll assembly. You can find this assembly in your installation folder's Bin folder. The default path of this assembly is C:\Program Files\Microsoft .NET\ OracleClient.NET\Bin. To add a reference to this assembly, you can use the Add Reference dialog box of VS .NET, as shown in Figure 12-1.

NOTE *In Microsoft VS .NET 2003, the* System.Data.OracleClient *namespace is already available without adding a reference to the* System.Data.OracleClient.dll.

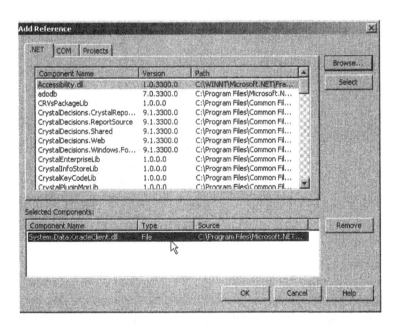

Figure 12-1. Adding a reference to System.Data.OracleClient.dll

Adding a reference to System.Data.OracleClient.dll adds the System.Data.OracleClient namespace to your project. To use the Oracle data provider classes, you must add the following line to your project:

```
Imports System.Data.OracleClient
```

Using the Oracle .NET Data Provider Classes

The Oracle data provider class hierarchy model is similar to other data providers. As with other data providers, it also has classes for Connection, Command, DataAdapter, DataReader, Transaction, Parameter, and so on. Table 12-1 describes the Oracle data provider common classes briefly.

Table 12-1. Oracle Data Provider Classes

CLASS	DESCRIPTION
OracleConnection	Connection class
OracleCommand	Command class
OracleCommandBuilder	CommandBuilder class
OracleDataAdapter	DataAdapter class
OracleDataReader	DataReader class
OracleParameter	Parameter class
OracleParameterCollection	ParameterCollection class
OracleTransaction	Transaction class
OraclePermission	Permission class
OracleException	Exception class
OracleBFile	Represents OracleBFile objects designed to work with the Oracle Binary File BFILE data type
OracleLob	Represents a Large Object Binary (LOB) data type

Creating the Connection: The First Step

The first step to access a database is to create a connection. The OracleConnection class of the Oracle data provider is responsible for opening and closing a connection with the database.

The OracleConnection class has four properties: ConnectionString, DataSource, ServerVersion, and State. The ConnectionString represents a connection string, which can contain data source or server name, security type, user ID, and password. Like the other data provider connection classes, the OracleConnection provides Open, Close, BeginTransaction, CreateCommand, and Dispose methods.

A typical connection string looks like the following:

```
"Data Source=Oracle8i;Integrated Security=yes"
```

where Oracle8i is the default Oracle database server instance.

NOTE *The Oracle .NET data provider works for Oracle 8i and later versions of Oracle.*

The following is another version of connection string with the user ID system and password manager for the database server instance MYDB:

```
"Data Source=MYDB;User ID=system;Password=manager;"
```

Listing 12-1 creates an OracleConnection, opens the connection, reads data, and closes the connection.

Listing 12-1. Connecting to an Oracle Database

```
Dim connectionString As String = _
    "Data Source=MYDB;User ID=system;Password=manager;"
Dim conn As OracleConnection = _
  New OracleConnection(connectionString)
Try
  If (conn.State = ConnectionState.Closed) Then
      conn.Open()
  End If

' Do something here

  Catch exp As Exception
    MessageBox.Show(exp.Message)
  Finally
        If (conn.State = ConnectionState.Open) Then
            conn.Close()
        End If
  End Try
```

NOTE *Remember that for the ODBC .NET data provider, Oracle 8i has different connection string than Oracle 9i. When you use the Oracle .NET data provider, the same connection string format works for all Oracle databases version 8i or later.*

Executing SQL Commands

In a similar manner to the other data providers (Sql, OleDb, and ODBC), the Oracle data provider's OracleCommand class represents a command object. The OracleCommand class provides the functionality to execute SQL queries directly or indirectly (through a DataAdapter).

The CommandText, CommandType, Connection, DesignTimeVisible, Parameters, Transaction, and UpdatedRowSource are OracleCommand properties. The CommandText property represents the SQL query or stored procedure to execute. The CommandType represents the type of command, which is of type System.Data.CommandType. The Connection property represents the connection associated with a command. By default OracleCommand isn't visible in the Toolbox, but if you want to make it visible and want to use it at design-time, you can set the DesignTimeVisible property to true. The OracleTransaction represents an Oracle transaction, and the UpdatedRowState property represents how the Update method should apply command results to the DataRow.

The OracleCommand methods include Cancel, Clone, CreateParameter, ExecuteNonQuery, ExecuteOracleNonQuery, ExecuteOracleScalar, ExecuteReader, and ExecuteScalar.

Apart from the ExecuteOracleNonQuery and ExecuteOracleScalar methods, other methods will look familiar to you.

Now let's create a sample application. Create a Windows application, add a reference to the Oracle .NET data provider, and import the System.Data and System.Data.OracleClient namespaces. After that, add three buttons and a DataGrid control to the form, and name the buttons InsertCmdBtn, UpdateCmdBtn, and DeleteCmdBtn. Then, we recommend you download the source code and open the project in VS .NET.

On the form's load event handler, you call the method FillDataGrid, which fills data from a database to the DataGrid control. Listing 12-2 shows the form's load event handler and the FillDataGrid method.

Listing 12-2. FillDataGrid *Method*

```
Private Sub Form1_Load(ByVal sender As System.Object, _
    ByVal e As System.EventArgs) Handles MyBase.Load
        FillDataGrid()
    End Sub


    Public Sub FillDataGrid()
        conn = New OracleConnection(connectionString)
        sql = "SELECT * FROM STDTABLE"
        Try
            ' Open the connection
            If (conn.State = ConnectionState.Closed) Then
                conn.Open()
            End If
            ' Create a command with SELECT query
            Dim cmd As OracleCommand = New OracleCommand(sql)
            cmd.Connection = conn
            ' Create a data adapter

Dim adapter As OracleDataAdapter = _
            New OracleDataAdapter(cmd)
            Dim builder1 As OracleCommandBuilder = _
            New OracleCommandBuilder()
            ' Create and fill a DataSet
            Dim ds As DataSet = New DataSet()
            adapter.Fill(ds, "STDTABLE")
            ' Bind DataSet with DataGrid
            DataGrid1.DataSource = ds.Tables(0)
            ' Close the connection

        Catch exp As Exception
            MessageBox.Show(exp.Message)
        Finally
            If (conn.State = ConnectionState.Open) Then
                conn.Close()
            End If
        End Try
    End Sub
```

In the FillDataGrid method, you create a connection and a DataAdapter, and then you call the Fill method of the DataAdapter to fill a DataSet with data from a database. You may also have noticed that you're reading data from STDTABLE. You may want to change this table name to the table that you want to access. If you want to use STDTABLE, create this table in an Oracle database with four columns named as STDNAME, STDADDRESS, STDDOB, and STDSRN of type varchar, varchar, datetime, and long, respectively.

The next step is to execute a SQL query using OracleCommand. The method ExecuteSqlQuery, shown in Listing 12-3, executes a SQL query. As you can see, the code opens a connection, creates an OracleCommand object, sets its connection, CommandText, and CommandType properties, and then calls ExecuteNonQuery method.

Listing 12-3. ExecuteSqlQuery *Method*

```
Public Sub ExecuteSqlQuery(ByVal sql As String)
    Try
        conn = New OracleConnection()
        conn.ConnectionString = connectionString
        If (conn.State = ConnectionState.Closed) Then
            conn.Open()
        End If
        Dim cmd As OracleCommand = New OracleCommand()
        cmd.Connection = conn
        cmd.CommandText = sql
        cmd.CommandType = CommandType.Text
        cmd.ExecuteNonQuery()

    Catch exp As Exception
        MessageBox.Show(exp.Message)
    Finally
        If (conn.State = ConnectionState.Open) Then
            conn.Close()
        End If
    End Try
End Sub
```

Now let's write the code for InsertCmdBtn, UpdateCmdBtn, and DeleteCmdBtn and construct SQL INSERT, UPDATE, and DELETE queues. Once the queries are constructed, you need to call ExecuteSqlQuery. Listing 12-4 shows the code for all three buttons.

Listing 12-4. Constructing SQL INSERT, UPDATE, *and* DELETE *Queries*

```
Private Sub InsertCmdBtn_Click(ByVal sender As System.Object, _
ByVal e As System.EventArgs) Handles InsertCmdBtn.Click
    sql = "INSERT INTO "
    sql += " STDTABLE(STDNAME, STDADDRESS, STDSRN) "
    sql += "VALUES('AName', 'Some Address', 3583)"
    ExecuteSqlQuery(sql)
    FillDataGrid()
End Sub
Private Sub UpdateCmdBtn_Click(ByVal sender As System.Object, _
ByVal e As System.EventArgs) Handles UpdateCmdBtn.Click
    sql = "UPDATE STDTABLE SET STDADDRESS = " & _
    "'New Address' WHERE STDNAME = 'AName' "
    ExecuteSqlQuery(sql)
    FillDataGrid()
End Sub
Private Sub DeleteCmdBtn_Click(ByVal sender As System.Object, _
ByVal e As System.EventArgs) Handles DeleteCmdBtn.Click
    sql = "DELETE STDTABLE WHERE STDNAME = 'AName' "
    ExecuteSqlQuery(sql)
    FillDataGrid()
End Sub
```

NOTE *You may also notice that you call the* FillDataGrid *method to update the* DataGrid *once a query is executed.*

Reading Fast Data Using a DataReader

The OracleDataReader class provides the DataReader functionality for Oracle data providers. Besides the methods to read generic data types, the OracleDataReader class also provides methods to read Oracle-specific data types. You can use all the methods of format ReadXXX to read general data types, and you can use methods that start with ReadOracleXXX to read Oracle-specific data types. GetOracleDbFile, GetOracleDateTime, GetOracleString, and GetOracleNumber are some of the Oracle-specific read methods.

The OracleDataReader has six properties: Depth, FieldCount, HasRows, IsClosed, Item, and RecordsAffected. The Depth property returns the depth of a row in a loop.

The FieldCount property returns the number of columns in a row. The HasRows and IsClosed properties represent whether the reader has any rows and closed, respectively. The Item property returns the value in a native format, and the RecordsAffected property returns the number of rows affected after the execution of a SQL query.

Listing 12-5 reads data from STDTABLE and adds it to a ListBox control. To test this code, create a Windows application and add a ListBox control to the form.

Listing 12-5. Reading Data Using OracleDataReader

```
Dim connectionString As String = _
    "Data Source=MYDB;User ID=system;Password=manager;"
    Dim conn As OracleConnection = _
    New OracleConnection(connectionString)
    Dim sql As String = "SELECT * FROM STDTABLE"
    Try
        If (conn.State = ConnectionState.Closed) Then
            conn.Open()
        End If
        Dim cmd As OracleCommand = New OracleCommand(sql)
        cmd.Connection = conn
        Dim reader As OracleDataReader = cmd.ExecuteReader()
        ListBox1.Items.Add("NAME     ADDRESS ")
        While (reader.Read())
            Dim str As String
            str = reader.GetString(0)
            Str += ", "
            str += reader.GetString(1)
            ' Read more fields depends on your table
            ' Do something here
            ListBox1.Items.Add(str)
        End While
        reader.Close()
Catch exp As Exception
        MessageBox.Show(exp.Message)
    Finally
        If (conn.State = ConnectionState.Open) Then
            conn.Close()
            conn.Dispose()
        End If
    End Try
```

Listing 12-5 used the generic data methods, but the code in Listing 12-6 demonstrates using the Oracle-specific DataReader methods. As you can see, the code uses the GetOracleString, GetOracleNumber, and GetOracleDateTime methods to read data in Oracle data types.

Listing 12-6. Using the Oracle-Specific DataReader Methods

```
While (reader.Read())
 Dim oraStr As OracleString
 oraStr = reader.GetOracleString(0)
 Dim str As String = oraStr.ToString()
 oraStr = reader.GetOracleString(1)
 Dim oraDtTime As OracleDateTime = _
 reader.GetOracleDateTime(2)
 Dim oraNum As OracleNumber = _
 reader.GetOracleNumber(3)
End While
```

Reading and Writing Data Using a DataAdapter

The OracleDataAdapter class represents the DataAdapter for the Oracle data provider. Like the other data provider's DataAdapter classes, this class also defines the Fill and Update methods. The Fill method fills a DataSet from a data source, and the Update method saves the changes made to a DataSet back to the database.

Listing 12-7 creates an OracleDataAdapter object from a command. After that, code fills a DataSet, adds a row by using the Update method, and displays the updated data in a DataGrid control. To test this code, create a Windows application, add a DataGrid control, and add this code on the form load or a button click event handler.

Listing 12-7. Reading and Writing Data Using OracleDataAdapter

```
Dim connectionString As String = _
    "Data Source=MYDB;User ID=system;Password=manager;"
      Dim conn As OracleConnection = _
      New OracleConnection(connectionString)
      Dim sql As String = "SELECT * FROM STDTABLE"
      Try
          ' Open the connection
          If (conn.State = ConnectionState.Closed) Then
              conn.Open()
```

```
            End If
            ' Create a command with SELECT query
            Dim cmd As OracleCommand = New OracleCommand(sql)
            cmd.Connection = conn
            ' Create a data adapter
            Dim adapter As OracleDataAdapter = _
                  New OracleDataAdapter(cmd)
            Dim builder1 As OracleCommandBuilder = _
                  New OracleCommandBuilder()
         builder1.DataAdapter = adapter
            ' Create and fill a DataSet
            Dim ds As DataSet = New DataSet()
            adapter.Fill(ds, "STDTABLE")
            Dim stdTable As DataTable = ds.Tables("STDTABLE")
            ' Add a row
            Dim row As DataRow = ds.Tables(0).NewRow()
            row(0) = "New Name"
            row(1) = "New Address"
            row(2) = DateTime.Today
            row(3) = "1234"
            stdTable.Rows.Add(row)
            adapter.Update(ds, "STDTABLE")
            ' Bind DataSet with DataGrid
            DataGrid1.DataSource = ds.Tables(0)
    Catch exp As Exception
            MessageBox.Show(exp.Message)
        Finally
            ' Close the connection
            If (conn.State = ConnectionState.Open) Then
                conn.Close()
            End If
        End Try
```

CAUTION *When it comes to performance, the* DataReader *should be your first choice over a* DataSet *when reading data from a database. Don't forget to close a* DataReader *when you're done accessing data.*

Reading BFILEs and LOBs

Reading Binary File (BFILE) and Large Object Binary (LOB) data types are two more tasks that Oracle developers don't encounter with other databases. The Oracle .NET data provider handles both of these data types wisely with the help of the OracleBFile and OracleLob classes.

The OracleLob class provides access to three Oracle data types: Blob, Clob, and NClob. The Blob data type contains binary data up to 4GB in the form of an array of bytes. The Clob data type contains character data up to 4GB in the form of a string. The NClob data type contains the character data based on the national character set of the server with up to 4GB.

The GetOracleBFile method of OracleDataReader returns an OracleBFile object. This code reads the BFILE data type from an Oracle database:

```
Dim bf As OracleBFile = reader.GetOracleBFile(1)
```

The GetOracleLob method of OracleDataReader returns an OracleLob object containing data. The following code uses the GetOracleLob method to read LOB data types:

```
reader.Read()
Dim blb As OracleLob = reader.GetOracleLob(1)
Dim buffer() As Byte = New Byte(100) {}
buffer(0) = 0xCC
buffer(1) = 0xDD
blb.Position = 0
Dim lob As OracleLob = CreateTempLob(cmd,blb.LobType)
Dim actual As Long = blb.CopyTo(lob)
```

> **NOTE** *If you want to know more about BFILE, LOB, and other data types and related classes, see the documentation of the Oracle .NET data provider.*

We could easily write more pages discussing other classes of Oracle data provider, but luckily, the documentation that comes with the Oracle data provider is full of samples. You shouldn't have to go anywhere else to find the solution for your problems.

Using the SQLXML and SQL XML .NET Data Providers

Chapter 6 discussed the major XML .NET-related classes found in the System.Xml namespace to read and write XML documents. We also discussed XML integration with ADO.NET. The .NET Framework Library also provides an XML .NET data provider to work with SQL Server 2000 and XML documents.

The .NET support was introduced in the SQLXML 2.0 library, which includes two data providers that can be used to read XML data and write XML from and into SQL Server 2000 databases. These two data providers are the following:

- The SQLXMLOLEDB provider, which is an OLE DB data provider that exposes SQLXML 2.0 functionality through ADO

- The SQLXML managed classes (the SQL XML .NET data provider) expose SQLXML 2.0 functionality through ADO.NET

NOTE *Currently, SQLXML 3.0 is available for download with Service Pack 1. This chapter uses SQLXML 3.0, which by default copies to the* C:\\Program Files\SQLXML 3.0\Bin *folder.*

In this chapter, we concentrate only on the SQL XML .NET data provider.

NOTE *To get the latest updates and downloads for SQLXML, visit* http://msdn.microsoft.com/sqlxml/.

The SXDP is an add-on; you can download and install it from Microsoft's site (http://msdn.microsoft.com/sqlxml/). Installing SXDP copies the Microsoft.Data.SqlXml.dll library, which you should add to an application before you start using it in an application. In VS .NET, you can add a reference to SXDP by using the Add Reference menu option and selecting the Browse button. The default path of SXDP is the C:\\Program Files\SQLXML 3.0\Bin folder (see Figure 12-2).

Figure 12-2. Adding a reference to Microsoft.Data.SqlXml.dll

Adding a reference to this library adds the Microsoft.Data.SqlXml namespace to the project. Obviously you include this namespace in your application to access the classes provided by the SXDP:

```
imports Microsoft.Data.SqlXml
```

Unlike other data providers, the SQLXMLDP model consists of only three classes: SqlXmlCommand, SqlXmlParameter, and SqlXmlAdapter.

Using the FOR XML Keyword

SQL Server 2000 provides a FOR XML keyword that you can use with the SELECT statement to read data from a SQL Server to XML format. Using this statement, you can generate XML in four formats: RAW, AUTO, NESTED, and EXPLICIT.

The syntax of FOR XML looks like the following:

```
FOR XML mode [, XMLDATA] [, ELEMENTS][, BINARY BASE64]
```

where mode specifies the XML mode. It can be RAW, AUTO, or EXPLICIT. XMLDATA specifies that an XML-Data schema should be returned. If ELEMENTS is specified, it produces columns as subelements; otherwise columns are mapped as XML attributes. This option is available for AUTO mode only. The choice of which to use is yours, as both options produce valid XML; however, using subelements is more like XML and may be especially useful if you need to share data across systems that may not have XML parsers that understand attributes. The BINARY BASE64 option specifies that any binary data retuned by the query will be in 64-bit encoded format.

The following examples use this syntax.

Using the SqlXmlAdapter Object

The SqlXmlAdapter object represents a partial DataAdapter. We said *partial* because unlike other data providers' DataAdapter object, it only provides two methods: Fill and Update.

You can create a SqlXmlAdapter from an XML document with arguments of a connection string and command type. These are two overloaded forms of the SqlXmlAdapter constructor:

```
Dim adapter As New SqlXmlAdapter(commandText, _
 SqlXmlCommandType, connectionString)
Dim adapter As New SqlXmlAdapter(commandStream, _
 SqlXmlCommandType, connectionString)
```

The connection string for a SqlXmlAdapter is a standard OleDb connection string; however, the provider must be SQLOLEDB, the SQL Server provider. You can also create a SqlXmlAdapter from a SqlXmlCommand:

```
Dim adapter As New SqlXmlAdapter(SqlXmlCommand)
```

You can also specify the command string and command type later using the CommandText and CommandType properties. You can use the SchemaPath property to read an XML document.

```
cmd.CommandText = "EmployeeElement"
cmd.CommandType = SqlXmlCommandType.XPath
cmd.SchemaPath = "xmlDoc.xml"
```

The Fill method takes a DataSet as an argument and fills it with the data specified in the SELECT command, and the Update method sends a DataSet to save the changes to a data source.

Listing 12-8 uses a SqlXmlAdapter to fill a DataSet and view data in a DataGrid control. The code also uses the Update method to add a new row to the database.

Listing 12-8. Using SqlXmlAdapter

```
Private Sub FillDataBtn_Click(ByVal sender As System.Object, _
  ByVal e As System.EventArgs) Handles FillDataBtn.Click
    Dim connectionString As String = _
    "provider=sqloledb;server=mcb;database=Northwind;uid=sa;password=;"
    Dim row As DataRow
    Dim adapter As SqlXmlAdapter
    Dim cmd As SqlXmlCommand = New SqlXmlCommand(connectionString)
    cmd.RootTag = "ROOT"
    cmd.CommandText = "EmployeeElement"
    cmd.CommandType = SqlXmlCommandType.XPath
    cmd.SchemaPath = "xmlDoc.xml"
    Dim ds As DataSet = New DataSet()
    adapter = New SqlXmlAdapter(cmd)
    adapter.Fill(ds)
    row = ds.Tables(0).Rows(0)
    row("FName") = "New FName"
    row("LName") = "New LName"
    adapter.Update(ds)
    DataGrid1.DataSource = ds.Tables(0)
  End Sub
```

Using the SqlXmlParameter Object

The SqlXmlParameter represents a parameter, which you can use in a SqlXmlCommand. The SqlXmlParameter object provides only two properties: Name and Value. The Name property represents the name of the parameter. The Value property represents the value of the parameter.

The CreateParameter method of the SqlXmlCommand object creates the parameter object. The following code creates a parameter:

```
Dim param As SqlXmlParameter
param = cmd.CreateParameter()
param.Name = "LastName"
param.Value = "Fuller"
```

Using the SqlXmlCommand Object

The SqlXmlCommand object represents the Command object of SXDP. It is usually used to execute SQL statements. The SqlXmlCommand constructor takes a connection string as its argument:

public SqlXmlCommand(string connectionString)

where connectionString is the ADO or OLEDB connection string identifying the server, database, and the login information. A typical connection string looks like following:

```
Dim connectionString As String = "Provider=SQLOLEDB; Server=(local); " & _
"database=Northwind; user id=UserLogin; password=UserPassword"
```

Using the SqlXmlCommand Methods

The ExecuteNonQuery method executes SQL statements that don't return any values such as INSERT, UPDATE, and DELETE statements. You can also use this method to execute an updategram or a DiffGram that updates records but returns nothing. A DiffGram is an XML format that identifies current and original versions of data elements. See Chapter 22 for more details.

NOTE *What are* updategrams? *Updategrams are a feature of SQL Server 2000 that allow SQL Server database updates to be defined in XML format. The updategrams format contains the XML nodes for each column of a database table.*

You can use the ExecuteStream and ExecuteToStream methods to write to streams. The ExecuteStream method returns a new Stream object, and the ExecuteToStream method writes the query results to an existing stream.

The ExecuteXmlReader method executes a query and returns results in an XmlReader object.

NOTE *To use* System.Xml *in your application, you need to add a reference to the* System.Xml *namespace.*

The CreateParameter method creates a parameter for SXDP, which can be used by SqlXmlCommand. You can set values for the Name and Value parameters of this object. The ClearParameter method removes all parameters associated with a Command object.

Using the SqlXmlCommand Properties

The SqlXmlCommand object supports many properties, which are defined in Table 12-2.

Table 12-2. The SqlXmlCommand *Properties*

ClientSideXml	When set to True, conversion of the rowset to XML occurs on the client instead of on the server. This is useful when you want to move the performance load to the middle tier. This property also allows you to wrap the existing stored procedures with FOR XML to get XML output.
SchemaPath	This is the name of the mapping schema along with the directory path (for example, C:\x\y\MySchema.xml). This property specifies a mapping schema for XPath queries. The path specified can be absolute or relative. If the path specified is relative, the base path specified in BasePath resolves the relative path. If the base path isn't specified, the relative path is relative to the current directory.
XslPath	This is the name of the XSL file along with the directory path. The path specified can be absolute or relative. If the path specified is relative, the base path specified in BasePath resolves the relative path. If the base path isn't specified, the relative path is relative to the current directory.
BasePath	This is the base path (a directory path). The value of this property resolves relative paths specified for the XSL file (using the XslPath property), the mapping schema file (using the SchemaPath property), or an external schema reference in an XML template (specified using mapping-schema attribute).

Table 12-2. The SqlXmlCommand *Properties (Continued)*

OutputEncoding	This specifies the requested encoding for the stream returned by the command execution. Some commonly used encodings are UTF-8, ANSI, and Unicode. UTF-8 is the default encoding.
Namespaces	XPath queries can include namespaces. If the schema elements are namespace-qualified (use a target namespace), the XPath queries against the schema must specify the namespace. This member enables the execution of XPath queries that use namespaces.
RootTag	This provides the single root element for the XML generated by the command execution. A valid XML document requires a single root-level tag. If the command executed generates an XML fragment (without a single top-level element), you can optionally specify the root element for the returning XML.
CommandText	This is the text of the command to execute.
CommandStream	This is the command stream to execute. This property is useful if you want to execute a command from a file (for example, an XML template). When using CommandStream, only Template, UpdateGram, and DiffGram CommandType values are supported
CommandType	This identifies the type of command being executed. This property is of type SqlXmlCommandType.

Table 12-3 describes the SqlXmlCommandType property.

Table 12-3. The SqlXmlCommandType *Members*

COMMANDTYPE	DESCRIPTION
Sql	Executes an SQL command (for example, SELECT * FROM Employees FOR XML AUTO).
XPath	Executes an XPath command (for example, Employees[@EmployeeID=1]).
Template	Executes an XML template.
UpdateGram	Executes an updategram.
DiffGram	Executes a DiffGram.
TemplateFile	Executes a template file. This allows you to execute updategrams and DiffGrams.

Seeing SqlXmlCommand in Action

Listing 12-9 uses different methods and properties of SqlXmlCommand to execute SQL queries.

Listing 12-9. Using SqlXmlCommand *to Execute Commands*

```
Imports System
Imports System.IO
Imports System.Xml
Imports Microsoft.Data.SqlXml


Module Module1

  Sub Main()
    ExecuteStreamMethod()
    ExecuteToStreamMethod()
    SqlParamExecuteMethod()
    ExecuteNonQueryMethod()
  End Sub


  Public Sub ExecuteStreamMethod()
    Dim connectionString As String = _
      "provider=sqloledb;server=mcb;database=Northwind;uid=sa;password=;"
    Dim sql As String = _
    "SELECT FirstName, Title, Address FROM Employees WHERE " & _
    "LastName = 'Fuller' FOR XML AUTO"
    Dim cmd As SqlXmlCommand = New SqlXmlCommand(connectionString)
    cmd.CommandText = sql
    Try
      Dim st As Stream = cmd.ExecuteStream()
      Dim stReader As StreamReader = New StreamReader(st)
      Console.WriteLine(stReader.ReadToEnd())
    Catch exp As Exception
      Console.WriteLine(exp.Message)
    End Try
  End Sub

  Public Sub ExecuteToStreamMethod()
    Dim connectionString As String = _
      "provider=sqloledb;server=mcb;database=Northwind;uid=sa;password=;"
    Dim sql As String = _
    "SELECT FirstName, Title, Address FROM Employees WHERE " & _
    "LastName = 'Fuller' FOR XML AUTO"
    Dim cmd As SqlXmlCommand = New SqlXmlCommand(connectionString)
    cmd.CommandText = sql
    Try
      Dim memStream As MemoryStream = New MemoryStream()
```

```vbnet
      Dim stReader As StreamReader = New StreamReader(memStream)
      cmd.ExecuteToStream(memStream)
      memStream.Position = 0
      Console.WriteLine(stReader.ReadToEnd())
    Catch exp As Exception
      Console.WriteLine(exp.Message)
    End Try
  End Sub


  Public Sub ExecuteNonQueryMethod()
    Dim connectionString As String = _
      "provider=sqloledb;server=mcb;database=Northwind;uid=sa;password=;"
    Dim sql As String = _
    "DELETE Employees WHERE LastName = 'tel'"
    Dim cmd As SqlXmlCommand = New SqlXmlCommand(connectionString)
    cmd.CommandText = sql
    Try
      cmd.ExecuteNonQuery()
    Catch exp As Exception
      Console.WriteLine(exp.Message)
    End Try
  End Sub


  Public Sub SqlParamExecuteMethod()
    Dim connectionString As String = _
      "provider=sqloledb;server=mcb;database=Northwind;uid=sa;password=;"
    Dim sql As String = _
    "SELECT FirstName, Title, Address FROM Employees " & _
    "FOR XML AUTO"
    Dim cmd As SqlXmlCommand = New SqlXmlCommand(connectionString)
    cmd.CommandText = sql
    Try
      Dim param As SqlXmlParameter
      param = cmd.CreateParameter()
      param.Name = "LastName"
      param.Value = "Fuller"
      Dim st As Stream = cmd.ExecuteStream()
      Dim stReader As StreamReader = New StreamReader(st)
      Console.WriteLine(stReader.ReadToEnd())
    Catch exp As Exception
      Console.WriteLine(exp.Message)
    End Try
  End Sub
End Module
```

CAUTION *You get an exception if you don't use the* FOR XML *directive in a SQL query and then try to use general SQL queries.*

Using a MySQL Database and the .NET Data Provider

In Chapter 10, we discussed how to access MySQL databases using the ODBC .NET data provider, but you can also access MySQL databases using different interfaces. Three common interfaces to access MySQL databases are as follows:

- Using the ODBC .NET data provider with the help of the MyODBC driver

- Using MySQL native .NET providers

- Using the OLEDB.NET solution, the MyOLDDB provider

To see more details about these interfaces, samples, links, and other resources, visit www.mysql.com/articles/dotnet/.

Summary

In this chapter, you added more data providers to your data provider list. You learned about various data providers to access Oracle databases. We discussed the Oracle .NET data provider in detail and showed you how you can access Oracle databases.

The SQLXML .NET data provider provides a fast and optimized way to communicate between SQL Server and XML. In this chapter, you saw how to install and work with the XML .NET data provider.

In the next chapter, you'll put all the data provider–related pieces together and work with some data provider internals. You'll also learn how to build your own custom data provider.

Developing a Custom Data Provider

ADO.NET ALLOWS developers as much flexibility in creating custom data providers as Microsoft had developing the SqlClient and OleDb data providers. In other words, you can create data providers for virtually any source of data you can think of, from file formats to Web services.

Think about some of the possibilities this presents. If you needed to create a database application that works on top of a number of different databases such as Microsoft SQL Server and IBM DB2, you could build a Web service that does the actual database access while your custom data provider provides the front end. Figure 13-1 shows such an application would work.

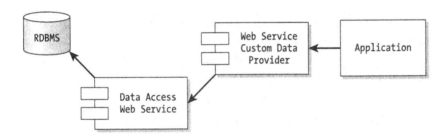

Figure 13-1. A Web-service-based data provider that accesses a Relational Database Management System (RDBMS)

Using an architecture like the one shown in Figure 13-1, you can have focused teams develop compatibility to the Web service you've created for data access. Your data provider only needs to know how to access the Web service, and you can build your application using the same Application Programming Interface (API) as you would for direct database calls.

The advantage of building a system like this is obvious—you can start building your application on top of the ADO.NET interfaces while the data provider, Web service architecture, and individual database compatibility gets worked out. This is more than a little helpful if you're working on a large project requiring cross-database compatibility.

This example highlights why the ability to write a custom data provider is truly beneficial; it's a way to provide standard access to a nonstandard source of data. In other words, this provides a way to normalize the way you work with data regardless of the source.

In this chapter you'll build a data provider that allows access to data in *pipe-delimited* format, and you'll provide a standard .NET API by implementing the Microsoft interfaces to create a custom data provider. The pipe-delimited format is common, especially to Unix systems, as a way to move data between systems. Many large Enterprise Resource Planning (ERP) systems support the ability to export data in this format. Another popular format you could build support for is the Comma Separated Values (CSV) format, which is more popular on Windows systems. This chapter begins with an overview of the data provider interfaces.

Overview of the Data Provider Interfaces

Figure 13-2 shows a custom data provider's interfaces, grouped by function, and shows how they use each other. As you can see, the custom data provider has four objects: Connection, Command, Reader, and Adapter. The following sections discuss these objects and how they work.

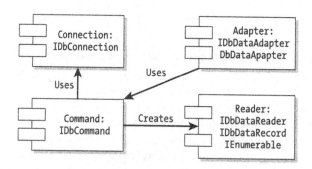

Figure 13-2. A custom data provider at a high level

Understanding the Connection Object

A `Connection` object is an individual session with a source of data. If it's a database connection, it's likely an open Transfer Control Protocol/Internet Protocol (TCP/IP) channel back to the server on a particular port that has been authenticated as having access to the database. If your data source is a file, it's likely a file handle on the file that will be read from. To fully understand how generic this interface is, take a look at the IDbConnection interface's properties in Table 13-1 and methods in Table 13-2.

Table 13-1. The Properties of the `IDbConnection` *Interface*

PROPERTY	DESCRIPTION
ConnectionString	This property represents how the data provider can find its data source. In the case of a file-based source, this could be the path to the file. If it's a Web service, it could be a Uniform Resource Indicator (URI).
ConnectionTimeout	This property represents the amount of time the object should try to connect before giving up.
Database	If connecting to a multiple data source such as an RDBMS, this is the name of the database to which it's connected. If connecting to an Extensible Markup Language (XML) file, it could potentially represent a section of the document.
State	This property represents the current state of the connection such as Open or Closed.

Table 13-2. The Methods of the `IDbConnection` *Interface*

METHOD	DESCRIPTION
BeginTransaction()	Starts a transaction
ChangeDatabase()	Changes from one database to another within the current connection
Close()	Closes the connection
CreateCommand()	Returns an uninitialized instance of a command that works with this connection
Open()	Opens the connection

After reading through the methods and properties of this interface, it should be obvious that you can use the IDbConnection interface to manage a connection to virtually any type of resource imaginable.

Understanding the Command Object

The second major component of an ADO.NET data provider is the Command object as represented by the IDbCommand interface. This interface represents a single action taken on the data source.

The IDbCommand interface gets data from a data source or performs alterations on the data source. Everything else about the behavior of your Command object is up to you. This means that you can, if you want, define your own data query language (or your own dialect of SQL) that's optimized for dealing with the specific type of data with which your provider is dealing. However, developers who use SQL should probably write a SQL-like language. If you have a complete meta-language that requires interpretation, you can interpret the CommandText string to execute whatever commands you need on the data source. If, for example, you're creating a Command object around selecting and altering text files, you can use a regular expression and execute it against the text file and then return the results in a custom implementation of IDbDataReader. Table 13-3 describes the IDbCommand interface's properties, and Table 13-4 describes its methods.

Table 13-3. The Properties of the IDbCommand Interface

PROPERTY	DESCRIPTION
CommandText	This property is a string that tells your Command object what to do. This can be SQL executed against the database, an XPATH query to choose a node in an XML document, or some other type of command that lets your command object know what it's expected to do.
CommandTimeout	This property represents the amount of time the command should wait before canceling its operation.
CommandType	This property represents the type of command this is, such as a stored procedure or a text command.
Connection	This property represents the IDbConnection that this object uses.
Parameters	This property represents a collection of IDbParameter objects. If your command requires any type of information from the calling program to know what to do, the Parameters collection is the place to do it.

Table 13-3. The Properties of the IDbCommand *Interface (Continued)*

PROPERTY	DESCRIPTION
Transaction	This property represents the Transaction object that provides the context for a given transaction.
UpdatedRowSource	This property represents the row in the DataRow or DataTable that's being altered.

Table 13-4. The Methods of the IDbCommand *Interface*

METHOD	DESCRIPTION
Cancel()	Stops the current command
CreateParameter()	Creates a new parameter in the Parameters collection
ExecuteNonQuery()	Executes the command with no expectation for a result set to be returned
ExecuteReader()	Returns an IDbDataReader object to iterate through the results of a query
ExecuteScalar()	Returns a single object from the execution of the command
Prepare()	Compiles or prepares the statement for execution if necessary

Understanding the Reader Object

The Reader object is a class that implements a number of interfaces; two interfaces are mandatory, and one interface is optional. The two required interfaces are IDataReader and IDataRecord, which provide the structure for iterating through any forward-only data collection. IDataReader allows for the iteration from one row to the next within your data source, and the IDataRecord object allows access to an individual row in the result set.

The optional interface to implement is the IEnumerable interface. If you choose to implement this interface, you can bind your IDataReader object directly to ASP.NET and Windows Forms controls. In practice, there really isn't any reason why you shouldn't implement this interface because you only have to implement one method that returns an instance of a DbEnumerator object.

As mentioned, to create a working data provider, you have to implement the IDataReader and IDataRecord interfaces. A little later in this chapter you'll see an example implementation of these methods coming together to provide a means of reading a pipe-delimited file. The DbEnumerator object already knows how to manipulate these interfaces and translate them into the behavior expected from a standard IEnumerable object. Think of implementing this interface as a no-pain, much-to-gain type of implementation. Listing 13-1 shows the implementation for an enumerator. Table 13-5 describes the IDataReader interface's properties, and Table 13-6 describes its methods.

Listing 13-1. The Implementation for an Enumerator

```
Public Function GetEnumerator() As IEnumerator Implements _
IEnumerable.GetEnumerator
Return New System.Data.Common.DbEnumerator(Me)
End Function
```

Table 13-5. The Properties of the IDataReader *Interface*

PROPERTY	DESCRIPTION
Depth	The level of nesting in the result sets
IsClosed	Returns true if the connection is closed
RecordsAffected	Returns the number of records affected

Table 13-6. The Methods of the IDataReader *Interface*

METHOD	DESCRIPTION
Close()	Closes the result set
GetSchemaTable()	Returns a table with the schema of the result set
NextResult()	Advances to the next result
Read()	Reads a single record

Using Visual Basic .NET, you'll find that creating the Reader object includes far more typing than actually thinking through the problem because of the level of verboseness required to implement an interface. Because the IDataRecord interface includes strongly typed methods to get a column's value, you have to create an implementation for each and every GetXXX method. Table 13-7 describes the IDataRecord interface's properties, and Table 13-8 describes its methods.

Table 13-7. The Properties of the IDataRecord *Interface*

PROPERTY	DESCRIPTION
FieldCount	The number of columns in the current row
Item	A collection of objects that represents the current row

Table 13-8. The Methods of the IDataRecord *Interface*

METHOD	DESCRIPTION
GetBoolean()	Gets a Boolean value for the specified column
GetByte()	Gets a byte value for the specified column
GetBytes()	Gets an array of bytes for the specified column
GetChar()	Gets a character for the specified column
GetChars()	Gets an array of characters for the specified column
GetData()	Gets an IDataReader for the specified column, which is useful for nested structures of data
GetDataTypeName()	Gets a string that represents the data type for the specified column
GetDateTime()	Gets a DateTime object for the specified column
GetDecimal()	Gets a decimal for the specified column
GetDouble()	Gets a double for the specified column
GetFieldType()	Gets a Type object for the specified column
GetFloat()	Gets a Float object for the specified column
GetGuid()	Gets a globally unique identifier for the specified column
GetInt16()	Gets a 16-bit integer for the specified column
GetInt32()	Gets a 32-bit integer for the specified column
GetInt64()	Gets a 64-bit integer for the specified column
GetName()	Gets a text name for the specified column
GetOrdinal()	Gets the column number of the column of a specified name
GetString()	Gets a string for the specified column
GetValue()	Gets an object for the specified column
GetValues()	Gets an array of objects for the specified column
IsDBNull()	Returns True if the current column is null

Understanding the Adapter Object

The Adapter object implements the IDbDataAdapter interface and inherits from the DbDataAdapter object. The purpose of this object is to glue together the four IDbCommand objects required to get and alter the database. It also defines how a DataSet should be filled and how to go about reflecting changes made in the DataSet back to your custom data source. Table 13-9 describes the properties of the IDbDataAdapter interface. Please note that this interface does not contain any methods, just properties.

Table 13-9. The Properties of the IDbDataAdapter *Interface*

PROPERTY	DESCRIPTION
SelectCommand	The IDbCommand that loads data from the data source
InsertCommand	The IDbCommand that inserts data into the data source
UpdateCommand	The IDbCommand that updates data in the data source
DeleteCommand	The IDbCommand that deletes data from the data source

The IDbDataAdapter interface simply defines the four IDbCommand objects and how they work with a DataSet. Depending on the requirements for your custom data provider, you can potentially set this in the constructor for your Adapter object. Table 13-10 describes the IDbDataAdapter interface's properties, and Table 13-11 describes its methods.

Table 13-10. The Properties of the IDbDataAdapter *Object*

PROPERTY	DESCRIPTION
DefaultTableSourceName	Provides the name of the table that this adapter will use to manage its mappings
AcceptChangesDuringFill	Determines if AcceptChanges is called on a DataRow when it's added to the DataSet
Container	Gets a reference to the IContainer for this adapter (primarily used in the visual builder)
ContinueUpdateOnError	Determines if the rest of a DataSet is updated when there's an error on a single row
MissingMappingAction	Determines what should be done if the adapter is unable to determine what action to execute
MissingSchemaAction	Determines what should be done if the DataSet's schema does not match the adapter's schema
Site	Returns the ISite of this component, which is similar to a namespace but is for the Internet. This is similar to an XML namespace.
TableMappings	A collection of mappings between the source table and this DataTable

Table 13-11. The Methods of the IDbDataAdapter *Object*

PROPERTY	DESCRIPTION
Fill()	Fills the DataSet using the SelectCommand of this adapter
FillSchema()	Creates a DataTable within a DataSet with the schema handled by this adapter
GetFillParameters()	Gets the parameters required for the SelectCommand to be properly called to fill up this data
Update()	Calls the appropriate InsertCommand, UpdateCommand, or DeleteCommand as required to update the data source to reflect the changes made in the DataSet
CreateRowUpdatedEvent()	Fills in the values of the RowUpdatedEventArgs object with the proper values for this adapter
CreateRowUpdatingEvent()	Fills in the values of a RowUpdatingEventArgs object with the proper values for this adapter
CreateTableMappings()	Creates an instance of the DataTableMappingCollection object
OnFillError()	Creates a FillError event
OnRowUpdated()	Creates a RowUpdated event
OnRowUpdating()	Creates a RowUpdating event
ShouldSerializeTableMappings()	If this object is serialized, determines whether the table mappings be serialized with it

As you can see, the DbDataAdapter object contains quite a few methods (Table 13-11 doesn't list all the methods, such as those inherited from MarshalByRefObject and Component). The good news is that you'll only have to override a few of them to create your custom data provider.

NOTE *Most of the methods you implement can throw a* NotSupportedException *if that particular property or method doesn't have any context with your particular data source. You'll see this used in several places in the PipedDataProvider application in the next section of this chapter.*

Building a Custom Data Provider

Now that you understand the data provider interfaces, you'll implement a custom data provider that has the ability to fill a DataSet from data in piped format. (This data provider will be read only for the sake of brevity.) Figure 13-3 shows the PipedDataProvider that you'll create in the following sections.

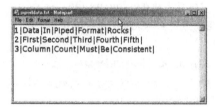

Figure 13-3. Data from pipeddata.txt *in Notepad*

As you can see from Figure 13-3, a *piped* format file is basically a series of columns separated by the pipe symbol (|). There's no data typing—or even the suggestion of data typing—other than what can be guessed from the strings between each pipe. For this reason, the object you'll implement will only support string data and not attempt to make a guess that the first column in the figure should be an integer.

Creating the PipedDataConnection Object

Because the data provider you're creating needs to access a file system object, the connection implemented in Listing 13-2 manages the file handle for the file provided to the object.

In the case of the PipedDataConnection object, the connection string is a complete path and filename of the file in piped format. As soon as you create a new FileStream object, the file handle opens; so, in the constructor for this object, you set the ConnectionState to Open. When the Close() method is called on the PipedDataConnection object, the FileStream closes and the handle to the file is released.

In the course of implementing this object, you'll find there are several methods that have no relevance to this particular type of data source. For example, ChangeDatabase() is meaningless because you're not working with a database or any other type of data source with named subsections. To avoid complexity, you can skip BeginTransaction(). With these methods you simply throw a NotSupportedException to let the data provider system know that this particular method or property isn't supported.

This may sound like it would cause this connection to create all kinds of problems, but in a practical application it doesn't. The portions of code in the PipedDataConnection object that throw the NotSupportedException will be understood and suppressed by the container they run in, assuming of course that you don't try to directly call them from your code.

Listing 13-2. The PipedDataConnection *Object*

```
Imports System
Imports System.Data
Imports System.IO

Namespace AppliedADO.DataProvider

    Public Class PipedDataConnection
        Implements System.Data.IDbConnection

        Public FileName As String
        Friend file As System.IO.StreamReader


        Public Sub New(ByVal fn As String)
            Me.FileName = fn
            file = New StreamReader(New FileStream(Me.FileName, FileMode.Open))
            _State = ConnectionState.Open
'The constructor for this connection opens a file handle
        End Sub

        Public Sub NotSupported()
            Throw New System.NotSupportedException()
        End Sub

        Public Function BeginTransaction(ByVal iso As IsolationLevel) _
As IDbTransaction Implements IDbConnection.BeginTransaction
            NotSupported()
            Return Nothing
        End Function

        Public Function BeginTransaction() _
As IDbTransaction Implements IDbConnection.BeginTransaction
            NotSupported()'We are not supporting transactions
            Return Nothing
        End Function
```

```vb
        Public Sub ChangeDatabase(ByVal newDB As String) _
Implements IDbConnection.ChangeDatabase
            NotSupported()'We are not supporting the ability to change databases
        End Sub


        Public Function CreateCommand() _
As IDbCommand Implements IDbConnection.CreateCommand
            Dim idbCmd As IDbCommand
            idbCmd = New PipedDataCommand()
            Return idbCmd
'Creates the command object
        End Function


        Public Sub Close() Implements IDbConnection.Close
            file.Close()
            _State = ConnectionState.Closed
'Closes the file handle and sets the state to closed
        End Sub


        Public Sub Open() Implements IDbConnection.Open
            _State = ConnectionState.Open
'Since we're opening the file handle in the constuctor, we're
'just setting the state here.
        End Sub


        Dim _State As ConnectionState


        Public ReadOnly Property State() As ConnectionState _
Implements IDbConnection.State
            Get
                Return _State
            End Get
        End Property


        Public Property ConnectionString() As String Implements _
IDbConnection.ConnectionString
            Get
                Return FileName
            End Get
            Set(ByVal Value As String)
                FileName = Value
            End Set
        End Property
```

```
        Private _ConnectionTimeout = 0

        Public ReadOnly Property ConnectionTimeout() As Integer Implements _
IDbConnection.ConnectionTimeout
            Get
                Return _ConnectionTimeout
            End Get
        End Property

        Private _Database = ""
        Public ReadOnly Property Database() As String Implements _
IDbConnection.Database
            Get
                Return _Database
            End Get
        End Property
    End Class
End Namespace
```

Creating the PipedDataCommand Object

The Command object for the piped data provider is the PipedDataCommand object. This object represents a single action taken against the data source; in this case, the PipedDataCommand object can only load the entire contents of the file named in the PipedDataConnection object, so it has no need to actually interpret the CommandText property.

When this object is created, it's passed a string for the CommandText of the command and the PipedDataConnection on which this command will take place.

The primary workhorse of this object is the ExecuteReader method. According to the interface it implements, the IDbCommand interface, this method should return something of the type IDataReader. In this case, a PipedDataReader is returned (PipedDataReader is defined in the next section of this chapter). Listing 13-3 shows the PipedDataCommand object.

Listing 13-3. The PipedDataCommand *Object*

```
Imports System
Imports System.Data

Namespace AppliedADO.DataProvider

    Public Class PipedDataCommand
        Implements System.Data.IDbCommand

        Public Sub New()

        End Sub

        Public Sub New(ByVal cmd As String, ByRef pdc As PipedDataConnection)
            _CommandText = cmd
            _Connection = pdc
        End Sub

        Public Sub NotSupported()
            Throw New NotSupportedException()
        End Sub

        Public Sub NotImpl()
            Throw New NotImplementedException()
        End Sub

        Public Sub Cancel() Implements IDbCommand.Cancel
            NotSupported()
        End Sub

        Public Sub Prepare() Implements IDbCommand.Prepare
        End Sub

        Public Function ExecuteNonQuery() _
    As Integer Implements IDbCommand.ExecuteNonQuery
            Return 0
        End Function

        Public Function CreateParameter()_
    As IDataParameter Implements IDbCommand.CreateParameter
            NotSupported()
            Return Nothing
        End Function
```

```vb
        Public Function ExecuteReader()_
As IDataReader Implements IDbCommand.ExecuteReader
            Dim reader As PipedDataReader
            reader = New PipedDataReader("ALL", _Connection)
            Return reader
        End Function


        Public Function ExecuteReader(ByVal b As CommandBehavior) _
As IDataReader Implements IDbCommand.ExecuteReader
            Return ExecuteReader()
        End Function


        Public Function ExecuteScalar() As Object Implements _
 IDbCommand.ExecuteScalar
            NotImpl()
            Return Nothing
        End Function


        Private _CommandText As String

        Public Property CommandText() As String Implements IDbCommand.CommandText
            Get
                Return _CommandText
            End Get
            Set(ByVal Value As String)
                _CommandText = Value
            End Set
        End Property


        Private _CommandTimeout = 0
        Public Property CommandTimeout()_
As Integer Implements IDbCommand.CommandTimeout
            Get
                Return _CommandTimeout
            End Get
            Set(ByVal Value As Integer)
                _CommandTimeout = Value
            End Set
        End Property


        Private _CommandType As CommandType

        Public Property CommandType() As CommandType  _
```

```vbnet
Implements IDbCommand.CommandType
        Get
            Return _CommandType
        End Get
        Set(ByVal Value As CommandType)
            If (Value <> CommandType.Text) Then
                NotSupported()
            End If
            _CommandType = Value
        End Set
    End Property


    Private _Connection As IDbConnection


    Public Property Connection() As IDbConnection _
Implements IDbCommand.Connection
        Get
            Return _Connection
        End Get
        Set(ByVal Value As IDbConnection)
            _Connection = Value
        End Set
    End Property


    Public ReadOnly Property Parameters() As _
IDataParameterCollection Implements IDbCommand.Parameters
        Get
            NotSupported()
            Return Nothing
        End Get
    End Property


    Public Property Transaction() As IDbTransaction _
Implements IDbCommand.Transaction
        Get
            NotSupported()
            Return Nothing
        End Get
        Set(ByVal Value As IDbTransaction)
            NotSupported()
        End Set
    End Property
```

```
        Public Property UpdatedRowSource() As UpdateRowSource    _
Implements IDbCommand.UpdatedRowSource
            Get
                Return UpdatedRowSource.None
            End Get
            Set(ByVal Value As UpdateRowSource)

            End Set
        End Property
    End Class
End Namespace
```

Creating the PipedDataReader Object

For the calling program to loop through and access the data in the piped data file, you have to implement a Reader object. The PipedDataReader object's responsibility is iterating through the data in the file and providing the data to the calling program in a strongly typed format.

Most of the work that this object does happens in the Read() method. This method reads the next line in the file and sets the internal object array _cols to the result. Once the _cols variable has been set, the different GetXXX methods can provide this information to the calling program.

In the constructor for this object, the Read() method is automatically called once and the connection is reset. The reason for this is so the object can "taste" the contents of the file and know how many columns to expect.

One of the traditional requirements of a file in piped format is that the column lengths be consistent. As an addition to the program in Listing 13-4, you could actually read through the whole file and verify that this is indeed the case and then throw an error if they aren't the same length.

There are portions of the object that are hard-coded such as the type of data supported. Because piped format contains no meta-data as to the data types of each column, you have to assume that they're all strings. Also, because there's no meta-data, the columns are not actually named, so the PipedDataReader has to invent a column name for each column based on its position.

The final item of interest in the PipedDataReader object is the IEnumerable interface and its related implementation. By implementing this interface, you allow your PipedDataReader to be bound directly to Web page and Windows Forms controls. In situations where performance is an absolute requirement down to the last processor cycle, Microsoft's tests show the DataReader to far outperform working with DataSets and XMLReaders.

The real joy of this is the simplicity of this implementation. All you have to do is implement the GetEnumerator() method and return a DbEnumerator object. Because you're implementing a standard .NET interface, there's a related object that knows how to work with it; therefore, there's no reason for you to implement a custom enumerator for your data provider.

Listing 13-4. The PipedDataReader *Object*

```
Imports System
Imports System.Data
Imports System.Data.Common
Imports System.IO
Imports PipedDataProvider

Namespace AppliedADO.DataProvider

    Public Class PipedDataReader
        Implements IDataReader, IDataRecord, IEnumerable

        Private _Command As String

        Public Sub New(ByVal cmd As String, ByRef conn As PipedDataConnection)
            _Command = cmd
            _Connection = conn
            'Taste The File To Fill In The Meta-Data
            Me.Read()
            'File Tasted, close and reopen the connection
            _Connection.Close()
            _Connection = New PipedDataConnection(_Connection.ConnectionString)
        End Sub

        Private Sub NotSupported()
            Throw New NotSupportedException()
        End Sub

        Public Function GetSchemaTable()_
As DataTable Implements IDataReader.GetSchemaTable
            Me.NotSupported()
        End Function
```

```vbnet
        Public Sub Close() Implements IDataReader.Close
            _isClosed = True
            If (Not _Connection Is Nothing) Then
                _Connection.Close()
            End If
        End Sub


        Public Function NextResult() As Boolean Implements IDataReader.NextResult
            Return False
        End Function


        Private splitter() As Char = {"|"}


        Public Function Read() As Boolean Implements IDataReader.Read
'This is the main method where a single line is read from the file and sets
'the value of the _cols collection.
            Dim line As String
            line = _Connection.file.ReadLine()
            If (line = "") Then
                Return False
            End If
            Dim tCols() As String
            tCols = line.Split(splitter)
            _cols = tCols
            Return True
        End Function


        Private _depth = 3
        Public ReadOnly Property Depth() As Integer Implements IDataReader.Depth
            Get
                Return _depth
            End Get
        End Property


        Private _isClosed = False
        Public ReadOnly Property IsClosed() As _
Boolean Implements IDataReader.IsClosed
            Get
                Return _isClosed
            End Get
        End Property
        Private _RecordsAffected As Integer
        Public ReadOnly Property RecordsAffected()_
```

```
As Integer Implements IDataReader.RecordsAffected
            Get
                  Return _RecordsAffected
            End Get
      End Property


      Public Function GetBoolean(ByVal i As Integer) _
As Boolean Implements IDataReader.GetBoolean
            Return CType(_cols(i), Integer)
      End Function


      Public Function GetByte(ByVal i As Integer) _
As Byte Implements IDataReader.GetByte
            Return CType(_cols(i), Byte)
      End Function


      Public Function GetBytes(ByVal i As Integer, ByVal _
fieldoffset As Long, ByVal bytes()_
As Byte, ByVal length As Integer, ByVal bufferoffset As Integer) _
As Long Implements IDataReader.GetBytes
            NotSupported()
            Return Nothing
      End Function


      Public Function GetChar(ByVal i As Integer) _
As Char Implements IDataReader.GetChar
            Return CType(_cols(i), Char)
      End Function


      Public Function GetChars(ByVal i As Integer, ByVal fieldoffset As Long, _
ByVal buffer As Char(), ByVal length As Integer, ByVal bufferoffset As Integer) _
As Long Implements IDataReader.GetChars
            NotSupported()
            Return Nothing
      End Function


      Public Function GetData(ByVal i As Integer) As  _
IDataReader Implements IDataReader.GetData
            NotSupported()
            Return Nothing
      End Function
```

```vb
        Public Function GetDataTypeName(ByVal i As Integer) _
As String Implements IDataReader.GetDataTypeName
            Return GetType(String).ToString()
        End Function


        Public Function GetDateTime(ByVal i As Integer) _
As DateTime Implements IDataReader.GetDateTime
            Return CType(_cols(i), DateTime)
        End Function


        Public Function GetDecimal(ByVal i As Integer) As _
Decimal Implements IDataReader.GetDecimal
            Return CType(_cols(i), Decimal)
        End Function


        Public Function GetDouble(ByVal i As Integer) As _
Double Implements IDataReader.GetDouble
            Return CType(_cols(i), Integer)
        End Function


        Public Function GetFieldType(ByVal i As Integer) As _
Type Implements IDataReader.GetFieldType
            Return GetType(String)
        End Function


        Public Function GetFloat(ByVal i As Integer) As _
Single Implements IDataReader.GetFloat
            Return CType(_cols(i), Single)
        End Function


        Public Function GetString(ByVal i As Integer) As _
String Implements IDataReader.GetString
            Return CType(_cols(i), String)
        End Function


        Public Function GetGuid(ByVal i As Integer) As _
Guid Implements IDataReader.GetGuid
            Return CType(_cols(i), Guid)
        End Function


        Public Function GetInt16(ByVal i As Integer) As _
Short Implements IDataReader.GetInt16
            Return CType(_cols(i), Short)
        End Function
```

```
        Public Function GetInt32(ByVal i As Integer) As _
Int32 Implements IDataReader.GetInt32
            Return CType(_cols(i), Int32)
        End Function


        Public Function GetInt64(ByVal i As Integer) As _
Int64 Implements IDataReader.GetInt64
            Return CType(_cols(i), Int64)
        End Function


        Public Function GetName(ByVal i As Integer) As _
String Implements IDataReader.GetName
            Return "COLUMN" + i.ToString()
        End Function


        Public Function GetOrdinal(ByVal name As String) As _
Integer Implements IDataReader.GetOrdinal
            NotSupported()
            Return Nothing
        End Function


        Public Function GetValue(ByVal i As Integer) As _
Object Implements IDataReader.GetValue
            Return CType(_cols(i), Object)
        End Function


        Public Function GetValues(ByVal values As Object()) As _
Integer Implements IDataReader.GetValues
            Dim i As Integer
            If (FieldCount < 1) Then
                Return 0
            End If
            For i = 0 To FieldCount - 1
                values(i) = _cols(i)
            Next
            Return FieldCount
        End Function


        Public Function IsDBNull(ByVal i As Integer) As _
Boolean Implements IDataReader.IsDBNull
            Return False
        End Function
```

```
        Public ReadOnly Property FieldCount() As Integer _
  Implements IDataReader.FieldCount
            Get
                Return _cols.Length - 1
            End Get
        End Property


        Default Public ReadOnly Property Item(ByVal name As String) _
  As Object Implements IDataReader.Item
            Get
                Me.NotSupported()
                Return Nothing
                'Return _cols(Array.IndexOf(_names, name))
            End Get
        End Property


        Default Public ReadOnly Property Item(ByVal i As Integer) _
  As Object Implements IDataReader.Item
            Get
                Return _cols(i)
            End Get
        End Property


        Public Function GetEnumerator() As IEnumerator Implements _
  IEnumerable.GetEnumerator
            Return New System.Data.Common.DbEnumerator(Me)
        End Function


        Private _Connection As PipedDataConnection


        Private _cols() As Object



    End Class
End Namespace
```

Creating the PipedDataAdapter Object

Finally, the PipedDataAdapter object is where it all comes together. This object provides the layer between the data source and the DataSet. This object also defines what operation should be performed to fill the DataSet with data and how to go about updating the data source to reflect changes made to the DataSet in your data source.

This object inherits DbDataAdapter to get the utility of methods such as Fill(). It also implements the IDbDataAdapter interface to define what IDbCommands (the interface that defines a single operation on the data source) perform operations on the DataSet.

The four main points of interest in this implementation are the SelectCommand, InsertCommand, UpdateCommand, and DeleteCommand properties. You'll probably recall the names of these commands from the first few chapters of this book. Each of these commands, once defined, allows any alteration made in the data source or DataSet to be reflected in the other. Listing 13-5 shows the PipedDataAdapter object.

Listing 13-5. The PipedDataAdapter *Object*

```
Imports System
Imports System.Data
Imports System.Data.Common
Imports System.IO
Imports PipedDataProvider

Namespace AppliedADO.DataProvider
    Public Class PipedDataAdapter
        Inherits DbDataAdapter
        Implements IDbDataAdapter
        Public Sub New()

        End Sub

        Public Sub New(ByRef cmd As PipedDataCommand)
            _SelectCommand = cmd
        End Sub

        Private Sub NotSupported()
            Throw New NotSupportedException()
        End Sub
```

```vbnet
        Protected Overrides Function CreateRowUpdatingEvent(ByVal row As DataRow, _
 ByVal cmd As IDbCommand, ByVal stmtType As StatementType, ByVal mapping  _
As DataTableMapping) As RowUpdatingEventArgs
            NotSupported()
        End Function
        Protected Overrides Function CreateRowUpdatedEvent(ByVal row As DataRow, _
ByVal cmd As IDbCommand, ByVal stmtType As StatementType, ByVal mapping  _
As DataTableMapping) As RowUpdatedEventArgs
            NotSupported()
        End Function

        Protected Overrides Sub OnRowUpdated(ByVal value As RowUpdatedEventArgs)

        End Sub
        Protected Overrides Sub OnRowUpdating(ByVal e As RowUpdatingEventArgs)
        End Sub

        Private _SelectCommand As IDbCommand
        Private _InsertCommand As IDbCommand
        Private _UpdateCommand As IDbCommand
        Private _DeleteCommand As IDbCommand

        Public Property SelectCommand() As IDbCommand Implements  _
IDbDataAdapter.SelectCommand
            Get
                Return _SelectCommand
            End Get
            Set(ByVal Value As IDbCommand)
                _SelectCommand = Value
            End Set
        End Property

        Public Property InsertCommand() As IDbCommand Implements  _
IDbDataAdapter.InsertCommand
            Get
                Return _InsertCommand
            End Get
            Set(ByVal Value As IDbCommand)
                _InsertCommand = Value
            End Set
        End Property
```

```
        Public Property UpdateCommand() As IDbCommand Implements _
IDbDataAdapter.UpdateCommand
            Get
                Return _UpdateCommand
            End Get
            Set(ByVal Value As IDbCommand)
                _UpdateCommand = Value
            End Set
        End Property

        Public Property DeleteCommand() As IDbCommand Implements _
IDbDataAdapter.DeleteCommand
            Get
                Return _DeleteCommand
            End Get
            Set(ByVal Value As IDbCommand)
                _DeleteCommand = Value
            End Set
        End Property

    End Class
End Namespace
```

Testing the PipedDataProvider Application

Creating a test case for the PipedDataProvider application is a simple one. It's
simply a DataGrid and a single button that loads the pipeddata.txt file, fills a
DataTable with its data, and then binds it to the DataGrid.

This example highlights how little is required in the front-end code that's
forever simplified by the encapsulated code in your custom data provider. A piped
data file is loaded, parsed, and displayed in just a few lines of code. Listing 13-6
shows the PipedDataProvider application.

Listing 13-6. The PipedDataProvider Test Case

```
    Private Sub LoadButton_Click(ByVal sender As System.Object, _
ByVal e As System.EventArgs) Handles LoadButton.Click
        Dim adapter As New PipedDataAdapter()
        adapter.SelectCommand = New PipedDataCommand("ALL", New _
PipedDataConnection("../../pipeddata.txt"))
        Dim reader As System.Data.IDataReader

        Dim data As New DataTable()
        adapter.Fill(data)
        DisplayGrid.DataSource = data
    End Sub
```

Figure 13-4 shows the output of this program.

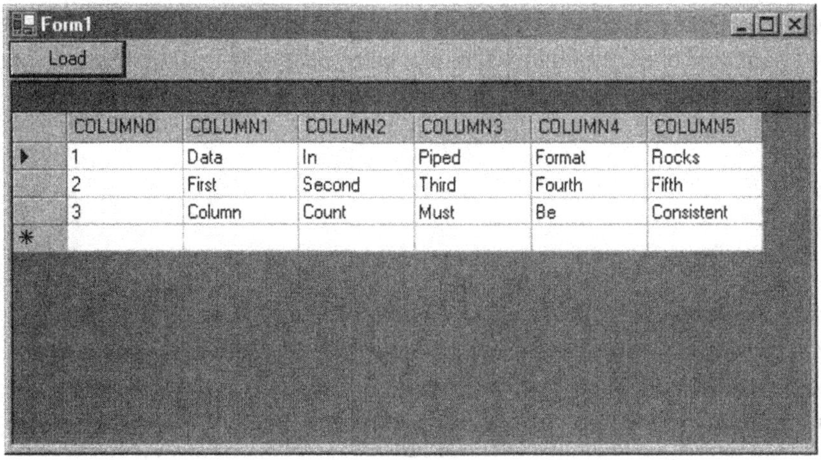

	COLUMN0	COLUMN1	COLUMN2	COLUMN3	COLUMN4	COLUMN5
►	1	Data	In	Piped	Format	Rocks
	2	First	Second	Third	Fourth	Fifth
	3	Column	Count	Must	Be	Consistent
*						

Figure 13-4. The output of the PipedDataProvider application

Debugging Your Custom Data Provider

The most common problem when you're trying to build your first data provider is simply getting all the interfaces implemented! Because of the strong interdependency among the interfaces, you won't have the luxury of starting with a small program that compiles, which you can then incrementally "grow."

One way to solve this problem is to make a note of what name you intend on giving each of your interfaces. Another helpful solution is to take a data provider implementation, such as the one in this chapter, and change each object to then work with your custom data source.

Additionally, you can also build in sections and wrap each object in a test case. For example, implement the Connection object first and write a test case that exercises each of the APIs to make sure you're getting predictable results. Then implement the IDbCommand object with a related test case to make it's working as well. Doing this will require a little more coding, but it will likely save you more time in debugging than trying to trace the needle in the haystack.

Finally, if you're serious about debugging your data provider, add trace logging at the entry and exit of each method. This can be as simple as writing to the debug stream or as sophisticated as writing to the Windows event log. This data can be valuable in performing a postmortem on your application when it crashes.

Summary

Developing a custom data provider can be a little difficult to understand at first because of the number of interfaces involved, but with an understanding of what each interface does, creating a custom provider is fairly easy.

With the ability to define a custom provider within the ADO.NET Framework, you can develop custom components to represent your custom data sources and leverage all of the .NET data technologies such as DataSets and data binding.

In the next chapter, we discuss the basics of writing Web applications using ASP.NET. As you read it, think through how you can use the PipedDataProvider application created in this chapter within your Web application.

CHAPTER 14

Developing Database Web Applications Using ASP.NET

AS THE PROGRAMMING world moves toward the Internet these days, it's becoming important for developers to be able to create Web applications and Web services. The Microsoft .NET Framework enables you to develop, maintain, and deploy reliable and high-performance Web applications and Web services.

This chapter starts with an overview of ASP.NET and how to install it, followed by a simple Web application development using Visual Studio .NET (VS .NET). After that it discusses the Web Forms controls and how to use them. The Web Forms' DataGrid control is a useful control to develop Web-based database applications. You can bind a DataSet to the DataGrid control as did for a Windows Forms' DataGrid control. This chapter also discusses how to fill data to a DataGrid and how to develop powerful Web-based database applications using the DataGrid control. It also discusses how to enable paging in a DataGrid control. At the end of the chapter you'll see how to develop a guest book for your Web site using ASP.NET.

Introducing ASP.NET

Writing database Web applications using ADO.NET in VS .NET is similar to writing Windows applications. The Microsoft .NET Class Library provides a set of server-side controls, which you can treat as Windows controls. To create a Web application, all you have to do is create a simple project, drag server-side controls onto a Web form, set their properties, and write event handlers. In this chapter, you'll first develop a simple Web application and see how the ASP.NET model works with Visual Basic .NET (VB .NET) and other .NET languages. After that you'll concentrate on ASP.NET and see how to write some real-world database Web applications using ADO.NET and VB .NET.

ASP.NET Platform Requirements

The following operating systems support ASP.NET: Windows XP, Windows 2000 Server, and Windows NT 4 (running Service Pack 6a) with Internet Information Services (IIS) 4 or later. Also, you must have the .NET Software Development Kit (SDK) installed on the server.

ASP.NET Language Support

You can use any .NET-supported language to write ASP.NET applications, including C#, VB .NET, and JScript. As this book is about VB .NET, the other languages are beyond the scope of this book.

Installing ASP.NET

You can develop and run ASP.NET applications on Windows 2000 or Windows XP operating systems. ASP.NET ships with VS .NET. For developers who don't have VS .NET, ASP.NET comes in a separate package, which can be downloaded from the Microsoft's Web site (www.microsoft.com). If you want to develop ASP.NET mobile-enabled applications for Pocket PC or cellular phones, you need to install ASP.NET Mobile Internet Toolkit, which you can also download from Microsoft Web site.

ASP.NET Editors

We'll be using VS .NET to develop the applications in this chapter. However, like most languages in the .NET family, you can develop ASP.NET applications using any text editor and command-line compiler. After compiling, you copy your file manually to IIS to deploy the application. The advantage of using VS .NET is that it provides you with a visual Integrated Development Environment (IDE) to drag and drop controls onto a page and view the Hypertext Markup Language (HTML) code in an HTML editor. Other features are IntelliSense and syntax checking. In summary, you can use VS .NET to compile, debug, and deploy your application.

NOTE *ASP.NET editors, including VS .NET, provide What-You-See-Is-What-You-Get (WYSIWYG) support for developing Graphical User Interface (GUI) applications by dropping controls on the Web Forms pages.*

Microsoft has also released a lightweight, easy-to-use, and free ASP.NET development tool (including editor) for non–VS .NET developers. You can find more details about this tool on the www.asp.net Web site.

ASP.NET: An Evolution of ASP

ASP.NET, previously called *ASP+*, is not just the next version of ASP. It is a new programming model based on Microsoft's .NET Framework for developing Web applications. Although ASP.NET syntaxes are taken from ASP, the ASP.NET model takes full advantage of Microsoft's Common Language Runtime (CLR) and its services. Therefore, developers have the flexibility to choose any .NET-supported language to write ASP.NET applications.

The main advantages of the ASP.NET model are the following:

ASP.NET is simple and flexible: Developing ASP.NET applications using VS .NET is similar to developing Windows applications. VS .NET offers you a set of controls to use with ASP.NET. You just need to drag and drop the controls onto a Web Form, write events corresponding to the controls, and compile and run the program. Other features include simple client authentication, security, deployment, and site configuration.

ASP.NET is language independent: You can choose any language that supports .NET, including C#, VB, VBScript, and JScript.

ASP.NET supports data binding: ASP.NET offers you a set of data-binding controls such as the DataGrid, DataList, and others. You can bind data with these controls in a similar fashion as you do in any Windows Forms application.

ASP.NET has enhanced performance and scalability: ASP.NET code is not interpreted like traditional ASP pages. ASP.NET pages are compiled on the server in a .NET assembly. It takes advantage of early binding, just-in-time compilation, native optimization, and caching services. ASP.NET also works in clustered and multiprocessor environments.

ASP.NET is browser independent: If you ever programmed in previous versions of ASP, you've probably had problems running ASP pages in browsers other than Internet Explorer. ASP.NET is browser independent. It automatically checks what browser you're using and produces HTML at runtime accordingly.

Web Forms and Web Services

Web Forms is a term Microsoft introduced when it released its ASP+ framework for developing Web applications using the ASP model.

Similar to Windows applications and services, you can also write Web applications and services. A *Web application* is a distributed application, which allows you to work and distribute functionality over the Web and provides user interfaces. Using Web Forms controls, you can write Web GUI applications similar to Windows applications.

ASP.NET's Web Forms provide you with the ability to build Web-based GUI applications. Web Forms include Web pages (also called *ASP.NET pages* or *Web Forms pages*) and *GUI components* (sometimes called *server controls*) such as a TextBox, Button, ListBox, DataGrid, and so on. ASP.NET provides the flexibility to add these controls to an ASP.NET page at runtime as well as at design-time. VS .NET provides design-time features to develop applications in no time. You add controls to a page by dragging controls from the Toolbox to the page and then setting the controls' properties and events. Web Forms also provide a method for using the Codebehind directive to separate your data from the code. In other words, you can write code in a separate file from the controls.

Web services are applications that perform a certain task; they can be used by a single application as well as distributed on the Web. However, Web services don't usually have a user interface like a normal application would. Chapter 15 covers Web services.

Developing Your First ASP.NET Web Application

Before discussing the ASP.NET model in more depth, we'll show you how to develop your first ASP.NET application using VS .NET. In this example, you'll create a simple Web application using VS .NET. You'll add a Button, a TextBox, and a ListBox control to a Web page and then add the TextBox contents to the ListBox on the button click event.

Creating a Web Application Project

Creating a new ASP.NET Web application using VS .NET is simple. First create a new project using File ➤ New ➤ Project ➤ Visual Basic Projects and then select the ASP.NET Web Application template (see Figure 14-1).

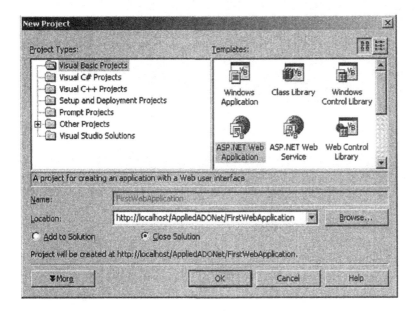

Figure 14-1. The FirstWebApplication project

As you see in Figure 14-1, the Location box shows you the default option of `http://localhost` and the application name. Here, `localhost` represents the default IIS server running on your local machine. The default virtual directory for `localhost` is `C:\Inetpub\wwwroot`.

Clicking the OK button creates a new directory, `FirstWebApplication`, in the server's virtual directory. It also creates a new Web application and sends you to the default `WebForm1.aspx` page, as shown in Figure 14-2.

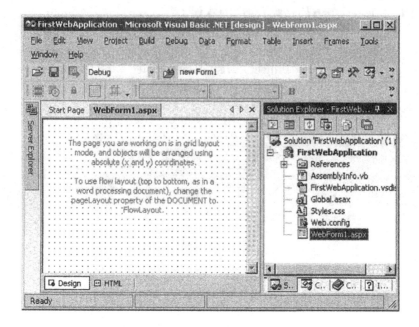

Figure 14-2. Default WebForm1.aspx *page*

From here you can edit your page's HTML. As you see in the left-bottom corner of Figure 14-2, there are two modes available: Design and HTML. Click the HTML button to edit the code, as shown in Figure 14-3.

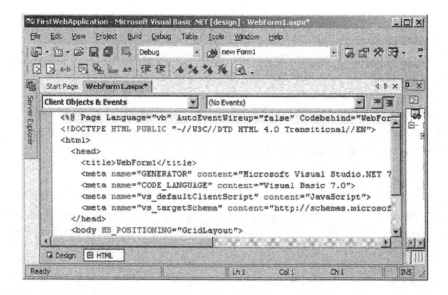

Figure 14-3. HTML view of WebForm1.aspx

The HTML view shows you the HTML code of a page, its controls, and control properties. The HTML editor also let you edit the HTML manually.

Now, if you switch to the design mode and right-click the page, you'll get several options: View HTML Source, Build Style, View in Browser, View Code, Synchronize Document Outline, and so on (see Figure 14-4).

Figure 14-4. An ASP.NET page's right-click options

You can set a page's properties by selecting Properties from the right-click menu. The Properties menu opens the Document Property Pages window. As you can see from Figure 14-5, there are three tabs available in the Properties window: General, Color and Margins, and Keywords. Most of the properties are self-explanatory. On the General tab, one merits explanation. The Page Layout property has two options, GridLayout and FlowLayout. GridLayout is when you want drop controls to the page and reposition them. If you want to add text to the page, you should set the page layout to FlowLayout; otherwise you won't be able to add text to the page. After setting the Page Layout property to FlowLayout, the editor works as a text editor.

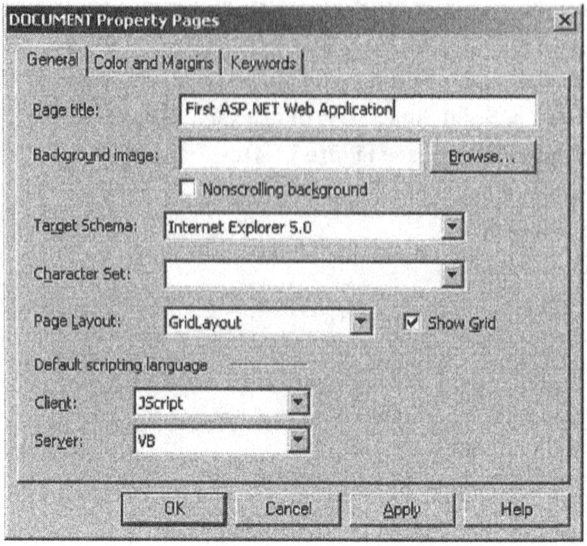

Figure 14-5. An ASP.NET document's page properties

Adding Web Controls to a Web Form

Similar to the Windows control Toolbox, VS .NET provides a Web Forms control Toolbox. You can open the Toolbox by selecting View ➤ Toolbox. The Web Forms Toolbox looks like Figure 14-6. The Web Forms category of the Toolbox contains form controls, and the HTML category contains HTML controls. The Data category provides the same data components you've seen in the Windows application Toolbox. It has the same ADO.NET data components, including Connection, DataAdapter, DataSet, DataView, and DataViewManager. Figures 14-6 shows the Web Forms controls. Similar to Web forms controls, if you click the HTML tab, you can see HTML controls.

For the applications in this chapter, we'll be using the Web Forms controls.

OK, now you can switch the page back to the design mode and GridLayout mode (if you changed its modes) and add a Button, a TextBox, and a ListBox to the form by dragging these controls from the Web Forms toolbox to WebForm1.aspx. The page should now look like Figure 14-7.

Figure 14-6. Web Forms controls

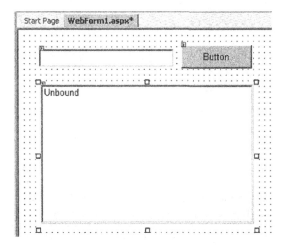

Figure 14-7. WebForms1.aspx *Design mode after adding Web Forms controls*

Setting Control Properties

The next step is to add some text to the page and change some of the controls'
properties. To add text to the page, first you need to change the page layout to
FlowLayout in the Properties window, which you open by right-clicking the page
and selecting Properties. Now add a heading to the page. For this example, add
two lines to the page and set different fonts and font sizes of these lines. You can
also set some of the Button control's properties (see Figure 14-8).

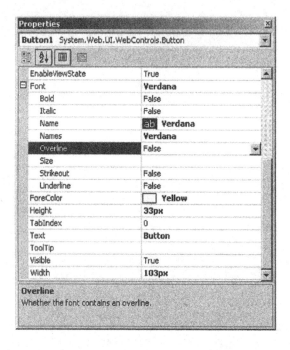

Figure 14-8. Properties window for the Web controls

Specifically, we changed the border, background color, font, and foreground
color of these controls. As you can see, changing these properties is similar to
changing them for Windows applications. The final page with these properties
looks like Figure 14-9.

Figure 14-9. Final page of the Web application after changing some control properties

Using Document Outline

Another nice feature of the VS .NET IDE is that you can synchronize a Web page's controls with its contents in the Document Outline viewer. This is useful when you're developing a Web application with hundreds of controls; it can be hard to keep track of all the controls, HTML tags, and other page contents. The Document Outline viewer enables you to manage a page's contents in a tree format. The tree format displays all the page elements in the order they're called in the page. You can open the Document Outline viewer by right-clicking a page and selecting Synchronize Document Outline. Clicking this menu item launches the Document Outline viewer in the left pane (see Figure 14-10). As you can see, the tree view displays the page contents, including the form, button, text box, and paragraph. If you click a control in the Document Outline viewer, it selects the corresponding control in the form. And, vice versa, if you select a control in the form, the viewer selects that control in the tree view.

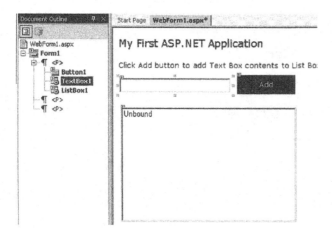

Figure 14-10. Document Outline viewer

You can also use the Document Outline viewer's right-click menu to cut, paste, delete, view the code, and view the properties of these controls. The right-click menu's View Code option displays the code of the page.

Not only that, but now you'll see one more thing. Select the HTML view of your page, and you can move to specific HTML tags using the Document Outline viewer. As you can see from Figure 14-11, the tree view displays all the code of an HTML page in a nested structure as they're organized in the original code.

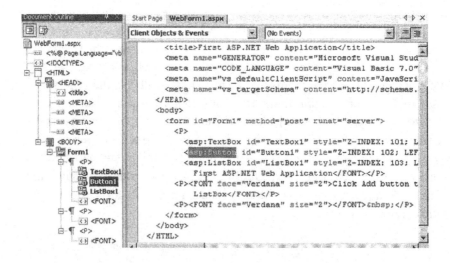

Figure 14-11. HTML view of the Document Outline viewer

So, the point is that you can find and organize your HTML code and controls from the Document Outline viewer instead of looking for a tag in the file manually.

Writing Code on the Button Click Event Handler

The last step of this tutorial is to add an event handler for the button and write code to add some TextBox text to the ListBox. You add a control event similar to Windows applications. You can just double-click the button to add a button click event handler.

This action adds the Button1_Click method to the WebForm1.aspx.vb class, which hosts the code for the page controls and events. Now write a line of code to add the TextBox contents to the list box. Specifically, add the bold line in the following section to the Button1_Click method:

```
Private Sub Button1_Click(ByVal sender As System.Object, _
  ByVal e As System.EventArgs) Handles Button1.Click
    ListBox1.Items.Add(TextBox1.Text.ToString())
End Sub
```

NOTE *You can also see the code using the View Code option of the page's right-click menu.*

Now compile and run the project. The output of the program looks like Figure 14-12. Clicking the Add button adds the TextBox contents to the list box.

Figure 14-12. Output of your first Web application

After finishing this application, you can see the power and flexibility of ASP.NET and the VS .NET IDE. You've just developed a nice ASP.NET Web application without any knowledge of ASP.NET and just by writing only one line of code.

Creating Your First ADO.NET Web Application

You've already seen how to develop an ASP.NET application using VS .NET. Now you'll see how to develop database applications using ADO.NET and ASP.NET. To start creating your first ADO.NET application, you'll create a Web Application project as you did in the previous tutorial. In this example, you'll read data from the SQL Server Northwind database and view data in few data-bound controls. After creating a Web application, add a ListBox and a DataGrid control to the Web page. In this application, you'll fill these controls with data from the database.

After dragging these controls from the Web Forms control Toolbox and dropping it on the page, you write the code in Listing 14-1 on the Page_Load event. You can add a Page_Load event by typing the code directly into the Codebehind.vb file or by double-clicking on the page.

 NOTE *We're using a SQL Server database and the SqlClient data provider, which means we import the* System.Data.SqlClient *namespace to the application.*

Listing 14-1. Filling Data from a Database to Data-Bound Controls

```
Private Sub Page_Load(ByVal sender As System.Object, _
  ByVal e As System.EventArgs) Handles MyBase.Load
    Dim ConnectionString As String = "user id=sa;password=;" & _
      "Initial Catalog=Northwind;" & _
      "Data Source=MCB;"
    Dim conn As SqlConnection = New SqlConnection(ConnectionString)
    ' Open the connection
    If (conn.State <> ConnectionState.Open) Then
      conn.Open()
    End If
```

```
    Dim adapter As SqlDataAdapter = New SqlDataAdapter _
    ("SELECT EmployeeID, LastName, FirstName FROM Employees", conn)
    Dim ds As DataSet = New DataSet()
    adapter.Fill(ds, "Employees")
    ' Bind data set to the control
    ' Set DataSource property of ListBox as DataSet's DefaultView
    ListBox1.DataSource = ds
    ListBox1.SelectedIndex = 0
    ' Set Field Name you want to get data from
    ListBox1.DataTextField = "FirstName"
    'DataGrid1.DataSource = ds.DefaultViewManager
    DataGrid1.DataSource = ds
    ' DataGrid1.DataBind()
    DataBind()
    '   Close the connection
    If (conn.State = ConnectionState.Open) Then
        conn.Close()
    End If
End Sub
```

As you can see, this code looks familiar. First you create a `Connection` object with the Northwind database. After that you create a `DataAdapter` and select the EmployeeID, FirstName, and LastName columns from the Employees table. Then you create a `DataSet` object and fill it using the `DataAdapter`'s `Fill` method. Once you have a `DataSet`, you set the `DataSet` as the `ListBox`'s `DataSource` property and set `SelectIndex` as 0. The `SelectIndex` property represents the index of the column from a `DataSet` you want to display in the control. The field name of the column is FirstName. You also set the `DataSource` property of `DataGrid` control as `DataSet`. At the end you call the `DataBind` method of the `ListBox`. This method binds the data to the data-bound controls.

The output looks like Figure 14-13. As you can see, the `ListBox` control displays data from the FirstName column of the Employees table, and `DataGrid` displays all three columns.

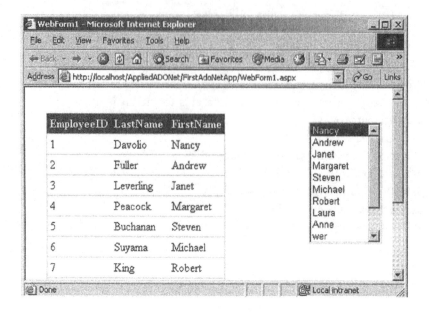

Figure 14-13. Your first ADO.NET Web application

In Figure 14-13, you may notice the DataGrid format looks different. You can set a DataGrid format by using the Auto Format option of the Properties window.

Using ASP.NET Server-Side Controls

The Microsoft .NET Framework provides a rich set of server-side controls for developing Web applications. You can add these controls to Web Forms pages just as you add Windows controls to a form. Server-side controls are often called *server controls* or *Web Forms controls*. There are four types of server controls: HTML server controls, Web server controls, validation controls, and user controls.

HTML Server Controls

HTML developers will be familiar with old HTML controls, which they use to write GUI applications in HTML. These controls are the same HTML controls; you can run these controls on the server by defining the runat="Server" attribute. Note that if you do not set this attribute, the HTML control acts as a normal HTML control. You may prefer this in some situations, as the HTML controls work without requiring a round-trip to the server. These control names start with Html. Table 14-1 defines some of these controls.

Table 14-1. HTML Server Controls

CONTROL	DESCRIPTION
HtmlForm	Creates an HTML form control, used as a placeholder of other controls
HtmlInputText	Creates an input TextBox control used to get input from user
HtmltextArea	Creates a multiline TextBox control
HtmlAnchor	Creates Web navigation
HtmlButton	Creates a Button control
HtmlImage	Creates an Image control that is used to display an image
HtmlInputCheckBox	Creates a CheckBox control
HtmlInputRadioButton	Creates a RadioButton control
HtmlTable	Creates a Table control
HtmlTableRow	Creates a row within a table
HtmlTableCell	Creates a cell within a row

Web server controls are more powerful than HTML controls because they provide more functionality and are easier to use. Besides some of the basic controls such as Button, TextBox, Label, and CheckBox, ASP.NET provides some more powerful controls such as DataGrid, DataList, and Calendar. You'll use these controls throughout this chapter. Table 14-2 describes some of these controls.

Table 14-2. Web Server Controls

CONTROL	DESCRIPTION
Label	Represents a label
ListBox	Represents a list box
CheckBox	Represents a check box
Calender	Represents a calendar
ImageButton	Represents an image button
TableCell	Represents a table cell
Panel	Represents a panel
DateList	Represents a data list
TextBox	Represents a text box
Image	Represents an image
CheckBoxList	Represents a list box with check boxes
Button	Represents a button
HyperLink	Represents a hyperlink
TableRow	Represents a row of a table
RadioButtonList	Represents a list box with radio buttons
DataGrid	Represents a data grid
DropDownList	Represents a drop-down list
AdRotator	Represents an ad rotator
RadioButton	Represents a radio button
LinkButton	Represents a link button
Table	Represents a table
Repeater	Represents a repeater

You'll see how to use these controls in example applications throughout this chapter.

Validation Controls

Validating user input is one of the important needs for Web applications. These controls provide features to validate user input. Using these controls you can check a required field, a value, a range, a pattern of characters, and so on. Table 14-3 describes validation controls.

Table 14-3. Validation Controls

CONTROL	DESCRIPTION
RequiredFieldValidator	Makes sure that the user does not skip an entry
CompareValidator	Compares user input with a value using a comparison operator such as less than, greater than, and so on
RangeValidator	Checks if the user's input falls within a certain range
RegularExpressionValidator	Checks if the user's input matches a defined pattern
CustomValidator	Creates your own custom logic

User Controls

Besides HTML server controls, Web server controls, and validation controls, you can also create your own controls by embedding Web Forms controls. These controls are called *custom controls*. You create custom controls when the available controls can't provide the functionality you need. For example, if you want to create a DataGrid control with check boxes, combo boxes, calendars, and date controls, you can create a custom control derived from the available controls and then write the additional functionality.

Server Controls and the .NET Framework Library

The .NET Framework Library provides the System.Web and its 15 supporting namespaces to define Web classes. These namespaces reside in the System.Web.dll assembly. Before you use any Web namespaces, though, you need to add a reference to the System.Web.Dll assembly and include the required namespace in the application. The five major namespaces of the Web series are System.Web, System.Web.UI, System.Web.UI.HtmlControls, System.Web.UI.WebControls, and System.Web.Services.

The System.Web Namespace

The System.Web namespace contains browser- and server-related classes and interfaces. For example, the HTTPRequest and HTTPResponse classes provide functionality to make requests for HTTP to retrieve and post data on the server through a browser. The HttpApplication class defines the functionality of an ASP.NET application. This namespace also contains the HttpCookie and HttpCookieCollection classes for manipulating cookies. The HttpFileCollection class provides access to and organizes files uploaded by a client. You can use the HttpWriter class to write to the server through HttpResponse.

The System.Web.UI Namespace

The System.Web.UI namespace contains classes and interfaces that enable you to develop Web-based GUI applications similar to Windows GUI applications. This namespace provides classes to create Web Forms pages and controls. The Control class is the base class for all Web control classes and provides methods and properties for HTML, Web, or user controls. The Page class represents a Web page requested by the server in an ASP.NET application. It also has classes for data binding with the data-bound controls such as DataGrid and DataList. You'll see these classes in the examples in this chapter. In addition to these classes, it also includes state management, templates, and validation-related classes.

The System.Web.UI.HtmlControls Namespace

This namespace contains HTML control classes (discussed in the "HTML Server Controls" section). Some of this namespace's classes are HtmlButton, HtmlControl, HtmlForm, HtmlImage, HtmlInputText, HtmlTable, and so on.

The System.Web.UI.WebControls Namespace

This namespace contains classes related to server controls and their supporting classes, as discussed in the "Web Server Controls" section of this chapter. Some of the classes are AddRotator, Button, Calendar, CheckBox, DataGrid, DataList, DropDownList, HyperLink, Image, Label, ListBox, ListControl, Panel, Table, TableRow, and TextBox. Besides the control classes, it also contains control helper classes. For example, the DataGridItem, DataGridColumn, and DataGridColumnCollection classes are helper classes of the DataGrid control, and TableRow, TableCell, TableCellCollection, TableHeaderCell, and TableItemStyle are helper classes of the Table control.

The System.Web.Services Namespace

A Web service is an application that sits and runs on the Web server. The System.Web.Service and its three helper namespaces— System.Web.Service.Description, System.Web.Service.Discovery, and System.Web.Service.Protocol—provides classes to build Web services. Chapter 15 covers Web services in more detail.

Why Are Web Forms Controls Called Server-Side Controls?

Microsoft's .NET Framework consists of powerful Web controls. By using these Web controls you can write powerful Web GUI applications similar to desktop applications. You can write code for these controls manually, or you can use VS .NET. VS .NET supports the *drag-and-drop* design-time feature. In other words, you can drag and drop Web Forms controls onto a Web form, set properties by right-clicking a control, and even write event handlers by double-clicking the control as you'd do in Windows GUI applications such as VB.

When a client (a Web browser) makes a call for a Web control such as a Button or a DataGrid, the runat="Server" attribute (discussed later in more detail) tells the Web server that the controls will be executed on the server and they'll send HTML data to the client at run-time after execution. Because the execution of these control events, methods, and attributes happens on the server, these controls are *server-side* Web controls. The main functionality of these controls includes rendering data from the server to the client and event handling. (The controls fire events and handle those events.)

Adding Server-Side Controls to a Web Form

You have two ways to add server controls to a Web form. You can use the VS .NET IDE to add server controls, or you can add controls manually by typing code using the <asp:..> syntax.

Adding Server Controls Using VS .NET

Adding server controls using VS .NET is pretty simple. As you have seen in the "Developing Your First ASP.NET Web Application" section of this chapter, you create a new ASP.NET application project, open the Toolbox, drag and drop controls from Toolbox, set properties, and write event handlers for the control.

Adding Server Controls Using ASP.NET Syntax

The other method of adding server controls to an application is writing the code manually. To add server controls manually, you create a text file and save it with an .aspx extension. .NET utilizes Extensible Markup Language (XML)–like tags to write server controls. A tag should follow XML syntaxes. Every ASP.NET control starts with asp: and a control name. For example, the following line creates a TextBox control:

```
<asp:textbox id=TextBox1 runat="Server" Text=""></asp:textbox>
```

This line creates a TextBox server control. Every control has a unique ID. In this sample the ID is TextBox1. The runat="Server" attribute represents that the control will run on the server.

The following code shows you can write the same code without the closing tag:

```
<asp:textbox id=Textbox1 runat="Server" />
```

OK, now let's get back to the first sample. Remember, you created your first application and added a TextBox, a Button, and a ListBox control to the Web page. Listing 14-2 shows the ASP.NET version of your first ASP.NET application (from Figure 14-12). You can see the ASP.NET version by using the HTML mode of the designer.

Listing 14-2. ASP.NET Version of Your First ASP.NET Application

```
<%@ Page Language="vb" AutoEventWireup="false" Codebehind="WebForm1.aspx.vb"
Inherits="FirstWebApplication.WebForm1"%>
<!DOCTYPE HTML PUBLIC "-//W3C//DTD HTML 4.0 Transitional//EN">
<HTML>
<HEAD>
<title>First ASP.NET Web Application</title>
<meta name="GENERATOR" content="Microsoft Visual Studio.NET 7.0">
<meta name="CODE_LANGUAGE" content="Visual Basic 7.0">
```

```
<meta name="vs_defaultClientScript" content="JavaScript">
<meta name="vs_targetSchema" content="http://schemas.microsoft.com/
intellisense/ie5">
</HEAD>
<body>
<form id="Form1" method="post" runat="server">
<P>
<asp:TextBox id="TextBox1" style="Z-INDEX: 101; LEFT: 16px;
POSITION: absolute; TOP: 80px" runat="server"></asp:TextBox>
<asp:Button id="Button1" style="Z-INDEX: 102; LEFT: 188px;
POSITION: absolute; TOP: 79px" runat="server" Text="Add"
Width="106px" Height="27px" Font-Names="Verdana"
ForeColor="Yellow" BackColor="#0000C0"></asp:Button>
<asp:ListBox id="ListBox1" style="Z-INDEX: 103; LEFT:
14px; POSITION: absolute; TOP: 121px" runat="server"
Width="284px" Height="170px"></asp:ListBox><FONT face="Verdana"
size="4">My First ASP.NET Web Application</FONT></P>
<P><FONT face="Verdana" size="2">Click Add button to add TextBox
contents to ListBox</FONT></P>
<P><FONT face="Verdana" size="2"></FONT> </P>
</form>
</body>
</HTML>
```

As you saw in Listing 14-2, asp:Button, asp:TextBox, and asp:ListBox are three server controls added using ASP.NET. In Listing 14-2, you probably noticed some unfamiliar keywords such as <%@Page, Language, and codebehind. The <%@Page Language is a page directive, which defines the language you're using in the page. You can use any .NET-supported language such as C# or VB .NET. The Codebehind directive separates code from the ASP.NET page. You can define a C# or VB .NET page as Codebehind, which hosts the code for ASP.NET controls for the page. As you can see from Listing 14-2, the WebForm1.aspx.vb file is a VB class, which hosts code for WebForm1 page.

Understanding Data Binding in ASP.NET

Web Forms provide many controls that support data binding. You can connect these controls to ADO.NET components such as a DataView, a DataSet, or a DataViewManager at design-time as well as at runtime. Data binding in Web Forms works in the same way as it does in the Windows Forms with a few exceptions. For example, to bind a DataSet to a DataGrid, you call the DataBind method of the

DataGrid control. We discuss all this in a moment. First let's see some basics of data-bound controls.

The following sections discuss data binding and how it works in ASP.NET.

Data-Bound Controls

ASP.NET provides a rich set of data-bound server-side controls. These controls are easy to use and provide a Rapid Application Development (RAD) Web development. You can categorize these controls in two groups: single-item data-bound controls and multi-item data-bound controls.

You use the single-item data-bound controls to display the value of a single item of a database table. These controls don't provide direct binding with the data source. The highlighted part of Figure 14-14 shows an *item* of a database table. You use the Text, Caption, or Value property of these controls to show the data of a field.

Mahesh	234, G. Road	12398
Mike	5443, NY	89433
AJ	P. Rd	54323

Figure 14-14. An item

Examples of single-item data-bound controls are a TextBox, Button, Label, Image, and so on.

You use the multi-item data-bound controls to display the entire table or a partial table. These controls provide direct binding to the data source. You use the DataSource property of these controls to bind a database table to these controls (see Figure 14-15).

Mahesh	234, G. Road	12398
Mike	5443, NY	89433
AJ	P. Rd	54323

Figure 14-15. Multi-item controls

Some examples of multi-item data-bound controls are DataGrid, ListBox, DataList, DropDownList, and so on. Figure 14-16 shows some of the data-bound controls.

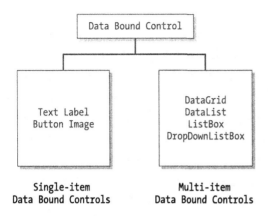

Figure 14-16. Data-bound controls

In ASP.NET, you create these controls using an <asp:controlName> tag. Table 14-4 describes some common data-bound server-side controls.

Table 14-4. ASP.NET Data-Bound Controls

CONTROL	ASP.NET CODE	DESCRIPTION
DataGrid	<asp:DataGrid>	This control displays a database (through ADO.NET) in a scrollable grid format and supports selection, adding, updating, sorting, and paging.
DataList	<asp:DataList>	This control displays data in templates and style format.
ListBox	<asp:ListBox>	This control can be associated to ADO.NET data fields to display data in a list format.
DropDownList	<asp:DropDownList>	This control displays ADO.NET data source data in a drop-down combo box format.
CheckBox	<asp:CheckBox>	This can be connected to an item of the ADO.NET data source.
CheckBoxList	<asp:CheckBoxList>	This control can be connected to the ADO.NET data source.
Repeater	<asp:Repeater>	A templated data-bound list.
TextBox	<asp:TextBox>	This control displays ADO.NET using its Text property.

DataGrid and DataList Controls

A DataGrid control is one of the most powerful Web controls. By using just a DataGrid control, you can write full-fledged Web applications for your Web site. In this section, you'll learn all about the DataGrid methods and properties. The following examples are heavily based on this control.

You can use a DataGrid control to display tabular data. It also provides the ability to insert, update, sort, and scroll the data. Using and binding a DataGrid control is easy with the help of the ADO.NET DataSets. This grid is capable of autogenerating the columns and rows depending on which data you're connecting.

Another control worth mentioning is the DataList control. A DataList control provides a list view of the data from a data source. These controls work similarly.

DataGrid and DataList controls have similar properties. Table 14-5 describes some of the common DataGrid properties.

Table 14-5. DataGrid *Control Properties*

PROPERTY	DESCRIPTION
AllowPaging, AllowCustomPaging	Boolean values indicate whether paging or custom paging are allowed in the grid. **SYNTAX** AllowPaging="true"
AllowSorting	Boolean value indicates whether sorting is allowed in the grid. **SYNTAX** AllowSorting="true"
AutoGenerateColumns	Gets or sets a value that indicates whether columns will automatically be created for each bound data field. **SYNTAX** AutoGenerateColumns="true"
BackColor, ForeColor, Font	Sets the background, foreground color, and font of the grid control. **SYNTAX** BorderColor="black"; ForeColor="green"; Font-Name="Verdana"; Font-Size="10pt"
BackImageUrl	Gets or sets the URL of an image to display in the background of the DataGrid.
BorderColor, BorderStyle, BorderWidth	Sets the border properties of the control. **SYNTAX** BorderColor="black"; BorderWidth="1"
CellPadding, CellSpacing	Sets the cell spacing and padding. **SYNTAX** CellPadding="10"; CellSpacing="5"
Columns	Gets a collection of column controls in the DataGrid.

Table 14-5. DataGrid *Control Properties (Continued)*

PROPERTY	DESCRIPTION
CurrentPageIndex	Index of the currently displayed page.
DataKeyField	Primary key field in the data source.
DataSource	Fills the grid with the data. **SYNTAX** DataGrid1.DataSource = ds.Tables["Student"].DefaultView;
EditItemIndex	Index of the item to be edited.
EditItemStyle	Style of the item to be edited.
HeaderStyle, FooterStyle	Header and footer styles. **SYNTAX** HeaderStyle-BackColor="#00aaaa"; FooterStyle-BackColor="#00aaaa"
GridLines	Gets or sets the grid line style. **SYNTAX** GridLines="Vertical"
Height, Width	Width and height of the control.
ID	ID of the control.
Page	Returns the Page object that contains the current control. **SYNTAX** Page.DataBind();
PageCount, PageSize	Returns the total number of pages and number of items in a page to be displayed. **SYNTAX** NumPages = ItemsGrid.PageCount; Items = ItemsGrid.PageCount
SelectedIndex	Index of the currently selected item.
SelectedItem	Returns the selected item in the DataGrid.
ShowFooter, ShowHeader	Shows header and footers. **SYNTAX** ShowFooter="true";; ShowHeader="true";
UniqueID	Returns the unique ID for a control.
VirtualItemCount	Total number of items on the page when AllowCustomPaging is true.

Setting DataGrid Control Properties at Design-Time

In VS .NET, you can set the DataGrid control's properties at design-time by right-clicking the control and selecting the Properties menu item. This displays the Properties window (see Figure 14-17).

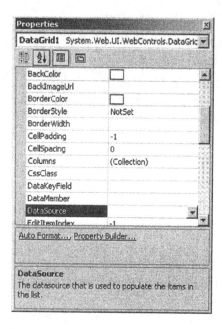

Figure 14-17. DataGrid *properties*

Most of these properties should look familiar to you by now. You can set the DataSource property to a DataView, DataSet, DataViewManager, or a DataReader. The DataMember property represents a column of a data table if you want to display only one column in the control.

AutoFormat

Besides the general properties of a DataGrid, in Figure 14-17, you see two links: Auto Format and Property Builder. The Auto Format option provides you with pre-defined formats for rows, columns, headers, footers, and so on (see Figure 14-18).

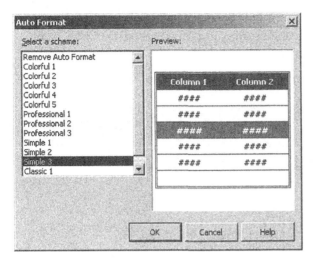

Figure 14-18. DataGrid*'s Auto Format dialog box*

Property Builder

The Property Builder option launches the Properties dialog box. Before setting the DataGrid properties, let's do one thing. Drag a SqlDataAdapter from the Toolbox's Data tab to the Web page, which launches the DataAdapter Configuration Wizard. Follow the steps and build a SQL query using SQL Query tool. Select EmployeeID, LastName, FirstName, and Title from Employees table.

After completing this step, generate a DataSet from the DataAdapter. You can right-click and select the Generate DataSet option to generate a DataSet from a DataAdapter. The Generate DataSet option asks you to use an existing DataSet or create a new DataSet.

This action asks the DataSet name and adds the DataSet11 DataSet object with a DataSet1 class derived from DataSet and DataSet1.xsd XML schema to the project.

Next, drop a DataView on the page and set DataSet11.Employees as its Table property. All these steps are explained in Chapter 2. Now you're all set to use the DataGrid Property Builder.

The first property page is General. This page lets you set a DataSource name at design-time. All available DataSet, DataView, and other data-bindable objects are available in the drop-down combo list. In this case, we have DataSet11 and DataView1. You can also set the DataMember and DataKeyField properties from this page. In this case, select DataSet11 as the DataSource option, Employees as the DataMember option (the only available option; if you have multiple tables in a DataSet, you'll have all tables listed here), and EmployeeID as the Data Key Field option. If you want to add headers and footers to the DataGrid control, you can set them by checking the Show Header and Show Footer check boxes on this page. The Allow Sorting check box enables sorting in a DataGrid control. Check all of these options as shown in Figure 14-19.

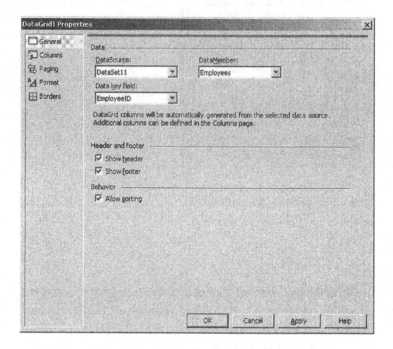

Figure 14-19. DataGrid *general properties*

Columns Property Page

By default, a DataGrid control adds columns at runtime depending upon the DataSource property of the grid. By using the Columns property page, you can add DataGrid columns at design-time by unchecking the Create Columns Automatically at Run Time check box (as shown in Figure 14-20). We also added four columns to the Selected Columns list: ID, LastName, FirstName, and Title. This page also lets you change the header text and footer text. Not only that, you can also define whether a column is read-only. The Header Image option allows you to set the image of a DataGrid header. We selected an image for the column headers.

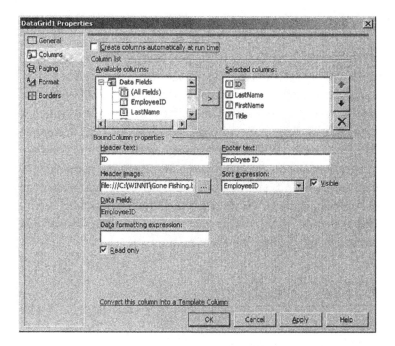

Figure 14-20. DataGrid *Columns properties page*

 NOTE *If you set the Header image option to some image, the header title will display as the image, not the text.*

If you scroll down your Available Columns list, you can even add DataGrid columns as a button, a hyperlink, or a template column.

Paging Property Page

The Paging page enables the paging feature in the grid control. The Paging page allows you to set the number of records per page in a DataGrid control. For example, if DataGrid grid control has 50 records and you set the Page Size as 5, the DataGrid will show all 50 records in 10 pages. The Paging page also allows you to navigate to the first page, next page, previous page, last page, and even to a particular page number. By using the Paging property page, you can set the number of pages viewed in a grid and the mode of navigation for navigating pages. In other words, you can either have previous and next options or have the number of pages option. As you can see from Figure 14-21, we check the Allow Paging check box and set the Page Size as 5 rows. We also set the page navigation buttons to include Next and Previous buttons and change the text of buttons.

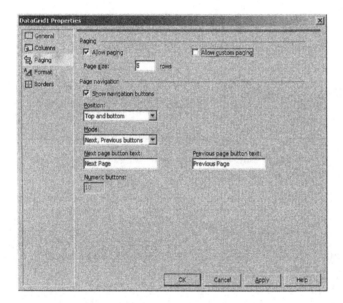

Figure 14-21. DataGrid *Paging properties page*

Format Property Page

If you don't want to use the Auto Format option, you can use the Format page. This page enables you to set the color and font of a DataGrid control. In fact, this page allows you control over every part of a DataGrid. You can set colors, fonts, style of the DataGrid, as well as its header and footers, page navigators, individual columns, and even column headers and footers (see Figure 14-22).

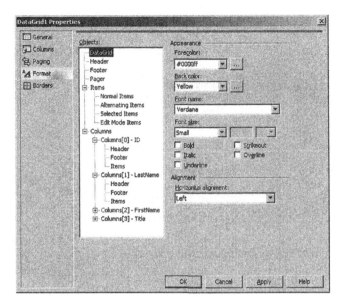

Figure 14-22. DataGrid *Format properties page*

Borders Property Page

The Borders page enables you to set the border, color, font, cell padding and spacing, and the type of lines in the grid (see Figure 14-23).

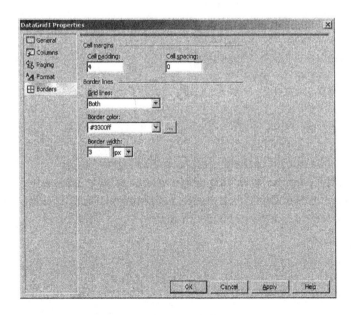

Figure 14-23. DataGrid *Border properties page*

The final DataGrid control looks like Figure 14-24.

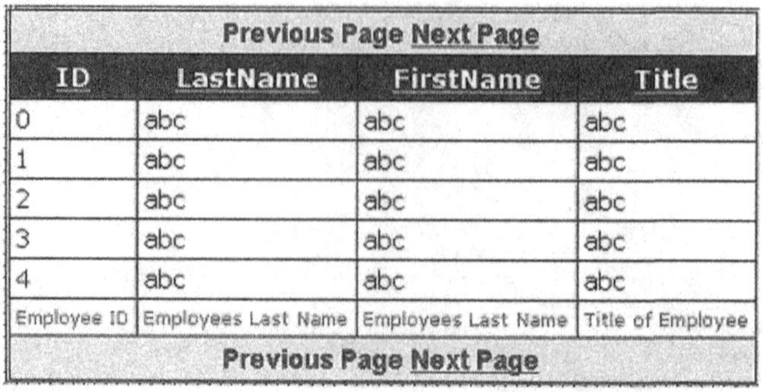

ID	LastName	FirstName	Title
\multicolumn{4}{Previous Page **Next Page**}			

	Previous Page **Next Page**		
ID	**LastName**	**FirstName**	**Title**
0	abc	abc	abc
1	abc	abc	abc
2	abc	abc	abc
3	abc	abc	abc
4	abc	abc	abc
Employee ID	Employees Last Name	Employees Last Name	Title of Employee
	Previous Page **Next Page**		

Figure 14-24. The final DataGrid *after setting various properties*

Filling a DataSet

You're almost there. Now the only thing you need to do is to call the DataAdapter's Fill method and fill the DataSet, and you're all set. Call the sqlDataAdapter1.Fill method with DataSet11 as the only argument on the Page_Load event and then call the DataGrid1.DataBind or Page.DataBind method to bind the DataGrid with the data. Listing 14-3 shows how do to this.

Listing 14-3. Filling the DataSet *from* DataAdapter

```
Private Sub Page_Load(ByVal sender As System.Object, _
   ByVal e As System.EventArgs) Handles MyBase.Load
     'Put user code to initialize the page here
     SqlDataAdapter1.Fill(DataSet11)
     Page.DataBind()
End Sub
```

Now run the project. The output of the project looks like Figure 14-25.

As you can see from this sample, by writing only two lines of code, you've developed a database application. Don't click the Next Page link just yet…it won't work right now. You need to add few lines of code for that.

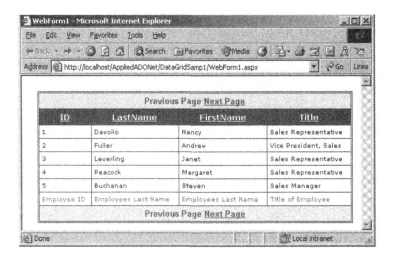

Figure 14-25. Viewing data in a DataGrid *using the design-time data binding method*

Paging in the DataGrid Control

As discussed earlier in the "Paging Property Page" section (Figure 14-24), using the Paging page of the Property Builder for a DataGrid controlyou can set paging options of a DataGrid at design-time as well as at runtime.

After enabling paging in a DataGrid, there's one more small addition you need to do to make the paging work. You need to write the PageIndexChanged event handler, which allows you to jump to a specific page by the page index. The easiest way to write a PageIndexChanged event handler is to set a method to the OnPageIndexChanged value, which you can do in the ASP.NET page itself. Add the bold part of the following line to <asp:DataGrid>

```
<asp:DataGrid id="DataGrid1" OnPageIndexChanged="Grid_Change" ..... >
```

Now write the Grid_Change method as shown in Listing 14-4. As you can see, we set DataGrid.CurrentPageIndex as DataGridPageChangedEventArgs's NewPageIndex and call the DataGrid1.DataBind method.

Listing 14-4. The PageIndexChanged *Handler of the* DataGrid *Control*

```
Sub Grid_Change(ByVal sender As Object, _
ByVal e As DataGridPageChangedEventArgs)
  DataGrid1.CurrentPageIndex = e.NewPageIndex
  DataGrid1.DataBind()
End Sub
```

Now, if you run the application, you'll find paging working for you. The first page of looks like Figure 14-26, and if you click the Next Page link, DataGrid loads the data, which after the first five records looks like Figure 14-26.

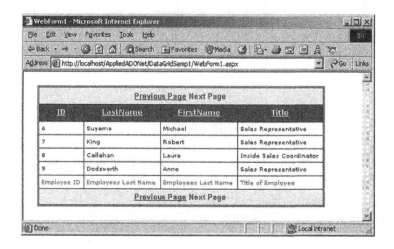

Figure 14-26. Paging option in a DataGrid

Now if you click the Previous Page link, the DataGrid loads the old data again.

Enabling Paging Programmatically

You can also enable paging programmatically from your .aspx file. Listing 14-5 shows the HTML code for a DataGrid control and its properties.

Listing 14-5. HTML View of asp:DataGrid

```
<asp:DataGrid id="DataGrid1" style="Z-INDEX: 101; LEFT: 204px;
POSITION: absolute; TOP: 174px" runat="server" Width="279px"
Height="212px" BorderStyle="None" BorderWidth="1px"
BorderColor="#CC9966" BackColor="White" CellPadding="4"
PageSize="5" AllowPaging="True">
<FooterStyle ForeColor="#330099" BackColor="#FFFFCC"></FooterStyle>
<HeaderStyle Font-Bold="True" ForeColor="#FFFFCC"
BackColor="#990000"></HeaderStyle>
<PagerStyle HorizontalAlign="Center" ForeColor="#330099"
BackColor="#FFFFCC"></PagerStyle>
<SelectedItemStyle Font-Bold="True" ForeColor="#663399"
BackColor="#FFCC66"></SelectedItemStyle>
<ItemStyle ForeColor="#330099" BackColor="White"></ItemStyle>
</asp:DataGrid>
```

The General paging properties include AllowPaging and PageSize. Both are pretty self-explanatory. Basically, AllowPaging enables paging, and PageSize sets the number of pages in a page. You can set these properties programmatically, as shown in Listing 14-6.

Listing 14-6. Setting the AllowPaging, PageSize, *and* AllowSorting *Properties*

```
DataGrid1.AllowPaging = True
DataGrid1.PageSize = 5
DataGrid1.AllowSorting = True
```

Like in the Property Builder, you can choose to have either the numeric page mode or the previous/next page mode. The numeric mode option shows you the number of pages to move to the previous or next pages (1, 2, and so on), and the previous/next mode displays angle brackets (< and >) to move to the previous and next pages. Listing 14-7 shows how to set the DataGrid control's page style modes to the Numeric and NextPrev styles.

Listing 14-7. Setting DataGrid's PageStyle *Modes*

```
DataGrid1.PagerStyle.Mode = PagerMode.NumericPages
DataGrid1.PagerStyle.Mode = PagerMode.NextPrev
```

You can even change the text of your previous/next mode from angle brackets to the text you want (see Listing 14-8).

Listing 14-8. Setting the DataGrid *Control's* PageStyle *Text*

```
DataGrid1.PagerStyle.NextPageText = "Go to Next Page"
DataGrid1.PagerStyle.PrevPageText = "Go to Previous Page"
```

If you want to use your own images for the Next and Previous buttons, you can do that as well. Just use the simple HTML <IMG> tag (see Listing 14-9).

Listing 14-9. Setting an Image as the DataGrid *Control's Next and Previous Page Text*

```
DataGrid1.PagerStyle.NextPageText = "<img srv=next.gif>"
DataGrid1.PagerStyle.PrevPageText = "<img srv=prev.gif>"
```

Adding, Editing, and Deleting Data in Web Forms

You'll now add more functionality to your application. In this application, you'll add options to add, delete, and update data. There are two ways you can add these options. One way is to use SQL statements and execute them with the help of SqlCommand, and other way is to do add, edit, and delete operations on a DataSet through DataTable objects. In this sample, you'll use the SqlCommand option. In the next chapter, you'll see the DataSet option to add, edit, and delete data in a DataGrid control.

Adding Web Forms Controls

To provide add, edit, and delete options, you add four TextBox, three Label, and three Button controls, as shown in Figure 14-27.

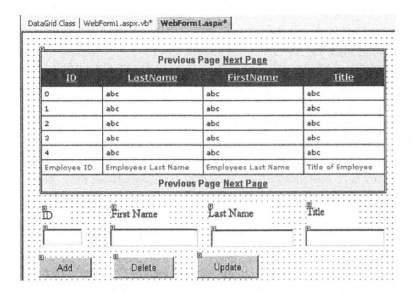

Figure 14-27. Adding, editing, and deleting pages

The Add button click adds data entered in the text boxes to the database. The Delete button click deletes the data based on the ID entered in the ID text box. The Update button updates the data of a record in the database based on the ID value.

The FillDataGrid Method

Before writing any code to add, update, or delete data, let's write a method that will refresh the DataGrid contents. Listing 14-10 shows the FillDataGrid method. As you can see from the code, this method just fills the DataSet from the DataAdapter and binds data to the DataGrid.

Listing 14-10. The FillDataGrid *Method*

```
' Refresh DataGrid
Private Sub FillDataGrid()
    SqlDataAdapter1.Fill(DataSet11)
    DataGrid1.DataBind()
End Sub
```

Executing SQL Queries

As discussed in Chapter 4, you can use the SqlCommand object's Execute and ExecuteNonQuery methods to execute SQL queries. If you want to add, update, or delete data from a database, executing SQL queries is one of the easiest ways to do so. It's fast and requires a minimum of code to write.

You use the SqlCommand object to execute a SQL command. The Execute and ExecuteNonQuery methods of SqlCommand execute a SQL query. The SqlCommand.Execute method executes the CommandText property and returns data in the SqlDataReader object. The SqlCommand.ExecuteNonQuery method executes CommandText and doesn't return any data. The logical time to use this method is when you're writing to the database or executing SQL statements that don't return any data, which works in this case when you need to add, update, and delete data from a database.

In this example, we've used the SqlCommand.ExecuteNonQuery() method to execute the INSERT, UPDATE, and DELETE SQL queries as obviously we don't need to return any data. This ExecuteSQL method wraps the execution of a SQL query, as shown in Listing 14-11.

Listing 14-11. The ExecuteSQL *Method*

```
Public Function ExecuteSQL(ByVal strSQL As String) As Boolean
    ' Creating a connection
    Dim conn As SqlConnection = New SqlConnection()
    conn = New SqlConnection(SqlConnection1.ConnectionString)
    Dim myCmd As SqlCommand = New SqlCommand(strSQL, conn)
    Try
        conn.Open()
        myCmd.ExecuteNonQuery()
    Catch exp As Exception
        'Error message
        Return False
    Finally
        ' clean up here
        conn.Close()
        conn.Dispose()
    End Try
    Return True
End Function
```

Adding Data

The Add button adds a new record to the database and calls the `FillDataGrid` method, which rebinds the data source and fills the `DataGrid` control with the updated data. Because the ID column of the database table is AutoNumber, you don't have to enter it. You only need to enter the first name, last name, and title. Listing 14-12 shows the Add button click event handler. As you can see, you create an `INSERT` SQL statement, call `ExecuteSQL`, and refill the data using the `FillDataGrid` method.

Listing 14-12. Add Button Click Event Handler

```
Private Sub AddBtn_Click(ByVal sender As System.Object, _
  ByVal e As System.EventArgs) Handles AddBtn.Click
    ' Build a SQL Statement
Dim SQL As String = _
  "INSERT INTO Employees(FirstName, LastName, Title)" & _
" VALUES('" + TextBox2.Text + "','" + TextBox3.Text + _
 "','" + TextBox4.Text + "')"    ' Execute SQL and refresh the data grid
    ExecuteSQL(SQL)
    FillDataGrid()
  End Sub
```

In Figure 14-28, we add a new record with first name as "Amy," the last name as "Sue," and the title as "Customer Support." Clicking the Add button adds data to the database and refreshes the `DataGrid` contents, as you can see from the figure.

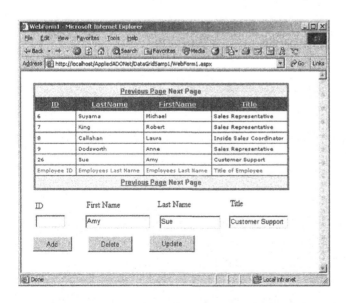

Figure 14-28. Adding a new record in the Web application

Updating Data

The Update button updates a record corresponding to an ID. This is where you build an UPDATE...SET SQL statement and execute it by calling the ExecuteSQL method, as shown in Listing 14-13.

Listing 14-13. Updating Data on the Update Button Click

```
Private Sub UpdateBtn_Click(ByVal sender As System.Object, _
ByVal e As System.EventArgs) Handles UpdateBtn.Click
    ' Build a SQL Statement
      Dim SQL As String = _
      "UPDATE Employees SET FirstName='" & _
    TextBox2.Text + "',LastName='" + TextBox3.Text + _
    "',Title='" + TextBox4.Text & _      "' WHERE EmployeeID=" + TextBox1.Text
    ' Execute SQL and refresh the data grid
    ExecuteSQL(SQL)
    FillDataGrid()
End Sub
```

Now to test the code, enter "Mel," "0Tel," and "Marketing Rep," in the First Name, Last Name, and Title text boxes (respectively) and ID = 26 and then click the Updated button. The result updates the row with ID=26, and the output looks like Figure 14-29. As you can see, that record is updated as Mel Tel.

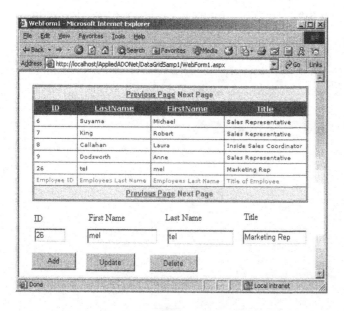

Figure 14-29. Updating records in a Web application

Deleting Data

The Delete button deletes a record corresponding with the ID from the database. You then build a DELETE SQL statement and execute it by calling the ExecuteSQL method, as shown in Listing 14-14.

Listing 14-14. Deleting Data on the Delete Button Click

```
Private Sub DeleteBtn_Click(ByVal sender As System.Object, _
ByVal e As System.EventArgs) Handles DeleteBtn.Click
 ' Build a SQL Statement
Dim SQL As String = "DELETE * FROM Employees WHERE EmployeeID= " + TextBox1.Text
 ' Execute SQL and refresh the data grid
ExecuteSQL(SQL)
FillDataGrid()
End Sub
```

To delete the newly added record, just enter 26 in the ID field or the ID of the record you want to delete and click the Delete button.

By using these insert, update, and delete data operations, you can write a full-fledged database application for your Web site.

Creating a Guest Book in ASP.NET

Today, a guest book is a common tool used on Web sites to gather information about visitors. In this example, you'll see how to create a guest book using ASP.NET and VB .NET. In this application, you'll use a Microsoft Access 2000 database to store the data submitted by site visitors. You can use even use a SQL Server database. The only reason this example uses an Access database is because it's easier to create and use than SQL Server. The database name is GuestBook.mdb. You can create this database in Access 2000. This database has only one table, Guest. Figure 14-30 shows the table schema. As you can see, ID is a unique auto number field. The Name, Address, Email, and Comments fields represent the name, address, email address, and comments of a visitor (respectively).

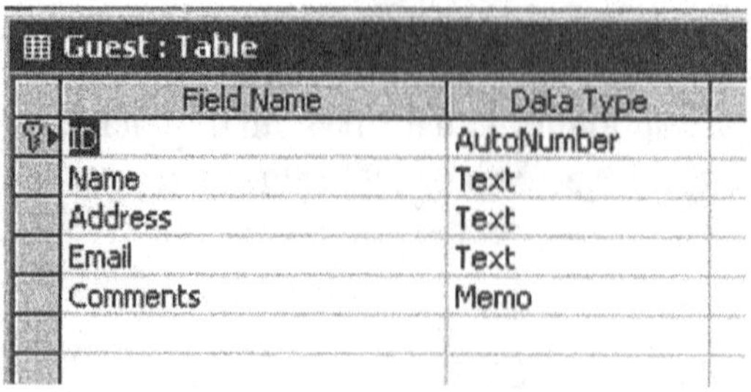

Figure 14-30. Table schema of Guest table of GuestBook.mdb

The following sections provide a simple tutorial that guide you through creating a guest book for your Web site step by step.

To create a guest book, first you create an ASP.NET Web Application project using the Visual Basic ➤ Web Application template from the available templates. Name the project MyGuestBook.

Default Web Form: MyGuestBook.aspx

When you create a new Web application project, the wizard adds one default Web Form to your project called WebForm1.aspx. You can see this page when you run your application. For this example, rename WebForm1.aspx to MyGuestBook.aspx. You can rename a page by right-clicking the .aspx file in the Solution Explorer and selecting the Rename option.

Next, add a few Web controls to the form. For this form, add the controls listed in Table 14-6.

Table 14-6. Web Controls on MyGuestBook.aspx *Page*

CONTROL	TYPE	DESCRIPTION
NameTextBox	<asp:TextBox>	Name text box
AddressTextBox	<asp:TextBox>	Address text box
EmailTextBox	<asp:TextBox>	Email text box
CommentsTextBox	<asp:TextBox>	Comments text box
Button1	<asp:Button>	Saves data to the database and calls Thanks.aspx
Button2	<asp:Button>	Calls ViewGuestBook.aspx

As you can see from Table 14-6, we added some text to the page, four text boxes, and two buttons and then renamed them accordingly by setting each one's properties. For example, we set the Comments TextBox control's TextMode property to Multiple. By changing the properties of the controls, MyGuestBook.aspx form looks like Figure 14-31.

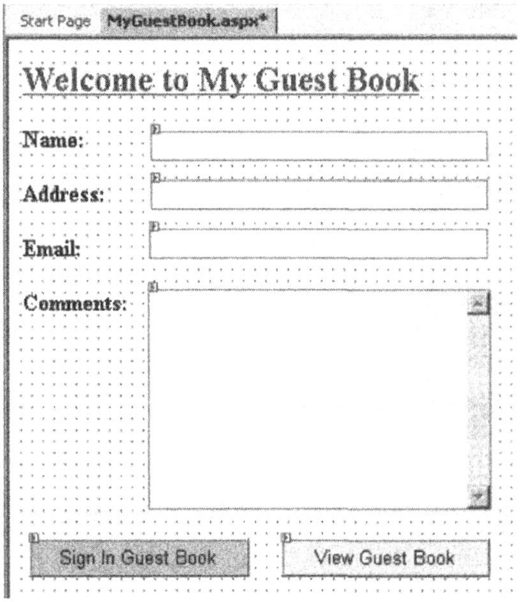

Figure 14-31. MyGuestBook.aspx *submission page*

Now double-click the Sign In Guest Book button and write the code in Listing 14-15. Don't forget to import System.Data.OleDb namespace in your application.

Listing 14-15. Adding Guest Data to the Database

```
Private Sub Button1_Click(ByVal sender As System.Object, _
   ByVal e As System.EventArgs) Handles Button1.Click
      ' set Access connection and select strings
      Dim strDSN As String = "Provider=Microsoft.Jet.OLEDB.4.0;" & _
            "Data Source=C:\\GuestBook.mdb"
      Dim strSQL As String = "INSERT INTO Guest" & _
                  "(Name, Address, Email, Comments )" & _
                  "VALUES('" + NameTextBox.Text.ToString() + "','" & _
                  AddressTextBox.Text.ToString() + "','" & _
                  EmailTextBox.Text.ToString() & _
                  "','" + CommentsTextBox.Text.ToString() + "')"

   ' create OleDbDataAdapter
   Dim conn As OleDbConnection = New OleDbConnection(strDSN)
   ' Create OleDbCommand and call ExecuteNonQuery to execute
   ' a SQL statement
   Dim myCmd As OleDbCommand = New OleDbCommand(strSQL, conn)
   Try
      conn.Open()
      myCmd.ExecuteNonQuery()
   Catch exp As Exception
      Console.WriteLine("Error: {0}", exp.Message)
   Finally
      conn.Close()
      conn.Dispose()
   End Try
   ' Open Thanks.aspx page after adding entries to the guest book
   Response.Redirect("Thanks.aspx")
End Sub
```

As you can see from Listing 14-15, you write the data entered into the Web Form to an Access database. Our database resides in the C:\ root dir. Obviously, if your database is somewhere else, you need to change this database path. After writing to the database's Guest table we continue the program by opening the Thanks.aspx page in your browser. (We discuss this page a little bit further in the "Thanks.aspx" section.)

Now, add the code in Listing 14-16 to the click event of the View Guest Book button. The View Guest Book click event opens the ViewGuestBook.aspx page in the browser.

Listing 14-16. Opening ViewGuestBook.aspx

```
Private Sub Button2_Click(ByVal sender As System.Object, _
  ByVal e As System.EventArgs) Handles Button2.Click
    ' View CiewGuestBook.aspx page
    Response.Redirect("ViewGuestBook.aspx")
  End Sub
```

Adding Forms to the Guest Book

Other than the MyGuestBook.aspx page, you'll add two more Web Forms to the project. The first form you'll add is called ViewGuestBook.aspx, and the second form is Thanks.aspx. The ViewGuestBook.aspx form reads the data from the database and enables you to view the contents in a DataGrid on a Web page. The Thanks.aspx form is, as you may have guessed, a simple "thank you" Web page shown to the guest, thanking them for registering on the site. Follow these steps:
To add a new Web form, right-click your project and select Add ➤ Add Web Form. Clicking this menu item opens a form, which lets you pick different types of items for your project. Choose the Web Form template, name it Thanks.aspx, and then click Open.

Using the same method, add one more Web page, ViewGuestBook.aspx, to the project.

ViewGuestBook.aspx

The ViewGuestBook.aspx form contains two controls, a DataGrid control and a Button control (see Table 14-7).

Table 14-7. Web Controls of ViewGuestBook.aspx

CONTROL	TYPE	DESCRIPTION
DataGrid1	<asp:DataGrid>	Displays guest book entries from the database
Button1	<asp:button>	Navigates to the home page

After setting the properties of controls, the page looks like Figure 14-32.

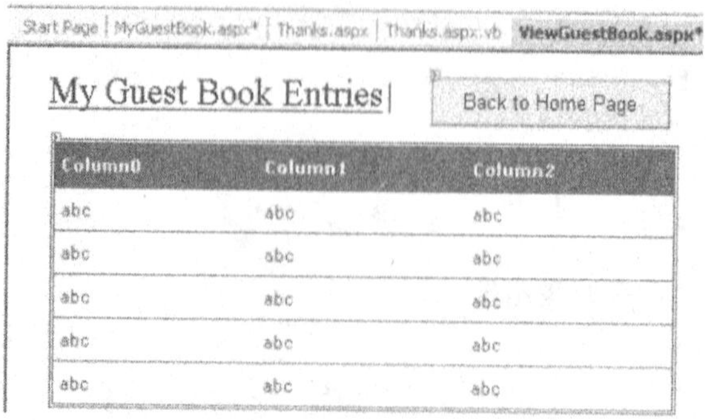

Figure 14-32. The ViewGuestBook.aspx *page*

The DataGrid control displays the guest book entries from the database. The code for populating the DataGrid from the database is on the Page_Load event of the form. The Back to Home Page button sends the browser to the site home page.

We've used the OleDbDataAdapter and DataSet to get the data from the database. As discussed, the DataSource property of the DataGrid takes care of rest. You just need to set the DataSource property as the DefaultView of the DataSet, like so:

```
DataGrid1.DataSource = ds.Tables("Guest").DefaultView
```

Listing 14-17 shows the Page_Load event and the Back to Home Page button click code.

Listing 14-17. Page_Load *Event Handler Code of* ViewGuestBook.aspx

```
Private Sub Page_Load(ByVal sender As System.Object, _
  ByVal e As System.EventArgs) Handles MyBase.Load
    ' Create a connection object
    Dim conn As OleDbConnection = New OleDbConnection()
    conn.ConnectionString = "Provider=Microsoft.Jet.OLEDB.4.0;" & _
              "Data Source=C:\\GuestBook.mdb"
    Dim sql As String = "SELECT * FROM Guest"
    ' Create a data adapter
    Dim da As OleDbDataAdapter = New OleDbDataAdapter(sql, conn)
    ' Create and fill data set and bind it to the data grid
    Dim ds As DataSet = New DataSet()
    da.Fill(ds, "Guest")
```

```
    DataGrid1.DataSource = ds.Tables("Guest").DefaultView
    DataGrid1.DataBind()
  End Sub
Private Sub Button1_Click(ByVal sender As System.Object, _
  ByVal e As System.EventArgs) Handles Button1.Click
    Response.Redirect("http://www.c-sharpcorner.com")
End Sub
```

Thanks.aspx

The Thanks.aspx page is merely a confirmation page that the user receives after adding data to the guest book. It has two buttons and a simple message. The buttons are responsible for navigating you through the ViewGuestBook.aspx page or to the site home page. Table 14-8 lists the controls for Thanks.aspx.

Table 14-8. Controls of Thanks.aspx Page

CONTROL	TYPE	DESCRIPTION
Button1	<asp:button>	Calls ViewGuestBook.aspx page
Button2	<asp:button>	Navigates the browser to the site home page

The Thanks.aspx page looks like Figure 14-33.

Figure 14-33. Thank you page

Listing 14-18 shows the My Home Page button and the View Guest Book button-click code. As you can see from the listing, the My Home Page button click calls www.c-sharpcorner.com. Obviously, you can call your Web site's home page. The View Guest Book button click calls ViewGuestBook.aspx.

Listing 14-18. My Home Page and View Guest Book Buttons

```
Private Sub Button1_Click(ByVal sender As System.Object, _
  ByVal e As System.EventArgs) Handles Button1.Click
    Response.Redirect("http://www.c-sharpcorner.com/")
  End Sub

  Private Sub Button2_Click(ByVal sender As System.Object, _
  ByVal e As System.EventArgs) Handles Button2.Click
    Response.Redirect("ViewGuestBook.aspx")
End Sub
```

NOTE *Don't forget to add a reference to the* System.Data.OleDb *namespace in the* ViewGuestBook.aspx *and* MyGuestBook.aspx *pages.*

Compiling and Running the Guest Book Project

Now you're all set to compile and run the project. You should be able to do everything you usually do in a guest book. The output of the program looks like Figure 14-34.

Figure 14-34. Welcome to my guest book

As you can see from Figure 14-34, we added a new record by filling data in the fields and clicking the Sign In Guest Book button. The next page displayed is the Thanks.aspx page, which looks like Figure 14-35.

Figure 14-35. The Thanks.aspx *page of the guest book*

Now, if you view the guest book, it looks like Figure 14-36. As you'll notice, there are a couple of extra records in this guest book.

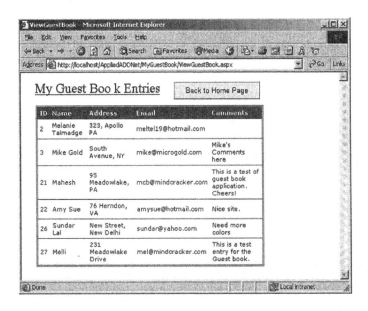

Figure 14-36. My guest book entries

Summary

ASP.NET is a new framework to write Web applications for the Microsoft .NET platform. ASP.NET supports a rich set of Web Forms controls. You can use these controls at runtime as well as design-time. In VS .NET, you can just drag these controls on a Web Form, set their properties and methods, and your application is ready to run on the Web.

You can also use ADO.NET components in Web Forms in the same way you use them in desktop applications. All ADO.NET components including the DataReader, DataSet, DataView, and DataCommand components work in the same way as they would in a desktop application. ASP.NET provides many data-bound controls you can directly bind to a data source with the help of DataSet and DataView. For example, DataGrid and ListBox are two common data-bound controls. You can use the DataSource property of these controls to bind to a DataSet.

The DataGrid is the most versatile control among all the Web controls. By using the DataGrid, you can write full-fledge database applications for your Web sites. The DataTable of the DataSet provides the programmer with a means of working with the data in these controls. A table is a collection of rows and columns. A DataTable represents a database table. With the help of the DataView class, you can bind a data table to a DataGrid or other data-bound controls.

The next chapter covers ASP.NET data-bound controls. You'll see some practical uses of these controls.

CHAPTER 15

Using ADO.NET in XML Web Services

WEB SERVICES PROVIDE a way to run a service on the Web and access its methods using standard protocols, including Simple Object Access Protocol (SOAP), Extensible Markup Language (XML), Web Service Description Language (WSDL), and Hypertext Transfer Protocol (HTTP). Technically, a Web service is nothing more than an application that exposes its interface over the Web to a client who wants to access the service's abilities. The uses of a Web service include validating credit cards, searching for data in a database, inserting an order into a shopping cart, and updating a guest list. The sky is the limit on what you can have your Web service do on your server.

In the past, JavaBeans, Component Object Model (COM) components, and other, nonstandard service components handled these services, which required specialized formats and/or extra specialist components to exchange data with the client. But Web services under .NET run by invoking methods in the service directly through HTTP or SOAP, so someone wanting to run your Web service from their computer can simply send a HTTP call to your service, passing the parameters in a standard Uniform Resource Locator (URL). You'll see how to do this later in the chapter.

Three components make up a Web service:

Discovery: First, you need to locate the Web service. You locate Web services through the Discovery Service Protocol. The discoverable information for a .NET Web service is stored in XML in a `.disco` file. This file contains references to all the Web services under your Web site's virtual directory. Visual Studio (VS) can automatically generate this file for you.

Description: Once you've discovered your service, you need a way to tell the client what methods, classes, and so on the Web service has and what wiring protocol (SOAP, HTTP, and so on) the services are using. You do this through WSDL, an XML format. VS provides a tool for generating WSDL files automatically from your services.

Wiring protocol: Web services under .NET use two main protocols: HTTP-post/HTTP-get and SOAP. HTTP-post and HTTP-get enable you to send and receive information via a URL by passing and receiving name-value pair strings. Unfortunately, HTTP can only pass strings that represent different data types. SOAP allows you to pass a richer type of information, such as DataSets. You can find more details and SOAP specifications at www.w3.org/TR/SOAP/.

Exploring Web Services and the .NET Framework Library

The .NET Framework Class Library provides four namespaces that contain Web service classes. These namespaces are System.Web.Services, System.Web.Services.Description, System.Web.Services.Discovery, and System.Web.Services.Protocol.

The System.Web.Services namespace provides classes that enable you to build and use Web services. It has four classes. The WebService class defines the optional base class for Web services, which provides direct access to an ASP.NET application. Server, Session, User, and Context are some of its properties. WebMethodAttribute, WebServiceAttribute, and WebServiceBindingAttribute are other classes of this namespace.

The System.Web.Services.Description namespace provides classes that enable you to describe a WSDL.

The System.Web.Services.Discovery namespace provides classes that enable Web service consumers to locate a Web service through discovery.

The System.Web.Services.Protocols namespace provides classes that define the protocols used to transmit data between a client and a Web service.

Creating a Web Service in VS .NET

To understand Web services better, you'll build a simple Web service. The Web service will receive an order ID and then query the Northwind database's Orders table for the correct order. It will then return the order in a DataSet.

The first step in creating the Web service is to select File ➤ New ➤ Project and choose the ASP.NET Web Service template, as shown in Figure 15-1.

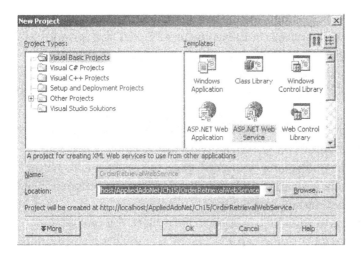

Figure 15-1. Creating a new Web service project

This creates a Web service project on the local Web server. By default, localhost is available as a Web server on your development machine. Alternatively you could use another Web server for your applications. After entering a server name, you enter a project name. In this sample, the project name is OrderRetrievalWebService. VS .NET creates a new folder with the project name on the Web server and keeps all project files under that folder.

First, the Web.config file is an XML file containing information on how to run the service under ASP.NET. Second, the Global.asax and Global.asax.vb files enable you to handle application-level events for the service. These event handlers include event handling pairs such as Application_Start/Application_End, Session_Start/Session_End, and Begin_Request/EndRequest. You can view Global.asax.vb by right-clicking the Global.asax file in the Solution Explorer and choosing View Code. Next, OrderRetrievalWebService.vsdisco is an XML file containing information for discovery of the service. You'll actually need to generate an OrderRetrievalWebService.disco file for your client to see the service (more on this later).

Finally, the Service1.asmx file serves as the entry point into the service. The code behind the service, Service1.asmx.vb, is where you'll place the method for retrieving the order. Right-click the Service1.asmx file in the Solution Explorer and choose View Code from the pop-up menu. Note that it looks like any other VB .NET component; it has a constructor, an InitializeComponent method, and a Dispose method.

Now you'll add database support to the Web service. Actually, adding database support to a Web service is quite easy using ADO.NET. You can add ADO.NET data components to a Web service by just dragging ADO.NET components from the Toolbox's Data tab to Web Forms. Similar to Windows or Web Forms, you can also use the Server Explorer to add database components to a Web service.

In this example, you'll use the SQL Server Northwind database. You won't use the design-time support for ADO.NET, for two reasons. Firstly, when you drop a table from the Server Explorer onto a Web page, the designer adds lots of unwanted code. Secondly, it's hard to understand and modify the designer-added code. We recommend writing code manually.

Now, the next step is to add a Web method to the project. You can use the Class Wizard to add a method, or you can add a method manually. If you examine the default code in Service1.asmx.vb, it has a method called HelloWorld, which looks like following:

```
'<WebMethod()> Public Function HelloWorld() As String
'HelloWorld = "Hello World"
' End Function
```

As you can see from this code, adding a Web method is simple. You just need to add the <WebMethod()> attribute in front of a method. Add a method called GetOrderFromDatabase. This method reads data from a database and returns the data as a DataSet object. The method takes an OrderID as an argument and returns all records related to that OrderID. Before you add the method, though, you also need to add the variables in the following code to the project:

```
Private ConnectionString As String = "user id=sa;password=;" & _
     "Initial Catalog=Northwind;" & _
     "Data Source=MCB;"
  Private conn As SqlConnection = Nothing
  Private adapter As SqlDataAdapter = Nothing
  Private sql As String = Nothing
```

The GetOrdersFromDatabase method fills data from the Orders table of the Northwind database and returns a DataSet that has records from the Orders table corresponding to an order ID. Listing 15-1 shows the GetOrdersFromDatabase method.

Listing 15-1. The GetOrdersFromDatabase *Method for Obtaining an Order from an Order ID*

```
<WebMethod()> Public Function GetOrderFromDatabase( _
  ByVal orderID As Integer) As DataSet
    Dim ds As DataSet = New DataSet()
    ' Create a new connection
    conn = New SqlConnection(ConnectionString)
    sql = "SELECT * FROM Orders WHERE OrderID = " + orderID.ToString()
    ' Open the connection
    If (conn.State <> ConnectionState.Open) Then
      conn.Open()
    End If
    ' Create a DataAdapter
    Dim adapter As SqlDataAdapter = New SqlDataAdapter(sql, conn)
    adapter.Fill(ds)
  '  Close the connection
    If (conn.State = ConnectionState.Open) Then
      conn.Close()
    End If
    ' Return DataSet
    Return ds
  End Function
```

As you can see from Listing 15-1, the method receives an order ID from a client and returns a DataSet to the client. It uses the DataAdapter to fill a DataSet with the row containing that order ID.

> **NOTE** *You have to add a* WHERE *clause onto the* SelectCommand *to filter the single row of data. Also, you must make all exposed methods in the Web service public, and they must contain a* [WebMethod] *attribute; otherwise, the client won't see them.*

Testing Your Web Service

Now you're actually ready to build and test your Web service. First, build the service using the Build menu option and then start it in Debug mode. This brings up the Web service's default page generated by VS .NET in your browser, as shown in Figure 15-2.

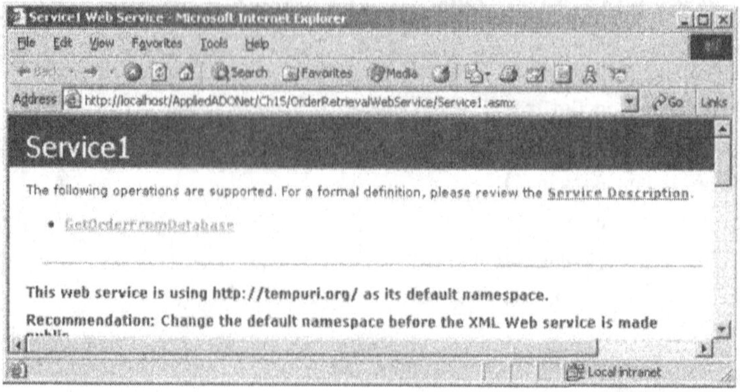

Figure 15-2. Initially running the Web service `Service1.asmx`

As you can see in Figure 15-2, one method, `GetOrderFromDatabase`, is available in the browser.

You can make this screen a bit more descriptive by adding a `WebService` attribute to the top of the class and then adding descriptions to both the `WebService` attribute and the `WebMethod` attribute. As you can see, Listing 15-2 adds a description to both.

Listing 15-2. Adding Descriptions to the `WebService` *and* `WebMethod` *Attributes*

```
<WebService(Namespace:="http://tempuri.org/", _
   Description:="Working with Orders in Northwind")> _
Public Class Service1
  Inherits System.Web.Services.WebService


      ....
<WebMethod(Description:="Retrieve an order from Northwind ")> _
 Public Function GetOrderFromDatabase( _
 ByVal orderID As Integer) As DataSet


End Function

End Class
```

The service now looks like Figure 15-3.

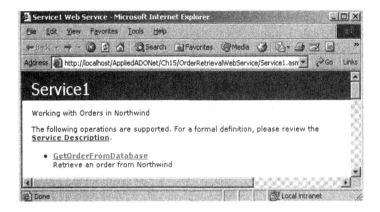

Figure 15-3. The Web service after you add attributes

If you click the link for the GetOrderFromDatabase method, you'll see a Parameter OrderID text box. Enter 10248 as the OrderID. After you click the Invoke button, the browser returns the XML data representing the DataSet, which contains the order with the order ID of 10248. Figure 15-4 shows a piece of the XML data representing the order and displayed by the browser.

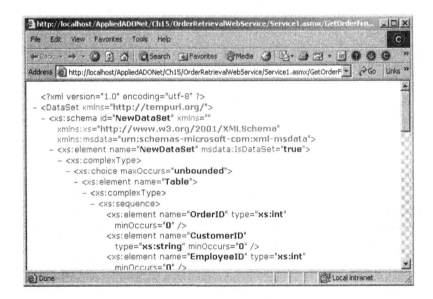

Figure 15-4. The Order DataSet displayed by the browser in XML format

As you can see from Figure 15-4, the default namespace for the DataSet xmlns is http://tempuri.org. You can use the WebService attribute to specify the namespace and description text for the XML Web service. As you can see, VS .NET doesn't generate this attribute by default. You have to write it manually. If you're specifying more than one property, you can separate them with a comma. For example, the following code sets the namespace and the description properties of the WebService attribute:

```
<WebService(Namespace:="http://servername/xmlwebservices/", _
    Description:="Working with Orders in Northwind")> _
Public Class Service1
  Inherits System.Web.Services.WebService
' code here
End Class
```

Creating the Web Service Consumer

Now that you've created a Web service, you should create a client to use it. In this tutorial, you'll create an ASP.NET Web Form application that accesses the Web service to retrieve an order. The client will then display the order in a DataGrid.

First, create an ASP.NET Web project by going to File ➤ New ➤ Project and choosing the ASP.NET Web Application template. For this example, we'll create the application on the localhost default Web server. If you're creating your application on a remote server, you may want to use the server name and an appropriate directory where you have read and write permissions. Call the Web application OrderLookupApp.

Creating a Web application adds a Web page to the project, which is the default gateway when VS .NET is done creating the project. As you saw in Chapter 14, you can use Web pages as Windows Forms. You can add Web and HTML controls to Web pages by simply dragging controls from Toolbox to the Web page.

In this example, add a Label, a TextBox, a Button, and a DataGrid control by dragging them from the ToolBox's Web Forms tab to the WebForm1.aspx Design View. Next, set the controls' properties. Figure 15-5 shows the final page after setting the properties.

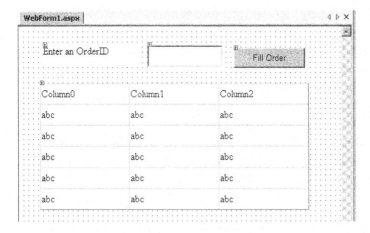

Figure 15-5. Design View for searching for and displaying an order

To use the Web service in the client application, you need to add a Web reference to the service. In the Solution Explorer, right-click the References option and choose Add Web Reference. This brings up the Add Web Reference page, as shown in Figure 15-6.

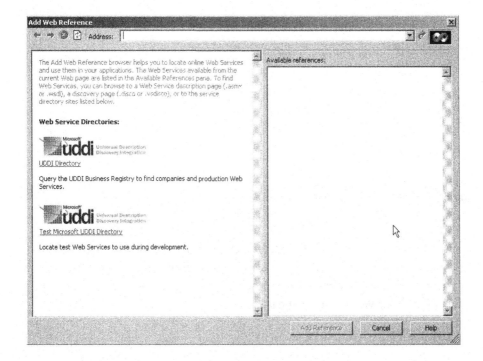

Figure 15-6. The Add Web Reference locator

As you can see from Figure 15-6, you can choose from any existing Web service. Those Web services can exist on your local Web server, in the Microsoft Universal Description, Discovery, and Integration (UDDI) Business Registry, or somewhere on the Internet. You just need to provide the URL of the service in the Address text box. In this case, you need to provide the URL of the OrderRetrieval-WebService service's .asmx page and then add ?wsdl at the end of URL. You can specify the .asmx file and URL path where the service entry point is located in the Address field of the wizard. As you can see, Figure 15-7 passes the URL of the service with localhost as the server. (You need to replace server name if you're accessing a remote server.) The contents of the service looks like Figure 15-7.

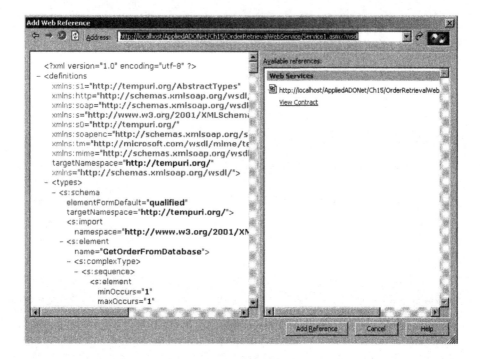

Figure 15-7. Web services available on the local server

Now you need to click the Add Reference button. To access Web services on the server, you need to use the server name as a namespace. You can even rename the namespace by right-clicking and choosing the Rename option. As you can see in Figure 15-8, the Web server name is localhost.

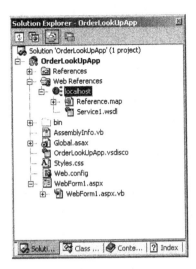

Figure 15-8. Adding Web references

Clicking the Add Reference button causes VS .NET to generate three files for referencing the service:

- A discovery file (Service1.disco)

- A WSDL file (Service1.wsdl)

- A proxy file (Service1.vb)

As already discussed, the discovery file is an XML file that helps the client to find the service. The WSDL file describes the methods and classes supplied by the service in XML and defines the format that messages need to adhere to when exchanging information with the client. The proxy file, although not displayed in the Solution Explorer, is a VB stub file generated so that the programmer can call the methods in the Web service with the same method names and method parameter structure as the Web service contains. These proxies wrap the method calls to the Web service so that the convoluted exchange of parameter passing and method invocation to the remote service is transparent to the programmer. If you expand the Web References node, you can see the files belong to a service. You can expand the server reference to see its files. Some files are hidden by default, but you can use the Show All button of the Solution Explorer to see all the files (see Figure 15-9).

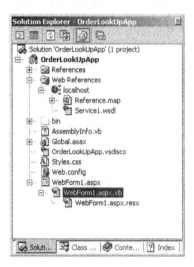

Figure 15-9. Files generated by the Web References Wizard to access the Web service

Now, everything is all set, and you're ready to call the Web service's method. In this sample, you'll call the GetOrderFromDatabase method from the Fill Order button click. So, double-click the button to write a click event handler for the button. As you probably noticed, the class in this example is Service1. So, that's the class of which you'll be creating an instance.

Once you have an instance to the service, you can call GetOrderFromDatabase in the service and assign it to a DataSet reference. To display the DataSet in a DataGrid, simply assign the DataSet to the DataGrid's DataSource and call DataBind on the DataGrid. Listing 15-3 shows the code for Fill the Order button-click handler.

Listing 15-3. Button-Click Event Handler That Calls the Order Retrieval Web Service

```
Private Sub Button1_Click(ByVal sender As System.Object, _
  ByVal e As System.EventArgs) Handles Button1.Click
    ' construct and call the web service with the order
    'id in the textbox
    Dim myWebService As localhost.Service1 = New localhost.Service1()
    Dim ds As DataSet = myWebService.GetOrderFromDatabase _
    (Convert.ToInt32(Me.TextBox1.Text))
    ' bind the data to the grid
    DataGrid1.DataSource = ds
    DataGrid1.DataBind()
  End Sub
```

As you can see, Listing 15-3 called `GetOrderFromDatabase` through `localhost.Service1`, which returns a `DataSet`. You use this database and bind to the `DataGrid` control and call `DataGrid`'s `DataBind` method.

Compile and run the Web application. Enter an order ID of 10248 and click the Fill Order button. Figure 15-10 shows the resulting output in Internet Explorer.

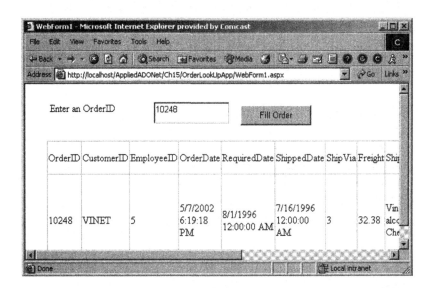

Figure 15-10. Result of the `Fill` *method in a DataGrid*

Actually, VS .NET takes away a lot of the WSDL, proxy, and discovery file coding so that you can concentrate on what you do best: coding the service. The truth is that without knowing anything about SOAP, XML, or even HTTP, you were able to develop this Web service. In the next section you'll create a Web service for entering an order into the database using this knowledge and what you know about ADO.NET.

Adding Data to a Database Through a Web Service

Now, why don't you ask the Web service to do some more than just return data from a database table?

This time you'll write to a database. You'll read data from a client in the form of an array, place it in a `DataSet`, and then add the data to the Orders table of the Northwind database.

Now, you add a new Web method called InsertOrder (see Listing 15-4). In this method, you read data from a database using a DataAdapter and fill a DataSet from the DataAdapter. As you can see, Listing 15-4 uses a SELECT * query with ORDER BY for the OrderId column value.

It gets the last OrderID in the table to determine what is the next available OrderID value. Then it creates a new DataRow in the dataset and populates the row with data passed in from the client. Finally, it calls the Update method of the DataAdapter to save the new row into the database.

Listing 15-4. Web Service Method for Populating an Order in the Database

```
<WebMethod(Description:="Insert Order from an Array")> _
Public Function InsertOrder(ByVal OrderInfo As String()) As Integer
    ' Create a new connection
    conn = New SqlConnection(ConnectionString)
    ' Open the connection
    If (conn.State <> ConnectionState.Open) Then
        conn.Open()
    End If
    'Create a DataSet
    Dim ds As DataSet = New DataSet()
    sql = "SELECT * FROM Orders ORDER BY OrderID"
    ' Create a data adapter with already opened connection
    Dim adapter As SqlDataAdapter = New SqlDataAdapter(sql, conn)
    ' Fill DataSet
    adapter.Fill(ds, "Orders")
    ' Get the last row
    Dim drLast As DataRow = _
    ds.Tables(0).Rows(ds.Tables(0).Rows.Count - 1)
    Dim LastOrderID As Integer = Convert.ToInt32(drLast("OrderID"))
    ' Create a new DataRow
    Dim row As DataRow = ds.Tables(0).NewRow()
    ' Set data row values
    row("OrderID") = LastOrderID + 1
    row("OrderDate") = Convert.ToDateTime(OrderInfo(0))
    row("ShipName") = OrderInfo(1)
    row("ShipAddress") = OrderInfo(2)
    row("ShipCity") = OrderInfo(3)
    row("ShipCountry") = OrderInfo(4)
    row("ShipPostalCode") = OrderInfo(5)
    ' Add DataRow to the collection
    ds.Tables(0).Rows.Add(row)
```

```
    ' Save changes back to data source
    adapter.Update(ds, "Orders")
    ' Return OrderID
    Return row("OrderID")
End Function
```

Now build and test the service. This service now has two methods, as shown in Figure 15-11.

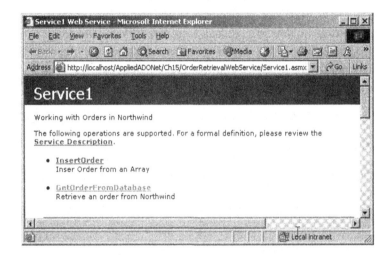

Figure 15-11. The InsertOrder *and* GetOrderFromDatabase *methods of* OrderRetrievalWebService

Now it's time to test your newly added Web method InsertOrder. To test this service, follow the same steps as previously when testing your GetOrderFromDatabase method.

Create a Web application project using VS .NET, or you can use the same client you used to test the GetOrderFromDatabase method. Create a new project called AddOrderClientApp.

The next step is to add a reference to the Web service by right-clicking the References node of a project in the Solution Explorer and clicking the Add Web Reference option.

NOTE *If you're using the same client application you used last time, you need to remove the namespace and then add it again by using Add Web Reference option to get the latest updated Web service contents.*

Again, follow the same steps as in the last example. Type the URL of your service in the Address text box and click the Add Reference button, which adds localhost (or YourRemoverServer if you're not using the default localhost as Web server) namespace to the project. The Add Reference option also generates the *.disco, *.wsdl, and proxy files. Now you can call your Web service. Add some controls to the page to make it look like Figure 15-12. We added six edit boxes to accept the order date, name, address, city, country, and zip of a customer. The Enter Order button submits the order to the service.

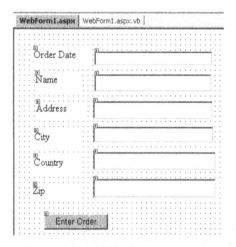

Figure 15-12. Design View of the order customer entry Web service

Again, double-click the Enter Order button and use the code in Listing 15-5 to populate the order array and pass it to the Web service. The Enter Order button event handler looks like Listing 15-5.

Listing 15-5. Client Event Handler for Executing the Web Service

```
Private Sub Button1_Click(ByVal sender As System.Object, _
  ByVal e As System.EventArgs) Handles Button1.Click

    Dim orderData() As String = New String(6) {}
    orderData(0) = TextBox1.Text
    orderData(1) = TextBox2.Text
    orderData(3) = TextBox4.Text
    orderData(4) = TextBox5.Text
    orderData(5) = TextBox6.Text
    ' Create Web serice instalce and call InsertOrder
    Dim myWebService As localhost.Service1 = New localhost.Service1()
    myWebService.InsertOrder(orderData)
  End Sub
```

The button event handler assigns a string array with information typed into the order form. You can create an instance of the service by direct using mcb.Service1 and calling the InsertOrder method.

Now build and run the application. The output looks like Figure 15-13. Now you enter customer data and clicking the Enter Order button adds the data to the Orders table.

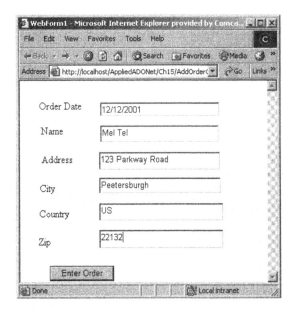

Figure 15-13. Adding an order to the database using Enter Order

Adding More Functionality to the Web Service

Now you've got a pretty good idea of how to develop a Web service and consume it in client applications. What else can a database Web service do? When it comes to databases, the only thing you can do is retrieve, add, update, and delete data. Earlier in this chapter, you saw how to retrieve and add data to a data source through Web service methods.

Now you just need to add functionality to update and delete data and you'll have a complete database Web service.

Actually, updating and deleting data is pretty simple. What you need to do is just create a new method for the Web service, which executes SQL statements. In the client application, you need to get data from the users, construct SQL UPDATE and DELETE statements, and then send this statement as a string to the Web service and let the Web service execute the SQL statement.

Listing 15-6 shows a method that executes a SQL statement by creating a SqlCommand and calling the ExecuteNonQuery method.

Listing 15-6. ExecuteQuery *Method*

```
' SaveChanges method saves a DataSet
  <WebMethod(Description:="Exceute SQL Statement")> _
Public Function ExecuteQuery(ByVal sql As String) As Integer
    Dim affectedRows As Integer = 0
    ' Open connection if already not open
    If conn.State <> ConnectionState.Open Then
      conn.Open()
    End If
    ' Create a SqlCommand and execute it
    Dim cmd As SqlCommand = New SqlCommand()
    cmd.Connection = conn
    cmd.CommandText = sql
    affectedRows = cmd.ExecuteNonQuery()
    ' Close and dispose connection
    If conn.State = ConnectionState.Open Then
      conn.Close()
    End If
    Return affectedRows
  End Function
```

Summary

In this chapter you learned what a Web service is and how you can set it up to perform services on the World Wide Web. You worked through a tutorial for creating a simple Web service for retrieving an order using ADO.NET and ASP.NET. You then created a Web service that allowed you to enter a customer for the order using XML and ADO.NET. In the end, you saw how to update and delete data from a database through a Web service. Using the same methodology, you can develop Web services, which can implement data access functionality for your clients. The next chapter covers data binding in ASP.NET. You'll see how to use different Web server controls in data binding operations. This chapter is based on real-world usage of Web server data-bound controls. So, you'll learn a lot of good stuff that you can use in your applications.

CHAPTER 16

ASP.NET Server Controls and Data Binding

Chapter 14 discussed the basics of data binding in Web Forms and ASP.NET data-bound controls. You also saw how to use data-bound controls in Web applications. Chapter 15 discussed how to develop data-driven Web services and how to access the functionality implemented in a Web service from Web Forms applications. This chapter is an extension of Chapter 14. This chapter concentrates on the more practical aspects of data binding and Web Forms data-bound controls.

Data Binding in Web Forms, Revisited

In Chapter 7, you learned about data binding in Windows Forms and the classes used in data binding. Data binding in Web Forms is totally different than in Windows Forms. Data binding in general is a process of binding some data to some property of a control at runtime. In other words, it allows you to set a value of some property of a control at runtime. The data being bound to a control doesn't have to be a database. It can be any data source including text, collections, expressions, methods, or even properties of other controls. Because this book is about ADO.NET, we'll use a database as our data source.

Before writing applications, you should understand the data-binding model in Web Forms. The following sections discuss the key concepts of Web Forms data binding.

Read-Only Data Binding

Windows Forms data binding is *bidirectional*, which means Windows Forms controls keep binding state with the data source and allow both read and write methods.

Unlike Windows Forms, the data binding in Web Forms is read only. Providing bidirectional data binding in Web Forms is costly, which is one of the main reasons Web Forms don't support bidirectional data binding.

Another reason why data binding in Web Forms is read only is because most of the data you access through Web applications is read only. For example, say you go to a site such as Microsoft, MSN, your bank, or Amazon. What you do? You search for the thing you're looking for, and then read it or print it. That's it. So who needs data write features? Only people who are responsible for updating the data need data write features. And most of the applications don't update data through the Web interface. Site administrators usually access data on their local servers through Windows Forms or other interfaces.

Even though Web Forms provide read-only data binding, you can't ignore the possibility that people may want to update (write) data through Web Forms applications. For instance, say a bookstore or an online newspaper agency has a Web site and its editors want to update the site content from all over the world.

So how do you provide this data update functionality in Web Forms? You have to implement your own logic. In this chapter, you'll not only see how to implement this logic, but you'll also see how to write some ready-to-run Web applications that you can use in your Web projects.

Simple and Complex Data Binding

Similar to Windows Forms data binding, Web Forms also support two types of data binding: *simple data binding* and *complex data binding*. In simple data binding, controls can bind and display one data value at a time. Some of the controls that participate in simple data binding are the TextBox, Button, Label, and Image controls. For example, these controls can only display a single value of a single column of a database table. On the other hand, complex data binding allows controls to bind and display multiple data records. For example, the Repeater, DataList, and DataGrid controls can display multiple records from multiple columns of a database table. The controls used in simple data binding are called *simple data-bound controls*, and the controls used in complex data binding are called *complex data-bound controls*.

 NOTE *See the "Understanding Data Binding in ASP.NET" section of Chapter 14 for more details on simple and complex data binding and data-bound controls.*

The Roles of the Control and Page Classes in Data Binding

The Control class defined in the System.Web.UI namespace provides the properties, methods, and events that are shared by all ASP.NET server controls. This is the control you would need when you develop your own custom controls. Even though this class is defined in the System.Web.UI interface, it doesn't have any User Interface (UI) functionality. You use this class when you're writing your own custom control that doesn't have a UI.

The Page class represents a Web page (an .aspx file) requested from a server that hosts other server controls and works as an ASP.NET Web application. The following class hierarchy shows the relationship between the Control and Page classes:

```
System.Object
    System.Web.UI.Control
        System.Web.UI.TemplateControl
            System.Web.UI.Page
            System.Web.UI.UserControl
```

Here you're only interested in two methods of the Control class: DataBind and OnDataBinding. The DataBind method is responsible for binding a data source to the server control and all its child controls.

 NOTE *When called on a server control, the* DataBind *method resolves all data-binding expressions in the server control and in any of its child controls. So, if you have a* DataGrid, *a* Label, *and a* TextBox *control bound to some data source and you call control's* DataBind *method, it also calls the* DataBind *methods of all the child controls. Usually you call this method through the* Page *class.*

The OnDataBinding method raises the DataBinding event, which occurs when the server control binds to a data source. A typical call to Page.DataBind method looks like this:

```
Sub Page_Load(Src As Object, e As EventArgs)
  If Not IsPostBack Then
      'Bind child controls here
  End If
  Page.DataBind()
End Sub
```

Data Binding in Simple Web Forms Controls

Chapter 14 discussed data-bound controls briefly. As mentioned, there are two types of data-bound controls: simple and complex. The Button, TextBox, and ListBox controls are simple data-bound controls, and the DataList and DataGrid controls are complex data-bound controls.

The following sections discuss data-bound Web server controls. The System.Web.UI.WebControls namespace provides a ton of classes for Web server controls. In fact, an entire book could be written on this namespace itself. Unfortunately, we won't be able to cover all of these controls in this chapter because this book targets ADO.NET-related controls. Because this book's scope is limited to data binding and data-bound controls, you'll see some of the most commonly used Web server controls in data-driven applications.

Using the Button Control

Similar to a Windows Forms Button control, a Web Forms Button control provides users with the ability to click the button and perform some action on the button click event. A Web Button control can be of three types: a button, a link button, and an image button. The Button, LinkButton, and ImageButton classes in the System.Web.UI.WebControls classes represent a button, link button, and image button, respectively.

The simple Button control is a standard command button, rendered as a Hypertext Markup Language (HTML) submit button. The LinkButton control represents a button with a hyperlink, and an ImageButton control represents a button with an image.

You can add the Button control to a Web page by dragging the control from the Toolbox to the page. For this example, drag a Button, LinkButton, and an ImageButton control to the page, as shown in Figure 16-1.

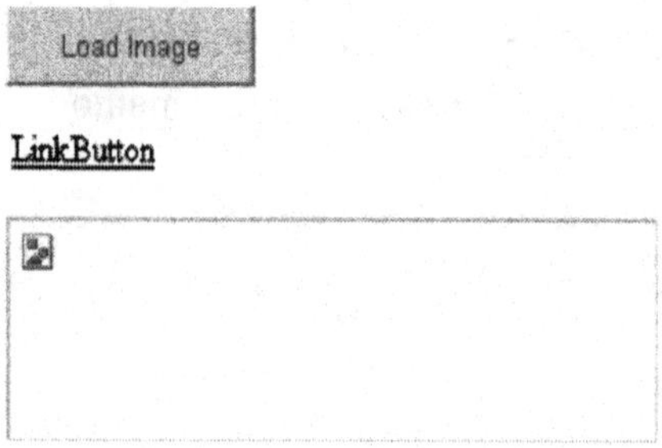

Figure 16-1. Adding Button *controls to a Web page*

Now, simply double-click the Button and LinkButton controls. This action adds button click event handlers. Use the ImageUrl property of ImageButton to set an image for the ImageButton control. Listing 16-1 shows the code of the button click event handlers for the Button and LinkButton controls.

Listing 16-1. Writing Button Click Handlers

```
Private Sub Button1_Click(ByVal sender As System.Object, _
  ByVal e As System.EventArgs) Handles Button1.Click
    ImageButton1.ImageUrl = _
    "http://www.c-sharpcorner.com/images/csLogo102.gif"
    ImageButton1.ImageAlign = ImageAlign.Baseline
  End Sub

  Private Sub LinkButton1_Click(ByVal sender As System.Object, _
  ByVal e As System.EventArgs) Handles LinkButton1.Click
    Response.Write("LinkButton clicked")
End Sub
```

If you click the Load Image button, the output looks like Figure 16-2.

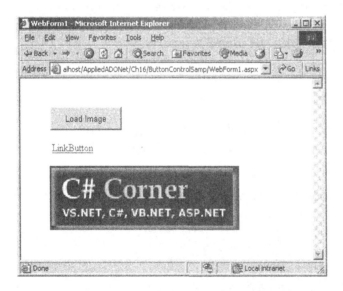

Figure 16-2. Loading an image in an ImageButton *control*

Using the Calendar Control

The Calendar control, represented by the Calendar class, displays a one-month calendar. A calendar on Web pages allows users to view and select dates such as in an airline reservation application. The Calendar control displays and selects dates, but it can also display appointments and other information.

The Calendar control is based on the DataTime data type of the .NET Framework, which displays any date between the years 0 and 9999 A.D.

NOTE *In VB .NET, the* Date *data type is equivalent to the .NET Framework's* DateTime *data type.*

To create a Calendar control, you simply drag a Calendar control from the Toolbox to the Web page. After that, if you run the application, it displays the current month and provides options to move to the next and previous months by default.

The default month for the Calendar control is the month of today's date represented by the TodaysDate property. If you want to change the starting month of a Calendar control, you can use the VisibleDate property. For example, the following line sets the visible month of a Calendar control to January 2002:

```
' Set VisibleDate to Dec 01, 2002
Calendar1.VisibleDate = New Date(2002, 12, 1)
```

After adding a Calendar control to a Web page, add a button called SelectedDate and write the code in Listing 16-2 on this button's click event.

Listing 16-2. Getting Selected Date of a Calendar Control

```
Private Sub GetPropsBtn_Click(ByVal sender As System.Object, _
  ByVal e As System.EventArgs) Handles GetPropsBtn.Click
    Label1.Text = "The selected date is " & _
    Calendar1.SelectedDate.ToShortDateString()
  End Sub
```

Setting the Calendar Class's Properties

Table 16-1 describes some of the common properties of the Calendar control.

Table 16-1. The Calendar Class Properties

PROPERTY	DESCRIPTION
DayHeaderStyle	This represents the style of the section that displays the day of the week. Read only.
DayNameFormat	This represents the style of the section that displays the day of the week. Read only.
DayStyle	This represents the style of the days in the displayed month. Read only.
FirstDayOfWeek	This represents the day of the week to display in the first day column. Both get and set.
NextMonthText	This represents the text of the next month navigation control. Both get and set.
NextPrevFormat	This represents the format of the next and previous month navigation elements in the title section. Both get and set.
NextPrevStyle	This represents the style of the next and previous month navigation. Both get and set.
OtherMonthDayStyle	This represents the style of the days that are not in the displayed month. Read only.
PrevMonthText	This represents the text of the previous month navigation control. Both get and set.
SelectedDate	This represents the selected date. Both get and set.
SelectedDates	This represents a collection of selected dates. Both get and set.
SelectedDayStyle	This represents the style of the selected dates. Read only.
SelectionMode	This represents the date selection mode. It represents whether a user can select a single day, a week, or an entire month. Both get and set.
SelectMonthText	This represents the text displayed for the month selection element in the selector column. Both get and set.
SelectorStyle	This represents the style of the week and month selector column. Read only.
SelectWeekText	This represents the text displayed for the week selection element in the selector column. Both get and set.

Table 16-1. The Calendar *Class Properties (Continued)*

PROPERTY	DESCRIPTION
ShowDayHeader	This value indicates whether the heading for the days of the week is displayed. Both get and set.
ShowGridLines	This value indicates whether the days are separated with grid lines. Both get and set.
ShowNextPrevMonth	This indicates whether the control displays the next and previous month navigation elements in the title section. Both get and set.
ShowTitle	This indicates whether the title section is displayed. Both get and set.
TitleFormat	This represents the title format for the title section. Both get and set.
TitleStyle	This represents the style properties of the title heading. Read only.
TodayDayStyle	This represents the style of today's date. Read only.
TodaysDate	This indicates the value of today's date. Both get and set.
VisibleDate	This date specifies the default month. Both get and set.
WeekendDayStyle	This represents the style of the weekend dates. Read only.

Now let's set some properties of the Calendar control (see Listing 16-3).

Listing 16-3. Setting a Calendar *Control's Properties*

```
' Set VisibleDate to Dec 01, 2002
Calendar1.ShowTitle = True
Calendar1.ShowGridLines = False
Calendar1.ShowNextPrevMonth = True
Calendar1.VisibleDate = New Date(2002, 12, 1)
Calendar1.NextMonthText = "Next"
Calendar1.PrevMonthText = "Back"
Calendar1.FirstDayOfWeek = _
System.Web.UI.WebControls.FirstDayOfWeek.Friday
Calendar1.ShowDayHeader = True
Calendar1.TitleFormat = TitleFormat.MonthYear
```

Navigating Months Programmatically

There will probably be cases when you'll want to customize the default behavior of the Calendar control. For example, say some airline only has flights between the 15th and 25th of the month. You'll want to develop a system so that the user can select dates between the 15th and 25th only. Set the control's VisibleDate property to a date in the month you want to display.

The control's VisibleMonthChanged event fires when a user moves to the next or previous months by using the Next and Back navigational links. Listing 16-4 shows the code for the VisibleMonthChanged event.

Listing 16-4. The VisibleMonthChanged *Event*

```
Public Sub Calendar1_VisibleMonthChanged(ByVal sender As Object, _
   ByVal e As System.Web.UI.WebControls.MonthChangedEventArgs) _
   Handles Calendar1.VisibleMonthChanged
   Calendar1.SelectedDates.Clear()
   Calendar1.SelectedDates.Add _
   (New DateTime(e.NewDate.Year, e.NewDate.Month, 15))
   Calendar1.SelectedDates.Add _
   (New DateTime(e.NewDate.Year, e.NewDate.Month, 25))
End Sub
```

When you run the Calendar control application, you'll see the Calendar control. When you select a date and click the Selected Date button, the output looks like Figure 16-3.

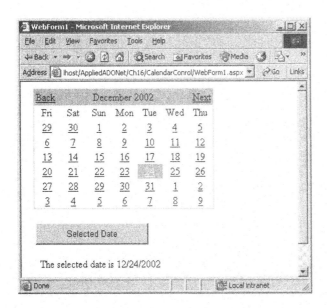

Figure 16-3. The Calendar *control in action*

Understanding Web Server Control Templates

Before discussing more controls, we'll first cover *templates.* Templates play a major role in managing the layout and format of the data being displayed in ASP.NET data-bound controls. You'll apply templates on various data-bound controls in this chapter. Before using templates, though, let's quickly look at template basics and how they work.

Templates provide a way to apply complex formatting to a control's parts such as the header, footer, and items (text being displayed by the control). A template is a set of HTML tags that define the layout for a particular part of a control. Besides HTML tags, a template can also contain other controls and ASP.NET inline code.

For a better understanding, let's take a look at a simple use of templates. Listing 16-5 uses templates in a Repeater control. As you can see, this listing uses the AlternatingItemTemplate and ItemTemplate templates. (We discuss the different types of templates in the following section.) Specifically, AlternatingItemTemplate, sets the font color to red, the font face to Verdana, and the font size to 3. ItemTemplate sets the font color to green, the font face to Tahoma, and the font size to 2. The listing also uses the HTML Table control to display items. As you probably can guess from this code, the items of a Repeater control will have a green color, the font face Tahoma with a size of 2. Alternating rows and their items will have the color red, the face Verdana, and a size of 3.

Listing 16-5. Applying a Simple Template on a Repeater *Control*

```
<ASP:Repeater id="repeaterControl" runat="server">
    <AlternatingItemTemplate>
      <font color="red" face = "verdana" size = 3>
      <table>
      <tr>
      alternating data
      </tr>
      </table>
      </font>
    </AlternatingItemTemplate>
    <ItemTemplate>
    <font color="green" face = "tahoma" size = 2>
      <table>
      <tr>
      some item
      </tr>
      </table>
```

```
            </font>
        </ItemTemplate>
        <FooterTemplate>
        </FooterTemplate>
</ASP:Repeater></P>
```

Using Different Template Types

A template describes the layout and formatting of the parts of a control. Similar to other control tags, templates have a starting and ending pair of tags. For example, HeaderTemplate describes the layout and format of header of a control, and the <HeaderTemplate></HeaderTemplate> pair represents a header template of a control. Table 16-2 describes the available templates.

Table 16-2. ASP.NET Templates

TEMPLATE	SYNTAX	DESCRIPTION
Header template	HeaderTemplate	Describes the layout and format of a control's header.
Footer template	FooterTemplate	Describes the layout and format of a control's footer.
Item template	ItemTemplate	Describes the layout and format of a control's items.
Alternating item template	AlternatingItemTemplate	Describes the layout and format of a control's alternating items.
Separator template	SeparatorTemplate	Describes the layout and format of a control's separator. (A *separator* separates two items of a control.)
Selected item template	SelectedItemTemplate	Describes the layout and format of a control's selected items.
Edit item template	EditItemTemplate	Some controls such as a DataGrid control allow users to edit items. EditItemTemplate describes the layout and format of the items being edited.

Table 16-2. ASP.NET Templates (Continued)

TEMPLATE	SYNTAX	DESCRIPTION
Pager template	Pager	The DataGrid control allows users to have a paging option through the pager. The Pager template describes the layout and format of the DataGrid control's pager.

Which Controls Support Templates?

Not all ASP.NET data-bound controls support templates. Only complex controls support templates. In addition, each control supports a different set of templates that specify layouts for different portions of the control, such as the header, footer, item, and selected items. The Repeater, DataList, and DataGrid controls utilize templates.

The Repeater control supports HeaderTemplate, FooterTemplate, ItemTemplate, AlternatingItemTemplate, and SeparatorTemplate.

The DataList control supports HeaderTemplate, FooterTemplate, ItemTemplate, AlternatingItemTemplate, SeparatorTemplate, SelectedItemTemplate, and EditItemTemplate.

The DataGrid control supports HeaderTemplate, FooterTemplate, ItemTemplate, EditItemTemplate, and Pager.

 TIP *Even though you can use the Visual Studio .NET (VS .NET) Integrated Development Environment (IDE) to create controls and add templates to the controls, you should add templates programmatically. Adding templates programmatically is simple. After completing the following section, you'll find out how easy working with templates is.*

Creating Templates Using the HTML View

You can create templates using template tags by simply editing your `.aspx` page in a text editor or in the HTML View of VS .NET.

In Listing 16-5, you saw how you can easily create and use templates in an ASP.NET page by defining template tags and specifying the formatting layout inside the tags. For example, say you want to add some templates to a `DataList` control. Well, what templates do you want to use? A `DataList` control supports header, footer, item, separator, alternating item, selected item, and edit item templates.

So, let's say you want to use header, item, alternating item, and footer templates. Listing 16-6 adds the header, item, alternating item, and footer templates to a `DataList` control. The `RepeatColumns` property of the `DataList` control represents how many columns appear in a row of a `DataList` control.

Listing 16-6. Adding Templates to a `DataList` *Control*

```
<ASP:DataList
id="dtList"
RepeatColumns="5"
RepeatDirection="Horizontal"
runat="server">
        <HeaderTemplate>
        </HeaderTemplate>
        <AlternatingItemTemplate>
        </AlternatingItemTemplate>
        <ItemTemplate>
        </ItemTemplate>
        <FooterTemplate>
        </FooterTemplate>
    </ASP: DataList >
```

So far, this code would do nothing. You need to add the format of the template within the template tags. Listing 16-7 adds content to the templates of a `DataList` control. As you can see from this code, the header, footer, item, alternating item templates have different formats. You can make these formats as complex as you want. You can even add Web controls to these templates.

Listing 16-7. Adding Formatting to the Templates of a DataList *Control*

```
<HeaderTemplate>
<font color =  #cc3333 face ="verdana" size = 3>
<b>DataList Control Header</b>
</font>
</HeaderTemplate>

<AlternatingItemTemplate>
<font face ="verdana" size = 2 color ="green" >
<br>
<b>Category ID: </b>
<%# DataBinder.Eval(Container.DataItem, "CategoryID") %>
<br>
<b>Category Name: </b>
<%# DataBinder.Eval(Container.DataItem, "CategoryName")%>
<br>
<b>Description: </b>
<%# DataBinder.Eval(Container.DataItem, "Description") %>
<br>
<b>Picture: </b>
<%# DataBinder.Eval(Container.DataItem, "Picture") %>
<p>
</div>
</font>
</AlternatingItemTemplate>

<ItemTemplate>
<font face ="verdana" size = 2>
<br>
<b>Category ID: </b>
<%# DataBinder.Eval(Container.DataItem, "CategoryID") %>
<br>
<b>Category Name: </b>
<%# DataBinder.Eval(Container.DataItem, "CategoryName")%>
<br>
<b>Description: </b>
<%# DataBinder.Eval(Container.DataItem, "Description") %>
<br>
<b>Picture: </b>
<%# DataBinder.Eval(Container.DataItem, "Picture") %>
<p>
</div>
```

```
</font>
</ItemTemplate>

<FooterTemplate>
<font color= #996600 face ="verdana" size = 1>
DataList Control footer
</font>
</FooterTemplate>
```

> **NOTE** *You may have noticed a line containing* DataBinder *and other syntaxes. You'll learn about this in the following sections.*

Creating Templates Using the Form Designer

Besides using the HTML View, you can create templates in VS .NET by using the form designer. You simply drag the control onto an ASP.NET page and right-click the control. For example, if you drag a DataList control and right-click it, you'll see the Edit Template menu item. The Edit Template menu item has three submenu items: Header and Footer Templates, Item Templates, and Separator Templates. Clicking any of these menu items opens the form designer.

Once you're in the form designer, you can enter HTML text and drop HTML or ASP.NET controls onto a data-bound control. You'll see how to use the form designer with data binding in the following sections.

> **TIP** *The Auto Format option of data-bound controls lets you select a format of the control from predefined formats.*

Working with Templates Programmatically

So far you've seen two methods for creating templates: using an HTML editor and the VS .NET IDE. Both of the methods force you to write code in an .aspx file at design-time. What if you're not sure what format of template you want to create, or you want to create an application where users can pick the format of template?

There are two ways to accomplish this. The first way is to provide prebuilt templates similar to the Auto Format option that the DataGrid control provides. In this method, you create and save the layout of the templates with an .ascx extension and load the file using the LoadTemplate method of the Page object. The second way is to create templates in memory based on the user selection.

Using the Repeater Control

The Repeater control is a data-bound container control that produces a list of individual items of a data source. By default the Repeater control doesn't support any style, formatting, or layout. To provide a layout to a Repeater control, you define the layout of individual items on a Web page using templates. If there's no template specified, the control does not appear on a Web page. The Repeater control supports HeaderTemplate, FooterTemplate, ItemTemplate, AlternatingItemTemplate, and SeparatorTemplate, as described in Table 16-3.

Table 16-3. Templates Supported by the Repeater Control

TEMPLATE	DESCRIPTION
ItemTemplate	Elements that are rendered once for each row in the data source.
AlternatingItemTemplate	Like the ItemTemplate element, but rendered for every other row in the Repeater control. You can specify a different look for the AlternatingItemTemplate element by setting its style properties.
HeaderTemplate	Header elements.
FooterTemplate	Footer elements.
SeparatorTemplate	Elements to render between each row, such as line breaks (tags), lines (<HR> tags), or commas.

Creating a Repeater Control

Unlike other Web server controls, the Repeater control doesn't have much design-time support from the IDE. You can only drag and drop a control onto the page and set its data-binding and data source properties. Everything else you have to do manually in the HTML View of the editor.

The best way to create a Repeater control is to just use the HTML syntax. For example, the following code creates a simple Repeater control with three templates:

```
<ASP:Repeater id="repeaterControl" runat="server">
<HeaderTemplate>
</HeaderTemplate>
<ItemTemplate>
</ItemTemplate>
<FooterTemplate>
</FooterTemplate>
</ASP:Repeater>
```

Data Binding and the Repeater Control

The DataSource property of the Repeater control binds data to the control. Like other controls, you can assign any data source that implements the IEnumerable interface. Some of the valid data sources are DataSet, DataView, and an Array. The syntax for binding the controls to the Repeater control uses "Container" as the data source because the Repeater is the container for all the controls. The following code binds the CategoryID column of a DataSource:

```
<%# DataBinder.Eval(Container.DataItem, "CategoryID") %>
```

NOTE *You can't bind controls in the header, footer, and separator templates using* DataBinder.Eval *expressions in HTML View. You must bind these controls in the code. Like other data-bound controls, you must call the* DataBind *method of the control to get the records to be displayed.*

Calling the Repeater Control Events

The Repeater.ItemCreated event is called each time the table is rendered. It allows you to customize the item-creation process. Similar to the other controls, the Repeater.ItemCommand event is raised in response to button clicks in individual items such as a Button, LinkButton, or ImageButton control. You use this event when you implement add, updated, and delete operations in a control.

Seeing the Repeater Control in Action

Listing 16-8 fills data from the Categories table of the Northwind database and displays it in a Repeater control.

Listing 16-8. Using the Repeater *Control*

```
<%@ Import Namespace="System.Data" %>
<%@ Import Namespace="System.Data.SqlClient" %>
<HTML>
<script language="VB" runat="server">
Sub Page_Load(sender As Object, e As EventArgs)
Dim conn As SqlConnection
Dim adapter As SqlDataAdapter
dim connectionString = _
"Data Source=MCB;Initial Catalog=Northwind;user id=sa;password=;"
conn = new SqlConnection(connectionString)
conn.Open()
dim sql = "SELECT * FROM Categories"
adapter = new SqlDataAdapter(sql, conn)
Dim ds As Dataset = new DataSet()
adapter.Fill(ds)
repeaterControl.DataSource = ds
repeaterControl.DataBind()
  End Sub
</script>
<body>
<P>
<ASP:Repeater id="repeaterControl" runat="server">
<HeaderTemplate>
<Table width="100%" style="font: 8pt verdana">
<tr style="background-color:DFA894">
<th>CategoryID</th>
<th>CategoryName</th>
<th>Description</th>
<th>Picture</th>
</tr>
</HeaderTemplate>
<ItemTemplate>
<tr style="background-color:FFECD8">
<td>
<%# DataBinder.Eval(Container.DataItem, "CategoryID") %>
```

```
</td>
<td>
<%# DataBinder.Eval(Container.DataItem, "CategoryName") %>
</td>
<td>
<%# DataBinder.Eval(Container.DataItem, "Description") %>
</td>
<td>
<%# DataBinder.Eval(Container.DataItem, "Picture") %>
</td>
</tr>
</ItemTemplate>
<FooterTemplate>
</FooterTemplate>
</ASP:Repeater></P>
</body>
</HTML>
```

Understanding the Role of the ListControl Class

The Web Controls namespace provides a rich set of list controls, and the ListControl class is the abstract base class for these controls. This class defines the properties, methods, and events common for all list controls. These controls are CheckBoxList, DropDownList, ListBox, and RadioButtonList.

This class defines the data-binding functionality of list controls. Similar to other data-bound controls, the DataSource property of the ListControl class represents the data source. This property has both get and set access.

A data source such as a DataSet can have multiple tables. The DataMember property of the ListControl class represents a table in a data source. This property also has both get and set access.

Normally, you bind list controls to a specific field of a table. The DataTextField represents the field of the data source. This property has both get and set access.

The DataTextFormatString property of ListControl represents the format of string, which presents how data that is bound to the list control is displayed. This property provides a custom display format for list control contents. This property also has both get and set access.

The data format string consists of two parts separated by a colon in the form { *A: Bxx*}, where *A* specifies the parameter number, which is 0 because there's only one item in a cell. Table 16-4 describes the B part of the string.

Table 16-4. The Values of the B Part of the Data Format String of ListControl

CHARACTER	DESCRIPTION
C	Currency format
D	Decimal format
E	Exponential format
F	Fixed format
G	General format
N	Number format
X	Hexadecimal format

See the help topic "Standard Numeric Format Strings" in the documentation for more details on these formats.

Using the ListBox Control

Similar to the Windows Forms ListBox control, the ListBox server control can display a list of items and allows single or multiple item selection. Because ListBox inherits from the ListControl, you can use the members discussed previously.

The easiest way to create a ListBox control is simply by dragging a control from the Toolbox to a page. To make the sample program interactive, add two Button controls and a Label control along with a ListBox control, as shown in Figure 16-4.

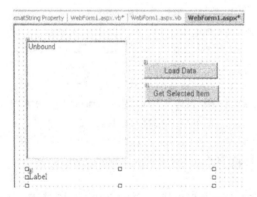

Figure 16-4. Using a ListBox Web server control

The Load Data button click reads data from the Northwind database and binds data to the ListBox control. The Get Selected Item button click returns the selected item. Listing 16-9 shows the code for both button click event handlers.

As you can see from this listing, it simply creates and fills a DataSet and sets the DataSource property of the ListBox control to DataSet. It also sets the DataTextField and DataTextFormatString properties of the ListBox control. DataTextField is the name of the table column, which you want to display in the control. This sample displays the UnitPrice column's data from the Products table. Format the data so it displays in currency format by using the DataTextFormatString property.

Listing 16-9. Data Binding in ListBox Control

```
Private Sub LoadDataBtn_Click(ByVal sender As System.Object, _
  ByVal e As System.EventArgs) Handles LoadDataBtn.Click
    Dim conn As SqlConnection = Nothing
    Dim adapter As SqlDataAdapter = Nothing
    Dim reader As SqlDataReader = Nothing
    Dim cmd As SqlCommand = Nothing
    Dim connectionString = _
    "Data Source=MCB;Initial Catalog=Northwind;user id=sa;password=;"
    conn = New SqlConnection(connectionString)
    conn.Open()
    Dim sql = "SELECT * FROM Products"
    ' Use DataSet
    adapter = New SqlDataAdapter(sql, conn)
      Dim ds As DataSet = New DataSet()
      adapter.Fill(ds)
    ListBox1.DataSource = ds
    ListBox1.DataTextFormatString = "Unit Price: {0:C}"
    ListBox1.DataTextField = "UnitPrice"
    ListBox1.DataBind()
End Sub

Private Sub GetSetBtn_Click(ByVal sender As System.Object, _
  ByVal e As System.EventArgs) Handles GetSetBtn.Click
    Label1.Text = "Selected Item: " & _
      ListBox1.SelectedItem.Value
End Sub
```

If you run the application and load the data, the output looks like Figure 16-5. As you can see from this figure, the data displays in currency format.

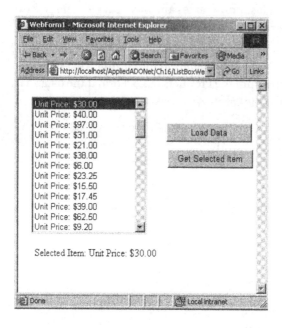

Figure 16-5. Data binding in a ListBox *control*

Using the DropDownList Control

The DropDownList control is a list control, which displays only the selected data. However, all data items are available when you drop the control. Data binding in the DropDownList control works in the same way as in the ListBox control. You simply set the DataSource, DataMember, and DataTextField properties and call the control's DataBind method.

> **NOTE** *Data binding works in a similar way with the* CheckBoxList *and* RadioButtonList *controls, too. You just need to set the* DataSource *and* DataTextField *properties and call the* DataBind *method.*

Let's create a similar application as in the last sample. To make the application little more interactive, add one CheckBox control to the page, as shown in Figure 16-6. As you can see from this figure, when you check the Use DataReader check box,

the Load Data button click reads data in a SqlDataReader and binds it with the
DropDownList control; otherwise it uses the DataSet.

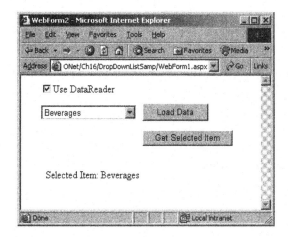

Figure 16-6. Data binding in a DropDownList *control*

Listing 16-10 shows the code for the Load Data and Get Selected Item button
click event handlers. As you can see, it binds the CategoryName column of the
Categories table to the control.

Listing 16-10. Data Binding in a DropDownList *Control*

```
Private Sub LoadDataBtn_Click(ByVal sender As System.Object, _
  ByVal e As System.EventArgs) Handles LoadDataBtn.Click
    Dim conn As SqlConnection = Nothing
    Dim adapter As SqlDataAdapter = Nothing
    Dim reader As SqlDataReader = Nothing
    Dim cmd As SqlCommand = Nothing
    Dim connectionString = _
    "Data Source=MCB;Initial Catalog=Northwind;user id=sa;password=;"
    conn = New SqlConnection(connectionString)
    conn.Open()
    Dim sql = "SELECT * FROM Categories"

    If CheckBox1.Checked Then
      ' Use DataReader
      cmd = New SqlCommand(sql, conn)
      reader = cmd.ExecuteReader()
```

```
        DropDownList1.DataSource = reader
        DropDownList1.DataTextField = "CategoryName"
        DropDownList1.DataBind()
        If Not reader.IsClosed Then
          reader.Close()
        End If
      Else
        ' Use DataSet
        adapter = New SqlDataAdapter(sql, conn)
        Dim ds As DataSet = New DataSet()
        adapter.Fill(ds)
        DropDownList1.DataSource = ds
        DropDownList1.DataTextField = "CategoryName"
        DropDownList1.DataBind()
      End If
    End Sub

    Private Sub GetSelItem_Click(ByVal sender As System.Object, _
    ByVal e As System.EventArgs) Handles GetSelItem.Click
      Label1.Text = "Selected Item: " & _
      DropDownList1.SelectedItem.Value
    End Sub
```

Data Binding in Other Simple Controls

How about data binding in simple TextBox, Button, and Image controls? These
controls don't provide a DataSource property. The ImageUrl property of the Image
control binds an image to the control. You use the Repeater control to bind data
with these controls.

 CAUTION *When binding data to a* TextBox *control, you must write
the* runat="server" *syntax after the* Text *property of these controls;
otherwise you'll get the error* "TextBox *cannot have children of*
DataBoundLiteralControl."

Listing 16-11 creates a TextBox, a Button, and an Image control and binds data
from the Employees table of the Northwind database.

TIP *If you want to bind data to a* LinkButton *control, just replace* asp:Button *with* asp:LinkButton *in Listing 16-10.*

Listing 16-11. Data Binding in the TextBox, Button, *and* Image *Controls*

```
<%@ Import Namespace="System.Data" %>
<%@ Import Namespace="System.Data.SqlClient" %>
<script language="VB" runat=server>
Sub Page_Load(sender As Object, e As EventArgs)
     Dim conn As SqlConnection
     Dim adapter As SqlDataAdapter
     dim connectionString = _
     "Data Source=MCB;Initial Catalog=Northwind;user id=sa;password=;"
     conn = new SqlConnection(connectionString)
     conn.Open()
     dim sql = "SELECT * FROM Employees"
     dim cmd as SqlCommand = new SqlCommand(sql, conn)
     Dim reader as SqlDataReader = cmd.ExecuteReader()
     repeaterControl.DataSource = reader
     repeaterControl.DataBind()
     reader.Close()
     conn.Close()
  End Sub

</script>

<HTML>
<HEAD><title>Other Controls Data Binding</title></HEAD>
<form id="Form1" method="post" runat="server">
<asp:Repeater
id="repeaterControl"
runat="server">
<ItemTemplate>
<asp:Button
id="Button1"
Text='<%# Container.DataItem("LastName") %>'
runat="server">
</asp:Button>
<asp:TextBox
```

```
id="TextBox1"
Text='<%# Container.DataItem("Title") %>'
runat="server">
</asp:TextBox>
<asp:Image
id="Image1"
ImageUrl='<%# Container.DataItem("Photo") %>'
runat="server">
</asp:Image>
</ItemTemplate>
</asp:Repeater>
</form>
</HTML>
```

Data Binding in Complex Web Forms Controls

The DataList and DataGrid controls are complex data-bound controls. These controls are capable of displaying multiple columns of a data source. The DataList and DataGrid controls share some common features. Before discussing each control, we'll discuss these common features.

Understanding the BaseDataList Class

Before discussing the DataList and DataGrid controls, let's take a look at the BaseDataList class. The BaseDataList class is an abstract base class for the DataList and DataGrid controls. Because it's an abstract base class, the functionality defined in this class can only be used through its derived classes. The class hierarchy is as follows:

```
System.Object
    System.Web.UI.Control
        System.Web.UI.WebControls.WebControl
            System.Web.UI.WebControls.BaseDataList
                System.Web.UI.WebControls.DataGrid
                System.Web.UI.WebControls.DataList
```

Table 16-5 describes the BaseDataList class properties.

Table 16-5. The BaseDataList *Class Properties*

PROPERTY	DESCRIPTION
CellPadding	This is the space between a cell and its border. Both get and set.
CellSpacing	This is the space between two cells. Both get and set.
DataKeyField	This is the key field in the data source. Both get and set.
DataKeys	This is the collection of data keys in the form of DataKeyCollection. Read only.
DataMember	This is the data member in a multimember data source. Both get and set.
DataSource	This is the data source. Both get and set.
GridLines	This is the border between the cells is displayed if true; otherwise false. Both get and set.
HorizontalAlign	This is the horizontal alignment of a data listing control within its container.

Using the DataKeyCollection Class

The DataKeyCollection object represents a collection of the key fields in a data source. Both the DataList and DataGrid controls provide access to the key fields through their DataKeyField properties.

The Count property returns the number of items in the collection. The IsReadOnly property returns true if the items in the collection are read only. If they aren't read only, the value of this property returns false.

The IsSynchronized property returns true if the collection is thread safe; otherwise it returns false.

The Item property gets the item from the collection at the specified index, and the SyncRoot property returns the object used to synchronize access to the collection.

The DataKeyCollection class provides two methods: CopyTo and GetEnumerator. The CopyTo method copies the contents of a collection to an array, and the GetEnumerator method creates an IEnumerator-implemented object that contains all key fields in the collection.

Using the DataList Web Server Control

The DataList control represents a data-bound list control that displays items using templates. You can create a DataList control by editing an .aspx file or by using the VS .NET IDE.

Before discussing DataList in more detail, let's look at a simple example. Listing 16-12 binds and displays data in a DataList control from the Categories table of the Northwind database.

Listing 16-12. Data Binding in a DataList Control

```
<%@ Import Namespace="System.Data" %>
<%@ Import Namespace="System.Data.SqlClient" %>
<HTML>
<BODY>
<font color="#006699" size="4" face="verdana">
DataList Server Control Sample
</font>
<script language="VB" runat="server">

Sub Page_Load(sender As Object, e As EventArgs)
Dim conn As SqlConnection
    Dim adapter As SqlDataAdapter
    dim connectionString = _
    "Data Source=MCB;Initial Catalog=Northwind;user id=sa;password=;"
    conn = new SqlConnection(connectionString)
    conn.Open()
    dim sql = "SELECT * FROM Categories"
    adapter = new SqlDataAdapter(sql, conn)
    Dim ds As Dataset = new DataSet()
    adapter.Fill(ds)
    dtList.DataSource = ds
    dtList.DataBind()
End Sub

</script>
<P>
```

```
<ASP:DataList
id="dtList"
RepeatColumns="1"
RepeatDirection="Horizontal"
runat="server">
<HeaderTemplate>
<FONT face="verdana" color="#cc3333" size="3">
<B>DataList Control Header</B></FONT>
</HeaderTemplate>

<FooterTemplate>
<FONT face="verdana" color="#996600" size="1">
DataList Control footer </FONT>
</FooterTemplate>

<ItemTemplate>
<FONT face="verdana" size="2">
<BR>
<B>Category ID: </B>
<%# DataBinder.Eval(Container.DataItem, "CategoryID") %>
<BR>
<B>Category Name: </B>
<%# DataBinder.Eval(Container.DataItem, "CategoryName")%>
<BR>
<B>Description: </B>
<%# DataBinder.Eval(Container.DataItem, "Description") %>
<BR>
<B>Picture: </B>
<%# DataBinder.Eval(Container.DataItem, "Picture") %>
<P>
<DIV></DIV>
</FONT>
</ItemTemplate>

</ASP:DataList>
</P>
</BODY>
</HTML>
```

The output of Listing 16-12 looks like Figure 16-7.

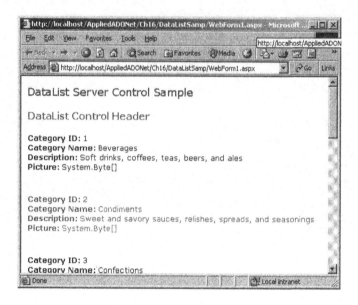

Figure 16-7. Data binding in a DataList *control*

Setting the DataList Properties

The DataList control is pretty useful and provides members to format the control's contents. Before discussing how to format a DataList control's contents, let's look at the DataList control properties. From these properties, you'll have an idea what a DataList control offers. Table 16-6 describes the DataList class properties.

Table 16-6. The DataList *Class Properties*

PROPERTY	DESCRIPTION
AlternatingItemStyle	This represents the style of alternating items. Read only.
AlternatingItemTemplate	This represents the template for alternating items. Both get and set.
EditItemIndex	This represents the index number of the selected item. Both get and set.
EditItemStyle	This represents the style of the item being edited. Read only.
EditItemTemplate	This represents the template for the items being edited. Both get and set.
ExtractTemplateRows	This represents the whether rows are extracted and displayed. Both get and set.
FooterStyle	This returns the style of the footer.

Table 16-6. The DataList *Class Properties (Continued)*

PROPERTY	DESCRIPTION
FooterTemplate	This represents the template for the footer. Both get and set.
GridLines	This represents grid lines: horizontal, vertical, both, or none.
HeaderStyle	This represents the style of the header. Both get and set.
HeaderTemplate	This represents the template for the header. Both get and set.
Items	This returns the collection of DataListItem objects.
ItemStyle	This returns the style of items.
ItemTemplate	This represents the template for DataList items. Both get and set.
RepeatColumns	This represents the represents the number of columns to display in a DataList. Both get and set. If you want to display 5 columns in a DataList, set it to 5.
RepeatDirection	The determines whether the DataList control displays vertically or horizontally.
RepeatLayout	This represents if the control is displayed in a table or flow layout.
SelectedIndex	This represents the index of the selected item. Both get and set.
SelectedItem	This returns selected item.
SelectedItemStyle	This returns the style of the selected item.
SelectedItemTemplate	This represents the template for the selected item.
SeparatorStyle	This represents the style of the border.
SeparatorTemplate	This represents the template for the border.
ShowFooter	If true, this shows the footer; otherwise it hides the footer. Both get and set.
ShowHeader	If true, this shows the header; otherwise it hides the header. Both get and set.

TIP *You can set most of the control properties at design-time as well as at runtime. To create and set a* DataList *control at design-time, just drag a control from the Toolbox to a page and use the Properties window to set its properties.*

Setting Multiple Columns, Grid Lines, and Alternating Rows

In Listing 16-12, you filled data from the Categories table and that data was listed in a single column. What if you want to display more than one column in a row? You can do that by setting the control's RepeatColumns property. You can even set the direction in which the control displays. The following code sets a DataList control to display five columns in a row in a horizontal direction with grid lines:

```
<ASP:DataList id="dtList"
RepeatColumns="5"
RepeatDirection="Horizontal"
GridLines="Both"
runat="server">
```

You can set the style of the alternating rows by using AlternatingItemTemplate. Listing 16-13 sets the format of alternating items in the controls.

Listing 16-13. Setting a DataList Control's Properties

```
<AlternatingItemTemplate>
<FONT face="verdana" color="green" size="2">
<BR>
<B>Category ID: </B>
<%# DataBinder.Eval(Container.DataItem, "CategoryID") %>
<BR>
<B>Category Name: </B>
<%# DataBinder.Eval(Container.DataItem, "CategoryName")%>
<BR>
<B>Description: </B>
<%# DataBinder.Eval(Container.DataItem, "Description") %>
<BR>
<B>Picture: </B>
<%# DataBinder.Eval(Container.DataItem, "Picture") %>
<P>
<DIV></DIV>
</FONT>
</AlternatingItemTemplate>
```

The output of this program looks like Figure 16-8. As you can see from this figure, each row of the DataList control has five columns with grid lines and alternating styles.

Figure 16-8. Multiple columns in a DataList *control*

Setting the Style and Templates of a DataList Control

As you saw in Table 16-6, the DataList class provides many style properties for different portions of the control. These properties are AlternatingItemStyle, EditItemStyle, FooterItemStyle, HeaderItemStyle, ItemStyle, SelectedItemStyle, and SeparatorStyle. Using these properties, you can set the style of the respective portion of the control.

In addition to the styles, you can hide or show the DataList control headers and footers by using the ShowHeader and ShowFooter properties. You can even set the layout of the DataList control by using the RepeatLayout property, which takes a value of the RepeatLayout enumeration, which has two values: Table and Flow. The Table layout is responsible for displaying items in a table. The Flow layout is responsible for displaying items without a table.

The DataList control supports many templates, even more than the DataGrid control. The templates supported by the DataList control are AlternatingItemTemplate, EditItemTemplate, FooterTemplate, HeaderTemplate, ItemTemplate, SelectedItemTemplate, and SeparatorTemplate. Using these templates you can set or get the format of different portions of the DataList.

NOTE *See the "Understanding Web Server Control Templates" section for more details about templates.*

Listing 16-14 sets the styles and templates of a DataList control and its portions manually. This code shows you how you can use templates. You can give them whatever format you want.

Listing 16-14. Setting a DataList Control's Styles

```
<asp:DataList
id=DataList1
runat="server"
GridLines="Both"
DataSource="<%# DataSet11 %>"
DataKeyField="CategoryID"
DataMember="Categories"
RepeatDirection="Horizontal"
RepeatColumns="5"
Font-Size="X-Small"
Font-Names="Verdana"
ForeColor="Navy"
BackColor="LightGray"
BorderColor="Black">
<SelectedItemStyle
ForeColor="#FF0033"
BackColor="#CCCC99">
</SelectedItemStyle>
<EditItemStyle
Font-Size="10pt"
Font-Names="Verdana"
Font-Bold="True"
BackColor="#FFE0C0">
</EditItemStyle>
<AlternatingItemStyle
ForeColor="#006600"
BackColor="Silver">
</AlternatingItemStyle>
<ItemStyle
ForeColor="Black"
BackColor="GhostWhite">
</ItemStyle>
<FooterStyle
Font-Size="8pt"
Font-Names="Tahoma"
ForeColor="White"
```

```
BackColor="Teal">
</FooterStyle>
<HeaderStyle
Font-Size="X-Small"
Font-Names="Verdana"
Font-Bold="True"
ForeColor="White"
BackColor="#003399">
</HeaderStyle>
</asp:DataList>
```

Using DataKeys

The DataKeys property of the BaseDataList class returns a collection of primary keys available in a data source. The DataKeys property accesses the key values of each row in a data listing control. The key field basically represents the primary key column value in a data source, which retrieves the data of other columns in a row based on the primary key. The DataKeyField property assigns the primary key of a data source.

What's the use of DataKeyField after setting its value to a primary key column of a data source? Well, let's say you want to retrieve, delete, and update a row in a data source bound to a DataList control. The only way to track down a row is through DataKeyField. DataKeyField is used in a handler for an event, such as ItemCommand or DeleteCommand, as part of an update query string to revise a specific record in the data source. So, DataFieldKey helps the update query string identify the appropriate row in a data source to modify.

The following code sets the DataKeyField property to the CategoryID column:

```
<ASP:DataList
id="dtList" RepeatColumns="5"
RepeatDirection="Horizontal"
GridLines="Both"
DataKeyField="CategoryID"
. . . . . . . . . . .
>
```

Understanding DataList Events

The DataList control supports events and provides method to raise events when items are being bound, edited, deleted, and created.

The ItemCreated event occurs when an item is created in the control. The event handler of the ItemCreated event receives an argument of type DataListItemEventArgs, which contains the data related to the event. You can use the OnItemCreated method to raise this event.

The ItemDataBound event occurs when an item is data bound to the control. You use this event to access the data item before it'll be displayed in the control. You can use the OnItemDataBound method to raise the ItemDataBound event.

A DataList control can have Update, Delete, and Cancel buttons, which can be used to update, delete, and cancel data in a DataList control, respectively. The ItemCommand event occurs when any button is clicked.

The CancelCommand event occurs when the Cancel button is clicked in a DataList control. You can use the OnCancelCommand method to raise this event.

The EditCommand event occurs when the Edit button of DataList is clicked. You can use the OnEditCommand method to raise this event.

The DeleteCommand event occurs when the Delete button of DataList is clicked. You can use the OnDeleteCommand method to raise this event.

The UpdateCommand event occurs when the Edit button of DataList is clicked. You can use the OnUpdateCommand method to raise this event.

The event handler of the ItemCreated, CancelCommand, EditCommand, DeleteCommand, and UpdateCommand events receive an argument of type DataListCommandEventArgs, which contains data related to this event. DataListCommandEventArgs provides information, which includes the argument for the command, the name of the command, the source of the command, and the item containing the command source in the control.

Listing 16-15 adds the Update, Delete, Cancel, and Edit command event handlers by using the OnUpdateCommand, OnDeleteCommand, OnCancelCommand, and OnEditCommand methods.

Listing 16-15. Adding Update, Delete, Cancel, *and* Edit *Command Handlers*

```
<asp:datalist
id="dtList" runat="server" CellPadding="4"
GridLines="Horizontal" RepeatColumns="5"
OnUpdateCommand="UpdateCommandHandler"
OnDeleteCommand="DeleteCommandHandler"
OnCancelCommand="CancelCommandHandler"
OnEditCommand="EditCommandHandler"
DataKeyField="CategoryID" BackColor="WhiteSmoke"
BorderColor="#CCCCCC" BorderStyle="Solid"
BorderWidth="1px" ForeColor="Black"
Font-Names="Verdana" Font-Size="8pt">
```

Listing 16-16 shows the code written on the event handlers for these commands.

Listing 16-16. The Code for the Update, Delete, Cancel, *and* Edit *Command Handlers*

```
Sub EditCommandHandler(sender as object, _
args as DataListCommandEventArgs)

End Sub

Sub CancelCommandHandler(sender as object, _
args as DataListCommandEventArgs)

End Sub

Sub DeleteCommandHandler(sender as object, _
args as DataListCommandEventArgs)

End Sub

Sub UpdateCommandHandler(sender as object, _
args as DataListCommandEventArgs)

End Sub
```

Editing, Updating, and Deleting Through a DataList Control

To see the real-world uses of DataKeys, templates, and DataList event handlers of a DataList control, let's write a useful editable DataList application. This application will display data from the Categories table of the Northwind database. The application will also allow you to edit, cancel, and delete data through the DataList control itself.

Actually writing an editable DataList control is little complex. So, you'll create a DataList by directly editing the code in an .aspx file. Once the DataList control is ready, you'll fill data to it and add event handlers for the Edit, Update, Cancel, and Delete buttons.

First, you create a DataList control and set its properties. You also make calls to the OnUpdateCommand, OnDeleteCommand, OnCancelCommand, and OnEditCommand methods, which raise the update command, delete command, cancel command, and edit command, respectively. The DataList control code is as follows:

```
<asp:datalist id="dtList" runat="server"
  CellPadding="4" RepeatDirection="Horizontal"
  GridLines="Horizontal" RepeatColumns="4"
  OnUpdateCommand="UpdateCommandHandler"
  OnDeleteCommand="DeleteCommandHandler"
  OnCancelCommand="CancelCommandHandler"
  OnEditCommand="EditCommandHandler"
  DataKeyField="CategoryID" BackColor="WhiteSmoke"
  BorderColor="#CCCCCC" BorderStyle="Solid" BorderWidth="1px"
  ForeColor="Black" Font-Names="Verdana" Font-Size="8pt">
```

Second, format and set a layout for the control. For this example, set the header, footer, selected item, item, alternating item, and edit item templates. On ItemTemplate and AlternatingItemTemplate, add a LinkButton control with a CommandName of Edit, which means it'll be responsible for raising the EditCommand event. The following code adds an Edit link button to the items of a DataList control:

```
<asp:LinkButton Text="Edit" CommandName="Edit"
  RunAt="server">
  </asp:LinkButton>
```

The code for ItemTemplate and AlternatingItemTemplate is as follows:

```
<ItemTemplate>
  <b>Category ID:</b>
  <%# Container.DataItem("CategoryID") %>
  <br>
  <b>Category Name:</b>
  <%# Container.DataItem("CategoryName") %>
  <br>
  <b>Description:</b>
  <%# Container.DataItem("Description") %>
  <br>
  <asp:LinkButton Text="Edit" CommandName="Edit"
  RunAt="server">
  </asp:LinkButton>
</ItemTemplate>
```

```
<AlternatingItemTemplate>
  <font face="verdana" color="green" size="1"><b>Category ID:</b>
   <%# Container.DataItem("CategoryID") %>
  <br>
  <b>Category Name:</b>
  <%# Container.DataItem("CategoryName") %>
  <br>
  <b>Description:</b>
  <%# Container.DataItem("Description") %>
  <br>
  <asp:LinkButton Text="Edit" CommandName="Edit"
  RunAt="server" ID="Linkbutton1" NAME="Linkbutton1">
  </asp:LinkButton>
  </font>
</AlternatingItemTemplate>
```

As you can see from the previous code, you simply display the contents of the Categories table and, in the end, add the Edit link button. You also set the header and footer styles of the control.

EditItemTemplate is another template that plays a major role in creating an editable DataList control. This is the template where you set the types of control being used when a DataList control is in edit mode. When a DataList control is in edit mode, you want to allow users to edit the CategoryName and Description columns of the Categories table. To do so, you need to create TextBox controls so the user can edit new values. Besides the TextBox controls, you need to allow options to save changes, cancel changes, and delete an item from the DataList. The following code snippet adds TextBox controls and link buttons to the edited item of the DataList control:

```
<EditItemTemplate>
  <b>Category Name:</b>
  <br>
  <asp:TextBox ID="catNameTextBox"
  Text='<%# Container.DataItem("CategoryName") %>'
  Runat="server"
  Font-Names="Verdana" Font-Size="8pt"
  BorderStyle="Groove" />
  <br>
  <b>Description</b>
  <br>
  <asp:TextBox ID="desTextBox"
  Text='<%# Container.DataItem("Description") %>'
  Runat="server"
```

```
    Font-Names="Verdana" Font-Size="8pt"
    BorderStyle="Groove" />
    <br>
    <asp:LinkButton Text="Cancel" CommandName="cancel" Runat="server" />
    <asp:LinkButton Text="Delete" CommandName="delete" Runat="server" />
    <asp:LinkButton Text="Update" CommandName="update" Runat="server" />
</EditItemTemplate>
```

The next step is to load data to the control. You create a method called FillDataList, which binds data to the DataList control based on the items specified in ItemTemplate and AlternatingItemTemplate, as shown earlier.

You call the FillDataList method on the Page_Load event, as shown in the following code:

```
Sub Page_Load
  If not IsPostBack
  FillDataList()
  End If
End Sub
```

Now you write the EditCommand event handler, where you set EditItemIndex of the DataList control to the ItemIndex of DataListCommandEventArgs.Item returned by the EditCommand handler. After setting EditItemIndex of DataList, you refill data to the control by calling the FillDataList method, as shown in the following code:

```
Sub EditCommandHandler(sender as object, _
args as DataListCommandEventArgs)
  dtList.EditItemIndex = args.Item.ItemIndex
  FillDataList()
End Sub
```

On the CancelCommand event handler, you simply set EditItemIndex of DataList to –1 and rebind the DataList control:

```
Sub CancelCommandHandler(sender as object, _
args as DataListCommandEventArgs)
  dtList.EditItemIndex = -1
  FillDataList()
End Sub
```

Writing code for the UpdateCommand and DeleteCommand handlers is little tricky. You probably can guess that on the UpdateCommand handler, you need to find out the index of the current item by using DataList.DataKeys, which returns the PrimaryKey column's value. Once you know the PrimaryKey, you can easily find out which record you want to update or delete. You can simply construct a SqlCommand and execute it.

The DeleteCommand event handler is as follows:

```
dim strId as string = dtList.DataKeys(args.Item.ItemIndex)
dim sql = "DELETE Categories WHERE CategoryID=@catID"
dim cmd as SqlCommand = new SqlCommand(sql, conn)
cmd.Parameters.Add("@catID", strId)
conn.Open()
cmd.ExecuteNonQuery()
conn.Close()
dtList.EditItemIndex = -1
FillDataList()
```

As you can see from the previous code, you simply get the CategoryID value for the edited item of the DataList control. Once you have the CategoryID value, you delete all records that match the CategoryID by constructing and executing a DELETE statement.

On the UpdateCommand event handler, you need to get the values of the CategoryName and Description columns and then construct and execute an UPDATE statement, as shown in the following code:

```
dim strId as string = dtList.DataKeys(args.Item.ItemIndex)
 dim strCatName as TextBox = args.Item.FindControl("catNameTextBox")
 dim strDesc as TextBox = args.Item.FindControl("desTextBox")
 dim sql = "UPDATE Categories SET CategoryName=@catName, " & _
 " Description=@desc WHERE CategoryID=@catID"
 dim cmd as SqlCommand = new SqlCommand(sql, conn)
cmd.Parameters.Add("@catID", strId)
cmd.Parameters.Add("@catName", strCatName.Text.ToString())
cmd.Parameters.Add("@desc", strDesc.Text.ToString())
conn.Open()
cmd.ExecuteNonQuery()
conn.Close()
dtList.EditItemIndex = -1
FillDataList()
```

NOTE *You also set the* EditItemIndex *of* DataList *to –1 and call the* FillDataList *method to refill the* DataList *control.*

Finally, Listing 16-17 shows the complete code.

Listing 16-17. Editable DataList *Control*

```
<%@ Import Namespace="System.Data" %>
<%@ Import Namespace="System.Data.SqlClient" %>
<HTML>
<HEAD>
<title>Editable DataList</title>
<script runat="server">

Sub Page_Load
If not IsPostBack
FillDataList()
End If
End Sub

Sub FillDataList()
Dim conn As SqlConnection
    Dim adapter As SqlDataAdapter
    dim connectionString = _
    "Data Source=MCB;Initial Catalog=Northwind;user id=sa;password=;"
    conn = new SqlConnection(connectionString)
    conn.Open()
    dim sql = "SELECT * FROM Categories"
    dim cmd as SqlCommand = new SqlCommand(sql, conn)
    dim reader as SqlDataReader = cmd.ExecuteReader()
    dtList.DataSource = reader
    dtList.DataBind()
    reader.Close()
    conn.Close()
End Sub

Sub EditCommandHandler(sender as object, _
args as DataListCommandEventArgs)
' code here
End Sub
```

```
Sub CancelCommandHandler(sender as object, _
args as DataListCommandEventArgs)
' code here
End Sub


Sub DeleteCommandHandler(sender as object, _
args as DataListCommandEventArgs)
' code here
End Sub


Sub UpdateCommandHandler(sender as object, _
args as DataListCommandEventArgs)
    ' code here
End Sub
</script>
</HEAD>
<body>
<form runat="server">
<asp:datalist id="dtList" runat="server"
  CellPadding="4" RepeatDirection="Horizontal"
  GridLines="Horizontal" RepeatColumns="4"
  OnUpdateCommand="UpdateCommandHandler"
  OnDeleteCommand="DeleteCommandHandler"
  OnCancelCommand="CancelCommandHandler"
  OnEditCommand="EditCommandHandler"
  DataKeyField="CategoryID" BackColor="WhiteSmoke"
  BorderColor="#CCCCCC" BorderStyle="Solid" BorderWidth="1px"
  ForeColor="Black" Font-Names="Verdana" Font-Size="8pt">
<SelectedItemStyle Font-Bold="True" ForeColor="White"
  BackColor="#CC3333">
</SelectedItemStyle>

<HeaderTemplate>
  <FONT face="verdana" color="#FFFFFF" size="3">
  <B>Editable DataList</B></FONT>
</HeaderTemplate>

<EditItemStyle BackColor="#FFC080"></EditItemStyle>

<FooterTemplate>
  <FONT face="verdana" color="#996600" size="1">
  DataList Control footer
  </FONT>
</FooterTemplate>
```

```
<ItemTemplate>
' item template code here
</ItemTemplate>

<AlternatingItemTemplate>
' alternative item template code here
</AlternatingItemTemplate>

<FooterStyle ForeColor="Black" BackColor="#C0FFC0">
</FooterStyle>

<HeaderStyle Font-Bold="True" ForeColor="#C04000" BackColor="#FF8000">
</HeaderStyle>

<EditItemTemplate>
' code here
</EditItemTemplate>

</asp:datalist></form>
</body>
</HTML>
```

If you run the application, the output looks like Figure 16-9.

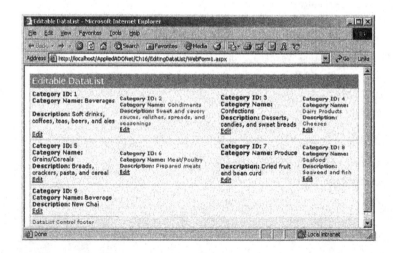

Figure 16-9. Editable DataList *control*

Now if you click an Edit link button, the item changes to editable form, which looks like Figure 16-10.

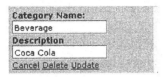

Figure 16-10. A DataList *control in editable mode*

The Update link button saves the changes, the Cancel link button ignores the changes and keeps the original values, and the Delete link button deletes the item.

Using the VS .NET IDE to Set a DataList's Properties

The VS .NET IDE provides limited support to the DataList control. There are two common ways to set a DataList control's properties. First, you can use the Properties windows; second, you can use the Property Builder. You call the Property Builder by right-clicking and selecting Property Builder or by clicking the Property Builder link at the bottom of the Properties window, as shown in Figure 16-11.

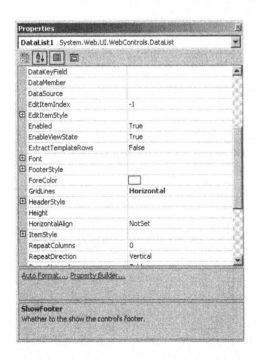

Figure 16-11. The Properties window of a DataList *control*

The first page of the Property Builder is the General page. On this page, you can set DataKeyField and other properties of the control. The Show Header and Show Footer check boxes indicate whether the header and footer will be displayed in the control. In the Repeat Layout section, you can set the Columns, Direction, and Layout properties.

The second page of the Property Builder is the Format page. On this page, you can set the format of the control, header, footer, items, and separators. From this page, you can set the properties such as background color, foreground colors, font, and alignment of each portion of the DataList control. You can even set the format of items, alternating items, selecting items, and edit mode items from this page.

The third page of the Property Builder is the Border Format page, which allows you to set the format of the DataList border. The properties on this page are cell padding, cell spacing, grid lines, border color, and border width.

Using the DataGrid Web Server Control

In Chapter 14, you learn about some DataGrid functionality. It discussed using data binding, setting a control's properties and styles using the Properties window as well as the Property Builder, writing event handlers, and implementing paging in a DataGrid control.

The DataGrid control's functionality doesn't end there; it provides much more than that. In this section, you'll see the rest of the functionality. You'll work in the HTML View because it's easy to understand and modify.

CAUTION *If you skipped Chapter 14, you should go back and read the "DataGrid and DataList Controls" section.*

The following code creates a DataGrid control programmatically:

```
<ASP:DataGrid id="dtGrid"
runat="server">
</ASP:DataGrid>
```

Similar to the DataList control, the DataGrid control provides a DataSource property, which binds data to the control. Once you have set the DataSource property, you call the DataBind method. Listing 16-18 reads data from the Categories table of Northwind and binds the filled DataSet to the DataGrid control.

Listing 16-18. Data Binding in a DataGrid Control

```vb
<%@ Import Namespace="System.Data.SqlClient" %>
<%@ Import Namespace="System.Data" %>
<HTML>
<script language="VB" runat="server">
  Sub Page_Load(sender As Object, e As EventArgs)
    If Not IsPostBack Then
      FillDataGrid()
    End If
  End SUb
  Sub FillDataGrid()
   Dim conn As SqlConnection
      Dim adapter As SqlDataAdapter
      dim connectionString = _
      "Data Source=MCB;Initial Catalog=Northwind;" & _
      "user id=sa;password=;"
      conn = new SqlConnection(connectionString)
      conn.Open()
      dim sql = "SELECT * FROM Categories"
      adapter = new SqlDataAdapter(sql, conn)
      Dim ds As Dataset = new DataSet()
      adapter.Fill(ds)
      dtGrid.DataSource = ds
      dtGrid.DataBind()
  End Sub
  </script>

  <body>
  <ASP:DataGrid id="dtGrid"
  runat="server">
  </ASP:DataGrid>
  </body>
</HTML>
```

The output of Listing 16-18 generates a page that looks like Figure 16-12.

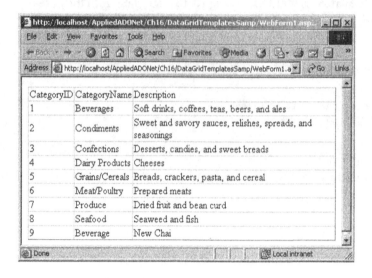

Figure 16-12. Data binding in a DataGrid *control*

Setting DataGrid Styles

Besides setting a DataGrid control's properties at design-time, you can always set a DataGrid control's properties (including style properties) from the .aspx page by simply editing the HTML code using the VS .NET IDE or a text editor.

The DataGrid control provides properties that can set the style of its various parts. The DataGrid style properties are AlternatingItemStyle, HeaderStyle, FooterStyle, EditItemStyle, ItemStyle, and SelectedItemStyle, which represent styles for alternating items, headers, footers, edit items, items, and selected items, respectively.

Each of these style properties is a type of the TableItemStyle class, which inherits from the Style class. The TableItemStyle class represents the style of properties for an element of a control. Table 16-7 describes the TableItemStyle class properties.

Table 16-7. The TableItemStyle *Class Properties*

PROPERTY	DESCRIPTION
BackColor	Background color of the item.
BorderColor	Border color of the item.
BorderStyle	Border style of the item. It can be Dashed, Dotted, Double, Groove, Inset, None, Notset, Outset, Ridge, or Solid.
BorderWidth	Width of the border.
CssStyle	Cascading style of the item.
Font	FontInfo, which defines how the font will be displayed.
ForeColor	Foreground color of the item.
Height	Height of the item.
HorizontalAlign	Horizontal alignment of the item.
VerticalAlign	Vertical alignment of the item.
Width	Width of the item.
Wrap	If true, items will be wrapped; otherwise not.

Listing 16-19 adds some colors to the DataGrid control by setting its ItemStyle, HeaderStyle, FooterStyle, AlternatingItemStyle, and EditItemStyle properties.

Listing 16-19. Setting a DataGrid *Control's Style Properties*

```
<ASP:DataGrid id="dtGrid"
HeaderStyle-BackColor=#003366
HeaderStyle-Font-Bold=True
HeaderStyle-Font-Name=verdana
HeaderStyle-ForeColor=white
HeaderStyle-Font-Size=10
ItemStyle-BackColor=black
ItemStyle-Font-Name=verdana
ItemStyle-Font-Size=8
ItemStyle-ForeColor=#ffcc33
AlternatingItemStyle-BackColor=LightSteelBlue
AlternatingItemStyle-ForeColor=black
FooterStyle-BackColor=#ffff99
FooterStyle-Font-Name=tahoma
FooterStyle-Font-Size=6
FooterStyle-Font-Italic=True
EditItemStyle-BackColor=red
EditItemStyle-Font-Size=8
```

```
EditItemStyle-ForeColor=#ccffff
ShowHeader=True
ShowFooter=True
runat="server">
```

Figure 16-13 shows the new DataGrid control.

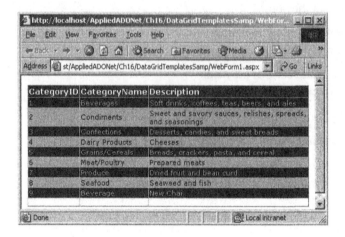

Figure 16-13. The DataGrid *control with the new styles*

Understanding a DataGrid's Columns

The DataGrid control provides control and manages a DataGrid's columns in different ways. You can manage a DataGrid control's columns at design-time as well as at runtime. The Columns property of the DataGrid control is the gateway to accessing and managing columns in a DataGrid at runtime. The Columns property represents a collection of DataGridColumn objects.

Using the AutoGenerateColumns Property

So far you've seen that if you bind a DataGrid control to a data source, the control displays all the columns available in a data source in the same order as they are defined in the data source. The AutoGenerateColumns property controls this behavior of the DataGrid control. If you want to change the order of the columns, or you want to customize a DataGrid control, you must set the AutoGenerateColumns property to false.

Actually, setting `AutoGenerateColumns` property to `true` automatically binds columns for all fields in the data source. Each field of the data source is rendered as a column of `DataGrid`. The `BoundColumn` class represents a bound column of a `DataGrid` control.

Using the DataGridColumn Class

The `DataGridColumn` class represents a column of a `DataGrid` control. A `DataGrid` control can have different kind of columns such as bound columns, button columns, edit command columns, hyperlink columns, and button columns. The `BoundColumn`, `ButtonColumn`, `EditCommandColumn`, `HyperlinkColumn`, and `TemplateColumn` classes represent the bound columns, button, edit command, hyperlink, and template column, respectively. The `DataGridColumn` class is the base class for all column classes.

The `DataGridColumn` class provides properties that can format a `DataGrid` column's header and footers. These properties are `FooterStyle`, `FooterText`, `HeaderImageUrl`, `HeaderStyle`, and `HeaderText`. The `ItemStyle` property gets the style of a column's items. The `SortExpression` property represents the name of the field or expressions, which are used in the `OnSortCommand` method when a column sorts its items.

Customizing and Rearranging a DataGrid's Columns

As you saw earlier, the `DataGrid` control generates a column for each column of a table in the data source in the same order as they're defined in the data source. But what if you don't want to display all the columns of a data source? One way to do this is to use a `SELECT` statement with the columns you want. There may be occasions when you want to control the column's display at runtime. For example, you may want to change the default order of the columns.

To allow the custom view and selection of columns, the first thing you need to do is disable the `AutoGenerateColumns` property:

```
AutoGenerateColumns=False
```

Now, because the `AutoGenerateColumns` property is false, you have to generate all the columns you want to display in a `DataGrid` control. You use `BoundColumn` for adding data-bound columns to the `DataGrid` control. You can use the `Columns` property of `DataGrid` and bind the `ASP:BoundColumn.DataField` property to the data source. Listing 16-20 displays the Description, CategoryName, and CategoryID columns of the Categories table in the same order.

Listing 16-20. Rearranging a DataGrid *Column's Sequence*

```
<ASP:DataGrid id="dtGrid"
AutoGenerateColumns=False
EnableViewState=False
runat="server">
<Columns>
<ASP:BoundColumn DataField="Description" />
<ASP:BoundColumn DataField="CategoryName" />
<ASP:BoundColumn DataField="CategoryID" />
</Columns>
</ASP:DataGrid>
```

The BoundColumn property provides the DataFormatString property, which can format the data of a column. You can even set the format of the BoundColumn header and footers. For this example, set the header and footer text for the columns by using the HeaderText and FooterText properties of BoundColumn. Listing 16-21 shows the final code.

Listing 16-21. Formatting BoundColumn's *Header and Footers*

```
<Columns>
<ASP:BoundColumn
DataField="Description"
HeaderText="Description"
FooterText="Category Description"/>
<ASP:BoundColumn
DataField="CategoryName"
HeaderText="Category Name"
FooterText="Name of Category"/>
<ASP:BoundColumn DataField="CategoryID"
HeaderText="ID"
FooterText="Category ID"/>
</Columns>
```

Figure 16-14 shows the updated DataGrid control.

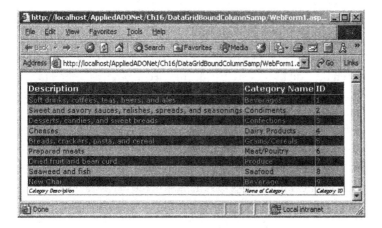

Figure 16-14. DataGrid *with* BoundColumns

Calling DataGrid Events

The DataGrid events play a major role in DataGrid customization. In this section, you'll learn about the DataGrid events, which you'll use in later examples. Table 16-8 describes the DataGrid control events.

Table 16-8. The DataGrid *Control Events*

EVENT	DESCRIPTION
CancelCommand	The Cancel button tells a DataGrid control not to save the changes made to the items. This event occurs when a Cancel button in a DataGrid is clicked. The OnCancelCommand method raises this event. The OnCancelCommand allows you to write a custom event handler for the CancelCommand, where you can get the data about a command. The CancelCommand event handler provides an argument of DataGridCommandArgs, which gets the data associated with a command.
DeleteCommand	The Delete button deletes an item of a DataGrid control. This event occurs when a Delete button is clicked. The OnDeleteCommand method raises this event. The OnDeleteCommand allows you to write a custom event handler for the DeleteCommand, where you can get the data about a command. The DeleteCommand event handler provides an argument of DataGridCommandArgs, which gets the data associated with a command.

Table 16-8. The DataGrid *Control Events (Continued)*

EVENT	DESCRIPTION
EditCommand	The Edit button edits a DataGrid control's items. This event occurs when the Edit button is clicked. The OnEditCommand method raises this event. The OnEditCommand allows you to write a custom event handler for the EditCommand, where you can get the data about a command. The EditCommand event handler provides an argument of DataGridCommandArgs, which gets the data associated with a command.
UpdateCommand	The Update button saves the changes made to a DataGrid. This event occurs when the Update button is clicked. The OnUpdateCommand method raises this event. The OnUpdateCommand allows you to write a custom event handler for the UpdateCommand, where you can get the data about a command. The UpdateCommand event handler provides an argument of DataGridCommandArgs, which gets the data associated with a command.
ItemCommand	This event occurs when any button on a DataGrid is clicked. The OnItemCommand method raises this event. Similar to previous event handler, the OnItemCommand event also provides an argument of DataGridCommandArgs, which gets the data associated with a command.
ItemCreated	This event occurs when the items of the control are created. The OnItemCreated method raises this event. This method also provides an argument of DataGridCommandArgs, which gets the data associated with a command.
ItemDataBound	This event occurs when an item is bound to a DataGrid control. The OnItemDataBound method raises this event. The ItemDataBound event handler provides an argument of DataGridItemEventArgs, which contains data related to this event.
PageIndexChanged	This event occurs when a paging selection of a DataGrid control is clicked. Chapter 14 covers this event in it "Paging in the DataGrid Control" section.
SortCommand	The DataGrid control has default built-in functionality for sorting. By writing a few lines of code, you can add the sorting functionality to a DataGrid control. First of all, you need to set the AllowSorting property of the DataGrid to true. Second of all, you need to write a SortCommand event handler. The SortCommand event handler provides an argument of DataGridSortCommandEventArgs, which returns data related to the sort command such as the column being used to sort the data.

Using the DataGridCommandEventArgs Class

This class provides data for the CancelCommand, DeleteCommand, EditCommand, ItemComand, and UpdateCommand events. The event handler of these events takes an argument of DataGridCommandEventArgs, which can be used to get the data about a command.

The CommandArgument property returns an argument for the command. The CommandName property returns the name of the command, which can be set by using a column's CommandName property. The CommandSource property returns the source of the command, and the Item property returns the item of the DataGrid that contains the command.

Using a DataGrid Control with Button Columns

The ButtonColumn class represents a button column. A button column can have two types: a push button or a link button. The ButtonType property of ButtonColumn represents the type of button.

The CommandName property is a string that represents the command to perform when the button is clicked. It's used to handle the button click event handler. The DataGridCommandEventArgs's CommandName property returns the CommandName of a column.

The DataTextField property binds a data source field to a button column, and DataTextFormatString represents the format of the column, which will be displayed in a DataGrid. The Text property represents the text of a column.

The following code creates two button columns:

```
<Columns>
<ASP:ButtonColumn
CommandName="Yes"
ButtonType=LinkButton
Text="Select">
</ASP:ButtonColumn>
<ASP:ButtonColumn
CommandName="No"
ButtonType=LinkButton
Text="UnSelect">
</ASP:ButtonColumn>
</Columns>
```

The next step is to handle the button click event. The following code adds an ItemCommand event handler to a DataGrid control:

```
<ASP:DataGrid id="dtGrid" OnItemCommand="dtGridItem" runat="server">
```

Now you'll change the format of the row clicked in a DataGrid control. Listing 16-22 shows the event handler of the button click. As you can see from this listing, you find out what command name was clicked and set the row's format accordingly.

Listing 16-22. The ButtonColumn *Click Event Handler*

```
Sub dtGridItem(obj as Object, args as DataGridCommandEventArgs)
  If (args.CommandName = "Yes") Then
    args.Item.BackColor = System.Drawing.Color.Gray
    args.Item.ForeColor = System.Drawing.Color.White
    args.Item.Font.Name = "tahoma"
  Else
    args.Item.BackColor = System.Drawing.Color.Black
    args.Item.ForeColor = System.Drawing.Color.LightSteelBlue
    args.Item.Font.Name = "verdana"
End If
End Sub
```

This DataGrid control looks like Figure 16-15 with the button columns. When you click the Select or UnSelect link button, you see the changes in the selected row.

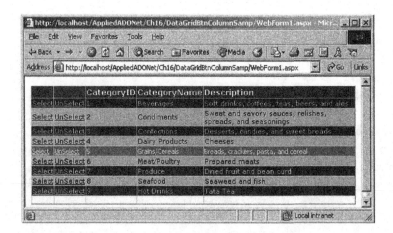

Figure 16-15. A DataGrid *control with button columns*

Listing 16-23 shows the complete code.

Listing 16-23. DataGrid *with Button Columns*

```
<%@ Import Namespace="System.Data" %>
<%@ Import Namespace="System.Data.SqlClient" %>
<html>
  <script language="VB" runat="server">
  Sub Page_Load(sender As Object, e As EventArgs)
    If Not IsPostBack Then
       FillDataGrid()
    End If
  End SUb

  Sub FillDataGrid()
   Dim conn As SqlConnection
      Dim adapter As SqlDataAdapter
      dim connectionString = _
      "Data Source=MCB;Initial Catalog=Northwind;" & _
      "user id=sa;password=;"
      conn = new SqlConnection(connectionString)
      conn.Open()
      dim sql = "SELECT * FROM Categories"
      adapter = new SqlDataAdapter(sql, conn)
      Dim ds As Dataset = new DataSet()
      adapter.Fill(ds)
      dtGrid.DataSource = ds
      dtGrid.DataBind()
  End Sub

  Sub dtGridItem(obj as Object, args as DataGridCommandEventArgs)
    If (args.CommandName = "Yes") Then
      args.Item.BackColor = System.Drawing.Color.Gray
      args.Item.ForeColor = System.Drawing.Color.White
      args.Item.Font.Name = "tahoma"
    Else
      args.Item.BackColor = System.Drawing.Color.Black
      args.Item.ForeColor = System.Drawing.Color.LightSteelBlue
      args.Item.Font.Name = "verdana"
    End If
  End Sub
```

593

```
    </script>
    <body>
      <form id="Form1" runat="server">
        <ASP:DataGrid id="dtGrid" HeaderStyle-BackColor="#003366"
        HeaderStyle-Font-Bold="True" HeaderStyle-Font-Name="verdana"
        HeaderStyle-ForeColor="white" HeaderStyle-Font-Size="10"
        ItemStyle-BackColor="black" ItemStyle-Font-Name="verdana"
        ItemStyle-Font-Size="8" ItemStyle-ForeColor="#ffcc33"
        AlternatingItemStyle-BackColor="LightSteelBlue"
        AlternatingItemStyle-ForeColor="black"
        FooterStyle-BackColor="#ffff99" FooterStyle-Font-Name="tahoma"
        FooterStyle-Font-Size="6" FooterStyle-Font-Italic="True"
        EditItemStyle-BackColor="red" EditItemStyle-Font-Size="8"
        EditItemStyle-ForeColor="#ccffff" ShowHeader="True"
        ShowFooter="True" OnItemCommand="dtGridItem" runat="server">
        <Columns>
          <ASP:ButtonColumn
          CommandName="Yes"
          ButtonType=LinkButton
          Text="Select">
          </ASP:ButtonColumn>
          <ASP:ButtonColumn
          CommandName="No"
          ButtonType=LinkButton
          Text="UnSelect">
          </ASP:ButtonColumn>
        </Columns>
        </ASP:DataGrid>
      </form>
    </body>
</html>
```

Using a DataGrid Control with Template Columns

Templates are one of the ways to customize DataGrid columns. The TemplateColumn
class represents a template column in a DataGrid control. A template column
allows you to customize a column's layout.

Similar to other column classes, this class also inherits from the DataGridColumn class. Besides the functionality provided by DataGridColumn, this class provides properties to set the layout of header, footer, item, and edit items of the control. The HeaderTemplate, FooterTemplate. ItemTemplate, and EditItemTemplate properties provide the custom appearance of the header, footer, items, and items that are being edited (respectively).

For example, Listing 16-24 creates a TemplateColumn and sets its ItemTemplate, HeaderTemplate, and FooterTemplates properties.

Listing 16-24. Using Template Columns

```
<Columns>

    <ASP:TemplateColumn>
    <ItemTemplate>
      <FONT face="verdana" size="2">
        <BR>
        <B>Category ID: </B>
        <%# DataBinder.Eval(Container.DataItem, "CategoryID") %>
        <BR>
        <B>Category Name: </B>
        <%# DataBinder.Eval(Container.DataItem, "CategoryName")%>
        <BR>
        <B>Description: </B>
        <%# DataBinder.Eval(Container.DataItem, "Description") %>
        <BR>
      </FONT>
    </ItemTemplate>
    <HeaderTemplate>
      <font face="verdana" size="3">
      DataGrid with Template Columns
      </font>
    </HeaderTemplate>
    <FooterTemplate>
      <font face="verdana" size="2">DataGrid Footer </font>
    </FooterTemplate>
  </ASP:TemplateColumn>
</Columns>
```

Figure 16-16 shows the result of using template columns.

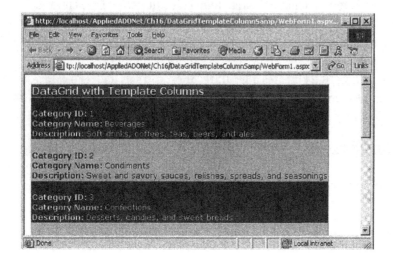

Figure 16-16. Using template columns

Listing 16-25 shows the complete code.

Listing 16-25. Using Template Columns in a DataGrid *Control*

```
<%@ Import Namespace="System.Data" %>
<%@ Import Namespace="System.Data.SqlClient" %>
<html>
  <script language="VB" runat="server">
  Sub Page_Load(sender As Object, e As EventArgs)
    If Not IsPostBack Then
        FillDataGrid()
    End If
  End SUb

  Sub FillDataGrid()
   Dim conn As SqlConnection
      Dim adapter As SqlDataAdapter
      dim connectionString = _
      "Data Source=MCB;Initial Catalog=Northwind;" & _
      "user id=sa;password=;"
      conn = new SqlConnection(connectionString)
      conn.Open()
```

```
    dim sql = "SELECT * FROM Categories"
    adapter = new SqlDataAdapter(sql, conn)
    Dim ds As Dataset = new DataSet()
    adapter.Fill(ds)
    dtGrid.DataSource = ds
    dtGrid.DataBind()
End Sub
</script>
<body>
  <form id="Form1" runat="server">
    <ASP:DataGrid id="dtGrid" HeaderStyle-BackColor="#003366"
    HeaderStyle-Font-Bold="True" HeaderStyle-Font-Name="verdana"
    HeaderStyle-ForeColor="white" HeaderStyle-Font-Size="10"
    ItemStyle-BackColor="black" ItemStyle-Font-Name="verdana"
    ItemStyle-Font-Size="8" ItemStyle-ForeColor="#ffcc33"
    AlternatingItemStyle-BackColor="LightSteelBlue"
    AlternatingItemStyle-ForeColor="black"
    FooterStyle-BackColor="#ffff99" FooterStyle-Font-Name="tahoma"
    FooterStyle-Font-Size="6" FooterStyle-Font-Italic="True"
    EditItemStyle-BackColor="red" EditItemStyle-Font-Size="8"
    EditItemStyle-ForeColor="#ccffff"
    ShowHeader="True" ShowFooter="True"
    AutoGenerateColumns="False"  runat="server">
      <Columns>

          <ASP:TemplateColumn>
          <ItemTemplate>
            <FONT face="verdana" size="2">
              <BR>
              <B>Category ID: </B>
              <%# DataBinder.Eval(Container.DataItem, "CategoryID") %>
              <BR>
              <B>Category Name: </B>
              <%# DataBinder.Eval(Container.DataItem, "CategoryName")%>
              <BR>
              <B>Description: </B>
              <%# DataBinder.Eval(Container.DataItem, "Description") %>
              <BR>
            </FONT>
          </ItemTemplate>
          <HeaderTemplate>
            <font face="verdana" size="3">
            DataGrid with Template Columns
```

```
          </font>
        </HeaderTemplate>
        <FooterTemplate>
          <font face="verdana" size="2">DataGrid Footer </font>
        </FooterTemplate>
      </ASP:TemplateColumn>
    </Columns>
  </ASP:DataGrid>
  </form>
 </body>
</html>
```

Creating an Editable DataGrid

Writing an editable DataGrid is one more useful feature of a DataGrid control.
You allow users to add, delete, edit, and save changes through a DataGrid control.
Adding data to a DataGrid is pretty simple; you don't need to use any special code.
You simply use some TextBox controls to get input from the user, construct a SQL
statement, execute the SQL statement, and refill the DataGrid control. When you
need to delete some data, you can simply find out the primary key of the row you
want to delete, construct a SQL statement, execute the statement, and refill the
DataGrid.

Editing, in other words, is no more difficult than adding and deleting the data.
Unlike the Windows Forms DataGrid control, the ASP.NET DataGrid control doesn't
have an edit mode. To make an ASP.NET DataGrid control editable, you need to
add TextBox controls and place them as the DataGrid items. Once the user is done
editing, you need to provide a mechanism to read the data from the TextBox
controls and then construct an UPDATE SQL statement, execute it, and refill the
DataGrid with new data.

So, the first thing you need to do is to provide some buttons for the DataGrid
control, which can set a DataGrid in editable mode. You can do this with the help of
EditCommand columns. The EditCommand column adds an Edit button to the DataGrid
control. When you click the Edit button, it changes the control's current cells into
TextBox controls and provides Update and Cancel buttons.

The `EditCommandColumn` class represents an `EditCommand` column. This class provides properties including `ButtonType`, `CancelText`, `EditText`, and `UpdateText`. The `ButtonType` property represents whether the buttons are hyperlink buttons or push buttons. The `CancelText`, `EditText`, and `UpdateText` properties represent the text of the Cancel, Edit, and Update buttons. For example, the following code sets the `EditCommandColumn` properties:

```
<asp:EditCommandColumn
ButtonType="LinkButton"
UpdateText="Save"
CancelText="Cancel"
EditText="Edit">
  <ItemStyle Font-Names="verdana" ForeColor="White"
  BackColor="Red">
  </ItemStyle>
</asp:EditCommandColumn>
```

The `DataGrid` control with an `EditCommandColumn` looks like Figure 16-17.

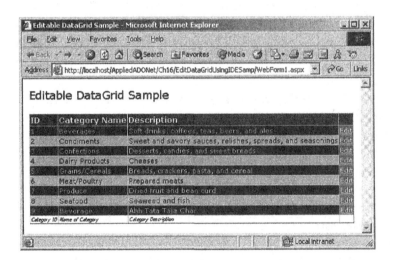

Figure 16-17. `DataGrid` *with* `EditCommandColumn`

If you click the Edit button, the current row of the `DataGrid` will have `TextBox` controls and the Edit button will be replaced with Save and Cancel buttons, as shown in Figure 16-18.

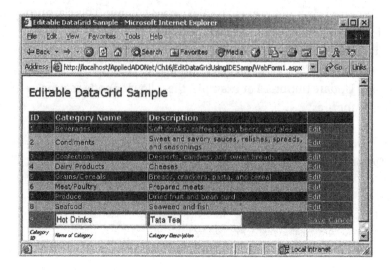

Figure 16-18. DataGrid *with Save and Cancel options*

 NOTE *You can change the text of the Update and Cancel buttons by setting the* EditText, UpdateText, *and* CancelText *properties.*

After setting the EditCommandColumn properties, you need to write the button click event handlers. The OnCancelCommand, OnUpdateCommand, and OnEditCommand methods of the DataGrid control are responsible for raising the Cancel, Update, and Edit button click events, respectively. The following code adds event handlers for these commands:

```
OnCancelCommand="dtGridCancel"
OnUpdateCommand="dtGridUpdate"
OnEditCommand="dtGridEdit"
DataKeyField="CategoryID"
```

Now you need to write the code for these command handlers. Editing in a DataGrid control works in a similar way to the DataList control. Listing 16-26 shows the complete code of an editable DataGrid.

Listing 16-26. Editable DataGrid

```vb
<%@ Import Namespace="System.Data.SqlClient" %>
<%@ Import Namespace="System.Data" %>
<HTML>
  <HEAD>
    <title>Editable DataGrid Sample</title>
    <script language="VB" runat="server">
Shared ConnectionString As String = "user id=sa;password=;" & _
    "Initial Catalog=Northwind;" & _
    "Data Source=MCB;"
  Shared conn As SqlConnection = Nothing
  Shared adapter As SqlDataAdapter = Nothing
  Shared sql As String = Nothing
  Shared cmd as SqlCommand = Nothing
  Shared ds as DataSet = Nothing

  Private Sub Page_Load(ByVal sender As System.Object, _
  ByVal e As System.EventArgs) Handles MyBase.Load
    'Put user code to initialize the page here
    If Not IsPostBack Then
      FillDataGrid()
    End If
  End Sub

  ' FillDataGrid method
  Private Sub FillDataGrid()
    conn = New SqlConnection(ConnectionString)
    If conn.State <> ConnectionState.Closed Then
      conn.Open()
    End If
    sql = "SELECT * FROM Categories"
    ds = New DataSet()
    adapter = New SqlDataAdapter(sql, conn)
    adapter.Fill(ds)
    dtGrid.DataSource = ds.Tables(0)
    dtGrid.DataBind()
    If conn.State = ConnectionState.Open Then
      conn.Close()
    End If
  End Sub
```

```vbnet
' EditCommand event handler
Sub dtGridEdit(obj as Object, args as DataGridCommandEventArgs)
  dtGrid.EditItemIndex = args.Item.ItemIndex
  FillDataGrid()
End Sub
' UpdateCommand Event handler
Sub dtGridUpdate(obj as Object, args as DataGridCommandEventArgs)
  Dim catId as Integer
  Dim strName as String
  Dim strDes as String
  Dim catNameTextBox as TextBox
  Dim desTextBox as TextBox
  ' Read text from text boxes
  catId = dtGrid.DataKeys(args.Item.ItemIndex)
  catNameTextBox = args.Item.Cells(1).Controls(0)
  desTextBox = args.Item.Cells(2).Controls(0)
  strName = catNameTextBox.Text
  strDes = desTextBox.Text
  ' Construct an UPDATE SQL statement
  sql = "UPDATE Categories SET CategoryName=@catName, " & _
  " Description=@desc WHERE CategoryID=@id"
  ' Construct a SqlCommand
  cmd = new SqlCommand(sql, conn)
  ' Add parameters to the command with the values
  ' read from text boxes and category ID
  cmd.Parameters.Add("@id", catId)
  cmd.Parameters.Add("@catName", strName)
  cmd.Parameters.Add("@desc", strDes)
  ' Open the connection
  conn.Open()
  ' Execute SQL statement
  cmd.ExecuteNonQuery()
  ' Close the connection
  conn.Close()
  ' Close editing mode of DataGrid
  dtGrid.EditItemIndex = -1
  ' Refill DataGrid with the updated data
  FillDataGrid()

End Sub
' CancelCommand Event handler
Sub dtGridCancel(obj as Object, args as DataGridCommandEventArgs)
  dtGrid.EditItemIndex = -1
  FillDataGrid()
End Sub
```

```
' Sort Event handler
Sub dtGridSort(obj as Object, args as DataGridSortCommandEventArgs)
  Dim sortExpr as String
  ' Open the connection
  If conn.State <> ConnectionState.Closed Then
    conn.Open()
  End If
  ' Get the column from SortCommand Event Args
  sortExpr = args.SortExpression
  ' Create a SELECT Statement with ORDER BY the expression
  sql = "SELECT * FROM Categories ORDER BY " + sortExpr
  ds = New DataSet()
  adapter = New SqlDataAdapter(sql, conn)
  adapter.Fill(ds)
  dtGrid.DataSource = ds.Tables(0)
  dtGrid.DataBind()
  If conn.State = ConnectionState.Open Then
    conn.Close()
  End If

End Sub

  </script>
</HEAD>
<BODY>
  <font face="verdana" size="4">Editable DataGrid Sample</font>
  <br>
  <form runat="server">
    <ASP:DataGrid id="dtGrid" HeaderStyle-BackColor="#003366"
    HeaderStyle-Font-Bold="True" HeaderStyle-Font-Name="verdana"
    HeaderStyle-ForeColor="white" HeaderStyle-Font-Size="10"
    ItemStyle-BackColor="black" ItemStyle-Font-Name="verdana"
    ItemStyle-Font-Size="8" ItemStyle-ForeColor="#ffcc33"
    AlternatingItemStyle-BackColor="LightSteelBlue"
    AlternatingItemStyle-ForeColor="black"
    FooterStyle-BackColor="#ffff99" FooterStyle-Font-Name="tahoma"
    FooterStyle-Font-Size="6" FooterStyle-Font-Italic="True"
    EditItemStyle-BackColor="red" EditItemStyle-Font-Size="8"
    EditItemStyle-ForeColor="#ccffff" ShowHeader="True"
    ShowFooter="True" OnCancelCommand="dtGridCancel"
    OnUpdateCommand="dtGridUpdate" OnEditCommand="dtGridEdit"
    DataKeyField="CategoryID" AutoGenerateColumns="False"
    AllowSorting="True" OnSortCommand="dtGridSort" runat="server">
```

```
        <FooterStyle Font-Size="6pt" Font-Names="tahoma"
        Font-Italic="True" BackColor="#FFFF99"></FooterStyle>

        <HeaderStyle Font-Size="10pt" Font-Names="verdana"
        Font-Bold="True" ForeColor="White" BackColor="#003366">
        </HeaderStyle>

        <EditItemStyle Font-Size="8pt" ForeColor="#CCFFFF" BackColor="Red">
        </EditItemStyle>

        <AlternatingItemStyle ForeColor="Black" BackColor="LightSteelBlue">
        </AlternatingItemStyle>

        <ItemStyle Font-Size="8pt" Font-Names="verdana" ForeColor="#FFCC33"
        BackColor="Black">
        </ItemStyle>

        <Columns>
            <asp:BoundColumn DataField="CategoryID" ReadOnly="True"
            HeaderText="ID" FooterText="Category ID">
            </asp:BoundColumn>
            <asp:BoundColumn DataField="CategoryName"
            HeaderText="Category Name" FooterText="Name of Category">
            </asp:BoundColumn>
            <asp:BoundColumn DataField="Description" HeaderText="Description"
            FooterText="Category Description">
            </asp:BoundColumn>
            <asp:EditCommandColumn
            ButtonType="LinkButton"
            UpdateText="Save"
            CancelText="Cancel"
            EditText="Edit">
              <ItemStyle Font-Names="verdana" ForeColor="White"
              BackColor="Red">
              </ItemStyle>
            </asp:EditCommandColumn>
        </Columns>
        </ASP:DataGrid>
      </form>
    </BODY>
  </HTML>
```

Sorting and Searching in a DataGrid

The DataGrid control provides partial built-in support for sorting. The AllowSorting property's true value makes DataGrid columns link buttons, which can sort a column's values. The OnSortCommand method raises the sort event of the control. The following code activates the sorting in a DataGrid:

```
<ASP:DataGrid id="dtGrid"
AllowSorting="True"
OnSortCommand="dtGridSort"
runat="server">
</ASP:DataGrid>
```

The OnSortCommand handler provides sorting data as the name of the column by using DataGridSortCommandEventArgs.SortExpression, as shown in the following code:

```
' Sort Event handler
Sub dtGridSort(obj as Object, args as DataGridSortCommandEventArgs)
  Dim sortExpr as String
  sortExpr = args.SortExpression
  FillDataGrid(sortExpr)
End Sub
```

NOTE *The default sorting order is ascending. If you want to provide descending order, you need to construct an* ORDER BY *query with a* DESCENDING *option.*

Once you know the column, you can simply construct an ORDER BY query and refill the data in the control. Listing 16-27 shows the complete code for sorting in a DataGrid control.

Listing 16-27. *Implementing Sorting in a* DataGrid *Control*

```vb
<%@ Import Namespace="System.Data.SqlClient" %>
<%@ Import Namespace="System.Data" %>
<HTML>
  <HEAD>
    <title>Editable DataGrid Sample</title>
    <script language="VB" runat="server">
Shared ConnectionString As String = "user id=sa;password=;" & _
    "Initial Catalog=Northwind;" & _
    "Data Source=MCB;"
  Shared conn As SqlConnection = Nothing
  Shared adapter As SqlDataAdapter = Nothing
  Shared sql As String = Nothing
  Shared cmd as SqlCommand = Nothing
  Shared ds as DataSet = Nothing

  Private Sub Page_Load(ByVal sender As System.Object, _
  ByVal e As System.EventArgs) Handles MyBase.Load
    'Put user code to initialize the page here
    If Not IsPostBack Then
     FillDataGrid("")
    End If
  End Sub

  ' FillDataGrid method
  Private Sub FillDataGrid(str as String)
    conn = New SqlConnection(ConnectionString)
    If conn.State <> ConnectionState.Closed Then
      conn.Open()
    End If
    if str = "" Then
        sql = "SELECT * FROM Categories"
    Else
      sql = "SELECT * FROM Categories ORDER BY " + str
    End If
    ds = New DataSet()
    adapter = New SqlDataAdapter(sql, conn)
    adapter.Fill(ds)
    dtGrid.DataSource = ds.Tables(0)
    dtGrid.DataBind()
    If conn.State = ConnectionState.Open Then
      conn.Close()
```

```
    End If
End Sub

  ' Sort Event handler
Sub dtGridSort(obj as Object, args as DataGridSortCommandEventArgs)
  Dim sortExpr as String
  sortExpr = args.SortExpression
  FillDataGrid(sortExpr)
End Sub

  </script>
</HEAD>
<BODY>
  <font face="verdana" size="4">Sorting in DataGrid</font>
  <br>
  <form runat="server" ID="Form1">
    <ASP:DataGrid id="dtGrid"
    AllowSorting="True"
    OnSortCommand="dtGridSort"
    runat="server">
    </ASP:DataGrid>
  </form>
</BODY>
```

CAUTION *You can't use the text, ntext, and image data types in an* ORDER BY *clause.*

To implement searching in a DataGrid control, you need to read the name of the column and a value for which you're searching. After that you can simply construct a SELECT..WHERE clause and refill the data. If you don't want to sort and read data from a data source, you can simply create a DataView control from a data source using a DataSet, apply sort and filter criteria on a DataView, and bind the DataView to the DataGrid control. (See the DataGrid and "Implementing Search in a DataGrid" sections of Chapter 7 for more information.) Sorting and searching works in both the controls in the same way because it's done through ADO.NET. The only difference is the data binding.

Summary

Even though the data-binding concept in ASP.NET server controls looks similar to Windows Forms data binding, they work in totally different ways. In this chapter, you learned the basic concepts of data binding in ASP.NET server controls and how to implement data binding in simple and complex data-bound controls.

Templates and columns play a major role in the formatting and data binding of controls. This chapter discussed how templates and columns work in ASP.NET. We also discussed the various functionality of the DataList and DataGrid ASP.NET server controls.

In the next chapter, you'll create a real-world data-driven Web application using ASP.NET. You'll use the major data-binding concepts discussed in this chapter.

CHAPTER 17

Building Real-World Web Applications

CHAPTER 14 DISCUSSED the basics of ASP.NET and how to write data-driven Web applications using ASP.NET and ADO.NET. Chapter 16 discussed data binding in ASP.NET and ASP.NET server controls and how to use these controls to develop data-bound Web applications.

In this chapter, we'll use the functionality discussed in Chapter 14 and 16. In this chapter, you'll see how you can write a real-world online job board where candidates can post their resumes, recruiters can post their jobs, recruiters can browse the available resumes, and job hunters can browse and apply for the available jobs on the site.

Introducing the Job Board Application Specifications

The Online Job Board is an ASP.NET application that allows users to post their resumes. Interface-wise, the application has three main modules: login, resumes, and jobs. The login module is a simple page that allows users to log in to the site. The resumes module allows users to post their resumes and view all the available resumes in the database. The jobs module allows users to post their jobs on the site and view all the available jobs in the database.

Figure 17-1 describes the application architecture. As you can see from Figure 17-1, the first page the user goes to is the login page. From there, the user either can log in to the site or can register if they aren't already a registered user. Once user is logged in, there are four options: Post Jobs, Post Resumes, View Jobs, and View Resumes.

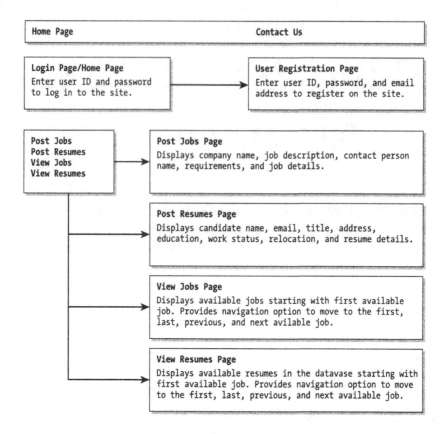

Figure 17-1. The Online Job Board application architecture

Understanding the Database Schema

For this application, we're using a SQL Server database to store the user, resume, and job-related information. To keep the application simple, we've used only three tables: Job, Resumes, and Users. The Job table has six columns (see Figure 17-2).

Column Name	Data Type	Length	Allow Nulls
Description	varchar	50	
Company	varchar	50	
Contacts	varchar	50	
Requirements	varchar	50	✓
Details	text	16	✓
PostingDate	datetime	8	✓

dbo.Job : Table (MCB.dnJobs)

Figure 17-2. Schema of the Job table

Figure 17-3 shows the Resumes table schema, which has 10 columns. These columns store the information about a candidate including a detailed resume.

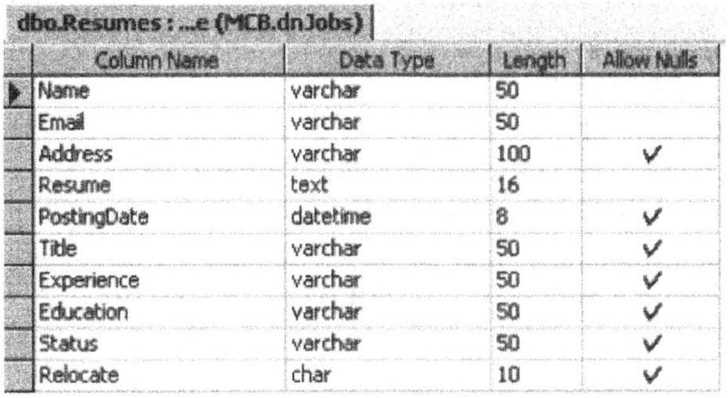

Column Name	Data Type	Length	Allow Nulls
Name	varchar	50	
Email	varchar	50	
Address	varchar	100	✓
Resume	text	16	
PostingDate	datetime	8	✓
Title	varchar	50	✓
Experience	varchar	50	✓
Education	varchar	50	✓
Status	varchar	50	✓
Relocate	char	10	✓

dbo.Resumes : ...e (MCB.dnJobs)

Figure 17-3. Schema of the Resumes table

Figure 17-4 shows the Users table schema, which has only three columns to store the user ID, password, and email address.

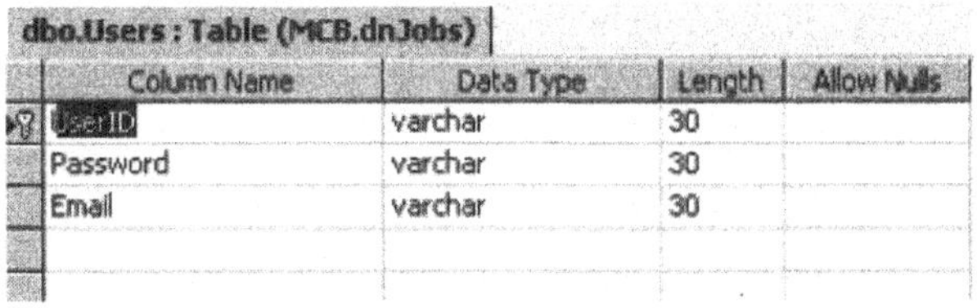

Column Name	Data Type	Length	Allow Nulls
UserID	varchar	30	
Password	varchar	30	
Email	varchar	30	

dbo.Users : Table (MCB.dnJobs)

Figure 17-4. Schema of the Users table

Developing the Online Job Board Application

When you start the application, the first page is Login.aspx. When you create an ASP.NET Web application, it adds WebForm1 as the first page of the application. You can simply change the name of this page to Login.aspx.

Creating the Login.aspx Page

The Login.aspx page allows users to enter their user ID and password and checks these against the data stored in the database. If the user ID and password are found in the database table, then you let them see the available options. Otherwise they need to register as a new user.

The Login.aspx page looks like Figure 17-5. As you can see from this page, it has two TextBox controls, one Hyperlink control, five Button controls, two Label controls, and a StatusBar control. When a user comes to this page, the buttons (Post a New Job, Post a New Resume, View Jobs, and View Available Resumes) are hidden. These buttons are visible when user successfully logs in to the site.

Figure 17-5. The Login.aspx *page*

Listing 17-1 shows the code for the Login button click event handler. Here you simply read the values entered in the User ID and Password TextBox controls and check if these values exist in the database. As you can see from this code, you create and open a connection, read UserID and Password from the Users table by creating a SqlCommand object, and call its ExecuteReader method that creates a SqlDataReader. You use only a single row because a single row will tell you whether the user exists in the table. After, that if the user exists, you display the Post a New Job, Post a New Resume, View Jobs, and View Available Resumes buttons and hide the TextBox, Label, and Hyperlink controls. You also display a message in the StatusBar control, if the user is logged in or not.

Listing 17-1. Login Button Click Event Handler Code

```
Private Sub LoginBtn_Click(ByVal sender As System.Object, _
ByVal e As System.EventArgs) Handles LoginBtn.Click

    ' Create and open a connection
    conn = New SqlConnection(connectionString)
    If (conn.State <> ConnectionState.Open) Then
        conn.Open()
    End If
    ' Construct a SQL string
    sql = "SELECT * FROM Users WHERE UserID='" + _
        IdTextBox.Text + _
        "' AND Password = '" + PassTextBox.Text + "'"
    ' and fill it
    Dim reader As SqlDataReader
    Dim cmd As SqlCommand = New SqlCommand(sql)
    cmd.Connection = conn
    reader = cmd.ExecuteReader(CommandBehavior.SingleRow)
    If (reader.Read()) Then
        PostJobBtn.Visible = True
        PostResumeBtn.Visible = True
        ViewJobsBtn.Visible = True
        ViewResumesBtn.Visible = True
        StatusBar.Text = "Logged In"
        Label1.Visible = False
        Label2.Visible = False
        IdTextBox.Visible = False
        PassTextBox.Visible = False
        NewUserLink.Visible = False
        LoginBtn.Visible = False
    Else
        StatusBar.Text = _
            "Enter a valid User ID and Password!"
    End If
    ' Close the connection
    If (conn.State = ConnectionState.Open) Then
        conn.Close()
    End If
End Sub
```

When you click the New User? Register Here HyperLink control, it simply opens the Register.aspx page. You do this by setting the NavigateUrl property of the HyperLink control as shown in Figure 17-6.

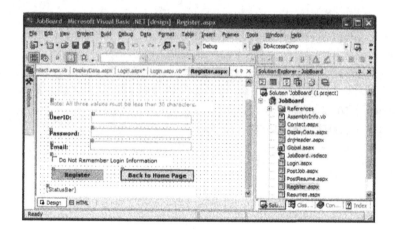

Figure 17-6. Setting the NavigateUrl *property of a* HyperLink *control*

The Post a New Job, Post a New Resume, View Available Resumes, and View Jobs button clicks simply open new Web pages: PostJob.aspx, PostResume.aspx, DisplayData.aspx, and Resumes.aspx, respectively (we'll discuss them in a moment). Listing 17-2 shows the code for these button click event handlers. As you can see, the code uses the Me.Response.Redirect method to open the new Web pages.

Listing 17-2. The Button Click Event Handlers

```
Private Sub PostResumeBtn_Click(ByVal sender As System.Object, _
    ByVal e As System.EventArgs) Handles PostResumeBtn.Click
        Me.Response.Redirect("PostResume.aspx")
End Sub

Private Sub ViewJobsBtn_Click(ByVal sender As System.Object, _
    ByVal e As System.EventArgs) Handles ViewJobsBtn.Click
        Me.Response.Redirect("DisplayData.aspx")
End Sub
```

```
Private Sub PostJobBtn_Click(ByVal sender As System.Object, _
    ByVal e As System.EventArgs) Handles PostJobBtn.Click
        Me.Response.Redirect("PostJob.aspx")
End Sub

Private Sub ViewResumesBtn_Click(ByVal sender As System.Object, _
  ByVal e As System.EventArgs) Handles ViewResumesBtn.Click
        Me.Response.Redirect("Resumes.aspx")
End Sub
```

Creating the Register.aspx Page

Now you add a new Web page called Register.aspx to the application. This page reads the user ID, password, and email address of the user. The page looks like Figure 17-7, where three TextBox controls are used to enter the user ID, password, and email address. The Register button click action saves these values to the database. The Back to Home Page button simply goes back to the Login.aspx page.

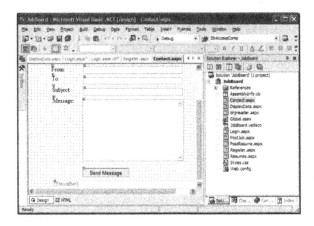

Figure 17-7. The Register.aspx *page*

Listing 17-3 shows the code for both of the button click event handlers. As you can see from this code, for the Register button, you construct a SqlCommand using an INSERT..INTO SQL query, add parameters and their values by reading from the TextBox controls of the page, and execute the query. This query adds a new record to the Users table of the database.

Listing 17-3. The Register.aspx *Code*

```vb
Private Sub RegisterBtn_Click(ByVal sender As System.Object, _
  ByVal e As System.EventArgs) Handles RegisterBtn.Click
    If IsValid Then
      ' Create a connection
      conn = New SqlConnection()
      conn.ConnectionString = connectionString
      'Open connection
      If conn.State <> ConnectionState.Open Then
        conn.Open()
      End If
      ' Construct an INSERT query with parameters
      sql = "INSERT INTO Users(UserID, Password, Email) " & _
      "VALUES (@id, @pass, @email)"
      cmd = New SqlCommand(sql, conn)
      cmd.CommandType = CommandType.Text
      ' Add parameters with values from text boxes
      cmd.Parameters.Add("@id", IdTextBox.Text)
      cmd.Parameters.Add("@pass", PassTextBox.Text)
      cmd.Parameters.Add("@email", EmailTextBox.Text)

      ' Execute the query
      Try
        cmd.ExecuteNonQuery()
      Catch exp As Exception
        StatusBar.Text = exp.Message.ToString()
      End Try
      ' Close connection
      If conn.State <> ConnectionState.Closed Then
        conn.Close()
      End If
      IdTextBox.Text = ""
      EmailTextBox.Text = ""
      StatusBar.Text = "Thank you registring with us."
    End If

End Sub

  Private Sub BackBtn_Click(ByVal sender As System.Object, _
  ByVal e As System.EventArgs) Handles BackBtn.Click
    Response.Redirect("Login.aspx")
End Sub
```

Creating the Contact.aspx Page

The next page you add to the application is the Contact.aspx page. This page sends a message. As you can see from Figure 17-8, you have TextBox controls for From, To, Subject, and Message. The From box takes the email address you're sending the message from; the To box takes the email address to which you are sending to the message. The Subject and Message boxes represent the title and the message body of the email, respectively. The StatusBar control displays the status of the message.

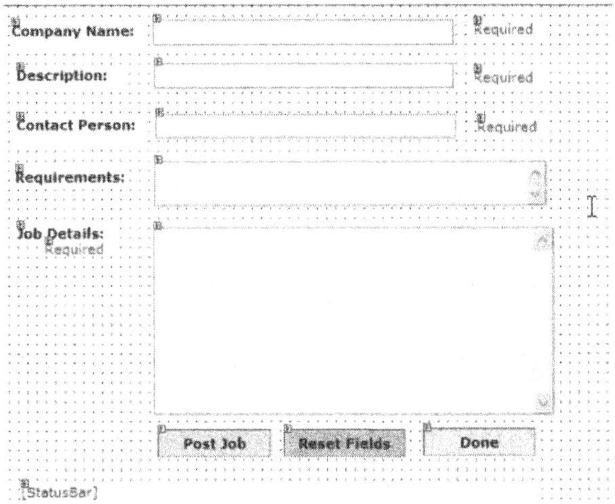

Figure 17-8. The Contact.aspx *page*

This page has only few lines of code for the Send Message click event handler, which is shown in Listing 17-4. As you can see from this code, you simply create a MailMessage that represents a mail message and set its From, To, Subject, and Body properties. After that we set SmtpMail.SmtpServer to the server, from which we're sending the email. Our mail server is mail5.fiberspeed.net. You must change it to your email server.

Listing 17-4. Send Message Click Event Handler

```
Private Sub SendMailBtn_Click(ByVal sender As System.Object, _
  ByVal e As System.EventArgs) Handles SendMailBtn.Click

    Dim msg As MailMessage = New MailMessage()
    msg.To = ToTextBox.Text
        msg.From = FromTextBox.Text
    msg.Subject = SubTextBox.Text
    msg.Body = MsgTextBox.Text
        SmtpMail.SmtpServer = "mail5.fiberspeed.net"
    SmtpMail.Send(msg)
    StatusBar.Text = "Message recieved. We will contact you soon. "
End Sub
```

Creating the PostJob.aspx Page

Now you add the PostJob.aspx page to the project. This page posts a new job to the job board. This page reads the information related to a job and adds to the Job table of the database. This page looks like Figure 17-9. As you can see from this page, there are five TextBox controls to read the company name, description of the job, contact person, requirements, and job details.

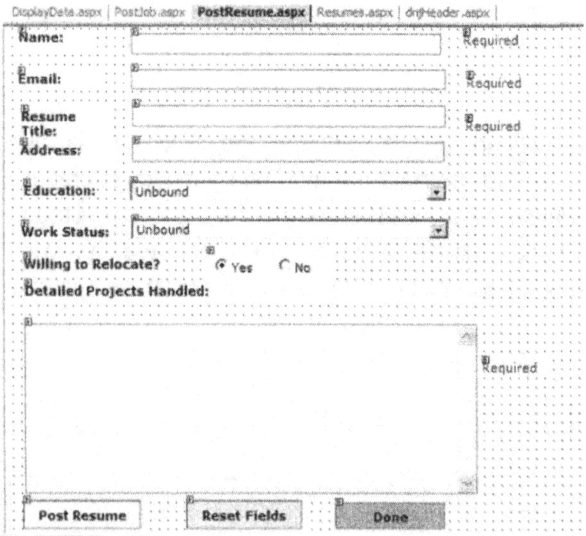

Figure 17-9. The PostJob.aspx *page*

Besides the `TextBox` controls, this page also has three `Button` controls and a `StatusBar` control. The Post Job button click event handler reads data from the `TextBox` controls and adds it to the Job database table. Listing 17-5 shows the code for the Post Job button click event handler. As you can see from this code, you simply construct a `SqlCommand` using an `INSERT..INTO` SQL query, add its parameters, and execute the query.

Listing 17-5. The Post Job Button Click Event Handler

```
Private Sub SaveBtn_Click(ByVal sender As System.Object, _
  ByVal e As System.EventArgs) Handles SaveBtn.Click
    conn = New SqlConnection()
    conn.ConnectionString = connectionString
    ' Construct an INSERT query with parameters
    sql = "INSERT INTO Job(Company, Contacts, Description, " & _
    "Requirements, Details, PostingDate) " & _
    "VALUES (@comp, @cont, @req, @des, @det, @post)"
    cmd = New SqlCommand(sql, conn)
    cmd.CommandType = CommandType.Text
    cmd.CommandText = sql
    ' Add parameters with values from text boxes
    cmd.Parameters.Add("@comp", CompanyTxtBox.Text)
    cmd.Parameters.Add("@cont", ContactsTxtBox.Text)
    cmd.Parameters.Add("@req", ReqTxtBox.Text)
    cmd.Parameters.Add("@des", DesTxtBox.Text)
    cmd.Parameters.Add("@det", DetailsTxtBox.Text)
    cmd.Parameters.Add("@post", _
    SqlDbType.DateTime).Value = DateTime.Today.ToString()
    ' Open connection
    If conn.State <> ConnectionState.Open Then
      conn.Open()
    End If
    ' Execute the query
    cmd.ExecuteNonQuery()
    ' Close connection
    If conn.State <> ConnectionState.Closed Then
      conn.Close()
    End If
    ClearFields()
    StatusBar.Text = "Thank you for Job Posting"
End Sub
```

The Reset Fields button simply clears the TextBox controls, as shown in Listing 17-6.

Listing 17-6. The Reset Fields Click Event Handler

```
Private Sub ClearFields()
    CompanyTxtBox.Text = ""
    ContactsTxtBox.Text = ""
    ReqTxtBox.Text = ""
    DesTxtBox.Text = ""
    DetailsTxtBox.Text = ""
  End Sub
  Private Sub ResetBtn_Click(ByVal sender As System.Object, _
  ByVal e As System.EventArgs) Handles ResetBtn.Click
    ClearFields()
End Sub
```

The Done button click event handler redirects the browser to the Login.aspx, as shown in Listing 17-7.

Listing 17-7. The Done Button Click Event Handler

```
Private Sub DoneBtn_Click(ByVal sender As System.Object, _
  ByVal e As System.EventArgs) Handles DoneBtn.Click
    Response.Redirect("Login.aspx")
End Sub
```

Creating the PostResume.aspx Page

The next page you add to the project is the PostResume.aspx page. This page allows candidates to post their resumes to the Job board. This page looks like Figure 17-10. As you can see from this page, you have a TextBox control for the name, email address, resume title, address, and detailed projects handled of a candidate. The Education and Work Status combo boxes list the options for candidate's education and work status. The Willing to Relocate radio buttons allow the candidate to set the option of whether he is willing to relocate.

Figure 17-10. The `PostResume.aspx` *page*

Now let's look at the code. You add the options to the Education and Work Status combo boxes. Listing 17-8 shows the code. As you can see, the `FillListBoxes` methods add options to the combo boxes.

Listing 17-8. Adding Options to Post Resume Page

```
Private Sub Page_Load(ByVal sender As System.Object, _
  ByVal e As System.EventArgs) Handles MyBase.Load
    'Put user code to initialize the page here
    FillListBoxes()
End Sub

Private Sub FillListBoxes()
    ' This method adds selection data to list boxes
    EduList.Items.Add("Master's Degree")
    EduList.Items.Add("Bachelor's Degree")
    EduList.Items.Add("Some College")
```

```
        EduList.Items.Add("2 Yrs Diploma")
        StatusList.Items.Add("US Citizen")
        StatusList.Items.Add("Green Card or Authorized to work")
        StatusList.Items.Add("H1 Visa")
        StatusList.Items.Add("Need Sponsorship")
End Sub
```

The Post Resume button click adds the contents of the page to the Resumes table of the database. Listing 17-9 shows the code for this button click event handler. As you can see, you again create a `SqlCommand` with an `INSERT..INTO` SQL query, sets its parameters by reading their values from the fields filled by the user, and execute the query. This option adds a new record to the Resumes table.

Listing 17-9. The Post Resume Button Click Event Handler

```
Private Sub PostResumeBtn_Click(ByVal sender As System.Object, _
  ByVal e As System.EventArgs) Handles PostResumeBtn.Click
    conn = New SqlConnection()
    conn.ConnectionString = connectionString
    ' Construct an INSERT query with parameters
        sql = "INSERT INTO Resumes(Name, Email, Address, Resume, " & _
        "Title, PostingDate, Education, Status, Relocate) " & _
        "VALUES (@nam, @mail, @add, @res, @tit, @post, @edu, @stat, @rel)"
    cmd = New SqlCommand(sql, conn)
    cmd.CommandType = CommandType.Text
    ' Add parameters with values from text boxes
    cmd.Parameters.Add("@nam", NameTxtBox.Text)
    cmd.Parameters.Add("@mail", EmailTxtBox.Text)
    cmd.Parameters.Add("@add", AddTxtBox.Text)
    cmd.Parameters.Add("@res", ResumeTxtBox.Text)
    cmd.Parameters.Add("@tit", TitleTxtBox.Text)
    cmd.Parameters.Add("@post", _
    SqlDbType.DateTime).Value = DateTime.Today.ToString()
    cmd.Parameters.Add("@edu", EduList.SelectedItem.Text.ToString)
    cmd.Parameters.Add("@stat", StatusList.SelectedItem.Text.ToString)


    If (RadioButtonList1.SelectedIndex = 1) Then
      cmd.Parameters.Add("@rel", "Yes")
    Else
      cmd.Parameters.Add("@rel", "No")
    End If
```

```
' Open connection
If conn.State <> ConnectionState.Open Then
   conn.Open()
End If
' Execute the query

Try
   cmd.ExecuteNonQuery()
Catch exp As Exception
   StatusBar.Text = exp.Message.ToString()
End Try

' Close connection
If conn.State <> ConnectionState.Closed Then
   conn.Close()
End If
ClearFields()
StatusBar.Text = "Thank you for posting your resume."
End Sub
```

The Done button click event handler simply redirects the browser to the Login.aspx page, as shown in Listing 17-10.

Listing 17-10. The Done Button Click Event Handler

```
Private Sub DoneBtn_Click(ByVal sender As System.Object, _
ByVal e As System.EventArgs) Handles DoneBtn.Click
    Response.Redirect("Login.aspx")
End Sub
```

Creating the DisplayData.aspx and Resumes.aspx Pages

The next two pages we'll discuss display the available resumes and jobs.
Add two Web pages to the project called DisplayData.aspx and Resumes.aspx.
The DisplayData.aspx page displays the available jobs, and the Resumes.aspx page displays the available resumes.

To display the data, you'll use the DataList control. (We discussed the DataList control and data binding in Chapter 16.) The final DisplayData.aspx page looks like Figure 17-11. On this page, the data is loaded when the page is loaded. The First Job, Previous Job, Next Job, and Last Job buttons move to the first, previous, next, and last jobs, respectively. The Home Page button redirects the browser to the Login.aspx page.

Figure 17-11. The DisplayData.aspx *page*

Listing 17-11 shows the complete code for the DisplayData.aspx page. As you can see from this code, you use templates to format and bind data to the template items. The tag <ItemTemplate> displays the data. (See Chapter 16 for more details about the DataList control and templates.)

Listing 17-11. DisplayData.aspx *HTML View*

```
<form id="Form2" method="post" runat="server">
    <ASP:DATALIST id="Datalist1" style="Z-INDEX: 100; LEFT: 1px;
     POSITION: absolute; TOP: 115px" runat="server" ShowFooter="False"
     Width="494px" BorderWidth="3px" GridLines="Horizontal" CellPadding="4"
     BackColor="White" BorderStyle="Double" BorderColor="#336666"
     RepeatDirection="Horizontal" RepeatColumns="1" Height="200px">
        <SelectedItemStyle Font-Bold="True" ForeColor="White"
            BackColor="#339966">
        </SelectedItemStyle>
        <HeaderTemplate>
```

```
    <FONT face="verdana" size="3"><B>.NET Jobs Listing</B></FONT>
</HeaderTemplate>
<FooterTemplate>
    <FONT face="verdana" color="#996600" size="1">
    DataList Control footer </FONT>
</FooterTemplate>
<ItemStyle HorizontalAlign="Left" ForeColor="#333333"
    VerticalAlign="Top" BackColor="White">
</ItemStyle>
<ItemTemplate>
    <FONT face="verdana" size="2">
    <BR>
    <B>Desciption ID:</B>
    <%# DataBinder.Eval(Container.DataItem, "Description") %>
    <BR>
    <B>Company Name:</B>
    <%# DataBinder.Eval(Container.DataItem, "Company") %>
    <BR>
    <B>Contact: </B>
    <%# DataBinder.Eval(Container.DataItem, "Contacts")%>
    <BR>
    <B>Requirements: </B>
    <%# DataBinder.Eval(Container.DataItem, "Requirements") %>
    <BR>
    <B>Posting Date: </B>
    <%# DataBinder.Eval(Container.DataItem, "PostingDate") %>
    <BR>
    <B>Job Details: </B>
    <%# DataBinder.Eval(Container.DataItem, "Details") %>
    <P>
    <b>
        <asp:HyperLink id="Hyperlink2" ImageUrl=""
        NavigateUrl="mailto:jobs@dnjobs.com"
        Text="Apply Now" runat="server" />
        <asp:HyperLink id="Hyperlink3" ImageUrl=""
        NavigateUrl="Login.aspx" Text="Home Page"
        runat="server" />
    </b>
    </FONT>
</ItemTemplate>
<FooterStyle ForeColor="#333333" BackColor="White">
</FooterStyle>
<HeaderStyle Font-Bold="True" ForeColor="White" BackColor="#336666">
```

```
            </HeaderStyle>
        </ASP:DATALIST></TD>
        <p></p>
        <asp:button id="Button1" style="Z-INDEX: 101;
            LEFT: 1px; POSITION: absolute; TOP: 91px"
            runat="server" Width="107px" BorderStyle="Groove"
            Font-Names="verdana" Font-Bold="True" Font-Size="8pt"
            Text="First Job">
        </asp:button>
        <asp:button id="Button2" style="Z-INDEX: 107;
            LEFT: 2px; POSITION: absolute; TOP: 56px"
            runat="server" Width="107px" BackColor="#C0FFC0"
            BorderStyle="Groove" Height="26px" Font-Names="Verdana"
            Font-Bold="True" Font-Size="8pt" Text="Home Page">
        </asp:button>
        <asp:button id="Button3" style="Z-INDEX: 103;
            LEFT: 108px; POSITION: absolute; TOP: 91px"
            runat="server" Width="115px" BorderStyle="Groove"
            Font-Names="verdana" Font-Bold="True" Font-Size="8pt"
            Text="Previous Job">
        </asp:button>
        <asp:button id="Button4" style="Z-INDEX: 104;
            LEFT: 223px; POSITION: absolute; TOP: 91px"
            runat="server" Width="105px" BorderStyle="Groove"
            Font-Names="verdana" Font-Bold="True"
            Font-Size="8pt" Text="Next Job">
        </asp:button>
        <asp:button id="Button5" style="Z-INDEX: 105;
            LEFT: 328px; POSITION: absolute; TOP: 91px"
            runat="server" Width="102px" BorderStyle="Groove"
            Font-Names="verdana" Font-Bold="True" Font-Size="8pt"
            Text="Last Job">
        </asp:button>
    </form>
```

Now you'll write code to load and navigate the data. Before you load the data, though, you define the following variables:

```
Public connectionString As String = _
  "Data Source=localhost;Initial Catalog=dnJobs; " & _
  "user id=mahesh;password=mahesh;"
  Public sql As String = Nothing
  Public conn As SqlConnection = Nothing
```

```
Public StartIndex As Integer = 0
Shared PageSize As Integer = 1
Shared CurrentIndex As Integer = 0
Shared TotalRecords As Integer = 0
Public ds As DataSet = Nothing
```

On the page's Load event handler, you call two methods: FillDataGrid and FillPartialData. The FullDataGrid method, shown in Listing 17-12, fills a DataSet from the Job table. On this method, you also count the total number of rows in the table and store them in the TotalRows variable, which helps you keep track of the rows.

Listing 17-12. The FillDataGrid *and* Page_Load *Methods*

```
Private Sub Page_Load(ByVal sender As System.Object, _
  ByVal e As System.EventArgs) Handles MyBase.Load
    FillDataGrid()
    FillPartialData(0)
End Sub

Private Sub FillDataGrid()
    ds = New DataSet()
    conn = New SqlConnection()
    conn.ConnectionString = connectionString
    ' Open connection
    If conn.State <> ConnectionState.Open Then
      conn.Open()
    End If
    sql = "SELECT * FROM Resumes"
    Dim adapter As SqlDataAdapter = _
      New SqlDataAdapter(sql, conn)
    adapter.Fill(ds, "Resumes")
    TotalRecords = ds.Tables(0).Rows.Count
    ' Close connection
    If conn.State <> ConnectionState.Closed Then
      conn.Close()
    End If
End Sub
```

The FillPartialData method reads data from the DataSet and creates a new DataSet based on the current index of the row and the page size. In this program, you only read one row at a time. Hence, the page size is 1. After copying data into a new temporary DataSet, this method binds this new DataSet to the DataList, called ResumeList, as shown in Listing 17-13.

Listing 17-13. The FillPartialData *Method*

```
Private Sub FillPartialData(ByVal start As Integer)
  Dim tempDs As DataSet = ds.Clone()
  Dim i As Integer = 0
  Dim range As Integer = start + PageSize
  For i = start To range - 1
    Dim row As DataRow = tempDs.Tables(0).NewRow()
    row(0) = ds.Tables(0).Rows(i)(0)
    row(1) = ds.Tables(0).Rows(i)(1)
    row(2) = ds.Tables(0).Rows(i)(2)
    row(3) = ds.Tables(0).Rows(i)(3)
    row(4) = ds.Tables(0).Rows(i)(4)
    row(5) = ds.Tables(0).Rows(i)(5)
    row(6) = ds.Tables(0).Rows(i)(6)
    row(7) = ds.Tables(0).Rows(i)(7)
    row(8) = ds.Tables(0).Rows(i)(8)

    tempDs.Tables(0).Rows.Add(row)
  Next
  tempDs.Tables(0).AcceptChanges()
  ResumeList.DataSource = tempDs
  ResumeList.DataBind()
End Sub
```

Now, on the First Job, Next Job, Previous Job, and Last Job button click event handlers, you simply call the FullPartialData method with a different index. As you can see from Listing 17-14, the First Job button click event handler passes the current index as 0, and the Last Job button click event handler passes the total rows minus the page size to read the last page. Similarly, the Next Job button click event handler passes the current index plus the page size, and the Previous Job button click event handler calls the current index minus the page size to the FillPartialData.

Listing 17-14. The FillDataGrid and Page_Load Methods

```
Private Sub FirstBtn_Click(ByVal sender As System.Object, _
  ByVal e As System.EventArgs) Handles FirstBtn.Click
    CurrentIndex = 0
    FillPartialData(CurrentIndex)
  End Sub
  Private Sub PrevBtn_Click(ByVal sender As System.Object, _
  ByVal e As System.EventArgs) Handles PrevBtn.Click
    CurrentIndex -= PageSize
    If (CurrentIndex < 0) Then
      CurrentIndex = 0
    End If
    FillPartialData(CurrentIndex)
End Sub
  Private Sub NextBtn_Click(ByVal sender As System.Object, _
  ByVal e As System.EventArgs) Handles NextBtn.Click
    CurrentIndex += PageSize
    If (CurrentIndex >= TotalRecords) Then
      CurrentIndex = TotalRecords - PageSize
    End If
    FillPartialData(CurrentIndex)
  End Sub
  Private Sub LastBtn_Click(ByVal sender As System.Object, _
  ByVal e As System.EventArgs) Handles LastBtn.Click
    CurrentIndex = TotalRecords - PageSize
    FillPartialData(CurrentIndex)
  End Sub
```

The Resumes.aspx page displays available resumes. You again use a DataList control to display the resumes. The final Resumes.aspx page looks like Figure 17-12. On this page, the data is loaded when the page is loaded. The First Resume, Previous Resume, Next Resume, and Last Resume buttons move to the first, previous, next, and last resume, respectively.

Figure 17-12. The `Resumes.aspx` *page*

Listing 17-15 shows the complete code for the `Resumes.aspx` page. As you can see from this code, you use templates to format and bind data to the template items. The `<ItemTemplate>` tag displays the data. (See Chapter 16 for more details about the `DataList` control and templates.)

Listing 17-15. `Resumes.aspx` *HTML View*

```
<form id="Form2" method="post" runat="server">
    <asp:datalist id="Datalist1" style="Z-INDEX:
    100; LEFT: 14px; POSITION: absolute; TOP: 124px"
    runat="server" Height="255px" Width="498px"
     BorderWidth="1px" GridLines="Both" CellPadding="4"
     BackColor="White" BorderStyle="None" BorderColor="#CC9966">

    <SelectedItemStyle Font-Bold="True" ForeColor="#663399"
        BackColor="#FFCC66">
    </SelectedItemStyle>
    <ItemStyle ForeColor="#330099" BackColor="White">
    </ItemStyle>
```

```
    <ItemTemplate>
        <FONT face="verdana" size="2">
        <BR>
        <B>Candidate Name:</B>
        <%# DataBinder.Eval(Container.DataItem, "Name") %>
        <BR>
        <B>Title: </B>
        <%# DataBinder.Eval(Container.DataItem, "Title") %>
        <BR>
        <B>Email:</B>
        <%# DataBinder.Eval(Container.DataItem, "Email") %>
        <BR>

        <B>Address: </B>
        <%# DataBinder.Eval(Container.DataItem, "Address")%>
        <BR>
        <B>Education: </B>
        <%# DataBinder.Eval(Container.DataItem, "Education")%>
        <BR>
        <B>Work Status: </B>
        <%# DataBinder.Eval(Container.DataItem, "Status")%>
        <BR>
        <B>Willing to Relocate? </B>
        <%# DataBinder.Eval(Container.DataItem, "Relocate")%>
        <BR>
        <B>Requirements: </B>
        <%# DataBinder.Eval(Container.DataItem, "PostingDate") %>
        <BR>
        <B>Resume Details: </B>
        <%# DataBinder.Eval(Container.DataItem, "Resume") %>
        /FONT>
    </ItemTemplate>
    <FooterStyle ForeColor="#330099" BackColor="#FFFFCC">
    </FooterStyle>
    <HeaderStyle Font-Bold="True" ForeColor="#FFFFCC" BackColor="#990000">
    </HeaderStyle>
</asp:datalist>
<asp:button id="Button1" style="Z-INDEX: 101; LEFT: 17px; POSITION:
    absolute; TOP: 101px" runat="server" BorderStyle="Groove"
    Width="107px" Font-Bold="True" Text="First Resume"
    Font-Names="verdana" Font-Size="8pt">
```

```
    </asp:button>
    <asp:button id="Button2" style="Z-INDEX: 103; LEFT: 124px;
        POSITION: absolute; TOP: 101px" runat="server"
        BorderStyle="Groove" Width="127px" Font-Bold="True"
        Text="Previous Resume" Font-Names="verdana" Font-Size="8pt">
    </asp:button>
    <asp:button id="Button3" style="Z-INDEX: 104; LEFT: 247px;
        POSITION: absolute; TOP: 101px" runat="server"
        BorderStyle="Groove" Width="105px" Font-Bold="True"
        Text="Next Resume" Font-Names="verdana" Font-Size="8pt">
    </asp:button>
    <asp:button id="Button4" style="Z-INDEX: 105; LEFT: 352px;
        POSITION: absolute; TOP: 101px" runat="server"
        BorderStyle="Groove" Width="102px" Font-Bold="True"
        Text="Last Resume" Font-Names="verdana" Font-Size="8pt">
    </asp:button>
    </form>
```

The code for filling data from the Resumes table to the DataList control and navigating through the resumes is the same as the code you saw on the DisplayData.aspx page for displaying a job. You just need to change the database table name from Job to Resumes in the FillDataGrid method. The rest is the same. For more details, download the source code from the Apress Web site (www.apress.com).

Creating the dnjHeader.aspx Page

There is one more thing left to do. To make the application a little more interactive, you'll design one more page called dnjHeader.aspx. This page has an image and two HyperLink controls: Home Page and Contact Us. The Home Page link simply redirects the browser to the Login.aspx page, and the Contact Us link redirects the browser to the Contacts.aspx page. This page works as a header of the job board. That means every page of the job board application includes this page. Figure 17-13 shows the dnjHeader.aspx page.

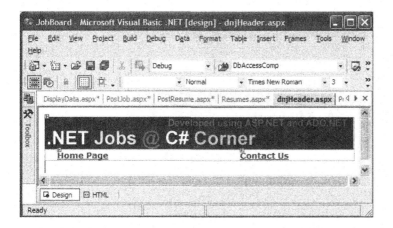

Figure 17-13. The dnjHeader.aspx *page*

To include the dnjHeader.aspx page, you use the INCLUDE keyword. The third line in the following code includes the page to other pages. You want to make sure you change the path of the page to your application's path:

```
<HEAD>
<title>Resumes</title>
<!-- #INCLUDE Virtual="/Ch17/JobBoard/dnjHeader.aspx" -->
</HEAD>
```

Running the Application

Now you're ready to run the application. When you run the application, the Login.aspx page will be the first page, which looks like Figure 17-14.

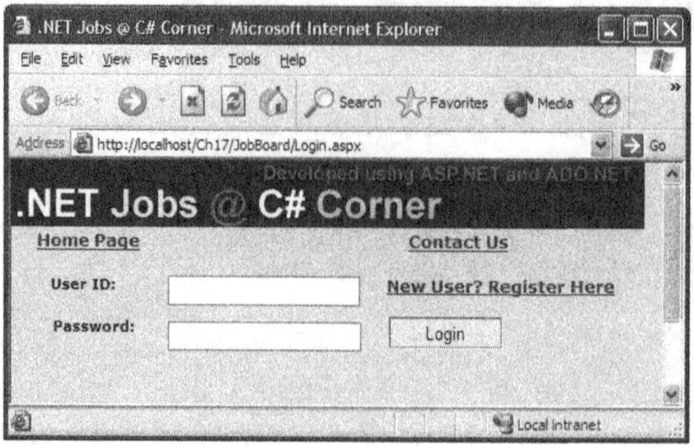

Figure 17-14. The job board

Once you register and log in to the site, you'll see job and resume options. You can test the application by posting a few resumes and jobs. After posting a few jobs and resumes, you can view the jobs and resumes by using the View Jobs and View Available Resumes buttons. The View Jobs page looks like Figure 17-15. You can use the buttons to move to the next, previous, first, and last job available in the database.

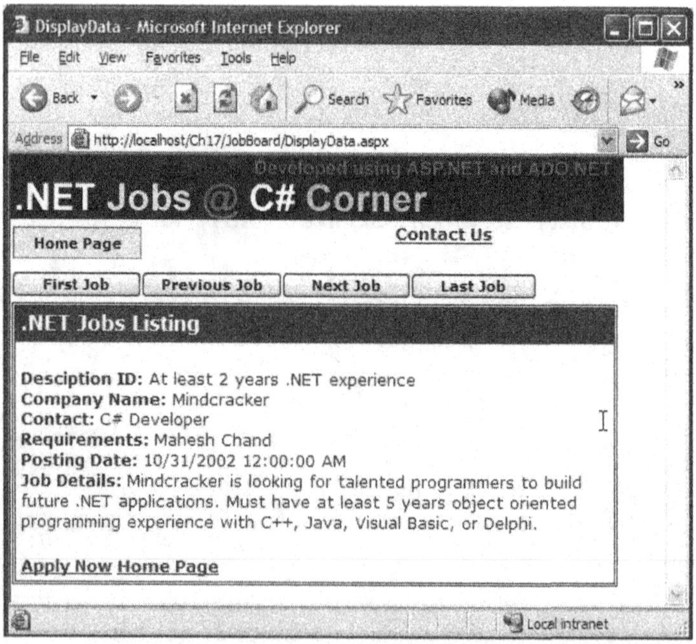

Figure 17-15. View Jobs page

The View Resumes page looks like Figure 17-16. You can use the buttons to move to the next, previous, first and last job available in the database.

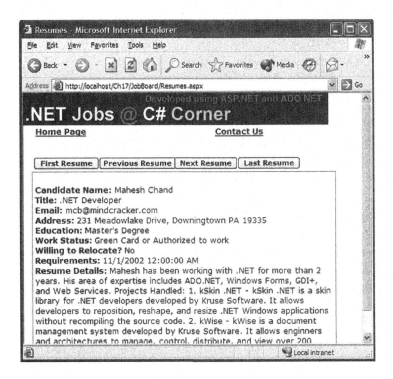

Figure 17-16. The View Resumes page

Improving and Modifying the Application

To keep in mind the size of this book and the chapter, we tried to limit the functionality of the Job Board application. However, you can modify the existing application to build a Job Board application with some more user-friendly features. Some of the possible improvements to the application could be the following:

- Adding the latest job listing on the home page

- Adding the latest resume listing on the home page

- Adding a search feature that can search jobs and resumes based on keywords

- Adding features such as a resume builder, search saves, personal pages, and other resources that can help candidates to build their resume online

- Categorizing jobs based on the state or country (if there is enough traffic on your site)

Summary

In this chapter, you learned how to build a real-world job application where employers can post their jobs and candidates can post their resumes. Object databases are quite useful in many situations, and as a developer there are quite a few situations when you need to deal with object databases as well as relational databases.

In the following chapter, we cover object and relational database mappings. You'll learn the basics of the object-mapped data model and how to create a simple video store application that allows users to load, create, and alter videos in the library as well as check in and out videos. You'll learn how to create mapped objects as well as workarounds for common pitfalls and quirks found in ADO.NET that can adversely affect your data model.

CHAPTER 18

Object-Relational Mapping in .NET

RELATIONAL DATABASES TREAT data in terms of rows and columns, and objects treat things in terms of arrays and properties. *Object-relational mapping* (OR mapping) bridges these two worlds so your code can look like object code and still store itself in a relational database.

In this chapter, you'll create a simple object data model for a video store application. You'll learn how to create mapped objects as well as workarounds for common pitfalls and quirks found in ADO.NET that can adversely affect your data model. Let's start by discussing why you may need to worry about OR mapping.

OR mapping provides three main benefits:

- **Encapsulation:** This is one of the primary pillars of object-oriented design, and OR mapping extends this concept to the database.

- **Identity:** A mapped object has an identity. In concrete terms it has a unique identifier. Most objects that are not mapped to a database lack a real identity independent of the data presented to the end user. Although it's possible to create an identity for the objects using hashcodes or a similar methodology, mapped objects take this to the next logical level.

- **Behavior:** Data in a database does not have behavior. By fusing the world of databases to software code, you have the unique opportunity to define how your data should interact with your system in a clean and reusable way.

Visual Basic .NET (VB .NET) takes the partial support for object-oriented programming found in VB 6 to the next level. By leveraging this expanded capability in VB .NET, you're presented with an opportunity to create powerful object systems with persistence into a medium that allows for easy integration with other systems and a simple way of reporting on that data.

Why Not Just Use a DataSet?

ADO.NET supplies you with a number of powerful objects including DataSet objects to provide a means of accessing and presenting data, but these objects fall short in situations where you need to provide a clear contract between the data and your object system. They also fall short in situations when you require complex validation, portability between multiple persistence mediums, or abstraction of data operation.

So, when does a programming problem require a clear contract to be defined between the data and the code? A good example is a situation where the data provides a means of recording history that then requires business logic to be applied to it before presenting it to the user or making a decision. For example, an order entry system requires that logic be applied to a user's entries before being stored into a database to determine if the user can purchase the selected items. This is a prime candidate for object-relational mapping.

Another situation when OR mapping can really help is when you have the need to enforce complicated data validation. Databases support enforcing relations and null vs. non-null values, but they do not (in general) have good support for complex validation. For example, if you need to make sure the user has provided at least one method of contact (such as a phone or email address), you can easily enforce this with a mapped object.

Many packaged applications need to be able to store the application data in multiple database systems and even be able to support situations where the user purchasing the software has no database at all (such as a flat text file). By keeping your application logic and data model in your objects, support for each persistence medium is as simple as adding handling in the data access components. If you use direct SQL or stored procedure calls throughout your code, you'll find portability a major problem.

The classic view of OR mapping involves abstracting a complex data model. A classic example is if you have the need to track employees, salespeople, and accountants. An employee is clearly the "base class" for the other types of employees. For example, all employees have name information, but only sales people have a sales territory code, and only accountants have a CPA certification flag. You would put the common parts in the Employee object (and related table in the database) and the task-specific information in a related object (and related table in the database).

In all of the previous cases, you'll find OR mapping beneficial in creating an easily manageable system.

Understanding Object Databases

Object databases such as Objectivity/DB, Poet, and Matisse started appearing in the 1980s as a proposed alternative to transaction-oriented relational database management systems. The idea was to treat data more intuitively as objects (Customer and Invoice objects, for example) instead of as a series of flat rows that have to be stored in tables and related via foreign keys. (For a good overview of object databases, see Doug Barry's site at www.odbmsfacts.com/articles/object-oriented_databases.html.)

A simple way of thinking about object databases is looking at how you would create a simple program that shows a list of all the users in your database.

Using SQL to get this data from your relational database, you would use the following statement:

```
SELECT * FROM Users
```

You would then have to take the data returned from the query, transform it into objects in your code, iterate through a list of users, and display the results. This is a hard-nosed look at the problem; technically you can just pipe the results directly out from the database, but in doing so you give up the encapsulation promised by object-oriented programming.

Using an object database, your code would look similar to the following statement:

```
Dim users As Users()
users = open('users').Load()
```

For listing all users, the object database wins in terms of simplicity. The data is acquired, and it's already an object with no need for a transformation to work with it. All you would need to do then is loop through the collection of users objects.

It gets a lot more complicated when you want to perform a "reporting" type of function on the database such as getting the total amount of orders to be shipped on a future date.

In SQL you can use the following syntax:

```
SELECT sum(Amount) FROM OrderedItems WHERE ShipDate > GetDate()
```

With an object database you would have to actually loop through all of the items in the OrderedItems collection and add each amount to the total. There are other options that different object database vendors support for summarizing data, but the options overall are not as simple and consistent as they are with SQL tables.

Ultimately, object databases never caught on for a variety of reasons. Some people feel strongly about to say that object databases are inferior to relational databases, but in the end the marketplace has spoken and the number of object databases in actual use in production systems is tiny.

So, although it's unlikely you'll ever run into a project that uses an object database, you can still work with objects in your code that store their properties in a database transparently, which allows you to focus on developing new functionality instead of worrying about breaking old code.

Why Object Relational Mapping?

OR mapping keeps the code in your application encapsulated and clean, and it makes it easy to manage changes in the database. By building an OR mapping component, your database logic will be encapsulated and hidden away from the rest of your system. Because the logic of loading and saving your object rests entirely in the OR mapping subsystem, the code in the rest of your program uses only clean object-oriented code. It also makes it far easier to make changes to the database later without having to alter every place you reference the data.

The core issue is short-term vs. long-term laziness. Using short-term laziness would probably put SQL queries directly in your Web pages and just use SqlDataReader objects to work with your data. Past the initial implementation, this method makes your code hard to maintain. If you add a column to the database, you'll have to find every reference to that table in your application and update it. Also, as the need to use the same table on multiple pages arises, you'll find yourself copying and pasting large sections of code to get the same functionality on these new pages as well.

Long-term laziness means taking the upfront time costs associated with building out the object relational mapping for your table. It will definitely take you longer to initially produce these objects, but in the long term it will mean much less work.

Creating the Basic Design of the Video Store Application

The OR mapping technique used in this chapter was inspired by a demo application from Microsoft intended to show best practices in .NET called *Duwamish7*. Downloading Duwamish7, reading through the source code, and truly understanding how it works can really help you become a much better .NET programmer. It covers topics such as statelessness, OR mapping, logical three-tier structures, and more. Download it from MSDN (http://msdn.microsoft.com) by searching for *Duwamish7*.

Understanding the Basic Architecture

Three objects make up a mapped object. These are the data object, the mapped object, and the Data Access Component (DAC). The DAC creates and fills the data object with data, then passes a single row of that data to create an instance of the mapped object.

The data object is simply an in-code representation of the database table you plan on using for an object. In .NET specifically, it's a subclassed DataTable or DataSet where you have defined what the columns names are as well as the data types. The application outside of the mapping never uses this object directly.

The mapped object uses your data object to point to a particular row of the DataTable found in the data object and maps the column names from the data object to easy-to-use property names. The mapped object is the primary interface between the rest of your application and your data.

The DAC is the glue that holds the data object and the mapped object together and persists the changes to the database. The DAC defines what stored procedures or database queries are necessary to load, insert, update, or delete your object's data from the database. Figure 18-1 shows the basic concept of OR mapping.

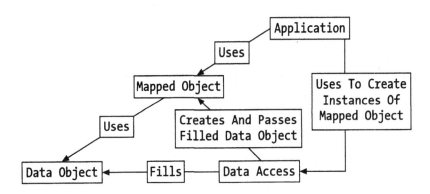

Figure 18-1. Basic concept of OR mapping

Creating the Database Design of the Video Store

The example for this chapter builds all of the data objects required for a simple video store application. It's probably too much to consider it a complete video store because you're not actually tracking money and late fees, but it'll do quite well to help you track your own video collection. It'll also come in handy if you have friends who borrow videos from you and you need to remember whom you let borrow what.

The design of the video store database is simple. At the core of this application is the VideoTape table, as shown in Table 18-1. The VideoTape table tracks only the title and description of the title in question. You could have quite a bit more information about a particular title and even expand the application to track DVDs as well as video tapes, but for this application, let's keep it simple. You can always expand this later to create a complete application.

Table 18-1. The VideoTape Table

COLUMN NAME	SQL SERVER DATA TYPE	.NET DATA TYPE
VideoTapeID	Numeric	Decimal
Title	Char (50)	String
Description	Text	String

The VideoTape table relates to the VideoCheckIn table (shown in Table 18-2) and the VideoCheckOut table (shown in Table 18-3) to model what is checked in and out. It also relates to the Users table to track who participated in the transaction. The information tracked in each table is the VideoTapeID, the date it was checked in or out on, the user who performed the check in or out, and the user to whom it was checked in or out.

Table 18-2. The VideoCheckIn Table

COLUMN NAME	SQL SERVER DATA TYPE	.NET DATA TYPE
VideoTapeID	Numeric	Decimal
CheckedInOn	Smalldatetime	DateTime
CheckedInByUserID	Numeric	Decimal
CheckedInFromUserID	Numeric	Decimal
VideoCheckOutID	Numeric	Decimal

Table 18-3. The VideoCheckOut Table

COLUMN NAME	SQL SERVER DATA TYPE	.NET DATA TYPE
VideoCheckOutID	Numeric	Decimal
VideoTapeID	Numeric	Decimal
CheckedOutOn	Smalldatetime	DateTime
CheckedOutByUserID	Numeric	Decimal
CheckedOutToUserID	Numeric	Decimal

The Users table tracks the people involved with the system (see Table 18-4). In a real-world situation, you would also provide a Login table so that the people involved with the system can log in and an access control system controls which users can actually check things in and out. Of course, to run a video store with this application, you'd also have to handle accounting and more, so don't get any ideas that this is a full-fledged application!

Table 18-4. The Users Table

COLUMN NAME	SQL SERVER DATA TYPE	.NET DATA TYPE
UserID	Numeric	Decimal
FirstName	Char (20)	String
LastName	Char (20)	String

We selected this particular application because it provides the opportunity to touch on many of the real-world issues you'll run in to when attempting to create a scalable Web application using .NET. Some of the topics ahead cover how to handle potentially large sets of data among dependant tables, how to manage the disconnects between the database's handling of null values, and how .NET handles null values. Additionally, you'll see some practical considerations to keep in mind when designing a scalable system with .NET.

Creating the Data Object

The data object represents what the table structure in the database is in your code. The data object is necessary for type safety and to provide a "bucket" for your data. You'll have to create a data object for each object in your database. You'll start by examining the VideoTapeData object, shown in Listing 18-1.

Listing 18-1. The VideoTapeData *Object*

```
Public Class VideoTapeData
    Inherits DataTable

    Public Sub New()
        MyBase.New("VideoTape")
        Me.Columns.Add("VideoTapeID", Type.GetType("System.Decimal"))
        Me.Columns.Add("Title", Type.GetType("System.String"))
        Me.Columns.Add("Description", Type.GetType("System.String"))

    End Sub
End Class
```

This code is fairly simple. You declare the VideoTapeData object as inheriting from the DataTable object. Basically what you're doing is taking the functionality of the existing DataTable object and turning it into a custom data type. Inside the constructor, you call the base class by calling MyBase.New to call the constructor of the DataTable object. The constructor for the DataTable object you're using in this example sets the table's name.

The rest of the constructor sets the names of each column as in the database and provides the .NET data types of each column. For example, the SQL Server data type Numeric is the Decimal object in .NET. The char and text fields both map to the same .NET type, String.

The reason for taking this extra step to create a "typed" DataTable instead of using a regular untyped table is to add one extra layer of data integrity. If a stored procedure returns more fields than this data object can handle, an error will be thrown immediately, highlighting that you've altered the data returned by a stored procedure without putting proper handling for it in your code.

Creating the Mapped Object

The mapped object is the front-end object that your application will use to interact with the database. The purpose of this object is to translate the data fields from the data object into easily managed fields in your object. This object is where you encapsulate the core logic of your object and what it's supposed to do.

Wherever possible, you should make your stored procedures as, well, "dumb" as possible. If a stored procedure has more logic than to save or get data, then there's likely a problem with your system design.

That said, sometimes it *does* make sense to put logic in your database where absolutely required for performance reasons. A common example is in the security management of your system. There are some situations where the security management part of your system needs to query across a large table and return only the results that the logged-in user has the access to see. In this case it may make sense to put a subset of your security system's logic in a subquery of your Select statement. Part of good design is knowing when to throw out an otherwise beautiful design for performance reasons. Any time you do this, always take a careful look at your design and try to come to a decision as to whether your design is flawed or this is just a sacrifice that has to be made for performance within the context of the situation (see Listing 18-2).

Listing 18-2. The VideoTape *Object*

```
Public Class VideoTape
```

```vbnet
    Protected data As DataTable
    Protected index As Integer


Protected Friend ReadOnly Property MyData() As DataRow()
        Get
            Dim myRow() As DataRow = {Me.data.Rows(index)}
            Return myRow
End Get
End Property


    Public Sub New(ByRef data As VideoTapeData, ByVal index As Integer)
        Me.data = data
        Me.index = index
        End Sub


        Public Function GetColumn(ByRef ColumnName As String) As Object
            Return data.Rows(index)(ColumnName)
        End Function


        Public Function SetColumn(ByRef ColumnName _
As String, ByRef ColumnValue As Object)
            data.Rows(index)(ColumnName) = ColumnValue
        End Function


        Public Property VideoTapeID() As Decimal
            Get
                If (GetColumn("VideoTapeID").GetType() Is _
Type.GetType("System.DBNull")) Then
                    Return -1
                End If
                Return CType(GetColumn("VideoTapeID"), Decimal)
            End Get
            Set(ByVal Value As Decimal)
                SetColumn("VideoTapeID", Value)
            End Set
        End Property


        Public Property Title() As String
            Get
                Return "" + GetColumn("Title")
            End Get
            Set(ByVal Value As String)
```

```
                SetColumn("Title", Value)
            End Set
        End Property


        Public Property Description() As String
            Get
                Return "" + GetColumn("Description")
            End Get
            Set(ByVal Value As String)
                SetColumn("Description", Value)
            End Set
        End Property



End Class
```

The constructor of the VideoTape object takes a VideoTapeData object and an integer as its arguments. The VideoTapeData object actually holds the data, and the integer index passed-in tells this object the row in the VideoTapeData DataTable for which this instance of the VideoTape object is mapping.

MyData is a read-only property that returns the DataRow that this object represents. The data access component uses MyData to get a reference to the VideoTape object's data. It was declared as a protected friend so that only other objects in this namespace can use it. The purpose of this is to hide this property from the rest of your program and remove the temptation other programmers might feel in trying to use the your object's data directly.

Each of the object's properties being mapped need the ability to get and set the values of the database field that corresponds with their values. To help with this task, we've included two functions, GetColumn and SetColumn, that allow the rest of the object's properties to avoid having to use the complete ADO.NET syntax for referencing a particular row and column. It's helpful to just think of the columns involved. By saving what row is being manipulated as plumbing that specifies the particular row of interest in this object, you can greatly simplify your code.

In the VideoTapeID property, do you notice the check to see if the value of the column is System.DBNull? This is an interesting disconnect between the database's view of values and .NET's. Because .NET's primitive types such as Integers, Decimals, Strings, DateTimes, and Guids are value types, they do not have a null state.

You can see an example of .NET's lack of null values for certain types with the DateTime object. If you declare a variable such as a DateTime and never initialize it with any given value, it's still given a value by .NET. The following statement prints 01/01/0001 even though myDate was never initialized:

```
Dim myDate As DateTime
Console.WriteLine(myDate.ToShortDateString())
```

In the VideoTape object, take a look at the checking it does to ensure that a null pointer exception doesn't occur. In the getter of the property, a check is made to see if the type of the column is System.DBNull. If it is, then it returns –1 to indicate that the value is not initialized to your .NET program. Otherwise, it casts the type of the column to a decimal and returns the result to the calling program:

```
        Public Property VideoTapeID() As Decimal
            Get
                If (GetColumn("VideoTapeID").GetType() Is _
Type.GetType("System.DBNull")) Then
                    Return -1
                End If
                Return CType(GetColumn("VideoTapeID"), Decimal)
            End Get
            Set(ByVal Value As Decimal)
                SetColumn("VideoTapeID", Value)
            End Set
        End Property
```

The database meanwhile treats data that hasn't been given a value as null. This becomes a problem when you try to move the content from the database into .NET because .NET needs to be able to represent the database's null value to the rest of your application in a way that lets your application know that a column has not been initialized. This includes things such as using –1 as a value for integers and decimals, an empty string for strings, and so on.

The trip back to the database compounds this problem. When the data is stored, if you have written a value to your data object such as an uninitialized DateTime, an error will occur. By handing these problems in the mapped object, you'll make the rest of your program more reliable by preventing value checks throughout your code.

The two string fields being mapped in this object are easier to handle. If the database has a character field, such as a Char or Text, that's null, it'll return a System.DBNull object. The handling on the .NET side is easier than with other value types.

The following statement returns the value if there is one:

```
Return "" + GetColumn("Description")
```

If the column is null in the database, it returns an empty string because ""+ calls the ToString method on the System.DBNull object. Either way, an acceptable .NET value is returned to the calling program.

Creating the Data Access Component

The DAC's responsibility is to fill your data objects with data from the database and create instances of your mapped object. It does this by defining what stored procedures should be used to load and save your data and makes them accessible to simple front-end methods. Once the DAC is done, the rest of your program will be able to get and set your mapped objects just as easy as calling a simple method (see Listing 18-3).

Listing 18-3. The VideoTapeDataAccess *Object*

```
Public Class VideoTapeDataAccess

    Public connectionString As String
        Protected adapter As SqlDataAdapter
        Protected loadAll As SqlDataAdapter

        Public Sub New()
            connectionString ="Your Connection String"


            adapter = New SqlDataAdapter()
            adapter.SelectCommand = New SqlCommand("ap_VideoTapeLoadByID", _
New SqlConnection(connectionString))
            adapter.SelectCommand.CommandType = CommandType.StoredProcedure
            adapter.SelectCommand.CommandType = CommandType.StoredProcedure
            adapter.SelectCommand.Parameters.Add _
            ("@VideoTapeID", SqlDbType.Decimal, 0, "VideoTapeID")
```

```
            adapter.InsertCommand = New SqlCommand("ap_VideoTapeInsert", _
New SqlConnection(connectionString))
            adapter.InsertCommand.CommandType = CommandType.StoredProcedure
            adapter.InsertCommand.Parameters.Add("@VideoTapeID", _
SqlDbType.Decimal, 0, "VideoTapeID")
            adapter.InsertCommand.Parameters("@VideoTapeID").Direction = _
ParameterDirection.Output
            adapter.InsertCommand.Parameters.Add("@Title", _
SqlDbType.Char, 50, "Title")
            adapter.InsertCommand.Parameters.Add("@Description", _
SqlDbType.Text, 0, "Description")

            adapter.UpdateCommand = New SqlCommand("ap_VideoTapeUpdate", _
New SqlConnection(connectionString))
            adapter.UpdateCommand.CommandType = CommandType.StoredProcedure
            adapter.UpdateCommand.Parameters.Add _
            ("@VideoTapeID", SqlDbType.Decimal, 0, "VideoTapeID")
            adapter.UpdateCommand.Parameters.Add _
            ("@Title", SqlDbType.Char, 50, "Title")
            adapter.UpdateCommand.Parameters.Add _
            ("@Description", SqlDbType.Text, 0, "Description")

            adapter.DeleteCommand = New SqlCommand("ap_VideoTapeDelete", _
New SqlConnection(connectionString))
            adapter.SelectCommand.CommandType = CommandType.StoredProcedure
            adapter.DeleteCommand.Parameters.Add("@VideoTapeID", _
SqlDbType.Decimal, 0, "VideoTapeID")

            loadAll = New SqlDataAdapter()
            loadAll.SelectCommand = New SqlCommand("ap_VideoTapeLoadAll", _
New SqlConnection(connectionString))
            loadAll.SelectCommand.CommandType = _
CommandType.StoredProcedure

        End Sub

        Public Function GetVideoTapeByID(ByVal vtID As Decimal) As VideoTape

            Dim data As New VideoTapeData()
            adapter.SelectCommand.Parameters("@VideoTapeID").Value = vtID
            adapter.Fill(data)
            If (data.Rows.Count < 1) Then
                Return Nothing
```

```vb
        End If
        Dim vt As New VideoTape(data, 0)
        Return vt
    End Function


    Public Function GetAllVideoTapes() As VideoTape()
        Dim data As New VideoTapeData()
        loadAll.Fill(data)
        Return GetVideoTapeArrayFromData(data)
    End Function


  Public Shared Function GetVideoTapeArrayFromData(ByRef data As VideoTapeData) _
As VideoTape()
        Dim vArray(data.Rows.Count - 1) As VideoTape
        Dim i As Integer
        For i = 0 To (data.Rows.Count - 1)
            vArray(i) = New VideoTape(data, i)
        Next i
        Return vArray
    End Function


    Public Function SetVideoTape(ByRef vTape As VideoTape)
        adapter.Update(vTape.MyData)
    End Function


    Public Function RemoveVideoTape(ByRef vTape As VideoTape)
        adapter.DeleteCommand.Parameters("@VideoTapeID").Value = _
vTape.VideoTapeID
        adapter.DeleteCommand.Connection.Open()
        adapter.DeleteCommand.ExecuteNonQuery()
        adapter.DeleteCommand.Connection.Close()
    End Function
End Class
```

The constructor of the VideoTapeDataAccess object initializes the SqlDataAdapters to use the stored procedures that handle the actual database access. The constructor initializes the Select, Insert, Update, and Delete stored procedures on the instance called adapter, but only the Select statement on the loadAll instance.

The reason for this is there are multiple ways you want to choose what data to get, but in the end there's only one way to update it in that database. Both adapters could have been fully initialized, but that would produce a large amount of redundant code. By only initializing one adapter for updates, inserts, and deletes, you're avoiding additional code that would needlessly slow down your program.

The GetVideoTapeByID method gets one VideoTape object out of the database. It sets the @VideoTapeID parameter on the stored procedure to the value passed in and fills the VideoTapeData object with data. If the database didn't find any records with the VideoTapeID passed in, then it returns Nothing, a null value. If there's at least one record returned, it creates an instance of the VideoTape object and initializes it with the data it loaded into the VideoTapeData object and sets the index to 0 so that the first record retuned is used by the mapped object. Because the VideoTapeID column is a unique identity column in the database, this stored procedure should never return more than one row.

The GetAllVideoTapes method is much simpler. It creates an instance of the VideoTapeData object and then uses the loadAll SqlDataAdapter to fill it. It then calls the GetVideoTapeArrayFromData method to turn the DataTable into an array of VideoTape objects.

The GetVideoTapeArrayFromData method creates an array of VideoTape objects the length of the number of results returned from the database and loops through the results, creating an instance of the VideoTape object for each row. As it goes through, it sets the index of each VideoTape object to a different row in the same result set. In the end it provides the array of VideoTape objects to the calling program.

The purpose of making the GetVideoTapeArrayFromData a separate method instead of simply putting this code inline with the GetAllVideoTapes method is to provide this method to other objects that may be attempting to create instances of VideoTape objects. You'll see this put to work later in the VideoCheckInCheckOut object.

If there are no video tapes in the database, it returns an array with no elements in it, not a null. This is, in general, good behavior for a DAC to have when it's expected to return an array of objects. In most situations the calling program will want to loop through however many elements are in the array, even if there are no elements. If the calling program wants to know if a null was returned, it can always check the length of the array to see if it's zero. In the end, returning a zero-length array should simplify your application's code.

The SetVideoTape object is amazingly short. It simply calls to update the row of the VideoTape object to the database. It automatically selects which stored procedure to call and then executes it with the corresponding data. If it was an insert call, the identity column will be automatically updated in the instance of the VideoTape object. This comes in handy when writing the front-end code of the application. There are many cases where the user will define the data for several related tables on one page, and you'll need a way to know the IDs of the related columns in order to allow the user to edit the data properly.

The one-line update call really highlights one of the core ideas of .NET: Hide as much complexity as possible. Your object builds on this principle to hide the rest of the database access functionality in your OR mapped component.

The RemoveVideoTape method actually uses the Delete command of the adapter directly. You could just remove the row in question from the VideoTapeData object and then call Update, but doing so could lose the isolation of the task to be performed. You would have to update the entire VideoTapeData set, which may include changes that the calling program doesn't want updated. This ensures that encapsulation is enforced and only the row you want to delete is deleted.

In most cases, it's a bad idea to actually delete rows from the database to remove an item from your application. What you would normally do is have a deleted field on the table that's flagged so you don't have to worry about maintaining your database's referential integrity or actually losing data. You would also modify your stored procedures that load data into your adapters to not return rows that are flagged as deleted unless it's referred to directly by its primary key.

Building the VideoTape Test Case

It's important to build a test case for an object relationally mapped system. A test case ensures that your component does what it's supposed to do and ensures that none of your changes have broken existing code. Each step of your test case should say what the expected output is and then show the output so that it's well marked in terms of what it's supposed to do in order to compare the output. It's even possible to build automated test cases that compare these types of things automatically, but that's not required for this particular system.

The VideoTapeTestCase object will do the following:

1. Load a VideoTape object from the database and display what its data is

2. Change the title and description

3. Store the object in the database

4. Reload the object and display what its data is

5. Restore the original VideoTape data and store it

6. Load all of the VideoTape objects from the database and show what each one is

Listing 18-4 shows the code for the test case.

Listing 18-4. The Test Case for the VideoTape *Component*

```vb
Imports VideoStoreDataModel.EnterpriseVB.VideoStore.Data

Module VideoTapeTestCase

    Sub Main()
        Dim vDAC As New VideoTapeDataAccess()
        Dim tVTape As VideoTape
        Console.WriteLine("Loading VideoTape")
        tVTape = vDAC.GetVideoTapeByID(1)
        Console.WriteLine("VideoTape Loaded:" + tVTape.GetType().ToString())
        DisplayVideoTape(tVTape)

        Dim origTitle = tVTape.Title
        Dim origDescription = tVTape.Description

        tVTape.Title = "TestTitle"
        tVTape.Description = "TestDescription"

        vDAC.SetVideoTape(tVTape)

        tVTape = vDAC.GetVideoTapeByID(1)
        Console.WriteLine _
("After alteration. Title=TestTitle  Description=TestDescription")
        DisplayVideoTape(tVTape)

        tVTape.Title = origTitle
        tVTape.Description = origDescription
        vDAC.SetVideoTape(tVTape)
        tVTape = vDAC.GetVideoTapeByID(1)
        Console.WriteLine _
("Restored to origional, should look like the first displayed VideoTape.")
        DisplayVideoTape(tVTape)

        Console.WriteLine("List all VideoTapes")

        Dim tVideos() As VideoTape
        tVideos = vDAC.GetAllVideoTapes()

        Dim i As Integer
        For i = 0 To tVideos.Length - 1
            DisplayVideoTape(tVideos(i))
```

```
        Next
        Console.WriteLine("Press Any Key To Quit...")
        Console.ReadLine()
    End Sub


    Sub DisplayVideoTape(ByRef tVTape As VideoTape)
        Console.WriteLine("--------------------------")
        Console.WriteLine("VideoTapeID:" + tVTape.VideoTapeID.ToString())
        Console.WriteLine("Title:" + tVTape.Title)
        Console.WriteLine("Description:" + tVTape.Description)
    End Sub

End Module
```

Figure 18-2 shows the VideoTape test case output.

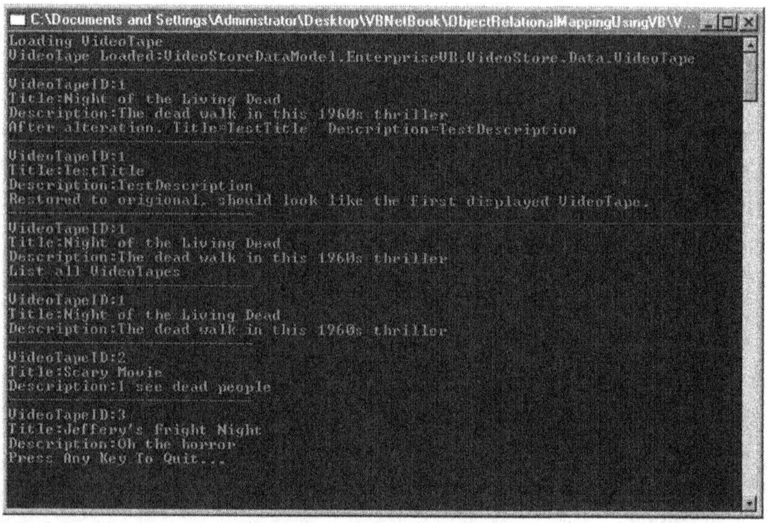

Figure 18-2. The VideoTape *test case output*

Using the User Component

The User component and the VideoTape component are virtually identical from the design point of view. The core requirements are the same—you want to be able to load one user record or all of them—and the basic data structure of both objects is the same. The purpose of the User component is to model the people involved with the application. The User is the one who can check in and out videos (see Listing 18-5).

Listing 18-5. The User *Object in the* User *Component*

```
Imports System
Imports System.Data
Imports System.Data.SqlClient
Imports System.Data.Common


Namespace EnterpriseVB.VideoStore.Data


    Public Class User

        Protected data As DataTable
        Protected index As Integer

        Protected Friend ReadOnly Property MyData() As DataRow()
            Get
                Dim myRow() As DataRow = {Me.data.Rows(index)}
                Return myRow
            End Get
        End Property

        Public Sub New(ByRef data As UserData, ByVal index As Integer)
            Me.data = data
            Me.index = index
        End Sub

        Public Function GetColumn(ByRef ColumnName As String) As Object
            Return data.Rows(index)(ColumnName)
        End Function

        Public Function SetColumn(ByRef ColumnName As String, _
ByRef ColumnValue As Object)
            data.Rows(index)(ColumnName) = ColumnValue
        End Function

        Public Property UserID() As Decimal
            Get
                If (GetColumn("UserID").GetType() Is _
Type.GetType("System.DBNull")) Then
                    Return -1
                End If
                Return CType(GetColumn("UserID"), Decimal)
            End Get    •
            Set(ByVal Value As Decimal)
                SetColumn("UserID", Value)
```

```
            End Set
        End Property

        Public Property FirstName() As String
            Get
                Return "" + GetColumn("FirstName")
            End Get
            Set(ByVal Value As String)
                SetColumn("FirstName", Value)
            End Set
        End Property

        Public Property LastName() As String
            Get
                Return "" + GetColumn("LastName")
            End Get
            Set(ByVal Value As String)
                SetColumn("LastName", Value)
            End Set
        End Property

    End Class
```

The User object is specifically designed to have as little logic as possible in it. As such, it has simple handling for null values and the ability to use values from the data object.

The "verb" types of actions concerning the user in relation to the rest of the system belong in the business objects, which you'll see later in the VideoCheckInCheckOut component.

Listing 18-6 shows the UserData object in the User component.

Listing 18-6. The UserData *Object in the* User *Component*

```
Public Class UserData
    Inherits DataTable

    Public Sub New()
        MyBase.New("Users")
        Me.Columns.Add("UserID", Type.GetType("System.Decimal"))
        Me.Columns.Add("FirstName", Type.GetType("System.String"))
        Me.Columns.Add("LastName", Type.GetType("System.String"))

    End Sub
End Class
```

The UserData object defines only three fields in the DataTable: UserID, FirstName, and LastName. Although much more data could be tracked on a user such as addresses and telephone numbers, let's keep it simple.

If you want to add this additional functionality, make sure you model it in separate tables. A common mistake beginners make is modeling all of a user's data in one giant table. Some systems go so far as having the person's name, address, phone numbers, credit card information, company, title, and more all in one table. This is bad both from a clean design sense and a performance sense. If a table has too many columns, SQL server handles it slowly.

Listing 18-7 shows the UserDataAccess object.

Listing 18-7. The UserDataAccess *Object in the* User *Component*

```
Public Class UserDataAccess
    Public connectionString As String
    Protected adapter As SqlDataAdapter
    Protected loadAll As SqlDataAdapter
    Public Sub New()
        connectionString = "Password=1deadrat;User ID=sa;" + _
"Initial Catalog=VideoStore;Data Source=grimsaado2k;" + _
"Workstation ID=GRIMSAADO2K;"
        adapter = New SqlDataAdapter()
        adapter.SelectCommand = New _
SqlCommand("ap_UsersLoadByID", New SqlConnection(connectionString))
        adapter.SelectCommand.CommandType = _
CommandType.StoredProcedure
        adapter.SelectCommand.CommandType = _
CommandType.StoredProcedure
        adapter.SelectCommand.Parameters.Add _
        ("@UserID", SqlDbType.Decimal, 0, "UserID")

        adapter.InsertCommand = New SqlCommand("ap_UsersInsert", _
New SqlConnection(connectionString))
        adapter.InsertCommand.CommandType = _
CommandType.StoredProcedure
        adapter.InsertCommand.Parameters.Add("@UserID", _
SqlDbType.Decimal, 0, "UserID")
        adapter.InsertCommand.Parameters("@UserID").Direction = _
ParameterDirection.Output
        adapter.InsertCommand.Parameters.Add("@FirstName", _
SqlDbType.Char, 50, "FirstName")
        adapter.InsertCommand.Parameters.Add("@LastName", _
SqlDbType.Text, 0, "LastName")
```

```
                    adapter.UpdateCommand = New SqlCommand("ap_UsersUpdate", _
        New SqlConnection(connectionString))
                    adapter.UpdateCommand.CommandType = CommandType.StoredProcedure
                    adapter.UpdateCommand.Parameters.Add("@UserID", _
        SqlDbType.Decimal, 0, "UserID")
                    adapter.UpdateCommand.Parameters.Add("@FirstName", _
        SqlDbType.Char, 50, "FirstName")
                    adapter.UpdateCommand.Parameters.Add("@LastName", _
        SqlDbType.Text, 0, "LastName")

                    adapter.DeleteCommand = New SqlCommand("ap_UsersDelete", _
        New SqlConnection(connectionString))
                    adapter.SelectCommand.CommandType = CommandType.StoredProcedure
                    adapter.DeleteCommand.Parameters.Add("@UserID", _
        SqlDbType.Decimal, 0, "UserID")

                    loadAll = New SqlDataAdapter()
                    loadAll.SelectCommand = New SqlCommand("ap_UsersLoadAll", _
        New SqlConnection(connectionString))
                    loadAll.SelectCommand.CommandType = _
        CommandType.StoredProcedure

            End Sub

            Public Function GetUserByID(ByVal userID As Decimal) As User

                Dim data As New UserData()
                adapter.SelectCommand.Parameters("@UserID").Value = userID
                adapter.Fill(data)
                If (data.Rows.Count < 1) Then
                    Return Nothing
                End If
                Dim vt As New User(data, 0)
                Return vt
            End Function

            Public Function GetAllUsers() As User()
                Dim data As New UserData()
                loadAll.Fill(data)
                Dim uArray(data.Rows.Count) As User
                Dim i As Integer

                For i = 0 To data.Rows.Count
```

```
            uArray(i) = New User(data, i)
        Next i


        Return uArray
    End Function


    Public Function SetUser(ByRef user As User)
        adapter.Update(user.MyData)
    End Function


    Public Function RemoveUser(ByRef user As User)
        adapter.DeleteCommand.Parameters("@UserID").Value = user.UserID
        adapter.DeleteCommand.Connection.Open()
        adapter.DeleteCommand.ExecuteNonQuery()
        adapter.DeleteCommand.Connection.Close()
    End Function
End Class


End Namespace
```

The DAC for the User component allows the calling program to look up a single user, list all of the users, update or insert a user, or delete a user. Once again the stored procedures are kept simple and the DAC itself is simple.

Creating the User Test Case

The User test case will verify that the User component works as expected. It will test your User component by doing the following:

1. Load a user from the database and display what its data is

2. Change the first name and last name

3. Store the object in the database

4. Reload the object and display what its data is

5. Restore the original user data and store it

6. Load all of the users from the database and show what each one is

Listing 18-8 shows the code for the UserTestCase object.

Listing 18-8. The UserTestCase *Object*

```
Imports VideoStoreDataModel.EnterpriseVB.VideoStore.Data

Module UserTestCase

    Sub Main()
        Dim uDAC As New UserDataAccess()
        Dim tUser As User
        Console.WriteLine("Loading User")
        tUser = uDAC.GetUserByID(1)
        Console.WriteLine("User Loaded:" + tUser.GetType().ToString())
        DisplayUser(tUser)
        Dim origFirstName = tUser.FirstName
        Dim origLastName = tUser.LastName

        tUser.FirstName = "TestFirst"
        tUser.LastName = "TestLast"

        uDAC.SetUser(tUser)

        tUser = uDAC.GetUserByID(1)
        Console.WriteLine _
("After alteration. FirstName=TestFirst LastName=TestLast")
        DisplayUser(tUser)
        Console.WriteLine _
("Restored to origional, should look like the first displayed user.")
        tUser.FirstName = origFirstName
        tUser.LastName = origLastName
        uDAC.SetUser(tUser)
        tUser = uDAC.GetUserByID(1)
        DisplayUser(tUser)

        Console.WriteLine("List all users")

        Dim tUsers() As User
        tUsers = uDAC.GetAllUsers()

        Dim i As Integer
        For i = 0 To tUsers.Length - 1
            DisplayUser(tUsers(i))
        Next
        Console.WriteLine("Press Any Key To Quit...")
```

```
        Console.ReadLine()
    End Sub


    Sub DisplayUser(ByRef tUser As User)
        Console.WriteLine("UserID:" + tUser.UserID.ToString())
        Console.WriteLine("FirstName" + tUser.FirstName)
        Console.WriteLine("LastName:" + tUser.LastName)
    End Sub
End Module
```

This program ensures that the component works as expected. You should run
this test case any time you've made changes to the User component to make sure
that it still works as expected. Figure 18-3 shows the output of the UserTestCase
program.

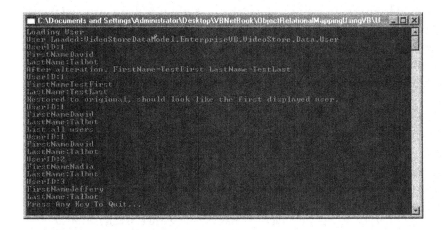

Figure 18-3. The output of the UserTestCase *program*

Managing Dependencies

Although the User component is similar to the VideoTape component, it's
important to talk about what isn't in the User object. Components that are at the
center of your system and relate to a number of other tables should wherever possible avoid referencing other components. The other components can reference
your core component, but by avoiding the core component referencing narrowly
scoped entities such as Check In/Check Out, you can keep your code portable to be
used in other projects that don't use Check In Check Out.

Figure 18-4 shows the dependencies within the video store application.

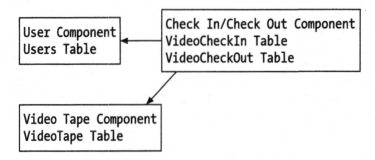

Figure 18-4. The dependencies in the video store application

In the design of this application, the Check In/Check Out component has all of the dependencies. You could easily move the VideoTape or User components to their own DLL and use them in other projects with or without each other, and nothing would be broken. The Check In/Check Out component, on the other hand, requires both the User component and VideoTape component.

When you're designing your next project, do some careful thinking about what components you plan on being able to use in other projects and think about what you need to do to make sure that core component is as independent as possible.

....

Paranoid Programming

In a perfect world, software has a specification that doesn't change, programmers produce the software, and it's done; there's no need for a second version. In reality, specifications change, goals change, and revisions happen faster than you intend. The only way to really manage this risk is what we like to call *paranoid programming*.

When designing your system, imagine what users *might* ask for next and try to anticipate it in your design and code. If the specification says that each user in the system has only one address, design the table schema and data objects to allow a one-to-many relationship because when users change their minds—and they will—it will be painful to make an alteration of this type if you did not allow for it in your original design.

The hardest part of being a professional programmer is managing expectations and exceeding them. A good design will help you manage the S.A.L.E.S. (Say Anything Let Engineering Sweat) part of the equation. Making sure your core components can easily be added to new projects will help this immensely.

To find out what specification for the next version of your product is, check the marketing brochures your sales team is showing to customers; this should give you a good idea of where the product is headed.

....

Creating the Check In/Check Out Component

The Check In/Check Out component allows the calling program to do the following:

1. List all of the video tapes currently checked out

2. Check out a video

3. Check in a video

4. Discover the status of a single video

This object is at the core of your system's functionality. The User and VideoTape components hold no real logic, but the Check In/Check Out component has enough to make up the rest of it. Although technically the VideoTape and User objects are business objects in that they hold some of the system's logic, the CheckInCheckOut object is where the vast majority of the job happens.

Death to N-Tier

Traditional thought is the only way to create a scalable system on the Web is the three-tier model (what academics call the *four-tier model* because they count the browser as a tier). The three-tier model is made up of a Web server, an application server, and a database server. The thinking goes that the code on your Web servers should only provide Hypertext Markup Language (HTML) generation and an interface back to the application server, which is actually running the code with the business logic in it. Of course, behind that is the database server, which should be treated as a dumb repository of data with no logic in it whatsoever (depending on the server you purchased, this may be a more truthful statement than with others).

The three-tier model has a number of problems, though. Every layer you add increases the likelihood of down time. If your application server cluster goes down, then your whole application will cease to function. Also, every incoming request goes from the Web server to the database server and on to the database server—and of course back again. The extra layer increases latency and adds to the complexity of your application. Complexity is inherently evil and must be destroyed; therefore, the physical two-tier model and logical three-tier model were born.

Under the 2/3 model, the database stays a dumb place where your data is stored, but the business logic objects live on the Web server. We're not saying your business logic should go in your code behind—far from it. What we're saying is that the data objects and logic objects you're creating in this chapter should live in nice, neat, compiled DLLs that your ASPX pages access.

This reduces latency as network usage goes down, this reduces complexity because you've cut a layer out of your application, and this significantly reduces the total cost of deploying your application.

The CheckInCheckOut object looks quite a bit like a function library and less like a real object. The reason is simple; this component defines the actions you're taking on the video tapes and users. By isolating the types of actions that can be taken with users and video tapes inside this object, the .aspx pages that use this business object layer have the ability to do amazing things in just a few lines of code:

```
VideosCheckedOutDataGrid.DataSource = (New _
VideoCheckInCheckOut(conn)). _
GetVideoTapesCheckedOutToUser(user)
```

This example shows how the VideoCheckInCheckOut component allows everything that's currently checked out to a single person to be listed in an .aspx page in one line of code. This truly comes in handy when you've got 20 different pages listing the videos checked out to a single user and the need arises to alter the actual logic behind it. One scenario where this might happen is if the checkout process allowed the user to choose how many days they wanted to pay for when they checked out the video. This would involve altering the data model and the logic concerning the data model, especially if a "list overdue" videos feature was added that would include even more dependant logic than just a simple check in/check out.

If you had embedded the call to a stored procedure directly into your page as you probably would have under the ASP model, you would have quite a task ahead of you! You would have to go to each page and add the handling for the new field now being returned from the stored procedure and take proper action on it to handle it. Obviously, this is a situation to avoid.

In the VideoCheckInCheckOut object, you'll notice a few things that are poorly coded in terms of good object-oriented principles, so be prepared. There's a conflict between good and fast under this model. You can have your code 90 percent well designed and easy to maintain, but sometimes you just have to break it a little to get the kind of performance you need.

Seeing How It Works

The VideoCheckInCheckOut component's workings are fairly simple. The design goal of this component is to provide the ability to check out a video tape to a user, check it back in, and be able to determine the state of this information in a few ways.

When a row is inserted into the VideoCheckOut table, a new VideoCheckOutID is "automagically" generated by SQL Server. The VideoCheckIn table has a VideoCheckOutID that references this ID. Anytime there's a VideoCheckOutID in the VideoCheckOut table that's not in the VideoCheckIn table, a video is currently checked out.

You can apply a few strategies on this data to determine if a video tape is checked out; you'll learn about this in the next section, which is about the design of the `Check In/Check Out` components.

Making Design Tradeoffs

There are three main tradeoffs to look at between good and fast design. Depending on the requirements for your application you'll have to make decisions on each of these items and evaluate the kinds of risks doing it the fast way pose to the design of your system.

The seemingly innocent code in Listing 18-9 has a number of implications you must be aware of when working with OR mapping in a system such as the video store application.

Listing 18-9. SelectVideosCheckedOutToUser

```
CREATE PROCEDURE dbo.SelectVideosCheckedOutToUser
@UserID decimal
AS
BEGIN
SELECT VideoTapeID, Title, Description FROM VideoTape WHERE
VideoTapeID  IN
(
SELECT VideoTapeID FROM VideoCheckOut  as vco WHERE
CheckedOutToUserID=@UserID AND VideoTapeID NOT IN
(SELECT VideoTapeID From VideoCheckIn as vci WHERE
vco.VideoCheckOutID=vci.VideoCheckOutID)
)
END
```

Understanding Logic in Stored Procedures

The first possible tradeoff is having anything resembling logic in your stored procedures. In the `SelectVideosCheckedOutToUser` stored procedure, a nested subquery finds out what VideoCheckOut entries don't have VideoCheckIn entries. An alternate approach to this is to load all VideoCheckOut entries and all VideoCheckIn entries using simple stored procedures, then make this comparison in your VB .NET code.

The advantage of using the stored procedure in Listing 18-9 is a much faster response time with only a small amount of data traveling over your network. Because the results are being filtered by the database server, only the small chunk of data you're looking for will be returned.

The disadvantage of placing this type of logic in a stored procedure is the maintainability of your code and the cost/scalability of your database server. When another programmer comes along and wants to alter the behavior of what the definition of CheckedOut is within your system, they'll have to trace your objects all the way back to the stored procedures to find out how you did this.

Another disadvantage is that your database is a finite resource. Running Microsoft SQL Server 2000 on .NET Server, you can cluster a maximum of eight machines together at an unbelievable hardware/software cost. Every bit of logic you have your stored procedures apply takes more resources from these machines. On the other hand, you can add Web servers almost indefinitely using a number of solutions available in the marketplace for a minimal cost (in comparison to expanding the database).

The other point of balance is large chunks of data. If the data to be returned is potentially large, it could be more of a burden on your database servers overall than having just sorted through it on its own. It'll take some time and thinking as to whether it's more database intensive one way or another. In the video store application, for example, most people in the system of an average video store have checked out more than 100 tapes but only have two checked out at a time. Some people have checked out more than 1,000, and returning all 2,000 (1,000 from the VideoCheckIn table and 1,000 from the VideoCheckOut table) could cause serious stress on the database server and the network.

Understanding Component Isolation

The next problem with the stored procedure in Listing 18-9 is the co-mingling of components. Notice how the stored procedure returns not only the VideoTapeID, but the Title and Description as well? This means that if an alteration is made to the VideoTape component's data model, the VideoCheckInCheckOut object will require reworking.

The only advantage of returning the data in line is speed. If only the was returned, then the calling program would likely make a separate call to the VideoTapeDataAccess object's GetVideoTapeByID, each in turn calling a stored procedure on its own to get the VideoTape referenced by the returned ID. By returning the data inline you're removing the need for the calling program to make separate round trips to the database.

The disadvantage of returning the data in line is that changes in your VideoTape component will likely break the VideoCheckInCheckOut component.

If you add a field to the VideoTape object such as YearReleased, you must alter the VideoCheckInCheckOut object and stored procedure as well. If these types of interdependencies are not well documented, you're well on your way to creating an unmaintainable system.

The good design way to do it is to have the stored procedure only return VideoTapeIDs and then leave the job of turning these IDs into objects in the VideoTape component's court.

If you employ a technique like this in your system, make sure that it's well documented within the VideoTape and the VideoCheckInCheckOut components. Both sides that are engaging in naughty behavior need to have a line drawn between them not only to let future programmers that come after you know what you've done, but also to help you keep track of what you've done.

Creating a Workaround on Part of the Problem

The component isolation part of the speed vs. design problem has a partial solution. You can take the specifics of turning the results of your VideoCheckInCheckOut stored procedure from data into objects and place it squarely on the shoulders of your VideoTape component. By designing the VideoTape component to include public methods for transforming VideoTapeData objects into VideoTape objects, you can bank on ADO.NET's SqlDataAdapter's ability to map the results of a stored procedure to fields in an ADO.NET DataSet. Listing 18-10 shows the VideoCheckInCheckOut object, found in ObjectRelationalMappingVB/VideoStoreDataModel/VideoCheckInCheckOut.vb.

Listing 18-10. The VideoCheckInCheckOut *Object*

```
        Public Function GetVideoTapesCheckedOutToUser(ByRef usr As User) _
As VideoTape()
            Dim cmd As New SqlDataAdapter("ap_SelectVideosCheckedOutToUser", _
New SqlConnection(connectionString))
            cmd.SelectCommand.CommandType = CommandType.StoredProcedure
            cmd.SelectCommand.Parameters.Add("@UserID", _
SqlDbType.Decimal)
            cmd.SelectCommand.Parameters("@UserID").Value = usr.UserID
            Dim data As VideoTapeData
            cmd.Fill(data)
            Return VideoTapeDataAccess.GetVideoTapeArrayFromData(data)
        End Function
```

In the `GetVideoTapesCheckedOutToUser` method, you use the `VideoTapeData` object to fill the result set and use the `GetVideoTapeArrayFromData` method on the `VideoTapeDataAccess` object to turn this data into an array of `VideoTape` objects. This means that any alterations made to the structure of the VideoTape table in the database will require fixing only the `VideoTape` component's code, not the `VideoCheckInCheckOut` component's code. The stored procedure that the `VideoCheckInCheckOut` component is using will still have to be altered to ensure it includes the new fields, but if you're careful in documenting your dependencies this should make it manageable (see Listing 18-11).

Listing 18-11. The `VideoCheckInCheckOut` *Object*

```
Public Class VideoCheckInCheckOut
    Private connectionString As String

    Public Sub New(ByVal connStr As String)
        Me.connectionString = connStr
    End Sub

    Public Function GetVideoTapesCheckedOutToUser(ByRef usr As User) _
As VideoTape()
        Dim cmd As New SqlDataAdapter("ap_SelectVideosCheckedOutToUser", _
New SqlConnection(connectionString))
        cmd.SelectCommand.CommandType = CommandType.StoredProcedure
        cmd.SelectCommand.Parameters.Add("@UserID", _
SqlDbType.Decimal)
        cmd.SelectCommand.Parameters("@UserID").Value = _
usr.UserID
        Dim data As New VideoTapeData()
        cmd.Fill(data)
        Return VideoTapeDataAccess.GetVideoTapeArrayFromData(data)
    End Function

    Public Function GetVideoTapesCheckedIn() As VideoTape()
        Dim cmd As New SqlDataAdapter("ap_SelectVideosCheckedIn", _
New SqlConnection(connectionString))
        cmd.SelectCommand.CommandType = CommandType.StoredProcedure
        Dim data As New VideoTapeData()
        cmd.Fill(data)
        Return VideoTapeDataAccess.GetVideoTapeArrayFromData(data)
    End Function
```

```
        Public Function CheckOutVideoToUser(ByRef usr As User, _
ByRef toUsr As User, ByRef vt As VideoTape)
            If (Me.IsVideoCheckedOut(vt)) Then
    Throw New Exception("Video is already checked out to another user.")
            End If
            Dim cmd As New SqlCommand("ap_CheckOutVideo", _
New SqlConnection(connectionString
            cmd.CommandType = CommandType.StoredProcedure
            cmd.Parameters.Add("@CheckedOutByUserID", _
SqlDbType.Decimal)
            cmd.Parameters.Add("@CheckedOutToUserID", _
SqlDbType.Decimal)
            cmd.Parameters.Add("@VideoTapeID", _
SqlDbType.Decimal)
            cmd.Parameters("@CheckedOutToUserID").Value = _
usr.UserID
            cmd.Parameters("@CheckedOutByUserID").Value = _
toUsr.UserID
            cmd.Parameters("@VideoTapeID").Value = _
vt.VideoTapeID
            cmd.Connection.Open()
            cmd.ExecuteNonQuery()
            cmd.Connection.Close()
        End Function


        Public Function CheckInVideoFromUser(ByRef usr As User, _
ByRef vt As VideoTape)
            Dim cmd As New SqlCommand("ap_CheckInVideo", _
New SqlConnection(connectionString))
            cmd.CommandType = CommandType.StoredProcedure
            cmd.Parameters.Add("@UserID", _
SqlDbType.Decimal)
            cmd.Parameters.Add("@VideoTapeID", _
SqlDbType.Decimal)
            cmd.Parameters("@UserID").Value = usr.UserID
            cmd.Parameters("@VideoTapeID").Value = _
vt.VideoTapeID
            cmd.Connection.Open()
            cmd.ExecuteNonQuery()
            cmd.Connection.Close()
        End Function


    Public Function IsVideoCheckedOut(ByRef vt As VideoTape) As Boolean
```

```
        Dim cmd As New SqlCommand("ap_IsVideoCheckedOut", _
New SqlConnection(connectionString))
        cmd.CommandType = CommandType.StoredProcedure
        cmd.Parameters.Add("@VideoTapeID", _
SqlDbType.Decimal)
        cmd.Parameters("@VideoTapeID").Value = _
vt.VideoTapeID
        cmd.Connection.Open()
        Dim isCheckedOut As Boolean
        isCheckedOut = cmd.ExecuteScalar()
        cmd.Connection.Close()
        Return isCheckedOut
    End Function
End Class
```

In the VideoCheckInCheckOut object you're modeling all of your "verbs." Each method of this object actually performs an action or describes a state as opposed to just returning data.

The two workhorses of this object are CheckInVideoFromUser and CheckOutVideoToUser. Each is a thin wrapper around calling a stored procedure but provides an important spot where future business logic can be added. If, for example, you chose to add accounting functionality to the system, it would be a simple matter of adding calls that code at this location.

Under that scenario, you would not need to change any of your front-end code to work with these enhancements to your system.

Creating the VideoCheckInCheckOut Test Case

To properly test the VideoCheckInCheckOut component, you'll need to do the following:

1. Check a video to see if it's checked out

2. Check out a video

3. Check the video's status

4. List all checked out videos for the user

5. List all the videos that are not checked out to anyone

6. Check in the video

7. Check the status of the video

8. List all the videos checked out to the user

9. List all the videos that are not checked out to anyone

As you can see, this test case is quite a bit more complicated than the test case for the User and VideoTape components! It's not enough to just test each method once; you have to verify that the listing methods actually get the right data when the video's state is displayed. Listing 18-12 shows the test case for the VideoCheckInCheckOut component.

Listing 18-12. The Test Case for the VideoCheckInCheckOut *Component*

```
Imports VideoStoreDataModel.EnterpriseVB.VideoStore.Data

Module VideoCheckInCheckOutTestCase

    Sub Main()

        Dim vDAC As New VideoTapeDataAccess()
        Dim uDAC As New UserDataAccess()
        Dim vciDAC As New VideoCheckInCheckOut(vDac.connectionString)
        Dim tTape As VideoTape
        tTape = vDAC.GetVideoTapeByID(1)
        Console.WriteLine("Is Tape Checked Out:" + _
vciDAC.IsVideoCheckedOut(tTape).ToString())

        Dim tUser As User
        tUser = uDAC.GetUserByID(1)
        Console.WriteLine("Checking out video.")
        vciDAC.CheckOutVideoToUser(tUser, tUser, tTape)
        Console.WriteLine("Is Tape Checked Out:" + _
vciDAC.IsVideoCheckedOut(tTape).ToString())

        Dim tapes() As VideoTape
        tapes = vciDAC.GetVideoTapesCheckedOutToUser(tUser)

        Console.WriteLine("Tapes Currently Checked Out To User:")
        DisplayTapeArray(tapes)
```

```
            Console.WriteLine("Tapes Not Currently Checked Out To Anyone")
            tapes = vciDAC.GetVideoTapesCheckedIn()
            DisplayTapeArray(tapes)
            vciDAC.CheckInVideoFromUser(tUser, tTape)

            Console.WriteLine("Video Checked In")
            Console.WriteLine("Is Tape Checked Out:" + _
    vciDAC.IsVideoCheckedOut(tTape).ToString())

            tapes = vciDAC.GetVideoTapesCheckedOutToUser(tUser)

            Console.WriteLine("Tapes Currently Checked Out To User:")
            DisplayTapeArray(tapes)
            Console.WriteLine("Tapes Not Currently Checked Out To Anyone")
            tapes = vciDAC.GetVideoTapesCheckedIn()
            DisplayTapeArray(tapes)

            Console.WriteLine("Press Any Key To Quit...")
            Console.ReadLine()
        End Sub
        Sub DisplayTapeArray(ByRef tapes() As VideoTape)
            Dim i As Integer
            For i = 0 To tapes.Length - 1
                Console.WriteLine("TAPE:" + tapes(i).Title)
            Next
        End Sub
    End Module
```

The test case correctly exercises each of the methods provided by the VideoCheckInCheckOut component. There's a caveat here, though; if the video (VideoTapeID 1) is already checked out, an exception will be thrown. Figure 18-5 shows the output of CheckInCheckOut test case.

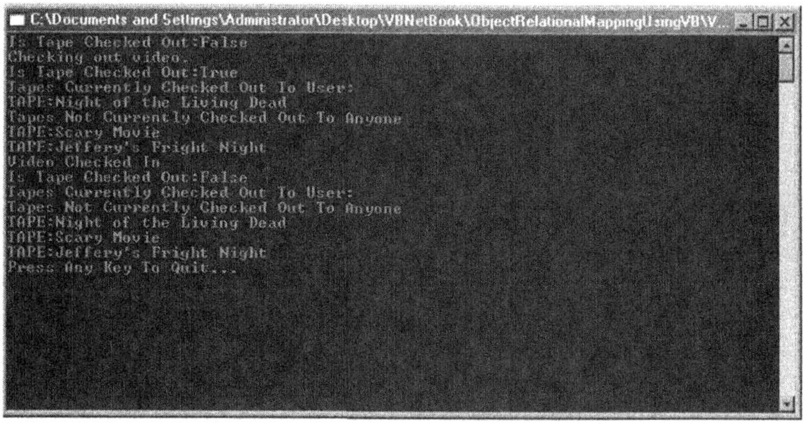

Figure 18-5. The output of the CheckInCheckOut *test case*

Summary

OR mapping affords the ability to hide data access completely from your application and greatly simplify the front-end code you write for your application. It allows you to write all of your data access logic once and allows significantly increased flexibility in your system.

In the next chapter, you'll look at how to use these mapped objects with ASP.NET widgets such as DataGrids. You'll also look at some additions to the performance end of your data model and implement a high-performance caching mechanism.

CHAPTER 19

Mapped Objects: Performance Considerations and Data Binding

IN THE LAST chapter you learned the basics of turning the data in your database into objects. Although basic Object-Relational (OR) mapping is simple, a number of issues become apparent when it comes time to actually put it to work.

In this chapter you'll learn how to put your objects to work in ASP.NET using data binding and how to solve the problems posed in relationships by working with master-detail relationships and building a tree structure for performance.

The chapter also covers how to implement a simple, near-zero-impact caching scheme for your objects and how to create business objects to further abstract your mapped objects.

These topics should help you solve common problems encountered when using OR mapping.

Using Data Binding and Mapped Objects

To get real use out of your mapped objects, you have to know how to leverage them with .NET's many server-side ASP.NET controls. The overall methodology of using data binding with mapped objects is similar to the technique you can use on a DataSet or DataTable yet it affords much greater flexibility.

You can bind all of the .NET controls that allow data binding to any object that implements IEnumerable. Don't panic, you don't have to actually implement IEnumerable and create custom collections for each group of mapped objects. Instead, Microsoft was kind enough to do that for you by implementing IEnumerable in all of their collections from ArrayList to Hashtable.

The ability to bind to virtually *any* .NET collection is liberating when you think about it. For example, if you store a number of objects in a Hashtable, you can actually bind it to a DataGrid control, work with the data, and then store it back in the database writing very little code. The advantage this affords you is the ability to enforce business logic in your objects while providing the ease of use of .NET data binding.

Using Connection Strings

The examples in the previous chapter and in this one use hard-coded database connection strings. This is something you should never do in a real application because you would have to recompile your program every time your application runs in a place where the database is different.

In a practical application this is generally the difference between your development environment and production environment. Granted, it's easy for you to change the connection string and then recompile and copy your files over if you're working in a small company. The problem is that your application will slowly start gaining more deployment-specific data in the code over time, and it will become difficult to maintain to say the least—not to mention that you'll likely forget to change it every time you get ready to deploy. So, it's generally a good idea to get it right the first time and put what .NET gives you to use with the web.config file.

The code-behind file of the TestDataGrid program highlights one of the advantages of OR mapping (see Listing 19-1). The amount of code you actually have to write is limited to just a few lines that list the contents of the VideoTape database.

Listing 19-1. The Code-Behind File of the TestDataGrid *Program*

```
Imports VideoStoreDataModel.EnterpriseVB.VideoStore.Data

Public Class WebForm1
    Inherits System.Web.UI.Page
    Protected WithEvents VideoTapesGrid As System.Web.UI.WebControls.DataGrid

    Private Sub Page_Load(ByVal sender As System.Object, _
ByVal e As System.EventArgs) _
Handles MyBase.Load
        Dim dac As New VideoTapeDataAccess()
        VideoTapesGrid.DataSource = dac.GetAllVideoTapes()
```

```
        If (Not IsPostBack) Then
            VideoTapesGrid.DataBind()
        End If
    End Sub

End Class
```

In the Page_Load method, first you create an instance of the VideoTapeDataAccess Data Access Component (DAC). Next, you set the DataSource of the VideoTapesGrid to the array of VideoTape objects returned from the GetAllVideoTapes() method of the VideoTapeDataAccess DAC. Finally, if the page request being served is not a postback, you call the DataBind method to update the User Interface (UI) of the VideoTapesGrid DataGrid.

The Hypertext Markup Language (HTML) side of this page is just as simple as the code-behind file using the syntax identical to the way you would bind to a DataSet or DataTable (see Listing 19-2).

Listing 19-2. The HTML Side of the TestDataGrid Page

```
<%@ Page Language="vb" AutoEventWireup="false"
Codebehind="TestGrid.aspx.vb" Inherits="TestDataGrid.WebForm1" %>
<!DOCTYPE HTML PUBLIC "-//W3C//DTD HTML 4.0 Transitional//EN">
<HTML>
<HEAD>
    <Title></Title>
    <meta name="GENERATOR" content="Microsoft Visual Studio.NET 7.0">
    <meta name="CODE_LANGUAGE" content="Visual Basic 7.0">
    <meta name="vs_defaultClientScript" content="JavaScript">
    <meta name="vs_targetSchema"
content="http://schemas.microsoft.com/intellisense/ie5">
</HEAD>
<body>
<form Id="Form1" method="post" runat="server">
<asp:DataGrid Id="VideoTapesGrid" runat="server" AutoGenerateColumns="false">
<Columns>
<asp:TemplateColumn HeaderText="Title">
<ItemTemplate>
    <%# DataBinder.Eval(Container.DataItem, "Title" ) %>
</ItemTemplate>
</asp:TemplateColumn>
<asp:TemplateColumn HeaderText="Description">
<ItemTemplate>
```

```
<%# DataBinder.Eval(Container.DataItem, " Description " ) %>
</ItemTemplate>
</asp:TemplateColumn>
</Columns>
</asp:DataGrid>
</form>
</body>
</html>
```

The call to `DataBinder.Eval` shows the way the `DataBinder` really works. When `DataBinder` processes the `Title` string, it's not actually binding directly to the underlying `DataTable` but actually calling your getter method on the `Title` . property. If you have logic in your `Title` property for example, to return what was in the database in uppercase, then the `DataGrid` would actually show the title in uppercase.

When a data-bound object such as a `DataGrid` is processing a collection of items—either your objects or a `DataTable`—it uses the `Reflect` architecture (found in `System.Reflection`) to make dynamic invocations on your code at runtime. This is the "secret sauce" that makes data binding in .NET so flexible.

Figure 19-1 shows the output of the page.

Title	Description
Night of the Living Dead	The dead walk in this 1960s thriller
Scary Movie	I see dead people
Jeffery's Fright Night	Oh the horror

Figure 19-1. The output of the TestDataGrid program

Directly Accessing a Bound Object's Properties

Using `DataBinder.Eval` is only one of the options available to you, but you're missing out on half of the power afforded by this flexible reflection-based architecture.

The more powerful way to work with bound objects is to get a reference to the objects themselves and use it to actually perform logic inline on your page. Listing 19-3 references the object itself and the number of characters in the Description field.

Functionality such as this is important in a number of situations. For example, if you added a derived field to the `User` object that concatenates the user's first name and last name and made sure they had initial caps, you could display it inline using this technique.

Listing 19-3. The HTML of the TestGridObjects Page

```
<%@ Page Language="vb" AutoEventWireup="false" Codebehind="TestGrid.aspx.vb"
Inherits="TestDataGrid.WebForm1" %>
<%@ import namespace="VideoStoreDataModel.EnterpriseVB.VideoStore.Data" %>
<!DOCTYPE HTML PUBLIC "-//W3C//DTD HTML 4.0 Transitional//EN">
<HTML>
<HEAD>
<Title></Title>
<meta name="GENERATOR" content="Microsoft Visual Studio.NET 7.0">
<meta name="CODE_LANGUAGE" content="Visual Basic 7.0">
<meta name="vs_defaultClientScript" content="JavaScript">
<meta name="vs_targetSchema"
content="http://schemas.microsoft.com/intellisense/ie5">
</HEAD>
<body>
<form Id="Form1" method="post" runat="server">
<asp:DataGrid Id="VideoTapesGrid" runat="server" AutoGenerateColumns="false">
<Columns>
    <asp:TemplateColumn HeaderText="Title">
        <ItemTemplate>
        <%# (CType(Container.DataItem, VideoTape)).Title%>
        </ItemTemplate>
    </asp:TemplateColumn>
    <asp:TemplateColumn HeaderText="Description">
    <ItemTemplate>
    <%# (CType(Container.DataItem, VideoTape)).Description %>
    ( <%# (CType(Container.DataItem, VideoTape)).Description.Length %> )
    </ItemTemplate>
</asp:TemplateColumn>
</Columns>
</asp:DataGrid>
</form>
</body>
</html>
```

The HTML for this page is fairly simple. You simply cast the `Container.DataItem` object to be a `VideoTape` object using `CType()`, and then you access the property the same way you would in regular compiled code.

To use an object such as `VideoTape`, you have to import the namespace in your HTML as well as in your code-behind file so that the HTML page will know what namespace to look in for your objects. If you don't do this, your application will compile successfully without any errors; however, when you try to actually view the Web page in your browser, you'll get a "BC30002: Type is not defined: 'VideoTape'" error. Figure 19-2 shows the output of the TestGridObjects page that utilizes object binding.

Title	Description
Night of the Living Dead	The dead walk in this 1960s thriller (36)
Scary Movie	I see dead people (17)
Jeffery's Fright Night	Oh the horror (13)

Figure 19-2. The output of the TestGridObjects page

The output of the TestGridObjects page shows the title, description, and description's character count of all of the video tapes in the database.

Using Logic with Bound Objects

It often isn't enough being able to just passively display data exactly as it is in the database. Quite often with a long field such as a description, you'll want to clip it off after a certain number of characters so the line won't wrap.

You'll likely run into a number of situations where you want to call a method on one of your bound objects and display the result inline in a list. There are basically two ways to apply logic to the cells in a bound collection.

The first, and simplest, method is to cast the Container.DataItem object to your object type and call a method on the object. This can be useful in a number of situations, especially if you have a method on your object that retrieves derived data. An example of where this might be useful is on a shopping cart object where you calculate the total of a person's order and want to display it in your grid (see Listing 19-4).

Listing 19-4. The Theoretical Shopping Cart Example

```
<asp:TemplateColumn HeaderText="Total">
<ItemTemplate>
    <%# (CType(Container.DataItem, ShoppingCart)).CalculateTotal().ToString() %>
</ItemTemplate>
</asp:TemplateColumn>
```

In Listing 19-4 you use the same syntax for casting Container.DataItem to your object type and then convert it to a string using the ToString() method. Everything you display in a bound collection must be converted to a string before it's sent to a browser, so keep this in mind anytime you call a method that returns anything other than a string.

The second method of applying logic to your grid is to pass your bound object to a function in your code-behind object, process it there, and then return a string to be displayed inline in the DataGrid. In the FancyBinding Web page example, a function is called in the code-behind object, which makes a decision as to whether it should clip the Description field to 10 characters (see Listing 19-5). Granted, this is a simple example, but it represents a common problem in data binding.

The FancyBinding page displays all of the video tapes in the database, applies some logic, and displays the object name. The Description field is clipped to 10 characters with an ellipsis (...) indicating that there's more text available in the description. When the user clicks the Show Description link, the description of the video tape displays in its entirety.

Listing 19-5. The HTML of the FancyBinding Page

```
<%@ Page Language="vb" AutoEventWireup="false" Codebehind="FancyBinding.aspx.vb"
Inherits="TestDataGrid.FancyBinding"%>
<%@ import namespace="VideoStoreDataModel.EnterpriseVB.VideoStore.Data" %>
<!DOCTYPE HTML PUBLIC "-//W3C//DTD HTML 4.0 Transitional//EN">
<HTML>
<HEAD>
    <title></title>
    <meta content="Microsoft Visual Studio.NET 7.0" name="GENERATOR">
    <meta content="Visual Basic 7.0" name="CODE_LANGUAGE">
    <meta content="JavaScript" name="vs_defaultClientScript">
    <meta content=http://schemas.microsoft.com/intellisense/ie5
 name="vs_targetSchema">
</HEAD>
<body>
<form id="Form1" method="post" runat="server">
<asp:datagrid id="VideoTapesDataGrid" runat="server"
BorderColor="Black" BorderWidth="2"
 AutoGenerateColumns="False">
<Columns>
<asp:BoundColumn DataField="VideoTapeID"></asp:BoundColumn>
<asp:TemplateColumn HeaderText="Title">
<ItemTemplate>
    <%# (CType(Container.DataItem, VideoTape)).Title %>
</ItemTemplate>
</asp:TemplateColumn>
<asp:TemplateColumn HeaderText="Description">
<ItemTemplate>
```

```
        <%# TrimDescription( CType(Container.DataItem, VideoTape), 20) %>
</ItemTemplate>
</asp:TemplateColumn>
<asp:ButtonColumn Text="Show Description" CommandName="Show"></asp:ButtonColumn>
<asp:TemplateColumn HeaderText="Object Type">
<ItemTemplate>
        <%# GetVideoTapeType( CType(Container.DataItem, VideoTape) ) %>
</ItemTemplate>
</asp:TemplateColumn>
</Columns>
</asp:datagrid>
</form>
</body>
</HTML>
```

The example in Listing 19-5 has five columns. The first column is the VideoTapeID column, which you have to have to set SelectedVideoTape, the second column simply displays the title of the video tape, and the third and fourth columns are where things get interesting.

The Description column's ItemTemplate calls the TrimDescription() method and passes a VideoTape object and the length to trim as a parameter. Because the HTML side of your page inherits from your code-behind object, you can call any method that's protected or public on your code-behind object from your HTML.

The Show Description column provides the user with a link to choose that they want the description of one of the lines to display in its entirety. There's a corresponding event handler in the code-behind object that makes this happen (covered shortly).

In the interest of simplicity, the video store example project keeps the mapped objects simple, so there's not a good method to call to show how to do an inline method call. Therefore, the FancyBinding page displays a text string representing the object type of the VideoTape object (see Listing 19-6).

Listing 19-6. The Code-Behind Object of the FancyBinding Page

```
Imports VideoStoreDataModel.EnterpriseVB.VideoStore.Data

Public Class FancyBinding
    Inherits System.Web.UI.Page
    Protected WithEvents VideoTapesDataGrid As System.Web.UI.WebControls.DataGrid

    Public Property ShowTapeID() As Decimal
        Get
```

```
            If (ViewState("ShowTapeID") = "") Then
                Return -1
            End If
            Return Convert.ToDecimal(ViewState("ShowTapeID"))
        End Get
        Set(ByVal Value As Decimal)
            ViewState("ShowTapeID") = "" + Value.ToString()
        End Set
    End Property


    Private Sub Page_Load(ByVal sender As System.Object, _
ByVal e As System.EventArgs) _
Handles MyBase.Load
        Dim dac As New VideoTapeDataAccess()
        VideoTapesDataGrid.DataSource = dac.GetAllVideoTapes()
        If (Not IsPostBack) Then
            VideoTapesDataGrid.DataBind()
        End If
    End Sub


    Public Function TrimDescription(ByRef tape As VideoTape, _
ByVal characters As Int32) As String
        If (tape.Description.Length < characters Or _
tape.VideoTapeID = ShowTapeID) _
Then
            Return tape.Description
        End If
        Return tape.Description.Substring(0, characters) + "..."
    End Function


    Public Function GetVideoTapeType(ByRef tape As VideoTape) As String
        Return tape.GetType().ToString()
    End Function


    Private Sub VideoTapesDataGrid_ItemCommand(ByVal sender As Object, ByVal e As _
DataGridCommandEventArgs) Handles VideoTapesDataGrid.ItemCommand
        If (e.CommandName = "Show") Then
            ShowTapeID = Convert.ToDecimal(e.Item.Cells(0).Text)
            VideoTapesDataGrid.DataBind()
        End If
    End Sub
End Class
```

The Page_Load method creates an instance of the VideoTapeDataAccess object, sets the DataSource of the VideoTapesDataGrid, and then if the page is not a postback it calls the DataBind() method to initially display the grid.

As the DataGrid is rendered it calls the TrimDescription() method for each row as it passes the current video tape. The TrimDescription() method checks the length of the string and if it's shorter, it's trimmed; otherwise it returns the full length of the string. If it's under the length and it tried to call Substring on it, an IndexOutOfRange exception would be thrown.

The DataGrid also returns the full-length description if the VideoTapeID matches the ShowTapeID property. The ShowTapeID property is a member of the FancyBinding object that stores its value in the ViewState so it can keep its state between page views.

If the description is longer than the length to be trimmed and the user hasn't chosen to have the full description displayed for that item, then the string is clipped and the shortened string is returned.

The event handler for VideoTapesDataGrid_ItemCommand checks to make sure the command matches up with the Show Description button and then sets the member property ShowTapeID to the VideoTapeID that the user selected. It then calls VideoTapesGrid.DataBind() to refresh the display.

Figure 19-3 shows the grid bound with the text description clipped, and Figure 19-4 shows the entire text.

Title	Description		Object Type
1 Night of the Living Dead	The dead walk in thi...	Show Description	VideoStoreDataModel.EnterpriseVB.VideoStore.Data.VideoTape
2 Scary Movie	I see dead people	Show Description	VideoStoreDataModel.EnterpriseVB.VideoStore.Data.VideoTape
3 Jeffery's Fright Night	Oh the horror	Show Description	VideoStoreDataModel.EnterpriseVB.VideoStore.Data.VideoTape

Figure 19-3. The output of the FancyBinding page with the description shortened

Title	Description		Object Type
1 Night of the Living Dead	The dead walk in this 1960s thriller	Show Description	VideoStoreDataModel.EnterpriseVB.VideoStore.Data.VideoTape
2 Scary Movie	I see dead people	Show Description	VideoStoreDataModel.EnterpriseVB.VideoStore.Data.VideoTape
3 Jeffery's Fright Night	Oh the horror	Show Description	VideoStoreDataModel.EnterpriseVB.VideoStore.Data.VideoTape

Figure 19-4. The output of the FancyBinding page with the description expanded

Understanding Problematic Master-Detail Relationships

Several types of master-detail and parent-child relationships pose unique challenges to creating a high-performance Web application. There are two main master-detail problems: highly nested structures such as category trees and large master-detail relationships.

Working with Highly Nested Structures

Most applications have a tree structure somewhere in them. Generally they are used as a method of navigating a Web site or organizing a collection. The data structure behind them is generally the same and usually wrong. Look at Table 19-1 and see if you can find the problem with this structure.

Table 19-1. The VideoCategory Table, the Poor Performance Way

DESCRIPTION	DATA TYPE
CategoryID	Int
Description	Char(20)
ParentCategoryID	Int

CategoryID is the primary key for this table. The Description field is the name of the category displayed to the user so they know what they're seeing. ParentCategoryID is a subcategory of CategoryID. Generally the root-level category has a ParentCategoryID of 0 or –1 to indicate that it's a root-level category and that there's no parent category.

The problem with Table 19-1 is that there isn't a way to get the entire tree without executing multiple Select statements. To get all of the categories in this tree you'll have to commit another scalability mistake—using recursion. The only way to successfully get the whole tree is to recursively select everything that has a ParentCategoryID equal to the current CategoryID and so on. If your tree structure gets malformed, major problems can happen on your Web server and/or database server depending on exactly how you coded your statement.

The second problem with Table 19-1 is that to get decent performance, you'll have to have an index for CategoryID and a clustered index for ParentCategoryID, which is unnecessary with the alternate method described in Table 19-2.

Don't despair if you're using a system that uses this technique; it's a common programming error. The important thing is that there's a solution. Table 19-2 shows a minor modification to the table that makes a major difference in performance.

Table 19-2. The VideoCategory Table, the High Performance Way

DESCRIPTION	DATA TYPE
CategoryID	Int
Description	Char(20)
ParentCategoryID	Int
RootCategoryID	Int

This structure adds a RootCategoryID column, which is the category at the base of this entire tree. This column gives you a simple way to load the entire tree in a single Select statement with no recursion needed on the database server, and with a little fancy code on your Web server, you can avoid recursion there as well.

An additional advantage of this structure is the level of optimization afforded by a single clustered index on the RootCategoryID. Because you won't be using the CategoryID in the WHERE clause of any of your Select statements, you won't even need it to be indexed—just the RootCategoryID column. Figure 19-5 shows a populated VideoCategory table, the high performance way.

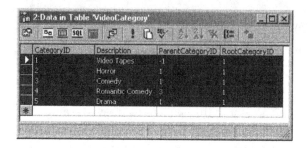

Figure 19-5. The data in the VideoCategory table

One of the mantras of good database design is to never have repetitive data, a mantra we're breaking here with good reason. In this case, it's necessary. Listing 19-7 shows the VideoCategory, VideoCategoryData, and VideoCategoryDataAccess objects.

Listing 19-7. VideoCategory *and Related Objects*

```
Imports System
Imports System.Data
Imports System.Data.SqlClient
Imports System.Data.Common

Namespace EnterpriseVB.VideoStore.Data


    Public Class VideoCategory

        Protected data As DataTable
        Protected index As Integer
        Protected subCategories As New ArrayList()
```

```vbnet
        Protected Friend ReadOnly Property MyData() As DataRow()
            Get
                Dim myRow() As DataRow = {Me.data.Rows(index)}
                Return myRow
            End Get
        End Property


        Public Sub New(ByRef data As VideoCategoryData, ByVal index As Integer)
            Me.data = data
            Me.index = index
        End Sub
        Public Sub New()
            Me.data = New VideoCategoryData()
            data.Rows.Add(data.NewRow())
            Me.index = 0
        End Sub


        Public Function GetColumn(ByRef ColumnName As String) As Object
            Return data.Rows(index)(ColumnName)
        End Function


        Public Function SetColumn(ByRef ColumnName As String, ByRef _
ColumnValue As Object)
            data.Rows(index)(ColumnName) = ColumnValue
        End Function


        Public Property CategoryID() As Int32
            Get
                If (GetColumn("CategoryID").GetType() Is _
Type.GetType("System.DBNull")) Then
                    Return -1
                End If
                Return CType(GetColumn("CategoryID"), Int32)
            End Get
            Set(ByVal Value As Int32)
                SetColumn("CategoryID", Value)
            End Set
        End Property


        Public Property Description() As String
            Get
                Return "" + GetColumn("Description")
            End Get
            Set(ByVal Value As String)
                SetColumn("Description", Value)
```

```
                End Set
            End Property


            Public Property ParentCategoryID() As Int32
                Get
                    If (GetColumn("ParentCategoryID").GetType() Is _
Type.GetType("System.DBNull")) Then
                        Return -1
                    End If
                    Return CType(GetColumn("ParentCategoryID"), Decimal)
                End Get
                Set(ByVal Value As Int32)
                    SetColumn("ParentCategoryID", Value)
                End Set
            End Property


            Public Property RootCategoryID() As Int32
                Get
                    If (GetColumn("RootCategoryID").GetType() Is _
Type.GetType("System.DBNull")) Then
                        Return -1
                    End If
                    Return CType(GetColumn("RootCategoryID"), Int32)
                End Get
                Set(ByVal Value As Int32)
                    SetColumn("RootCategoryID", Value)
                End Set
            End Property


            Public Function AddSubCategory(ByRef subCat As VideoCategory)
                Me.subCategories.Add(subCat)
            End Function


            Public Function FindCategoryByID(ByVal catID As Integer) As VideoCategory
                Return Me.FindCategoryByID(Me, catID)
            End Function


            Friend Function FindCategoryByID(ByRef cat As VideoCategory, _
ByVal catID As Integer) As VideoCategory

                If (catID = cat.CategoryID) Then
                    Return cat
                End If
```

```
        Dim i As Integer
        For i = 0 To cat.CountSubCategories() - 1
            If (FindCategoryByID(cat.GetSubCategory(i), catID) Is Nothing) Then
            Else
                Return cat.GetSubCategory(i)
            End If
        Next
        Return Nothing
    End Function


    Public Function CountSubCategories() As Int32
        Return Me.subCategories.Count
    End Function


    Public Function GetSubCategory(ByVal i As Int32) As VideoCategory
        Return CType(Me.subCategories(i), VideoCategory)
    End Function



End Class

Public Class VideoCategoryData
    Inherits DataTable

    Public Sub New()
        MyBase.New("VideoCategory")
        Me.Columns.Add("CategoryID", Type.GetType("System.Int32"))
        Me.Columns.Add("Description", Type.GetType("System.String"))
        Me.Columns.Add("ParentCategoryID", Type.GetType("System.Int32"))
        Me.Columns.Add("RootCategoryID", Type.GetType("System.Int32"))
    End Sub
End Class

Public Class VideoCategoryDataAccess

    Public connectionString As String
    Protected adapter As SqlDataAdapter
    Protected loadAll As SqlDataAdapter

    Public Sub New()
        connectionString = "Your Connection String;"
```

```
        adapter = New SqlDataAdapter()
        adapter.SelectCommand = New SqlCommand("VideoCategoryGetTree", New _
SqlConnection(connectionString))
        adapter.SelectCommand.CommandType = CommandType.StoredProcedure
        adapter.SelectCommand.Parameters.Add _
        ("@RootCategoryID", SqlDbType.Decimal, 0, "RootCategoryID")

    End Sub

    Public Function GetCategoryTree(ByVal rootCategoryID As Int32) _
As VideoCategory
        Dim data As New VideoCategoryData()
        adapter.SelectCommand.Parameters("@RootCategoryID").Value = _
rootCategoryID
        adapter.Fill(data)

        Dim categories As VideoCategory()
        categories = GetVideoCategoryArrayFromData(data)

        Dim i As Integer
        Dim x As Integer

        If (categories.Length = 0) Then
            Return Nothing
        End If

        For i = 0 To categories.Length - 1
            For x = 0 To categories.Length - 1
                If (categories(i).CategoryID = _
categories(x).ParentCategoryID) Then
                    categories(i).AddSubCategory(categories(x))
                End If
            Next
        Next
        Return categories(0)
    End Function

    Public Shared Function GetVideoCategoryArrayFromData(ByRef data As _
VideoCategoryData) As VideoCategory()
        Dim vArray(data.Rows.Count - 1) As VideoCategory
        Dim i As Integer
        For i = 0 To (data.Rows.Count - 1)
            vArray(i) = New VideoCategory(data, i)
```

```
        Next i
        Return vArray
    End Function
  End Class
End Namespace
```

The real magic of this object happens in the GetCategoryTree() method of the DAC. It's here that the category tree is assembled without recursion and with a single query. The DAC returns a single VideoCategory object that you can then work with and display. The net effect of this is you have a high-performance category tree and you'll never have to write and data access methods for the VideoCategory object no matter how many times you use it.

The VideoCategory object models the complete tree by providing a GetSubCategory() method to retrieve the subcategories of the current category. Internally, the VideoCategory object stores its subcategories in an ArrayList that it manages.

The VideoCategory object also provides a FindCategoryByID() method that does a search on the tree and returns the requested VideoCategory object. When a specific category gets referenced, either by the user selecting something or by some other method, it will likely be by the CategoryID. Without a method such as this, you would likely have to make another round trip to the database to load a category again that you already have in memory.

Figure 19-6 shows the output of a test harness. A test harness is a simple application used to exercise the features of a component. Test harnesses can be helpful in doing object-level or component-level debugging.

```
☐ Video Tapes
☐☐ Horror
☐☐ Comedy
☐☐☐ Romantic Comedy
☐☐ Drama
```

Figure 19-6. The output of the test harness

Working with a Much Larger Tree

The method described in the "Highly Nested Structures" section works great on most category trees with a reasonable amount of categories, but if you have a tree with potentially hundreds of categories, you'll need to use an alternate method.

For large structures you need to be able to load the tree in logical blocks. For example, look at the large structure-optimized version of the category tree in Table 19-3.

Table 19-3. The BlockedTree Table

DESCRIPTION	DATA TYPE
CategoryID	Int
Description	Char(20)
ParentCategoryID	Int
GroupID	Int

In this table's structure you can load the tree one block at a time and assemble the tree structure using your mapped objects in memory.

The stored procedure in Listing 19-8 allows you to request all the children of a specific category and get all of the categories in that group in a single block. The result is you can display a collapsed tree to the user, and as they expand the tree, the server won't have to hit the database for each expanded category.

Listing 19-8. The GetBlockedCategory *Stored Procedure*

```
CREATE PROCEDURE dbo. GetBlockedCategory
@CategoryID int
AS
BEGIN
SELECT CategoryID, Description, ParentCategoryID, GroupID
FROM BlockedTree WHERE GroupID=
    (SELECT GroupID FROM Category WHERE
ParentCategoryID=@CategoryID)
END
```

The only additional concern you have is writing the corresponding Visual Basic .NET code to take these blocks and dynamically assemble them on to your tree using a simple lazy-loading technique. (If you don't know what lazy loading is, don't worry—we cover it in the "Implementing Lazy Loading" section.)

Figure 19-7 shows the data in the BlockedTree table. Seeing this table with a sample of data in it should help you understand the intent of the structure.

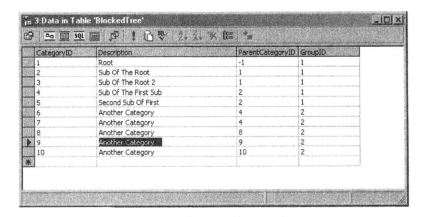

Figure 19-7. The BlockedTree table with data

Using a Better Tree Control

The test harness in this example uses a simple custom-coded method of displaying a tree, but there's a better way to do it. Microsoft provides the outstanding TreeView control for just this task in their Internet Explorer Web controls package at `http://msdn.microsoft.com/library/default.asp?url=/workshop/webcontrols/overview/treeview.asp`. Don't let the name fool you—it's not only for Internet Explorer. In fact, it works quite well in Netscape 4.*x* and 6, thanks to some clever coding by Microsoft.

The Internet Explorer Web controls package is free and includes several other useful Web components, such as a tabbed view and a docking-capable toolbar that will have your Web applications looking like desktop applications!

A Final Note on Tree Optimization

Using recursion to walk through the tree is not the most high-performance method of moving through a tree structure. As an alternative, you can create an index that looks like Table 19-4.

Table 19-4. An Indexed Table

CATEGORYID	DESCRIPTION	PARENTCATEGORYID	INDEX
1	Video Tapes	−1	1.0.0
2	Horror	1	1.2.0
3	Comedy	1	1.3.0
4	Romantic Comedy	3	1.3.4
5	Drama	1	1.5.0

The index is a string that shows the category at each stop of the tree. In Table 19-4, the root CategoryID is 1; therefore, all of the first numbers in the index are 1. The second number is the next level down in the tree, which is different for everything except the Romantic Comedy category. Romantic Comedy is a subcategory of Comedy, so they share the second number 3. The last number is 0 for everything but Romantic Comedy because only it is nested three levels deep.

The index would not actually be stored in the database but instead assembled in memory as a way to quickly iterate through the tree without recursion. The reason why it's not a good idea to necessarily store the index in the database is because you would have to use the substring function as part of your subquery, which would cause a table scan.

Implementing an index such as this is both a good and a bad thing depending on how you look at it. The good part is that once the tree is assembled, the tree can be iterated through and searched quickly and without recursion. The bad part is there's a small upfront cost in building the index. Because .NET is stateless and will forget the tree as soon as it's assembled, we included the "quick-and-dirty" method over building the full index for the examples in this chapter.

If you plan on caching a tree or implementing some type of method that reuses the same structure, we recommend adding an index.

Working with Large Master-Detail Relationships

One of the most common issues with OR mapping is how to handle large master-detail relationships without degrading performance. There are several ways to handle these types of relationships. You'll have to decide what works best for the application you're building because the best method depends on how your data will actually be used; also, some of it may require some experimentation.

There are three primary approaches to this problem:

- Implementing a lazy loading scheme

- Implementing an incremental lazy loading scheme

- Loading the detail when the master is loaded

Implementing Lazy Loading

Large master-detail relationships can be problematic in any relationship but even more so with OR mapping. The primary goals of OR mapping is to hide anything even vaguely resembling data access and to enable a clean object-oriented Application Programming Interface (API) that's easily usable by anyone.

With these design points in mind, ideally you would like your API to work something like the following:

```
myCategory.Videos(0).Title
```

Because a group of VideoTape objects belong to a category, you want to be able to access the VideoTape objects that belong to the category using an array. The problem is that you don't always want to load all of the VideoTape objects from the database. In most cases, you load all of the categories and likely only one collection of VideoTape objects belonging to a category.

The solution to this problem is to implement an old programming trick called *lazy loading*. Lazy loading means not actually loading the detail data until the program tries to use it the first time. This is most advantageous in a situation such as the one in Listing 19-9, namely when you're only displaying the detail table on one or two of the master items.

Listing 19-9. The Addition of the Videos() *Array to the* VideoCategory *Object*

```
Dim vids As VideoTape()
      Public ReadOnly Property Videos() As VideoTape()
         Get
             If (vids Is Nothing) Then
                 Dim vDAC As New VideoTapeDataAccess()
                 vids = vDAC.GetAllVideoTapesInCategory(Me.CategoryID)
             End If
             Return vids
         End Get
      End Property
```

A VideoTape array called vids is added to the object. Because this array hasn't been initialized, its default value is Nothing. The read-only property Videos provides access to the VideoTape objects that belong in this category.

When the calling program accesses the Videos array, the VideoCategory object checks to see if vids hasn't been initialized. If it hasn't, then the VideoCategory creates an instance of the VideoTapeDataAccess DAC and initializes vids with the array of VideoTapes that belong in this category. Listing 19-10 shows the HTML side of the LazyLoading page.

Listing 19-10. The HTML Page of the LazyLoading Page

```
<%@ Page Language="vb" AutoEventWireup="false"
Codebehind="LazyLoading.aspx.vb" Inherits="LazyLoadingWeb.WebForm1"%>
<!DOCTYPE HTML PUBLIC "-//W3C//DTD HTML 4.0 Transitional//EN">
<HTML>
<HEAD>
     <title></title>
     <meta content="Microsoft Visual Studio.NET 7.0" name="GENERATOR">
     <meta content="Visual Basic 7.0" name="CODE_LANGUAGE">
     <meta content="JavaScript" name="vs_defaultClientScript">
     <meta content=http://schemas.microsoft.com/intellisense/ie5
 name="vs_targetSchema">
</HEAD>
<body>
<form id="Form1" method="post" runat="server">
<table cellSpacing="0" cellPadding="0" width="100%" border="0">
<tr>
     <td vAlign="top" align="left">
     <asp:table id="CategoryTree" runat="server"></asp:table>
</td>
<td vAlign="top" align="left" width="100%">
     <asp:DataGrid id="VideoTapesGrid" runat="server"
AutoGenerateColumns="False" Width="100%">
     <Columns>
     <asp:BoundColumn DataField="VideoTapeID"></asp:BoundColumn>
     <asp:BoundColumn DataField="Title"></asp:BoundColumn>
     </Columns>
     </asp:DataGrid>
</td>
</tr>
</table>
</form>
</body>
</HTML>
```

The HTML of this page consists of two main elements. The first is a server-side table that renders the category tree, and the second is a DataGrid that displays the VideoTapes that belong in the category.

Server-side table generation in the code-behind object is obviously not the best solution for rendering a tree control. When implementing these techniques on an actual system, please be a responsible programmer and implement your tree views using a Web custom control or subclass Microsoft's Internet Explorer TreeView object. Listing 19-11 shows the code-behind object of the LazyLoading page.

Listing 19-11. The Code-Behind Object of the LazyLoading Page

```
Imports VideoStoreDataModel.EnterpriseVB.VideoStore.Data

Public Class WebForm1
    Inherits System.Web.UI.Page
    Protected WithEvents VideoTapesGrid As System.Web.UI.WebControls.DataGrid
    Protected WithEvents CategoryTree As System.Web.UI.WebControls.Table

    Public Property SelectedCategoryID() As Integer
        Get
            If (("" + ViewState("SelCatID")) = "") Then
                Return -1
            End If
            Return Convert.ToInt32("" + ViewState("SelCatID"))
        End Get
        Set(ByVal Value As Integer)
            ViewState("SelCatID") = "" + Value.ToString()
        End Set
    End Property
    Private Sub Page_Load(ByVal sender As System.Object, ByVal e As _
System.EventArgs) Handles MyBase.Load
        DisplayCategoryTree()
    End Sub

    Private Sub DisplayCategoryTree()
        CategoryTree.Rows.Clear()
        Dim dac As New VideoCategoryDataAccess()
        Dim category As VideoCategory
        category = dac.GetCategoryTree(1)
        Dim depth As Integer
        depth = GetDepth(category, 0)
        RenderTree(category, depth, 0)
```

```
            If (SelectedCategoryID <> -1) Then
                Dim cCat As VideoCategory
                cCat = cCat.FindCategoryByID(SelectedCategoryID)
                VideoTapesGrid.DataSource = cCat.Videos
                VideoTapesGrid.DataBind()
            End If
        End Sub
        Public Function RenderTree(ByRef cat As VideoCategory, _
    ByVal depth As Integer, _
    ByVal currentDepth As Integer)
            Dim tr As New TableRow()

            Dim i As Integer
            For i = 0 To currentDepth
                Dim spacerCell As New TableCell()
                spacerCell.Text = " "
                spacerCell.Width = Unit.Pixel(10)
                spacerCell.Height = Unit.Pixel(10)
                spacerCell.BorderWidth = Unit.Pixel(0)
                tr.Cells.Add(spacerCell)
            Next

            Dim descCell As New TableCell()
            descCell.ColumnSpan = (depth - currentDepth) + 1

            Dim lb As New LinkButton()
            lb.Text = cat.Description
            lb.ID = "CAT" + cat.CategoryID.ToString()
            AddHandler lb.Click, AddressOf Category_Selected

            descCell.Controls.Add(lb)
            If (Me.SelectedCategoryID = cat.CategoryID) Then
                descCell.BackColor = Color.Yellow
            Else
                descCell.BackColor = Color.White
            End If
            descCell.Style.Add("white-space", "nowrap")

            tr.Cells.Add(descCell)
            CategoryTree.Rows.Add(tr)

            currentDepth = currentDepth + 1
            For i = 0 To cat.CountSubCategories() - 1
```

```
                RenderTree(cat.GetSubCategory(i), depth, currentDepth)
        Next

    End Function

    Public Sub Category_Selected(ByVal sender As Object, ByVal e As EventArgs)
        Me.SelectedCategoryID = _
Convert.ToInt32((CType(sender, LinkButton)).ID.Substring(3))
        Me.DisplayCategoryTree()
    End Sub

    Public Function GetDepth(ByVal cat As VideoCategory, _
ByVal depth As Integer) As Integer

        Dim tDepth As Integer
        Dim deepest As Integer
        deepest = depth

        Dim i As Integer
        For i = 0 To cat.CountSubCategories() - 1
            tDepth = GetDepth(cat.GetSubCategory(i), depth + 1)
            If (tDepth > deepest) Then
                deepest = tDepth
            End If
        Next
        Return deepest
    End Function
End Class
```

You can break the code-behind object of the LazyLoading page into two primary functional parts: the tree rendering portion and the VideoTape listing.

The DisplayCategoryTree() method delegates the task of building the table to RenderTree() and GetDepth() methods after loading the data from the database. The GetDepth() method is needed so you know how deep the deepest element is in the tree to determine what the ColSpan needs to be for each category to achieve a nice tabbed look for the tree. As the tree is being rendered, it checks each VideoCategory to see if it matches the SelectedCategoryID property. If it does, it highlights that category.

At the end of the DisplayCategoryTree() method, it checks to see if SelectedCategoryID has a value provided. If it does, the program makes a call to the FindCategoryByID() method of the VideoCategory object to get the category that the user has selected. It then sets the DataSource of the VideoTapesGrid to the Videos array of the VideoCategory object and calls DataBind() to update the display.

As the Videos array is accessed for the first time, behind the scenes the
VideoCategory object loads the array of VideoTapes from the database and returns
it. Subsequent attempts to the Videos collection of the VideoCategory object will
use the version already in memory without having to make another round trip to
the database. Figure 19-8 shows the LazyLoading page in action.

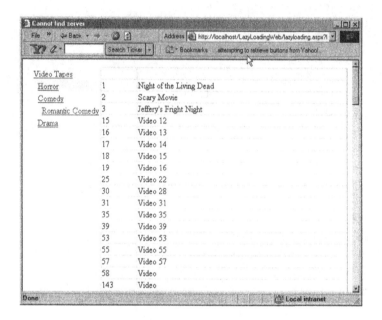

Figure 19-8. The output of the LazyLoading page

Implementing an Incremental Lazy Loading Scheme

Lazy loading as described in the previous section works for most purposes, but if
you're in a situation where the detail set is potentially hundreds or thousands of
records, then it becomes necessary to implement an incremental lazy loading
technique.

In a nutshell, when the information is first requested from the detail set, a
small number of records will be retrieved along with the count of the total number
of records. If a request is made for one of the records that's out of range of what
was loaded, the rest of the records will be loaded.

An example of where this technique is useful is on a "summary page" that displays the first 10 records on the front page and allows the user to click for more
information. Most of the time the user will not click the link to see the additional
records, so it doesn't make any sense to load them and incur the network overhead
between your Web server and database to fetch the entire result set if it's not necessary.

To implement the incremental lazy loading scheme, you must modify both the stored procedure and the VideoCategory component. The VideoCategory object needs to get the first 10 records from the database, and it also needs to know how many records there are total in the database, so the VideoCategory object will know if and when an additional round trip to the database is necessary. Listing 19-12 shows the VideoTapeLoadByCategoryIncrID stored procedure, which loads the first 10 video tapes for a given category.

Listing 19-12. The Incremental Lazy Loading Stored Procedure

```
CREATE PROCEDURE dbo.VideoTapeLoadByCategoryIncrID
@CategoryID int,
@TotalRows int out
AS
BEGIN
SELECT @TotalRows = (SELECT count(*) FROM VideoTape WHERE CategoryID=@CategoryID)
SELECT  TOP 10 VideoTapeID,  CategoryID, Title, Description FROM
VideoTape WHERE CategoryID=@CategoryID
END
```

The VideoTapeLoadByCategoryIncrID stored procedure first gets the total number of records that are in the result set and stores it in an output variable. The second Select statement actually loads the first 10 rows from the database.

To put this stored procedure to work, you need a custom indexer smart enough to transparently know when it needs to return to the database to get the remaining records. Listing 19-13 shows the VideoCategoryIndexer.

Listing 19-13. VideoCategoryIndexer

```
    Public Class VideoCategoryIndexer

        Private vids As ArrayList
        Private cnt As Integer

        Public Sub New(ByVal catID As Integer, ByRef conn As SqlConnection)
            vids = New ArrayList()
            Dim sda As New SqlDataAdapter()
            sda.SelectCommand = New SqlCommand(_
"VideoTapeLoadByCategoryIncrID", conn)
            sda.SelectCommand.CommandType = _
CommandType.StoredProcedure
```

```
            sda.SelectCommand.Parameters.Add( _
    "@CategoryID", SqlDbType.Int, 0, "CategoryID")
            sda.SelectCommand.Parameters.Add( _
    "@TotalRows", SqlDbType.Int)
            sda.SelectCommand.Parameters("@TotalRows").Direction = _
    ParameterDirection.Output
            sda.SelectCommand.Parameters("@CategoryID").Value = catID
            Dim data As New VideoTapeData()
            sda.Fill(data)
            cnt = Convert.ToInt32(sda.SelectCommand.Parameters("@TotalRows").Value)
            vids.AddRange(VideoTapeDataAccess.GetVideoTapeArrayFromData(data))
        End Sub


        Public Function Count() As Integer
            Return cnt
        End Function


        Public Property Videos(ByVal index As Integer) As VideoTape
            Get
                If (index >= vids.Count) Then
                    FullLoad()
                End If
                Return CType(vids(index), VideoTape)
            End Get
            Set(ByVal Value As VideoTape)
                vids(index) = Value
            End Set
        End Property


        Public ReadOnly Property LoadedCount() As Integer
            Get
                Return vids.Count
            End Get
        End Property


        Private Function FullLoad()
            Dim dac As New VideoTapeDataAccess()
            vids.Clear()
            vids.AddRange(dac.GetAllVideoTapes())
        End Function
    End Class


End Namespace
```

VideoCategoryIndexer immediately loads the first 10 records in the constructor using an inline call to the VideoTapeLoadByCategoryIncrID stored procedure. The stored procedure also returns a count of the number of records that existed in the database in the @TotalRows output variable, which VideoCategoryIndexer then stores in the member variable cnt.

The Videos() indexed property accesses the internal ArrayList to get the requested VideoTape object. If the calling program requests one of the VideoTapes within the rage that's loaded, it returns it immediately. If the calling program requests one of the VideoTape objects that has not been loaded yet, it transparently loads the entire collection.

VideoCategoryIndexer would not normally include a public LoadedCount property simply because the point of an object such as this is to make the incremental lazy loading transparent to the calling program. It's only included in this example to provide "proof" to the test case that it's indeed working. Listing 19-14 shows the test case for VideoCategoryIndexer.

Listing 19-14. The VideoCategoryIndexer *Test Case*

```
Imports VideoStoreDataModel.EnterpriseVB.VideoStore.Data

Module IncLoadTestCase

    Sub Main()

        Console.WriteLine("Starting IncLoadTestCase")
        Dim iLoadCat As New VideoCategoryIndexer(3, _
New SqlClient.SqlConnection(VideoCategoryDataAccess.connectionString))
        Console.WriteLine("Loaded " + iLoadCat.LoadedCount.ToString() _
+ " out of " + iLoadCat.Count().ToString() + ".")

        Console.WriteLine("Displaying First 10")
        Dim i As Integer
        For i = 0 To iLoadCat.LoadedCount - 1
            Console.WriteLine("Item:" + iLoadCat.Videos(i).Title)
        Next

        Console.WriteLine("Displaying All")
        For i = 0 To iLoadCat.Count() - 1
            Console.WriteLine("Item:" + iLoadCat.Videos(i).Title)
        Next

        Console.WriteLine("Test Complete.")
```

```
        Console.WriteLine("Press enter key to quit.")
        Console.ReadLine()

    End Sub

End Module
```

The incremental lazy loading test case first creates an instance of VideoCategoryIndexer. Second, it displays the number of items loaded as well as the total count of items to be found in the database. Next, it displays all of the VideoTape objects currently loaded. Finally, it displays all of the items in the collection. As it does this final step, it reaches out into the database and loads the remaining VideoTape objects as soon as the requested index is outside of the loaded range. Figure 19-9 shows the output of the incremental lazy loading test case that tests the LazyLoading component.

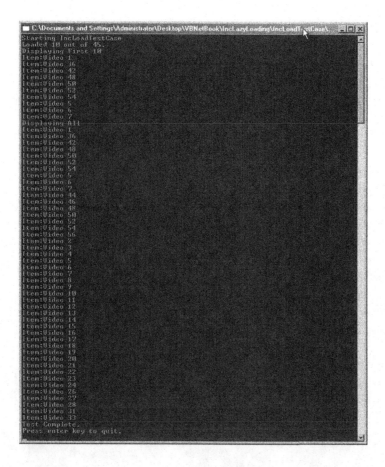

Figure 19-9. The incremental lazy loading test case output

The amazing thing about this test case is that the object's lazy loading functionality is completely transparent. That said, you can do certain things to enhance the functionality of this system.

If you were to implement IEnumerable, this collection would be capable of being data bound to any of .NET's many controls. You would also be able to use it transparently as you would any other array.

Another thing you can do to enhance the functionality of VideoCategoryIndexer is to integrate it into the VideoCategory object to use it as its internal means of loading the VideoTape objects that belong in the category. This, combined with implementing the IEnumerable interface, would allow you to use incremental lazy loading without modifying any code you may have written for the VideoCategory object.

You'll want to consider your own problem carefully before using lazy loading. If parts of your application will always need the whole table, you need to keep VideoCategoryIndexer as a separate object only to be used when you truly intend to do incremental lazy loading; otherwise you'll have code that calls two stored procedures instead of one.

Loading the Detail When the Master Is Loaded

The third main tool at your disposal when working with potentially large master-detail relationships is loading the detail table when the master table is loaded. The advantages of doing this are minimizing the round trips required to the database to load and work with your objects.

The situation where this strategy is beneficial is when you need to be able to display the master as well as most, or all, of the detail. A good example is a page that displays 10 orders per page, and each order has 1 to 20 line items. The master table Order will always display the detail table Selection every time the master is displayed throughout the application.

The solution is to implement a GetOrdersByDay() method (or whatever method of choosing the orders you need to provide) that automatically calls the stored procedures to load the Orders and the Selections for that day and then assemble them into your mapped objects in memory.

Loading the detail automatically in situations where it's not needed increases the round trips to the database and increases application latency. Always make sure that this is what your users will be doing most of the time when using this technique.

In situations where you're loading more detail records than you'll be displaying, but you know that the user will be asking to see them fairly quickly, makes this technique a good fit if you have a simple high-performance caching mechanism.

Using a Near-Zero-Impact Caching Mechanism

When working with mapped objects, a number of places and situations call for a fast but not necessarily reliable caching mechanism. Although .NET is built to be a highly scalable stateless model, it doesn't hurt to use a little caching at the Web server as long as it doesn't consume unnecessary resources.

A good example of where this is helpful is loading something such as an object for the currently logged-in user. For each page view you get a cookie from the user that's their user ID, query the database, load it into the mapped object, and then display their first and last name in the header of the page. Using a simple caching mechanism eliminates many of these round trips and thus boosts scalability and reducing latency.

The problem with using a traditional cache that keeps items cached for a set amount of time is the amount of memory consumed by the server increases for each user. The entire point of a stateless model is to avoid situations where memory usage increases for all of the incoming connections to the Web server.

In most situations you can use what Microsoft gives you by putting the Cache object to work. In situations where you have a layer of abstraction between what you're caching and ASP.NET, this simply isn't possible without explicitly passing a reference to the Cache object to your data access components. Using good OR mapping practices such as abstracting your objects from the presentation layer make the Cache object unusable in a mapped application. This unfortunately means that if you need a caching mechanism available in any situation where your code isn't executing on a Web server, you'll need to buy or write your own caching object. Because you can't use the Cache object in your data access components, the solution to implementing a caching system in the stateless model is to use weak references to your objects. A weak reference is a way of referring to an object that tells the .NET runtime that if it needs the memory for something else to go ahead and overwrite the space where your object is in memory. If you attempt to access your weak referenced object after its memory has been consumed by another process, it will return the Visual Basic null constant Nothing. Listing 19-15 shows the WeakCache object, a cache that won't consume resources needed by other parts of the application.

Listing 19-15. The WeakCache *Object*

```vb
Imports System
Imports System.Collections


Namespace EnterpriseVB.VideoStore.Data

    Public Class WeakCache

        Private hash As Hashtable
        Private lastCleared As DateTime

        Public Sub New()
            hash = New Hashtable()
            lastCleared = DateTime.Now
        End Sub

        Public Property Items(ByVal key As String) As Object
            Get
                Dim ref As WeakReference
                If (hash(key) Is Nothing) Then
                    Return Nothing
                End If
        If (lastCleared.Ticks + 1000000 < DateTime.Now.Ticks) Then
                    Dim temp As Object
                    lastCleared = DateTime.Now
                    temp = CType(hash(key), WeakReference).Target
                    hash.Clear()
                    lastCleared = DateTime.Now
                    Return temp
                End If
                Return CType(hash(key), WeakReference).Target
            End Get
            Set(ByVal Value As Object)
                hash(key) = New WeakReference(Value)
            End Set
        End Property

    End Class


End Namespace
```

The WeakCache object creates an instance of a Hashtable and sets the lastCleared property to the current time. When the calling program sets a value in the Items indexed property, the WeakCache object stores it as a WeakReference.

When the calling program tries to get a value from the indexed property, a few things happen. As the property is accessed, the WeakCache object checks to make sure the value being requested is not Nothing. If it's Nothing, it returns immediately to avoid a NullReferenceException.

Next, it checks to see if 1,000,000 ticks have passed since the lastAccessed time. If they have, the WeakCache object clears the entire cache after updating the lastCleared time to the currentTime and returning the value for which the calling program has asked. You may be asking yourself the question, "If weak references don't hog memory, why ever clear the cache?"

There are two primary reasons why an occasional clearing of the cache is necessary. First, there has to be a check to make sure that cached objects have some kind of expiration date. It would be bad if a user whose account you locked out didn't expire until you rebooted the server. The second reason is that although the object is weak referenced, the key isn't. If you don't clear the Hashtable from time to time, these tiny little keys will pile up and consume a noticeable amount of memory toward a collision course with the greatest fear of all Web applications— paging. (Paging is when a machine runs out of available RAM memory and has to start writing to disk, which is substantially slower than RAM.)

The final thing the getter method of the Items property indexer does is actually return the value. All of the checks prior to this step are necessary to guard against NullReferenceExceptions, keeping the data fresh and avoiding a memory leak.

Optimal areas to put a weak cache in your code are areas where large amounts of data, such as a detail table, are loaded. Generally, in situations such as these, you want to cache the entire collection as a single entry in the WeakCache object so if one of the objects in the detail collection gets overwritten, the whole thing returns null. If you just cache the individual objects and scan through the collection to load the details, some records may have disappeared. You want an all-or-nothing situation.

Summary

In this chapter you learned how to use data binding with your mapped objects and how to overcome common performance problems that arise when working with mapped objects. You can enhance the performance of your application in a number of ways that are far easier to implement if you put OR mapping to work than if you use simple DataSet objects.

CHAPTER 20

COM Interoperability and ADO.NET

THE COMPONENT OBJECT Model (COM) has been around for many years and is used by many Windows applications. Eventually the .NET platform will replace COM, but until then you may need to develop COM components from .NET and access them from unmanaged code, or you may want to use COM components in .NET applications. *COM interoperability* (also referred to as *COM Interop*) enables you to use existing COM components in .NET applications or use .NET components in unmanaged code.

 NOTE *In this chapter you'll see how to use ADO and other COM-based data access technologies through COM Interop in your .NET applications. However, COM interoperability is a wide area. If you want to learn about COM interoperability in more detail, you may want to read* COM and .NET Interoperability *by Andrew Troelsen (Apress, 2002).*

The code written for the .NET Framework is also referred to as *managed code*, and the code written for traditional Windows applications (previous to the .NET Framework) is called *unmanaged code.* Managed code contains metadata used by the Common Language Runtime (CLR).

In COM, type libraries stored metadata for a COM component and described the characteristics of a COM component. In .NET, an *assembly* is the primary building block of a .NET application. An assembly is a collection of functionality that's built, versioned, and deployed as a component. An assembly contains an assembly manifest, which performs similar functions to a COM type library. The assembly manifest includes information about an assembly such as the identity, version, culture, digital signature, compile-time dependencies, files that make up the assembly implementation, and permissions required to run the assembly properly.

In brief, COM understands the language of type libraries, and the .NET Framework understands the language of assembly manifests. So converting a type library into an assembly manifest provides accessibility to COM components from the managed code, and converting an assembly manifest to a COM type library provides accessibility to .NET assemblies in unmanaged code.

Interop assemblies are .NET assemblies that act as a bridge between managed and unmanaged code. Interop assemblies provide mapping COM object members to equivalent .NET managed members.

The .NET Framework defines a common set of data types. All .NET programming languages use these common data types. During the import process of a COM type library, there may be cases when the parameters and return values of COM objects use data types that do not correspond to .NET data types. The Interop marshaler handles these conversions for you. *Interoperability marshaling* is the process of packaging parameters and returning values into equivalent data types during conversion of a COM type library to an assembly manifest and an assembly manifest to a COM type library.

TIP *If you're looking for more COM- and Interop-related answers, you may want to look at the* System.Runtime.InteropServices *namespace and its classes in the MSDN documentation.*

Exploring the .NET Interop Tools

The .NET Framework provides many tools for runtime as well as Visual Studio .NET (VS .NET) users. We'll use VS .NET for the applications in this chapter, but it doesn't hurt to take a look at these options. It's easy to convert a COM library into a .NET assembly using these tools. There are three different ways to do so.

Using Visual Studio .NET

VS .NET provides a pretty simple way to import a type library in a managed application. The Project ➤ Add Reference menu option allows you to access a COM library and add it to the project. This adds a namespace to the project, so you can access the library members through that namespace.

Using the Type Library Importer and Exporter (Tlbimp.exe)

The Type Library Importer, known as Tlbimp or Tlbimp.exe, is a command-line utility to convert a COM type library into a .NET assembly. Why a command-line utility? Well, this is an obvious question if you're using VS. You can ignore this option if you use VS.NET for your development. This option is useful for developers who don't have VS.NET.

Tlbimp.exe takes as a minimum one argument, the filename of the COM type library that you want to convert to an equivalent .NET Runtime assembly. The output of Tlbimp.exe is a binary file that contains runtime metadata for the types defined in the original COM type library.

This is the syntax:

```
tlbimp  tlbFile [options]
```

where tlbFile is the name of the COM type library.

Table 20-1 describes some of the Tlbimp.exe options.

Table 20-1. Tlbimp.exe *Options*

OPTION	DESCRIPTION
/asmversion:versionNumber	Specifies the version of the assembly to produce
/help	Displays the available help commands
/namespace	Specifies the namespace in which to produce the assembly
/out:filename	Specifies the name of output assembly
/references:filename	Specifies the namespaces to use to resolve references to types defined outside the current type library
/?	Displays syntaxes and options for the tool

You can find Tlbimp.exe in the FrameworkSDK\Bin directory of your VS .NET or .NET Software Development Kit (SDK) installation.

Using the Type Library Exporter (Tlbexp.exe)

The Type Library Exporter (Tlbexp.exe) does the reverse job of Tlbimp.exe. It generates an equivalent type library for a .NET assembly. This utility is useful when you need to use a managed code assembly in unmanaged code. Similar to Tlbimp, this utility also has options. The default command is as follows:

```
tlbexp assemblyName
```

where assemblyName is the name of the assembly for which you want to convert an equivalent type library.

Table 20-2 describes some of the options.

Table 20-2. Tlbexp.exe *Options*

OPTION	DESCRIPTION
/help	Shows command syntax and options.
/out:file	Specifies the name of the type library to generate equivalent to an assembly. If there are no options, the default name of the type library is the same as the assembly.
/?	Shows command syntax and options.

You can find Tlbexp.exe in the FrameworkSDK\Bin directory of your VS .NET or .NET SDK installation.

CAUTION *You can't use* Tlbexp.exe *to produce a type library from an assembly that was imported using* Tlbimp.exe.

Using the ADO Recordset in ADO.NET

In this example, you'll see how to import the ADO type library and use the ADO recordset to access a database. After that, you'll fill data to a DataSet from the ADO recordset using a DataAdapter.

CAUTION *There's a cost involved in terms of performance when you use ADO in managed code because of COM Interop. Using ADO in managed code doesn't give you the same performance you can get using and ADO.NET* DataSet *and* DataReader. *We use an ADO recordset only when we have no other option--for example, when you have a library that uses ADO and you need to use this library in managed applications.*

To test this application, create a Windows application and drag a DataGrid control to the form from Toolbox. To add a reference to a COM type library, go to the Add Reference option from the Project menu and select the COM tab in the Add Reference dialog box. As you can see from the Figure 20-1, we selected Microsoft ActiveX Data Objects 2.7 Library. Click Select to add the selection to the Selected Components list. Now click OK.

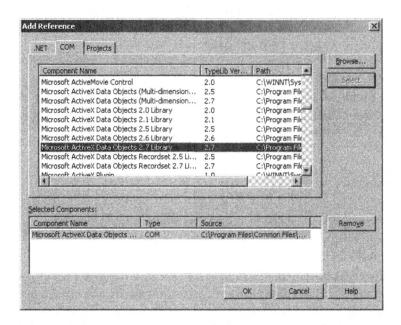

Figure 20-1. Adding a reference to a COM library

This action adds the ADODB namespace to the project. You can see this namespace now listed in the project's namespaces (see Figure 20-2).

Figure 20-2. Namespace after adding ADODB namespace to the project

After adding a namespace reference to a project, its members are available for use in your project. You include this namespace in your application by calling Imports. You also should add a reference to the System.Data.OleDb namespace because you'll use the OleDb DataAdapter to fill a DataSet. So, add these two name-space references to the project with this:

```
Imports ADODB
Imports System.Data.OleDb
```

Now you can use the ADO recordset and connection to access a database. As you can see from Listing 20-1, you create a Connection object and set the con-nection mode and cursor location. After that, you call the connection's Execute method to execute a SQL statement that returns the _Recordset object. The Fill method of the DataAdapter reads data from a recordset and fills data to a DataSet. As you can see from this code, you create a DataSet and DataAdapter and call the DataAdapter's Fill method. The Fill method takes three parameters: a DataSet, a recordset, and a DataSet name. Finally, you bind the DataSet to a DataGrid to fill data from the DataSet to the DataGrid.

Listing 20-1. Using an ADODB Namespace to Access a Database

```
Private Sub Form1_Load(ByVal sender As System.Object, _
ByVal e As System.EventArgs) Handles MyBase.Load
' Create SQL and Connection strings
Dim ConnectionString As String = "Provider=Microsoft.Jet.OLEDB.4.0;" & _
"Data Source=c:\\Northwind.mdb"
Dim sql As String = "SELECT CustomerId, CompanyName, ContactName From Customers"
' Create a Connection object and open it
Dim conn As Connection = New Connection()
Dim connMode As Integer = CType(ConnectModeEnum.adModeUnknown, Integer)
conn.CursorLocation = CursorLocationEnum.adUseServer
conn.Open(ConnectionString, "", "", connMode)
Dim recAffected As Object = Nothing
Dim cmdType As Integer = CType(CommandTypeEnum.adCmdText, Integer)
Dim rs As _Recordset = conn.Execute(sql, recAffected, cmdType)
' Create dataset and data adapter objects
Dim ds As DataSet = New DataSet("Recordset")
Dim da As OleDbDataAdapter = New OleDbDataAdapter()
' Call data adapter's Fill method to fill data from ADO
' Recordset to the dataset
da.Fill(ds, rs, "Customers")
' Now use dataset
DataGrid1.DataSource = ds.DefaultViewManager
End Sub
```

The output of Listing 20-1 looks like Figure 20-3.

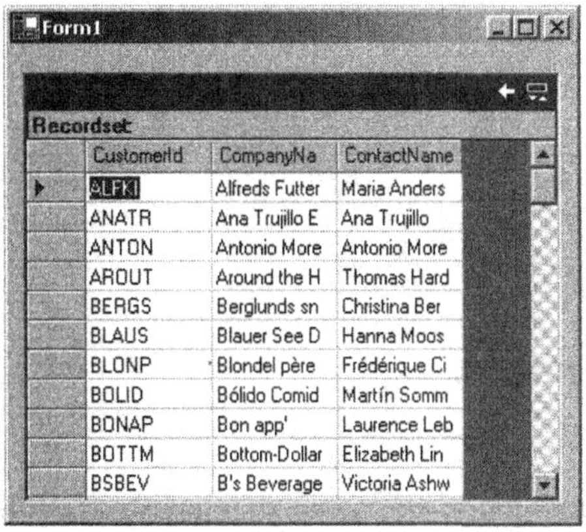

Figure 20-3. Displaying data from an ADO recordset to a DataGrid

Once you know to access ADO in managed code, you can do anything you want including adding, updating, and deleting data using an ADO recordset.

Using ADOX with ADO.NET

Microsoft ActiveX Data Objects Extensions for Data Definition Language and Security (ADOX) is an extension to ADO that provides an object model to manipulate data definition and security.

You can use ADOX in managed code in a similar way that you used an ADO recordset in the previous section. Just add a reference to ADOX type library using VS .NET's Add Reference option and use the namespace and its members as you would in unmanaged code.

To test this, create a new Windows application. After that, add a reference to the Microsoft ADO Ext. 2.7 for DLL and Security component to the project (see Figure 20-4).

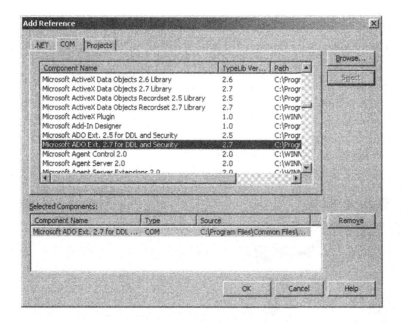

Figure 20-4. Adding a reference to ADOX library

After adding the reference, you'll see that the ADOX namespace is listed in the available namespaces in your application (see Figure 20-5).

Figure 20-5. ADOX namespace listed in project references

Now, the only thing you need to do is to use the namespace and its members. The ADOX classes should be available in your application after adding Imports ADOX to the project. ADOX provides objects that you can use to create databases, tables, and columns. The Catalog object represents a database and its Create method creates a new database. The Table object represents a database table. You can add columns to a Table object using the Columns collection's Append method. Listing 20-2 creates a new Microsoft Access database called Test.mdb with the table MyTable and two columns, col1 and col2, in it.

Listing 20-2. Using ADOX from Managed Code

```vb
Private Sub Form1_Load(ByVal sender As System.Object, _
  ByVal e As System.EventArgs) Handles MyBase.Load
    ' Create SQL and Connection strings
    Dim ConnectionString As String = _
    "Provider=Microsoft.Jet.OLEDB.4.0; Data Source=c:\\Test.mdb"
    Try
      ' Create a Catalog object
      Dim ct As Catalog = New Catalog()
      ct.Create(ConnectionString)
      ' Create a table and two columns
      Dim dt As Table = New Table()
      dt.Name = "MyTable"
      dt.Columns.Append("col1", DataTypeEnum.adInteger, 4)
      dt.Columns.Append("col2", DataTypeEnum.adVarWChar, 255)
      ' Add table to the tables collection
      ct.Tables.Append(CType(dt, Object))
```

```
    Catch exp As Exception
        MessageBox.Show(exp.Message.ToString())
    End Try
End Sub
```

Accessing OLAP Server Data with ADO.NET

On-Line Analytical Processing (OLAP) is a service that represents raw data in a variety of views of information that's easily understandable by the users. OLAP provides consistent and fast access to the data, which can be represented in personalized views in the real world without considering the size and complexity of the database. For example, OLAP can represent data in the form of three-dimensional cubes and cells. The server involved in this processing is called an *OLAP server*. The OLAP server is a high-capacity, multiuser data manipulation engine specifically designed to work on multidimensional data structures. The ActiveX Data Objects Multi-Dimensional Library (ADOMD) provides access to OLAP server data. OLAP services extract, summarize, organize, and store data warehouses in multidimensional structures, also known as OLAP *server cubes*.

To test this OLAP sample, you'll use the FoodMart 2000 database that comes with Microsoft SQL Server Analysis Server. Before testing this sample, you must have SQL Server 2000 Analysis Server running. If you don't have SQL Server 2000 Analysis Server running, you can install it from Microsoft SQL Server CD by selecting SQL Server 2000 Components ➤ Install Analysis Services. This option installs SQL Server 2000 Analysis Server on your machine.

NOTE *Installing Analysis Services may not install the FoodMart 2000 database. You may need to restore the database from the* `C:\Program Files\ Microsoft Analysis Services\Samples\ foodmart 2000.cab` *file. You can restore a database by using Analysis Manager ➤ Meta Data ➤ Restore option.*

ADOMD functionality is defined in the `msadomd.dll` library. If this library is not listed in your COM components list, you can use the Browse button on the Add Reference dialog box to browse for it. The default path for this library is `C:\Program Files\Common Files\System\ADO` (see Figure 20-6).

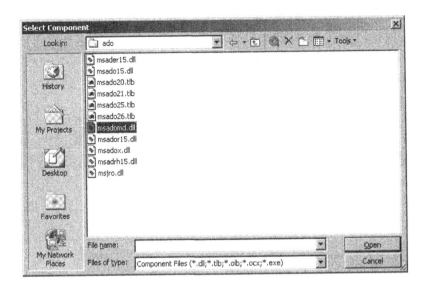

Figure 20-6. Browsing the msadomd.dll *library*

After adding a reference to the msadomd.dll, the Add Reference dialog box looks like Figure 20-7.

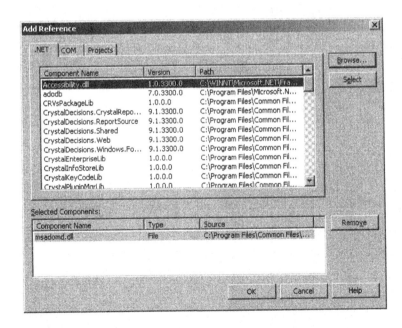

Figure 20-7. Adding a reference to msadomd.dll *library*

Now click the OK button to add the reference. This action adds the ADOMD namespace to the project (see Figure 20-8).

Figure 20-8. ADOMD namespace listed in the project namespaces

Now you can use the `Imports` directive to include the ADOMD namespace in your project and use ADOMD classes.

To test the source code, create a Windows application and add two `ListBox` controls, two `Button` controls, a `TextBox` control, and a `Label` controls and set their properties (see Figure 20-9).

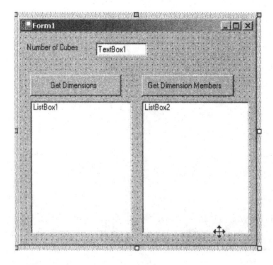

Figure 20-9. Windows form to test ADOMD

Next, add references of ADOMD and ADODB in the application as follows:

```
Imports ADODB
Imports ADOMD
```

Also, add the following variables in the beginning of the form class:

```
Private strConn As String
Private dbConn As Connection
Private dtCatalog As Catalog
Private cubes As CubeDefs
```

After that, create `Connection` and `Catalog` objects on the form load and use `CubeDefs` of `Catalog` to get all the cubes. As you can see from Listing 20-3, you then add all cubes to the `ListBox` and the number of cubes to the `TextBox`.

Listing 20-3. Getting All Available Cubes from the FoodMart 2000 Database

```
Private Sub Form1_Load(ByVal sender As System.Object, _
  ByVal e As System.EventArgs) Handles MyBase.Load
    ' Construct connection string
    strConn = "Provider=msolap; Data Source = MCB;" & _
    "Initial Catalog = FoodMart 2000; User ID =sa; Pwd="
    ' Create and open a connection
    dbConn = New Connection()
    dbConn.Open(strConn, "", "", _
      CType(ConnectModeEnum.adModeUnknown, Integer))
    ' Create a Catalog object and set it's active connection
    ' as connection
    dtCatalog = New Catalog()
    dtCatalog.ActiveConnection = CType(dbConn, Object)
    ' Get all cubes
    cubes = dtCatalog.CubeDefs
    ' Set text box text as total number of cubes
    TextBox1.Text = cubes.Count.ToString()
    Dim cube As CubeDef
    For Each cube In cubes
      Dim str As String = ""
      ListBox1.Items.Add(cube.Name.ToString())
      str = "Cube Name :" + cube.Name.ToString() + ", "
      str += "Description :" + cube.Description.ToString() + ", "
      str += "Dimensions :" + cube.Dimensions.Count.ToString()
    Next
    ListBox1.SetSelected(0, True)
  End Sub
```

If you run the application, the output looks like Figure 20-10.

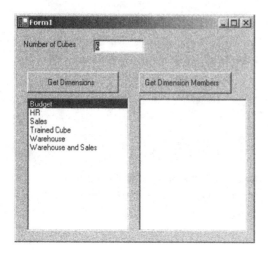

Figure 20-10. All available cubes in the FoodMart 2000 database

The Get Dimensions button gets the dimensions of the selected cube in the left box in Figure 20-10. Listing 20-4 returns the dimensions of a cube and adds it to the right box of Figure 20-10.

Listing 20-4. Getting All Dimensions of a Cube

```
Private Sub Button1_Click(ByVal sender As System.Object, _
  ByVal e As System.EventArgs) Handles Button1.Click
    ' Get the selected cube
    Dim cube As CubeDef = cubes(ListBox1.SelectedItem.ToString())
    ' Get all the dimensions of the selecte cube
    Dim i As Integer
    For i = 0 To cube.Dimensions.Count - 1 Step i + 1
      Dim dimen As Dimension = cube.Dimensions(i)
      ListBox2.Items.Add(dimen.Name.ToString())
    Next
    ListBox2.SetSelected(0, True)
End Sub
```

The output of the Get Dimensions button fills the right box with the dimensions (see Figure 20-11).

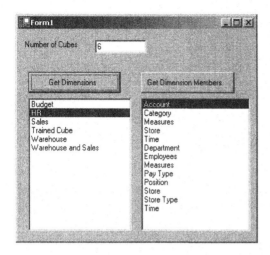

Figure 20-11. Getting dimensions of a cube

The Get Dimension Members button returns the properties of a dimension such as name, hierarchies, UniqueName, and Properties (see Listing 20-5).

Listing 20-5. Getting Dimension Members

```
Private Sub Button2_Click(ByVal sender As System.Object, _
  ByVal e As System.EventArgs) Handles Button2.Click
    ' Get the selected cube
    Dim cube As CubeDef = cubes(ListBox1.SelectedItem.ToString())
    ' Get the selected Dimension
    Dim dimen As Dimension = cube.Dimensions(ListBox2.SelectedItem.ToString())

    MessageBox.Show("Dimension Properties :: Name=" + dimen.Name.ToString() & _
        ", Description=" + dimen.Description.ToString() + ", Hierarchies=" & _
        dimen.UniqueName.ToString())
  End Sub
```

The output of Listing 20-5 looks like Figure 20-12.

Figure 20-12. Viewing dimension properties

Summary

Even though the .NET Framework uses a new approach to access data sources (through ADO.NET), it provides COM interoperability services to access previous data access libraries. In this chapter, you learned how to use ADO, ADOX, ADOMD, and OLAP services in managed applications using the COM Interop services.

Messaging service is one more popular topic these days. In the next chapter, you'll get a brief overview of messaging services and learn how you can access them in the .NET Framework.

CHAPTER 21

Messaging

MESSAGING SERVICES ARE one of the most effective and popular mediums to communicate between two machines. It doesn't matter if you're a high-tech developer, a stockbroker, a high-school student, or a businessperson. In some way, you use messaging services. Some of the common messaging services are electronic mail (email), instant messenger services, text messaging via phones, or messaging used in complex distributed applications.

We could easily write a book on messaging itself. In this chapter, we'll give you a brief overview of messaging services and how you can access them in the .NET Framework.

The messaging functionality in the .NET Framework Library is accessible through the System.Messaging namespace. This chapter starts by introducing you to the basics of messaging and the System.Messaging namespace. After that, we'll show you how to use messaging classes to write real-world distributed messaging applications.

So, what is messaging? A *message* is some data transferred between two machines. These machines can be two computers or other devices such as cell phones. These machines may be attached to each other via the Internet, a local area network, or a wireless network. A message can be a simple text message, a string, some streaming data, some live streaming data, or some complex objects. *Messaging* is the process of sending and receiving messages from one machine to another.

A *message queue* is a mediator between two machines. When a sender sends a message, it goes to a queue that holds the message and makes sure the receiver gets the message. A message queue also guarantees the delivery of the message. One of the simplest examples of this is email exchange using Microsoft Outlook. If you have any message in your Outbox, Outlook will try to send it until it leaves. The messaging service that handles message queues in Microsoft Windows is called *Microsoft Message Queuing* (MSMQ).

Introducing Types of Queues

You can divide queues in two categories: user and system. The user queues are used by a group of network users, and system queues are used by the system.

Using User Queues

You can further categorize the user queues into four categories: public, private, administration, and response queues.

The public queues are published on the network's shared areas, which are available to all the valid users of the network. In other words, all of the authorized users of the network can access these queues.

Unlike public queues, the private queues are not published on the network. Instead, they are published and available only on the local machine that contains them. Only the workgroup users can access this type of queue. To access private queues, a user has to pass the path and label of the queue. A path of the queue is a folder where queues are stored.

The administration queues contain messages acknowledging the receipt of messages, and the response queues contain messages received by the destination applications.

Using System Queues

You can also divide the system queues into four categories: journal, dead letter, report, and private system queues.

The journal queues can store copies of messages that applications send by using a queue. They also store the messages removed from a queue. Each client machine maintains a journal queue for outgoing messages, and the server also maintains a journal queue for each individual queue.

The dead letter queues stores undelivered and expired messages. This queue is maintained on the client machine only.

The report queues contain messages that store the route of a message. These queues are also stored on the client machine, and the private system queues store administrative and notification messages.

Installing Message Queuing

Before you start working with MSMQ, you must ensure that you've installed MSMQ on the server. You can install MSMQ by selecting Control Panel ➤ Add/Remove Programs ➤ Message Queuing Services. If you aren't running Windows 2000 or later versions, the installation may ask you to insert your Windows CD. Windows 2000 (Professional and Server) installs MSMQ with the operating system by default.

To see if you have MSMQ installed your machine, you can select Control Panel ➤ Administrative Tools ➤ Computer Management and then expand the Message Queuing node, as shown in Figure 21-1.

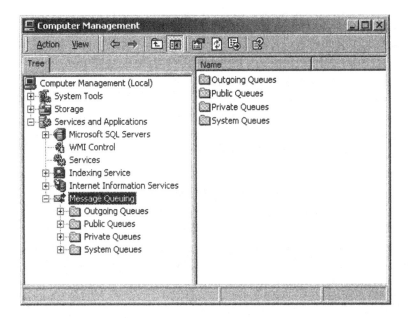

Figure 21-1. Viewing the Messaging Queuing node from Computer Management

 CAUTION *If you don't see the Message Queuing option here, you must install it.*

Using the System.Messaging Namespace

Before writing messaging applications, let's take a quick look at the key classes provided by the System.Messaging namespace.

The MessageQueue class is the most important class in the System.Messaging namespace. This class represents a messaging queue in a messaging queuing server. This class provides members to send messages to and receive messages from MSMQ. The Create and Delete static methods of this class create and delete message queues, respectively. This class also provides methods to retrieve and filter private and public queues available on the server.

The `Message` class is another important class of the `System.Messaging` namespace. The `Message` object represents a message in message queuing. This class provides access to messages of a message queue. It provides properties that you can use to read a message body, label, priority, posting time, sender, authentication mode, and so on.

The `MessageEnumerator` class represents an enumeration, which provides a forward-only cursor through messages in a message queue, which you can use to navigate through from the first message to the last in a message queue. An enumerator returns information about the message at the current cursor position. It doesn't remove the message from the queue.

The `MessagePropertyFilter` class controls and filters messages from a message queue. The `MessageReadPropertyFilter` property of `MessageQueue` uses the `MessagePropertyFilter` object.

The `MessageQueueEnumerator` class provides a forward-only cursor that you can use to enumerate (loop) through the messages in a server.

The `MessageQueueTransaction` class represents a transaction in message queuing. A complete messaging transaction contains a successful send and successful receive. The `MessageQueueTransaction` can commit or roll back transactions. Messages sent to transactional queues are removed if a transaction is rolled back, and messages received from transactional queues are returned to the queue if the transaction is rolled back.

The `Trustee` class represents a user or a group account with a set of access rights that is trying to access a messaging item. The `AccessControlEntry` class allows, denies, or revokes access rights to a trustee.

The `AccessControlList` class represents a loss of access control entries that specify access rights for trustees. It's a collection of `AccessControlEntry` objects.

The `System.Messaging` namespace also provides some formatting-related classes. These classes are `ActiveXMessengerFormatter`, `BinaryMessageFormatter`, and `XmlMessageFormatter`.

Messaging in .NET is compatible with previous versions of MSMQ. `ActiveXMessengerFormatter` provides interoperability functionality, so you can use MSMQ ActiveX controls in the .NET Framework.

The `BinaryMessageFormatter` class serializes and deserializes objects to or from the body of a message in a binary format.

XML is the default format used by MSMQ and messaging services. `XmlMessageFormatter` is responsible for serializing and deserializing objects to or from the body of a message in Extensible Markup Language (XML) format using XML Schema Definition (XSD).

Finally, the `System.Messaging` namespace also provides one messaging-related exception handling class: `MessageQueueException`. This class represents the exception that is thrown if an MSMQ internal error occurs.

Working with Message Queues

The MessageQueue class is a wrapper around MessageQueuing, which defines functionality to access and manage a queue on an MSMQ server. This class also provides methods to create and delete queues, send and receive messages, and retrieve queues and messages.

Using the MessageQueue Properties

It's always a good idea to know what functionality is provided by a class before using the class. Table 21-1 describes the MessageQueue class properties.

Table 21-1. The MessageQueue *Class Properties*

PROPERTY	DESCRIPTION
Authenticate	This property represents whether a queue will accept only authenticated messages. The queue will reject nonauthenticated messages. Both get and set.
BasePriority	This property represents the base priority of messages. Both get and set.
CanRead	This property is true if a message queue can be read; otherwise, it's false. Both get and set.
CanWrite	This property is true if a message queue can be written to; otherwise, it's false. Both get and set.
Category	This property represents the queue category. Both get and set.
CreateTime	This property gets the time and date the queue was created.
DefaultPropertyToSend	This represents the default message property when an application sends a message. Both get and set.
DenySharedRecieve	This property is true if the queue has exclusive access to receive messages from the MSMQ queue; otherwise, it's false. Both get and set.
EnableConnectionCache	When this property is true, a cache of connections will be maintained by the application; otherwise, they won't. Both get and set.
EncryptionRequired	If this property is true, the queue accepts only nonprivate (nonencrypted) messages. Both get and set.

Table 21-1. *The* MessageQueue *Class Properties (Continued)*

PROPERTY	DESCRIPTION
FormatName	This property represents the unique queue name generated by MSMQ when queue was created. Read only.
Formatter	This property represents the formatter used to serialize and deserialize. Both get and set.
Id	This property represents the unique queuing identifier. Read only.
Label	This property represents the queue description. Both get and set.
LastModifyTime	This property represents the last time the properties on a queue were modified. Read only.
MachineName	This property represents the name of the computer where queue is located. Both read and write.
MaximumJournalSize	This property represents the maximum size of the journal queue. Both get and set.
MaximumQueueSize	This property represents the maximum size of the queue. Both get and set.
MessageReadPropertyFilter	This is the property filter for receiving or peeking messages. Both get and set.
Path	This property represents the queue path. Both get and set.
QueueName	This property represents the queue's user-friendly name. Both get and set.
ReadHandle	This property represents the native handle used to read messages from the queue. Read only.
SynchronizingObject	This property represents the object that marshals the event handler calls resulting from a ReceiveCompleted or PeekCompleted event. Both get and set.
Transactional	When this property is true, the queue accepts only transactions.
UseJournalQueue	If this property is true, received messages are copied to the journal queue. Both get and set.
WriteHandle	This property represents the native handle used to send messages to the queue. Read only.

Managing Queues Using VS .NET

In Visual Studio .NET (VS .NET), the Server Explorer provides options to manage messaging queues in the messaging server. You can see all available queues by expanding the Servers\MachineName\Message Queues node. The Message Queues node has three children—Private Queues, Public Queues, and System Queues—that list private, public, and system queues, respectively. You can see the corresponding available queues by expanding these nodes (see Figure 21-2).

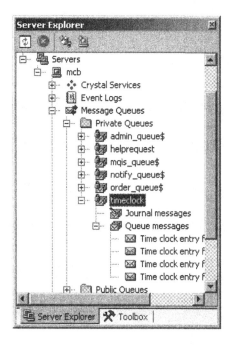

Figure 21-2. Managing message queues through the Server Explorer

The Server Explorer also allows you to create and delete queues. To create a queue, right-click the Private Queues or Public Queues node and select the Create Queue option.

NOTE *You may not be able to view or create public queues if you're a member of a proper domain or working on a WORKGROUP computer.*

Now if you expand an available queue, you'll see children: Journal Messages and Queue Messages. You can also delete messages from a queue by simply right-clicking and selecting the Clear Messages menu option.

 TIP *After creating a message queue using the Server Explorer, you can easily add it to your application by simply dragging the queue from the Server Explorer to a form. This action adds an object of type* MessageQueue *to your project.*

Retrieving Available Queues

The MessageQueue class provides six methods, which you can use to retrieve private and public queues.

The GetPrivateQueuesByMachine method retrieves private queues available on the server (see Listing 21-1).

Listing 21-1. Retrieving Private Queues

```
Dim queList As MessageQueue() = _
    MessageQueue.GetPrivateQueuesByMachine(".")
Dim que As MessageQueue
For Each que In queList
 Console.WriteLine(que.Path)
Next que
```

The GetPublicQueues method returns public queues on the server (see Listing 21-2).

Listing 21-2. Retrieving Public Queues

```
Sub GetPublicQueuesMethod()
    Try
      Dim queList As MessageQueue() = _
    MessageQueue.GetPublicQueues()
      Dim que As MessageQueue
      For Each que In queList
        Console.WriteLine(que.Path)
```

```
        Next que
    Catch exp As Exception
      Console.WriteLine(exp.Message)
End Try
End Sub
```

The GetPublicQueuesByCategory method returns public queues that belong to the specified category. This method takes the ID of the queue as an argument, which can be retrieved by using the Id property of MessageQueue.

The GetPublicQueuesByMachine method returns public queues that belong to the specified machine. This method takes the machine name as an argument.

The GetPublicQueuesByLabel method returns public queues that have the specified label.

NOTE *All* GetPublicXXX *and* GetPrivateQueuesByMachine *methods are static methods. Hence, they can't be used through the* MesssageQueue *class instances.*

Listing 21-3 retrieves public queues based on the specified category, machine, and label.

Listing 21-3. Filtering Queues Based on Category, Machine Name, and Label

```
Sub GetQueuesByCategoryMethod()
    Try
      Dim queList As MessageQueue() = _
    MessageQueue.GetPublicQueuesByCategory(New _
        Guid("{00000000-0000-0000-0000-000000000001}"))
      Dim que As MessageQueue
      For Each que In queList
        Console.WriteLine(que.Path)
      Next que
    Catch exp As Exception
      Console.WriteLine(exp.Message)
    End Try
  End Sub

  Public Sub GetQueuesByLabelMethod()
    Try
      Dim queList As MessageQueue() = _
```

```
MessageQueue.GetPublicQueuesByLabel("LabelName")
    Dim que As MessageQueue
    For Each que In queList
        Console.WriteLine(que.Path)
    Next que
  Catch exp As Exception
    Console.WriteLine(exp.Message)
  End Try
End Sub


Public Sub GetQueuesByMachineMethod()
    Try
      Dim queList As MessageQueue() = _
    MessageQueue.GetPublicQueuesByMachine("MCB")
      Dim que As MessageQueue
      For Each que In queList
        Console.WriteLine(que.Path)
      Next que
    Catch exp As Exception
      Console.WriteLine(exp.Message)
    End Try
End Sub
```

Filtering Queues Using MessageQueueCriteria

You can even filter public queues by using GetPublicQueues. This method takes an argument of type MessageQueueCriteria. The MessageQueueCriteria class provides properties you can use to filter queue types (see Table 21-2).

Table 21-2. The MessageQueueCriteria *Class Properties*

PROPERTY	DESCRIPTION
Category	Filters queues based on this category (both get and set)
CreatedAfter	Filters queues created after this time (both get and set)
CreatedBefore	Filters queues created before this time (both get and set)
Label	Filters queues based on this label (both get and set)
MachineName	Filters queues based on this machine name (both get and set)
ModifiedAfter	Filters queues based on the queues modified after this time (both get and set)
ModifiedBefore	Filters queues based on the queues modified before this time (both get and set)

Using `MessageQueueCriteria`, you can simply filter the queues. The following code filters queues based on a machine name and label:

```
Dim filter As New MessageQueueCriteria()
Filter.MachineName = "MCB"
filter.Label = "LabelName "
Dim queList As MessageQueue() = _
    MessageQueue.GetPublicQueues(filter)
```

TIP *To remove all filters set by the* `MessageQueueCriteria` *class, call the* `RemoveAll` *method.*

Creating and Deleting Message Queues Programmatically

The `Create` method of `MessageQueue` creates a queue on the server. This method has two overloaded forms. The first form takes only one argument of the path of the queue, and the second form takes a path with a Boolean argument, which represents whether the queue will be created as a transactional queue. The following shows both forms of the `Create` method:

```
Overloads Public Shared Function Create(String) As MessageQueue
Overloads Public Shared Function Create(String, Boolean) As MessageQueue
```

The `Create` method returns an object of type `MessageQueue`. You can create a public queue or a private queue using the `Create` method. The type of queue created depends on the path of the queue. For a public queue, the path syntax is *MachineName\QueueName;* for a private queue, the path syntax is *MachineName*`Private$`*\QueueName.*

The following code creates one public and one private queue:

```
MessageQueue.Create(".\MyPubQ")
MessageQueue.Create(@".\Private$\MyPrivatQ")
```

The `Delete` method of `MessageQueue` deletes a queue on the server. Similar to the `Create` method, the deletion of the public or private queue depends on the path of the queue. The following code deletes a public and a private queue from the server:

```
MessageQueue.Delete(".\MyPubQ")
MessageQueue. Delete (@".\Private$\MyPrivatQ")
```

The `Exists` method checks whether a queue path is available.

NOTE *The* `Create`, `Delete`, *and* `Exists` *methods are static methods and hence can't be used through the* `MessageQueue` *class instances.*

Creating a Sample Application

Now let's create a sample application. Create a Windows application and add controls to the form so that the final form looks like Figure 21-3.

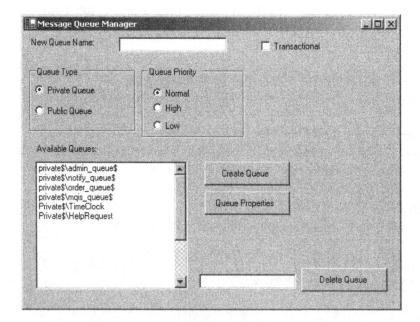

Figure 21-3. Message Queue Manager form

The Create Queue button reads the name from New Queue Name text box and creates a new queue on the server. Listing 21-4 shows a Create Queue button event handler, which reads the queue name from a text box and creates a private queue. It also sets the priority of the queue based on the user's option selected on the form. The Transactional check box is responsible for creating a transactional queue.

Listing 21-4. Creating a Queue

```
Private Sub CreateQueueBtn_Click(ByVal sender As System.Object, _
  ByVal e As System.EventArgs) Handles CreateQueueBtn.Click
    Dim str As String = String.Empty
    Dim trn As Boolean = False
    ' If transactional type is true
    If CheckBox1.Checked Then
      trn = True
    End If
    ' If queue is private
    If RadioButton1.Checked Then
      str = ".\Private$\"
    End If
    str += TextBox1.Text
    If Not MessageQueue.Exists(str) Then
      currentQueue = MessageQueue.Create(str, trn)
      If currentQueue Is Nothing Then
        ' Set priority
        If RadioButton4.Checked Then
          currentQueue.BasePriority = _
          Convert.ToInt16(MessagePriority.High)
        ElseIf RadioButton5.Checked Then
          currentQueue.BasePriority = _
          Convert.ToInt16(MessagePriority.Low)
        Else
          currentQueue.BasePriority = 0
        End If
        ListBox1.Items.Add(TextBox1.Text)
        ListBox1.Update()
      End If
    End If
End Sub
```

The Delete Queue button deletes the queue from the server (see Listing 21-5).

Listing 21-5. Deleting a Queue

```
Private Sub DeleteQueBtn_Click(ByVal sender As System.Object, _
  ByVal e As System.EventArgs) Handles DeleteQueBtn.Click
    Dim str As String = String.Empty
    ' If queue is private
    If RadioButton1.Checked Then
      str = ".\Private$\"
    End If
    str += TextBox2.Text
    ' Create and connect to a public Message Queuing queue.
    If MessageQueue.Exists(str) Then
      MessageQueue.Delete(str)
    End If
End Sub
```

The Queue Properties button simply returns the current queue properties (see Listing 21-6).

Listing 21-6. Getting a Queue's Properties

```
Private Sub QuePropsBtn_Click(ByVal sender As System.Object, _
  ByVal e As System.EventArgs) Handles QuePropsBtn.Click
    Dim props As String = "Format Name: " + currentQueue.FormatName
    props += ", Base Priority:" + currentQueue.BasePriority.ToString()
    props += ", Create Time:" + currentQueue.CreateTime.ToString()
    props += ", ID:" + currentQueue.Id.ToString()
    props += ", Path:" + currentQueue.Path.ToString()
    props += ", Max Size:" + currentQueue.MaximumQueueSize.ToString()
    props += ", Transaction:" + currentQueue.Transactional.ToString()
    MessageBox.Show(props)
  End Sub
```

Creating a MessageQueue Instance

The simplest way to create a MessageQueue instance is just drag a queue from the Server Explorer to a form in the form designer. This action adds a MessageQueue component to the form.

But most of the time you'll be creating a MessageQueue instance programmatically. For that, you create a MessageQueue object and set its path. For example, the following code creates a MessageQueue instance programmatically:

```
Dim mq = new MessageQueue()
mq.Path = ".\mcbQueue"
```

Alternatively, you can also pass the path in the MessageQueue constructor as follows:

```
Dim mq = new MessageQueue(".\mcbQueue")
```

Setting a Queue's Path

You can create a MessageQueue instance from a path, from a format name, or from a label. Each of these methods has their advantages. For example, in XML Web services, the format name method gives you better performance than the path method. When a queue is disconnected, the path method won't work. You have to use the format method.

The path of queue takes the form *servername\queuename*. Each type of queue has a unique path. Actually, the path is the combination of machine name and queue name of a queue. You can use the MachineName and QueueName properties of MessageQueue and combine them to get the path of a queue.

Table 21-3 describes the paths for different types of queues.

Table 21-3. Path for Different Types of Queues

QUEUE TYPE	PATH
Public queue	MachineName\QueueName
Private queue	MachineName\Private$\QueueName
Journal queue	MachineName\QueueName\Journal$
Machine journal queue	MachineName\Journal$
Machine dead-letter queue	MachineName\Deadletter$
Machine transactional dead-letter queue	MachineName\XactDeadletter$

TIP *The dot (.) represents the current machine in a path. For example,*
`MessageQueue1.Path=".\mcbQueue"` *represents the* `mcbQueue` *queue on the*
current machine.

The following code uses the path of the queue:

```
MessageQueue1.Path=".\mcbQueue"
```

You can use format names to indicate whether a queue is public or private.
The `FORMATNAME:PUBLIC=QueueGUID`, `FORMATNAME:PRIVATE=MachineGUID\QueueNumber`,
and `FORMATNAME:PUBLIC=QueueGUID;JOURNAL` names represent public, private, and
journal queues, respectively.

The following code sets the path of the queue as a public queue using format
names:

```
MessageQueue1.Path = "FORMATNAME:PUBLIC=queueGUID"
```

You can also use a label name to refer to a queue. The `Label` property of
`MessageQueue` represents the label of a queue:

```
MessageQueue1.Path="LABEL:mcbQueue"
```

Sending and Receiving Messages

The `Send` method of `MessageQueue` is responsible for sending a message to the
queue. Using these forms, you can even specify the type of MSMQ transaction.
The `Send` message takes the first argument of type `Object`, which can be a `Message`
object, a text string, or any other message. The `Send` method has six overloaded
forms:

```
Overloads Public Sub Send(Object)
Overloads Public Sub Send(Object, _
MessageQueueTransaction)
Overloads Public Sub Send(Object, _
MessageQueueTransactionType)
Overloads Public Sub Send(Object, String)
Overloads Public Sub Send(Object, String, _
 MessageQueueTransaction)
Overloads Public Sub Send(Object, String, _
 MessageQueueTransactionType)
```

The Receive method receives the first message in the queue and removes it from the queue. If there's no message available in the queue, you can even specify a time span, and the method will wait for that interval or until the next message is available in the queue. The Receive method has six overloaded forms:

```
Public Overloads Function Receive() As Message
Overloads Public Function Receive _
(MessageQueueTransaction) As Message
Overloads Public Function Receive _
(MessageQueueTransactionType) As Message
Overloads Public Function Receive(TimeSpan) As Message
Overloads Public Function Receive(TimeSpan, _
MessageQueueTransaction) As Message
Overloads
Public Function Receive(TimeSpan, _
 MessageQueueTransactionType) As Message
```

Both the Send and Receive methods take an argument of type MessageQueueTransactionType enumeration, which specify the type of transaction. It can be Automatic, None, or Single. The None type transaction represents that the operation will not be transactional. The Single option is for single internal transactions, and the Automatic type is used for Microsoft Transaction Server (MTS) or COM+ 1.0 services.

Walking Through Simple Messaging Application

Before discussing messaging any further, let's create a simple messaging application using VS .NET. In this application, you'll send and receive messages using a Windows application.

First, add two Label controls, two TextBox controls, two Button controls, and a DataGrid control to the form. Second, set the second TextBox control's Multiline property to true. The final application looks like Figure 21-4. As you can see, you'll read the title and body of a message. The Send Message button will send message to the queue, and the Receive Messages button will read all the messages from the queue and display them in the DataGrid control.

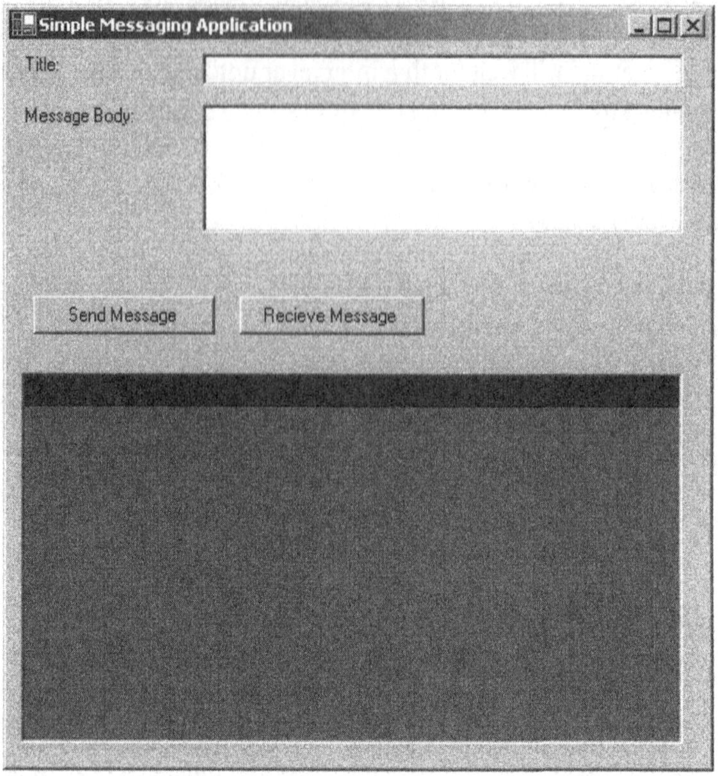

Figure 21-4. A simple messaging application

After creating a Windows application, open the Server Explorer and expand the Message Queues node. Right-click the Private Queues node and click the Create Queues menu item. Type *mcbQ* in the text box and then click OK. Don't select the Transactional check box. To verify the action, you should now have a mcbQ queue listed under your Private Queues node.

Now drag the mcbQ queue to the form. This action adds a reference to the System.Messaging namespace and adds an object of type MessageQueue called MessageQueue1.

Finally, the only thing you need to do is add code to send and receive messages. Listing 21-7 shows the code of the Send Message button click event handler. As you can see, the code simply reads the title and body text, creates a Message object, sets its Label and Body properties, and then calls the MessageQueue.Send method.

NOTE *We'll discuss the* Message *class in more detail in the following sections.*

Listing 21-7. Sending Messages to a Queue

```
Private Sub SendMsgBtn_Click(ByVal sender As System.Object, _
   ByVal e As System.EventArgs) Handles SendMsgBtn.Click
     Dim msg As System.Messaging.Message = _
        New System.Messaging.Message(titleTextBox.Text)
     msg.Label = titleTextBox.Text
     msg.Body = bodyTextBox.Text
     MessageQueue1.Send(msg)
End Sub
```

Listing 21-8 reads messages from a queue and adds them to the DataGrid control. As you can see, this code calls the GetAllMessages method of MessageQueue, which returns an array of Message objects. After that it simply reads the Label and Body properties of a Message and adds them to a DataTable. This DataTable is bound to the DataGrid control to display the results.

Listing 21-8. Receiving Messages from a Queue

```
Private Sub RecMsgBtn_Click(ByVal sender As System.Object, _
   ByVal e As System.EventArgs) Handles RecMsgBtn.Click
     ' Create a DataTable in memory
     Dim dtTable As New DataTable()
     dtTable.Columns.Add("Title")
     dtTable.Columns.Add("Message Body")
     Dim messages() As System.Messaging.Message
     messages = MessageQueue1.GetAllMessages()
     ' Need a formatter to get the text of the message body.
     Dim stringFormatter As System.Messaging.XmlMessageFormatter = _
        New System.Messaging.XmlMessageFormatter(New String() _
        {"System.String"})
     Dim index As Integer
     Dim msg As System.Messaging.Message

     For index = 0 To messages.Length - 1
       messages(index).Formatter = stringFormatter
```

```
        msg = messages(index)
        Dim row As DataRow = dtTable.NewRow()
        row(0) = msg.Label
        row(1) = msg.Body.ToString()
        dtTable.Rows.Add(row)
    Next
    DataGrid1.DataSource = dtTable
End Sub
```

Now, run the application, enter the title and body of the messages, and click Send Message to send messages to the queue. When you're done sending messages, click the Receive Messages button to read all the messages from the queue (see Figure 21-5).

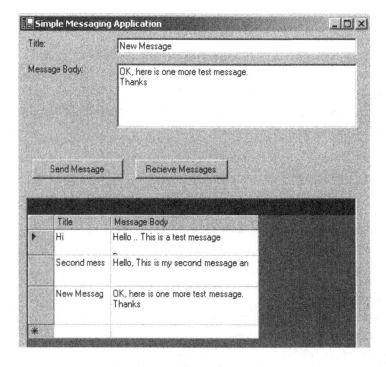

Figure 21-5. Messaging application in action

Working with Messages

The Message class represents a message in MSMQ. The Message class provides one static method called InfiniteTimeout that specifies that no timeout exists. This class provides more than 40 properties and some of them represent the body text, format, security, ID, and priority of the message. You'll see this class's properties in the sample applications throughout this chapter.

Creating and Removing Messages

You can use the Message class to create a message. Once you have created a message, you can use it as an argument of the Send and Receive methods of MessageQueue to send and receive messages. The following code creates a message and sets its priority, body, and label:

```
Dim msg1 As Message = New Message()
msg1.Priority = MessagePriority.High
msg1.Body = "Body of first message"
msg1.Label = "First Message"
```

The Purge method of MessageQueue removes all the messages from a queue. The following code removes messages from MessageQueue1:

```
MessageQueue1.Purge()
```

You can remove a single message from the queue by calling the Receive method of MessageQueue. You can also use the ReceiveById method to remove a message identified by the ID. You can also call the PeekById method to find a specific message and then use the RecieveById method to remove it.

TIP *You can always remove messages manually from the Server Explorer by selecting the Queue Messages ➤ Clear Messages menu option. There's no way you can remove a single message from a queue manually.*

Setting Queue and Message Priorities

You can set both a queue's and a message's priority. Both MessageQueue and Message classes provide properties to set their priorities. You can use the BasePriority property of MesssageQueue to get and set a priority of a queue. It's only applied on public queues. The BasePriority of a private queue is always 0.

You can use the Priority property of the Message class to get and set the priority of a message. The MessagePriority enumeration specifies the value of the Priority property. Table 21-4 describes the MessagePriority enumeration members.

Table 21-4. The MessagePriority *Enumeration Members*

PROPERTY	DESCRIPTION
Lowest	Lowest priority
VeryLow	Between Low and Lowest message priority
Low	Low priority
Normal	Normal priority
AboveNormal	Between High and Normal message priority
High	High priority
VeryHigh	Between Highest and High message priority
Highest	Highest priority

The following code creates two messages and sets their priority, body, and label properties:

```
Dim msg1 As Message = New Message()
Dim msg2 As Message = New Message()
msg1.Priority = MessagePriority.High
msg1.Body = "Body of first message"
msg1.Label = "First Message"
msg2.Priority = MessagePriority.Normal
msg2.Label = "Second Message"
msg2.Body = "Body of second message"
```

Understanding Transactional Messaging

Transactional messaging is the process of sending and receiving messages in transactions. A *transaction* is a set of one or more messages. Transactional messages are grouped inside a *transaction context*, which keeps track of the transaction states.

Transaction processing ensures two things: that all messages bundled in a transaction either are delivered together in order or that none of the messages participating in a transaction are sent if there's a failure in transaction. The success of a transaction is called a *committed transaction*, and the failure of a transaction is called an *aborted transaction*.

In message queuing, there are two types of transactions: internal and external. In the internal transaction process, the message transfer happens between two queues belonging to a queuing server. On the other hand, an external transaction involves message transfer between a queue and other resources (not related to queuing) such as a database. This chapter discusses internal transactions only.

Using the MessageQueueTransaction Class

The MessageQueueTransaction class represents an internal transaction. This class has a property called Status, which represents the status of the transaction. The status of a transaction is of type MessageQueueTrasactionStatus enumeration type. It has four values: Aborted, Committed, Initialized, and Pending.

The Aborted value represents the transaction has been aborted, and there will be no changes in the current state of the messages. The Committed value indicates that the transaction has been committed and all message were sent as expected. The Initialized value indicates that the transaction has been initialized but not started yet. The Pending value represents that the transaction has been started and is still in process.

Besides the Status property, the MessageQueueTransaction has three methods: Abort, Begin, and Commit. The Abort method rolls back the pending transaction. The Begin method starts a transaction, and the Commit method saves the pending transactions.

To create an internal transaction, you can use the Create method of MessageQueueTransaction, and when you're sure you want to commit or roll back the transaction, you call Commit or Abort methods.

Creating Transactional Queues

Do you remember when you created a new message queue in the Server Explorer using the Create Queue menu option? When you create a queue using the Server Explorer, there's a check box on the dialog box that allows you to create a transactional queue (see Figure 21-6).

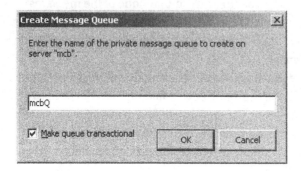

Figure 21-6. Creating a transactional queue using the Server Explorer

Creating a transactional message queue programmatically is pretty simple. When you use the Create method of MessageQueue, you pass the second argument as true to create a transactional message queue. For example, the following code creates a transactional queue:

```
Dim mq as New MessageQueue
mq =MessageQueue.Create(".\mcbTransQueue", True)
```

Sending and Receiving Transactional Messages

When creating a transactional queue, the Send and Receive methods of MessageQueue take the last argument as the transaction object. Listing 21-9 shows how to send and receive transactional messages. As you can see from this code, the transaction is only committed where there were no errors; otherwise, the transaction is aborted.

Listing 21-9. Sending and Receiving Transactional Messages

```vbnet
Imports System
Imports System.Messaging

Module Module1

  Sub Main()
    'SendTransactionalMessages()
    RecieveTransactionalMessages()
  End Sub

  Public Sub SendTransactionalMessages()
    Dim mq As MessageQueue = New MessageQueue()
    mq = MessageQueue.Create(".\Private$\mcbTQ", True)
    Dim tran As MessageQueueTransaction = _
    New MessageQueueTransaction()
    Try
      tran.Begin()
      mq.Send("Body of first message", "Message1", tran)
      mq.Send("Body of second message", "Message2", tran)
      mq.Send("Body of third message", "Message3", tran)
      tran.Commit()
      Console.WriteLine("Transaction committed!")
    Catch
      tran.Abort()
      Console.WriteLine("Transaction Aborted!")
    End Try
  End Sub

  Public Sub RecieveTransactionalMessages()
    Dim mq As MessageQueue = New MessageQueue()
    mq.Path = ".\Private$\mcbTQ"
    Dim tran As MessageQueueTransaction = _
    New MessageQueueTransaction()
    Try
      tran.Begin()
      Dim messages() As System.Messaging.Message
      messages = mq.GetAllMessages()
      ' Need a formatter to get the text of the message body.
      Dim stringFormatter As System.Messaging.XmlMessageFormatter = _
        New System.Messaging.XmlMessageFormatter(New String() _
        {"System.String"})
```

```
        Dim index As Integer
        Dim msg As System.Messaging.Message

        For index = 0 To messages.Length - 1
          messages(index).Formatter = stringFormatter
          msg = messages(index)
          Console.WriteLine(msg.Label + "," + msg.Body)
        Next
        tran.Commit()
        Console.WriteLine("Transaction committed!")
      Catch
        tran.Abort()
        Console.WriteLine("Transaction Aborted!")
      End Try
    End Sub
End Module
```

 TIP *Transactional processing is useful when you want to make sure that all messages in a transaction are delivered or none of them are.*

Encrypting Messages

There are certain requirements when you need to send encrypted messages to make sure the data you're sending is secure. You can use encryption in two ways. First, you can encrypt a message itself. Second, you can use queuing services to encrypt a message through the MessageQueue class.

To encrypt a message, you can use the DestinationSymmetricKey property of a message and then send this message to the queue. The DestinationSymmetricKey property represents the symmetric key used to encrypt application-encrypted messages.

The EncryptionRequired property of MessageQueue sets whether a queue accepts nonencrypted or encrypted messages. The EncryptionRequired enumeration provides the value of the EncryptionRequired property, which has three values: Body, None, and Optional. The Body option makes sure the queue only accepts private (encrypted) messages. The None option means the queue accepts only nonencrypted messages. The Optional option means the queue accepts both encrypted and nonencrypted messages.

The `EncryptionAlgorithm` property of the `Message` class represents the type of encryption applied on a message. This property is represented by the `EncryptionAlgorithm` enumeration, which has three values: `None`, `RC2`, and `RC4`. The value `None` means no encryption. `RC2` is a 64-bit block encryption, and `RC4` is the stream encryption. The block mode encrypts a block of data at a time, and the stream mode encrypts a bit at a time.

Listing 21-10 sends encrypted messages. As you can see, it sets the `UseEncryption` property of a `Message` object to activate the encryption.

Listing 21-10. Sending Encrypted Messages

```
Try
    Dim msg As System.Messaging.Message = _
      New System.Messaging.Message(titleTextBox.Text)
    MessageQueue1.EncryptionRequired = _
    Messaging.EncryptionRequired.Body
    msg.UseEncryption = True
    If (rc4RadioBtn.Checked) Then
      msg.EncryptionAlgorithm = Messaging.EncryptionAlgorithm.Rc4
    ElseIf (rc2RadioBtn.Checked) Then
      msg.EncryptionAlgorithm = Messaging.EncryptionAlgorithm.Rc2
    Else
      msg.EncryptionAlgorithm = Messaging.EncryptionAlgorithm.None
    End If

    msg.Label = titleTextBox.Text
    msg.Body = bodyTextBox.Text
    MessageQueue1.Send(msg)
Catch exp As Exception
    MessageBox.Show(exp.Message)
End Try
```

Summary

In this chapter, we covered some basic programming of messaging services. The System.Messaging namespace offers much more than we're able to discuss in this chapter. Still, this chapter should give you a quick jump start on MSMQ using .NET.

We also discussed the classes provided by the .NET Framework Library to work with messaging services. We discussed how to create, delete, and manage queues. Additionally, we discussed how to send and receive normal messages and transaction messages. Finally, we discussed the security, encryption, and authentication issues involved in messaging and the classes provided by the .NET Framework Library to implement messaging.

In the next chapter, we cover performance and optimization issues and how to handle these issues when working with ADO.NET and SQL Server.

CHAPTER 22

SQL Server and ADO.NET: Notes on Performance

EVER SINCE THE early days of relational databases, optimizing database performance has always been as much an art as a science. Even today, you'll often hear of new "secrets" through professional relationships that take on the air of furtive back-alley exchanges more reminiscent of a Le Carré novel than a sober discussion between colleagues. This chapter discusses some SQL Server and ADO.NET performance issues. It also discusses some best practices to make sure you get the most out of your code.

Improving SQL Server Performance

The following sections provide some of the "back-alley" secrets we've accumulated over the years, as well as some of the more methodical approaches for examining your database and determining the best course of action to achieve the best performance.

Using Indexes

Properly selecting and managing your indexes can have the single biggest impact on performance using any database—and Microsoft SQL Server is no different. Indexes are like little optimized tables that organize the data you'll most commonly use so that you can find rows in the main table optimally.

To manage the indexes on a table, simply right-click the table in Enterprise Manager, choose All Tasks from the menu that pops up, and then select Manage Indexes (see Figure 22-1).

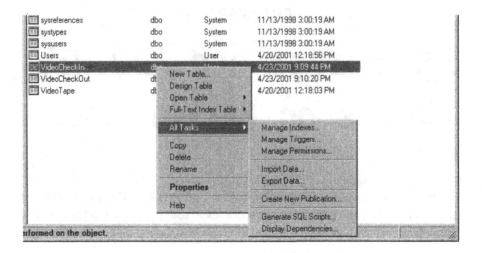

Figure 22-1. The Manage Indexes menu in Enterprise Manager

From the dialog box that appears, you can manage any of the tables in any of the databases running in the current instance of Microsoft SQL Server (see Figure 22-2). You can change databases by choosing a different database from the Database drop-down list, or you can change the table you're managing your indexes on by choosing another table from the Table drop-down list.

Once you have the database and table selected that you would like to manage the index on, the current indexes that exist on the table display in the Existing Indexes area.

To add a new index to the table, click the New button at the bottom of this dialog box. This opens the Create New Index dialog box (see Figure 22-3). Having a good understanding of this dialog box and its implications is critical to creating a top-performing application. Determining which columns you should index in different contexts will be covered later in this chapter, so for now you'll focus on the options for determining the behavior of the index you'd like to create.

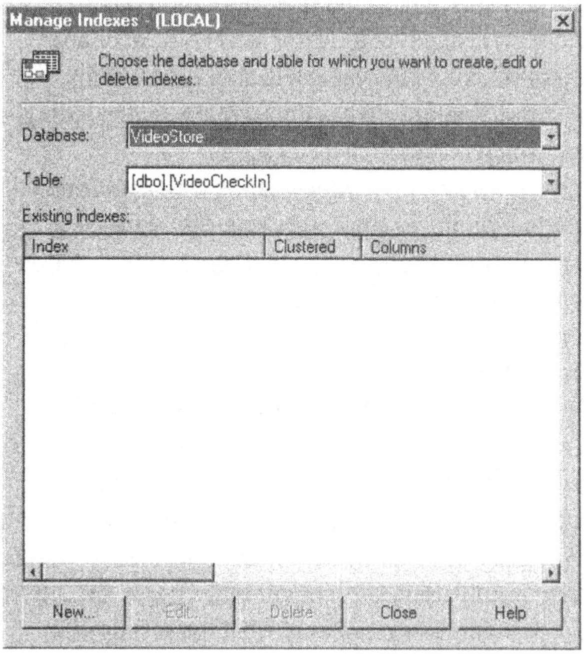

Figure 22-2. The Manage Indexes dialog box

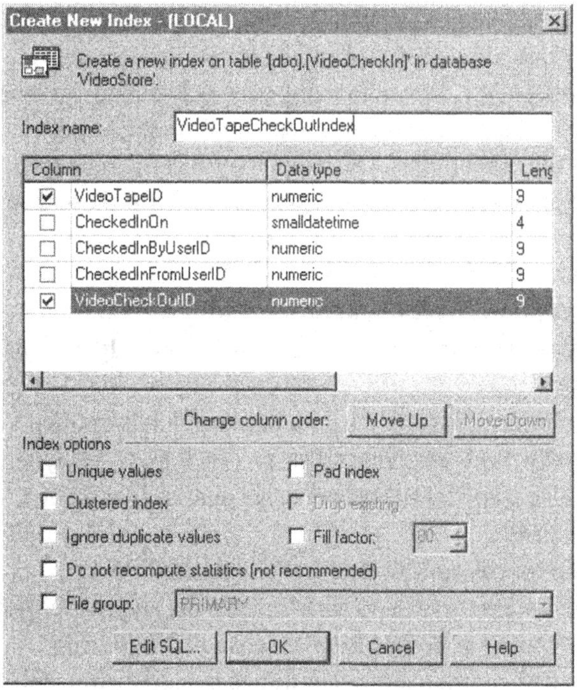

Figure 22-3. The Create New Index dialog box

Checking the Unique Values box tells SQL Server that this index will be unique. If you're creating an index on a single-column identity column or any other type of single column where you know the value will always be unique, check this box. The index then knows that once it has found the item it's looking for, it shouldn't look any further, which makes for a faster index.

The real value of this option comes into play when dealing with a multiple-column index that, when combined, produces a unique value. For example, a complicated join table may not have any single column that represents a unique value, but a combination of two of the columns is unique.

The Pad Index and Fill Factor options are related. When you build an index, the index pages contain as much data as possible by default. However, if you subsequently add data to the table, then it takes a little longer because new index pages have to be created from scratch. Setting the Fill Factor option allows you to control how much spare space is left in each index page; a frequently updated table might have a Fill Factor option as low as 20 or even 10 percent. An index with a lower Fill Factor takes up more space, but it provides better performance. Note, though, that once the spare space is fully used, subsequent index pages are completely filled as if their Fill Factor was zero—regardless of what the setting was when the index was created. At this point, you should recompile the index to recover the performance enhancement. At installation, the default Fill Factor option for a server is set at 0, meaning each index page is completely filled, but you can alter this either through the SQL Server Enterprise Manager Server Properties dialog box or by using the `sp_configure` system stored procedure.

The Pad Index option performs a similar function and in fact uses the same percentage as the Fill Factor option. SQL Server indexing uses an indexing method called *b-trees*, which means the index contains a number of nodes where each node acts as a parent to two or more subnodes. The lowest pages of the index, beyond which there are no further nodes, are called *leaf pages*, and it is these that the Fill Factor option affects. Padding the index allocates spare space in the intermediate nodes, allowing for much greater expansion to the table's data than the Fill Factor option alone would support. Typically, however, setting the Fill Factor option provides enough optimization, and you should pad the index only in high-use scenarios.

The Clustered Index option internally sorts the data in a way that is optimal for a number of queries, especially those involving GROUP BY, ORDER BY, BETWEEN, or join clauses. A clustered index also provides a large boost for queries that involve aggregate functions such as MIN or MAX.

Clustered indexes don't help on columns that contain data with little variability such as bit columns or columns that join to something finite such as values representing states. Unless the country goes on a huge annexation binge, this number will remain relatively small compared to other things that are better candidates for your clustered index.

You can have only one clustered index on any given table, so think about what you want to take advantage of the potential performance boost. This may sound trivial; however, if you closely examine a table, you'll see a number of options. You'll have to determine which ones your queries will use the most.

The Do Not Recompute Statistics option comes with a warning that it is not recommended. In almost all circumstances, heed this warning or you could get some unexpected results. The only situation where you should use this option is where a table is read only and will never be altered.

Choosing Which Columns to Index

Knowing which columns to index is as important as knowing what options to use when indexing them. This is a good place to start: Any column you frequently query is probably a good candidate for an index.

The best candidates for indexes are usually the primary keys of your tables. The reason for this is when you're doing a multiple table join, you'll usually do the join on your primary key. If most of your queries use a particular column, then it's probably optimal to make that column a clustered index. It's never necessary to create an index for your primary keys because of the nature of how SQL Server stores data relating to auto-numbered primary keys.

How SQL Server Stores Your Data

SQL Server works well when storing data. Its overall goal is to make sure that when a row is inserted, it can be placed physically between rows above and below your primary key in terms of sort order. By ensuring that the rows are stored in the order of your primary key, primary key searches are very fast. For tables where you're providing your own value for your primary key, you'll want to use table padding.

If your table uses an auto-numbered primary key, your records will automatically be in the correct order as you insert them because of the auto numbering that SQL Server uses to store your data. In this case, it's not beneficial to use table padding.

Also, when choosing what columns to index, remember that you only get one clustered index. The clustered index groups and orders your index in a manner that it can quickly find what is being queried against.

Also, don't waste your clustered index on a finite state column. This includes bits and numbers with little variance (for example, an integer between 1 and 10). The clustered index shines on columns with broad variances in data, not in situations where most of the data in the column is the same from row to row.

Understanding the SQL Server Profiler

You can learn quite a few things about how to optimize your database by using the SQL Server Profiler. The SQL Server Profiler allows you to see what the database is doing, when it is doing it, and how long it takes.

You can launch the SQL Server Profiler from the Microsoft SQL Server submenu in the Start menu or from the Tools menu of Enterprise Manager. Once you've launched the SQL Server Profiler, you can start a new trace by choosing File ►New ►Trace. This opens the Trace Properties dialog box (see Figure 22-4).

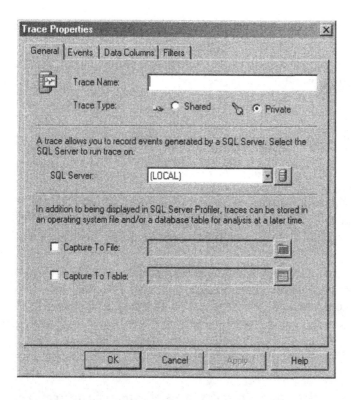

Figure 22-4. The Trace Properties dialog box

Once you've launched the Trace Properties dialog box, you'll see a number of important options. If you intend on being able to run the optimizer (which can automatically perform a number of optimizations on your database), you'll need to save the output to a trace file. You can do this by checking the Capture to File box and then choosing a file by clicking the folder icon to the right of the box.

The Events tab allows you to manually choose the events you'd like to include in the trace. These events include table scans, stored procedures being called, and more. It's worth your time to look through this menu and identify the types of events in which you're interested.

The Data Columns tab provides you with the ability to choose the kind of information you want captured when each of the selected events occurs. Some of the options included are the Application Name, CPU Time Used, IO, and Duration.

The Filters tab allows you to choose the items you would like excluded from your trace. Generally, you don't need this tab when working against a development database whose traffic is limited to your usage, but it's helpful in building a trace against a large server that has multiple databases on it. In other words, it's helpful to be able to filter out the "noise."

Once you've started your trace, you'll be able to watch the activity on your database in real time and understand how long each query and stored procedure takes to execute (see Figure 22-5).

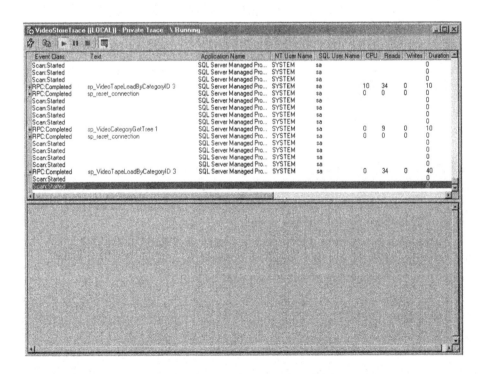

Figure 22-5. The SQL Server Profiler with a trace running

If you're watching a trace on a live production system, you should be able to quickly identify any stored procedures that are taking a long time to run by looking at the Duration column. Any stored procedure taking longer than 50 milliseconds is a potential danger to your application's scalability.

Optimizing Automatically with the SQL Server Profiler

The SQL Server Profiler also provides an outstanding tool that can automatically optimize your database for you. Database veterans are probably cringing as they read this after having been burned by one of the variety of applications that promised to do this and delivered marginal results. However, SQL Server's Index Tuning Wizard provides most of the optimization that applications need as long as you understand a few caveats.

Foremost, it's important to keep in mind that the Index Tuning Wizard does nothing for optimizing the database for queries contained in stored procedures. This is a bit of a problem given that it's a good practice to keep all of your database queries wrapped in stored procedures for optimal performance.

NOTE *For more information about SQL Server performance, see Brad M. McGehee's site at* www.sql-server-performance.com. *You can also refer to William R. Vaughn's books, notably* ADO.NET and ADO Examples and Best Practices for VB Programmers, Second Edition *(Apress, 2002) or the classic* Hitchhiker's Guide to Visual Basic and SQL Server *(Microsoft Press, 1998), which discusses Visual Basic 6, SQL Server 7, and SQL Server 2000, Microsoft Data Engine (MSDE), and ADO 2.0.*

Fortunately, there are some workarounds to this particular problem. You can copy and paste queries from your stored procedures into the Query Analyzer and have it assess the load you're putting on the database and make an informed decision on what indexes should be added.

Once you've pasted your query into the Query Analyzer, choose Query ➤ Perform Index Analysis, and the Query Analyzer will use the SQL Server Profiler to show you the best course of action (see Figure 22-6).

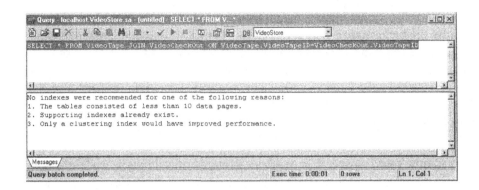

Figure 22-6. The Query Analyzer's recommendations for the current query

If the Query Analyzer has recommendations on what you should do, a second dialog box will pop up and ask if you want it to automatically implement the recommendations. Often, it recommends adding an index to a particular column that is causing a table scan because table scans take significantly longer to run than indexed queries (see Figure 22-7).

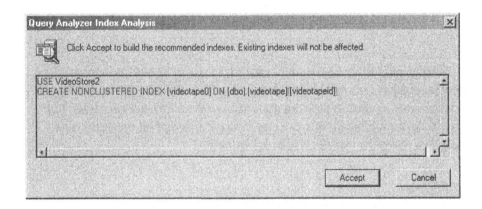

Figure 22-7. The Query Analyzer's recommendation to create an index that would help the query run faster

You can also attach the SQL Server Profiler to run a trace against your production database to identify stored procedures that are taking longer to execute than you would like. Then, launch the wizard and choose Profile the Performance of a Stored Procedure; the tool will test that particular stored procedure and recommend what you can do to optimize its performance.

It's largely a matter of personal preference as to how you want to work to improve the performance of your stored procedures. Although the wizard makes suggestions, you don't have the opportunity to tweak and alter the stored procedure the way you do with the Query Analyzer.

Optimizing Your Transact-SQL Queries for Performance

You can tune your Transact-SQL queries and stored procedures for performance in a number of ways. Think of your queries as asking the database a question and think of the optimizations you make on the query as asking the question in a way that requires the database less thought. Listing 22-1 shows an inefficient query that you can optimize.

Listing 22-1. The Query from SelectVideosCheckedIn, *Not Optimized*

```
SELECT VideoTapeID, Title, Description FROM VideoTape WHERE VideoTapeID NOT IN
    (
    SELECT VideoTapeID FROM VideoCheckOut  as vco WHERE VideoTapeID NOT IN
        (SELECT VideoTapeID From VideoCheckIn as vci WHERE
        vco.VideoCheckOutID=vci.VideoCheckOutID)
    )
```

The query in Listing 22-1 took 15 seconds to return 42,000 rows from the VideoStore2 database available in the downloadable code for this book. Most of this is the time required to pipe out that many rows to the Query Analyzer. But even with factoring that in, there's a way to shave a second off the query time. Figure 22-8 shows the execution plan of Listing 22-1.

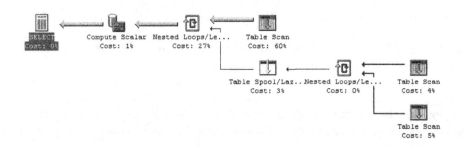

Figure 22-8. The estimated execution plan of the query in Listing 22-1

By using NOT IN to test the subqueries, SQL Server has to do a comparison to make sure that the VideoTapeID doesn't match at each level of the subquery. To understand what SQL Server is doing to perform this query, it's helpful to be able to see the execution path and examine it for comparisons and table scans that you can eliminate.

You can view this in the Query Analyzer by choosing Query ➤Display Estimated Execution Path. This tool is an especially powerful weapon in the war against inefficient queries.

Next to each item in the execution path is a cost in terms of the percentage of the overall execution time (always adding up to 100 percent). As you follow the execution path and move your mouse over each item, you should pay attention to a few key items in the pop-up text. The three most critical factors to pay attention to are Estimated Number of Executes, Estimated CPU, and Estimated IO.

Estimated Number of Executes lets you know how many times the comparison will be performed. If you can think of a way to keep the logic of your query and still reduce the number of times this comparison must be performed, you can have an excellent impact on performance.

The Estimated CPU and Estimated IO columns let you know how much CPU usage and disk IO is resulting for a single step in the process of executing your stored procedure.

Using the information derived from the estimated execution plan, you can identify a few areas that are ripe for optimization. You can significantly reduce the table scan icon that is taking up 60 percent of the execution time if you use a narrowing item in the WHERE clause.

One of the biggest impacts you can have on the speed of your query execution is keeping the result set as small as possible. To this end, you can modify the SelectVideosCheckedIn stored procedure to include a simple way to reduce the number of rows that must be compared to the subquery. In this case, narrowing the results based upon the CategoryID vastly reduces the number of rows that will be analyzed and returned. Listing 22-2 lists an optimized version of SelectVideosCheckedIn.

Listing 22-2. An Optimized Version of the SelectVideosCheckedIn *Query*

```
SELECT VideoTapeID, Title, Description FROM VideoTape WHERE
    CategoryID=5 AND
    VideoTapeID NOT IN
    (
    SELECT VideoTapeID FROM VideoCheckOut  as vco WHERE VideoTapeID NOT IN
        (SELECT VideoTapeID From VideoCheckIn as vci WHERE
vco.VideoCheckOutID=vci.VideoCheckOutID)
    )
```

Another effect of narrowing the results from the VideoTape table before performing the subquery comes from the Estimated Number of Executions that are now expected to run on the Table Spool step and its related substeps. Without narrowing the results by CategoryID first, this step executed 42,000 times—one for each row in the database. With the VideoTape table narrowed by CategoryID, this number drops to a few thousand, providing an enormous boost to the performance of the SQL statement. Figure 22-9 shows the execution plan of Listing 22-2.

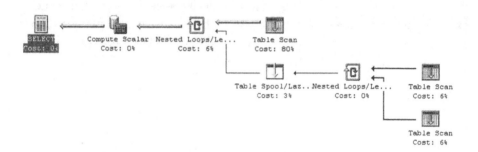

Figure 22-9. The estimated execution plan of the query in Listing 22-2

A second strategy you can use to reduce the number of rows returned is to use SELECT TOP to reduce the number of rows you expect to be returned. This can provide an enormous performance boost, especially in situations where you don't care precisely what records from the larger result set are required.

An example of where this behavior is beneficial is in an unordered queue situation. For example, if you had a table that tracks tasks for employees to perform and you wanted a query that would return 10 tasks for the employee to do, you could write a query like this one:

```
SELECT TOP 10 TaskID, Name FROM Tasks WHERE Assigned=0
```

The performance increase comes from two elements. First, the number of rows that have to be piped across the network is significantly less. Second, the query can stop running as soon as it has any 10 records that meet the criteria.

If the query had to have the tasks in some type of order, such as Date Due column, then the query would lose the benefit of being able to stop executing as soon as it identified 10 items meeting the criteria. Adding an ORDER BY clause forces the query to completely execute to return the top 10 items in the correct order in which you expect them.

Understanding the execution plans of your queries can help you devise effective strategies for producing better stored procedures.

Avoiding Excessive Stored Procedure Recompilation

One of the reasons stored procedures are faster than simply executing SQL directly against the database is that stored procedures are interpreted and compiled into a structure that SQL Server can execute efficiently. The danger that comes from this is excessive recompilation if SQL Server thinks something has changed in your stored procedure.

A simple way to avoid excessive recompilations is to keep all of your variable and temporary table declarations together in your stored procedure. Some types of declarations, such as the creation of a temporary table, cause the stored procedure to recompile, but if it surrounded by other such statements, they will all be compiled at the same time instead of breaking execution as each statement is compiled.

Another cause of your stored procedure being frequently recompiled is if the contents of the tables the stored procedure is querying change frequently. If you have a table that is constantly changing, using sp_executesql can keep your stored procedure from recompiling (see Listing 22-3). The downside of this particular approach is that SQL Server won't be able to cache the execution plan of the query you run in your stored procedure.

Listing 22-3. Using sp_executesql *to Execute a Database Query*

```
EXEC dbo.sp_executesql N'
SELECT VideoTapeID, Title, Description FROM VideoTape WHERE
    VideoTapeID NOT IN
    (
    SELECT VideoTapeID FROM VideoCheckOut  as vco WHERE VideoTapeID NOT IN
        (SELECT VideoTapeID From VideoCheckIn as vci WHERE
vco.VideoCheckOutID=vci.VideoCheckOutID)
    )'
```

To identify what stored procedures in your database are recompiling excessively, use the SQL Server Profiler and make sure you have the SP:Recompile event selected. The SQL Server Profiler shows you when each recompilation occurs. If you're able to identify any stored procedures that recompile often, you'll have an excellent place to start tuning your database performance.

Avoiding Locks

To avoid two threads accessing the same resource at the same time, SQL Server has a locking system. If your CPU usage and IO are low but your database is performing slowly, it's likely you have some bad locking conditions occurring.

If you have a stored procedure that needs frequent recompilation, make sure you include the table owner in all of your statements. When a stored procedure is being recompiled, it's in a locked state and can't be called by another process until it has finished recompiling. If it has to look up who owns each table as it does the recompile, it'll take longer.

Also, avoid using cursors at all costs. A cursor allows row-by-row processing on a result set. Sometimes a cursor is necessary, but it can put a lock on the table while it executes. You can rewrite most queries that use a cursor using either a CASE clause or at least a TABLE variable if you're using SQL Server 2000.

Finally, only use transactions when you need to—and keep transactions short. Because a transaction can't have any data modified outside of the transaction while it's occurring, it'll lock almost everything it touches. If you think through the execution of your transaction and come up with any way to keep your transactional integrity without actually using a transaction, then you can reduce the number of locks that occur.

Designing Your Tables for Optimal Performance

To achieve the best performance from your database, you'll need to start thinking about performance as you design your table schema. In every step of the process, think about how you'll query the data in the table and how you'll run updates on it. Unfortunately, sometimes you'll have to break away from clean design and choose one that is not as clean as you would like it to be to achieve optimal performance.

A common myth in designing a database for performance is that every table must have a primary key. In general, it's a good idea for every table to have a primary key—unless the primary key will never be used. A good example of this is a join table that sits between two tables and expresses a relationship between the two. Adding an extra column to a table that represents a many-to-many relationship is like having a fifth wheel on your car—it won't break anything, but it might hurt your gas mileage just a little. Figure 22-10 shows a join table.

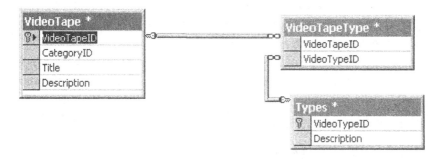

Figure 22-10. A join table that doesn't need a primary key

In the table structure shown in Figure 22-10, the VideoTapeType table doesn't need a primary key. If you added another VideoTapeTypeID column as an auto-numbered primary key, it would be completely superfluous and add a useless piece of data to the database.

If performance is absolutely critical down to the last cycle and you're willing to commit to an unclean database design, denormalizing your data can be an effective means of achieving that performance. This type of situation comes up fairly often when dealing with a system that allows people to log in and search for companies. In this situation, you're working on a database that has two types of companies—companies with people who can log into your system and companies that are just searchable data. It'll provide better performance for the companies that can log in to have the companies that can't in a separate table. The reason for this is it's likely that the number of companies that can't log in is significantly greater than those that can, but at the same time you'll likely be doing many more queries on the companies that can log in. It's definitely a convoluted situation and bad practice to track the same data in two places. However, if you can keep the amount of data in one table that will be frequently accessed small to the detriment of good design, it can help quite a bit.

Checking the Size of Database Pages

In SQL Server 2000, data is internally stored as a collection of 8KB pages. The more rows that can be stored on a single 8KB page, the faster all queries run on the database will be and the less space the table will take up.

A simple way to find out how many bytes each row takes up is to look at the Size column in design view. If you add up the size of each of these columns and it's perfectly divisible by 8KB, then you have a perfect situation where no space will be wasted in the pages. This doesn't mean you should intentionally make your tables larger just to be divisible by 8KB—but in general smaller tables are better for your application's design. If you have a table with more than 10 columns, make sure your requirements are best served by what you're doing.

Database page size is one of the reasons why it's generally better to have multiple small tables as opposed to a denormalized table that contains a large number of columns.

Understanding Denormalization

The opposite of normalization is denormalization, which essentially amounts to creating large, flat table structures that have all of the columns you need on a single row. Denormalized tables are generally used for reporting, for derived tables, or for data warehousing. In general, it's not recommended to use a denormalized schema unless it's for one of those reasons—generally in a data warehouse or "business intelligence" environment.

The performance benefit of these tables comes from the fact that the database doesn't need to join multiple tables together. Denormalization is useful for situations where you need most of the data that's in the table. If a denormalized table has 40 columns, and you really only need the data in two of the columns the majority of the time, you're likely better off just using a regular normalized table schema to achieve optimal performance.

Understanding the Dangers of Database Design Slippage

You have to maintain a fine balance when creating a database schema between three main elements:

- Clean normalized design

- Performance

- Speed of development

If you're designing a large, complicated application, a good normalized design is probably the way to go. If scalability is the prime consideration, then performance comes first. If the application you're developing is small and doesn't have scalability requirements, obviously speed of development is at the top of your list.

Above all, make sure you're designing the application the way it's needed, and as with all professional applications, make the right tool for the job and avoid architectural "gold plating" (creating a system that is beautifully geeky to a programmer but doesn't solve the business problem any better than a less-geeky solution). The people who pay your salary probably don't know or care that your application uses an absolutely perfect normal form.

With this consideration, you have to be careful when you start slipping from clean design because without discipline it can become a "slippery slope." Sometimes doing the "wrong" thing because it's fast can make development slow later as you work to cover up the sins of your past. Always think in terms of both long-term lazy and short-term lazy (described in Chapters 18 and 19).

Understanding ADO.NET Performance Issues and Using Best Practices

The following sections discuss some performance strategies and best practices when working with ADO.NET.

Selecting Data Providers

Many data providers are available to work with a single database, and selecting a best-suited data provider is the first step to designing performance-oriented, data-driven solutions. Some of the common data providers discussed in this book are Sql, OleDb, ODBC, OracleClient, and SQLXML.

Each data provider acts in a different way because of its internal architecture and the way it's designed. For example, the ODBC data provider uses ODBC drivers, and the OleDb data provider uses OLE DB providers to connect to different data sources. Each of these technologies works differently internally.

Selecting a data provider depends on your application's requirements. This section discusses the different scenarios and the best solutions.

To work with SQL Server databases, you can use any of these three data providers: Sql, OleDb, and ODBC. But when working with SQL Server 7.0 or later databases, the Sql data provider is the best choice. No other data provider can beat the performance of the Sql data provider in this case. The Sql data provider can provide much faster data access than the OleDb and ODBC data providers. That said, the Sql data provider isn't the best choice to work with SQL Server 6.5 or prior versions of SQL Server.

When working with Access databases, OleDb is the obvious choice. You can even use ODBC data providers, but OleDb provides better performance.

The ODBC data provider is useful when your application needs to access an ODBC data source or there aren't OleDb or other providers available. For example, if you need to access Excel or text data sources, you can simply do this using ODBC data sources.

Now let's say your application needs to access an Oracle database. There are different ways you can work with Oracle databases. You can use the ODBC data provider. Microsoft already has released an Oracle .NET data provider called OracleClient. Oracle offers another .NET provider developed for Oracle databases. Besides these three data providers, CoreLab offers an Oracle .NET data provider called OraDirect. So, now the question is this: Which one do you choose? Obviously, using an Oracle .NET data provider (either Microsoft, Oracle, or CoreLab) is better than using an ODBC data provider to access Oracle databases. Performance-wise, the Oracle data provider is faster than the ODBC data provider because there's no overhead ODBC layer.

NOTE *The .NET Framework 1.1 (or Visual Studio 2003) installs the Oracle and ODBC data providers. The OleDb, Sql, Odbc, and Oracle data providers are defined in the* System.Data.OleDb, System.Data.SqlClient, System.Data.Odbc, *and* System.Data.OracleClient *namespaces (respectively).*

Choosing from different Oracle .NET data providers depends on your options. Microsoft's Oracle .NET data provider is available free as a part of ADO.NET. If you want to use a third-party data provider such as OraDirect, you need to pay for it.

So, what's the solution when you need to work with different databases? Developing custom data access code is definitely a good idea. A custom data provider can consume all data providers to find out the best solution. Because all data providers implement ADO.NET interfaces, you can write some generic code based on the interfaces that will work with any data provider. The following section shows you how to write a generic data access component that utilizes multiple data providers to give you the best options.

Writing a Generic Data Access Component

In this section, you'll create a simple generic data access class that allows you to select a DataAdapter at runtime. Based on the similar theory, you can extend this class by adding other common functionality to it.

Listing 22-4 lists the generic class. As you can see, this code uses interfaces to create a connection and DataAdapter objects. This class has two methods: GetConnection and GetDataAdapter. The GetConnection method returns an IDbConnection object created using different data providers based on the connection type and connection string passed in the method. The code also provides functionality for the Sql, OleDb, ODBC, and Oracle data providers.

The GetDataAdapter method returns an IDbDataAdapter object created based on the connection and connection type variables passed in the method. You can also add methods to return a DataSet, a DataReader, and other objects from this class.

Listing 22-4. Generic Data Access Class

```
' Generic Data Access component class
Public Class GenericDataAccessComp
  Private idbConn As IDbConnection = Nothing
  Private idbAdapter As IDbDataAdapter = Nothing
  Private dbAdapter As DbDataAdapter = Nothing
  ' Default connection type exposed through
  ' ConnectionType
  ' 1 - Sql; 2 - OleDb, 3 - Odbc
  ' 4 - Oracle
  Private DefConnType As Int16 = 1
  ' Default connection string exposed through
  ' ConnString property
  Private DefConnStr As String


  Public Sub GenericDataAccessComp()

  End Sub


  ' GetConnection returns IDbConnection
  Public Function GetConnection(ByVal connType As Integer, _
  ByVal connString As String) As IDbConnection
    Select Case connType
      Case 1
        ' OleDb Data Provider
        idbConn = New SqlConnection(connString)
      Case 2
        ' Sql Data Provider
        idbConn = New OleDbConnection(connString)
      Case 3
        ' ODBC Data Provider
```

```
            idbConn = New OdbcConnection(connString)
        Case 4
          ' Oracle data provider
          idbConn = New OracleConnection(connString)
        Case Else
          Exit Function
      End Select
      Return idbConn
    End Function


  ' GetDataAdapter returns IDbDataAdapter
  Public Function GetDataAdapter(ByVal connType As Integer, _
  ByVal conn As IDbConnection, ByVal sql As String) _
  As IDbDataAdapter

      Select Case connType
        Case 1
          ' OleDb Data Provider
          idbAdapter = New SqlDataAdapter(sql, conn)
        Case 2
          ' Sql Data Provider
          idbAdapter = New OleDbDataAdapter(sql, conn)
        Case 3
          ' ODBC Data Provider
          idbAdapter = New OdbcDataAdapter(sql, conn)
        Case 4
          'Oracle data provider
          idbAdapter = New OracleDataAdapter(sql, conn)
        Case Else
          Exit Function
      End Select
      Return idbAdapter
    End Function
End Class
```

Now you're going to create a Windows application that consumes the class in Listing 22-4. Add a GroupBox control, four RadioButton controls, a DataGrid control, and a Button control. After changing the properties of these controls, the final form looks like Figure 22-11. When you select a data provider and click the Connect button, the program uses the selected data provider.

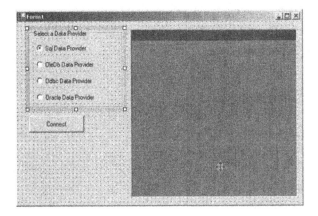

Figure 22-11. Generic data access class consumer application

First, define some variables that you use in the application (see Listing 22-5). As you can see, this code defines connection strings for different data providers.

Listing 22-5. User-Defined Variables

```
' User defined variables
  Private connString As String = Nothing
  Private sql As String = Nothing
  Private conn As IDbConnection = Nothing
  Private adapter As IDbDataAdapter = Nothing
  Private OleDbConnString As String = _
   "Provider=Microsoft.Jet.OLEDB.4.0;" & _
   "Data Source=c:\\Northwind.mdb"
  Private SqlConnString As String = _
    "Integrated Security=SSPI; Initial Catalog=Northwind;" & _
    "Data Source=localhost;"
  Private OdbcConnString As String
  Private OracleConnString As String
```

Second, on the Connect button click event handler, you check what data provider is selected and based on that selection, you create a connection using the GetConnection method of the previously discussed class. You also call the GetDataAdapter method that returns a DataAdapter.

Once data is in a DataAdapter, you simply call its Fill method to fill data from the DataAdapter to a DataSet. As you can see, the code opens a connection, creates and fills a DataSet, and then binds the DataSet to the DataGrid. In this case, you have limited the functionality to Sql and OleDb data providers, but you can also specify the connection strings for Oracle and ODBC data providers. Listing 22-6 shows how to use the generic data access class.

Listing 22-6. Using the Generic Data Access Class

```
Private Sub ConnectBtn_Click(ByVal sender As System.Object, _
  ByVal e As System.EventArgs) Handles ConnectBtn.Click
    ' Construct SQL statement
    sql = "SELECT * FROM Employees"
    Dim daComp As GenericDataAccessComp = _
    New GenericDataAccessComp
    ' SQL data adapter
    If SqlRadioButton.Checked Then
      conn = daComp.GetConnection(1, SqlConnString)
      adapter = daComp.GetDataAdapter(1, conn, sql)
      ' OleDb data adapter
    ElseIf OleDbRadioButton.Checked Then
      conn = daComp.GetConnection(2, OleDbConnString)
      adapter = daComp.GetDataAdapter(2, conn, sql)
    End If
    ''' Add code for other data adapters

    ' Open connection. If you don't open it explicitly,
    ' calling DataAdapter will open it internally
    If conn.State <> ConnectionState.Open Then
      conn.Open()
    End If
    ' Create and fill a DataSet
    Dim ds As DataSet = New DataSet
    adapter.Fill(ds)
    ' Display DataSet in DataGrid
    DataGrid1.DataSource = ds.Tables(0)
    ' Close connection
    If conn.State = ConnectionState.Open Then
      conn.Open()
    End If

  End Sub
End Class
```

Now if you run the application and click the Connect button, you'll see data in the DataGrid.

You can extend the functionality of this generic data access component by adding various methods and their overloaded forms. You can also add functionality for other data providers including Oracle, MySql, and WinCE.

Choosing a Development Mode: Designer vs. Manual

This book covered both designer and manual approaches for adding data components to applications. The designer approach is easy to use and takes less time to write data-driven applications. (See Chapter 2 for more details.) You simply drag and drop data components to a form and follow simple steps using wizards, and the application is ready in few minutes. For example, say you want to write a Windows application that allows users to view, delete, edit, update, and navigate data through DataGrid controls and you already know the database and database tables. In this scenario, using the Data Form Wizard isn't a bad idea. However, you have no idea what happened under the hood; further, this approach is rigid, and there's no flexibility. You can go and edit code by hand, but the queries written by the designer are a big headache if you try to update them manually. On the other hand, if you write code manually, you know what code is where and how it works. Writing code manually may be time consuming, but it's worth it for experienced developers who know how and where to write code.

Alternatively, you can mix the approaches to get the best out of both worlds. You can use the designer to add some controls, and you can write some code manually.

Again, it depends on you to decide what approach to adapt. We prefer the manual approach over the designer approach because the designer writes lots of unwanted code and leaves no option to modify it. For beginners, it's better to use a designer rather than writing bad code. (But if you're already on Chapter 22 of this book, then you're not a beginner anymore!)

Retrieving Data: DataReader, XmlReader, and DataSet

One of the most frequently asked questions on discussion forums and newsgroups relates to whether you should use a DataReader or a DataSet. You can use a DataReader, XmlReader, and DataSet to retrieve data from a database. When reading hundreds of records, the DataReader is twice as fast as an XmlReader or DataSet. This difference gets bigger when there's higher user load and more records.

Now, the question is this: Which one do you use? Obviously, the XmlReader has no competition. The competition is between the DataReader and the DataSet. You use a DataReader when you need to simply read data in data types or streams—for example, when you need to display data on a system console. You use a DataSet when you need to display data in data-bound controls and do something more with the data such as editing and deleting data through a DataGrid control.

NOTE *For more information, read "Building Distributed Applications with Microsoft .NET" at* http://msdn.microsoft.com/library/default.asp?url=/library/en-us/dnbda/html/bdadotnetarch13.asp.

Updating a Data Source: Command vs. DataSet

You have two approaches for adding and updating data to a data source: using commands or using a DataSet. For example, if you want to use a command, you construct a SQL statement (INSERT, UPDATE, or DELETE) and execute the command using SqlCommand or another data provider's Command object. If you want to use a DataSet, you go through the DataSet and call the AddNew, Edit, or Delete members of a DataTable to add, update, and delete (respectively). Both of the approaches have their uses. Executing commands give you control over the entire table, and using the DataSet approach limits you to a record. For example, you can construct UPDATE and DELETE SQL statements and execute them using commands to update and delete all records of a table. On the other hand, a DataTable provides a way to access all records in the form of a collection, where you can loop through these records one by one and do whatever you want to do with them.

So, again, which one should you choose? It depends on your application requirements. If you're using a DataGrid bound to a DataSet and want to delete a particular record, your obvious choice would be to use the DataTable.Rows.Delete method. But if there's no DataSet available in your application and you want to delete a record based on some criteria, you can simply construct a DELETE statement with a WHERE clause and execute it using the Command object.

If you want to add a record to a database, executing a command is faster than a DataSet. This is also the case with delete and update operations.

Saving Data and Using GetChanges

When using a DataAdapter.Update method, it's a good idea to send only updated records back to the database. The GetChanges method of the DataSet returns the updated records. See FAQ 18 of Appendix C for more details.

Retrieving Data with the SELECT Statement

Using SELECT * FROM TableName is a common statement to retrieve data from a database. It doesn't matter whether you read data through a DataReader or a DataSet. You don't even have to think about what columns a database table has.

In most of the cases, you don't need all the columns of a table. Don't use SELECT * unless you really need all data. Instead, use your column names. For example, if you want to select only the FirstName and LastName columns of the Employees table, use SELECT FirstName, LastName FROM Employees instead of SELECT * FROM Employees.

Using Stored Procedures

Stored procedures are highly optimized objects and reduce network traffic, code size, execution time, and server overhead. Use store procedures instead of creating SQL commands if possible.

Using Connection Strings and Pooling

ADO.NET sends all Connection objects to a pool after a connection closes. When there's a need for a connection, instead of creating a new connection, you use a connection from the pool. But there's a limitation in connection pooling: The connection string must be the same. This means, if possible, you should store a connection string as a program-level scope variable and use it instead of creating a dynamic connection string each time you create a connection.

Summary

Getting good performance out of SQL Server is not as hard as many people believe. It's largely a matter of knowing what tools are available to you and knowing a few small tricks of the trade. In this chapter, you saw some tricks related to SQL Server. You also learned about some tricks and performance issues with different objects of ADO.NET.

APPENDIX A

Relational Databases: Some Basic Concepts

THIS APPENDIX DISCUSSES some key concepts of relational databases, including normalization, sets, cursors, and locking.

A *relational database* is a collection of tables, and a *table* is a set of columns and rows. A table's columns can be referred to as *columns*, *fields*, or *attributes*, and each column in a table requires a unique name and a data type. The datum in a given row is generally referred to as a *record*. (The term *recordset* refers to a set of records, reminding you that relational databases use set-based operations rather than row-at-a-time, pointer-based operations.)

In relational databases, each table needs to have a key, which is associated with a column. There are two important types of keys: primary keys and foreign keys. A *primary key* is a column of a table with a unique value for each row, which helps ensure data integrity by (theoretically) eliminating duplicate records. A *foreign key* takes care of the *relational* in relational databases and provides a link between related data that are contained in more than one table. For example, in a classic parent-child relationship such as customers and orders, if CustomerId is the primary key in the Customers table, it'll need to occur in the Orders table as a foreign key to associate each order with an individual customer. The customer/order relationship is a one-to-many relationship because each *one* customer can have *many* orders. That relationship is sometimes depicted as *1:n*.

 NOTE *A primary key can also be a combination of several columns of a table, where one of those columns is a foreign key. For example, in an example database table, one table can have a primary key that's a combination of the Path and File columns to avoid duplicate file records. The File column is a foreign key.*

A *database* is a collection of tables, indexes, constraints, and other objects. The definition of these objects is known as the database's *schema*, which can be represented in a graphical way using various diagrams.

Meta-data refers to the collection of data that describes the content, quality, relations, and other characteristics of data. A database's meta-data includes information that ranges from table definitions to users and their permissions.

Understanding Normalization

If you've been working with databases for a while, you're probably familiar with the term *normalization*. Database designers or developers often ask whether a database is normalized. So, what's normalization? Normalization is a process of eliminating data redundancy (except for the redundancy required by foreign keys) in multiple relational tables, and it ensures that data is organized efficiently. When you normalize a database, you basically have three goals:

- Ensuring you've organized the data correctly into groups that minimize the amount of duplicate data stored in a database

- Organizing the data such that, when you (or your users) modify data in it (such as a person's address or email), the change only has to be made once

- Designing a database in which you can access and manipulate the data quickly and efficiently without compromising the integrity of the data in storage

E. F. Codd first proposed the normalization process in 1972. Initially, he proposed three normal forms, which he called *first, second,* and *third normal forms* (1NF, 2NF, and 3NF). Subsequently, he proposed a stronger definition of 3NF, known as *Boyce-Codd Normal Form* (BCNF). Later, others proposed fourth normal form (4NF) and fifth normal form (5NF). Most people agree that a database that's in 3NF is probably good enough—in other words, normalized enough.

First Normal Form (1NF)

A table is in 1NF if the values of its columns are *atomic*, containing no repeating values. Applying 1NF on a table eliminates duplicate columns from the same table, which creates separate tables for each group of related data, and adds a primary key to the table to identify table rows with a unique value. For example, say you have a Customers table (see Figure A-1). The Customers table stores data about customer orders. The columns store data about a customer such as name, address, and order description.

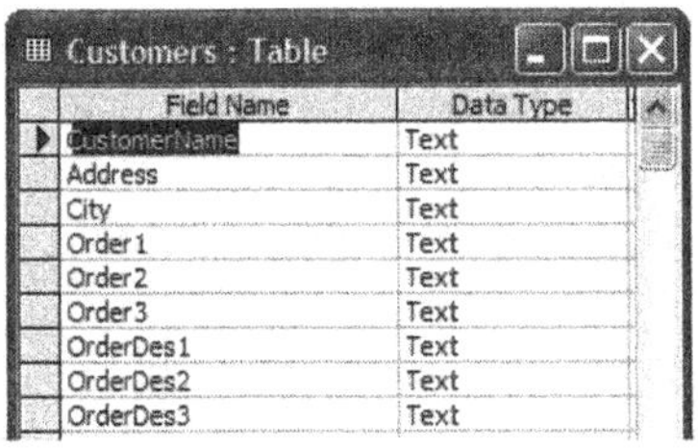

Customers : Table

Field Name	Data Type
CustomerName	Text
Address	Text
City	Text
Order1	Text
Order2	Text
Order3	Text
OrderDes1	Text
OrderDes2	Text
OrderDes3	Text

Figure A-1. Customers table before normalization

The data of the Customers table looks like Figure A-2.

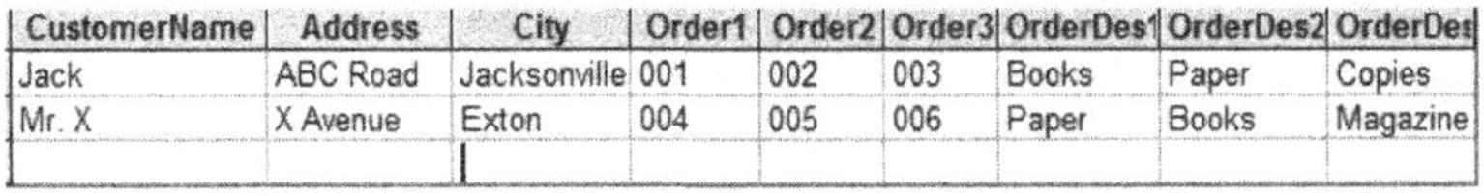

CustomerName	Address	City	Order1	Order2	Order3	OrderDes1	OrderDes2	OrderDes
Jack	ABC Road	Jacksonville	001	002	003	Books	Paper	Copies
Mr. X	X Avenue	Exton	004	005	006	Paper	Books	Magazine

Figure A-2. Two rows of data from the Customers table

Figure A-1 shows the design of a Customers table. As you can see, it's been designed to store up to three orders for any customer—sort of mimicking an array structure in spreadsheet format. There are obvious problems with this design. As you can see from Figure A-2, there are many columns related to orders (that's a classic giveaway of a poorly designed table—mixing two or more *entities*, or kinds of data). Whenever a customer posts a new order, a new column will be added to the table. Not only that, if the same customer posts more than one order, the duplicate Address and City column data will be added to the table. This scenario adds duplicate data to the table. This table isn't in 1NF because the 1NF rule says that a table is in 1NF if and only if a table's columns have no repeating values.

You apply 1NF on this table by eliminating the details about the orders, providing just enough relational information to link the Customers table with a new Orders table. The new format of this table after 1NF looks like Figure A-3. You still have some information about orders in this Customers table but only basic link information: OrderNumber. You've fixed the repeating fields problem by jamming all the other order information into a single OrderDescription field.

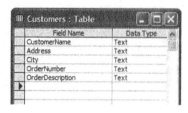

Figure A-3. Customers table schema after 1NF

The data of the table now looks like Figure A-4.

CustomerName	Address	City	OrderNumber	OrderDescription
Jack	ABC Road	Jacksonville	001	Books
Jack	ABC Road	Jacksonville	002	002
Jack	ABC Road	Jacksonville	003	Copies
Mr. X	X Avenue	Exton	004	Paper
Mr. X	X Avenue	Exton	005	Books
Mr. X	X Avenue	Exton	006	Magazine

Figure A-4. Data of the Customers table after 1NF

Second Normal Form (2NF)

2NF eliminates redundant data. A table is in 2NF if it's in 1NF and every *nonkey* column (not a key column—primary or foreign) is fully dependent upon the primary key.

Applying 2NF on a table removes duplicate data on multiple rows, places data in separate rows, places grouped data in new tables, and creates relationships between the original tables and new tables through foreign keys. As you can see from Figure A-4, there are six records for two customers and three columns—CustomerName, Address, and City has the same information three times. 2NF eliminate these cases. Under 2NF, you separate data into two different tables and relate these tables using a foreign key. Records in tables should not depend on anything other than the table's primary key.

In this example, you now create a separate Orders table. As you can probably guess, the Orders table stores information related to customer orders. It *relates* back to the correct customer via the CustomerId column. Now the two tables, Customers and Orders, look like Figure A-5 and Figure A-6.

⊞ Customers : Table	
Field Name	Data Type
CustomerName	Text
Address	Text
City	Text
🔑 CustomerId	AutoNumber ▾
	Field Properties

Figure A-5. Customers table after 2NF

⊞ Orders : Table	
Field Name	Data Type
🔑 OrderId	AutoNumber
OrderNumber	Text
OrderDescription	Text
CustomerId	Text
	Field Proc

Figure A-6. Orders table after 2NF

As you can see from Figures A-5 and A-6, both tables now have a primary key—denoted by the key icon to the left of the column name. This key will be unique for each record. The CustomerId column of the Customers table is mapped to the CustomerId column of the Orders table. The CustomerId column of the Orders table is a foreign key. The relationship between the Customers and Orders tables looks like Figure A-7.

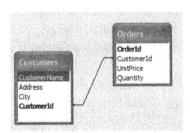

Figure A-7. Relationship between the Customers and Orders tables

Now the data in these tables look like Figure A-8 and Figure A-9.

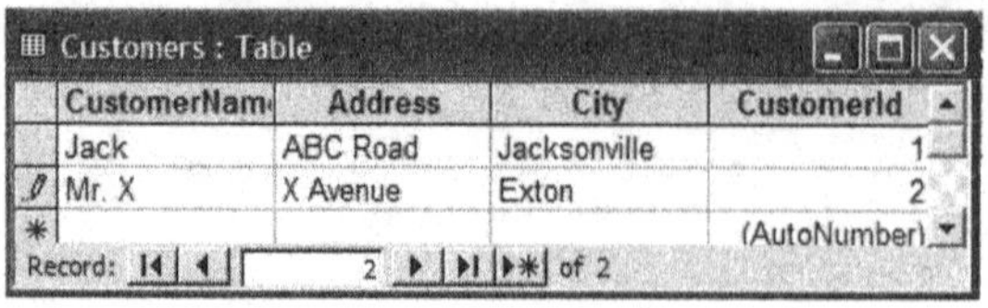

Customers : Table

CustomerNam	Address	City	CustomerId
Jack	ABC Road	Jacksonville	1
Mr. X	X Avenue	Exton	2
			(AutoNumber)

Record: 2 of 2

Figure A-8. Customers table after 2NF

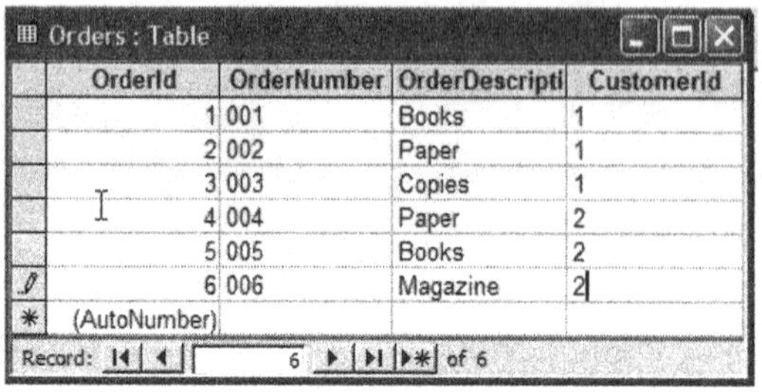

Orders : Table

OrderId	OrderNumber	OrderDescripti	CustomerId
1	001	Books	1
2	002	Paper	1
3	003	Copies	1
4	004	Paper	2
5	005	Books	2
6	006	Magazine	2
(AutoNumber)			

Record: 6 of 6

Figure A-9. Orders table after 2NF

Third Normal Form (3NF)

A table is in 3NF if all columns of a table depend upon the primary key. 3NF eliminates columns that don't depend on the table's primary key. (Note that primary keys don't have to be single columns as shown in these simple examples.)

For example, as you can see from Figure A-10, CustomerId, UnitPrice, and Quantity depend on OrderId (the primary key). But the Total column doesn't depend on the OrderId column; it depends upon the UnitPrice and the Quantity columns.

The data of the Orders table look like Figure A-11 after applying the 3NF rule on it, and you can calculate Total as the multiplication of UnitPrice and Quantity in your SQL statement.

For example:

```
SELECT UnitPrice * Quantity AS Total FROM Orders
```

Orders : Table

OrderId	CustomerId	UnitPrice	Quantity	Total
1	1001	$3.00	6	$18.00
2	1002	$2.50	4	$10.00
3	1002	$4.00	2	$8.00
4	1003	$12.00	2	$24.00
(AutoNumber)		$0.00	0	$0.00

Record: 5 of 5

Figure A-10. Orders table after 3NF

Orders : Table

OrderId	CustomerId	UnitPrice	Quantity
1	1001	$3.00	6
2	1002	$2.50	4
3	1002	$4.00	2
4	1003	$12.00	2

Record: 1 of 4

Figure A-11. Data of the Orders table after 3NF

Boyce-Codd Normal Form (BCNF)

A *determinant* column is the column on which other columns are fully dependent. BCNF is an extended version of 3NF. A database is in BCNF if and only if every determinant is a candidate key. A *candidate key* is a combination of columns that can be uniquely used to identify a row. Each table may have one or more candidate keys.

Fourth Normal Form (4NF)

4NF and 5NF seem to be of interest only in computer science classes and in the academic world in general. But, if you're really interested, a database is in 4NF if and only if it's in BCNF and all multivalued dependencies are also functional dependencies. For example, a customer can have multiple orders and multiple addresses. This data (the customer having multiple addresses and multiple orders) can be stored in a single table, but after applying 4NF, the data will be stored in two tables. The first table stores the CustomerId with addresses, and the second table stores the CustomerId with orders.

Fifth Normal Form (5NF or PJ/NF)

A database is in 5NF—or Projection/Join Normal Form (PJ/NF)—if it can't have a lossless decomposition into any number of smaller tables. In other words, this means a table that has been decomposed into three or more smaller tables must be capable of being joined again on common keys to form the original table.

NOTE *This ends the quick overview of normal forms. SQL Server Magazine has numerous articles about database design and normal forms that you might find helpful at* www.sqlmag.com/Articles/Index.cfm?AuthorID=436.

NOTE *If you've heard about database normal forms and normalization, chances are you've also heard about* denormalization, *which basically refers to the process of embracing a less than rigorously perfect relational design in favor of performance. You might, for example, include calculated fields or aggregations in your design. By including redundant information in your design, you denormalize it.*

Introducing Sets, Cursors, and ADO.NET

Cursors were basically added to SQL to accommodate programmers who preferred row-at-a-time, pointer-style processing. *Real* relational databases don't even have a notion of record number, for example; you use a SELECT statement to obtain record sets.

The ADO.NET model has been redesigned from scratch. There's no explicit support for cursors in ADO.NET. Why do you need cursors? This is a good question. To get your answer, first you have to find out what cursors do.

In ADO, a *recordset* represents the set of rows returned from a data source after executing a SQL statement. A recordset uses a *cursor* to keep track of the current location and navigate through rows.

ADO supports four types of cursors: static, forward-only, keyset, and dynamic. The static cursors are a static copy of records on the client side. Static cursors are either read-only or read/write and provide both backward and forward navigation by using the MoveFirst, MoveNext, MovePrevious, MoveLast, and Move methods of the recordset. Also, you can bookmark records using this type of cursor. The AbsolutePosition property provides the row number of a cursor.

Forward-only cursors are similar to static cursors except they support forward-only navigation from the first to the last record in the cursor. You can update records, insert new records, and delete records, but you can't move backward. The forward-only cursor supports only the MoveNext method of the recordset.

Keyset cursors support both backward and forward navigation through the recordset object's Move methods. In addition to that, they also reflect changes made by other users. Dynamic cursors provide dynamic navigation and reflect all changes immediately. They're useful when your application allows multiple users to add, update, delete, and navigate records simultaneously. Dynamic cursors are flexible, but they don't support absolute positioning and bookmarks.

In ADO, when you create a recordset, you can specify the type of cursors to use. Table A-1 represents the cursor types and their values.

Table A-1. Recordset Cursor Type and Their Values in ADO

CONSTANT	VALUE	DESCRIPTION
adOpenForwardOnly	0	Forward-only recordset cursor (the default)
adOpenKeyset	1	Keyset recordset cursor
AdOpenDynamic	2	Dynamic recordset cursor
AdOpenStatic	3	Static recordset cursor

As you can see, ADO uses cursors to navigate, to position, and to bookmark records in a recordset. ADO.NET represents a new approach. To be blunt, recordsets are history! The DataTable and DataReader have replaced them. Under ADO.NET, a DataReader enables you to perform the function of the forward-only, server-side cursor. However, a DataReader doesn't have a MoveNext method, which moves to the next record of a recordset. But it provides a Read method, which reads all the records until the end of the records. A DataReader is useful when you need to read data fast with no updates and you're not using data-bound controls.

The DataSet and Command objects enable you to work with data as a disconnected source, which is similar to ADO client-side behavior. This method is useful when you need to write data-bound, control-based applications.

ADO.NET doesn't support server-side cursors. However, you can use server-side cursors through ADO by adding a reference to the ADODB type library by generating a .NET wrapper for its objects.

Using Locking

In database terms, *locking* is a mechanism used to avoid inconsistency when multiple users access and update data simultaneously. Using the locking technique, you can lock records or a database table when a user is modifying the records or table, and the data will be unavailable for other users until the current user calls the update method to make final changes. For example, say user A is updating a record. During this operation, user B deletes that record. This scenario may lead to inconsistency in the table. You can avoid this inconsistency by making that record unavailable when user A is updating it and make it available when user A is done updating it. The only drawback of this is user B has to wait until user A is done updating the record. Oh well, waiting is better than having inconsistencies and inaccurate data.

Isolation Levels

An *isolation level* represents a particular locking strategy applied on a database. It's basically a way of representing the stages of locking depending on the complexity of locking. There are four isolation levels, starting from level 0 to 3. Applying these levels on transactions is also called determining *Transaction Isolation Levels* (TILs).

TILs provide consistency during data manipulation when multiple users are accessing data simultaneously. There are three cases that apply to the transactions:

Dirty read: A *dirty read* occurs when a user reads data that have not yet been committed. For example, user 1 changes a row. User 2 reads the row before user 1 commits the changes. What if user 1 rolls back the changes? User 2 will have data that never existed.

Nonrepeatable read: A *nonrepeatable read* occurs when a user reads the same record twice but gets different data each time. The simple case for this situation is when user 1 reads a record. User 2 goes and either changes a record or deletes a record and commits the changes. Now if user 1 tries to read the same records again, user 1 gets different data.

Phantom: A *phantom* is a record that matches the search criteria but isn't initially seen. For example, say user 1 searches for records and gets some records. Now user 2 adds new rows with user 1's search criteria. Now if user 1 searches again using the same criteria, user 1 gets different results than the previous one.

Table A-2 describes the isolation levels defined by OLE DB.

Table A-2. Isolation Levels

LEVEL	DEFINITION
Read Uncommitted	A user can read uncommitted changes made by other users. At this level all three cases (dirty reads, nonrepeatable reads, and phantoms) are possible.
Read Committed	A user can't see changes made by other users until the changes are committed. At this level of isolation, dirty reads aren't possible, but nonrepeatable reads and phantoms are possible.
Repeatable Read	A user can't see the changes made by other users. At this level of isolation, dirty reads and nonrepeatable reads aren't possible, but phantoms are possible.
Serializable	A user sees only changes that are finalized and committed to the database. At this isolation level, dirty reads, nonrepeatable reads, and phantoms aren't possible.

NOTE *The definitive book on transaction processing is* Concurrency Control and Recovery in Database Systems *by Philip A. Bernstein, Vassos Hadzilacos, and Nathan Goodman (Addison-Wesley, 1987). You can download it in its entirety as a 22.9MB self-extracting ZIP file from* http://research.microsoft.com/pubs/ccontrol/. *You can also find related information at* http://research.microsoft.com/~philbe/.

Table A-3 summarizes the data consistency behaviors and isolation level relationship. (Read Committed is SQL Server's default isolation level.)

Table A-3. Isolation Levels and Data Consistency

LEVEL	DIRTY READ?	NONREPEATABLE READ?	PHANTOM?
Read Uncommitted (0)	Yes	Yes	Yes
Read Committed (1)	No	Yes	Yes
Repeatable Read (2)	No	No	Yes
Serializable (3)	No	No	No

Locking Modes

In general, locking avoids the consequences of multiple users accessing the same data simultaneously and tries to maintain the data's consistency and integrity. There are two locking modes: shared and exclusive. The shared mode lets multiple users access the same data simultaneously. However, an exclusive mode won't let user 2 access the data until user 1 unlocks the data. Depending on the database, you can implement locking on a record, a table, or a page level. In table locking, a user can lock the entire table until he commits the changes and unlocks the table. The same method applies on a page as well as on a record for page-level and record-level locking.

NOTE *Chapters 4 and 5 discuss ADO.NET concurrency.*

Based on these general locking modes, ADO provides two different types of locking on recordsets and the combination of them: optimistic locking and pessimistic locking. Optimistic locking is based on the assumption that there won't be any other users when a user is accessing some records of a table.

In optimistic locking, locking only occurs during the final update of records. If any changes were made to the data since it was last accessed, the application must read data again and update the data.

In pessimistic locking, records are unavailable to other users when a user is accessing records until the user makes the final changes.

You can pass an argument when you create a recordset to specify the type of locking. Table A-4 describes these values.

Table A-4. Locking Types

CONSTANT	VALUE	DESCRIPTION
adLockReadOnly	1	Read-only
adLockPessimistic	2	Pessimistic locking
adLockOptimistic	3	Optimistic locking
adLockBatchOptimistic	4	Optimistic locking with batch updates

You set the LockType variable in the recordset to 1 when you need to read data. It doesn't allow you to add or update data.

You use LockType=3, or optimistic locking, when you need to lock records and only when ADO physically updates the record. Otherwise, records are available when you're editing them. In contrast to the optimistic locking, pessimistic locking locks the records when you start editing records. You set LockType=2 in that case. Before applying optimistic locking, you need to make sure that database manufacturer supports it. Some database manufacturers don't support optimistic locking.

Optimistic locking with batch updates, LockType=4, enables you to access multiple records, update them locally, and update the database as a single batch operation. Again, before using this type of locking, you need to make sure the database manufacturer supports this type of locking. Many don't.

NOTE *For more information on locking and concurrency levels, you may want to read Jim Gray's article on isolation levels at* http://research.microsoft.com/~gray/Isolation.doc *or* Transaction Processing: Concepts and Techniques *by Jim Gray and Andreas Reuter (Morgan Kaufmann, 1993).*

What Are Deadlocks?

If you've heard about concurrency and different kinds of locks, you've probably also heard about *deadlocks*. Unfortunately, they're an inevitable fact of life in the database world. But, fortunately, today's Database Management Systems (DBMSs) are typically designed to handle deadlocks—usually by selecting a "victim" whose transaction gets rolled back (or undone).

When users share access to database tables, they may prevent each other from completing transactions. That's because a user who locks a table or a single record during an update may prevent other transactions from acquiring the locks they need to complete their task. As a result, the other transactions enter a wait state, waiting their turn. Sometimes, the locks are unresolvable, though. For example, if transaction A can't complete until it acquires a lock being used by transaction B, and transaction B can't complete until it acquires a lock being used by transaction A, the transactions enter a deadlock state and neither can complete unless the other is terminated.

Microsoft describes deadlocks by noting the following: "A deadlock occurs when there is a cyclic dependency between two or more threads for some set of resources." It adds that deadlocks can occur on any system with multiple threads, not just on a relational DBMS.

Summary

In this appendix, we discussed some of the basic concepts of relational databases. To learn more, you can access the following resources online:

- "Database Normalization Basics":
  http://support.microsoft.com/default.aspx?scid=KB;en-us;q209534

- "Database Normalization Tips" by Luke Chung:
  http://msdn.microsoft.com/library/default.asp?url=/library/
  en-us/dnacc2k2/html/odc_FMSNormalization.asp

- "Database Normalization and Design Techniques" by Barry Wise:
  www.devarticles.com/art/1/321

- *Concurrency Control and Recovery in Database Systems* by
  Philip A. Bernstein, Vassos Hadzilacos, and Nathan Goodman:
  http://research.microsoft.com/pubs/ccontrol/

- "Denormalization Guidelines" by Craig S. Mullins:
  www.tdan.com/i001fe02.htm

- "Getting Down to Data Basics" by Craig S. Mullins:
  www.dbazine.com/edba4.html

- "Transaction Isolation Levels" by Kalen Delaney:
  www.sqlmag.com/Articles/Index.cfm?ArticleID=5336

- "Responsible Denormalization" by Michelle A. Poolet:
  www.sqlmag.com/Articles/Index.cfm?ArticleID=9785

- SQLCourse: www.sqlcourse.com

- Free online version of *Teach Yourself SQL in 21 Days*, Second Edition:
  www8.silversand.net/techdoc/teachsql/index.htm

- Free PowerPoint tutorial on Transact-SQL by Michael R. Hotek:
  www.mssqlserver.com/tsql/

Commonly Used SQL Statements

STRUCTURED QUERY LANGUAGE (SQL) is a language you use to work with relational databases. In this appendix, we'll discuss some commonly used SQL queries and show how to construct them. To test the SQL statements, we'll use the familiar Northwind database—specifically, its Customers and Orders tables.

NOTE *SQL queries are also referred to as* SQL statements.

Understanding SQL References

For the most part, we used Access 2000's Northwind database to illustrate the SQL statements discussed in this appendix, but you can also use the Northwind database that's in SQL Server. (We use the SQL Server version in the examples in the "Understanding Views" section because Access doesn't support the SQL concept of views as virtual tables.) To test SQL statements, you can open the Northwind database in Access and create a new query by selecting Queries and clicking the New button. This opens the New Query dialog box, as shown in Figure B-1.

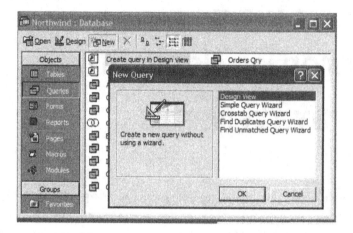

Figure B-1. Creating a new query in Access 2000

The Show Table dialog box displays all the tables in the database and lets you pick the tables with which you want to work (see Figure B-2). Click the Close button.

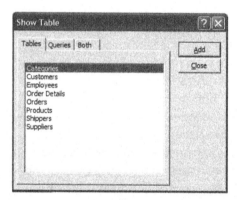

Figure B-2. Selecting database tables

Now, you can open the Query Editor by simply right-clicking the query pane and selecting the SQL View menu item. The Query Editor is basically a blank screen that appears when you're creating a new query, but you can also use it to examine the contents of existing queries (see Figure B-3). In this case, you can either type in a SQL statement directly or paste one in and then choose Query ➤ Run Query to execute the statement.

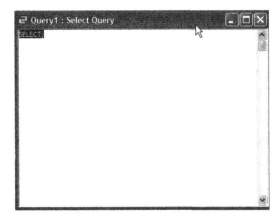

Figure B-3. The Query Editor of Access 2000

Now let's take a look at the Northwind database's Customers table. Figure B-4 shows the table schema (the structure) with its column names and their data types (all of type Text in this case). Note that the CustomerID field is the primary key field.

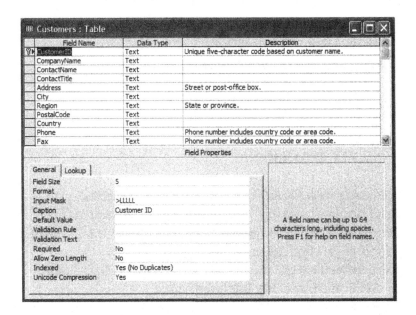

Figure B-4. Customers table schema of the Northwind database

The Orders table columns and their data types look like Figure B-5. OrderID is the primary key in the Orders table. CustomerID and EmployeeID function as foreign keys and provide the "glue" that links data in the Customers table to data stored in Orders and Employees. (Employees is another table in the Northwind database that stores employee records.)

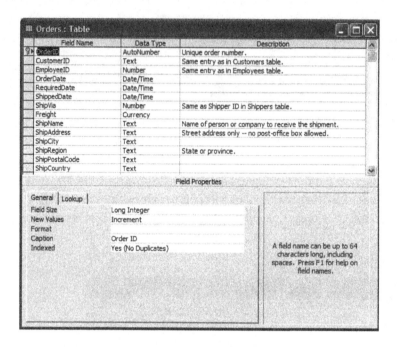

Figure B-5. Orders table schema of the Northwind database

Using the SELECT Statement

The SELECT statement is the workhorse of the SQL language; it enables you to retrieve data from database tables and views. If you want to retrieve data from selected columns, you list the column names in the SELECT statement. You use the WHERE clause to retrieve data from selected rows.

The simplest form of the SELECT statement is SELECT...FROM, which returns records from a table defined after FROM. This is the syntax:

```
SELECT column1, column2, .., FROM table
```

For example, the following SELECT statement returns all records from the CustomerID, CompanyName, Address, and City columns of the Customers table:

```
SELECT CustomerID, CompanyName, Address, City FROM Customers
```

The output looks like Figure B-6.

Customer ID	Company Name	Address	City
1400	Xerox	111 Broad St.	NY
ALFKI	Alfreds Futterkiste	Obere Str. 57	Berlin
ANATR	Ana Trujillo Empareda	Avda. de la Constituci	México D.F.
ANTON	Antonio Moreno Taque	Mataderos 2312	México D.F.
AROUT	Around the Horn	120 Hanover Sq.	London
BERGS	Berglunds snabbköp	Berguvsvägen 8	Luleå
BLAUS	Blauer See Delikatess	Forsterstr. 57	Mannheim
BLONP	Blondel père et fils	24, place Kléber	Strasbourg
BOLID	Bólido Comidas prepa	C/ Araquil, 67	Madrid
BONAP	Bon app'	12, rue des Bouchers	Marseille
BOTTM	Bottom-Dollar Markets	23 Tsawassen Blvd.	Tsawassen
BSBEV	B's Beverages	Fauntleroy Circus	London
CACTU	Cactus Comidas para	Cerrito 333	Buenos Aires

Record: 14 4   1 ▶ ▶I ▶✱ of 93

Figure B-6. Output of the SELECT *statement*

NOTE *You can switch back to the SQL view be selecting View ➤ SQL View.*

You use SELECT * to return all columns from a table (the asterisk is a handy wildcard character in most dialects of SQL). For example, the following statement returns all records from the Customers table:

```
SELECT * FROM Customers
```

The output looks like Figure B-7.

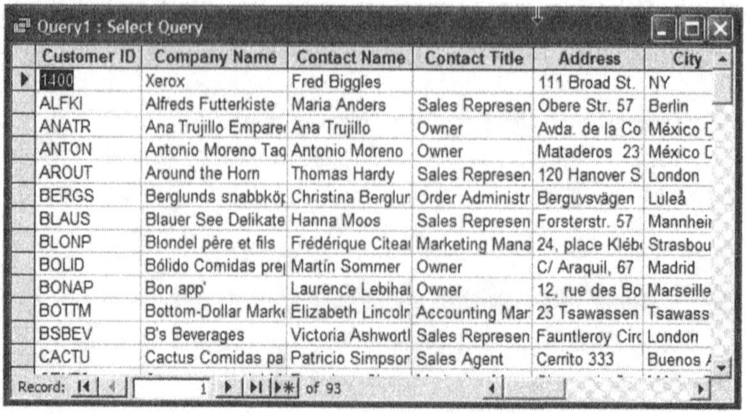

Customer ID	Company Name	Contact Name	Contact Title	Address	City
1400	Xerox	Fred Biggles		111 Broad St.	NY
ALFKI	Alfreds Futterkiste	Maria Anders	Sales Represen	Obere Str. 57	Berlin
ANATR	Ana Trujillo Empare	Ana Trujillo	Owner	Avda. de la Co	México D
ANTON	Antonio Moreno Taq	Antonio Moreno	Owner	Mataderos 23	México D
AROUT	Around the Horn	Thomas Hardy	Sales Represen	120 Hanover S	London
BERGS	Berglunds snabbköp	Christina Berglur	Order Administr	Berguvsvägen	Luleå
BLAUS	Blauer See Delikate	Hanna Moos	Sales Represen	Forsterstr. 57	Mannheir
BLONP	Blondel père et fils	Frédérique Citeai	Marketing Mana	24, place Klébe	Strasbou
BOLID	Bólido Comidas pre	Martín Sommer	Owner	C/ Araquil, 67	Madrid
BONAP	Bon app'	Laurence Lebiha	Owner	12, rue des Bo	Marseille
BOTTM	Bottom-Dollar Mark	Elizabeth Lincolr	Accounting Mar	23 Tsawassen	Tsawass
BSBEV	B's Beverages	Victoria Ashwortl	Sales Represen	Fauntleroy Circ	London
CACTU	Cactus Comidas pa	Patricio Simpsor	Sales Agent	Cerrito 333	Buenos A

Record: 1 of 93

Figure B-7. Output of `SELECT * FROM Customers` *statement*

There are some occasions when the database table stores redundant records, but you generally don't want duplicate records returned. You can use the `SELECT DISTINCT` statement for this purpose. This is the syntax:

```
SELECT DISTINCT column1, column2, .., FROM table
```

For example, the following statement returns only unique records from the Customers table:

```
SELECT DISTINCT CompanyName FROM Customers
```

In addition to restricting columns to those you're interested in, you can also restrict rows by using the `SELECT...FROM...WHERE` statement. The `WHERE` clause takes a conditional statement:

```
SELECT column1, column2, .., FROM table WHERE condition
```

For example, the following query:

```
SELECT * FROM Customers WHERE CustomerID = "BOTTM"
```

returns records only having a CustomerID that equals `BOTTM`. The output of the Northwind database's Customers table looks like Figure B-8.

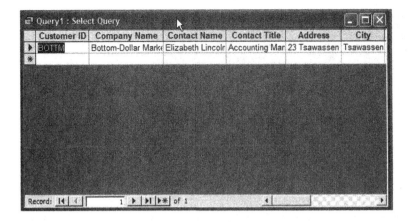

Figure B-8. Output of the SELECT...WHERE *statement*

Table B-1 summarizes the conditional statements used in SQL.

Table B-1. Conditional Statements Used in SQL

OPERATOR	MEANING
<	Less Than
>	Greater Than
<>	Not Equal To
=	Equal To

You can also use the SUM and AVG functions to return the sum and average of numeric columns, respectively:

```
SELECT function(column) FROM table
```

For example, the following query returns the sum of the Freight column in the Orders table:

```
SELECT SUM(Freight) FROM Orders
```

See Figure B-9 for the output of this statement.

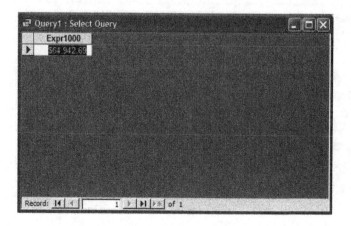

Figure B-9. Output of query that uses the SQL SUM *function*

The following query returns the average of the Freight column:

```
SELECT AVG (Freight) FROM Orders
```

You can use SELECT COUNT to return the number of rows in a table (based on a column). This is the syntax:

```
SELECT COUNT(column) FROM table
```

For example, the following statement returns the number of rows in the Customers table:

```
SELECT COUNT(CustomerID) FROM Customers;
```

The output of this statement looks like Figure B-10.

Figure B-10. Output of COUNT

GROUP BY is another handy clause that returns results grouped by the
mentioned column. This is the syntax:

```
SELECT column1, SUM(column2) FROM table GROUP BY column1
```

For example, the following statement returns the number of rows grouped by
OrderDate from the Orders table:

```
SELECT OrderDate, SUM(Freight) FROM Orders GROUP BY(OrderDate)
```

The output of the query looks like Figure B-11.

Order Date	Expr1001
	$0.00
04-Jul-1996	$32.38
05-Jul-1996	$11.61
08-Jul-1996	$107.17
09-Jul-1996	$51.30
10-Jul-1996	$58.17
11-Jul-1996	$22.98
12-Jul-1996	$148.33
15-Jul-1996	$13.97
16-Jul-1996	$81.91
17-Jul-1996	$140.51
18-Jul-1996	$3.25
19-Jul-1996	$58.14

Record: 1 of 481

Figure B-11. Output of GROUP BY

The HAVING clause limits output based on a criterion. You can use it with or without the GROUP BY clause. This is the syntax:

```
SELECT column1, column2 FROM table GROUP BY column1 HAVING condition
```

For example, the following statement returns records of the OrderDate column that have a total freight of more than 900:

```
SELECT OrderDate FROM Orders GROUP BY(OrderDate) HAVING SUM(Freight) > 900
```

Using the UPDATE Statement

The UPDATE statement makes changes to existing records in a database table. The UPDATE statement takes database table names and table columns and their values.

The syntax for UPDATE statement is as follows:

```
UPDATE table SET column1 = [new value],  column2 =[new value],.,WHERE {condition}
```

For example, the following query updates the Freight column value to 500 in the Orders table where OrderId is 10248:

```
UPDATE Orders SET Freight = 500 WHERE OrderId = 10248
```

Using a comma, you can update as many as columns as you want. If you want to update all the rows of a column or more than one column, you don't use the WHERE clause. For example, the following query updates all the rows of the Freight column with the value of 500:

```
UPDATE Orders SET Freight = 500
```

Using the DELETE Statement

The DELETE statement removes records from a database table. Using the DELETE statement, which is dangerously simple, you can either delete records based on certain criteria or delete *all* the records of a database table.

The syntax of the DELETE statement is as follows:

```
DELETE FROM table WHERE {condition}
```

For example, the following statement deletes all rows of OrderId 10248 (there should be only one because OrderID is the primary key):

```
DELETE FROM Orders WHERE OrderID = 10248
```

If you want to delete all of a table's rows, retaining an empty table, you can use the following statement:

```
DELETE FROM Orders
```

(In Access, DELETE statements can impact more than one table's rows depending on whether cascading deletes are enabled.)

Using the CREATE TABLE Statement

A database table is a collection of rows and columns. Each field in a table is represented as a column. Each field of a table must have a defined data type and a unique name. You can use the CREATE TABLE statement to create database tables programmatically.

The syntax for CREATE TABLE is as follows:

```
CREATE TABLE table (column1 column1_datatype,
column2 column2_datetype, .., column column_datatype)
```

The following statement creates a myTable table with the columns myId, myName, myAddress, and myBalance, which can store integer, character 50, character 255, and floating values, respectively. The CONSTRAINT...PRIMARY KEY syntax makes a column a primary key column:

```
CREATE TABLE myTable (myId INTEGER CONSTRAINT PKeyMyId PRIMARY KEY,
myName CHAR(50), myAddress CHAR(255), myBalance FLOAT)
```

Using the DROP TABLE Statement

There might be some occasions when either you need to delete a table permanently or you need to create temporary, "scratch" tables and then delete them. The DROP TABLE statement deletes a database table.

The syntax for DROP TABLE is as follows:

```
DROP TABLE table
```

For example, the following statement deletes myTable from the database:

```
DROP TABLE myTable
```

Using the TRUNCATE TABLE Statement

DROP TABLE deletes all records of a table and the table itself from the database. But what if you don't want to delete the table, just its records? One way of doing this is to use the DELETE FROM query. TRUNCATE TABLE is another way to remove the data of a table without getting rid of the table itself. TRUNCATE TABLE removes all records from a table without logging the individual record deletes. The DELETE statement removes records one at a time and makes an entry in the transaction log for each deleted record. TRUNCATE TABLE is faster than DELETE because it removes the data by deallocating the database table data pages, and only deallocations of the pages are recorded in the transaction log.

TRUNCATE TABLE doesn't remove the table structure, columns, constraints, or indexes. If you want to remove a table definition and its data, use DROP TABLE instead.

The syntax of this statement is simple:

```
TRUNCATE TABLE table
```

For example, the following statement truncates the Customers table:

```
TRUNCATE TABLE Customers
```

NOTE *Access databases don't natively support* TRUNCATE TABLE.

Using the INSERT Statement

In the previous sections you saw how to retrieve information from tables. But how do these rows of data get into the tables in the first place? This is what this section, covering INSERT INTO, and the next section, covering UPDATE, are about.

There are basically two ways to insert data into a table. One way is to insert them one row at a time, and the other way is to insert the data several rows at a time. First let's look at how you can insert data one row at a time.

The syntax for inserting data into a table one row at a time is as follows:

```
INSERT INTO table (column1, column2, .., columnn)
VALUES (value1, value2, ..., valunen)
```

For example, the following query adds a new record to the Customers table columns with their corresponding values:

```
INSERT INTO Customers(CompanyName, ContactName, ContactTitle,
Address, City, Phone) VALUES ("New Name","New Contact","New Title",
"New Address", "New City", "New Phone" )
```

You can also insert records in a table by selecting records from another table. You can do that by mixing INSERT INTO and SELECT statements. The only condition is that the data type of the columns must match in both tables.

The syntax for this is as follows:

```
INSERT INTO table1 (column1, column2, ...)
SELECT column1, column2, ... FROM table2
```

The previous syntax selects data from table2 and inserts it in table1. The data types of column1 in table1 must match with the data type of column1 in table2 and so on.

The following query reads CustName and ContName from NewTable and inserts data to the Customers table:

```
INSERT INTO Customers (CustomerName, ContactName)
SELECT CustName, ContName FROM NewTable
```

You can also apply WHERE and other clauses on this query as you have applied them on the previous SELECT statements.

Using Joins and Aliases

You can represent a table and column in a SQL statement using their alias names. Aliases are frequently used as shorthand—especially in join queries. This is the syntax:

```
SELECT aliastable.column1 aliascolumn FROM table aliastable
```

For example, this code uses A1 as the alias for the Customers table:

```
SELECT A1.CustomerID FROM Customers A1;
```

Figure B-12 shows the output of this statement. You can use the same syntax for multiple tables by separating them with commas.

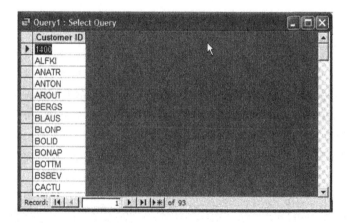

Figure B-12. Output of the Alias *statement*

Joins are useful when you need to select data from multiple tables based on selection criteria from more than one table. For example, you want to select data from the Orders and Customers tables where the CustomerID column in the Customers table exists in the CustomerID column of the Orders table as a foreign key. The following statement returns you the result:

```
SELECT DISTINCT Orders.OrderID, Orders.CustomerID, Orders.EmployeeID,
Customers.CompanyName, Customers.Address, Customers.City
FROM Customers INNER JOIN Orders ON Customers.CustomerID = Orders.CustomerID;
```

The output of this statement looks like Figure B-13.

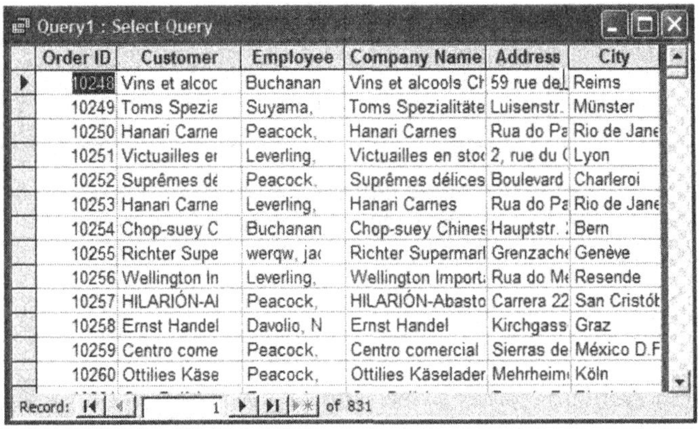
Query1 : Select Query

Order ID	Customer	Employee	Company Name	Address	City
10248	Vins et alcoc	Buchanan	Vins et alcools Ch	59 rue de l	Reims
10249	Toms Spezia	Suyama,	Toms Spezialitäte	Luisenstr.	Münster
10250	Hanari Carne	Peacock,	Hanari Carnes	Rua do Pa	Rio de Jane
10251	Victuailles en	Leverling,	Victuailles en stoc	2, rue du (	Lyon
10252	Suprêmes dé	Peacock,	Suprêmes délices	Boulevard	Charleroi
10253	Hanari Carne	Leverling,	Hanari Carnes	Rua do Pa	Rio de Jane
10254	Chop-suey C	Buchanan	Chop-suey Chines	Hauptstr. :	Bern
10255	Richter Supe	werqw, jac	Richter Supermarl	Grenzache	Genève
10256	Wellington In	Leverling,	Wellington Import:	Rua do Me	Resende
10257	HILARIÓN-Al	Peacock,	HILARIÓN-Abasto	Carrera 22	San Cristób
10258	Ernst Handel	Davolio, N	Ernst Handel	Kirchgass	Graz
10259	Centro come	Peacock,	Centro comercial	Sierras de	México D.F
10260	Ottilies Käse	Peacock,	Ottilies Käselader	Mehrheim	Köln

Record: 1 of 831

Figure B-13. Output of the `JOIN` *statement*

There are a handful of different types of joins, the most important of which are inner joins, outer joins, and cross joins.

Inner joins return records when both tables have at least one row that satisfies the join condition.

Outer joins work with `LEFT (OUTER) JOIN`, `RIGHT (OUTER) JOIN`, and `FULL (OUTER) JOIN` clauses. `OUTER JOIN` with `RIGHT JOIN` return all records from the right table and null values for the unmatched records in the left table. The `OUTER JOIN` with `LEFT JOIN` clause is the reverse of the `OUTER JOIN` with `RIGHT JOIN` clause. It returns all records from the left table and null values for the unmatched records in the right table. The `OUTER JOIN` with the `FULL JOIN` clause returns all records from both tables. If there's no match for a record of the left table in the right table, the right table returns null values and vice versa.

Cross joins return all records from the left table, and each row of the left table is combined with all records of the right table.

Understanding Views

A *view* is a virtual table that represents data from one or more than one database table. You can select data from single or multiple tables based on the sort and filter criteria (using `WHERE` and `GROUP BY` clauses) and save data as a view. You can also set permissions on views to control access to sensitive data. For example, a manager, an accountant, and a clerk of a company can all use the same database. The manager can access all data from different tables of the database, the accountant can access only some of the data from multiple tables, and the clerk can access only some of a single table's data. The easiest way to do this is with SQL views; you create three different views based on the user rights and let the user access these views based on their rights.

 NOTE *Access databases don't natively support SQL views. You'll need to use a "true" relational database to explore views, such as SQL Server and its copy of Northwind.*

The CREATE VIEW SQL statement creates a view. The simple format of the CREATE VIEW statement is as follows:

CREATE VIEW viewname AS selectstatement

where viewname is the name of the view and selectstatement is the SELECT statement used to select data from one or more table.

The following CREATE VIEW statement creates myView with records as a result of SELECT myName FROM myTable:

CREATE VIEW myView AS SELECT myName FROM myTable

The following two CREATE VIEW statements create the View1 view and the View2 view from the Orders table based on different criteria:

```
CREATE VIEW "View1" AS
SELECT OrderID, OrderDate, ShippedDate
FROM Orders
WHERE (Freight < 10)
```

```
CREATE VIEW "View2" AS
SELECT OrderID, OrderDate, ShippedDate
FROM Orders
WHERE (Freight > 1000)
```

You can also create views by selecting data from multiple tables. For example, the following view selects data from the Products and Categories tables. By using views this way, you can essentially "save" frequently used queries:

```
CREATE VIEW "Products by Category" AS
SELECT Categories.CategoryName, Products.ProductName, Products.QuantityPerUnit,
Products.UnitsInStock, Products.Discontinued
FROM Categories INNER JOIN Products ON Categories.CategoryID
= Products.CategoryID
WHERE Products.Discontinued <> 1
ORDER BY Categories.CategoryName, Products.ProductName
```

NOTE *You may have heard the term* materialized view *and wondered what it was. Basically, a materialized view is a view that's been stored (in many ways defeating the original goal of views as being virtual tables, but that's another issue). SQL Server calls its materialized views* indexed views, *and although you can create indexed views with any version of SQL Server, only the enterprise, developer, and evaluation editions use them. A SQL Server indexed view is essentially a view that has had a set of unique values "materialized" into the form of a clustered index, thereby providing a quick lookup in terms of pulling the information behind a view together.*

Using SQL Server's SELECT...FOR XML Clause

Most of today's databases support Extensible Markup Language (XML). In SQL Server, for example, you can execute SQL queries to return results as XML rather than standard rowsets. You can execute these queries directly or from within stored procedures. To retrieve results directly, you use the FOR XML clause of the SELECT statement. Within the FOR XML clause, you specify one of three XML modes: RAW, AUTO, or EXPLICIT. (You can also work with XML data in Access, Oracle, MySQL, and other databases, but the techniques vary.)

For example, this SQL Server SELECT statement retrieves information from the Customers and Orders tables in the Northwind database:

```
SELECT Customers.CustomerID, ContactName, CompanyName,
     Orders.CustomerID, OrderDate
FROM Customers, Orders
WHERE Customers.CustomerID = Orders.CustomerID
AND (Customers.CustomerID = "NALFKI"
   OR Customers.CustomerID = "NXYZAA")
ORDER BY Customers.CustomerID
FOR XML AUTO
```

Understanding SQL Injection

SQL injection is the process of using SQL queries and failing because of invalid user input. SQL injection is usually caused by the code written by developers. For example, let's say a form has a TextBox1 control and developers use the text of TextBox1 as one of the SQL query variables:

```
string str = "SELECT * FROM Table WHERE Name ='"
+ TextBox1.Text + "'";
```

Now, what happens when Amie O'Donell enters her name in TextBox1? The execution of the SQL query will fail because of invalid SQL syntax. You have to be careful when building and executing direct SQL queries. You can simply avoid this by checking if the user input has an invalid character in it.

Another common scenario is when the database server is expecting a number value and the user enters a string value or vice versa. This could lead to a failure if you don't have a check in the code. For example, you could use the ToString method to make sure the input is a valid query (using the Convert class to convert from one data type to another).

Summary

In this appendix, we discussed some commonly used SQL statements. You can access the following resources online:

- "A Gentle Introduction to SQL" by Andrew Cumming: http://sqlzoo.net

- Microsoft SQL Server product documentation:
  www.microsoft.com/sql/techinfo/productdoc/2000/default.asp

- Peter Gulutzan's Ocelot SQL site: www.ocelot.ca

- "SQL Tutorial" at W3Schools: www.w3schools.com/sql/default.asp

- "Trees in SQL" by Joe Celko:
  www.intelligententerprise.com/001020/celko1_1.shtml

- The SQL Tutorial site by Chuo-Han Lee: www.1keydata.com/sql/sql.html

ADO.NET Frequently Asked Questions

IN THIS APPENDIX, we'll answer some of the commonly asked questions related to ADO.NET. Most of these questions were originally asked on C# Corner discussion forums (www.c-sharpcorner.com) or other newsgroups.

FAQ 1: How can I obtain a database schema programmatically?

If you're using the OleDb data provider, you can use the GetOleDbSchemaTable method of the OleDbConnection object. Unfortunately, the Sql data provider doesn't support this method. However, you can use sysobjects as a table name in your SELECT statement, which returns all the tables stored in a database for SQL Server.

FAQ 2: How can I obtain table schema using a Command object?

You can get a database table schema by executing a SqlCommand object. Actually, the IDataReader object helps you to return a table schema with the help of its GetSchemaTable method. You know that the ExecuteReader method of SqlCommand returns an IDataReader (or SqlDataReader) object. When you want a table schema, you need to pass CommandBehavior.SchemaOnly as the only argument of ExecuteReader, which returns a DataTable with the schema of a database table.

Listing C-1 reads a database table schema, displays it in a DataGrid control, and lists all the columns of a table in a ListBox control.

Listing C-1. Getting a Database Table Schema Using SqlCommand

```
conn = New SqlConnection(connectionString)
conn.Open()
sql = "SELECT * FROM Employees"
Dim cmd As SqlCommand = New SqlCommand(sql, conn)
Dim reader As IDataReader = _
cmd.ExecuteReader(CommandBehavior.SchemaOnly)
```

```
Dim schemaTable As DataTable = New DataTable()
schemaTable = reader.GetSchemaTable
DataGrid1.DataSource = schemaTable
Dim rowCollection As DataRowCollection = _
reader.GetSchemaTable().Rows
Dim row As DataRow
For Each row In rowCollection
    str = row("ColumnName")
    ListBox1.Items.Add(str)
  Next
conn.Close()
```

The GetSchemaTable method returns meta-data about each column. Table C-1 defines the metadata and column order.

Table C-1. IDataReader *Meta-Data*

COLUMN NAME	DESCRIPTION
ColumnName	This is the name of the column.
ColumnOrdinal	This is the ordinal of the column. This is zero for the bookmark column of the row, if any. Other columns are numbered starting with one. This column can't contain a null value.
ColumnSize	This is the length of the column.
NumericPrecision	If ProviderType is a numeric data type, this is the maximum precision of the column.
NumericScale	If ProviderType is DBTYPE_DECIMAL or DBTYPE_NUMERIC, this is the number of digits to the right of the decimal point. Otherwise, this is a null value.
DataType	This is the data type of the column (the .NET Framework data type).
ProviderType	This is the indicator of column's data type.
IsLong	You can use this to find out if a column contains a Binary Long Object (BLOB) that contains very long data.
AllowDBNull	This is true if a column can contain null values; otherwise, it's false.
IsReadOnly	This is true if a column is read only; otherwise, it's false.
IsRowVersion	This is true if the column contains a persistent row identifier that can't be written to, and it has no meaningful value except to identity the row.

Table C-1. IDataReader *Meta-Data (Continued)*

COLUMN NAME	DESCRIPTION
IsUnique	This is true if the column has unique values, which means no two rows can have same values
IsKeyColumn	This is true if the column is one of a set of columns in the rowset that, taken together, uniquely identify the row.
IsAutoIncrement	This is true if a column is auto-incrementing.
BaseSchemaName	This is the name of the schema in the data store that contains the column. This is a null value if you can't determine the base schema name.
BaseCatalogName	This is the name of the catalog in the data store that contains the column. This is a null value if you can't determine the base catalog name.
BaseTableName	This is the name of the table or view in the data store that contains the column. This is a null value if you can't determine the base table name.
BaseColumnName	This is the name of the column in the data store. This might be different from the column name returned in the ColumnName column if you used an alias.

FAQ 3: How can I get rid of the plus (+) sign in a DataGrid?

When you fill a DataGrid control using a DataSet's DefaultViewManager, the DataGrid control displays a plus (+) sign, which lets you expand it and see all the available tables in a collection. You can easily avoid the + sign by not binding a DataGrid with the DefaultViewManager. Instead, you can read each DataTable from the collection and bind them programmatically.

Say you have a DataSet called ds. You can use the following method:

```
dataGrid1.DataSource = ds.Tables["TableName"];
```

or you can use the following:

```
dataGrid1.DataSource = ds.Tables[index];
```

FAQ 4: How do I hide a DataTable column?

The Columns property of a DataTable represents a collection of columns in a DataTable. You can get a DataColumn from this collection by using a column index or the name of the column. Setting the Visible property to false hides a column, and setting it to true displays the column:

```
DataTable.Columns(index).Visible = false;
```

FAQ 5: How can I insert dates in a SQL statement?

The following code shows how to construct a SQL statement with date values in it. You can simply execute this query:

```
Dim sql As String = "INSERT INTO Table (col1, [date], col2)" & _
    " VALUES(4588, #01/02/02#, 'some value')"
```

FAQ 6: How can I get columns names and their data types from a DataSet?

It's a common need when you want to find out how many columns (and their names and data types) that a DataSet or a DataTable contains. You can get DataTable columns through the Columns property, which returns all columns as a collection. If a DataSet has multiple tables, you use the DataSet.Tables property, which returns a collection of DataTable objects as a collection of DataTables. To get a DataTable from a collection, you can either use the table name or use the table index.

Once you get a collection of columns of a DataTable, you can read each column one by one and get DataColumn member values. To find out the data type of a DataColumn, you can use the DataType property. If you want to compare whether a column is a string, integer, or other type, you can compare its DataType property with Type.GetType().

Listing C-2 reads a DataTable's columns and checks if a column is a string type.

Listing C-2. Reading DataSet Columns and Their Data Types

```
' Add Table columns to the dropdownlistbox
Dim cols As DataColumnCollection = ds.Tables(0).Columns
Dim col As DataColumn
For Each col In cols
  searchDropDown.Items.Add(col.ColumnName)
```

```
      ' add only string type columns, otherwise
      If (col.DataType Is Type.GetType("System.String")) Then
        ' do something
      Else
        ' else do something
      End If
Next
```

FAQ 7: How can I find out how many rows are in a DataGrid?

Each control has a `BindingManager` object associated with it. You can use the `Count` property of `BindingManager`:

```
  Dim rows As Integer = _
    dtGrid.BindingContext(dtGrid.DataSource, _
    dtGrid.DataMember).Count
```

FAQ 8: How do I implement paging in ADO.NET?

Paging is a processing of fetching a number of rows as a page (a subset of data) instead of all rows from a data source. You can achieve paging in two ways in ADO.NET: by using a `DataAdapter` and by using a SQL statement.

Paging Using a DataAdapter

The `Fill` method of `DataAdapter` provides an overloaded form where you can ask the `DataAdapter` to return only a selected number of rows in a `DataSet`. The overloaded form of the `Fill` method is as follows:

```
Overloads Public Function Fill(ByVal dataSet As DataSet, _
    ByVal startRecord As Integer, _
    ByVal maxRecords As Integer, _
    ByVal srcTable As String _
) As Integer
```

where `dataSet` is a `DataSet` to fill with records and, if necessary, schema; `startRecord` is the zero-based record number to start with; `maxRecords` is the maximum number of records to retrieve; and `srcTable` is the name of the source table to use for table mapping. Listing C-3 shows a function that returns a `DataSet` filled with the records based on the page size passed in the method.

Listing C-3. GetPageData *Method*

```
Function GetPagedData(ByVal da As SqlDataAdapter, _
   ByVal idx As Integer, ByVal size As Integer) As DataSet
      Dim ds As DataSet = New DataSet()
      Try
        da.Fill(ds, idx, size, "Orders")
      Catch e As Exception
        MessageBox.Show(e.Message.ToString())
      End Try
      Return ds
End Function
```

Paging Using the SELECT TOP SQL Statement

Besides the Fill method of a DataAdapter, you can even use a SELECT SQL statement to retrieve the number of records from a table. You use the SELECT TOP statement for this purpose. The following statement selects the top 10 records from the Customers table. You set the SELECT statement as the SELECT TOP statement:

```
"SELECT TOP 10 CustomerID, CompanyName, " & _
    " ContactName FROM Customers ORDER BY CustomerID"
```

Implementing Paging

Finally, let's see how to use both the previously discussed methods to implement paging in ADO.NET. The sample application looks like Figure C-1. In this figure, you can enter the number of rows you want to load in a page. The Load Page button loads the first page. The Previous Page and Next Page buttons load those pages from database. When you check the SELECT TOP check box, the program uses the SELECT TOP method; otherwise, it uses the DataAdapter's Fill method.

Listing C-4 implements paging using both methods. As you can see from this code, the Load Page button click event handler reads the page size, creates and opens a new connection, and checks whether the SELECT TOP check box is checked. If it is, it calls the GetTopData method; otherwise, it calls the GetPagedData method.

The GetTopData method uses the SELECT TOP SQL query to get the top records, creates a DataTable custTable, and reads data in this table from the main DataTable tmpTable, which has all records from the database table.

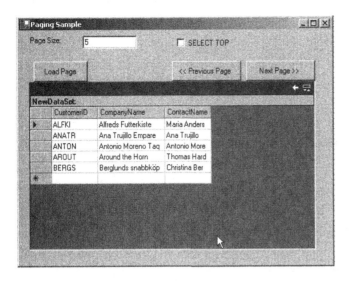

Figure C-1. Paging in an ADO.NET application

Now, if you see the Previous Page and Next Page button click handlers, you'll see that it's just a matter of calling GetTopData and GetPagedData with the current record number and number of records to be fetched.

Listing C-4. Implementing Paging in ADO.NET

```
Private Sub LoadPageBtn_Click(ByVal sender As System.Object, _
ByVal e As System.EventArgs) Handles LoadPageBtn.Click
  pageSize = Convert.ToInt32(TextBox1.Text.ToString())
  ' Create and open a connection
  conn = New SqlConnection(connectionString)
  conn.Open()
  ' Find out total number of records
  Dim cmd As SqlCommand = New SqlCommand()
  ' Assign the SQL Insert statement we want to execute to the CommandText
  cmd.CommandText = "SELECT Count(*) FROM Customers"
   cmd.Connection = conn
  ' Call ExecuteNonQuery on the Command Object to execute insert
  totalRecords = cmd.ExecuteScalar()
  ' Create data adapter
  sql = "SELECT CustomerID, CompanyName, ContactName " & _
  "FROM Customers ORDER BY CustomerID"
  adapter = New SqlDataAdapter(sql, conn)
  ds = New DataSet()
```

```vbnet
    ' If SELECT TOP check box is checked
    If CheckBox1.Checked Then
      selectTop = True
    Else
      selectTop = False
    End If


    ' if SELECT TOP is checked
    If selectTop Then
      GetTopData("", 0)
      DataGrid1.DataSource = custTable
    Else
      ds = GetPagedData(adapter, curIndex, pageSize)
      curIndex = curIndex + pageSize
      DataGrid1.DataSource = ds.DefaultViewManager
    End If
End Sub


' Get a page using SELECT TOP statement
Public Shared Sub GetTopData(ByVal selectCmd As String, ByVal type As Integer)
  ' First time load first TOP pages
  If (selectCmd.Equals(String.Empty)) Then
    selectCmd = "SELECT TOP " & pageSize & " CustomerID, CompanyName, " & _
    " ContactName FROM Customers ORDER BY CustomerID"
  End If


  totalPages = CInt(Math.Ceiling(CDbl(totalRecords) / pageSize))
  adapter.SelectCommand.CommandText = selectCmd
  Dim tmpTable As DataTable = New DataTable("Customers")
  Dim recordsAffected As Integer = adapter.Fill(tmpTable)
  ' If the table does not exist, create it.
  If custTable Is Nothing Then custTable = tmpTable.Clone()
  ' Refresh the table if at least one record is returned.
  If recordsAffected > 0 Then
    Select Case type
      Case 1
        currentPage = currentPage + 1
      Case 2
        currentPage = currentPage - 1
      Case Else
        currentPage = 1
    End Select
    ' Clear the rows and add new results.
    custTable.Rows.Clear()
```

```vbnet
    ' Import rows from temp tabke to custTable
    Dim myRow As DataRow
    For Each myRow In tmpTable.Rows
      custTable.ImportRow(myRow)
    Next
    ' Preserve the first and last primary key values.
    Dim ordRows() As DataRow = custTable.Select("", "CustomerID ASC")
    firstVisibleCustomer = ordRows(0)(0).ToString()
    lastVisibleCustomer = ordRows(custTable.Rows.Count - 1)(0).ToString()
  End If
End Sub


' Previous page button click
Private Sub PrePageBtn_Click(ByVal sender As System.Object, _
ByVal e As System.EventArgs) Handles PrePageBtn.Click
  ' if SELECT TOP is checked
  If selectTop Then
    sql = "SELECT TOP " & pageSize & " CustomerID, CompanyName, " & _
    " ContactName FROM Customers " & _
    "WHERE CustomerID < '" & firstVisibleCustomer & "' ORDER BY CustomerID"
    GetTopData(sql, 1)
  Else
    ds = GetPagedData(adapter, curIndex, pageSize)
    curIndex = curIndex - pageSize
    DataGrid1.DataSource = ds.DefaultViewManager
  End If

End Sub


' Next page button click
Private Sub NextPageBtn_Click(ByVal sender As System.Object, _
ByVal e As System.EventArgs) Handles NextPageBtn.Click
  ' if SELECT TOP is checked
  If selectTop Then
    sql = "SELECT TOP " & pageSize & " CustomerID, CompanyName, " & _
    " ContactName FROM Customers " & _
    "WHERE CustomerID > '" & lastVisibleCustomer & "' ORDER BY CustomerID"
    GetTopData(sql, 2)
  Else
    ds = GetPagedData(adapter, curIndex, pageSize)
    curIndex = curIndex + pageSize
    DataGrid1.DataSource = ds.DefaultViewManager
  End If
End Sub
```

You can download the complete source code from the Downloads section of the Apress Web site (www.apress.com) for more details.

FAQ 9: How do I implement transactions in the OleDb data provider?

A transaction is a set of SQL SELECT, INSERT, UPDATE, and DELETE statements that are dependent on one another. For instance, say you can't delete and update some data until it's added to the database. So, you combine all required SQL statements and execute them as a single transaction. If there are no errors during the transaction, all modifications in the transaction become a permanent part of the database. If errors are encountered, none of the modifications are made to the database. If a transaction was successful, the transaction was *committed*; otherwise, the transaction was *rolled back.*

For example, in a banking application where funds are transferred from one account to another, one account is credited an amount and another account is debited the same amount simultaneously. Because computers can fail because of power outages, network outages, and so on, it's possible to update a row in one table but not in the related table. If your database supports transactions, you can group database operations into a transaction to prevent database inconsistency resulting from these outages.

In ADO.NET, the Connection and Transaction objects handle transactions. Follow these steps to perform transactions:

1. After creating an instance of a Connection class (no matter what data provider you choose), you call the BeginTransaction method to start a transaction. The BeginTransaction method returns a Transaction object:

   ```
   Dim tran As OleDbTransaction = conn.BeginTransaction()
   ```

2. Create Command objects with the active transaction, set its Transaction property as the current transaction, and call its Execute method:

   ```
   Dim cmd As OleDbCommand = New OleDbCommand()
   cmd.Connection = conn
   cmd.Transaction = tran
   ```

3. Call the Commit and Rollback methods to commit and roll back transactions using this code:

   ```
   tran.Commit()
   tran.Rollback()
   ```

Listing C-5 shows you how to use transactions in the OleDb data provider.

Listing C-5. Transactions in the OleDb Data Provider

```
Sub Main()
Dim str As String
Dim connectionString As String = _
    "Provider=Microsoft.Jet.OLEDB.4.0; Data Source=F:\\AppliedAdoNet.mdb"
' Create and open a connection
Dim conn As OleDbConnection = _
  New OleDbConnection(connectionString)
conn.Open()
' Start a transaction
Dim tran As OleDbTransaction = conn.BeginTransaction()
Dim cmd As OleDbCommand = New OleDbCommand()
cmd.Connection = conn
cmd.Transaction = tran
Try
    str = "INSERT INTO Users (UserName, UserDescription)" & _
    " VALUES ('New User', 'New Description')"
    cmd.CommandText = str
    cmd.ExecuteNonQuery()
    str = "UPDATE Users SET UserName = 'Updated User' WHERE " & _
        " UserName = 'New User'"
    cmd.CommandText = str
    cmd.ExecuteNonQuery()
    str = "DELETE * FROM Users WHERE UserName = 'Updated User'"
    cmd.CommandText = str
    cmd.ExecuteNonQuery()
    ' Commit transaction
    tran.Commit()
    Console.WriteLine("Changes saved.")
    Catch e As Exception
     ' Rollback transaction
     tran.Rollback()
     Console.WriteLine(e.Message.ToString())
     Console.WriteLine("No changes were made to database.")
    Finally
      conn.Close()
      conn.Dispose()
    End Try
End Sub
```

FAQ 10: How can I create AutoIncrement columns?

Auto-incrementing columns are columns whose value increases automatically when a new record is added to the table. To create an auto-incrementing column, you set the DataColumn.AutoIncrement property to true. The DataColumn will then start with the value defined in the AutoIncrementSeed property, and with each row added, the value of the AutoIncrement column increases by the value held in the AutoIncrementStep property of the column:

```
Dim col1 As DataColumn =
DataTable.Columns.Add("CustomerID", typeof(Int32))
workColumn.AutoIncrement = true
workColumn.AutoIncrementSeed = 1000
workColumn.AutoIncrementStep = 10
```

FAQ 11: How can I copy a DataSet's contents?

There are occasions when you don't want to mess with the original DataSet's data and instead want to copy data somewhere and work with it. The DataSet provides a Copy method that you can use to copy the data of a DataSet to a second DataSet. When you copy data, you can copy in different ways: You can create an exact copy of a DataSet including its schema, data, row state information, and row versions. You can also copy only affected rows of a DataSet to a second DataSet. Another case may be when you only want to copy a DataSet schema, not the data.

To create an exact copy of the DataSet including a DataSet schema and data, you can use the Copy method. For example:

```
Dim ds2 As DataSet = ds1.Copy()
```

The GetChanges method gets the affected rows of a DataSet. The GetChanges method takes a DataRowState object, which has members including Added, Modified, and Deleted. Using this method, you can create a new DataSet from an existing DataSet with all rows that have been modified, or you can specify new added, deleted, or modified rows.

To create a copy of a DataSet that includes schema and only the data representing the Added, Modified, or Deleted rows, use the GetChanges method of the DataSet. You can also use GetChanges to return only rows with a specified row state by passing a DataRowState value when calling GetChanges. The following code shows how to pass a DataRowState when calling GetChanges:

```
' Copy all changes.
Dim ds2 As DataSet = ds1.GetChanges()
' Copy only new rows.
Dim ds2 As DataSet = ds1.GetChanges(DataRowState.Added)
' Copy only updated rows.
Dim ds2 As DataSet = ds1.GetChanges(DataRowState.Modified)
' Copy only deleted rows.
Dim ds2 As DataSet = ds1.GetChanges(DataRowState.Deleted)
```

The Clone method of a DataSet creates a new DataSet from an existing DataSet without copying its data:

```
Dim ds2 As DataSet = ds1.Clone()
```

FAQ 12: How can I use Count (*) to count number of rows?

Getting the number of records using a DataSet is pretty simple. A DataSet is a set of DataTable objects, and a DataTable's Rows property represents the number of records in a DataTable. The following code retrieves the number of rows of the first table of a DataSet. Similarity, you can retrieve the number of records from other tables if a DataSet contains more than one DataTable object:

```
Dim ds As DataSet = New DataSet()
adapter.Fill(ds, "Employees")
Dim counter As Integer = ds.Tables(0).Rows.Count
MessageBox.Show(counter.ToString())
```

Retrieving the number of records using a DataReader is little tricky. You use the SELECT Count * SQL statement and execute the SQL statement using the ExecuteScalar method of the Command object. The following code returns the number of records using the Count * statement:

```
Dim cmd As OleDbCommand = _
  New OleDbCommand("SELECT Count(*) FROM Orders", conn)
Dim counter As Integer = CInt(cmd.ExecuteScalar())
MessageBox.Show(counter.ToString())
```

FAQ 13: How do I get a database schema using a DataSet programmatically?

Usually when you work with databases, you already know the database schema such as database tables, table columns, and column properties. What if you don't know the database schema, and you need to get a database's tables, columns, and column properties programmatically?

In this sample we show you how to access a database schema programmatically. As you can see from Figure C-2, we created a Windows application with one TextBox control, three Button controls, and two ListBox controls. The Browse button lets you browse .mdb databases on your machine. The Get Tables button then reads the database tables and adds them to the first list box. The Get Table Schema button returns the table columns and the properties of the selected table in list box.

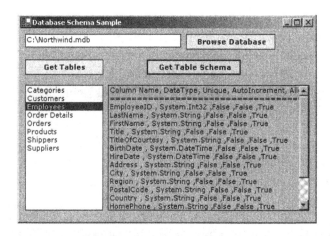

Figure C-2. Getting a database schema programmatically

Listing C-6 shows the source code for this application. As you can see, the BrowseBtn_Click handler browses Access databases on the machine, fills the selected database name to the text box, and sets dbName as the database name, which is a string type of variable defined as follows:

```
private string dbName = "";
```

Listing C-6. Reading a Database Schema Programmatically

```
Private Sub Browse_Click(ByVal sender As System.Object, _
  ByVal e As System.EventArgs) Handles Button1.Click
    Dim fdlg As OpenFileDialog = New OpenFileDialog()
    fdlg.Title = "C# Corner Open File Dialog"
    fdlg.InitialDirectory = "c:\\"
    fdlg.Filter = "All files (*.*)|*.mdb|" & _
  "MS-Access Database files (*.mdb)|*.mdb"
    fdlg.FilterIndex = 2
    fdlg.RestoreDirectory = True
    If fdlg.ShowDialog() = DialogResult.OK Then
      TextBox1.Text = fdlg.FileName
      dbName = fdlg.FileName
    End If
  End Sub
```

The GetOleDbSchemaTable method of OleDbConnection returns a DataTable object containing database tables. As you can see from the GetTableBtn_Click handler listed in Listing C-7, we set the DataSet to the left list box with the DisplayMember property set to TABLE_NAME. We also set DisplayMember because we show only one column of the DataTable in the list box.

Listing C-7. Getting a Database's Tables from a SQL Server Database

```
Private Sub GetTables_Click(ByVal sender As System.Object, _
  ByVal e As System.EventArgs) Handles GetTables.Click

    ' Connection string
    Dim strDSN As String = "Provider=Microsoft.Jet.OLEDB.4.0;" & _
    "Data Source=" + dbName
    ' Create a connection and open it
    Dim conn As OleDbConnection = New OleDbConnection(strDSN)

    Try
      conn.Open()
      ' Call GetOleDbSchemaTable to get the schema data table
      Dim dt As DataTable = _
      conn.GetOleDbSchemaTable(OleDbSchemaGuid.Tables, New Object() _
                 {Nothing, Nothing, Nothing, "TABLE"})
      ' Set DataSource and DisplayMember properties
      ' of the list box control
```

```
            ListBox1.DataSource = dt.DefaultView
            ListBox1.DisplayMember = "TABLE_NAME"

        Catch exp As Exception
          MessageBox.Show(exp.Message.ToString())
        Finally
          ' Close the connection
          conn.Close()
          conn.Dispose()
        End Try
    End Sub
```

Listing C-8 shows the GetSchemaBn_Click event handler that returns the columns and properties of a database table. You read the database table using SELECT * and use a DataTable to get columns. The DataColumn class defines the member for a table column properties such as allow null, auto number, unique, column data type, column name, and so on.

Listing C-8. Getting a Database Table Schema

```
Private Sub GetTableSchema_Click(ByVal sender As System.Object, _
  ByVal e As System.EventArgs) Handles GetTableSchema.Click
    ' Get the selected item text of list box
    Dim selTable As String = ListBox1.GetItemText(ListBox1.SelectedItem)
    ' Connection string
    Dim strDSN As String = "Provider=Microsoft.Jet.OLEDB.4.0;" & _
        "Data Source=" + dbName
    ' Create and open connection
    Dim conn As OleDbConnection = New OleDbConnection(strDSN)
    Try
      conn.Open()
      Dim strSQL As String = "SELECT * FROM " + selTable
      ' Create data adapter
      Dim adapter As OleDbDataAdapter = New OleDbDataAdapter(strSQL, conn)
      ' Create and fill data set
      Dim dtSet As DataSet = New DataSet()
      adapter.Fill(dtSet)
      Dim dt As DataTable = dtSet.Tables(0)

      ' Add items to the list box control
      ListBox2.Items.Add("Column Name, DataType, Unique," & _
              " AutoIncrement, AllowNull")
      ListBox2.Items.Add("=====================================")
```

```
      Dim i As Integer
      For i = 0 To dt.Columns.Count - 1
        Dim dc As DataColumn
        dc = dt.Columns(i)
ListBox2.Items.Add(dc.ColumnName.ToString() + _
    " , " + dc.DataType.ToString() + _
        " ," + dc.Unique.ToString() + " ," + dc.AutoIncrement.ToString() & _
        " ," + dc.AllowDBNull.ToString())
      Next

    Catch exp As Exception
      MessageBox.Show(exp.Message)
    Finally
      conn.Close()
      conn.Dispose()
    End Try
  End Sub
```

FAQ 14: How does SELECT DISTINCT work, and how is it related to duplicates?

It's not a big deal to select unique rows from a database table using SELECT DISTINCT, but somehow this question gets asked a lot. So, it's not a bad idea to talk about procedure.

You can use the SELECT DISTINCT SQL statement to select distinct records from a database. This is useful when you want to return only one record corresponding to a criterion. Listing C-9 returns distinct records from the Employees table ordered by the last name.

Listing C-9. Selecting Distinct Rows from a Database Table

```
Private Sub DistinctRows_Click(ByVal sender As System.Object, _
  ByVal e As System.EventArgs) Handles DistinctRows.Click
    ' Connection string
    Dim strDSN As String = "Provider=Microsoft.Jet.OLEDB.4.0;" & _
    "Data Source=C:\\Northwind.mdb"
    ' Create a connection and open it
    Dim conn As OleDbConnection = New OleDbConnection(strDSN)
    Try
      conn.Open()
      ' Call GetOleDbSchemaTable to get the schema data table
```

```
        Dim sql As String = "SELECT DISTINCT(LastName)" & _
            "FROM Employees ORDER BY LastName"
        Dim adapter As OleDbDataAdapter = New OleDbDataAdapter(sql, conn)
        Dim ds As DataSet = New DataSet()
        adapter.Fill(ds, "Employees")
        DataGrid1.DataSource = ds.DefaultViewManager
    Catch exp As Exception
        MessageBox.Show(exp.Message.ToString())
    Finally
        ' Close the connection
        conn.Close()
        conn.Dispose()
    End Try
End Sub
```

FAQ 15: How do I read and write to the Windows Registry in .NET?

There are many cases when you need to read and store data in the Windows Registry. A common case is storing your program's serial number and activation code in the Windows Registry. The installation package of your program writes a serial number and activation code to the Windows Registry, and when the user runs program, it checks whether the code matches and runs the program.

The Windows Registry is a central database for application configuration settings and other information required by the applications. Actually, there's nothing else you can do with the Windows Registry besides reading its data and writing data to it.

.NET Framework Library provides two classes (Registry and RegistryKey) to work with the Registry.

NOTE *The Registry classes are defined in the* Microsoft.Win32 *namespace. Before using these classes, you need to add a reference to this namespace.*

Using the Registry Class

The Registry class contains members to provides access to Registry keys. Table C-2 described the Registry class members.

Table C-2. The Registry *Class Members*

MEMBER	DESCRIPTION
CurrentUser	Stores information about user preferences
LocalMachine	Stores configuration information for the local machine
ClassesRoot	Stores information about types (and classes) and their properties
Users	Stores information about the default user configuration
PerformanceData	Stores performance information for software components
CurrentConfig	Stores non-user-specific hardware information
DynData	Stores dynamic data

For example, if you want to access the HKEY_LOCAL_MACHINE key, you need to call the Registry.LocalMachine member, which returns a RegistryKey type:

```
RegistryKey pRegKey = Registry.LocalMachine;
```

Using the RegistryKey Class

The RegistryKey class contains members to add, remove, replace, and read Registry data. Table C-3 defines some of its common properties.

Table C-3. The RegistryKey *Class Properties*

PROPERTY	DESCRIPTION
Name	Name of the key
SubKeyCount	Number of children of the key
ValueCount	Count of values in the key

Table C-4 describes the RegistryKey class methods.

Table C-4. The `RegistryKey` *Class Methods*

METHOD	DESCRIPTION
Close	Closes the key
CreateSubKey	Creates a new subkey if not in existence or opens it
DeleteSubKey	Deletes a subkey
DeleteSubKeyTree	Deletes subkey and its children
DeleteValue	Deletes the value of a key
GetSubKeyName	Returns an array of strings that contains all the subkey names
GetValue	Returns the value of a subkey
GetValueName	Retrieves an array of strings that contains all the value names associated with a key
OpenSubKey	Opens a subkey
SetValue	Sets the value of a subkey

Adding a Key and Value to Registry

Let's see how to add data to the Registry. You use `CreateSubKey` to add a new key to the Registry and call the `SetValue` method to write a value and key. The following code does this:

```
' Create a new key under HKEY_LOCAL_MACHINE\Software as MCBInc
Dim key As RegistryKey = Registry.LocalMachine.OpenSubKey("Software", True)
' Add one more sub key
Dim newkey As RegistryKey = key.CreateSubKey("MCBInc")
' Set value of sub key
newkey.SetValue("MCBInc", "NET Developer")
```

Retrieving Data from the Registry

Now let's see how to use these remove the keys and their values from the Registry.

The `GetValue` method returns the value of a subkey in the form of `Object`. The following code reads the value of the `CenteralProcessor\0` subkey and writes it to the console:

```
' Retrieve data from other part of the registry
' find out your processor
Dim pRegKey As RegistryKey = Registry.LocalMachine
pRegKey =
 pRegKey.OpenSubKey("HARDWARE\\DESCRIPTION\\System\\CentralProcessor\\0")
```

```
Dim val As Object = pRegKey.GetValue("VendorIdentifier")
Console.WriteLine("The central processor of this machine is:" + val)
```

Deleting Data

You can use the DeleteValue method to delete the value of a subkey. DeleteSubKey deletes the defined subkey. DeleteSubKey deletes the subkey with its data:

```
Dim delKey As RegistryKey = Registry.LocalMachine.OpenSubKey("Software", True)
delKey.DeleteValue("MCBInc")
Dim delKey As RegistryKey = Registry.LocalMachine.OpenSubKey("Software", True)
delKey.DeleteSubKey("MCBInc")
```

Examining the Final Source Code

Listing C-10 shows the entire source code for reading and writing to and from the Windows Registry.

Listing C-10. Reading and Writing to and from the Windows Registry

```
Public Sub ReadWriteRegistry()
    ' Create a new key under HKEY_LOCAL_MACHINE\Software as MCBInc
    Dim key As RegistryKey = _
    Registry.LocalMachine.OpenSubKey("Software", True)
    ' Add one more sub key
    Dim newkey As RegistryKey = key.CreateSubKey("MCBInc")
    ' Set value of sub key
    newkey.SetValue("MCBInc", "NET Developer")
    ' Retrieve data from other part of the registry
    ' find out your processor
    Dim pRegKey As RegistryKey = Registry.LocalMachine
    Dim keyPath As String = _
      "HARDWARE\\DESCRIPTION\\System\\CentralProcessor\\0"
    pRegKey = pRegKey.OpenSubKey(keyPath)
    Dim val As Object = pRegKey.GetValue("VendorIdentifier")
    Console.WriteLine("The Processor of this machine is:" + val)
    ' Delete the key value
    Dim delKey As RegistryKey = _
    Registry.LocalMachine.OpenSubKey("Software", True)
    delKey.DeleteSubKey("MCBInc")
  End Sub
```

FAQ 16: How can I obtain ODBC Data Source Names (DSNs)?

Do you remember programming ODBC before .NET was introduced? The best way to access databases through ODBC was to use ODBC Data Source Names (DSNs). You still use ODBC DSNs to access a database by using the ODBC data provider. How do you read all available ODBC DSNs? You do this through the Windows Registry. All ODBC data sources are stored in the Windows Registry under `LocalMachine\ODBC\ODBC.INI\ODBC Data Sources` and `CurrentUser\Software\ODBC\ODBC.INI\ODBC Data Sources` keys. You use the following code:

```
Imports Microsoft.Win32
```

You just saw how to read and write to the Windows Registry in FAQ 15. Listing C-11 shows the code module that reads the ODBC system and user DSNs and adds them to a `ListBox` control.

Listing C-11. Reading ODBC DSNs

```
Private Sub ReadODBCSNs()
    Dim str As String
    Dim rootKey As RegistryKey, subKey As RegistryKey
    Dim dsnList() As String
    rootKey = Registry.LocalMachine
    str = "SOFTWARE\\ODBC\\ODBC.INI\\ODBC Data Sources"
    subKey = rootKey.OpenSubKey(str)
    dsnList = subKey.GetValueNames()
    ListBox1.Items.Add("System DSNs")
    ListBox1.Items.Add("================")
    Dim dsnName As String
    For Each dsnName In dsnList
      ListBox1.Items.Add(dsnName)
    Next
    subKey.Close()
    rootKey.Close()
    ' Load User DSNs
    rootKey = Registry.CurrentUser
    str = "SOFTWARE\\ODBC\\ODBC.INI\\ODBC Data Sources"
    subKey = rootKey.OpenSubKey(str)
    dsnList = subKey.GetValueNames()
    ListBox1.Items.Add("================")
    ListBox1.Items.Add("User DSNs")
    ListBox1.Items.Add("================")
```

```
  For Each dsnName In dsnList
    ListBox1.Items.Add(dsnName)
  Next
  subKey.Close()
  rootKey.Close()
End Sub
```

FAQ 17: How can I read and write bitmaps or BLOB data?

Often you may need to save user images in a database and then read back from a database when needed. For an example, we'll save an author's photo in a database so it can be read later to display in the author's article.

The Northwind database's Employees table has a Photo field that stores images of employees. You can use this table for testing your code if you want. For this example, though, we'll create our own database.

To make it simple, we created a new AppliedAdoNet.mdb Access database and added a Users table to it. The database table schema looks like Figure C-3. Access stores BLOB objects as OLE Object data types.

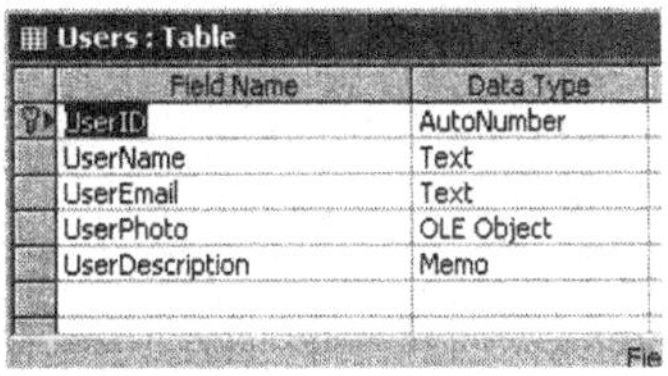

Figure C-3. Users table schema

To make the application a little more interactive and user friendly, we created a Windows application, added a TextBox control, three Button controls, and a PictureBox control. The final form looks like Figure C-4. As you can pretty much guess from this figure, the Browse Image button allows users to browse for bitmap files. The Save Image button saves opened file in the database, and the Read Image button reads the first row of the database table, saves binary data as a bitmap, and displays the image in a PictureBox control.

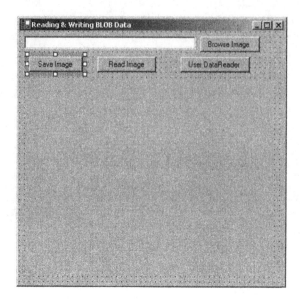

Figure C-4. Reading and writing images in a database final form

Before writing code on the button clicks, define following variables:

```
' User defined variables
  Private curImage As Image = Nothing
  Private curFileName As String = Nothing
  Private connectionString As String = _
    "Provider=Microsoft.Jet.OLEDB.4.0; " & _
    "Data Source=C:\\AppliedAdoNet.mdb"
  Private savedImageName As String _
    = "C:\\ImageFromDb.BMP"
```

Also, don't forget to add references to the System.IO and System.Data.OleDb namespaces:

```
Imports System.Data.OleDb
Imports System.IO
```

Listing C-12 shows the Browse button click code, which simply browses bitmap files and saves the filename in the curFileName variable.

Listing C-12. Browse Button Click Event Handler

```vb
Private Sub BrowseBtn_Click(ByVal sender As System.Object, _
ByVal e As System.EventArgs) Handles BrowseBtn.Click
    Dim openDlg As OpenFileDialog = New OpenFileDialog()
    openDlg.Filter = "All Bitmap files|*.bmp"
    Dim filter As String = openDlg.Filter
    openDlg.Title = "Open a Bitmap File"
    If (openDlg.ShowDialog() = DialogResult.OK) Then
      curFileName = openDlg.FileName
      TextBox1.Text = curFileName
    End If
  End Sub
```

The Save Image button code shown in Listing C-13 first creates a `FileStream` object from the bitmap file, opens a connection with the database, adds a new `DataRow`, set its values, and saves the row back to database.

Listing C-13. Save Image Button Click Event Handler

```vb
Private Sub SaveImageBtn_Click(ByVal sender As System.Object, _
  ByVal e As System.EventArgs) Handles SaveImageBtn.Click

    If TextBox1.Text Is String.Empty Then
      MessageBox.Show("Browse a bitmap")
      Return
    End If
    ' Read a bitmap contents in a stream
    Dim fs As FileStream = New FileStream(curFileName, _
FileMode.OpenOrCreate, FileAccess.Read)
    Dim rawData() As Byte = New Byte(fs.Length) {}
    fs.Read(rawData, 0, System.Convert.ToInt32(fs.Length))
    fs.Close()
    ' Construct a SQL string and a connection object
    Dim sql As String = "SELECT * FROM Users"
    Dim conn As OleDbConnection = New OleDbConnection()
    conn.ConnectionString = connectionString
    ' Open connection
    If conn.State <> ConnectionState.Open Then
      conn.Open()
    End If
    ' Create a data adapter and data set
```

```vb
Dim adapter As OleDbDataAdapter = _
    New OleDbDataAdapter(sql, conn)
Dim cmdBuilder As OleDbCommandBuilder = _
    New OleDbCommandBuilder(adapter)
Dim ds As DataSet = New DataSet("Users")
adapter.MissingSchemaAction = MissingSchemaAction.AddWithKey

' Fill data adapter
adapter.Fill(ds, "Users")

Dim userDes As String = _
    "Mahesh Chand is a founder of C# Corner "
userDes += "Author: 1. A Programmer's Guide to ADO.NET;"
userDes += ", 2. Applied ADO.NET. "

' Create a new row
Dim row As DataRow = ds.Tables("Users").NewRow()
row("UserName") = "Mahesh Chand"
row("UserEmail") = "mcb@mindcracker.com"
row("UserDescription") = userDes
row("UserPhoto") = rawData
' Add row to the collection
ds.Tables("Users").Rows.Add(row)
' Save changes to the database
adapter.Update(ds, "Users")
' Clean up connection
If conn Is Nothing Then
    If conn.State = ConnectionState.Open Then
        conn.Close()
    End If
    ' Dispose connection
    conn.Dispose()
End If
MessageBox.Show("Image Saved")
End Sub
```

Once data is saved, the next step is to read data from the database table, save it as a bitmap again, and view the bitmap on the form. You can directly view an image using the Graphics.DrawImage method or by using a PictureBox control. In this case, we'll use a PictureBox. Listing C-14 shows the code for reading binary data. As you can see, the code simply opens a connection, creates a DataAdapter, fills a DataSet, and gets the first row of the Users table. Now if you want to read all images, you may want to modify your application or make a loop through all rows.

Once a row is read, you get the data stored in the UserPhoto column (Image column) in a stream and save it as a bitmap file. Later you can view that bitmap file in the PictureBox control by setting its Image property to the filename.

Listing C-14. Reading Binary Data

```
Private Sub UseReaderBtn_Click(ByVal sender As System.Object, _
ByVal e As System.EventArgs) Handles UseReaderBtn.Click

    ' Construct a SQL string and a connection object
    Dim sql As String = "SELECT UserPhoto FROM Users"
    Dim conn As OleDbConnection = New OleDbConnection()
    conn.ConnectionString = connectionString
    ' Open connection
    If conn.State <> ConnectionState.Open Then
        conn.Open()
    End If

    Dim cmd As OleDbCommand = New OleDbCommand(sql, conn)
    Dim fs As FileStream
    Dim bw As BinaryWriter
    Dim bufferSize As Integer = 300000
    Dim outbyte(300000 - 1) As Byte
    Dim retval As Long
    Dim startIndex As Long = 0
    Dim pub_id As String = ""
    Dim reader As OleDbDataReader = _
        cmd.ExecuteReader(CommandBehavior.SequentialAccess)
    ' Read first record
    reader.Read()
    fs = New FileStream(savedImageName, _
    FileMode.OpenOrCreate, FileAccess.Write)
    bw = New BinaryWriter(fs)
    startIndex = 0
    retval = reader.GetBytes(0, 0, outbyte, 0, bufferSize)
    bw.Write(outbyte)
    bw.Flush()
    ' Close the output file.
    bw.Close()
    fs.Close()
    reader.Close()
    ' Display image
```

```
            curImage = Image.FromFile(savedImageName)
            PictureBox1.Image = curImage
            PictureBox1.Invalidate()
            ' Clean up connection
            If conn.State = ConnectionState.Open Then
              conn.Close()
              ' Dispose connection
              conn.Dispose()
            End If
        End Sub
```

Now, you probably want to see this program in action. You can select any image by clicking the Browse Image button, which lets you browse images. Once you've selected a file, you need to save it by clicking the Save Image button. To read the image, simply click the Read Image button. This creates a temporary bitmap file named `ImageFromDb.BMP` file in `c://` folder. You may want to change your path to `C:\\`. The final output looks like Figure C-5.

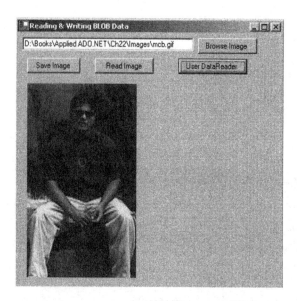

Figure C-5. Displaying a bitmap after reading data from a database

FAQ 18: What are DiffGrams and how do they relate to DataSets? How do I read and write DiffGrams using a DataSet?

The following sections discuss the basics of DiffGrams and how a DataSet utilizes the DiffGram format in this context.

DiffGrams and DataSet

There are occasions when you want to compare the original data with the current data to get the changes made to the original data. A common example of this is saving data on Web Forms applications. When working with Web-based data-driven applications, you read data using a DataSet, make some changes to the data, and send data back to the database to save the final data. Sending an entire DataSet may be a costly affair, especially when there are thousands of records in a DataSet. In this scenario, the best practice is to find out the updated rows of a DataSet and send only those rows back to the database instead of the entire DataSet. This is where the DiffGrams are useful.

NOTE *Do you remember the* GetChanges *method of a* DataSet*? This method returns the rows that have been modified in the current version in the form of a* DataSet*. This is how a* DataSet *knows the modified rows.*

A DiffGram is an XML format used to identify the current and original versions of data elements. Because the DataSet uses XML to store and transfer data, it also uses DiffGrams to keep track of the original data and the current data. When a DataSet is written as a DiffGram, not only does the DiffGram stores original and current data, it also stores row versions, error information, and their orders.

DiffGram XML Format

The XML format for a DiffGram has three parts: data instance, DiffGram before, and DiffGram errors. The <DataInstance> tag represents the data instance part of a DiffGram, which represents the current data. The DiffGram before is represented by the <diffgr:before> tag, which represents the original version of the data. The <diffgr:errors> tag represents the DiffGram errors part, which stores the errors and related information. The DiffGram itself is represented by the tag <diffgr:diffgram>. Listing C-15 represents the XML skeleton of a DiffGram.

Listing C-15. A DiffGram *Format*

```
<?xml version="1.0"?>
<diffgr:diffgram
        xmlns:msdata="urn:schemas-microsoft-com:xml-msdata"
        xmlns:diffgr="urn:schemas-microsoft-com:xml-diffgram-v1"
        xmlns:xsd="http://www.w3.org/2001/XMLSchema">

    <DataInstance>
    </DataInstance>

    <diffgr:before>
    </diffgr:before>

    <diffgr:errors>
    </diffgr:errors>
</diffgr:diffgram>
```

The <diffgr:before> sections only store the changed rows, and the <diffgr:errors> section only stores the rows that had errors. Each row in a DiffGram is identified with an ID, and these three sections communicate through this ID. For example, if the ID of a row is Id1, and it has been modified and has errors, the <diffgr:errors> stores those errors. Besides the previously discussed three sections, a DiffGram uses other elements (see Table C-5).

Table C-5. The DiffGram *Elements*

ELEMENT	DESCRIPTION
id	This is the DiffGram ID, which is usually in the format of [TableName][RowIdentifier]. For example: <Customers diffgr:id="Customers1">.
parented	This is the parent row of the current row, which is usually in the format of [TableName][RowIdentifier]. For example: <Orders diffgr:parentId="Customers1">.
hasChanges	This identifies a row in the <DataInstance> block as modified. The hasChanges element can have one of the three values: inserted, modified, or descent. The value inserted means an added row, modified means a modified row, and descent means the children of a parent row have been modified.
hasErrors	This identifies a row in the <DataInstance> block with a RowError. The error element is placed in the <diffgr:errors> block.
error	This contains the text of the RowError for a particular element in the <diffgr:errors> block.

There are two more elements a DataSet-generated DiffGram can have, and these elements are RowOrder and Hidden. RowOrder is the row order of the original data and identifies the index of a row in a particular DataTable. Hidden identifies a column as having a ColumnMapping property set to MappingType.Hidden.

Listing C-16 reads data from the Employees tables and writes in an XML document in DiffGram format.

Listing C-16. Reading DiffGrams

```
Dim connectionString As String = _
    "Provider=Microsoft.Jet.OLEDB.4.0; Data Source=c:\\Northwind.mdb"
    Dim sql As String = _
    "SELECT EmployeeID, FirstName, LastName, Title FROM Employees"
    Dim conn As OleDbConnection = Nothing
    Dim ds As DataSet = Nothing
    ' Create and open connection
    conn = New OleDbConnection(connectionString)
    If conn.State <> ConnectionState.Open Then
        conn.Open()
    End If
    ' Create a data adapter
    Dim adapter As OleDbDataAdapter = New OleDbDataAdapter(sql, conn)
    ' Create and fill a DataSet
    ds = New DataSet("TempDtSet")
    adapter.Fill(ds, "DtSet")
    ' Write XML in DiffGram format
    ds.WriteXml("DiffGramFile.xml", XmlWriteMode.DiffGram)
    ' Close connection
    If conn.State = ConnectionState.Open Then
        conn.Close()
    End If
MessageBox.Show("Done")
```

The output of Listing C-16 looks like Figure C-6.

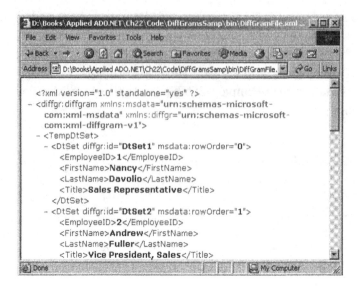

Figure C-6. DiffGram *format*

Now if you update data, you'll see new additions to the XML file with `<diffgr:before>` and `<DataInstance>` tags; if any errors occur during the update, the entries will go to the `<diffgr:errors>` section.

You can use the ReadXml method to read XML documents in DiffGram format. The first parameter of ReadXml is the XML document name, and the second parameter should be XmlReadMode.DiffGram:

```
' Create a DataSet Object
Dim ds As DataSet = New DataSet()
' Fill with the data
ds.ReadXml("DiffGramFile.xml", XmlReadMode.DiffGram)
```

Using the GetChanges Method

The GetChanges method of DataSet can retrieve the rows that have been modified since the last time DataSet was filled, saved, or updated. The GetChanges method returns a DataSet's objects with modified rows.

The GetChanges method can take either no argument or one argument of type DataRowState. The DataRowState enumeration defines the DataRow state, which can be used to filter a DataSet based on the types of rows. Table C-6 describes the DataRowState members.

Table C-6. The `DataRowState` *Members*

MEMBER	DESCRIPTION
Added	Add added rows to a `DataRowCollection` of a `DataSet` and `AcceptChanges` has not been called.
Deleted	All the deleted rows.
Detached	Rows were created but not added to the row collection. Either waiting for the addition to or removal from the collection.
Modified	Modified rows and `AcceptChanges` has not been called.
Unchanged	Unchanged rows since last `AcceptChanges` was called.

Listing C-17 copies only modified rows of `ds` to a new `DataSet` called `tmpDtSet`.

Listing C-17. Reading Only Modified Rows of a `DataSet`

```
' See if DataSet has changes or not
    If Not ds.HasChanges(DataRowState.Modified) Then Exit Sub
    Dim tmpDtSet As DataSet
    ' GetChanges for modified rows only.
    tmpDtSet = ds.GetChanges(DataRowState.Modified)
    If tmpDtSet.HasErrors Then
      MessageBox.Show("DataSet has errors")
      Exit Sub
    End If
    adapter.Update(tmpDtSet)
```

Now you can use the new `DataSet` to bind it to data-bound controls or send back to the database to store results.

FAQ 19: How does CommandBehavior work?

Besides the default `ExecuteReader` method of `SqlCommand` or other data provider command objects, an overloaded form of `ExecuteReader` takes an argument of type `CommandBehavior` enumeration. The `CommandBehavior` enumeration provides a description of the results of the query and its effect on the database. We've used the `SchemaOnly` and `SequentialAccess` members of `CommandBehavior` members in the samples discussed in FAQ 2. However, the `CommandBehavor` enumeration has few more members (see Table C-7).

Table C-7. The CommandBehavior *Enumeration*

MEMBER	DESCRIPTION
CloseConnection	The Connection object associated with the DataReader is closed when the DataReader is closed.
Default	Default option. No effects. Hence, calling ExecuteReader with CommandBehavior.Default returns the same result as calling ExecuteReader with no parameters.
KeyInfo	Returns column and primary key information. You should use this option when you need to read the information about a table's columns and primary key.
SchemaOnly	Returns column information only. Useful when you want to know a table schema. We used this option in FAQ 2 to read a database table schema.
SequentialAccess	Used to read rows that contain columns with large binary values. The SequentialAccess option allows the DataReader to read data in a stream. We use this option in Listing C-14, where we read binary data.
SingleResult	Returns a single result set.
SingleRow	Returns a single row.

FAQ 20: How can I count total number of records in a DataReader?

Unlike an ADO recordset, the DataReader doesn't provide any property or method that returns the total number of records fetched through a SELECT statement. There are two common ways to find out the total number of records fetched by a DataReader. First, you can use a SELECT COUNT * statement, which was discussed in FAQ 12. Second, you can loop through all the records and store the value in an increment counter. This method is not recommended when there are thousands of records.

FAQ 21: How can I find out the end of file in a DataReader?

Unlike an ADO recordset, the DataReader doesn't support EOF either. If there aren't any records left in a DataReader, the Read method of the DataReader returns false.

FAQ 22: How can I sort records using a DataReader?

A DataReader doesn't provide any property or method to sort the records. The easiest way to sort DataReader records is using the ORDER BY clause with the SELECT statement. The ORDER BY clause followed by ASC or DESC sorts in ascending or descending order, respectively. For example, if you want to sort records based on the Name column in descending order, you use the following SQL statement:

```
SELECT * FROM Table ORDER BY NAME DESC
```

FAQ 23: What's the fastest way to figure out connection strings for different data providers?

The following Uniform Resource Locator (URL) lists the connection string for different data providers: www.able-consulting.com/ado_conn.htm.

Summary

In this appendix, we discussed some of the ADO.NET frequently asked questions. There could be a never-ending list of FAQs related to ADO.NET. We've tried to cover almost every aspect of ADO.NET programming, but if you don't find the answer to your question in this book, you can go to the FAQ section of C# Corner (www.c-sharpcorner.com) where there are hundreds of FAQs.

Index

Numbers

About Apress

Apress, located in Berkeley, CA, is a fast-growing, innovative publishing company devoted to meeting the needs of existing and potential programming professionals. Simply put, the "A" in Apress stands for *The Author's Press™*. Apress' unique approach to publishing grew out of conversations between its founders, Gary Cornell and Dan Appleman, authors of numerous best-selling, highly regarded books for programming professionals. In 1998 they set out to create a publishing company that emphasized quality above all else. Gary and Dan's vision has resulted in the publication of over 70 titles by leading software professionals, all of which have *The Expert's Voice™*.

Do You Have What It Takes to Write for Apress?

Apress is rapidly expanding its publishing program. If you can write and you refuse to compromise on the quality of your work, if you believe in doing more than rehashing existing documentation, and if you're looking for opportunities and rewards that go far beyond those offered by traditional publishing houses, we want to hear from you!

Consider these innovations that we offer all of our authors:

- **Top royalties with *no* hidden switch statements**
  Authors typically receive only half of their normal royalty rate on foreign sales. In contrast, Apress' royalty rate remains the same for both foreign and domestic sales.

- **Sharing the wealth**
  Most publishers keep authors on the same pay scale even after costs have been met. At Apress author royalties dramatically increase the more books are sold.

- **Serious treatment of the technical review process**
  Each Apress book is reviewed by a technical expert(s) whose remuneration depends in part on the success of the book since he or she too receives royalties.

Moreover, through a partnership with Springer-Verlag, New York, Inc., one of the world's major publishing houses, Apress has significant venture capital and distribution power behind it. Thus, we have the resources to produce the highest quality books *and* market them aggressively.

If you fit the model of the Apress author who can write a book that provides *What The Professional Needs To Know™*, then please contact us for more information:

editorial@apress.com

ted in the United States
Bookmasters